Margins and Metropolis

❧

MARGINS AND METROPOLIS

ↄ⌒

AUTHORITY ACROSS THE BYZANTINE EMPIRE

Judith Herrin

PRINCETON UNIVERSITY PRESS

PRINCETON AND OXFORD

press.princeton.edu

Library of Congress Cataloging-in-Publication Data

Herrin, Judith.
    Margins and metropolis : authority across the Byzantine Empire /
Judith Herrin.
        pages cm
    Includes bibliographical references and index.
    ISBN 978-0-691-15301-8 (acid-free paper) 1. Authority—
Social aspects—Byzantine Empire—History. 2. Byzantine
Empire—Provinces—History. 3. Borderlands—Byzantine
Empire—History. 4. City and town life—Byzantine Empire—
History. 5. Byzantine Empire—Social life and customs. 6. Byzantine
Empire—Social conditions. 7. Byzantine Empire—Politics and
government. 8. Christianity and politics—Byzantine Empire—
History. 9. Byzantine Empire—Intellectual life. I. Title.
DF531.H47 2013
949.5′02—dc23   2012038201

British Library Cataloging-in-Publication Data is available

This book has been composed in Sabon

Printed on acid-free paper. ∞

Printed in the United States of America

10 9 8 7 6 5 4 3 2 1

For

PATRICIA CRONE

Inspiring scholar and best of friends

☙

CONTENTS
༄

Abbreviations   ix

Introduction   xiii

MARGINS

1. A Christian Millennium: Greece in Byzantium—
   How the Empire Worked at Its Edge   3

2. Aspects of the Process of Hellenization in the
   Early Middle Ages   33

3. Realities of Provincial Government: Hellas and Peloponnesos,
   1180–1204   58

4. The Ecclesiastical Organization of Central Greece
   at the Time of Michael Choniates: New Evidence
   from the *Codex Atheniensis 1371*   103

5. The Collapse of the Byzantine Empire in the Twelfth
   Century: A Study of a Medieval Economy   111

6. Byzantine Kythera   130

METROPOLIS

7. Byzantium: The Palace and the City   159

8. Philippikos and the Greens   179

9. Philippikos "the Gentle"   192

10. The Historical Context of Iconoclast Reform   206

11. Constantinople, Rome, and the Franks in the Seventh
    and Eighth Centuries   220

12. The Pentarchy: Theory and Reality in the Ninth Century   239

13. From Bread and Circuses to Soup and Salvation:
     The Origins of Byzantine Charity   267

14. Ideals of Charity, Realities of Welfare: The Philanthropic
     Activity of the Byzantine Church   299

15. Mathematical Mysteries in Byzantium: The Transmission
     of Fermat's Last Theorem   312

16. Book Burning as Purification in Early Byzantium   335

Index   357

Abbreviations

ℰℬ

AB: *Analecta Bollandiana*

ABSA: *Annual of the British School at Athens*

ACO: *Acta conciliorum oecumenicorum*

AD: *Archaiologikon Deltion*

AE: *Archaiologike Ephemeris*

AP: *Anthologia Palatina*, in the *Greek Anthology*, trans. W. Paton, 5 vols. (London/New York, 1969, repr. Cambridge, MA, 1993)

B: *Byzantion*

BCH: *Bulletin de correspondance hellénique*

BF: *Byzantinische Forschungen*

BMGS: *Byzantine and Modern Greek Studies*

BS: *Byzantinoslavica*

BZ: *Byzantinische Zeitschrift*

CahCM: *Cahiers de civilisation médiévale*

CFHB: *Corpus Fontium Historiae Byzantinae*

Cod. Just.: *Codex Justinianus*, ed. P. Krüger, Corpus Iuris Civilis, vol. 2 (Berlin, 187; repr. 1967)

Cod. Theod.: *Codex Theodosianus*, ed. T. Mommsen with P. Meyer and P. Krüger (Berlin, 1905; repr. 1962); Eng. trans., *The Theodosian Code and Novels* (Princeton, 1952; repr. New York, 1969)

CSCO: *Corpus Scriptorum Christianorum Orientalium*

CSHB: *Corpus Scriptorum Historiae Byzantinae*, Bonn corpus (Bonn edition and dates)

DC: Constantine Porphyrogenitus, *De cerimoniis aulae byzantinae*, ed. J. J. Reiske, 2 vols. (Bonn, 1829–30); and partial Fr. trans., A. Vogt, *Le livre des cérémonies*, 2 of 4 vols. (Paris 1967)

DOC: A. R. Bellinger and P. Grierson, *Catalogue of the Byzantine Coins in the Dumbarton Oaks Collection and in the Whittemore Collection*, 3 vols. (Washington, DC, 1966–73)

DOP: *Dumbarton Oak Papers*

EcHB: *The Economic History of Byzantium: From the Seventh through the Fifteenth Century*, ed. Angeliki Laiou, 3 vols. (Washington, DC, 2002); available at http://www.doaks.org/publications/doaks_online_publications/EconHist with many specialist contributions

EEBS: Ἐπετηρὶς Ἑταιρείας βυζαντινῶν Σπουδῶν (*Epeteris Hetaireias Byzantinon Spoudon*)

EHR: *English Historical Review*

EM: Εὐθυμίου τοῦ Μαλάκη Μητροπολίτου Νέων Πατρῶν τὰ σωζόμενα (*Euthymiou tou Malake Metropolitou Neon Patron ta sozomena*), ed. K. G. Mponès, 2 vols. (Athens, 1937–49)

ÉO: *Échos d'Orient*

GRBS: *Greek, Roman and Byzantine Studies*

JHS: *Journal of Hellenic Studies*

JÖB: *Jahrbuch der österreichischen Byzantinistik* (previously *Jahrbuch der österrechischen byzantinischen Gesellschaft*)

JRS: *Journal of Roman Studies*

JTS: *Journal of Theological Studies*

JusGR: K. E. Zachariae von Lingenthal, *Jus Graecoromanum*, ed. I. and P. Zepos, 8 vols. (Athens, 1931; repr. Aalen, 1962)

LP: *Le Liber pontificalis*, text, intro., and comm., L. Duchesne, 2 vols. (Paris, 1884–92); Bibliothèque des Ecoles françaises d'Athènes et de Rome, 2nd ed., C. Vogel, 3 vols. (Paris, 1955–57); Eng. trans., R. Davis, *Book of the Pontiffs (Liber pontificalis to AD 715)*, TTH 6 (Liverpool, 1989; with 2nd and 3rd eds. 2000 and 2010); *The Lives of the Eighth-Century Popes*, TTH 13 (Liverpool, 1992; rev. ed. 2007); *The Lives of the Ninth-Century Popes*, TTH 20 (Liverpool, 1995)

Mansi: J. D. Mansi, *Sacrorum conciliorum nova at amplissima collectio*, 53 vols. (Florence, 1759–98; repr. Paris/Leipzig, 1901–27, and Graz, 1960)

M. Ch.: Μιχαὴλ Ἀκομινάτου τοῦ Χωνιάτου τὰ σωζόμενα (*Michael Akominatou tou Choniatou ta sozomena*), ed. S. Lampros, 2 vols. (Athens, 1878–80)

MEFR: *Mélanges de l'école française de Rome*

MGH: *Monumenta Germaniae Historica*: *AA* = *Auctorum antiquissimorum*, 15 vols. (Berlin, 1877–1919) (this now includes *Auctores antiquissimi*); *Concilia* = *Concilia Aevi Karolini*, vol. 2 (Hannover, 1893), and vol 2., suppl. = *Libri Carolini* (Hannover, 1924) (includes *Concilia Aevi Karoli*); *Ep.* = *Epistolarum*, 8 vols.

(Berlin, 1887–1939) (includes *Epistulae*); *SS* = *Scriptorum*, 32 vols. (Hannover, 1826–1934) (includes *Schriften*)

MM: F. Miklosich and J. Müller, *Acta et diplomata graeca medii aevi sacra et profana* (Vienna, 1860–90)

N. Ch.: Nicetas Choniates, *Historia*, Bonn ed. (1835); see the new Greek edition, ed. J. L. Van Dieten, *Nicetae Choniatae Historia* (Berlin/New York, 1975), and the Eng. trans., H. Magoulias, *O City of Byzantium: Annals of Niketas Choniates* (Detroit, 1984)

Nikephoros: *Nicephori opuscula historica*, ed. C. de Boor (Leipzig, 1880); new ed. with Eng. trans., Cyril Mango, *Nikephoros, Patriarch of Constantinople, Short History*, Dumbarton Oaks Texts 10 (Washington, DC, 1990)

OC: *Orientalia Christiana*

OCA: *Orientalia Christiana Analecta*

OCP: *Orientalia Christiana Periodica*

ODB: Alexander Kazhdan et al., eds., *Oxford Dictionary of Byzantium*, 3 vols. (Oxford, 1994)

Peira: I. and P. Zepos, eds., *Peira of Eustathios Romaios*, in *JusGR*, vol. IV (Athens, 1931)

PG: J. P. Migne, ed., *Patrologiae cursus completus, series graeco-latina*, 161 vols. (Paris, 1857–94)

PL: J. P. Migne, ed., *Patrologia cursus completus, series latina*, 225 vols. (Paris, 1844–64)

PO: *Patrologia Orientalis*

PBW: *Prospography of the Byzantine World*

REB: *Revue des études byzantines*

ROChr: *Revue de l'Orient chrétien*

RSBN: *Rivista di studi bizantini e neoellenici*

Theophanes: *Theophanis Chronographia*, ed. C. de Boor, 2 vols. (Leipzig, 1883–85; repr. Hildesheim, 1963, New York, 1980); Eng. trans. with intro. and commentary, Cyril Mango and Roger Scott, *The Chronicle of Theophanes Confessor: Byzantine and Near Eastern History AD 284–813* (Oxford, 1997)

TM: *Travaux et Mémoires*

TT: G.L.F. Tafel and G. M. Thomas, eds., *Urkunden zur älteren Handels—und Staatsgeschichte der Republik Venedig* (Vienna, 1856–57)

TTH: *Translated Texts for Historians*

VizVrem: *Vizantijskij Vremennik*

ZRVI: *Zbornik Radova Vizantološkog Instituta*

INTRODUCTION

❧

THIS BOOK AND ITS COMPANION VOLUME, *Unrivalled Influence: Women and Empire in Byzantium*, bring together forty years of research and writing about the Byzantine Empire. Each chapter has been very lightly edited and notes selecting some of the most important, relevant new publications have been added. At my publisher's suggestion I have also introduced each essay with a personal account of how I came to write it and who and what influenced me in doing so.

Each volume traces a historian's journey across the Byzantine Empire. This one maps my research into its political and intellectual power and authority, the other my discoveries of the role and influence of women. The request to situate each chapter throws some personal light on each particular step of my journey, but it also seems to demand this overall introduction about how I decided to pursue these interests and to write the books I have. The double trek began in the 1960s, at Cambridge, when I chose to become a historian. They were radical and innovative times that naturally left their influence. I still feel myself linked to that period, am proud to have contributed to its spirit, and am happy to say that it has marked my work ever since.

At that time there was a very strong tradition in Britain of historians working from primary material, archives, and documentary evidence. Sometimes this led to narrow, empirical parochialism. But it could also be combined with efforts to build up a large picture, seeking to embrace the totality and to understand the underlying explanation for what happened, especially by scholars on the left. These ambitious aims were invigorated by the anti-authoritarian, anti-hierarchy radicalism of the 1960s. E. H. Carr's *What Is History?* (1961) questioned many assumptions and stimulated as many unanswered issues but made us think. For historians, Marx was perhaps the dominant theorist, whose ideas were taken up and applied by Christopher Hill, for example, in his work on the English Civil War. His *Century of Revolution* was a compelling read. I was also deeply influenced by R. W. Southern, whose book, *The Making of the Middle Ages*, opened at St. Martin du Canigou, a spectacular monastery in the Eastern Pyrenees that I knew from several visits.

At Newnham College, Cambridge, I was taught by inspiring figures like Kathleen Hughes, Margaret Aston, and Betty Behrens, who introduced me to Carr. I read very widely in modern Russian and American history, as well as taking in the Marxists. I wrote a study of Jane Addams and Hull House in Chicago that won a University prize and chose the church in the French Revolution along with the Expansion of Medieval Europe as special subjects. In the latter Philip Grierson introduced me to Byzantine coin finds, scattered across the Mediterranean, western Europe, and as far north as Russia and Scandinavia, which indicated a major force at work. This inspired me to investigate the Eastern Empire, then totally unfamiliar to me—it drew me to Byzantium. At the same time, the nascent student movement, the Vietnam Solidarity Campaign, and the New Left were major influences. In addition to demonstrations against the American war in Indochina, feminism arrived to gladden many young women (and men).

This heady mixture of political awareness, theoretical writing about history, and practical efforts to change the university's traditional and patronizing attitudes developed when I moved to Birmingham to master Greek and start work on the Byzantine Empire. I found a strong dedication to Marxist analysis among professors like Rodney Hilton, Roy Pascal, and George Thomson. Among the students there was a widespread interest in the events of 1968 as well as the work of Althusser. In the Spring of 1969 we organized a sit-in at Birmingham, one of many university occupations. It was one of the largest in Britain at the time and was run by a Committee of Ten, of which I was a member.

Amidst the rather sterile rivalry of established leftist groups, Trotskyist and Maoist, I was more concerned to test Marxist analysis, by trying to apply it to the medieval empire of Byzantium. We formed a reading group and tackled the first volume of *Das Kapital*. I found Marx's *Pre-Capitalist Economic Formations* with Eric Hobsbawm's introduction more helpful for the medieval period, and it led me to Barrington Moore and Shmuel Eisenstadt's work on comparative transformations of preindustrial societies and the political systems of empires.

As I began the process of becoming a professional Byzantinist, there was a moment when I understood that a Marxist analysis didn't deliver what I was looking for to explain the development of the empire. Marxism insists that all history is the history of class struggle and that economic relations determine the growth, development, and decline of societies. All other activities, politics, religion, social relations are "super-structures" with limited influence. In modern capitalist societies the dynamics of forces and relations of production are a massively shaping force, but this didn't appear to hold up for precapitalist societies, such as Byzantium. The medieval empire I was studying had a written legal code and a centralized administration capable of issuing a gold coinage that remained stable for over 700 years. None of this fitted with the feudal mode of production as conceived by Marxists.

Much later I argued in *Byzantium: The Surprising Life of a Medieval Empire* (2007) that Byzantium was "born old" out of a unique combination of established traditions; these created a powerful imperial system that directed the economy rather efficiently and maintained both the collection of taxes and the reliability of the coinage until the eleventh century. Strikingly, the devaluation of the gold standard appeared to coincide with developments that could be linked to a more feudal society, analyzed by George Ostrogorsky. But overall, the feudal mode of production as a concept prevented rather than illuminated an understanding of the dynamics of change within imperial Byzantium, where arguments over Christian theology and belief were shaping forces that couldn't be reduced to a function of class interest, profit, and gain. Others, however, pursued a more theoretical approach to Byzantium, which has always proved a challenge to Marxist historians.[1]

In addition to the constant interest in relating Western medieval feudalism to Byzantine society, there is currently a revival of interest in Marxist analysis of Byzantium, for example, the work of Telemachos Lounghis in Greece and Peter Sarris in Cambridge, from rather different perspectives.[2] I wish them good fortune but do not share their starting point, nor do I regard myself as a Marxist historian. Which is not to say that inequality and exploitation didn't exist in Byzantium, and the clash of interests occasionally made this explicit. Appeals to the high courts in Constantinople by provincial communities often reflected unjust demands for additional taxation, or failures to abide by agreed tax exemptions. When the "Zealots" of Thessalonike rebelled against the city government and established their own council from 1341–50, they presented their case as a justified correction of entrenched aristocratic power. In *Byzantium* I was delighted to give them the attention they are due, for there was always antagonism to the accumulated wealth of large landowners and conflict over economic resources. But it rarely assumed the high profile of "class warfare," as maintained by the Zealots, who were overthrown after a brief rule.

The other major theoretical influence of the 1960s and 1970s was feminism, which I embraced and continue to do so without regret. Feminism is a different kind of "ism" to Marxism. It does not offer a theory of determination but rather an analysis of an unacceptable state of affairs that arises in the deeply unfair, unequal patriarchal societies in which men exploit women. Feminists campaign to reverse this condition. As a historian, feminism alerted me to the weight of patriarchal power in Byzantine society, which produces deeply embedded prejudices in the male-authored sources. These have to be unpicked if the texts are to be used, a process that sometimes leads to the almost total "deconstruction" of the women who form the supposed subject matter. Learning to read such texts critically, avoiding a naïve acceptance of statements about women, is an essential task for all historians.

The significance of women's contribution to society informed my effort to understand Byzantium as a whole with its underlying structures of power and authority. The imperial court with its insistent feminine component immediately attracted my attention, which led to a broader study of Byzantine women from all social strata, including their influence even on orthodox Christianity. Byzantium was a thoroughly patriarchal society, but as I worked out in the studies now collected in *Unrivalled Influence: Women and Empire in Byzantium,* the unique Byzantine combination of Roman law (which gave women property rights), of Christianity (with its insistence on monogamy that underwrote maternal and wifely influence, especially important for the ruling dynasty), and of Greek education (with its commanding literacy) made it possible for them to break through patriarchal constraints. I did not have to look far to identify women in urban and rural settings, from shopkeepers and nuns to peasant heads of household, whose awareness of their potential power and authority could be studied beyond the scorn and dismissal of male authors, and it was thrilling to be a pioneer in this field.

From the first, my interest in Byzantium was that of a Western historian aware of the empire's larger influence and seeking a comparative perspective. Since the empire shared features with other medieval states, such an approach would help to identify its specific characteristics, such as landholding, social strata, economic control of resources. I decided to try and compare one particular region of Byzantium with an area of western Europe and draw out the differences. Historians often point to the difficulty of exploring how medieval rule was experienced. The aims and intentions of governments as recorded in laws and official regulations assume a uniform administration in all regions. But clearly this was not always the case. Not only were such written instructions interpreted in a variety of ways, but in addition particular provinces under individual administrators, taking account of their own relations with forces in the capital city, might undermine or reinforce what they read. It is quite inappropriate to assume that imperial government in far-flung regions was the same, and this is as true of the medieval empire of the Han in China as the empire of Charlemagne.

As this thought became clearer in my mind, I decided that the Fourth Crusade of 1204 might be the watershed that would allow me to compare the region of central Greece before and after the arrival of the crusader conquerors. In that way I could compare the two societies, Byzantine and Frankish, and assess the impact of 1204 in the mixed society that resulted. And so I embarked on a doctoral thesis on the provinces of Hellas and Peloponnesos, using the letters and speeches of Michael Choniates, Archbishop of Athens from 1182–1205, as a key source. Ever since I have been struck by the contrasts between his life in the province and his previous training in the metropolis before he was sent, as he saw it, to the margins of empire. His letters provided ample evidence of the administration of the region by civilian and military dignitaries sent from the center and local church officials, many of whom were drawn from notable families. I found some of the same family names in documents relating to the numerous small village churches, with elegant brickwork and marble decoration that dot the region. Toward the end of the twelfth century, pressures exacerbated relations between the margins and the metropolis, leading in some cases to separatist movements. Central Greece thus shared in the general deterioration of imperial control, which is also visible in Cyprus, northwestern Asia Minor, and Trebizond on the far eastern border.

The arrival of the Frankish conquerors was disastrous for Choniates. He was exiled from Athens and moved from place to place until he eventually settled on the barren island of Kea. His account of this period is full of complaints about the Latin clergy who had displaced him, as well as the western knights who took over the region and adapted its monasteries and churches to their Catholic rite. With the help of a loyal team of Orthodox clerics, Choniates tried to look after the needs of the indigenous Greek population, now reduced to servile status. My study of Hellas and Peloponnesos gave me considerable insight into the state of one particular province of the Byzantine Empire at the turn of the thirteenth century as well as the critically important role of the Constantinopolitan-educated bishops. Unlike civil and military officials, who held temporary appointments usually for three years, these ecclesiastics who had been trained in the patriarchate with the resources of the metropolis were sent to administer the chief sees of the Byzantine church for life. They also maintained their links with Constantinople, returning to attend councils or court cases or to consult the patriarch about problems. In this way men like Michael Choniates of Athens and his teacher, Eustathios of Thessalonike, brought the highest standards of twelfth-century education and clerical training to provincial capitals. They attracted local men who wanted to learn and transmitted their knowledge and wisdom to younger generations, who had not had the same opportunities. The church of Constantinople thus sustained a spider-web of connections between the center and the provinces, which were maintained by letters often exchanged over decades. This provided a much firmer and more deeply embedded clerical culture, a solid support for Byzantine imperial values as well as correct definitions of Orthodoxy, than civilian or military administration could manage.

While it is clearly erroneous to talk or argue about the nature of a city-based empire like Byzantium as if it was uniform, the network of church leadership did provide a common overlay of cultural expression that overcame some of the obvious differences among the provinces. The writings of officials based in the regions provided a vital source of information, although it varied according to region. The archaeology and development over ancient sites through centuries was another. Yet despite the obvious differences between naval and landlocked cities, frontier castles and market centers on main trade routes, their inclusion within the Byzantine Empire clearly created some degree of unity of purpose and activity. When I wrote *Byzantium*, one of the most striking aspects of the empire that came to me as a discovery, even though I had been studying it for many years, was the intensity of its self-belief and the wealth of its traditions and resources at the local city level. These not only gave even its remote provinces direct links to the center that could be adapted to circumstances, particularly by ecclesiastical leaders, they also encouraged local forces to create a miniature Byzantium of their own when the Queen City was occupied by western forces in 1204.

Thus, it was from working on Choniates for my doctorate under the inspiring supervision of Anthony Bryer that I learnt at first hand the immense importance of Christianity not as a belief but as a formative force. Clearly, beliefs mattered, especially for those who believed in them. But the disputes over theological definitions and the way Christianity was organized and practiced influenced, sometimes decisively, the entire direction of empires—and would-be empires—across the entire period of the Middle Ages. At the same time I was taking every opportunity to work on archaeological excavations in Greece, Cyprus, and Turkey, where the Turkish/American restoration of Kalenderhane Camii brought me closer than ever to my chosen subject. The mosque, situated beside the Aqueduct of Valens, was a converted twelfth-century church, itself built onto the apse of an earlier Byzantine church.[3]

An invitation from Franz-Georg Maier to contribute to the Fischer Weltgeschichte volume devoted to Byzantium broadened my approach to the religious foundations of the empire. Since the tenth to twelfth centuries were already being covered, I was asked to undertake the earlier period of iconoclasm, the battle over icons. Partly as a result of this interest, in 1975 Bryer and I decided to devote the Spring Symposium to the same topic, later published as *Iconoclasm*, and I began to research the much broader Christian development, which eventually became *The Formation of Christendom* (1987).

Iconoclasm, however, led me immediately to the heart of the empire and to imperial policies decided in Constantinople. It was encouraged by the seminar on the *Parastaseis Syntomoi Chronikai*, a curious text that Professors Alan and Averil Cameron had selected for group study at King's College London. After several years of teaching and archaeological research I had the privilege of becoming a Senior Research Fellow of the Warburg Institute and was able to assist Averil in the publication. We decided that this collection of stories largely about the capital city Constantinople should be dated to the early eighth century, which fitted into my study of the battle over icons.[4] The investigation of methods used by the government to maintain its authority also led to closer analysis of the life of the capital itself.

Taking account of the significance of religion from a secular perspective was essential, as Christian practice and doctrine was clearly a decisive influence in Byzantium. I examined how the Byzantine church took over responsibility for organizing charity, previously the duty of city councils and private benefactors, and made itself an indispensable ally of imperial government. Increasing attention to the care of the poor, who had never been the beneficiaries of official, charitable donations, demanded more efficient measures from patriarchs, bishops, and monastic communities throughout the empire. At the same time it was essential to study the institutional development of the universal church, as the concept of the pentarchy of five great centers was challenged by claims of bishops of Rome, leaders of the expanding Christian regions of the West.

Finding a satisfying explanation of the Byzantine totality remained my goal, using a materialist approach that was open to different forms of evidence, notably archaeological, and to novel arguments in favor of Byzantine feudalism that developed in the 1970s and were then rebutted. I remained resistant to high theory of the "Linguistic Turn" variety (I'd read enough Althusser), and I'm intolerant of theoretical jargon that fails to deliver understanding of the human experience. The same attitude informed my exploration of the forces that shaped Christianity across its first millennium; I concentrated on the practices of Christian believers rather than the most sophisticated theologians. My research on iconoclasm and the opposition to it, visible in the commitment of ordinary people to iconophile practice, thus became the lynch-pin of a longer study of how Christendom developed, and how the Western half of the universal church created its distinct traditions, independently of the East. Gradually, I realized that the eighth century was the most significant period in relations between East and West during the early Middle Ages.

In the course of reading many decrees of church councils, held in different regions of the Christian world, I realized how bishops had responded to the ideas of their congregations in the course of developing ecclesiastical government. The growth of canon law and books of penance owed much to the input of regular believers, who often found new ways of expressing their faith when left to their own devices. Practices based on erroneous interpretations of scripture or on local traditions that owed more to pre-Christian cults had to be condemned, while scales of penance for personal sins had to be drawn up. Despite the absence of records on the side of regular believers, it was clear that ecclesiastical government in the early medieval period developed through debates between Christians and their leaders. Both reciprocity and mutual influence lay behind the driving forces that molded the Christian universe. As a result, I find it vexing when *The Formation of Christendom* is shelved with Theology rather than Medieval History.

That book turns on an interpretation of iconoclasm but is devoted to the entire early medieval world. It has remained in print for twenty-five years, and I will discuss how it has stood up in an introduction to a new edition that Princeton University Press is planning to publish. Here I should alert readers to some highlights, as they reflect on my general approach. Pirenne argued that without Muhammed, Charlemagne was inconceivable.[5] I argue that without Byzantium, Muhammad's followers would have conquered the entire Roman world and there would have been no Charlemagne. For the development of western medieval Europe came about thanks both to the rise of Islam, and as important, the frustration of the Arab conquests by Byzantium, which created the three-way division of the Mediterranean that survives until today. I don't wish to play down the role of the Franks in successfully opposing Muslim forces in the West, but the Arabs' failure to capture Constantinople proved the more important overall: with the resources of the Queen City behind them, they would probably have conquered Rome.

A critical part of the process was the consolidation of the much reduced eastern half of the Roman Empire after the Arab conquests, shorn of its granaries in Egypt and North Africa, and the pilgrim centers of the holy land—in constant contest with its Islamic enemy. In the 730s, after a century of conflict across a vast and fluid frontier area, Leo III launched an official policy of iconoclasm to bolster his military campaigns. For over a century a furious argument raged within Byzantium until icons were restored in 843. Women were a decisive influence in this outcome, as I show in *Unrivalled Influence*: both in homes, where they devoted themselves and their children, boys as well as girls, to domestic shrines, and in the imperial court itself, where two female emperors were responsible for both the initial and then the ultimate victory over the iconoclasts (aided by a significant but ignored go-between, Empress Euphrosyne).[6] In *The Formation of Christendom* I stress that this immense theological-imperial battle over the definition of the legitimacy and place of holy images was part of the formation of Christendom as a whole, shared by all regions around the Mediterranean: the early medieval West, the Byzantine East, and the world of Islam that stretched across the southern shore.

In their recent sweeping and detailed study of the period, *Byzantium in the Iconoclast Era*, Leslie Brubaker and John Haldon restate the view that the dispute over icons was a relatively superficial contest in comparison with the challenges to Byzantium's military and economic base.[7] This is repeated in his magnificent survey of the early medieval West by Chris Wickham, who declares: "there is absolutely no sign that the Byzantine Iconoclasts were influenced by the Arabs."[8] I think it is impossible to sustain this claim. The two societies were deeply embroiled, the Byzantines well aware that Muslim opposition to graven images was based on the authority of the tablets of Moses, and that Muslims claimed to be the true followers of the same God as the Christians. Thus even if iconoclasm had emerged spontaneously within Byzantium, it would immediately have been opposed by those saying it was based on the arguments of the infidel and was essentially heretical. But I think it more likely that the first iconoclasts were forced to question the Christian use of icons by the pervasive triumphs of the rival faith. Both the rise of iconoclasm and the beliefs of iconophiles were "influenced" by the challenge of Islam. Here I draw attention to this contrast of views in order to illustrate more clearly my own approach: that the powers of organized belief and the developments of its institutions are formative. I feel I should alert readers that while I do not hesitate to state my approach firmly, it is contested.

While I constantly try to study Byzantium from a broad comparative approach, I like to respond to current events that connect to public interest. The discovery in the 1990s of a proof of Fermat's last theorem provoked my curiosity about how the theorems of Diophantos were communicated from second-century AD Alexandria to seventeenth-century France. I had been exploring the ways in which the empire displayed its power to the wider world, and now I found a fascinating example in the transmission of ancient mathematics. There were two routes of transmission, the Byzantine and the Arab, which created two distinct manuscript traditions. The Byzantine reached out to puzzles recorded in Armenian to enhance mathematical knowledge in Constantinople (an unusual link between margins and metropolis) and to enrich the Greek tradition. Its conscious effort to remain "the center" of the world—of maintaining a defining tradition—did not, however, depend on the imperial court and official hierarchy of power. It was internalized thanks to the wider traditions of Greek authority and learning, which in due course provided copies of Diophantos's theorems to Bessarion, who took them to the West.

My anger at the burning of Salman Rushdie's *The Satanic Verses* stimulated another response. It prompted me to consider the determination of religious authorities to burn texts considered heretical, and this led into a wider consideration of such bonfires. Books were expensive to produce, so the instruction to condemn them to the flames sprang from a serious attempt to remove their contents from circulation. Such destruction is not always successful because authors and readers alike remember what they learned from books. "Books don't burn!" Yet the practice was ancient and apparently continued unabated, a paradox I explored in "Book Burning as Purification in Early Byzantium."

On looking back over these contributions to the relations between margins and metropolis, I'm struck by their interdependence. The capital may have been a dominant force in Byzantine life, but relations with the margins of empire were often critical. Isolated frontier zones such as the Crimea, Peloponnesos, islands like Kephalonia, or castles in the Taurus region of eastern Anatolia, were used as areas of imprisonment, and gave those who were banished a sense of extreme distance and isolation from the capital. But the same regions provoked rebellions that might prove fatal to the ruling emperor. It was essential for Constantinople to be well informed about such potential opposition movements, which might swell into serious military threats. By the same token those living in border regions wanted to know what was happening in the Queen City, where they often had relatives or allies, who could send news. As I've argued elsewhere the idea of a "bride show," to select a wife for the future emperor, was exploited by the imperial court to strengthen provincial loyalty to the ruling family, focusing the attention of provincial families on the once-in-a-lifetime opportunity to win the ultimate prize. This was one method that appears to have been quite successful in creating hopes among those who lived in the margins of the possibility of promotion to the very center of empire.

In the era of "World History" Byzantium can claim a significant place as the medieval empire that developed out of the Greek world of Alexander of Macedon and the Roman Republic and Empire of the Caesars, and went on to endow both the Russian and the Ottoman Empires with traditions that survived into the twentieth century. In religious terms Greek Orthodoxy played a critical role in the maintenance of the Byzantine Empire, and links vast territories and time-spans that may be compared with the greatest empires of Asia. This volume aims to contribute to further comparative history, which will place Byzantium within a context of influential medieval societies. Taken together these sixteen chapters offer an overview of Byzantium, from its outlying regions to the hub of the Queen City, and thereby present an insight into the dynamic character of an empire tremendously focused on itself and what it stood for in a way that was at once defining and flexible.[9]

ACKNOWLEDGMENTS

In the writing and preparation for republication of these essays I want to thank many who have supported my work: the A. G. Leventis Foundation, the Hellenic Foundation, and the Michael Marks Charitable Trust; Anthony Barnett; Alexandros Kedros; Edmée Leventis; Marina Marks; Rick Trainor, the Principal of King's College London; and my colleagues in the departments of Classics, Byzantine and Modern Greek Studies, and History at King's. These essays complement a second volume, *Unrivalled Influence: Women and Empire in Byzantium*.

New bibliography in both volumes is signaled in the notes by **Update**. In preparing these notes, I thank Andreia Carvalho and Rupert Smith for their skill in scanning, editing, and entering Greek text, and Alessandra Bucossi and Alex Rodrigues for introducing me to the wonders of Endnote. The photographs in chapter 6 of this volume, "Byzantine Kythera," are reproduced with the kind permission of George Huxley and the approval of the original publisher, Faber and Faber. Jennifer Harris's careful copyediting saved me from many inconsistencies and non sequiturs. I'm most grateful to Brigitta van Rheinberg for her enthusiastic acceptance of the idea of these volumes, to Larissa Klein for her help in putting them together, and to Heather Roberts for compiling the index.

NOTES

1. The enforced Marxist historiography of the Soviet Union and East European bloc until the fall of the Berlin Wall produced many useful studies but no compelling explanation. George Ostrogorsky's *History of the Byzantine State*, originally published in German (1940) and translated into more than a dozen languages, remains a very useful, basic textbook, but is singularly devoid of Marxist ideology. His *Pour l'histoire de la féodalité byzantine* (Fr. trans. Brussels, 1954) is a more serious, though not convincing, study of the feudal mode. E. Patlagean adopted a very successful comparative perspective in her classic study of poverty, *Pauvrété économique et pauvrété sociale à Byzance 4e–7e siècles* (Paris, 1977), followed by *Un moyen âge grec. Byzance IXe–XVe siècles* (Paris, 2007).

2. T. Lounghis, *E Ideologia tes Vyzantines istoriografias* (Athens, 1993), and P. Sarris, "The Early Byzantine Economy in Context: Aristocratic Property and Economic Growth Reconsidered," *Early Medieval Europe* 19, no. 3 (2011), 255–84.

3. The final reports of the restoration of the building are now published in two large-format volumes, ed. C. L. Striker and D. Kuban, *Kalenderhane in Istanbul: The Buildings, Their History, Architecture and Decoration . . .* (Mainz, 1997–2007).

4. This date has been modified to the later eighth or early ninth century by many commentators, notably Otto Kresten, "Leon III und die Landmauer von Konstantinopel. Zur Datierung von c. 3 der Παραστάσεις σύντομοι χρονικαί," *Römische Historische Mitteilungen* 36 (1994), 21–52.

5. Henri Pirenne, *Mohammad and Charlemagne* (Eng. trans. London, 1954)

6. She is the central figure in *Women in Purple: Rulers of Medieval Byzantium* (London/Princeton, 2001).

7. Leslie Brubaker and John Haldon, *Byzantium in the Iconoclast Era ca. 680–850: A History* (Cambridge, 2011), esp. 790–92.

8. Chris Wickham, *The Inheritance of Rome: A History of Europe from 400–1000* (London, 2009), 278.

9. For a more detailed account of the authorities who influenced my development as a historian, see my introduction to *Authority in Byzantium*, ed. P. Armstrong (Farnham, 2013), 1–11.

MARGINS
ᘒ

1

A CHRISTIAN MILLENNIUM

GREECE IN BYZANTIUM—HOW THE
EMPIRE WORKED AT ITS EDGE

❧

Robert Browning commissioned this chapter for his elegant compendium, *The Greek World: Classical, Byzantine and Modern*, published by Thames and Hudson in 1985. In those days publishers had picture researchers who scoured unusual photo collections for suitable material to illustrate what the publishers conceived as a brilliant coffee-table book. Robert, however, had planned an overview of the entire history of Greece written to his specifications by experts in their fields. His own introduction sets the scene and lays out his Marxist interpretation in very clear terms. Even if all the contributors did not share these views, they prepared chapters on their periods of Greek history with care, and the whole volume has a greater coherence and quality than many multi-authored books. References were not footnoted and have not been added, as most recur updated in later chapters.

It was an honor to participate, and I enjoyed the challenge of covering the period when Greece was effectively a rather minor province of the great empire of Byzantium. The problems of imposing Christian belief on a population deeply rooted in traditional rituals dedicated to the pagan gods, of converting temples to Christian use and adapting pilgrimage and miraculous cures to novel ends are not tackled as directly as I would now wish. But the overview of Byzantine Greece stands as an introduction to the Christian Millennium, and many of its distinct features are treated in greater detail in the following chapters. The chapter is reprinted by kind permission of Thames and Hudson.

AT THE TURN OF THE SIXTH and seventh centuries AD the history of Greece enters a period that is perhaps the least well documented since the development of Greek script and written records. The early medieval period has been aptly characterized as the "Great Breach" in Greek history. For the first time historical documents are almost completely lacking; archaeological evidence is also sparse; outside sources present little information. While a similar trend is clear throughout the Mediterranean world from the late sixth to the late eighth centuries, giving rise to the epithet "The Dark Ages," the label does not assist our understanding of developments in Greece. For what is witnessed during this period is the very slow and uncertain shift from a society organized according to the principles of the ancient world—a world of half-autonomous cities—to one dominated by a peculiarly medieval concept of empire, the Christian Roman empire of Byzantium.

PRECARIOUS SURVIVAL

During the first half of the seventh century the great empire built up by Justinian was subjected to a series of devastating blows from which it barely recovered. Among the newly reconquered lands in western Europe, southeast Spain and much of Italy succumbed to the Visigoths and the Lombards. From the 580s onward, the Slavs from across the Danube swept through the Balkans, reaching as far south as the Peloponnese and sailing to Crete. Finally, in the east, no sooner had the threat of the Persian invasion been removed by Heraclius (628) than it was replaced by the far more irresistible advance of Islam, which deprived Byzantium of its Near Eastern provinces—Syria, Palestine, and Egypt—in one decade (following the death of Muhammad in 632).

The effect of these upheavals, combined with the changes already underway within the empire, was traumatic. The first evidence of fundamental change is the marked decline of urban life: there was a radical break with the traditions of the ancient Greek *polis* and an increasing ruralization of areas previously dominated by cities. The second, related, aspect lies in the movements of population that forced Greeks away from their cities, scattering them to Sicily, southern Italy, small Greek islands, and fortified refuges in the eastern Peloponnese, while newcomers from the north settled in the fertile agricultural areas. The Slavonic tribes who raided, plundered, and finally occupied parts of the Balkan peninsula from the late sixth century onward undoubtedly contributed to these upheavals.

Major sites such as Athens, Corinth, and Thessalonike shrank to smaller areas within defensible walls, reflecting this process of adaptation. Similarly, ancient cities often associated with riverine trade were replaced by settlements on inaccessible mountain peaks. Among the Greeks, withdrawal, circumspection, and self-protection imposed themselves in place of outgoing contacts, open access, and confident self-assertion.

For many years during this breach, numerous Greek communities existed sometimes in self-imposed exile, sometimes in enforced flight. They were directed by their elders and religious leaders, in isolation, beyond the authority of any ruler. But many survived and in due course returned to their regions, as Arethas, bishop of Caesarea (in Cappadocia) describes. His ancestors had sailed from Patras to avoid the incursions of non-Christian "barbarians." They settled in Calabria, where many generations had lived, until his own grandparents learned that the emperor in Constantinople could guarantee their safety. Then they returned to repopulate the city of Patras in the early ninth century.

Such turbulent uprooting, resettlement, and mobility of population was indeed characteristic of the entire Byzantine Empire at this time. From Palestine, Egypt, and Syria large numbers of Christians fled the Persian and Islamic invaders of the early and mid-seventh century to occupy safer lands behind the natural frontier of the Taurus mountains; island populations harried by Arab pirates similarly sought refuge elsewhere. Through these movements the inhabitants of Sicily and Syria were brought into much closer contact than usual; Greek colonies once again dotted the Italian landscape, reinforced by refugees from North Africa. But in the east Mediterranean these political changes were accompanied by a total eclipse of Greek culture; Arabic gradually replaced even Syriac, the *lingua franca* of a vast area in northern Syria, and endowed some of the Christian communities that remained behind with a new language for their worship. The Coptic churches of Egypt and the Greek monasteries near Jerusalem succeeded in maintaining their own identity but had progressively less and less influence over the Islamic environment in which they survived. Knowledge of Greek and observance of Christianity remained the preserve of a tiny minority; in general the dominance of Islam became undisputed.

In contrast, the Slavonic invaders of the Balkan peninsula failed to preserve their own distinct identity. They may have disrupted the political and military control of Constantinople for many years, but they could not dislodge the Greek tongue or the Christian faith. Instead, the Slavs gradually embraced both, adopting in addition the medieval Byzantine style of city life (as cities slowly revived), of coinage, trading organization, ecclesiastical structure, and Hellenic culture. So while the Great Breach divided ancient from medieval Greek, it did not involve a fundamental linguistic loss. Certainly changes occurred in the Greek tongue between the sixth and ninth centuries, but the process of "hellenization" predominated: the newcomers were converted to Christianity and inducted into

Hellenic culture to become the not-always obedient subjects of the Byzantine emperors.

STABILITY RESTORED

During the late seventh and eighth centuries the Byzantine state slowly imposed its authority upon nearly all the Slav tribes that had crossed the Danube. This process will be described in more detail in a later section; it was not finally complete until 1018. By about 800, too, what seemed to be a reliable defense system against Islam had been established in the east.

For the next 400 years, from ca. 800 to 1204, the Greek world was governed by the emperors of Constantinople, who extended their own political system throughout the east Mediterranean and as far west as Palermo. Administered through a series of large provinces (called *themata*, singular *thema*) embracing Cyprus, the Aegean islands, the northern Balkans, Thrace, and the mainland, Greece was subordinated to the needs of the imperial capital in the same way as the rest of the empire. Thus it was expected to provide naval and military forces, manpower for the industries of the capital, taxation in kind and coinage, as well as to act as a place of exile for dissidents. These duties were balanced by an imperial responsibility for the well-being of provincial inhabitants, not only in the form of an often rhetorical philanthropy, but sometimes in direct assistance. When the people of Tenedos, Imbros, and Samothrace were taken prisoner by Slavs, Constantine V (741–75) ransomed 2,500 by sending an embassy laden with silk clothing. The internal development and organization of Greece, however, were geared to that of an empire, whose center lay on the Bosphorus, on the site of a colony established by Greeks from Megara in the seventh century BC.

It is no exaggeration of the conflict between center and periphery to say that an element of competitiveness governed the relationships between Constantinople and all its provinces. And everywhere the tedium of provincial life was contrasted, unfavorably, with life in the metropolis—the Queen of cities, Empress, as Constantinople was called. This reflected both the fact that Constantinople had remained a great urban center, while other famous cities had declined, and also an extreme centralization that had concentrated power and influence in the capital. Provincial inhabitants understandably looked to it as if to a city whose streets were paved with gold. One, the future Basil I (867–886), even made good that dream, in a career from "stable-boy" to emperor, assisted by his wealthy patron, the widow Danelis from Patras. Another, Rendakis, rose to be a senator, and married his daughter to the heir presumptive in the early tenth century.

Metropolitan disdain for provincial life, however, should not be allowed to obscure the fact that the Greek provinces became relatively prosperous in the eleventh and twelfth centuries. This development was related both to the decline of imperial power in Anatolia and to the inherent resources of Greece. A clear demographic increase accompanied greater economic activity; there was a more rapid circulation of coinage and local products, which included silk spun in central Greece on mulberry farms established by Justinian. While internal demand accounts for some of the expansion, the role of Italian merchants in stimulating greater production may be significant. There can be no doubt that the appearance of Venetian, Amalfitan, and Genoese traders in the ports of Methone, Korone, Nauplion, Thebes, Corinth, Halmyros, and of many islands attracted additional commerce. They took a larger share of Byzantine foreign trade than the Greek merchants of the time. And their presence was to be formally recognized by treaties that gave them a privileged position in Byzantine commerce—for example, the charters of 1084, 1126, or 1147. They established landing stages in many harbors and set up warehouses, depots, and offices. Eventually, by the mid-twelfth century, there were Italian residential quarters in several major export centers, each patterned on the extensive communities of Constantinople, which were strung along the Golden Horn and in Pera (Galata), the Genoese enclave.

The penetration of Byzantine commercial life by western merchants was paralleled by a military threat from the west. While it may not have been as dangerous as the challenge from the east, posed by the Seljuk Turks, it was still a constant worry. For many years the Normans had threatened Byzantine possessions in southern Italy; from the late eleventh century they extended their attention to Greece. Ports on the Adriatic littoral and round the Peloponnese—Dyrrachion, Korone, and Methone—were attacked. Although the Norman naval force of 1147 was beaten off by Monemvasia, it proceeded to sack both Corinth and Thebes, carrying off as booty their skilled artisan populations as well as much woven cloth and embroidered silk. In 1185 the great city of Thessalonike succumbed to a Norman attack. Imperial military and naval weakness (and reliance on Italian mercenary forces) were partly to blame for this increasing Norman presence in the empire, but it was also part of a continuous western push to establish states in the east, on the model of the kingdom of Jerusalem, set up after the First Crusade (1098–99).

In both a military and an economic sense, therefore, western activities in Greece during the twelfth century foreshadowed the occupation that followed the Fourth Crusade of 1201–4. This ill-fated attempt to recover the holy places from Islamic control, preached by Pope Innocent III and accompanied by many pilgrims and feudal princes of the west, also brought the Venetians permanently into the Eastern Empire. Under the combination of military challenge and economic rivalry Byzantium collapsed.

THE DISASTER OF THE FOURTH CRUSADE

Some powers in Constantinople had no doubt hoped to use the crusade for their own, more local, concerns: ever since the first expedition of westerners it had been Byzantine policy to assist crusading troops on the march farther east while forcing them to participate in imperial campaigns of reconquest, unrelated to the holy places. This tactic had caused bad feeling in the past. When it appeared to be surfacing again in 1203—as Alexios III refused to honor the terms of an agreement made with the Venetians—the crusaders quickly decided to assist the Doge in taking revenge, and captured and plundered Constantinople. The Byzantine court and many metropolitan inhabitants fled to Asia, some to Trebizond, others to Nicaea, where they gradually regrouped under the leadership of Theodore Laskaris (son-in-law of Alexios III and emperor 1204–22). The sack of Constantinople in April 1204, which lasted for twelve days and denuded the city of many of its finest antiquities (the four gilded bronze horses now at San Marco, Venice, for example), set a new precedent in crusader brutality toward Christians. Possession of the city then permitted Doge Andrea Dandolo and the crusaders to implement their planned division of the empire; Baldwin of Flanders was elected Latin Emperor of Constantinople, while all the possessions of the Orthodox patriarch were assigned to Venice. Booty was divided and lands allotted to the crusader knights, who set out eagerly to conquer them. Mainland Greece and the islands thus became the preserve of a variety of Western rulers, most of them feudal vassals of the Latin emperor, or of the Lombard Boniface of Montferrat (who had married the Emperor Isaac II's widow).

Opposition to the crusaders was led by local Greek *archontes*, Leon Sgouros in Corinth and Nauplion, and the chief families of cities like Monemvasia in the far south. Only in Epiros, however, was an independent Greek state established by Michael Komnenos Doukas, cousin of the Emperors Alexios III and Isaac II. In the Peloponnese the Burgundians

Guillaume de Champlitte and Geoffroi de Villehardouin succeeded in imposing their own authority, forming the principality of Achaia in an area that had been given to Venice in the partition plan. The Venetians concentrated initially on gaining firm possession of those ports and harbors in the Ionian and Aegean seas which would guarantee their commercial dominance. Most importantly, Marco Sanudo assumed the title "duke of the Archipelago," and set up his own Venetian authority in the Aegean, from which west/east shipping could be regulated.

At a gathering held in Ravennika in 1209 the occupying forces reviewed their position and reaffirmed their loyalty to the Latin emperor, Henri de Hainault (1206–16). Boniface was already dead, killed in a battle with the Bulgars (1207); control in the Thessalonike region remained tenuous rather than firm and would be largely destroyed in 1224 when Theodore, despot of Epiros, recaptured it. But in central and southern Greece, Othon de la Roche, Nicolas de St. Omer (a newcomer), and Geoffroi de Villehardouin had established principalities that would endure through most of the fourteenth century. In Thebes, Athens, and Clermont (the site chosen by Geoffroi for the capital of Achaia) crusader culture intermingled with that of the occupied Greeks to form a flourishing hybrid, aware and relatively tolerant of the differences between Greek and Latin, Orthodox and Catholic, eastern imperial and western feudal traditions.

The scene was thus set for a complex development of political, military, and economic rivalry, with crusader princes, Byzantine emperors and despots, and Venetian dukes as the main protagonists. In 1261 Constantinople was recaptured by Michael Palaiologos (emperor 1259–82), thus effectively removing the claims of Epiros to represent Byzantium. Imperial authority was quickly established in northern Greece, Thessalonike again serving as the administrative center, and in 1263 Michael VIII sent his brother Constantine to recapture several fortresses in Achaia (Morea). The Greek residents, of Monemvasia in particular, assisted in reoccupation of parts of the Peloponnese, which resulted in the Byzantine province (later despotate) of Mistra. Meanwhile, to counter Venetian domination in the east Mediterranean, the emperor granted extensive privileges to the Genoese, who effectively monopolized Black Sea trade from their important base in Pera/Galata (Constantinople).

Venice, however, remained entrenched in Greece and even extended its authority during the fourteenth century—taking Pteleon in 1323; Cerigo (Kythera) in 1363; Argos, Nauplion, and Corfu in the 1380s; and Tinos and Mykonos from 1390. (Cyprus was added in 1489.) In some of these colonies Venetian control was still exercized in the eighteenth century—Cerigo and Corfu only becoming briefly part of the Ottoman Empire in 1917.

THE FINAL ACT

The Turkish advance had been felt in mainland Greece centuries before, as Moslem pirates from Anatolia harassed mercantile activity, raided coastal towns, and took prisoners among the local Greek population. Acre, the last stronghold of the Latin kingdom of Jerusalem, was stormed by the Mamluk Sultan, al-Asraf, in 1291. And thirty-five years later (1326), the Ottoman Turks captured Bursa in western Asia Minor and made it their capital. The Byzantine Empire was therefore much less extensive in the late thirteenth century than in the twelfth century, and was progressively reduced in the east, regular contact with the independent empire of Trebizond being lost by the Turkish conquests.

From 1353, when they crossed the Dardanelles and captured Gallipoli, the Turks of Bursa had a European center from which to direct their conquest of the Balkans and Greece. Leaving Constantinople in an isolated position, Murad I, the first Ottoman ruler to use the title Sultan (1359–89), pursued a westward thrust into Thrace against both Byzantine and Serbian authorities. He forced the Byzantine emperor, John V, to campaign with him. His son Bayezid I accomplished the conquest both of other Turkish principalities in Anatolia and of Bulgaria (1393), but when the Mongol forces of Timur (Tamerlane) advanced from Samarkand and defeated Bayezid at Ankara (1402), Ottoman authority in Anatolia was destroyed, making the European capital at Adrianople (Edirne) a city of great significance.

It was from this base that the final Turkish assault on Byzantium was launched, the campaign that resulted eventually in the fall of Constantinople (1453) and the conversion of Hagia Sophia to a mosque. All those who had a stake in the empire had long realized that they had to fight or come to terms with the forces of Islam. Encouraged by Pope Eugenius IV, a crusading movement had sailed from Venice in June 1444, only to be crushingly defeated by Murad II. Venice itself made peace and offered tribute in order to preserve at least some colonies in the east, but the rest of Greece remained open to the conqueror.

In 1446 Murad embarked on this campaign, breaching the newly fortified defenses at the Isthmus of Corinth and forcing the two despots of Mistra and Patras—Demetrios and Constantine—to flee. All of central Greece, including Corinth and Patras, was subjected in this attack. A revolt against Turkish authority in Albania, led by George Castriota (Iskender Bey or "Skanderbeg") was successful for a brief period and was supported by dissident Greeks in the Morea. But the momentum of the Ottoman advance was not to be checked. Despite Genoese assistance, the Byzantine capital was taken (1453) and the Albanian revolt suppressed. The last despots of Mistra (Thomas and Demetrios, brothers of Constantine XI, the final Byzantine emperor) were effectively tributaries of the Sultan, then vassals, and, finally, were forced into exile (1460). Apart from a few Venetian colonies, the whole world of Greece had been incorporated into the Ottoman Empire.

This brief sketch must suffice as an outline of Byzantine history from the death of Justinian in 565 to the fall of Constantinople in 1453. To offer any meaningful generalization on the political and religious structure, the culture and thought of a period of nearly 900 years is not easy, but in the pages that follow the nature of the Byzantine state as a whole will be discussed, concentrating specifically on the story of Greece during the vital period when it was laboriously and painfully restored to the Byzantine world, and concluding with a necessarily condensed account of some of the larger issues—economic, social, and cultural—that affected Greece in common with the rest of the empire.

Byzantium—A Medieval Theocracy

As heir to both ancient Greece and Rome, the Byzantine Empire preserved the Hellenic culture of the former and the imperial organization—military, legal, and administrative—of the latter. In addition, however, by promoting the Christian faith to an absolute dominance within Byzantine society, these ancient traditions were further transformed to serve a medieval purpose. Under the leadership of "the most pious, Christ-loving emperors" (as they were styled), pagans, Jews, nonbelievers, schismatics, and heretics were all subjected to the full weight of official attempts to impose uniformity of belief. Although patriarchs claimed an independent control in the ecclesiastical domain, emperors continued to intervene in church affairs, debating theological problems, defining dogma, presiding over ecumenical councils, and deposing and appointing clergy at will. So while secular rulers ceded the ritual functions of *pontifex maximus* to ecclesiastics (normally the patriarchs of Constantinople), they retained nearly all the authority implied by the ancient title. Only in matters relating to moral standards and the application of canon law could the church overrule an emperor, as Nicolas Mystikos (Patriarch, 901–7) tried to do over Leo VI's fourth marriage. And even then he was unsuccessful.

Church and state were therefore intimately connected through their dual administration and hierarchies, which culminated in the patriarchal chancellery and imperial court. A double network of control spreading outward from Constantinople established representatives of each throughout the empire—metropolitans in charge of ecclesiastical dioceses, military and civilian officials with responsibility for provincial administration. Normally the two collaborated to ensure that central policy was thoroughly enforced. But there were always gray areas and local elements that escaped such rigorous control—in the form of pirates, bandits, soothsayers, or holy men, who maintained a limited independence. Their activities occasionally led to open revolt—as in the case of Thomas the Slav, whose ascent to the throne had been predicted by an Anatolian monk—but usually they coexisted under nominal imperial rule, a thorn in the flesh of local bishops and administrators. Naturally the network was most efficient in the capital, where the presence of crack troops (the *tagmata*) and police (under the city prefect, the *eparch*) deterred opposition, and grew progressively weaker as the distance from Constantinople increased. In frontier areas this structural weakness permitted adventurers as well as heretics to flourish, as the epic stories of Digenes Akritas reveal.

GREECE RECLAIMED FOR BYZANTIUM

In Greece itself this frontier mentality remained a permanent feature of certain mountainous areas even after imperial rule was reestablished: the northern Rhodopes (straddling the border with medieval Bulgaria), parts of the Pindos settled by Vlachs, and areas of the Taygetos range in the southern Peloponnese, where Slavonic tribes maintained their separate identity into the tenth century. But from the reign of Nikephoros I (802–11) onward, the pattern of dual control was enshrined, with the clear aim of maintaining uniformity of administration and belief. It had taken an exceptionally long time to win back the provinces of Greece, because Slavonic tribes continued to move south during the seventh and eighth centuries, filling every void in imperial authority, sometimes in alliance with other antagonistic forces—Arab, Bulgar, or internal rebel.

The first stage of reconquest involved limited military actions against specific targets, often Slav settlements in Thrace and Macedonia. In 657/68 Constans II campaigned in this region. Five years later he successfully marched a considerable imperial force through Thessalonike, Athens (where they wintered in 662/63), and Patras, where the emperor embarked for Sicily in his ill-fated attempt to move the imperial capital back to the west. (He was murdered in his bath in the palace at Syracuse in 668.) His son, Constantine IV, also attempted to check the ravages of Bulgar tribes in Thrace, an important grain-producing area of increasing significance to Constantinople as supplies from Egypt declined (due to the Arab occupation of the 640s). A further campaign in 688 by Justinian II succeeded in clearing the main route from Constantinople to the west (the Via Egnatia) of Slavonic settlements. The emperor was welcomed into Thessalonike in triumph and celebrated by granting privileges to the city and its churches. The success was only partial, however, for the western sector of the Via Egnatia, which ran through the Balkans to Dyrrachion on the Adriatic and had formerly provided the chief method of communication with Italy, had passed irretrievably out of imperial control. For many centuries Slavonic settlements would render this route unusable.

The second stage of reconquest developed from the campaigns of the first, as permanent forces of occupation were established under Byzantine control. Thrace was the first of the European *themata*—it is recorded together with the four Asian ones in a letter of Justinian II to Pope John V sent in 687. Probably created after the Bulgarian incursions of 679, which routed the Byzantine cavalry and caused serious damage, it became the major base for operations against these hostile forces to the north, for instance during Justinian II's campaign of 706.

Hellas was the next *thema* to be set up; it comprised the area of central Greece and Thessaly. The first mention of its *strategos* (military governor) occurs in 695. Some military and naval forces were attached to the new province, for in 727 Agallianos, a subordinate officer (*tourmarches*), led a detachment of local people (*Helladikoi*) in an unsuccessful attempt to replace Leo III by their own imperial candidate. The civilian aspect of provincial administration in Hellas may be deduced from the existence of seals belonging to the officials responsible: for example, that of a *protonotarios*, Nikephoros (dated to the eighth or ninth century). The *protonotarios* supervised the surveys of land and population on which tax returns were based. The seals of customs and excise officers (*kommerkiarioi*) may not reflect provincial administration, but certainly imply an imperial presence in the region. *Thema* administration was probably facilitated by a policy of Constantine V introduced in the 750s. Constantinople, like Greece, had been attacked by an outbreak of plague and its population reduced. To increase the number of inhabitants, people from the islands, Hellas, and the *katotika mere* (Peloponnese) were moved to the capital. Ten years later the decision to restore the major aqueduct of the metropolis involved a similar procedure: construction workers were summoned from all parts of the empire, including 500 potters from Hellas and the islands and 5,000 workmen and 200 ceramic craftsmen from Hellas and Thrace. Such directions could not have been implemented had not there been a definite degree of imperial control in the European provinces. A further indication of such control may be deduced the fact that both Thessalonike and Kephalonia served as places of exile in the early eighth century.

THE EMPIRE OF THE CHURCH

The process of restoring imperial control in Greece was also assisted by a reorganization of the church. Until the early eighth century the ecclesiastical diocese of East Illyricum, which included the entire Balkan peninsula, the Aegean islands, Crete, Sicily, and southern Italy, had formed part of the territory of the west and fell under Roman control. Popes maintained their own vicars in Thessalonike (normally metropolitans of that city) and exercised certain rights of jurisdiction within the diocese. In 668, for instance, the bishop of Lappa (Crete) appealed to Pope Vitalian against his deposition by a local synod. The pope judged the decision uncanonical and ordered the metropolitan, Paul of Gortyna, to reinstate the bishop and to hand back two monasteries wrongly removed from his control. Similarly, disputes over the see of Larissa and among its suffragan clergy were resolved by appeal to Rome. Under Leo III (717–41) this somewhat anomalous situation was altered by the emperor's unilateral decision to place the diocese of East Illyricum under Constantinople. Church leaders were thereby brought into much closer contact with the capital, and the patriarch gained a firmer say in the ecclesiastical organization of Greece—both in elections and in disputes; appeals were henceforth directed to Constantinople not Rome. Later popes, notably Nicholas I (858–67), greatly resented this imperial coup, which deprived them of a good deal of revenue from church patrimonies, as well as the right, for example, to nominate the metropolitans of Syracuse. In Greece, however, the change stimulated a rapid growth of episcopal sees, from about 18 bishops (recorded in the late seventh century) to the 46 who attended the Council of 787. This not only increased the Christian presence, especially important at inland sites previously occupied by Slavs, but also involved greater communication between the metropolis and provincial cities.

A further significant bond was established in 768 by the marriage of Irene, a member of the Sarandapechys family of Athens, to the son of Constantine V, the future Leo IV (775–80); this united a local family from Hellas with the ruling dynasty. Although Irene is most renowned for the restoration of icon veneration by the second Council of Nicaea (787), her attention to Greece was of equal importance. Members of her family were favored with imperial appointments and involved in the detention and blinding of political rivals held in exile in Greece. In 783 her general, Stavrakios, was sent on the first major expedition against Slav communities in the Peloponnese. His victory was celebrated in a ceremonial triumph at Constantinople and an imperial tour in the following year to Berroia in Thrace (Stara Zagora). In classical fashion the city was renamed Irenopolis after the empress, who observed the Byzantine reconquest from her litter. Macedonia became a separate *thema* between 789 and 802. The return of imperial authority was commemorated in the rebuilding of Hagia Sophia, Thessalonike, which Irene and her son, Constantine VI, endowed with new mosaics. Finally, at the empress's insistence, Athens was raised to metropolitan status and thus given the same rank as Thessalonike and Corinth, the two established archiepiscopal sees in Greece.

Although Irene's successor, Nikephoros I (802–11), is not known to have shared her personal commitment, he did continue the work of pacification in the Peloponnese. When Patras was threatened, the emperor sent imperial forces under a *strategos* to relieve the city. It was rebuilt, repopulated and promoted to a metropolitan see. The *thema* administration of the Peloponnese probably dates from his reign. Greek communities then returned from southern Italy and Sicily to the region—the family of Athanasios, later bishop of Methone, moved back to Patras in about 826. Greek-speaking Christians from other parts of the empire were also transplanted to the *Sklaviniai* (Slav settlements in Greece) and the Peloponnese to support the process of "byzantinization." This forced movement of population was another imperial method of consolidating control. With imperial aid the churches of Lakedaimonia were reconstructed and bishoprics were established in Lakedaimonia, Korone, and Methone.

AN INTEGRATED STATE

Nikephoros also adopted a novel method designed to integrate the Slavs into Byzantine society. After their defeat at Patras in about 807, he issued a chrysobull (golden charter) setting out the conditions for their continued residence in Patras. All their property, wealth, and children were given in perpetuity to the cathedral church of the city, dedicated to its patron, St. Andrew. As servants of the saint, the Slavs were to maintain the governor's residence (where imperial agents, distinguished visitors, and envoys from abroad might stay). While the metropolitans of Patras were forbidden to interfere in these arrangements, their tenth-century successors clearly did, and Leo VI (886–912) had to issue another charter specifying the duties and the autonomy of the cathedral servants.

Similar methods were used by Michael III (843–67) after the Slav revolt of 840–42, in which two tribes in the southern Peloponnese played a prominent part. The Melingoi and Ezeritai were forced to pay an annual tribute of 60 and 300 gold coins (*nomismata*), respectively. And 80 years later, when they began to act in a thoroughly independent fashion, refusing to obey the governor, to perform military or other public duties, or to pay the tribute, another campaign was launched. After a decisive Byzantine victory by the *strategos*, Krinites Arotras, in ca. 921, 600 *nomismata* each was fixed as a new level of payment. But on their appeal to Romanos I (920–44) the old sums were restored and confirmed in a new chrysobull. One reason for the apparent climb-down by imperial officials was that an incursion of Bulgars in 922 threatened the Peloponnese, and it was deemed essential to prevent any alliance between the newcomers and the Melingoi and Ezeritai. So even in the tenth century imperial authority was regularly disturbed. Nonetheless, the arrangements set out in the charters appear to have been largely successful; they permitted the gradual incorporation of the Slavs into imperial society.

Less official but equally effective methods of integration arose from the trading contacts between the Slavs and the indigenous population. In the fourth century such activity across the Danube frontier had familiarized the Visigoths with Roman customs and Christian beliefs. During the "Dark Ages" it once again became a factor of importance, as the Slavs settled to agricultural occupations and sought to exchange their crops for objects of Byzantine manufacture. In the course of one of the many sieges of Thessalonike that occurred in the seventh century, the inhabitants sent an embassy to a Slav tribe in Thessaly, and successfully purchased corn from them. Similarly, at the end of the ninth century John Kameniates describes the relations between Greeks and Slavs near Thessalonike. Around Berroia Slavs traded with local inhabitants and brought fish to sell in Thessalonike. They made profits and cooperated with the city people. Some lived in mixed villages such as those that were already established near Patras prior to the great siege of ca. 807. But in contrast to the Slavs of the Peloponnese, the Slavonic tribes had all adopted Christianity by John's time. Yet he insists that it was through commercial activity that Greek and Slav became familiar and learned to live in the same villages.

Not all economic activity was purely spontaneous, however. From the eighth century onward emperors appointed *kommerkiarioi* to collect the customs and excise dues on the sale and transport of goods. Bronze coinage was also struck by imperial mints at Thessalonike, Corinth, and possibly another in central Greece, at Patras, Thebes, or Athens. Archaeological finds tend to confirm the impression that imperial coinage circulated more widely in Greece from the reign of Theophilos (829–42). In this way local exchange was regulated and long-distance commerce taxed by imperial agents while the Slavs were gradually drawn into a commercial network based on a monetary economy and an urban way of life. Increasing supplies of silver and bronze coins satisfied the economic expansion of the eleventh and twelfth centuries, some of the smaller denominations being produced for central Greece probably at Thebes. Gold tended to be restricted to a cyclical movement through the Byzantine provinces: it went out in the form of soldiers' pay and was returned to the capital as taxation (such as the tribute paid by the Melingoi and Ezeritai). Only when hoarded for a particular purpose (marriage dowry, for instance) does any quantity of gold appear in provincial finds.

The chief means of incorporation, however, was neither political nor economic but religious. It was through a combination of official and unofficial missionary work that the Slavs were converted to Christianity—a development that probably did more than anything else to transform them into Byzantine citizens. The construction of numerous new churches, frequently at sites apparently unconnected with episcopal activity, confirms the spontaneous and local initiative behind such building. Ecclesiastical complexes grew up around monastic retreats and tombs of holy men such as St. Nikon of Lakedaimonia or Hosios Lukas (Holy Luke) of Steiris (near Delphi). In the case of one particularly fine monument, the great domed church of the Virgin at Skripou (near Lamia), Leo the *protospatharios*, a military official, is known as patron. He probably served in the *thema* administration in central Greece, for which he was rewarded with lands near Lake Kopais. These formed the basis of his local property, on which his church and attached monastery were built in 873/74. Perhaps like many officials with sufficient means he wished to retire to the monastic community when his active military service ended.

While private foundations of this type account for a good deal of Byzantine ecclesiastical building, at both Skripou and Steiris a quite exceptional initiative in both architecture and decoration is observable. The earlier church was adorned with particularly fine sculptures that appear to indicate the existence of a team of skilled local carvers. Their work can be traced in later monuments, extending as far west as Corfu, and including the twin churches at Steiris. At these eleventh-century foundations, however, expertise in stone sculpture is matched by unusual decoration in carved tiles, fresco, and mosaic. These monuments established a distinctive school of Middle Byzantine architecture, responsible for many important churches of the eleventh to thirteenth centuries. Those at Daphni (near Athens), in the Argolid, Messenia, Epiros, and at Kastoria reflect the wide dissemination and development of this independent style in Byzantine art. And it was in these magnificent surroundings that the hellenized Slavs and medieval Greeks forgot their origins in a common devotion to their faith.

From the reign of Nikephoros I, therefore, *thema* administration appears to have been securely established in parts of Greece and would cover the entire region by the end of the ninth century. Dyrrachion and Kephalonia became separate provinces by 809; Thessalonike between 796 and 824; the Aegean and Samos (both specifically naval units) in 843 and 899, respectively; Nicopolis and Strymon are also first mentioned in 899. Ecclesiastical control was similarly extended, with a large number of new sees being created in remoter inland sites—Bolaina, Zemaina, and Maina in the Peloponnese, and Stagoi, Loidorikion, Ezeros, and Trikkis in Thessaly, for example. Other bishoprics were established on islands such as Corfu, Zakynthos, Leukas, Skopelos, and Aigina. Through a number of mechanisms the mixed population of Greece was being integrated and unified.

These achievements did not remove the threat of revolt, whether by Slavs subjected to imperial rule, by Bulgars and Arabs from beyond the frontiers, or by disaffected sectors of the local population. In the 790s the sons of Constantine V, banished to central Greece for conspiring against their nephew, the young Emperor Constantine VI, received support from Greeks as well as from the Slavs of Belzetia in their unsuccessful revolt. Arab pirates were active in at least one attack on Patras (ca. 807) and became a menace to the entire Aegean after their capture of Crete in 827.

Two years later the population of Aigina was forced to flee; at the end of the century Demetrias, on the Gulf of Volos, was captured and occupied (897–902), and in 904 Thessalonike was sacked. This hostility was subsequently contained by Byzantine campaigns to recapture Crete, which finally succeeded in 961.

Throughout the tenth century, however, Bulgar inroads disturbed the empire. In 917/18 Tsar Symeon raided as far south as the Isthmus of Corinth, after inflicting a serious defeat on imperial forces near Anchialos, on the Black Sea. He even besieged Constantinople (without success). Another raid into central Greece in 943 made it necessary for Holy Luke to leave his ascetic retreat for a more inaccessible one. And in the 980s Larissa, a well-fortified stronghold, was plundered by Tsar Samuel, who removed the precious relics of St. Achilleos.

To put an end to this continuous instability, Basil II (998–1025) directed several campaigns against the Bulgars with the aim of incorporating their independent state within the empire. His victories and reprisals earned him the nickname *Boulgaroktonos*, "the Bulgar-slayer." After a long struggle Byzantine forces defeated Samuel's in the Struma Valley (1014) and imposed a terrible punishment on the vanquished: 99 out of every 100 survivors were blinded; the last retained the sight of one eye to guide the rest back home. The arrival of this unseeing procession is said to have caused the tsar's death. Basil reorganized imperial administration in Kastoria, Serbia, and Berroia, creating three small *themata* to protect the western approaches to Thessalonike, and established direct rule in Bulgaria proper. After the final victory in 1016 he made a special pilgrimage to Athens, to give thanks in the church of the Virgin on the Acropolis (the converted Parthenon). He endowed it with new plate and ecclesiastical decorations and confirmed its privileges as a metropolitan see. The spectacular silk hanging (now known as the Gunther silk because it was used as the shroud of Bishop Gunther of Bamberg in the eleventh century) may have been woven to commemorate this visit. It depicts a mounted horseman flanked by the symbolic representations of cities—Constantinople and Athens—in female form.

This was the last direct military intervention by a Byzantine emperor in the provinces of Greece. Subsequent revolts were dealt with by governors or generals dispatched from the capital. But it was by no means the last instance of imperial patronage, which had already created many major monuments of Byzantine art in Greece. For later in the eleventh century Constantine IX Monomachos constructed an enormous new basilica over the holy spring at Nea Moni on Chios. The mosaics of the

New Monastery brought to the Aegean islands that style of metropolitan art then being exported to Kiev, Jerusalem, Venice, Torcello, Palermo, and Cefalù (to name only the most important sites graced with Byzantine mosaics). Throughout the twelfth century imperial patronage consolidated the monastic foundations of Mount Athos, extending their properties and privileges in charters. The same pattern of endowment encouraged the later Byzantine communities of Meteora, Mistra, and Monemvasia, while provincial officials and local notables emulated the imperial style of patronage in their own churches and monasteries. The well-documented monastic complex at Bačkovo (northern Macedonia), established by the Georgian aristocrat, Pakourianos, illustrates the wealth that might be transferred to ecclesiastical institutions in this way. Similarly, thirteenth-century Serbian and Bulgar princes commemorated their own Christian faith in foundations such as Mileševa (King Vladislav, 1235) and Boiana (Tsar Kaloyan, 1259). Metropolitan artists or local artists trained in the style of the capital were employed to execute the fine frescos that adorned these churches. In their thoroughly Byzantine celebration of orthodoxy, the erstwhile enemies of the empire revealed what a complete integration had taken place over the centuries. As in so many other cases (Russia, Venice, the south Italian trading communities, for instance), the Hellenic culture of medieval Byzantium won allies and devotees through its artistic skills.

Byzantine Economy and Society

The material base for this flourishing provincial society lay in the village communities of Greece, which developed during the poorly documented period from AD 600–900. As in Roman times, rural and agricultural property continued to be the most significant source of personal wealth, but its distribution was completely altered by the breakdown of traditional patterns of cultivation. The villas and extensive private estates, typical of Late Antiquity, began to collapse under the impact of Slavonic incursions and the failure of Justinianic administration, and were replaced by smaller and more collective forms of agriculture. From the Farmers' Law (late seventh or early eighth century) and the fragmentary tax-rolls of Thebes and Athens (late eleventh and twelfth centuries), it is possible to reconstruct the new village system that developed.

The organization of the village, as reflected in the Farmers' Law, was structured round a collective responsibility for the total land tax paid to the central treasury. Villagers farmed the surrounding land in strip cultivation. Individual members owned strips (on which their tax contribution was assessed), rented land from their neighbors, or in turn rented out their land to others; all shared in the communal grazing and facilities like watermills, ovens, and wine and olive presses. Stringent regulations governed situations that might cause friction between members, such as the straying of flocks into vineyards or cornfields, or the killing of a sheep dog. This possibly idealized picture of rural life is not identified with any particular area; the Farmers' Law is ubiquitous and universal, and probably sprang from an experience common to all parts of the empire. Because the village combined two essential functions, cultivation and self-government, this form of settlement was used to establish foreigners (such as the Mardaites from Syria), prisoners-of-war, and populations transplanted to different provinces. Such villages were later incorporated into *thema* institutions, although their autonomy was sometimes threatened by the centralized control of government agents.

Nonetheless, after three or four centuries the tax-rolls of Thebes and Athens confirm the persistence of scattered land ownership and strip cultivation. As these are basically fiscal records, revised every twenty-five years to list the taxes due on each strip, they provide evidence of each owner's resources: his titles, family, property, and livestock. They thus indicate changes in land ownership through inheritance, sale, gift, or exchange, which in turn make it possible to trace variations in family fortunes. While one might prosper and acquire additional land, another could find itself unable to cultivate its strips and be forced to sell them. Gradually, such differences resulted in extremes of poverty and wealth—creating the opposition between poor and rich well known to Byzantines. The Theban records, in particular, reveal the economic base of richer families: from increased land ownership and rents they were able to move from a village to a town, where they built houses and obtained posts in local administration. Samuel Gerontas commanded a small detachment of the local militia as *drouggarios* and lived in Thebes, although his strips were far away. Similarly, a member of the Pothos family had become a monk in Euripos. In contrast, one of the villagers had become so poor that he was qualified as *ptochos* (destitute) and was probably unable to pay any taxes. Such a process of differentiation lies behind the emergence of identifiable local families such as the Sarandapechys, from whose ranks Irene rose to be empress, or the Pardos and Chalkoutzes, who had been settled in central Greece for many years. The source of their power stemmed from their considerable control of landed property.

Emperors, however, tried repeatedly to check the domination of these families (called *dynatoi*, powerful) by legislation designed to protect the less powerful and to maintain a more equitable distribution of village lands. But they were unsuccessful. A combination of factors, not least the imperial use of land grants as a reward for military service, permitted certain families to form a provincial aristocracy. The Xeros family of Lakedaimonia, the Kamateroi of central Greece, or Choirosphaktoi of Thessaly were part of an indigenous nobility, which then intermarried with representatives of the Anatolian *dynatoi* settled in the west, the Tornikai, Kantakouzenoi, and Branades, for instance. By the time of the Fourth Crusade the countryside was divided between such families (who enjoyed tax exemptions and other privileges), while the surviving village communities were expected to bear an increasing tax burden.

Imperial concern for the weaker members of village communities was not a purely philanthropic matter, whatever rhetoric might be used in the preamble of such laws; it sprang from the need to maintain a taxpaying capacity throughout the empire. Since local notables frequently obtained imperial titles and administrative positions that carried an immunity from certain taxes, it was essential to preserve the village communities that remained collectively responsible for the basic one—the direct tax on land. They were also forced to make contributions toward the upkeep of public services—castles, roads, bridges, and so on—as well as payments for military defense and the governor's expenses (a much abused privilege). During the eleventh century, when a number of such taxes in kind and *corvées* (in the form of labor services or the provision of food and transport animals for the governor) were commuted to money payments, the entire population of Epiros (the *thema* of Nicopolis) rose in revolt. Their antagonism was directed especially against John Kontzomytes, the *praktor* (chief tax collector) whose method of commutation had resulted in excessive sums, harshly extracted. A generation later, in 1066, even the Vlachs (transhumant shepherds of the Pindos range) joined in a more serious rebellion against a new tax. Nikoulitzas, a local leader, was elected to represent the Thessalians at court and obtained a remission, whereupon a deputation of Vlachs and inhabitants of Larissa accompanied him to Constantinople to express their appreciation. Such extreme opposition to treasury demands heralds a new phase in the underlying hostility between capital and province. It also reveals the degree of autonomy exercised by individual officials, which might well border on an intolerable degree of exploitation.

That these changes sprang from an economic crisis at the heart of the empire is clear from the accompanying devaluation of the gold coinage.

For close on 700 years the Constantinian gold *solidus* (in Greek, *nomisma*) had maintained its dominance. As a reliable currency, it exercised a profound influence in the medieval west, draining gold from all available sources and leaving silver as the supreme precious metal there. The power of Byzantine gold can be traced through hoards excavated over a wide area of European Russia, Scandinavia, and throughout the west. Many had found their way to such findspots as pay packets for mercenary soldiers, notably the Varangians (Norsemen from Scandinavia who traveled to Byzantium through Kievan Russia and served as a special imperial bodyguard). From the reign of Constantine IX (1042–55) this gold coinage was debased by the introduction of silver alloys that reduced both its value and fineness. As a measure intended to spare the treasury much needed funds for the increasing demands of military activity against the Turks in Asia Minor, devaluation may have been temporarily successful. But in the long term it had disastrous results, which eventually permitted the new gold currencies of Italian city-states to replace the Byzantine *nomisma* as the most acceptable trading coin.

The overall economic crisis of the eleventh century arose from a series of pressures, military, political, and economic, that placed enormous strains on the imperial system. In an empire that ran most industry as a state monopoly and kept a tight control over all commercial transactions, urban resources could never compete with rural ones. Employment in the imperial administration and the purchase of court sinecures might enable the wealthy to reside in the capital, but ownership of land provided the essential base. So it is hardly surprising that the empire found itself in financial difficulties when its land base began to be eroded. Military failures to maintain the expanded eastern frontier were matched by a rapid Seljuk advance into Anatolia after the Battle of Mantzikert (1071). Simultaneously, more of the remaining agricultural land passed out of imperial and village control into the hands of tax-exempt individuals.

Such a reduction in rural resources might have been balanced by an increase in urban profits from trade, for Byzantine cities recovered and prospered from the tenth century onward. But the restrictive nature of imperial control of commerce effectively prevented this. An urban bourgeoisie comparable to the Islamic and Jewish middle classes of medieval cities of the east Mediterranean was inconceivable in Byzantium. Instead, strict regulations over all guild activity in the capital (recorded in the tenth-century *Book of the Eparch*) stifled economic initiatives. In particular, the production of luxury goods exported or presented as diplomatic gifts to foreign potentates, especially silk, remained a state preserve. In Greece the results of this imperial stranglehold can be seen in different fields. As silk was one of the prestige manufactures of Greece, the cultivation of mulberries and weaving of cloth played an important part in the local economy, for instance, in Stagoi (in Thessaly). Regrettably, very little is known of the organization of this crop, though documents from southern Italy may be typical of provincial silk production. Carpets and other woven materials, some embroidered with gold thread, appear to have constituted a second valuable sector of Greek production. Such activity implies increased trade and prosperity for the region, which was reflected in the annual fairs held on local saints' days, for example, of St. Spiridon at Corfu and St. Demetrios at Thessalonike. From accounts preserved by twelfth-century travelers, such as the anonymous Cappadocian author who visited Thessalonike and described local events in the *Timarion*, or the diary of Benjamin of Tudela, it is clear that Greece was prosperous. To some observers, however, the central administration appeared to drain local wealth away from the provinces to the metropolis. As Michael Choniates, bishop of Athens (1182–1205), complained:

> What do you (in Constantinople) lack? Not the wheat-bearing plains of Macedonia, Thrace and Thessaly, which are farmed by us; nor the wine of Ptelion, Chios and Rhodes, pressed by us; nor the fine garments woven by our Theban and Corinthian fingers, nor all our wealth, which flows, as many rivers flow into one sea, to the Queen City.

This policy of extraction, combined with a traditional determination to manage all aspects of the economy, impoverished and limited provincial life. It was also consonant with the imperial habit of balancing the budget through currency manipulation and tax reform. By these methods the twelfth-century dynasties of Komnenos and Angelos attempted to tap the growing wealth of Greece.

Their efforts were hampered by local opposition that increasingly took the form of separatist movements, led by local notables such as Leo Sgouros in Corinth in 1203. Other prominent families (*archontes*) or castle inhabitants (*kastrenoi*) participated in revolts to establish independent principalities. This splintering prefigured the post-1205 division of Greece among crusader knights, in the same way that growing social stratification among the rural population prepared it for feudal relations. Although the distinction between rich and poor had arisen from entirely different processes, it produced a strange effect when taken in conjunction with the disintegration of imperial control and appearance of local rulers: the poorer inhabitants of Greece had been assimilated to a position similar to that of western medieval serfs.

The mixed crusading society documented by the fourteenth-century *Assizes of Romania* reveals how western social relations had been introduced to the Morea. But in Thrace and Macedonia apparently similar institutions developed within the imperial framework. Village communities continued to exist as before but many of their members sought the patronage and protection of aristocratic landowners or large monasteries. As dependent laborers (*paroikoi*) they then paid their taxes to the state via intermediary *dynatoi*. These changes were a natural consequence of the pressure of the powerful and the imperial failure to preserve a free peasantry.

During the civil war of 1341–47 the anti-aristocratic faction of Zealots seized control of Thessalonike, proclaimed its independence and opened a campaign against the local nobility. Although the commune of Thessalonike drew on popular peasant support in a rare example of political democracy in Byzantium, it was destined to fail. A firmly aristocratic administration was reestablished by the coronation of John VI Kantakouzenos (1347) as emperor and regent for John V Palaiologos (reigned 1354–91). For the peasantry, however, the civil war, Zealot commune, and expansion of Serbian domination in the Balkans brought little change. They remained the serfs of feudal landowners, chiefly monastic. A similar dependence on ecclesiastical patronage is clearly visible throughout Greece. The monasteries of Meteora in Thessaly, constructed from the fourteenth century onward, and of Mistra and Mega Spelaion in the Peloponnese, occupied a privileged place in Late Byzantine society. And it was these ecclesiastical institutions—now strengthened by the patronage of Russian, Georgian Serbian, and other non-Greek Orthodox—that survived the Ottoman conquest.

BYZANTINE CULTURE

Throughout the Byzantine world, intellectual activities declined during the seventh and early eighth centuries. In education even the schools of Constantinople failed to provide an adequate training, and students sought out the few individuals who maintained the old traditions. One of these, Tychikos, gave instructions in Trebizond; another (unnamed) on the island of Andros. It was to the latter that Leo "the Mathematician" turned for lessons in rhetoric, philosophy, and arithmetic in the early

ninth century. And when he had mastered the principles of these disciplines, Leo pursued his interest in ancient wisdom in the monasteries of
Andros (and in mainland Greece, probably). Classical manuscripts, therefore, were to be found in religious communities, an indication of the shift
of intellectual work into the ecclesiastical domain. Despite the church's
hostility to aspects of ancient learning, such manuscripts continued to be
copied, studied, and annotated by clerics to the end of the empire and
beyond.

During the "Dark Ages," however, there is little evidence of manuscript production, profane or spiritual. Threatened by the rapid expansion of Islam, both empire and church fought to survive. And it was in
the struggle with the Muslims (who observed the prohibition of graven
images) that the rejection of icons attained a popular support and an imperial champion in the person of Leo III (717–41). Iconoclasm developed
in reaction to the veneration of these pictures of divine and saintly figures, which had assumed a central position in Christian worship. While
the iconoclast party felt that only the removal and destruction of icons
would prevent idolatry and return the church to the observance of Old
Testament law, the iconophiles justified the cult as a long-established
Christian tradition. Because Leo III came from the eastern frontier region
and Empress Irene, who restored icon veneration in 787, was a native of
Greece, a polarity between the iconoclast east and iconophile west has
often been assumed. But there is insufficient evidence to justify this dichotomy; supporters and detractors of icons can be found in most parts.
A more interesting aspect of the iconoclast debate lies in the stimulus
it provided for intellectual work and for closer relations between the
iconophile party and the church of Rome. Both sides plundered the Bible
and patristic writings for arguments in favor of their views; they traveled
(often illicitly) between isolated communities to give encouragement, and
composed tracts against each other. In the journeys of St. Gregory the
Dekapolite and the correspondence of St. Theodore of the Stoudios monastery in Constantinople, an iconophile network stretched beyond the
empire (evidence for a comparable iconoclast organization was destroyed
after 843). The Byzantine cursive script (minuscule), which evolved at the
turn of the eighth–ninth centuries, was a lasting result.

In Greece itself indirect evidence for iconophile sympathies is found in
Thessalonike, where the sixth-century mosaic of Ezekiel's Vision in the
apse of Hosios David was boarded up for protection. When other figural
representations were destroyed, this one was saved and still exists today.
Official iconoclasm in the same city is marked by traces of a monumental

cross in the apse of St. Sophia. Thessalonike was obviously a center of intellectual aspiration, for it was here that Constantine (later St. Cyril) and his brother Methodios received their elementary schooling and knowledge of the Slavonic vernacular. Still, Constantine had to go to the capital for training in grammar and philosophy, which prepared him for his life's work as the "Apostle of the Slavs." Before 862, when he and Methodios left Constantinople for Moravia at the invitation of Prince Rastislav, they had already devised a script (Glagolitic, later replaced by Cyrillic) and were able to make translations of the Greek liturgy, lectionary, and Bible into Slavonic. The Moravians, thus presented with the possibility of worshipping in their own language, turned against the Frankish missionaries (who employed Latin) and rejected Roman authority. Through the use of the new alphabets large areas of central Europe and Russia were converted to Christianity and Byzantine influence was enormously extended.

This attention to Slavonic needs was not matched by a comparable concern to render the Greek liturgy more easily comprehensible. Apart from the relatively uncomplex congregational responses and some of the older hymns, ecclesiastical Greek used in sermons conformed to the sophisticated Attic employed in intellectual circles. From the early ninth century onward this official language was enriched and developed by scholars such as Leo the Mathematician, who taught the traditional trivium and quadrivium in the Magnaura School in the 850s. The achievements of these early humanists can be illustrated by the career of Photios, twice patriarch of Constantinople, polymath, and bibliophile extraordinary. His sermons, for instance, full of classical allusions, rhetorical devices, and ancient techniques, must have been hard for any but the most educated to understand. They established models (in addition to ancient exercises) for the Greek taught in institutions of higher education for centuries, and thus shaped the language used by historians like Anna Komnene (daughter of Alexios I), lawyers, and administrators.

Photios also demonstrates the tendency for intellectual work to be combined with a clerical career. While secular education continued and the civilian administrators provided posts of high status for laymen, a great number of scholars entered the church. Many became monks, like Constantine, who took the name Cyril shortly before his death in Rome— he was buried in the church of San Clemente in 869. Others assumed leading positions as bishops, like Arethas of Patras, for instance, who was appointed to the foremost metropolitan see of Caesarea in 902/3. But he had already acquired an interest in classical learning before joining the clergy. In 888 he commissioned a copy of Euclid's works (the manuscript survives in the Bodleian Library at Oxford, d'Orville 301), the first of many ancient authors he studied and wrote about in important marginal notes (*scholia*). Aristotle, Plato, Aelius Aristides, Lucian, the Chaldaic oracles, Pausanias, and many others followed. Arethas probably received a regular classical training, partly in Patras, partly in Constantinople. But even in the alternative schools, run by monasteries (notably the Stoudios foundation in the capital), the same essentially secular lessons were taught.

With this foundation of humanist study, tenth-century Byzantium witnessed an artistic and cultural revival (known as the "Macedonian Renaissance"). Constantine VII Porphyrogennitos's personal interests and patronage were responsible for some of the finest artifacts produced, the gold reliquary of the True Cross now in Limburg, for example, and for new standards of historical research and encyclopedic scholarship. While the resources of the capital and the imperial workshops ensured the employment of precious metals, jewels, ivory, enamel, and silk, a similar spirit inspired less extravagant products made far from the capital. It was not only a case of manuscripts copied in Constantinople being decorated with motifs taken directly from their classical ancestors: in provincial *scriptoria* the same rediscovery of ancient art took place.

In addition to its Hellenistic inspiration, tenth-century art is characterized by a reduced scale. The change in dimension constitutes a major transformation of ecclesiastical architecture, from Late Antique basilicas to Middle Byzantine cross-in-square churches. Churches were increasingly built as private chapels for family use. Even in vast public churches like Hagia Sophia, the liturgy was often celebrated in side chapels. Icons also encouraged an individual style of devotion, a more personal form of worship. Such features resulted in a plethora of smaller foundations, for instance in Kastoria or Cappadocia, which were lavishly decorated, often with portraits of their donors. In northern Greece a quite distinctive style of brick, stone, and tile construction developed, with domes raised on high drums and ornate carved decoration. In Cappadocia the rock-cut churches permitted few architectural features but a complex program of fresco decoration. Their small scale and provincial origin does not, however, imply a "provincial" style in the pejorative sense, one inevitably inferior to the higher metropolitan style of the capital. For these individual styles were to develop into a number of particular schools that produced the frescoes of Asinou and Lagoudera (Cyprus), and of Nerezi (Macedonia); the mosaics of Hosios Lukas and Daphni, and the finely proportioned churches of the Chalkoprateia at Thessalonike and Porta Panaghia at Arta. These are without doubt some of the masterpieces of Byzantine art and stand comparison with the greatest monuments of Constantinople constructed at the same time.

Nor should the degree of interaction between different parts of the empire be overlooked, even if it frequently took the form of a rivalry between metropolis and province. During the eleventh and twelfth centuries the cultural life of Greece was greatly influenced by some of the ecclesiastics appointed to its bishoprics. They brought not only theological expertise but also intellectual interests and artistic concepts. Theophylact of Ohrid was distinguished by his observations of the Bulgarian people; Eustathios of Thessalonike by his commentaries on Homer; Demetrios Chomatenos by his concern for canon law. In addition, they all expressed themselves to their friends and ecclesiastical colleagues in letters that form a fascinating branch of Byzantine literature. Of course, their letters carry complaints about the unsophisticated conditions of provincial life, but they also reveal a concern to correct injustice, to train the local clergy and supervise the copying of manuscripts. Through the work of these bishops a wide range of religious experiences could be shared between all levels of society—the 1054 schism with Rome (a political decision taken in the capital) as well as the growth of religious confraternities, such as the one in central Greece centered on the "Naupaktitissa" icon of the Virgin (an indigenous expression of devotion).

Bishops nonetheless constituted a literary elite in a largely nonliterate world and employed the stylized Attic Greek of ruling circles for their correspondence. It was very rare for a general like Kekaumenos (eleventh century) to master the skill of writing, and even more unusual for a military official to record his memoirs in a simpler form of Greek. The dichotomy between official and spoken language became more marked from the twelfth century, when a written vernacular developed. The introduction of new literary forms—satire, romance, and verse histories—in a demotic Greek readily understood by one and all made a profound change. Whether this literature was stimulated by a new audience, the growing numbers of urban dwellers, or by new patrons, the western princesses who had difficulty in mastering classical Greek, it found a broad popular response. In Frankish Morea, particularly, the new medium was put to use to record the conquest and history of the crusaders. The *Chronicle of Morea* survives in vernacular Greek, French, Italian, and Spanish versions, which were declaimed at feasts in castles throughout the Mediterranean. Like the earlier Greek epic of Digenes Akritas (the eastern border hero) it combined accessibility and contemporary relevance. While it never removed the dominance of official Greek, the new demotic encouraged romances like *Kallimachos and Chrysorrhoe*, satirical tales by Theodore Prodromos and the development of different vernaculars—for example, the Cypriot dialect used in the chronicles of Leontios Makhairas and George Boustronios. And through these literary works demotic Greek established its own history, so that when the battle with *katharevousa* (pure) Greek was joined in the modern period it could draw on a rich tradition.

While the events of 1204 brought eastern and western cultures together in a stimulating fashion in parts of the Morea, elsewhere an ingrained hostility was merely confirmed. From the schism of 1054 onward, the Byzantine church was very torn, one party striving for unity with Rome while another clung to independence. The custom of holding theological debates at court, if necessary with translators for the western representatives, encouraged both factions but induced a feverish agitation in the reign of Michael VIII (1259–82). Largely for political and military reasons the emperor negotiated with the papacy for reunion, which was finally achieved in 1274 at the Council of Lyons, but immediately repudiated by significant sections of the Byzantine clergy and laity. Although diplomatically advantageous, the union never commanded popular support.

In Greece an uneasy symbiosis had developed. The Byzantine clergy maintained their church in exile while a Latin hierarchy was established: Cistercians took over Daphni, for instance, and William of Moerbeke assumed the archbishopric of Corinth (1278–?86). In contrast to the Holy Land and Cyprus, however, no Gothic cathedrals were built; western influence is far more visible in the castles of the Peloponnese and in a few churches with arched windows. Byzantine art flourished under both Latin and Greek patrons and is especially evident in the city of Mistra, capital of the Byzantine despotate.

The Late Byzantine period was marked by a renewed concern for spiritual values and a vigorous interest in Neoplatonist philosophy. Both contributed to the development of Byzantine mysticism, which bore fruit in the Hesychast movement of contemplation and silent prayer. The work of scholars such as George Pachymeres and Maximos Planoudes at Nicaea (1204–61) and later at Constantinople established a pattern of outstanding scholarship. For the first time major works of western thought in Latin were translated, including parts of St. Augustine. Planoudes also prepared new editions of classical authors, notably Plutarch, and revived Byzantine interest in ancient epigrams. Under Manuel II (1391–1425), who was himself a gifted humanist, Demetrios Kydones of Thessalonike was encouraged to prepare a Greek edition of Aquinas's *Summa Theologiae*, a project related to the effort to renew union with Rome. But the philosophical interest in Neoplatonism was most characteristic of the period, and culminated in the work of Gemistos Plethon, who established a Platonic Academy in Mistra. Ancient Greek philosophy, as well as religion, brought Byzantine intellectuals into close contact with Italian Renaissance scholars and transmitted much eastern learning to the west even before the fall of Constantinople.

THE BYZANTINE LEGACY

Because of its long history spanning the ancient and early modern worlds, Byzantium was bound to influence neighboring states. This influence—with its Hellenistic component—can be traced particularly in those that adopted an imperial form. In tenth-century Germany, for instance, the court of the Holy Roman Empire adopted Byzantine ceremonial and political ideology with the encouragement of the Empress Theophano. As the niece of John I Tzimiskes (969–76), she was married to Otto II in a diplomatic alliance and brought up her son, Otto III, in the traditions of a Byzantine prince. Under Theophano's tutelage he tried to rebuild an empire in the west following the Byzantine model. Although this project failed, it left an important tradition that lived on into the days of Frederick II and Charles V.

A more profound adaptation of imperial ideals occurred in the Slavonic lands converted to Orthodoxy by Byzantine missionaries. In medieval Bulgaria and Serbia, but especially in Russia, theocratic systems proved long-lasting. The roles of prince and tsar (itself a corruption of the Latin, *caesar*, which had passed into Byzantium as the official term for a co-emperor) drew upon ancient types. State hierarchies of both honorary and active positions emulated the Byzantine system and were similarly distinguished by special costumes made from materials reserved for the ruler.

The greatest contribution of Byzantium to the world, however, lies in its legal, literary, devotional, and, above all, artistic traditions. By conservation, interpretation, and commentary, the Byzantines elaborated the inheritance of Roman law. The systematic edition made by Constantine Harmenopoulos of Thessalonike in 1345, the *Hexabiblos*, was widely used in eastern Europe during the late medieval period and into modern times. Similarly, the *Syntagma* (Constitution) of Matthew Blastares (1335), which consisted of secular and ecclesiastical rulings arranged in alphabetic order, was translated into Serbian at Stephan Dušan's order.

The Byzantine liturgy also played a decisive role not solely in the Orthodox churches of the east but also in literary culture. Traditions of icon painting, fresco decoration, and architecture formed another common inheritance, as many sixteenth- and seventeenth-century monuments of purely Byzantine character testify.

In Greece particularly, the Byzantine domination bequeathed a rich heritage to the Hellenic world. Through many of its distinctive features, aspects of ancient and classical learning were preserved and transmitted together with a particular medieval contribution to the modern era. In the mid-fourteenth century, for instance, a cleric of the Orthodox bishop of Athens, then under Catalan domination, could copy and illustrate a medical manuscript of ancient origin for a local doctor (this is preserved in the Bibliothèque National in Paris). By maintaining the language and literature of ancient Hellas, and encouraging the development of a lively written vernacular, the medieval inhabitants of Greece ensured a continuity in their own history. Byzantine forms of intellectual, artistic, and religious expression added invaluable strength to this tradition. And when it was put to test by the Turkish occupation, it was not found wanting.

2

ASPECTS OF THE PROCESS
OF HELLENIZATION IN THE
EARLY MIDDLE AGES

ⲥⲟ

An invitation from the Hibernian Hellenists Association in 1972 prompted this investigation of early medieval Hellenization, later published in *ABSA* 68 (1973). I thank George Huxley for arranging this exciting meeting and Nobert Elias for his critical and constructive discussions of the text. In the medieval history of Greece the influence of the Slavic invaders who swept into the country from the north from the late sixth century onward is a vexed problem. Nineteenth-century German historians seized on the discovery of Slavic place names in southern Greece to argue that the Greek people had been severely or even entirely replaced by northern non-Greek tribes. The resulting claim that the modern Greeks had no connection with the ancient Greeks provoked an inevitable riposte from Greek historians, anxious to reassert their distinguished ancestry. The debate grew out of a greater emphasis on ethnicity associated with the racist aspects of European culture in the nineteenth and twentieth centuries, emphasized by Fallmerayer and recapitulated by Vasmer in 1941. For many decades it diverted attention from the medieval history of Greece but has now been replaced by more balanced analysis of the precise influence brought by Slavic tribes who occupied the central and southern parts of the peninsula.

There can be no doubt that these non-Greek invaders caused quite significant disruption to imperial rule. Regardless of the precise value to be attached to the texts, for example, the so-called Chronicles of Monemvasia and of Galaxeidi, it's clear that for over a century (from ca. 580 to ca. 680) Constantinople had limited control over the Aegean coastal areas and none over parts of the interior. Few bishops remained in the sees established before the invasions; famously, the inhabitants of the city of Patras sailed to a more secure home in Sicily and other bishops led their communities to mountain refuges like Monemvasia, founded in 587, and Orove, an island in the Gulf of Corinth. Monastic communities do not appear to have survived. Military defense clearly failed to sustain many cities and even major centers like Corinth, Athens, and Patras were attacked.

The purpose of this chapter was to draw attention to the inherent forces that remained to sustain medieval Hellenism. Despite the "grande brèche" in continuous imperial rule, the inhabitants of Greece were able to reassert their identity as citizens of the empire of Constantinople. If many of them had come as invaders, they were converted to Greek-speaking subjects of the emperor, and eventually began to live by imperial laws, pray according to the Byzantine liturgy, and pay their taxes to Constantinople. A precise study of their DNA, were that possible, might reveal their Slavic origins beyond Greece. But their activity once settled on Greek soil reveals the gradual adoption of the language, religion, and cultural inheritance of Byzantium. This argument, written in the heat of youthful research, may now seem rather naïve, but it has the merit of emphasizing neglected features of medieval Hellenism.

IN THE WINTER MONTHS of AD 905–6 Arethas, Archbishop of Caesarea, unwillingly made the difficult journey from Constantinople to the Byzantine province of Hellas, central Greece.[1] The official reason for this visit was to reconsecrate several churches that had been defiled and pillaged by raiders, probably Bulgars, but there was another reason why the vociferous archbishop should be removed from the capital. In September 905 Zoe, mistress of the Emperor Leo VI, had given birth to a child Constantine, Leo's first son and heir.[2] While this event was joyfully celebrated by the entire court, it provoked dismay and alarm among ecclesiastics such as Arethas. For the emperor had already been married three times and to take a fourth wife was against the canons of the Orthodox Church.[3]

Over the question of the christening of the young prince and the emperor's fourth marriage (τετραγμία), the church divided. The majority of bishops supported Patriarch Nikolaos in his efforts to find a compromise that would admit the legitimacy of Leo's heir without raising the excessively embarrassing question of a fourth marriage. But a few clerics, led by Arethas of Caesarea, stubbornly refused to accept this subordination of ecclesiastical law to imperial pressures. For his opposition Arethas was sent off to Hellas. In his absence the patriarch agreed to perform the christening ceremony, and Constantine was duly baptized on 6 January 906.[4] He survived a difficult childhood to reign in the mid-tenth century as Constantine VII Porphyrogennetos—the emperor who did so much to encourage the revival of classical culture in Byzantium.[5]

Patriarch Nikolaos, however, made one condition about the christening: the emperor was to end his liaison with Zoe immediately, and she was to enter a nunnery. But Leo refused to adhere to this condition.

Shortly after the baptism of his son his fourth marriage was celebrated by a priest in a private chapel of the palace. The emperor introduced Zoe, his new Augusta, to the court, igniting one of the most lasting scandals in Byzantine history. Paradoxically Leo, who was known as Leo the Wise, was a pious, moderate, and unselfish emperor. His first three wives had all died young and through no fault of his own he had no heir, a serious disadvantage for any emperor. So it was only natural that he should do everything possible to legitimize Constantine, even appealing to Pope Sergius III for a dispensation to marry for the fourth time. As the canons of the Western Church were not so strict, this could be granted—in addition the Papacy could never resist an opportunity to intervene in the East as the superior of the Patriarch of Constantinople. After this appeal to Rome and many months of wrangling over Empress Zoe, Patriarch Nikolaos resigned and went into exile.[6]

These were the important matters that brought Arethas to Greece. But the visit itself has great significance. By a strange coincidence this journey took Arethas back home. He was born in Patras, in the northwest corner of the Peloponnese, and was familiar with the insecurity of provincial existence. As a result of Slavonic incursions into this area his family had been forced to emigrate from Patras to Calabria in southern Italy, along with others who could afford this course of action. They returned to Patras only after the defeat and conversion of the Slavs there at the beginning of the ninth century.[7] As a young man Arethas was sent to the capital, where he lived until he was about forty, collecting manuscripts, commissioning copies of classical texts, and studying commentaries. His library was famous, and the marginalia of its manuscripts reveal Arethas's many interests and intellectual curiosity.[8] It is not clear whether he was ever taught by Photios, the great classical scholar who was patriarch from 858 to 867 and 878 to 886, but he was certainly influenced by the older man's work and interests.[9] In 888 Arethas paid fourteen gold solidi for a copy of Euclid, and by 895 he had entered the church and become a deacon, the first step in his ecclesiastical career.[10] So although he had experienced provincial life in a limited way, Arethas represented a brand of scholarship found only in the capital, nurtured in libraries and discussion circles. What did he make of life in this particularly isolated and backward outpost of the empire in the early tenth century?

Despite the fact that the inhabitants of central Greece spoke the same language as Arethas (though he probably used a more literary and classical form of speech), recognized the same secular authority, the emperor, and worshipped according to the same rite, the province was in every way deprived. For centuries the Balkan peninsula had been cut off from the political, cultural, and religious center of the empire. According to a Chronicle written before AD 932 and a report compiled by Constantine VII, Greece had been "slavicized" by 218 years of foreign occupation, when it was subject to no Roman emperor.[11] Only in coastal towns and settlements along the littoral or in the islands had contact been maintained through maritime routes.

A comparable development had taken place earlier in western Europe, where Germanic invaders overran Gaul and Italy and captured Rome. The imperial Roman system of education and government was destroyed. Knowledge of classical Greek and study of Greek texts declined, until by AD 600 neither Gregory of Tours nor Pope Gregory the Great could use it.[12] The fact that Gregory served as papal legate in Constantinople for many years before he was elected to the see of St. Peter, and still learnt no Greek, was symptomatic of the growing separation between East and West. This process of separation was undoubtedly encouraged by the gradual establishment of a Slavonic bloc in the Balkans, which effectively cut land communication between Constantinople and Italy.[13]

The Eastern Empire was also threatened by extinction under the pressure of the barbarians; from the late sixth century onward numerous Avar, Slavonic, and Bulgar tribes crossed the Danube frontier and established themselves in the Balkan peninsula. To the emperors at Constantinople this movement became an insidious infiltration, for the enemy advanced with women, children, and livestock in tow, often in small bands. Few pitched battles were fought in the course of this disorganized invasion; the barbarians avoided fortified towns and drove the indigenous population from their villages by burning, looting, and raiding. Over generations this movement from north to south continued, and slowly the Slavonic peoples, who were chiefly farmers and shepherds, took over the countryside. They all shared a pagan background, and lacked a written language, the use of coinage, and certain building skills. Although they organized sieges of some major cities, including Constantinople, they were unable to capture the capital of the East Roman Empire. Their presence, however, meant that the Balkan peninsula passed out of Byzantine control.[14] In the north Bulgar tribes maintained a highly aggressive attitude; their very militaristic society gradually became a rival to Byzantium. In contrast, the Slav settlements farther south had no definite social form that can be clearly identified and did not share the ambitious political aims of the Bulgars.

From the late eighth century these differences became clearer. The Bulgars began to challenge Byzantium directly; under Khan Krum the

Emperor Nikephoros I was killed in battle and Constantinople was blockaded. At exactly the same time Byzantine commanders began to undertake campaigns of pacification among the Slavonic settlements (Σκλαυινίαι).[15] Within fifty years the central and southern parts of Greece were effectively under Byzantine control again, Greek was spoken and Orthodox churches were being founded, whereas in the north Saints Cyril and Methodios found the Bulgars still pagan, illiterate, and jealous of Byzantine political power.[16] Why had this integration taken place only in south? And how had this transformation occurred?

It was result of a hellenizing process that was at work in parts of the Balkan peninsula during the "Dark Ages" of Byzantine history.[17] In this period, from the late sixth to the end of the eighth century, the Slavonic peoples established in central Greece appear to have adopted the language, culture, and religion of the Byzantines. Because there are so few recorded events we can only surmise how this process worked. But this has to be attempted if we are to account for the rehellenization of Slav-occupied territory. There were at least two aspects to this process, each helping to preserve distinct parts of the Hellenistic tradition: the continued use of spoken Greek, and the preservation of Byzantine political, cultural, and religious practices[18] The first was probably the precondition for the second. In both cases the agents of this process were the indigenous population of Greece, who sought refuge from the Slavs on Aegean islands, in mountain fortresses, and along the littoral.[19] It is clear that they gradually established a *modus vivendi* with the invaders, chiefly through commercial transactions. During a siege of Thessalonike by the Slavs, the Greek inhabitants sent boats to Thessaly to purchase and bring back grain for the city. Supplies were bought from the Velegetzitai, a Slavonic people settled farther south.[20] In addition to these indigenous Greeks, many who had fled abroad, like Arethas's family, returned from Sicily, southern Italy, and the Aegean islands in the course of this period, reinforcing Greek as the everyday language. The isolated activity of holy men, hermits, and stylites also influenced this trend.

Second, these Greek-speaking inhabitants identified themselves as Byzantine, and defined themselves as such in contrast to foreigners, pagans, and barbarians. Although they were often out of touch with the capital, they continued to acknowledge the authority of the emperor and patriarch. In coastal towns such as Athens and Corinth bishops appointed from Constantinople occasionally resided; a slight trace of imperial authority might also survive in the person of a κομμερκιάριος, customs' official.[21] But the most important quality in this aspect of the process of hellenization was that the local Greeks valued their Byzantine culture; they considered it far superior to any aspects of Slavonic society and clung to it. The appeal of this culture for the Slavs is also documented.[22] It was this unplanned, almost unconscious, activity of anonymous provincials that proved decisive in the rehellenization of southern parts of the Balkan peninsula.

Such a thesis must, of course, remain hypothetical. Yet it is clear that the Slavs established themselves in a distinctive fashion—they penetrated and settled by unorganized infiltration. While they fought and pillaged, they never presented a direct political challenge to Constantinople. This in turn permitted the Greek population to reestablish its dominance by a long and piecemeal recuperation, also assisted by military victories. The relative absence of a direct threat, which in the long run seems to have favored Byzantine supremacy in the area, was reinforced by the fact that Constantinople did not organize swift military action against the Slavs.

When the Slavs first overran the Balkan peninsula, successive Byzantine emperors were preoccupied by Persian military activity in the East. Later the rapid Arab conquest of Syria, Palestine, and Egypt again demanded a vigorous defense in the surviving eastern provinces. The western half of the empire remained deprived of troops and was imperceptibly taken over by another enemy. During the seventh century emperors tried to keep the main route from the capital to Thessalonike open, and made brief campaigns against the *Sklaviniai*, but they could not maintain a permanent Byzantine military presence in the Balkans.[23] By a policy of enforced resettlement, various Christian communities were moved from their homes in the East to western regions of the empire, while Slavonic prisoners-of-war were established in Asia Minor. Although they were not always successful, these resettlement programs brought further Greek-speakers into the Balkans, underlining the significance of everyday language.[24] In this situation the practice of spoken Greek, the first of the hellenizing factors, became of prime importance: gradually the European parts of the empire underwent an internal hellenization. The example of medieval Sicily will illustrate this process.

Several theories have been put forward to explain the survival of Greek in Sicily. They are, briefly, first that the language of the first Greek colonizers was maintained throughout the period of Roman domination and into the medieval period. This opinion has been critically received, though it still has energetic supporters.[25] The second postulates an injection of Greek-speakers from Egypt, Syria, and parts of North Africa following the seventh-century Arab conquests. While this is very possible, many remained behind to form the independent Monophysite and Coptic Churches that continued to exist under Arab rule.[26] Third, it has been suggested that during the eighth and ninth centuries "thousands of Greek monks fleeing from the iconoclast persecution settled in southern Italy and penetrated as far north as Rome. It is not going too far to say that Rome was hellenized afresh between 600 and 750."[27] The author goes on to say that the Exarchs of Ravenna and the Greek-speaking Popes were chiefly responsible for this hellenization; this is certainly closer to the truth. In the second half of the eighth century, that is from 750 onward, when persecution of iconophiles became severe, Rome was indeed the goal of some refugees from iconoclasm, just as it had been for those who opposed monothelitism in the seventh. There is little indication, however, that Sicily or southern Italy was much affected by this supposed exodus.[28] Finally, there is a theory that large-scale emigration from the Balkans to Sicily and southern Italy took place in the late sixth and seventh centuries under the pressure of barbarian invasions.[29]

The first two of these suggestions are perfectly plausible. But the fourth is substantiated by a ninth- or early tenth-century source and by the evidence of Arethas that has already been mentioned. The Chronicle records:

> And the city of Patras emigrated to the country of Reggio of the Calabrians and the Argives to the island called Orove and the Corinthians to the island which is called Aigina. Now at the time the Laconians left the land of their fathers; they sailed away to the island of Sicily. And those who even now live in the place called Demenna have changed their name from "Lakedai-monitai" to "Demenetai," and they preserve the speech of the Laconians.[30]

The scale of this emigration may be exaggerated, but there can be no doubt that many Greeks abandoned their homes and settled in southern Italy and Sicily.[31] The Chronicle also records what happened to those who could not escape by sea—they sought refuge in the most inaccessible parts of the Peloponnese, where they built new fortified sites, such as the city of Monemvasia, so called because it was only one entrance, μονὴ ἔμβασις. It is situated on a huge rock off the southeast coast of the Peloponnese and is joined to the mainland by a narrow causeway. Recently the foundation of the city has been dated to the years 582–83 by a combination of archaeological and documentary evidence.[32] The chief coastal cities managed to maintain some sort of existence behind their fortifications, but from all evidence city life was much reduced.[33]

During the late sixth and seventh centuries there were other elements that reinforced knowledge of Greek in Sicily. Syrian merchants were still active; the episcopal hierarchy was basically Greek-speaking; there were several Greek monasteries and probably many more unrecorded hermitages and cave-churches; and among educated people a tradition of classical learning was still very much alive.[34] Even if the intellectual powers of Cosmas, the Sicilian monk captured by Arab pirates and ransomed in Damascus by the father of Saint John Damascenus, are a posterior invention, his life provides a fascinating piece of evidence. It shows that at the end of the seventh century a monk from Sicily could, through his knowledge of Greek and of Eastern Orthodoxy, adapt to the routine of the monastery of Saint Sabas near Jerusalem.[35] That Sicily was entirely hellenized is confirmed by the Emperor Constans II's project of 662 to move his capital to Syracuse.[36] At this time Rome was undergoing a fresh hellenization through the energies of a series of Greek-speaking popes who held the see of Saint Peter between 645 and 751.[37] But Latin remained the language of administration in both Rome and Ravenna. Despite some contact between the Exarchate and Constantinople, knowledge of Greek and of ancient culture declined throughout the seventh century.[38] It was only in southern Italy and Sicily that hellenization had lasting and permanent effects.

From the 730s Eastern influence in this region was consolidated when the churches there were brought under the direct control of the Patriarch of Constantinople; they had previously been subject to Rome.[39] While the Greeks from Greece were no more than one factor in the process of hellenization, they helped considerably to keep the language alive. It was the establishment of whole communities using everyday Greek that preserved Greek-speaking villages in parts of southern Italy into the twentieth century.[40] Farther north, in Rome, Greek was no longer a living language by the eighth century, but the city had resources that attracted Orthodox refugees from iconoclasm. Foremost among these were the Greek monasteries and libraries. In 761 Pope Paul I founded a new Greek monastery for the refugees, but the Greek-speaking community of Rome did not know enough Latin to have much influence on the local inhabitants.[41] For those who could read Greek, however, Rome was a great center. Between 815 and 821 the Sicilian Methodios, who was to become Patriarch of Constantinople after the restoration of icons in 843, lived in Rome copying manuscripts.[42] All the same, most Orthodox monks must have returned to the East when the iconoclast doctrine was finally banished, for by 869 none of the papal delegates to the Photian Council understood Greek.[43]

The hellenization of Sicily in the early Middle Ages appears to be rather partial, but it was to have repercussions in other parts of the empire, most significantly in the Balkan peninsula. In the late eighth century, when

Byzantine emperors directed campaigns of reconquest in the Balkans, central Greece and the Peloponnese were gradually reincorporated into the empire's political structure. These campaigns were greatly facilitated by the hellenization that had already taken place in central Greece. In addition, after the defeat of a Slavonic and Arab attack on Patras in 805–7, the Emperor Nikephoros I ordered the Greeks of Sicily and southern Italy to return to their former home. As the Chronicle records the event:

> When he learnt of the defeat of the Slavs, the Emperor Nikephoros was filled with joy. He ordered the cities which had been levelled to the ground by the barbarians to be rebuilt; and the churches to be built and the barbarians to be made Christian. And when he heard about the migration of the people of Patras he ordered that they should return to their original land, with their leader who was called Athanasios.[44]

Patras was made a metropolitan see, and the city of Lakedaimonia, similarly rebuilt, was made a bishopric under Patras together with two more, Korone and Methone. Nikephoros collected a mixture of Orthodox believers from many eastern parts of the empire and forced them to settle in Lakedaimonia to swell the Greek-speaking Christian population. The Chronicle concludes, "In this way, the barbarians were instructed in the will and joy of God and were baptised and brought into the Christian faith."[45]

Later in the ninth century intensified Arab piracy and the eventual conquest of Sicily forced some of the Greek population there to move north into Calabria or to return to Greece. The family of Saint Athanasios, who was then a young boy and later became Bishop of Methone, left Catania for Patras at this time. There was a similar exodus from the Aegean islands to the Greek mainland.[46] Through this movement knowledge of Greek was strengthened. In Sicily the fruits of this long process were reaped much later, when the island passed under the political control of the Normans. Greek was maintained as one of the three official languages of the Norman kingdom, which patronized the translation of texts from Greek into Arabic and Latin.[47] When Charles of Anjou offered the Papacy the corpus of Greek manuscripts from Sicily, the Vatican Library acquired those twenty-three that formed the core of its collection for many years. Of these only two were theological texts; all the rest contained philosophical, scientific, and grammatical works.[48] In southern Italy the process of hellenization was expanded by the Byzantine reconquest of Calabria and Longobardia under Basil I (867–86). The monastery of Monte Cassino was probably the most striking achievement of medieval Hellenism in Italy, but the medical school of Salerno and students of Homer, Aristotle, and many less famous authors were greatly indebted to anonymous medieval Greek copyists.[49] In the field of art, architecture, and administration ninth-century Venice embodied traditions of Hellenism handed down intact by the Byzantines, and many little-known buildings, frescoes, and mosaics display this influence in a less direct form.[50]

In central Greece close contacts with Sicily and southern Italy reinforced imperial conquest and the conversion of the Slavs. But the area was already largely hellenized, not by Byzantine troops or civilian officials, but by unofficial policies pursued by the local inhabitants over centuries. Although it is generally assumed that the few urban centers that survived were vital to the hellenization and christianization of the Slavs, this view underestimates the role of indigenous Greeks living in the countryside. (It is perhaps based on an analogy with the earlier conversion of pagan rural areas of the Roman Empire.)[51] But by the eighth century conditions had changed greatly. The influence of the ecclesiastical hierarchy, based in the cities, was an important factor, but not the most significant. The activities that encouraged the process of hellenization were primarily rural rather than urban. They can be characterized as follows: the intellectual pursuits of isolated scholars; the ascetic practices of holy men, and the building of churches—the "scientific," "ascetic," and "architectural" contributions to this process. During the "Dark Ages," a remarkable mobility of population facilitated the spread of these practices throughout the countryside, where the Slavs were established. Later, when long-distance trade and economic activity revived, the attractions of urban life drew the Slavs into the cities. Here different factors came into play.

In the seventh and eighth centuries the exemplary lives of scholars and holy men, each dedicated to the pursuit of different ideals, had an important influence on the generally uneducated population. Although Justinian's Edict of 529 has often been regarded as the deathblow to pagan philosophy, there is a little evidence that classical teaching continued in Athens. Even in the eighth century the fame and reputation of the "city of the philosophers" lingered on.[52] It was said of many scholars that they had studied in Athens, for example, of Theodore of Tarsus, later Archbishop of Canterbury, but their teachers are never named.[53] In fact, the only securely dated reference is to an anonymous Athenian professor who taught at Constantinople in the early part of the seventh century. Together with Stephen of Alexandria, he was responsible for part of the ancient cycles of learning, both the literary and scientific.[54] Some teachers in Athens may have continued even in the most limited capacity to pass on the classical tradition. It is quite reasonable to suppose that the last teachers at the Academy did not disappear without trace, but sought refuge with their manuscripts in safe places where they continued to study. One may have gone to the capital, another to the island of Andros, where in the early ninth century another anonymous professor had the reputation of being an expert in ἑλληνικὴ σοφία.[55] Such teachers and their manuscripts were greatly respected, even by churchmen who deeply distrusted pagan philosophy.

In the unsettled conditions of this period mobility of population, which is a common feature of medieval life, has a particular role. Throughout, and sometimes because of, Slavonic invasions and Arab raids, educated people traveled far more widely than they might have done in times of peace. Trade continued, though on a smaller scale than in the late Roman Empire. Pilgrimages became more common, especially to Rome and Jerusalem, and students traveled far to find teachers.[56] Although the anonymous professor of Andros remains an exceptional figure, and Leo the Mathematician, the great ninth-century scholar, is his sole identified pupil, other students must have helped to build up their teacher's reputation.[57] The constant movement of these enthusiastic students from one teacher to another, which is so evident in the "Autobiography" of Anania, an Armenian scholar, is paralleled by the journeys of iconophiles from one center of faith to another.[58] In both cases there were discussions between Greek-speakers from Sicily, southern Italy, Greece, and all parts of the east Mediterranean, not only about political events, but also monastic training, availability of texts, and quality of teachers. This mobility undoubtedly strengthened the process of hellenization.

The "Life" of Saint Elias of Sicily provides an example. Like Cosmas, the Sicilian monk and teacher of Saint John Damascenus, Elias was captured by Arab raiders and spent many years in North Africa and the Near East. He eventually returned to Sicily and became a hermit. But as the danger of Muslim piracy persisted, in about 880 he decided to visit the Peloponnese. At Lakedaimonia he stopped at the church of Saints Cosmas and Damian; in Epiros he was arrested as an Arab spy; in Corfu he stayed with the Bishop Pachomios; and in every place he is reported to have performed miracles and driven out demons. After some time in Rome, where he was received by Pope Stephen V (885–91), he returned to Palermo. Soon he was off again, this time to Constantinople at the invitation of Emperor Leo the Wise. But on the way through central Greece Elias fell ill and died in Thessalonike before reaching the Byzantine capital.[59] This sort of constant mobility is extremely common among saints of the iconoclast period. Many suffered persecution as devoted iconophiles and made the journey to Rome visiting other refugees on the way. Among them Gregory of Dekapolites in Isauria spent a lifetime of travel, starting at the tender age of eight when he was sent to school. This was probably the local teacher's home, where Gregory could live as a student. Many events in the saint's "Life" are mirrored in other hagiographies; some features, for example, the threat of an arranged marriage, are so common as to become suspect. Other details, especially those concerning movement from one iconophile center to another, are of considerable historical significance. When Gregory fled from his parents to avoid the proposed marriage, he sought the local bishop, who was living in hiding in the mountains of Isauria to escape iconoclast persecution. He advised the saint to join a monastic community, but to Gregory's horror the monks supported the destruction of icons, so he became a hermit and lived a solitary life. He braved Slav brigands, Arab pirates, and the usual quota of demons and devils in his pilgrimage to Rome and returned unscathed to Constantinople. What is interesting is that Gregory was hospitably received wherever he went by local bishops, monks, ascetics, and groups of hermits. At every stage of his journey he exchanged information about persecution and the fate of iconophiles, and also about the organization of monasteries, preaching, and education in general.[60]

At a time of severe geographical and social isolation, this interchange among churchmen helped to keep alive many Greek and Christian traditions. It reinforced, and was in turn reinforced by, the exemplary activity of holy men, who continued to follow ascetic practices and to build shrines, chapels, and hermitages. In contrast to the official hierarchy of bishops and well-endowed monastic communities holy men sought isolated retreats in inaccessible regions, where they devoted themselves to a rigorous ascetic life. Feats of self-denial were by no means restricted to the first hermits of Egypt, Palestine, and Syria. That these unofficial representatives of the church had an important influence on local rural inhabitants has been carefully documented.[61] Their advice was sought on many occasions, for example, in the sixth century the people of Thessalonike chose Saint David to represent them at the court of Emperor Justinian. Although the Saint had lived for many years in an almond tree ignoring worldly matters, he finally agreed to go to Constantinople on their behalf.[62] Such holy men were not only significant as examples of a special Christian tradition, they also filled the roles of teacher, missionary, and doctor. In the "Lives" of the Saints these roles are mentioned again and again. When Saint Athanasios left his home in Patras, he was attracted to the ascetic life of hermits in the region. He later joined a monastic community and then became Bishop of Methone, converting the whole area to Christianity.[63] Few holy men were well trained; their powers derived from years of contemplation and disciplined ascetic living rather than from books. Their medical skills were certainly exaggerated by hagiographers, but they were not doubted by contemporaries.

Whenever there was any question about the powers attributed to a holy man, a special test was devised, such as the expulsion of well-established devils. This happened to Saint Elias the cave-monk when he arrived in Patras. He asked the people for a retreat where he could stay, and they offered him a haunted tower. According to the "Life," he installed himself in this tower and successfully drove out the devils. His fame spread through the neighborhood; people came from far and wide to have their diseases cured; many stayed to be converted and baptized Christian. After eight years Saint Elias was forced to move away from the tower to find a more isolated spot. He returned to Calabria and established a monastery in a large cave. It was run on the most ascetic lines; even the monastic animals were not allowed to eat meat, and Elias ate only one meal a day when he was not fasting completely. He continued to work miraculous cures, to tame bears, and to copy manuscripts until he reached a great age.[64]

This most austere activity played a particularly important role in hellenizing the Slavs settled in central Greece.[65] Even though it was usually spontaneous and unsponsored by local authorities, it was bound to carry more weight than the activity of established church leaders. For most of the seventh and eighth centuries few bishoprics existed in Greece and ecclesiastical activity was confined to the main coastal towns. Later the episcopacy expanded considerably: by the Photian Council of 879 central Greece was represented by twelve metropolitans and bishops, some from newly created sees at Neai Patrai (New Patras, in Thessaly) and Ezeros, others from sees recently divided, such as Demetrias, Naupaktos, and Pharsala.[66] But the church was regularly split over serious matters: the end of iconoclasm and restoration of icons; the deposition of Patriarch Photios, followed by that of his successor, Ignatios; and finally the tetragamy of Leo VI. The whole Church was torn into opposing camps by Patriarch Nikolaos's final acceptance of Empress Zoe, and the division continued to be felt long into the tenth century. In Greece there were fights between rival ecclesiastics, one group appointed by Nikolaos, the other by his successor Euthymios.[67] Because bishops were empowered to appoint abbots to monasteries under their jurisdiction and most clerical staff, the quarrel involved a large number of people. None of this in-fighting could have made a very good impression on the Slavs. Of course there were individual bishops who rose above the disturbances: Saint Athanasios of Methone devoted himself to preaching and converting the inhabitants of the southwest Peloponnese, while Saint Peter of Argos looked after those who had been attacked by raiding Bulgars or Arab pirates.[68]

During the first centuries of Slavonic settlement in the Balkans the Slavs, who were essentially farming people who avoided towns, came into contact with ascetic hermits seeking a retreat from the world. In the rich agricultural areas this particular example of Byzantine civilization must have had a profound effect on the barbarians. But it was through urban life and commercial transactions that the Slavs were gradually drawn from the countryside and into the towns. From barter exchange they learned to use coins, weights, and numerals for counting. The major cities of Greece, far more than rural areas, represented Byzantine abilities that the Slavs lacked. These included building in stone, fortifying cities and castles, constructing roads and bridges, recording agreements in written documents, observing certain laws, and a general ordering of society that the Slavs regarded as superior to their own. As they had no developed social organization, they were attracted by this order in Byzantine society. At the same time they were impressed by the missionary activity of holy men and ecclesiastics who won them to Orthodox belief and taught them to read and write. In contradistinction to the first wave of Christian missionary work, which went from the cities to the country, this medieval process of hellenization was predominantly a movement from the countryside to the cities. While the urban centers represented a decisive factor in the final political and religious integration of the Slavs, this assimilation would not have been possible without linguistic and cultural preparation in the countryside.

From the third quarter of the ninth century a new secular patronage of culture is documented by the foundation of churches in central Greece. There is no evidence that people of Slavonic origin were responsible for these particular buildings, but their construction was an important part of the hellenization of the region. An imperial dignitary, Leo the πρωτοσπαθάριος, endowed the church of the Dormition at Skripou erected in 873–74. An inscription records that Leo's wealth came from the fertile lands round Lake Kopais and the ancient site of Orchomenos.[69] He may have been given estates there by Basil I as a reward for military service. With his resources he built an impressive domed church, decorated with frescoes and high-quality stone carving, which is also found in the church of St. Gregory the Theologian at Thebes, dating from 876–77.[70] In 871 an Athenian church dedicated to St. John the Baptist was constructed at the orders of three men, Konstantinos, Anastasios, and Ioannes the δρουγγάριος, and in 895 an anonymous donor founded the church at Episkope on Skyros.[71] These buildings were not at all primitive or provincial in the pejorative sense; Middle Byzantine architecture in Greece has been characterized as a particular school, independent from that of the capital and in some ways superior to it.[72] Certainly the fame of Skripou church reached Constantinople, where a follower of Photios composed an epigram on the building.[73]

In conclusion, what did Arethas find on his visit to Hellas in 905–6? The province had been devastated, not only by Bulgar raiders who had attacked churches among other targets, but also by Arab pirates. During the reign of Michael II (820–29) Crete was occupied by Arabs who used it as a base for their raids against the Aegean islands and the coasts of Greece and Asia Minor. Aigina was one of the first to suffer. In 901–2 Demetrias in the Gulf of Pagasai was reduced despite strong resistance, but an attack on the coast of Attica was repelled.[74] Arethas made much of this minor victory in an official speech, but the Arabs were not deterred. In 904 they blockaded Thessalonike, the second city of the empire, which was well fortified and had resisted many sieges. Under the Arab attack the defenses of the city crumbled and almost the entire population was taken prisoner.[75] So for Arethas the first difficulty about his journey to Greece was the simple fact of getting there safely. He perhaps took a ship to Thessalonike, which had been refortified immediately after the 904 attack, and then proceeded by land down the coast road through Tempe, Larissa, Zetouni (medieval Lamia), and Thermopylai to Thebes and Athens. But on land the danger of Bulgar military activity persisted. Under Tsar Symeon (893–927) the Bulgars plundered as far south as the Peloponnese and sailed to the islands and Euboia.[76]

Unfortunately we know nothing about Arethas's stay in Greece. But as senior metropolitan of the Orthodox Church (πρωτόθρονος), he must have been the most distinguished visitor to the area since the Emperor Constans II.[77] A major reception would have been arranged by the governor of the province (στρατηγὸς τῆς Ἑλλάδος) and by the highest ranking ecclesiastic of the region, the Archbishop of Corinth. Other church leaders, bishops, abbots, monks, and holy men would certainly have attended. From the Parthenon inscriptions the names of some of them are known: Archbishop Sabas of Athens, Bishops Sabas of Skyros and Germanos of Diauleia.[78] In addition to the clerics, Arethas would have met the secular leaders of provincial society. First and foremost, the military governors of Hellas and the Peloponnese, both preoccupied by the problem of defending their provinces against Arab attacks. At about this time Konstantinos Tessarakontapechys, στρατηγός in the south, captured a Cretan pirate who was blown on shore; the attack on Attica had recently been beaten off.[79] After the στρατηγοί with their military attendants, came the judges, κριταί. Only a few years after this visit, the κριτής of Hellas made complicated arrangements for troops from Greece to participate in a major attempt to regain Crete.[80] Behind the κριταί would come the numerous junior officials concerned with the day-to-day administration of the province.

The highlight of the visit must have been the ceremony of reconsecration performed by Arethas in those churches that had been plundered. In the course of these celebrations he would probably have met the founders and restorers of these buildings, the new secular patrons of Byzantine culture. He would also have observed the piety of the local population, whatever its ethnic origin. Hellas was clearly a Byzantine province with a familiar Byzantine culture and normal provincial government. In sharp contrast to the situation farther north, where Saints Cyril and Methodios had to devise a new script to represent the language of the pagan Bulgars, the population of Hellas spoke Greek. Not all the Slavs had been peacefully integrated—there were revolts later in the tenth century—but in central Greece most of the Slavs had become Christian and were accepted in provincial society. If their Slavic origin was noticed and sometimes commented on court writers, it was because the Byzantines were often identified by their origin, as "Armenian," "Paphlagonian," or "Cappadocian." To have Slav ancestors was not considered a bar to high office: Patriarch Niketas (776–80) and Empress Sophia, daughter-in-law of Romanos I, both came from Slavic families.[81] Cultural life in central Greece, which had been retarded by intermittent warfare, must have seemed undeveloped in comparison with the intellectual climate of Constantinople, but it drew on the same practices and Hellenistic traditions.

This tenth-century Hellenism was not the same as that of the fourth century BC. It was not as significant as the movement unleashed by Alexander the Great and his successors. But it preserved Greek as a living language in areas outside Greece proper, and it won to Orthodox faith, imperial control, and Byzantine culture a vast population previously pagan. Like the earlier Hellenism, it had the function of integrating and civilizing non-Greeks tribes. And during the early Middle Ages it performed this function most effectively, not least in Greece itself.

NOTES

1. R.J.H. Jenkins and Basil Laourdas, "Eight Letters of Arethas on the Fourth Marriage of Leo the Wise," Ἑλληνικά xiv (1956), 293–372, esp. 332, 335–36. Reprinted in R.J.H. Jenkins, *Studies on Byzantine History of the Ninth and Tenth Centuries* (London, 1970).

2. Ibid., 305. On the event see, R.J.H. Jenkins, *Byzantium: The Imperial Centuries* (London, 1966), 214–16.

3. *JusGR*, vol. 2, 128–29; P. Noailles and A. Dain, *Les Novelles de Léon VI le Sage* (Paris, 1944), 296–99. **Update** Shaun Tougher, *The Reign of Leo VI (886–912)* (Leiden, 1997), 133–63.

4. V. Grumel, *Les Regestes des actes du Patriarchat de Constantinople*, vol. 1, pt. 2 (Kadiköy, 1936), nos. 602, 603, 635. On the violent opposition of Arethas, see Jenkins and Laourdas, "Eight Letters of Arethas," 298–322, 329–30 (nos. 2, 3, 4, 6).

5. A. Rambaud, *L'Empire grec au dixième siècle: Constantin Porphyrogénète* (Paris, 1870), 51–174; R.J.H. Jenkins, *Byzantium: The Imperial Centuries*, 256–67; P. Lemerle, *Le premier humanisme byzantin* (Paris, 1971), 267–300. **Update** Now available in English, *Byzantine Humanism:The First Phase*, translation by Helen Lindsay and Ann Moffatt (Canberra, 1986).

6. Grumel, *Les Regestes des actes*, nos. 811, 612, 613, 614, 635; F. Dölger, *Regesten der Kaiserurkunden des oströmischen Reiches*, vol. 1 (Munich/Berlin, 1924), no. 545.

7. P. Lemerle, "La Chronique, improprement dite de Monemvasie: le contexte historique et légendaire," *Revue des Études Byzantines* xxi (1963), 5–49 (hereafter cited as *Chronique de Monemvasie*); Σ. Κουργέας "Ἐπὶ τοῦ καλουμένου χρονικοῦ, "Περὶ τῆς κτίσεως τῆς Μονεμβασίας"," Νέος Ἑλληνομνήμων ix (1912), 473–80; N. Βέης, "Αἱ ἐπιδρομαὶ τῶν Βουλγάρων ὑπὸ τὸν Τζάρον Συμεὼν καὶ τὰ σχετικὰ σχόλια τοῦ Ἀρέθα Καισαρείας," Ἑλληνικά (1928), 337–70. **Update** N. Oikonomides, "St Andrew, Joseph the Hymnographer and the Slavs of Patras," in ΛΕΙΜΩΝ: *Studies Presented to L. Rydén on His Sixty-fifth Birthday*, ed. J. O Rosenqvist (Uppsala, 1996), 71–78.

8. Σ. Κουργέας, Ὁ Καισαρείας Ἀρέθας καὶ τὸ ἔργον αὐτοῦ (Athens, 1913), 40–63, 97–138; E. Zardini, " Sulla biblioteca dell'arcivescovo Areta di Cesarea," *Akten des XI internationalen Byzantinisten-kongresses* (Munich, 1960), 671–78; R.J.H. Jenkins, *Byzantium: The Imperial Centuries*, 219–22; L. G. Westerink and B. Laourdas, "Scholia by Arethas in Vindob. phil. gr. 314," Ἑλληνικά xvii (1962), 105–31; L. G. Westerink, "Marginalia by Arethas in Moscow Gr. ms. 231," *B* xlii (1972), 196–244. **Update** Michael Share, *Arethas of Caesarea's Scholia on Porphyry's Eisagoge and Aristotle's Categories* (Athens, 1994).

9. F. Dvornik, *The Photian Schism: History and Legend* (Cambridge, UK, 1948, reprinted 1970), 386–87; S. Impellizzeri, "L'umanesimo bizantino del IX secolo e la genesi della 'Biblioteca' di Fozio," *RSBN* N.S. vi–vii (1969–70) 9–69. On the interest in pagan learning at Constantinople, see C. A. Mango, *The Homilies of Photius Patriarch of Constantinople* (Cambridge, MA, 1958), 161–76; R.J.H. Jenkins, B. Laourdas, and C. A. Mango, "Nine Orations of Arethas from Cod. Marcianus gr. 524," *BZ* xlvii (1954), 28–32 (reprinted in R.J.H. Jenkins, *Studies*).

10. Κουργέας, Ὁ Καισαρείας Ἀρέθας καὶ τὸ ἔργον αὐτοῦ, 3–9; Lemerle, "La Chronique," 207–8.

11. *Chronique de Monemvasie*, 10; Constantine Porphyrogenitus, *De Thematibus*, ed. A. Pertusi (Rome, 1952), 91.

12. P. Riché, *Éducation et culture dans l'occident barbare (VI–VIII siècles)* (Paris, 1962), 189–90; P. Courcelle, *Late Latin Writers and Their Greek Sources* (Cambridge, MA, 1969), 412. **Update** Chris Wickham, *The Inheritance of Rome: A History of Europe from 400–1000* (London, 2009), 99–108.

13. G. Ostrogorsky, "The Byzantine Empire in the World of the Seventh Century," *DOP* xiii (1959), 1–12.

14. Miracula Sancti Demetrii, ed. J. P. Migne, *PG*, cxvi, col. 1325; Paul Lemerle, *Les plus anciens recueils des miracles de Saint Démétrius et la pénétration des Slaves dans les Balkans*, 2 vols. (Paris 1979–81); John of Ephesos, *Ecclesiastical History*, translated into English by R. Payne Smith (Oxford, 1860), 432–33; *Chronique de Monemvasie*, 9. Cf. the accounts given by A. Bon, *Le Péloponnèse byzantin jusqu'en 1204* (Paris, 1951), esp. 31–64; V. Tapkova-Zaimova, "Sur les rapports entre la population indigène des régions balkaniques et les "barbares" aux 6e–7e siècles," *Byzantino-Bulgarica* i (1962), 67–78. Reference will not be made to the mass of secondary material on this subject, much of which is distorted by the attempt to minimize or to exaggerate the extent of Slav occupation.

15. *Theophanes*, 456, 485, 486, 490–91, 495–96, 497–503.

16. S. Runciman, *A History of the First Bulgarian Empire* (London, 1930), 25–43, 47–70, esp. 93–96; F. Dvornik, *Byzantine Missions among the Slavs* (New Brunswick, NJ, 1970), 71–104. **Update** A. P. Vlasto, *The Entry of the Slavs into Christendom* (Cambridge, UK, 1970).

17. D. Zakythinos has indicated the significance of this period; see "La grande brèche dans la tradition historique de l'Hellénisme du 7e au 9e siècles," Χαριστήριον εἰς Ἀ. Ὀρλάνδον iii (Athens, 1966), 300–327. **Update** E. Kountoura-Galake, *O vyzantinos kleros kai e koinonia ton skoteinon aionon* (Athens, 1996), and eadem, ed., *Ta skoteine aiona sto Vyzantio/The Dark Centuries of Byzantium* (Athens 2001).

18. These two aspects were of particular importance in the Hellenization of the Slavs; other aspects that are not treated here, for example, the preservation of ancient Greek learning, will form the subject of a separate article.

19. To speak of the "extermination" of the Greek race is incorrect, as it is quite clear from the sources that the indigenous Greeks did not simply disappear forever. Cf. Sinclair Hood, "Isles of Refuge in the Early Byzantine Period," *ABSA* lxv (1970), 37–44, and see the following. **Update** Vasso Penna, "The Island of Orovi in the Argolid: Bishopric and Administrative Center," in *Studies in Byzantine Sigillography*, vol. 4, ed. N. Oikonomides (Dumbarton Oaks, 1995), 163–73. J. Rosser, "Byzantine 'Isles of Refuge' in the Chronicle of Galaxeidi" in *The Archaeology of Medieval Greece*, eds. P. Lock and G.D.R. Sanders (Oxford/Oakville CT, 1996); I. Anagnostakis, *To chronikon tou Galaxeidiou*, rev. ed. (Athens 2004).

20. A. Tougard, *De l'histoire profane dans les actes grecs des Bollandistes* (Paris, 1874), 166.

21. The existence of several bishops of Corinth and Athens is recorded in their attendance at Church Councils, for example, at the Sixth Ecumenical Council of 680–81: see *Mansi* xi, 669, 689 (Stephanos of Corinth), 672–73 (Ioannes of Athens); cf. Zakythinos, "La grande brèche," 303. The so-called Notitia episcopatuum of Leo III has frequently been used to prove the survival of many inland bishoprics in eighth-century Greece, despite the fact that since 1895 it has been identified as a list of cities similar to the Synekdemos of Hierokles; see L. Duchesne, "Les anciens évêchés de la Grèce," *MEFR* xv (1895), 375–85, emphatically confirmed by Bon, *Le Péloponnèse byzantin*, 22–25. **Update** See now Kountoura-Galake, *O vyzantinos kleros* (n17 earlier), 127; eadem, "Symvole sten melete tes vyzantines ekklesiastikes hierarchias . . . ," *Vyzantiaka* 14 (1994), 67–80. On the presence of κομμερκιάριοι in the area, see H. Antoniadis-Bibicou, *Recherches sur les douanes à Byzance* (Paris, 1963), 157–91; in the list of seals, nos. 17, 42, 56, 58, 67, 82, 83, 85, and 86 indicate the existence of these officials, though not all these seals can be securely dated.

22. A tenth-century oration recounts, "We are no longer called 'Scythian' or 'barbarian' or I know not what, but may be named and shown to be Christians and sons of God and travail of the Spirit." The complete text was published by F. Uspensky, *Letopis of the Historico-Philological Society of the University of Novorossiya* iv (Byzantine section 2) 1894, 55–94, relevant passage 67–68. The oration was formerly attributed to Arethas but has now been shown to be the work of Theodoros Daphnopates; see R.J.H. Jenkins, "The Peace with Bulgaria (927) celebrated by Theodore Daphnopates," *Polychronion. Festschrift F. Dölger* (Heidelberg, 1966), 287–303 (reprinted in the author's *Studies*). The relevant passage is reproduced on 289 and translated on 293.

23. *Theophanes*, 347–48, 364, 374; Eng. trans., Mango and Scott, 483–87, 507–8, 521.

24. *Nikephoros*, 66; Eng. trans., Mango, para. 73, 144. *Theophanes*, 359, 429, 432; Mango and Scott, 499, 593, 599.

25. The theory of linguistic continuity was first developed by G. Rohlfs, *Scavi linguistici nella Magna Graeca* (Rome, 1933), and ever since it has aroused great controversy; see the works of O. Parlangèli, particularly "L'importanza dell'elemento greco nella storia linguistica dell'Italia meridionale," *Akten des XI internationalen Byzantinisten-Kongresses* (Munich, 1960), 445–49. S. Karatzas, *L'Origine des dialectes néo-grecs de l'Italie méridionale* (Paris, 1958), has summarized the arguments and concluded in support of Rohlfs, but this position is not universally accepted; see, for example, P. Courcelle, *Late Latin Writers*, 336–38.

26. A. J. Butler, *The Arab Conquest of Egypt and the Last Thirty Years of Roman Domination* (Oxford, 1902), 439–64.

27. J. Wallace-Hadrill, *The Barbarian West 400–1000* (London, 1952), 64, reproduced in K. F. Drew, *The Barbarian Invasions* (New York, 1970), 68–69.

28. "Life of S. Stephen the Younger," *PG*, 100, col. 1117; A. Guillou, "Grecs d'Italie du sud et de Sicile au Moyen Âge: les moines," *MEFR*, lxxv (1963), 79–110, esp. 83 n. 2 (reprinted in the author's *Studies on Byzantine Italy* [London, 1970]).

29. This theory has been championed for many years by P. Charanis; see "On the Question of the Hellenization of Sicily and Southern Italy during the Middle Ages," *American Historical Review* lii (1946–47), 74–86. The author was one of

the first to support N. Βέης in his belief that the so-called Chronicle of Monemvasia was a reliable historical source. P. Lemerle has confirmed this, but he doubts that a large-scale emigration took place; see Lemerle, *Les plus anciens recueils*, 19, n. 30. In the context of greater mobility than is generally appreciated, I think that the Chronicle deserves credence; see the following.

30. *Chronique de Monemvasie*, 9–10. A possible identification of Orove is Ὀροβίαι (modern Rovies), in northern Euboia: L. H. Sackett et al., *ABSA* lxi (1966), 48; J. Koder, *Negroponte* (Vienna, 1973) 114–15 and pls. 43–45. **Update** But see now the evidence of a bishop of Orove, found on an island in the Gulf of Corinth, which confirms the Chronicle, Penna, as earlier.

31. The migration of the city of Patras with its bishop, mentioned in the Chronicle (*Chronique de Monemvasie*, 10) is confirmed by the acts of the Seventh Ecumenical Council held in Nikaia in 787. This Council was attended by bishops from several Aegean islands, including Aigina, Euboia, and Skopelos, but not from the mainland centers, Thessalonike, Larissa, Athens, and Corinth. Patras, however, was represented by Ἰωάννης μοναχὸς καὶ ἐκ προσώπου Πατρῶν, who signed after the Bishop of Reggio (Calabria) and before the group of Sicilian bishops; see Mansi xiii, col. 365. I am most grateful to Paul Speck, who brought this important evidence to my attention. **Update** Speck went on to explore the Acta of 787; see *Die Interpolationen in den Akten des Konzils von 787 und die Libri Carolini* (Bonn, 1998). E. Lamberz is preparing a new edition and has examined the subscription lists; see *Die Bischoflisten des VII. Ökumenischen Konzils (Nicaenum II)*, Abh. Der Bayer. Akad. der Wissen., phil.-hist Kl. Neue Folge, Heft 124 (Munich, 2004).

32. P. Schreiner, "La Fondation de Monemvasie en 582/3," *TM* iv (1970), 471–76. **Update** H. Kalligas, *Byzantine Monemvasia: The Sources* (Monemvasia, 1990).

33. E. Kirsten, "Die Byzantinische Stadt," *Berichte des XI internationalen Byzantinistenkongresses* (Munich, 1960), 19–23. Coin evidence is here very useful, although difficult to interpret; see D. Metcalf, "The Aegean Coastlands under Threat," *ABSA* lvii (1962), 14–24; S. Vryonis, "An Attic Hoard of Byzantine Gold Coins (668–741) from the Thomas Whittemore Collection and the Numismatic Evidence for the Urban History of Byzantium," *ZRVI* viii (1963), 291–300, reprinted in the author"s *Byzantium: Its Internal History and Relations with the Muslim World* (London, 1971); Bon, *Le Péloponnèse byzantin*, 53, tabulates the coin finds from Athens and Corinth. **Update** V. Penna, "E zoe stis Vyzantines poleis tes Peloponnesou: e nomismatike martyria (8os–12os ai M.X.)," in *Mneme Martin J. Price* (Athens, 1996), full account in Greek, 195–226; shorter version in English, 265–88.

34. On Syrian merchants and oriental trade, see H. Pirenne, *Mohammed and Charlemagne* (London, 1939), 79–96; L. Bréhier, "Les colonies d'Orientaux en Occident au commencement du moyen-âge," *BZ* xii (1903), 1–39: F. Vercauteren, "La circulation des marchands en Europe occidentale du VIe au Xe siècles: aspects économiques et culturelles," *Settimane di studio del Centro italiano di Studi sul'Alto Medioevo* xi (Spoleto, 1964), 393–412. On the Greek-speaking ecclesiastics and Orthodox monasteries, see A. Guillou, "Grecs d'Italie du sud et de Sicile," 81–82; S. Borsari, *Il monachesimo bizantino nella Sicilia e nell'Italia meridionale pre-normanno* (Naples, 1963), 32–46.

35. The "Life of S. John Damascenus," *PG*, 94, cols. 440–49, recounts how the Arab captive, Cosmas, was employed by John's father as teacher, and imparted to the young saint the complete cycles of classical learning. But the "Life" was written many centuries later and is not a reliable source; see M. Jugie, "La vie de Saint Jean Damascène," *ÉO* xxvii (1924), 137–61. **Update** C. Mango, "Greek Culture in Palestine after the Arab Conquest," in G. Cavallo et al., eds., *Scritture, libri e testi nelle aree provinciali di Bisanzio* (Spoleto, 1991), vol. 1, 149–60.

36. *LP*, vol. 1, 343; *Theophanes*, 348; Mango and Scott, 486; Georgius Cedrenus, *Synopsis Historion*, ed. I. Bekker (Bonn, 1839), vol. 1, 762–63.

37. J. Gay, "Remarques sur les papes grecs et syriens avant l'Iconoclastie," *Mélanges G. Schlumberger* (Paris, 1924), vol. 1, 40–54; A. Pertusi, "Bisanzio e l'irridazione della sua civiltà in occidente nell'Alto Medioevo," *Settimane di studio... xi* (Spoleto, 1964), 75–133, esp. 117–19; P. Riché, *Éducation et culture*, 393–96, 467–72.

38. A. Guillou, *Régionalisme et indépendence dans l'Empire byzantin au 7e siècle. L'exemple de l'Exarchat et de la Pentapole d'Italie* (Rome, 1969), 77–88, 112–16, 231–34.

39. M. Anastos, "The Transfer of Illyricum, Calabria and Sicily to the Jurisdiction of the Patriarchate of Constantinople," *Studi bizantini e neoellenici 9* (1957), 14–31. **Update** The date of this transfer is disputed; see V. Prigent, "Les empereurs isauriens et la confiscation des patrimoines pontificaux d'Italie du sud," *MEFR*, Moyen Age, 116 (2004), 557–94. H. Ohme considers that it may have been anticipated by Justinian II at the Council in Trullo; see *Das Concilium Quinisextum und seine Bischofsliste* (Berlin/New York, 1990), 208–28.

40. S. Karatzas, *L'Origine des dialects néo-grecs*, 17–18, 239–51.

41. *LP*, 1, 465; P. Riché, *Éducation et culture*, 398–400; J. Irigoin, "L'Italie méridionale et la tradition des texts antiques," *JÖB* xviii (1959), 37–55, esp. 41. **Update** J.-M. Sansterre, *Les moines grecs et orientaux à Rome aux époques byzantine et carolingienne (milieu du VIe siècle–fin du IXe siècle)* (Brussels, 1983); and "Le monachisme byzantin à Rome," in *Bisanzio, Roma e l'Italia nell'alto medioevo, Settimane di studi* 34 (Spoleto, 1988), 701–46.

42. "Life of S. Methodios," *PG* 100, col. 1248; R. Devreesse, *Le Fonds grec de la Bibliothèque Vaticane des origins à Paul V* (Vatican, 1965), 2.

43. A. Pertusi, "Bisanzio e l'irridazione," 118.

44. *Chronique de Monemvasie*, 10; cf. Constantine Porphyrogenitus, *De Administrando Imperio*, ed. G. Moravcsik and R.J.H. Jenkins (Budapest/London, 1949–62), i, 228–30; ii, 184–85; and notes 7, 29, and 31 earlier.

45. *Chronique de Monemvasie*, 10–11; P. Charanis, "Nicephorus I, the Savior of Greece from the Slavs (810 AD)," *Byzantina-Metabyzantina* i (1946), 75–92, reprinted in the author's *Studies on the Demography of the Byzantine Empire* (London, 1972).

46. F. Gabrieli, "Greeks and Arabs in the Central Mediterranean Area," *DOP* xviii (1964), 59–65; A. Vasiliev, "The 'Life' of Saint Peter of Argos and Its Historical Significance," *Traditio* v (1947), 163–91. On the alleged movement of population north into Southern Italy, see L. R. Ménager, "La 'byzantinisation' religieuse de l'Italie méridionale (IXe–XIIe siècles) et la politique monastique des Normans d'Italie," *Revue d'Histoire ecclésiastique* liii (1958), 747–74; liv (1959), 5–40;

and the criticism of A. Guillou, "Inchiesta sulla populazione greca della Sicilia e della Calabria nel Medio Evo," *Rivista Storica Italiana* lxxv (1963), 53–68, reprinted in the author's *Studies*. The return of Athanasios is recorded in an epitaph composed by St. Peter of Argos; see J. Cozza-Luzi, *Nova Patrum Bibliotheca* (Rome, 1888), ix, sec. 3, 33–35; on the family of St. Joseph the Hymnographer, see A. Papadopoulos-Kerameus, *Monumenta graeca et Latina ad historiam Photii patriarchae pertinentia* (St. Petersburg, 1901), ii, 3. On the inhabitants of Aigina, see the "Life of Holy Luke," ed. Γ. Κρέμος, Φωκικά (Athens, 1874), i, 132. **Update** Carolyn L. and W. Robert Connor, *The Life and Miracles of Saint Luke of Steiris: Text, Translation, and Commentary* (Brookline, MA, 1994).

47. J. Irigoin, "L'Italie méridionale," 37–51; R. Weiss, "The Greek Culture of South Italy in the Middle Ages," *Proceeding of the British Academy* xxxvii (1951), 23–50.

48. R. Devreesse, *Le Fonds grec*, 2–4; J. Irigoin, "L'Italie méridionale," 54, points out the importance of Byzantine gifts to the Norman kings of Sicily; these were often manuscripts of a technical nature that were added to the Sicilian collection of texts.

49. H. Bloch, "Monte Cassino, Byzantium and the West," *DOP* iii (1946), 156–224; J. Irigoin, "L'Italie méridionale," 46–47, 54–55, on the copying done at the Orthodox monasteries.

50. R. Cessi, *Venezia Ducale: I. Duca e Populo* (Venice, 1963), 155–221.

51. See, for example, E. Kirsten, "Die byzantinische Stadt," 25; P. Charanis, "Ethnic Changes in the Byzantine Empire in the Seventh Century," *DOP* xiii (1959), 41, reprinted in the author's *Studies*. On the importance of cities in the earlier period, see W.H.C. Frend, "The Winning of the Countryside," *Journal of Ecclesiastical History* xviii (1967), 1–14.

52. *Cod. Just.*, I. 5, 18; I. 11, 10. A. Cameron, "The Last Days of the Academy at Athens," *Proceedings of the Cambridge Philological Society* N.S. xv (1969), 7–29, but cf. P. Lemerle, *Les plus anciens recueils*, 70–73. In the mid-eighth century Stephen of Surož, future Bishop of Sougdaia, is said to have made a pilgrimage to Athens, "where he found native inhabitants, traditional philosophers and orators, and he conversed and discussed with them, all at length." This evidence comes from the Greek Synaxarion edited by V. Vasilievskii, *Trudy*, iii (St. Petersburg, 1915), 73, but it is not found in the Russian version of the Saint's "Life," ibid., 77–78. **Update** Nor does it occur in the Armenian and Slavonic versions, newly edited by Azat Bozyan and Sergey A. Ivanov; see Constantin Zuckerman, ed., *La Crimée entre Byzance et le Khaganat Khazar* (Paris, 2006).

53. This claim was made nearly a century later by Pope Zacharias in a letter written to Saint Boniface; see M. Tangl, *Monumenta Germania Historiae: Epistolae selectae* (Berlin, 1916), i, 80. It was not known to the Venerable Bede, who recorded Theodore's activity in England, including his teaching of Latin and Greek, but it is generally accepted; see, for example, J. B. Bury, *A History of the Later Roman Empire 395–800* (London, 1889), ii, 280, 392. **Update** Recent study of the life of Theodore has corrected this; see Michael Lapidge, ed., *Archbishop Theodore: Commemorative Studies on His Life and Influence* (Cambridge, UK, 1994).

54. On the anonymous professor, see H. Berberian, "Autobiographie d'Anania Širakac'i," *Revue des études arméniennes* N.S. i (1964), 189–94; on Stephen of Alexandria, L. G. Westerink, *Anonymous Prolegomena to Platonic Philosophy* (Amsterdam, 1962), xxiv–xxv. **Update** Tim Greenwood, "A Reassessment of the Life and Mathematical Problems of Anania Širakac'i," *Revue des études arméniennes* 32 (2011), 129–84.

55. *Theophanes*, 192; Georgius Cedrenus, *Synopsis Historion*, ii, 170. **Update** See "Mathematical Mysteries in Byzantium," chapter 15 in this volume.

56. On mercantile activity, see F. Vercauteren, "La circulation des marchands." On the attraction of Rome, see F. Dvornik, *Les Légendes de Constantin et de Méthode vues de Byzance* (Prague, 1933), 291–93; A. Michel, *Ostkirchliche Studien* i (1952), 32–45. **Update** On travel in general, see Elisabeth Malamut, *Sur la route des saints byzantins* (Paris, 1993).

57. E. Lipchits, "Vizantiiskii uchenyy Lev Matematik," *Vizantiiskii Vremennik* N.S. ii (1949), 106–49; P. Lemerle, *Les plus anciens recueils*, 148–65; J. Irigoin, "Survie et renouveau de la littérature antique à Constantinople," *Cahiers de Civilisation médiévale* v (1962), 287–302. **Update** On the possible misunderstanding of the alleged teacher in Andros, see "Mathematical Mysteries in Byzantium," chapter 15 in this volume.

58. H. Berberian, "Autobiographie d'Anania Širakac'i," 189–94. **Update** See now, Tim Greenwood, "A Reassessment . . . " (as earlier), with a new translation of the text of the autobiography.

59. G. Rossi Taibbi, *Vita di Sant'Elia il Giovane* (Palermo, 1962), 40–44, 54–56, 104–14.

60. F. Dvornik, *La vie de Saint Grégoire le Décapolite et les Slavs Macédoniens au IXe siècle* (Paris, 1926), 48–62; cf. P. Karlin-Hayter, *Vita Euthymii patriarchae CP* (Brussels, 1970), 181, who refers to Gregory as a "leader and organiser of iconodule resistance." **Update** C. Mango, "On Re-reading the Life of St Gregory the Decapolite," *Byzantina* 13 (1985), 633–46.

61. On the effects of these unofficial missionaries, see H. G. Beck, "Christliche Mission und politische Propaganda im byzantinischen Reich," *Settimane di studio* . . . xiv (Spoleto, 1967), 649–74, esp. 654–74 (reprinted in the author's *Ideen und Realitaeten in Byzanz* [London, 1972]); cf. E. A. Thompson, "Christianity and the Northern Barbarians," in *The Conflict between Paganism and Christianity in the Fourth Century*, ed. A. Momigliano (Oxford, 1963), 56–78; and particularly the powerful analysis by P. Brown, "The Rise and Function of the Holy Man in Late Roman Society," *JRS* lxxi (1971), 80–101; idem, "A Dark-Age Crisis: Aspects of the Iconoclastic Controversy," *EHR* lxxviii (1973), 1–34, esp. 12–21. **Update** Richard E. Sullivan, *Christian Missionary Activity in the Middle Ages* (Aldershot, UK, 1994).

62. A. Vasiliev, "The Life of Saint David of Thessalonica," *Traditio* iv (1946), 115–47; ibid., v (1947), 191.

63. J. Cozza-Luzi, *Nova Patrum Bibliotheca*, 36–40.

64. G. da Costa-Louillet, "Saints de la Grèce aux VIIIe, IXe et XIe siècles," *B* 31 (1961), 115–16, 118, 121, 309–39; cf. the forthcoming edition of the "Life" of Saint Elias by M. V. Strazzeri. I would like to thank Signorina Strazzeri for

showing me the photographs of the manuscript Cod. Messinensis gr. 30 on which her new edition is based.

65. In other parts of the empire different agencies brought about the integration of the Slavs. In the case of Saint Ioannikios the army played as important a role as the church; see S. Vryonis, "St Ioannicius the Great (754–846) and the 'Slavs' of Bithynia," *B* xxxi (1961), 245–48, reprinted in the author's *Byzantium*.

66. *Mansi* xvii, 373–77. **Update** Eleonora Kountara-Galake, cited earlier.

67. V. Grumel, *Les Regestes des actes*, nos. 636, letter of Patriarch Nikolaos to the governor of Hellas; 706, to Archbishop Niketas of Athens; 735, to Archbishop Andreas of Patras; and 745, to Archbishop Philippos of Larissa. When his brother Paul was appointed to the see of Corinth, Saint Peter of Argos decided to go with him to the Peloponnese to avoid further disputes with the patriarch.

68. J. Cozza-Luzi, *Nova Patrum Bibliotheca*, 39–42; A. Vasiliev, *The "Life" of Saint Peter of Argos*, 176. Both men had established a reputation for holiness as ascetics before they were appointed bishops; cf. *The Life of Saint George of Amastris*, ed. V. Vasilievskii, *Trudy*, 17–25.

69. M. Σωτηρίου, "Ὁ ναὸς τῆς Σκριποῦς τῆς Βοιωτίας," *AE* (1931), 119–57; A.H.S. Megaw, "The Skripou Screen," *ABSA* lxi (1966), 1–32; J. Strzygowski, "Inedita der Architektur und Plastik aus der Zeit Basilios I," *BZ* iii (1894), 1–16, esp. 3–12. **Update** Amy Papalexandrou, "Memory Tattered and Torn: Spolia in the Heartland of Byzantine Hellenism," *Archaeologies of Memory*, ed. Susan Alcock and Ruth van Dyke (Oxford, 2003), 56–80.

70. *Corpus Inscriptionum Graecarum*, ed. A. Boeckh (Berlin, 1877) iv, no. 8686; Γ. Σωτηρίου, "Ὁ ἐν Θήβαις Βυζαντινὸς ναὸς Γρηγορίου τοῦ θεολόγου," *AE* 1924, 1–26.

71. Κ. Κωνσταντόπουλος, "Ἐπιγραφὴ ἐκ τοῦ ναοῦ τοῦ ἁγίου Ἰωάννου Μαγκούτη," *EEBS* viii (1931), 252–54; Β. Ἀτέσης, "Ἡ ἐπισκοπὴ Σκύρου ἀνὰ τοὺς αἰῶνας," ibid., xv (1939), 103–4.

72. G. Millet, *L'École grecque dans l'architecture Byzantine* (Paris, 1916). **Update** Charalambos Bouras, *Byzantine and Post-Byzantine Architecture in Greece* (Athens, 2006), 67–77.

73. C. A. Trypanis, *Medieval and Modern Greek Poetry* (Oxford, 1951), 43–44.

74. John Cameniates, *De excidio Thessalonicensi*, ed. I. Bekker (Bonn, 1838), 506; Theophanes Continuatus, *Chronographia*, 364. For the attack on the coast of Attica, see R.J.H. Jenkins, B. Laourdas, and C. A. Mango, "Nine Orations of Arethas" (note 9 earlier), 13–14, 31.

75. An eyewitness account is given by John Cameniates, *De excidio Thessalonicensi*.

76. Ν. Βέης, "Αἱ ἐπιδρομαὶ τῶν Βουλγάρων" (note 7 earlier); Κ. Σάθας, *Χρονικόν ἀνέκδοτον Γαλαξιδίου...* (Athens, 1865), 192–95; Γ. Κρέμος, *Φωκικά*, 148. **Update** C. and W. R. Connor (as earlier).

77. Cf. note 36 earlier.

78. A. Boeckh, *Corpus Inscriptionum Graecarum*, nos. 9358, 9378; Β. Ἀτέσης, "Ἡ ἐπισκοπὴ Σκύρου ἀνὰ τοὺς αἰῶνας," 103–4.

79. Genesius, *Regna*, ed. C. Lachmann (Bonn, 1838), 47–48.

80. Constantine Porphyrogenitus, *De Cerimoniis Aulae Byzantinae*, ed. J. J. Reiske (Bonn, 1829), i, 657.

81. *Theophanes*, 440, 453; Mango and Scott, 608, 625. People at court made fun of Sophia's father, Niketas Rendakis, not because he was a Slav but because of his pretensions to high-born status; see Theophanes Continuatus, *Chronographia*, 413; Constantine Porphyrogenitus, *De Thematibus*, 91. Sophia not only established herself at court, she also retained the title of Empress after the premature death of her husband; see "Life of S. Luke the Stylite," ed. H. Delehaye, *Les Saints Stylites* (Brussels, 1923), 214.

3

REALITIES OF PROVINCIAL GOVERNMENT

HELLAS AND PELOPONNESOS, 1180–1205

❧

The research presented here formed the central part of my PhD thesis approved by the University of Birmingham in 1972. Anthony Bryer supervised it and I was the first in a long line of his doctoral students who have gone on to make careers in the field. John Haldon and Margaret Mullett graduated directly after me, followed by John Smedley (who has built Ashgate into a formidable publishing venture), Catia Galatariotou, Wesam Farag (Kuwait), Jim Crow (Edinburgh), Alan Harvey (Newcastle), Archie Dunn (Birmingham), and many others.

As recorded in the introduction to this volume, I originally intended this research on central Greece in the twelfth century to be completed by a parallel investigation of the western background of the Frankish knights who occupied the region after the Fourth Crusade. In this way I hoped to achieve a comparative study of the overall impact of Northern European traditions in the Byzantine world. I'm pleased to see that others have pursued this ambitious project. Encouraged by David Jacoby's edition of the *Assizes de Romanie*, the combination of western and Byzantine legal traditions that guided the Frankish principalities established in central and southern Greece can now be studied, and has led to renewed interest in the *gasmouloi*, children of mixed parentage, the Gothic features of churches erected by the Friars, and the relations of local with incoming peoples.

The examiners of my thesis, Robert Browning and Ralph Davis, had recommended its publication as a monograph, but I preferred to divide it into articles, and this one was lavishly published in *Dumbarton Oaks Papers*. Provincial administration and how it worked on the ground proved the most difficult subject, because there were very few studies of local and ecclesiastical government at the time. Fortunately, Michael Choniates's letters provided a rich source of details about his own government, which I could link to the few references to Hellas and Peloponnesos in Constantinopolitan texts. I added what information could be gleaned from excavation reports and the existence of churches and monasteries scattered throughout the region. My efforts to assess how well Byzantine administration worked on the ground did not resolve the problem of how local law courts functioned. It was clear from appeals to the Patriarch in Constantinople that decisions taken by Choniates were disputed, but the lack of court records leaves a serious gap. Only by looking at the thirteenth-century accounts of Ioannes Apokaukos and Demetrios Chomatanos can we imagine how twelfth-century metropolitans handled legal problems.

The publication of prosopographical material, including many new seals, and above all the new edition of Choniates's writings by Photeine Kolovou, has facilitated much closer investigation of Athens in the late twelfth century. Together with additional archaeological evidence, this seems to confirm the framework I established.

THE BYZANTINE EMPIRE was governed through a complex administrative system, predominantly military in nature, within which civilian and ecclesiastical sectors played a significant role, though one definitely subordinated to the essential needs of the empire's defense. Studies of the administrative structure rely heavily on lists of officials and their honorary titles, and on records of persons attending important functions at court, which reflect the significance attached to particular posts and the seniority of offices. Based on these lists, a whole hierarchy of ranks can usefully be drawn up, but little about the working of Byzantine administration can be reconstructed. Even when the existence of certain positions is confirmed by persons holding the appropriate title, there is often no evidence that the formal role assigned to them was being executed.

Because of the almost total lack of sources and documentary evidence about everyday business in most parts of the empire, twelfth-century provincial administration is largely unrecorded. The absence of basic data on population, land holding, judicial proceedings, taxation, commercial activity, social relations, and so on, severely limits the social historian. To rely only on records kept by officials in the capital produces merely an ideal picture, one negated by numerous protests and revolts against corrupt and inefficient administrators. Although complaints from the provinces are so common that they should not always be taken literally, it is clear that specific disorders provoked serious antagonism toward the capital. This must be related to the notional ideal of administration developed in Constantinople. Only by combining official sources with a thorough investigation of practical effects of provincial administration (however scrappily recorded) and of all local sources (however insufficient and unclear) can one begin to gain a wider picture of provincial reality. Even though local events are usually recorded by people educated at the capital, whose reports are inevitably biased toward the imperial ideal, this evidence can reveal several little-known aspects of provincial life: the interaction of different spheres of authority; the activities of administrators, civil, military, and ecclesiastical, nominated by Constantinople; the degree of local involvement in provincial government; and rural attitudes toward the capital. These aspects of provincial life suggest in particular that during the latter part of the twelfth century there was a significant change in provincial government. Constantinople failed to maintain administration, both military and civilian authorities transformed their appointed roles, the nature of their command altered. Only the ecclesiastical sector of imperial administration retained its coherence and given function. Through the new role imposed on it by failures in other sectors, it gained strength and became an outstanding force for the unity of the empire at a time of disintegration and separatist movements.

While this pattern was fairly general, it took rather different forms in different parts of the empire. For Central Greece the position of the church is especially highlighted in the letters of Michael Choniates, Metropolitan of Athens from 1182 to 1205.[1] His diocese formed part of the theme of Hellas and Peloponnesos, which had its own character defined by geographical and historical particularities. From its strategic position it served as a port of call for trade and as a base for negotiations between Constantinople and the West. Despite this geographical advantage, the area never rated very highly in military terms, nor did the theme enjoy a high status within Byzantine administration. Distance from the capital and rather poor resources reduced the desirability of appointments in Hellas and Peloponnesos. Both churchmen and civilian governors were hesitant to accept positions, but their reaction may be partly attributed to cosmopolitan distaste for the provinces.[2]

In the twelfth century, however, the region was by no means poverty-stricken. The seat of administration was at Thebes, a well-fortified city situated in the fertile Kephissos plain. Some of the finest Byzantine silks were woven and embroidered there by skilled craftsmen from the large Jewish community. Thebes also attracted a great number of foreign merchants and was the chosen residence of many landowners in central Greece.[3] In contrast, Athens was no longer the grand city of classical proportions, but a relatively small town based on the slopes of the Acropolis. The port facilities at Piraeus sustained some commercial life, but it was not a noted social or intellectual center. Unlike the well-watered areas of Boiotia, Euboia, and Thessaly, Attica was notoriously hot and dry. But the vine, olive, pistachio, and citrus fruits flourished in its stony, sandy soil. Overall the theme was self-sufficient in basic necessities, though they were considered primitive by Constantinopolitan standards.[4]

The theme of Hellas and Peloponnesos was created in the first half of the eleventh century when the two provinces were combined into one unit. It was administered by both military and civil appointees.[5] Among them Nikèphoros Botaneiatès, *prôtoproedros* and *doux* of Hellas and Peloponnesos, clearly reflected the former.[6] Another Nikèphoros, nicknamed Nikèphoritzès because of his precocious career in the administration, held the three equivalent titles *dikastès*, *kritès*, and *praitôr*, all belonging to the civil sector of the Constantinopolitan bureaucracy.[7] However, as a result of the reforms—ca. 1094—of Alexios I, the *megas doux* (μέγας δούξ) took charge of all maritime parts of the empire, including Hellas and Peloponnesos. To the most strategic he appointed subordinate officers as military governors (*doukes*).[8]

In this new arrangement the theme of Hellas and Peloponnesos held an anomalous position: it fell under the authority of the *megas doux*, but continued to be governed by a civilian official, *praitôr* (πραίτωρ). Some of these governors were drawn from the judiciary and were also known as *kritès*, while others held the title ἀνθύπατος (*anthypatos*, proconsul), which was often used in other European provinces in association with *pronoètès* and *praitôr*.[9] This was probably an honorific title; it had always been connected with the patriciate and it declined rapidly after Alexios I introduced a new hierarchy of titles.[10] While the *megas doux* remained in overall control, these civilian officials were nominated from Constantinople through other channels. Officers responsible for naval affairs were active in the province, and the *megas doux* could assert his authority within the province by a personal visit. But there is no evidence that governors were normally his appointees. Despite these regional particularities the area fell into the general pattern of twelfth-century military administration; it suffered the same stresses and pressures as other themes, and in this sense developments in Hellas and Peloponnesos can be seen as reflecting those of the whole empire.

THE HIERARCHY OF ADMINISTRATION

In order to examine the administrative structure of provincial government, the triad of military, civilian, and ecclesiastical sectors from the reforms of Alexios I to the end of the twelfth century is plotted in table 3.1.[11] This is not at all complete, as is evident from many gaps; further

Table 3.1. Administration in Twelfth-Century Greece

Naval/military Grand Duke—Μέγας Δούξ		Civilian Governor—Πραίτωρ		Ecclesiastical Archbishop—Μητροπολίτης	
1. ca. 1085	Anonymous	15. ca. 1088–1105	Κωνσταντῖνος Χοιροσφάκτης	30. ca. 1086–1103	Νικήτας
2. ca. 1089/90	Ἰωάννης Δούκας	16. before 1105	Ἐπιφάνιος Καματηρός		
3. ca. 1104	Landulf	17. before 1105	Λέων Νικερίτης		
4. ca. 1107	Ἰσαάκιος Κοντοστέφανος	18. before 1105	Βάρδας Ἰκανάτος		
5. ca. 1109	Μαριανὸς Μαυροκατακαλών	19.	Βασίλειος Ἐρωτικός	31. ca. 1103–1121	Νικηφόρος
6. ca. 1111/12–1118	Εὐμάθιος Φιλοκάλης	20.	Πέτρος Σερβλίας		
7.	Νικηφόρος Βατάτζης	…	Εὐμάθιος Φιλοκάλης		
8. ca. 1148	Στέφανος Κοντοστέφανος	21. ca. 1140–50	Ἰωάννης Ἁγιοθεοδωρίτης		
9.	Ἀλέξιος Κατακουριανός	22. inter 1143–80	Βασίλειος Ξηρός	32. d. 1153	Λέων Ξηρός
		23. before 1161	Ἀλέξιος Ἀριστηνός		
10. ca. 1156–61	Ἀλέξιος Κομνηνὸς Βρυέννιος	…	Ἀλέξιος Κομνηνὸς Βρυέννιος	33. 1153–60	Γεώργιος Βούρτζης

11. ca. 1169–82	Ἀνδρόνικος Κοντοστέφανος	24. ca. 1167	Ἀλέξιος Κοντοστέφανος	34. 1160–75	Νικόλαος Ἁγιοθεοδωρίτης
12.	Ἰωάννης Κομνηνός	25. ca. 1182–83	Νικηφόρος Προσοῦχ	35. ca. 1175–82	Ἰωάννης
		26. ca. 1183–85	Δημήτριος Δριμύς		
13.	Ἰσαάκιος	27. ca. 1186–87	Νικόλαος Τριψυχός		
				36. ca. 1182–1205	Μιχαὴλ Χωνιάτης
		28.	Κωνσταντῖνος Μαυρικᾶς		
		29.	Anonymous		
14. ca. 1198–1204	Μιχαὴλ Στρυφνός	. . .	Μιχαὴλ Στρυφνός		

1. The first *megas doux* is known only through his official, *pronoētēs tōn ktēmatōn tou megalou doukos*, active in the region of Hierissos; see *Actes de Xéropotamou*, ed. J. Bompaire, *Archives de l'Athos*, III (Paris, 1963), no. 7. This document is dated ca. 1085, i.e., at least five years before the title of *megas doux* is recorded. As a close relative of the emperor, Iōannēs Doukas might have been given properties near Mt. Athos. In 1085 he was probably commander of the naval post at Dyrrachion, but he did not become *megas doux* until ca. 1090; see infra. In the first decade of Alexios's reign there were many *doukes tou stolou*; see R. Guilland, *Recherches sur les institutions byzantines* (Berlin/Amsterdam, 1967), I, 542–43.

2. On Iōannēs Doukas, son of Andronikos, *prōtobestiarios*, and brother-in-law of Alexios I, see D. Polemis, *The Doukai* (London, 1968), 66–70; A. Hohlweg, *Beiträge zur Verwaltungsgeschichte des oströmischen Reiches unter den Komnenen, Miscellanea Byzantina Monacensia*, 1 (Munich, 1965), 17, 23, 142–47; cf. P. Gautier, "L'obituaire du typikon du Pantocrator," *REB* 27 (1969), 254.

3. Landulf was one of the most successful non-Greek commanders of the Byzantine navy; see Anna Comène, *Alexiade*, ed. and trans. B. Leib (Paris, 1937–45), III, 42–47, 81–82; F. Chalandon, *Essai sur le règne d'Alexis Ier Comnène (1081–1118)* (Paris, 1900), 215, 235, 243.

4. On Isaac Kontostephanos, the first of this celebrated family to hold the position, see H. Grégoire, "Notes épigraphiques XII," *Revue de l'instruction publique en Belgique* 52 (1909), pt. 3, 152–61; Hohlweg, *Verwaltungsgeschichte*, 147–48; and notes 8, 11, and 24 infra.

(continued)

Table 3.1. (*Continued*)

5. Marianos Maurokatakalón also came from a distinguished military family. The son of another naval commander, Nikolaos, he married the sister of Nikèphoros Bryennios. He appears to have been appointed *megas doux* when Alexios I was angered by Isaac Kontostephanos, who was effectively demoted; see Anna Comnène, *Alexiade*, II, 216–20; III, 111–15.

6. Eumathios Philokalès gained prominence as *stratopedarchès* of Cyprus after the revolt of 1092; he had previously been *stratègos* of Crete; see S. Marinatos, Εὐμάθιος ὁ Φιλοκάλης, τελεύταιος στρατηγὸς τοῦ θέματος τῆς Κρήτης in Ἐπ. Ἑτ. Βυζ. Σπ., 7 (1930), 388–93. He was twice *doux* of Cyprus before 1118, when he held the highest naval post as *megas doux*. In this capacity he took over the government of Hellas and Peloponnesos as *praitôr*, a title recorded on his seal; see A. Bon, *Le Péloponnèse byzantin jusqu'en 1204* (Paris, 1952), 197–99, no. 48. On his career and his association with the monastery of St. Chrysostom in northern Cyprus, see C. Mango and E.J.W. Hawkins, "Report on Field Work in Istanbul and Cyprus, 1962–1963," *DOP*, 18 (1964), 335–39; and on his family, see A. P. Každan, *Social'nyj sostav gospodstvujuščego klassa Vizantii XI–XII vv.* (Moscow, 1974), 161–62.

7. Nikèphoros Batatzès is known as *megas doux* only from his seal; see B. A. Pančenko, "Katalog' molivdovulov'," *IRAIK* 9 (1904), 376, n. 241, which also records his position as *praitôr* of the Aegean, another maritime region that fell under the control of the *megas doux*. On his family, see K. Amantos, Ἡ οἰκογένεια Βατάτζη, in Ἐπ. Ἑτ. Βυζ. Σπ. 21 (1951), 174–78.

8. Stephanos Kontostephanos, brother-in-law of Manuel I, died at the siege of Corfù in 1149 after only two years as *megas doux*.

9. Alexios Katakourianos is another official known only by his seal; see G. Schlumberger, *Sigillographie de l'Empire byzantin* (Paris, 1884), 670.

10. Alexios Komnènos Bryennios, the son of Anna and Nikèphoros Bryennios, made a successful career under Manuel I, rising to become *megas doux* in ca. 1156; see Joannes Cinnamos, *Epitome*, Bonn ed. (1836), 165–68; Hélène Ahrweiler, *Byzance et la Mer* (Paris, 1966), 254. Michael Choniates records that as *megas doux* Alexios, taking the title *anthypatos*, governed Hellas and Peloponnesos, and claims that he was an exceptionally good governor; see Μιχαὴλ Ἀκομινάτου τοῦ Χωνιάτου τὰ σωζόμενα, ed. S. Lampros (Athens, 1878–80), I, 336, 338.

11. Andronikos Kontostephanos, son of Stephanos, held the post of *megas doux* for a long time, from ca. 1169 until after the accession of Andronikos I in 1182; see C. M. Brand, *Byzantium Confronts the West, 1180–1204* (Cambridge, MA, 1968), 38–46. Ahrweiler, *Byzance et la Mer*, 259, 265–66, 281. On his decisive role in 1182, see C. M. Brand, *Byzantium Confronts the West, 1180–1204* (Cambridge, MA, 1968), 38–46.

12. Under Manuel I there are at least two characters called Ioannès Komnènos, and sorting out their careers is extremely difficult. From a poem of Theodóros Prodromos it appears that Ioannès, *prôtosebastos* and *megas doux*, son of a *sebastokratôr*, restored the monastery of Christ "tou Euergetou," and retired there, taking the monastic name of Ignatios; see Νέος Ἑλλ, 8, pt. 1 (1911), 19–20; R. Janin, *La géographie ecclésiastique de l'empire byzantin*, I, 3: *Les églises et les monastères* (2nd ed., Paris, 1969), 508f. This cannot be the same person who served in Cyprus and was killed at the battle of Myriokephalon, but there are many complications in the identification; see V. Laurent, "Andronikos Synadenos, ou la carrière d'un haut fonctionnaire byzantin au XIIe siècle," *REB* 20 (1962), 212f.

13. Theodóra Komnènè must have taken great pride in her father, Isaac, commander of the navy, to judge from her seal; see Schlumberger, *Sigillographie*, 644–45. On the problem of his identity, see Guilland, *Recherches sur les institutions*, I, 547.

14. On Stryphnos, brother-in-law of Alexios III, see pp. 87–88.

15. Kónstantinos Choirosphaktès held several important positions at court before he was appointed *praitôr* to Hellas and Peloponnesos; he served as ambassador for Nikèphoros III, and became the *oikeios anthrôpos* of Alexios I; see Anna Comnène, *Alexiade*, I, 133–34; Nicephorus Bryennius, *Commentarii*, Bonn ed. (1836), 130. His title of *praetor* is recorded in the *Life of Hosios Meletios*, ed. V. Vasil'evskij, *Pravoslavnyj Palestinskij Sbornik'* 17 (1886), 34; and on his seal, see Schlumberger, *Sigillographie*, 188, 636. The family had connections with Greece; see Bon, *Le Péloponnèse*, 195–96, no. 44; N. Bees, "Zur Sigillographie der byzantinischen Themen Hellas und Peloponnesos," *VizVrem* 21 (1914), 224–26; Každan, *Social'nyj sostav*, 91, 135, 203.

16. Epiphanios Kamatèros came from another family with property in central Greece; see J. Darrouzès, *Georges et Dèmètrios Tornikès. Lettres et Discours* (Paris, 1970), 48–49; Každan, *Social'nyj sostav*, 89. He governed Hellas and Peloponnesos with the title of *anthypatos* (*Life of Meletios*, 53), and two seals that might belong to him carry the titles *proedros* and *eparchos*, and *spatharokandidatos kai tourmarchès*; see Bon, *Le Péloponnèse*, 196–97, no. 47.

17. Leòn Nikeritès is known from the *Life of Meletios* as *stratègos* of Peloponnesos and probably governed both themes; he also served as *prôtoproedros* and *anagrapheus* in Peloponnesos and as *anagrapheus* in Cyprus; see Bees, "Zur Sigillographie," 96–98, 233–34; *Life of Meletios*, 60–62. While it is quite clear that he held high positions under Alexios I, it is not certain that he ever became *megas doux* as Bees claimed, "Zur Sigillographie."

18. Bardas Hikanatos governed Hellas and Peloponnesos three times and was known both as *anthypatos* and *praitôr*; see *Life of Meletios*, 59; Schlumberger, *Sigillographie*, 188. In a document dated 1094 he held the title of *megalepiphanestatos kouropalatès*, indicating that he held a significant position at court; see F. Miklosich and J. Müller, *Acta et diplomata graeca meddi aevi sacra et profana* (Vienna, 1860–90), VI, 93.

19. Two seals record the position of Basileios Eròtikos as *kritès epi tès Hellados kai Peloponnèsou*; see Bon, *Le Péloponnèse*, 194–95, no. 41.

20. Petros Serblias is also known from seals that give him the titles *magistros bestitôr kai kritès* of Hellas and Peloponnesos; see Schlumberger, *Sigillographie*, 190, 698. Other members of the family are recorded but not in the same region; see PG, 126, col. 321; Anna Comnène, *Alexiade*, II, 37; G. G. Litavrin, *Sovety i rasskazy Kekaumena* (Moscow, 1972), 152; Schlumberger, *Sigillographie*, 270, 698; Ahrweiler, *Byzance et la Mer*, 146.

21. Iòannès Hagiotheodòritès came from a well-known family (see note 34 infra) and held a charge connected with imperial domains, *hypodrestèr tôn oikeiakôn*. He was clearly an influential adviser of Manuel I, and was only supplanted by Theodòros Styppeiòtès, who arranged for him to be sent to govern Hellas and Peloponnesos, a considerable demotion; see Nicetas Choniates, *Historia*, Bonn ed. (1835), 77–78; *Synopsis Chronikè*, ed. K. Sathas, Μεσαιωνικὴ Βιβλιοθήκη, 7 (1897), 220–21.

22. Basileios Xèros was an ambassador of Manuel I to Sicily in the early part of the reign (1146–47); see Cinnamos, *Epitome*, 91–92; Bees, "Zur Sigillographie," 228; Schlumberger, *Sigillographie*, 189, 715. The family was well established in central Greece; see *Life of Meletios*, 59–60; Miklosich and Müller, *Acta*, IV, 324; Anna Comnène, *Alexiade*, III, 70; Michael Psellos, *Epistulae*, ed. K. Sathas, Μεσαιωνικὴ Βιβλιοθήκη, 5 (1876), 279, 282; Každan, *Social'nyj sostav*, 135, 203; and note 32 infra.

23. Alexios Aristènos appears to have held an appointment in the province, but his exact title is not preserved; see a letter of Theodôros Prodromos, PG, 133, col. 1274, *megistos hègemòn*. He was one of the many clerics who combined civilian duties with ecclesiastical functions until such dual careers were banned in 1157; see V. Grumel, *Les regestes des Actes du patriarcat de Constantinople*, I, fasc. 3 (Paris, 1947), no. 1048. His position in Greece must be dated before 1161 when he either died or became a monk; see Darrouzès, *Georges et Dèmètrios Tornikès*, 53–57; cf. Každan, *Social'nyj sostav*, 39, 65.

24. The post of Alexios Kontostephanos, brother of the *megas doux*, note 11 supra, is recorded in a monody composed after his death in 1176 by Euthymios Malakès; see A. Papadopoulos-Kerameus, *Noctes Petropolitanae* (St. Petersburg, 1913), 145, 151; Darrouzès, *Georges et Dèmètrios Tornikès*, 57–62.

25. On Nikèphoros Prosouch, see p. 76.

26. On Dèmètrios Drimys, see also p. 76.

27. On Nikolaos Tripsychos, see p. 76 and note 77.

28. Kònstantinos Maurikas ruled Hellas and Peloponnesos as *praitôr*; see his seal, Schlumberger, *Sigillographie*, 54, 189; cf. Michael, *bestarchès kai katepanô Dyrrachiou*, ibid., 677; Každan, *Social'nyj sostav*, 146.

29. Choniates frequently refers to *praitores* who are unidentified except as agents of unjust administration. Unfortunately, it is impossible to tell how many governors were appointed to the province between Tripsychos and Stryphnos, but one features most prominently in the *Hypomnèstikon* (of ca. 1198); the same official may also be recorded in letters; see Μιχαὴλ Ἀκομινάτου τοῦ Χωνιάτου, I, 307–11; II, 103, 105, 106–7, 110, 131, 137.

(*continued*)

Table 3.1. (*Continued*)

30. Nikètas is recorded as Metropolitan of Athens in the *Synodikon*, first published by V. Laurent, "La liste épiscopale de la Métropole d'Athènes, d'après le Synodicon d'une de ses églises suffragantes," *Mémorial L. Petit* (Bucharest, 1948), 272–91, esp. 285; and most recently by G. Nowack, *REB* 19 (1961), 227–38. His death is known from inscriptions on the Parthenon columns; see A. K. Orlandos and L. Branouses, Tὰ Χαράγματα τοῦ Παρθενώνος (Athens, 1973), nos. 62, 222; and his seal is published in V. Laurent, *Le Corpus des sceaux de l'Empire byzantin. V: L'Eglise* (Paris, 1972), no. 601.

31. On Nikèphoros, see Laurent, "La liste épiscopale," 285–86; Orlandos and Branouses, Tὰ Χαράγματα, no. 47.

32. Lean Xèros came from a family well known in Greece; see note 22 supra; Orlandos and Branouses, ibid., no. 39; Laurent, *Le Corpus des sceaux*, no. 602; J. Darrouzès, "Obit de deux Métropolites d'Athènes, Léon Xèros et Georges Bourtzès, d'après les inscriptions du Parthenon," *REB* 20 (1962), 195.

33. On the Bourtzès family, see Darrouzès, ibid., 190–95; B. Georgiadis, Μιχαὴλ Ακομνάτου τοῦ Χωνιάτου καὶ Γεωργίου Βουρτζοῦ λόγοι (Athens, 1882), introduction, 10–19; Každan, *Social'nyj sostav*, 142; and on George, see Orlandos and Branouses, Tὰ Χαράγματα, no. 40; Laurent, *Le Corpus des sceaux* no. 603.

34. Nikolaos Hagiotheodôritès was the most distinguished ecclesiastical representative of this famous twelfth-century family, which included Iôannès (note 21 supra) and Michael, *logothetès tou dromou*; see A. P. Každan, "Brat'ja Ajofeodority pri dvore Manuila Komnina," *ZRVI* 9 (1966), 85–94. On Nikolaos, see V. Grumel, "Titulature de métropolites byzantins. II: Les métropolites hypertimes," *Mémorial L. Petit* (Bucharest, 1948), 159–63; Darrouzès, *Georges et Dèmètrios Tornikès*, 14, 204, n. 2; Orlandos and Branouses, Tὰ Χαράγματα, no. 48; Laurent, *Le Corpus des sceaux*, nos. 604, 605.

35. Iôannès is known only from his seals, one of which was excavated in the Athenian Agora; see Laurent, ibid., no. 606.

36. On Michael Choniates, see H.-G. Beck, *Kirche und Theologische Literatur im byzantinischen Reich* (Munich, 1959), 637–38; G. Stadtmüller, "Michael Choniates, Metropolit von Athen (ca. 1183–ca. 1222)," *OC* 33 (1934), 138–43; I. C. Thallon, "A Mediaeval Humanist: Michael Akominatos," *Vassar Mediaeval Studies* (New Haven, 1923), 275–314; Laurent, *Le Corpus des sceaux*, no. 607.

research will certainly add many entries. However, it does correlate the different spheres of administration, and it emphasizes a basic feature that was to become most significant in the period: the relatively brief duration of civilian and military appointments in comparison to ecclesiastical. Following the table, the three sectors will be discussed in sequence in order to contrast their specific characters, effectiveness, and particularly their relationship to each other. In this fashion it may be possible to elucidate some of the complexities of Byzantine provincial government in the twelfth century. Many remain, for it is the social and economic aspects of provincial life, from the level of external trade to the wealth and poverty of domestic existence, that provide the essential basis for any complete study of administration. But these lie beyond the scope of this chapter.

To emphasize the contrast between the three sectors of government, the order of table 3.1 is reversed in the following discussion: first, metropolitan administration, which presented the greatest continuity; second, the civilian sector; and third, the military/naval authority, which, although it was the most powerful, probably had the least influence in day-to-day matters of provincial government.

METROPOLITAN ADMINISTRATION

Whatever the nominal control of the *megas doux* and the claims made by civil officials, ecclesiastical administration was probably the most efficient in the province. As Constantinople's grasp over the outlying regions of the empire diminished through the twelfth century, churchmen increasingly took over the difficult task of maintaining imperial authority. They replaced weak and corrupt provincial governors as the main force for law and order, constituting the most reliable and immediate influence over local inhabitants. This development should be related to the ancient custom of the patriarchal defense of the capital in the emperor's absence. But in the provinces rather more decisive initiatives were sometimes called for. The examples of Michael Italikos, Nikètas of Chônai, and Eustathios of Thessalonike indicate that Michael Choniates's defense of Athens under siege was by no means exceptional.[12] It was an action typical of concerned ecclesiastics throughout the empire.

Unlike the other two sectors of administration, ecclesiastical government had always been based on the lengthy residence of metropolitans in provincial centers and on long continuous service by lesser officials. Although many churchmen preferred to spend as much time as possible in the capital, others developed a proprietary concern for their dioceses and established a position of great personal authority there. Metropolitans held lifelong appointments and normally built up a good relationship with their provincial parishioners. In every major city they could be seen to represent the authority of the patriarch, of the ecumenical church, and of the emperor whose name was always mentioned in prayers and sermons. Whereas governors might change every three years or more frequently, or might be permanently absent—an unseen force—ecclesiastics embodied an element of continuity in provincial administration. During the twelfth century this factor took on new significance.

THE DIOCESE OF ATHENS

Under the metropolitan of Athens a large diocese extended over central Greece, bordering on those of Thebes and Neopatras (Νέαι Πάτραι) to the north, Naupaktos in the west, and Corinth to the south. Corinth retained the highest position as twenty-seventh in the hierarchy of metropolitan sees; Athens came next as twenty-eighth; then Naupaktos, thirty-fifth; Neopatras, fiftieth; and Thebes, fifty-seventh.[13] At the end of the twelfth century Athens had twelve suffragan sees of which the last two, "Kea kai Thermia" and Megara, were created in the course of that century, probably in response to a growing population.[14] In addition it controlled many important monasteries, Daphnè, Hosios Loukas, and Kaisareianè among them. Since its creation in 806 the metropolitan see of Athens had accumulated property beyond its diocesan boundaries and certainly appeared to Pope Innocent III as a wealthy see.[15] By Byzantine standards it did not compare favorably with major sees in Asia Minor; Theodore Pantechnès dissuaded George Tornikès from accepting the nomination to Corinth on these grounds.[16] Nonetheless, among European sees Athens was not that poor, as it owned estates (προάστεια) and properties, irrigated fields, ponds, mills, and gardens scattered through at least twenty-five villages. These possessions, recorded in official registers (πρακτικά), furnished the metropolitan with produce—honey from the monastery of Kaisareianè, corn from the region of Karystos in Euboia—and they brought in a certain amount of revenue.[17] All the clergy and provincial institutions under the metropolitan's authority also paid the ecclesiastical tax, κανονικόν. But undoubtedly the greatest privilege of Athens was the possession of an imperial chrysobull issued in the twelfth century, which particularly protected its church and lands from external pressures.[18] It specifically prevented the civil governor based in Thebes from making unsolicited visits to Athens, thereby confirming the undisputed authority of the metropolitan. This charter gave Athens privileges similar to those enjoyed by very few cities and churches—Ohrid and Corfù, for example.[19] In practice, however, the charter, though important, was a paper privilege, as the metropolitan was quite unable to enforce its terms: armed with soldiery and under the pretext of worshiping at the Parthenon church, governors continued to enter the city uninvited.

The duties of a metropolitan were basically fivefold: to manage the election of bishops and lesser clergy, to preach regularly in the metropolitan church, to ensure high standards of learning and discipline among the clergy and parish, to collect taxes destined for the patriarch, and to implement any decisions of the patriarch and synod affecting provincial churches. Naturally, the routine business of any metropolitan also included performing the ecclesiastical services associated with local births, marriages, deaths, and other events recorded in church registers, maintaining church property, settling disputes that fell under ecclesiastical jurisdiction, and representing the patriarch in the province (or elsewhere) whenever necessary.[20] To carry out these services metropolitans employed a team of clerical officials modeled on the staff of the patriarch, ecclesiastical *archontes*.[21] From the ranks of these Constantinopolitan clerics many patriarchs and metropolitans were recruited; it was the most prestigious training ground.[22] The same pattern was often found in the provinces, although local *archontes* were usually less well educated and much less powerful. They regularly combined several offices and sometimes held part-time civilian jobs in addition to these clerical duties. The number of *archontes* and their efficiency varied considerably from one diocese to another; there was no uniformity.

In the twelfth century the diocese of Athens was governed by a series of very capable men, most of them trained at Constantinople in the patriarchal chancellery and fully aware of the methods and practices followed at the capital. George Bourtzès and Nikolaos Hagiotheodôritès in particular, were familiar not only with patriarchal administration, but also with the nonecclesiastical duties often demanded of metropolitans.[23] Michael Choniates fitted into this tradition perfectly. He had spent many years at the patriarchate, chiefly as secretary (ὑπογραμματεύς), writing and editing material for speeches and orations. From this position he got to know the *archontes*, some of whom had a strong influence on him—Theodosios Boradiôtès (patriarch from 1178 to 1185), George Xiphilinos (*megas skeuophylax* and subsequently patriarch, 1191–98), Michael Autôreianos (patriarch at Nicaea after the fall of Constantinople), and particularly Eustathios Kataphlôrôn, his teacher who became metropolitan of Thessalonike in 1175. He kept up a correspondence with many of them.[24]

Metropolitans of Athens officiated from the Acropolis using the converted Parthenon as the metropolitan church dedicated to the Mother of God. It formed an exceptionally large church, richly decorated and endowed by many benefactors, among them Basil II, the most celebrated of pilgrims to Athens.[25] For centuries it had commanded the services of a large clergy whose deaths were recorded in graffiti scratched on the original temple columns—for example Theodôros, monk and *skeuophylax* (died 1055); Iôannès, *prôtopapas* (1041), son of Pothos, *oikonomos*; Nikètas, *presbyteros* (1072); Iôannès, *prôtopsaltès* (1063/64), and David, *domestikos* (1071). The columns of the Propylaia, walled up to form the metropolitan residence, also carry these coarse inscriptions.[26] On the edge of the ancient Agora, the Theseion, similarly converted to a church dedicated to St. George, seems to have provided additional assistants to metropolitans, such as one Leontios, probably secretary to Iôannès Blachernitès.[27] Local involvement in church matters was common throughout the empire. In Athens the Pleuritès/Pleurès family was one of those that regularly committed members to ecclesiastical duties and to monasteries in the area.[28]

From writings dating after his appointment to Athens it appears that Michael Choniates inherited several assistants and maintained quite a large staff. The chief offices of *oikonomos*, *sakellarios*, *skeuophylax*, *chartophylax*, and *prôtekdikos* are mentioned, but not that of *sakelliou*.[29] Among the junior offices, only those of *hypomnèmatographos* and of *repherendarios* are known.[30] Although it is not clear that these few offices were always filled, the team probably compared favorably with those of other sees. Euthymios Malakès mentions only one *chartoularios* and one deacon and *kouboukleisios* among his assistants at Neopatras.[31] The fact that several of the Athenian *archontes* are recorded after 1205 does not mean that the titles were necessarily honorary, for Michael Choniates's officials were active under the Frankish occupation. Orthodox clergy were by no means excluded from Greece by the Latin conquest even though their leaders were forced into exile.[32]

The activity of this provincial clergy is somewhat sketchily illustrated in Choniates's letters. But it is possible to reconstruct the roles of the chief officials. The *oikonomos* is mentioned only once in a letter to Manuel, metropolitan of Thebes, concerning a monastery called "tou Myrriniou" (or "tôn Myrriniôtôn"), which may have been situated nearer Thebes than Athens. Michael writes that his official, the *megas oikonomos*, will be visiting the area to announce a synodal decision to those monasteries under the church of Athens.[33] As the *oikonomos* was normally responsible for financial matters, he would probably have collected rents, looked after the resources, and kept the accounts of the see. The post was usually reserved for deacons and was an important one for any see with property. Numerous graffiti indicate previous *oikonomoi* of Athens.[34]

Shortly after his arrival in Athens, Choniates was forced to explain his reasons for not granting the request of one of his deacons, Phôkas, to be promoted from *sakellarios* to *skeuophylax*. As *sakellarios* he would probably have been in charge of the chapels and monasteries in the diocese, and for their financial contribution to ecclesiastical funds.[35] The post of *skeuophylax* was more prestigious in that it involved custody of all the sacred vessels, liturgical books, and vestments that at Athens must have constituted a valuable treasury.[36] Phôkas, however, was elderly and blind, and as it was against canon law for a blind or deaf person to hold such a post, his request for promotion was firmly refused. Later the post of *sakellarios* was filled by Pleurès.[37] *Skeuophylakes* are often recorded in Parthenon graffiti, usually in connection with the diaconate, and sometimes held together with the post of first chanter (πρωτοψάλτης).[38]

Before the Latin conquest there is no evidence of a *chartophylax* of Athens, but at some time after his departure from the Acropolis Choniates appointed George Bardanès as *hypomnèmatographos*, assistant to an unidentified *chartophylax*.[39] George, the son of Dèmètrios, bishop of Karystos, was a pupil of Michael in Athens, and became a great friend. The anonymous *chartophylax* whom George had to assist was clearly a mutual friend who failed to organize the transport of wheat and barley harvested from estates in Euboia belonging to Athens to the island of Kea, where the metropolitan had established his exile. Evidently Michael was dissatisfied with his official and asked George and his father to help, instructing that as much grain as could be carried by boat should be sent and the rest be sold. As *hypomnèmatographos* George was expected to assist the *chartophylax* in issuing and countersigning documents; keeping metropolitan records, including the register of births, marriages, and deaths; and looking after the library.[40] Choniates loved books and constantly desired to add to his collection; he himself had made a copy of Theophylact's exegesis on the Epistles of St. Paul and expected his pupils to do likewise.[41] It was possibly under Michael's orders that the *Synodikon* of Athens was brought up to date; in the form in which it survives, it concludes with the death of Metropolitan Nikolaos Hagiotheodôritès in 1175.[42]

It is difficult to illustrate the exact role of *chartophylax* from George's activity, because he was promoted to that position in new and delicate circumstances created by the Frankish occupation.[43] Michael expected George to keep him informed of all developments on the mainland and to represent him abroad. But he realized the problems of working under foreign domination and eventually transferred George to the bishopric of Grevena, south of Kastoria. The *chartophylax* finally relinquished his title on his election to the see of Kerkyra (Corfù) in 1219.[44] By then Michael had given up his skeletal administrative staff and had retired to the Prodromos monastery at Bodonitza near Thermopylai. In his old age he was only anxious to obtain good positions for his pupils in the flourishing Orthodox communities at Nicaea and in Epiros.[45]

The last office in the group of chief *archontes* was that of *prôtekdikos*, again recorded by Michael only in the context of Latin occupation. The official, Orphanos, wished to join the monastery of Hosios Meletios and his application was supported by the metropolitan.[46] At Constantinople the *prôtekdikos* was the first of several judges (ἔκδικοι) presiding over a special public tribunal for criminals who sought religious asylum.[47] Provincial *prôtekdikoi* probably had a comparable judicial function, though this is not well illustrated by the few sources.[48]

The junior *archontes* of the capital were divided into a group of four who assisted in the work of the *chartophylakion* of the patriarch and into another separate group connected with other aspects of administration.[49] In the provinces their counterparts appear rarely and have a less well defined role. Of those attached to the *chartophylax* of Athens, only the *hypomnèmatographos* is mentioned by Choniatès, but provincial *hieromnèmones* and *logothetai* are elsewhere.[50] The other junior staff seem to act as general assistants and scribes, but they are not recorded in Athens. The one reference to a *repherendarios* is certainly to the patriarchal official from Constantinople. He is associated with another high-ranking figure from the capital, the *mystikos*, a civilian officer, and both are accused of plundering and ruining Athens.[51] Among various clerics definitely attached to the Metropolitan church there were several concerned with liturgical matters, *domestikoi* and *deutereuontes*, and chanters, *psaltai*; others were involved more in administration, including scribes and recorders (*chartoularioi*), among them lay officials (*kouratores*). But most of them were deacons and monks.[52] Shortly before Michael's arrival in Athens, Kosmas Kampokilos, *chartoularios* of the metropolitan, had died.[53] The unfamiliar patronyms of these officials confirm their local origin—Oxeidas, Tyropoulès, Leichènarès, Mamounès, Syleôtès and Chrysochos (from the Parthenon), and Satôreianos and Kampoki-los (from the Propylaia).[54] When taken together with the few patrons whose names are preserved in Athenian churches, for example, Nikolaos Kalommalos, founder of the church of St. Theodore, and Germanos Spor-gitès who restored the Prodromos church, devout but otherwise quite unknown families begin to take on real flesh and blood.[55]

Finally, Michael Choniates had two secretaries who probably filled the role of additional scribes in the metropolitan administration. Nikolaos Antiocheitès may well have been recruited in the province to be secretary for local affairs.[56] For the vital task of messenger Michael had a trusted *grammatikos*, Thomas, clearly a devoted friend also, who carried bundles of letters from Athens to the capital and back even after 1205.[57]

With this relatively small staff Choniates ran the see of Athens. As its possessions were scattered all over central Greece, the metropolitan was often in touch with other ecclesiastics. A long and interesting cor-respondence with Euthymios Malakès at Neopatras was provoked by the behavior of Balsam, bishop of Euripos, the first suffragan see of Athens.[58] Michael also used to consult the metropolitan of Thebes when he needed the governor's advice. Despite its proximity no correspondence between Athens and Corinth is recorded, though Michael noted with horror Met-ropolitan Nikolaos's death at Sgouros's hands.[59] Similarly, there is no evidence of contact with Larissa, and it was only after 1205 that Michael began to communicate with Iôannès Apokaukos of Naupaktos.[60]

Matters of discipline lay behind the relatively few letters to suffragan bishops and diocesan monasteries.[61] Only with Dèmètrios of Karystos was there an immediate link through his son, George Bardanès. Other bishops may have visited Athens from time to time, but they are not mentioned by the metropolitan. It was not until the period of foreign domination, when Michael was forced to write to his abbots and to support them against Frankish pressures, that he developed a close re-lationship with some.[62] This minimal contact with subordinate institu-tions before 1205 may be due to the fact that Michael came to know his diocese and its population through his officials who were sent on par-ticular missions. He must have met local people and visitors from farther afield who came on pilgrimages to the church of the Theotokos, and all those who petitioned him for assistance or who found their way into the ecclesiastical courts. Through his preaching and catechisms he became known as a teacher—he probably had other pupils besides Georges Bardanès and the Hagiosophitai, a group of deacons from the capital.[63] The affectionate correspondence he maintained with local inhabitants, doctors, and friends suggests that he was held in high esteem in Hellas and Peloponnesos.[64]

No doubt the charitable organizations of the church locked the metropolitan into a very close contact with people in the diocese, but it is clear that Michael also tried to understand and to relieve particular problems of the locality. Even though his letters to influential contacts in Constantinople may not always have produced the desired effect, people in the capital were certainly kept aware of Athens's difficulties. The fact that Michael took the initiative in beating off Sgouros's attack on the city illustrates his total involvement in provincial life, his commitment to his parish as well as to the emperor, and his concomitant influence in regional life.[65]

CIVILIAN ADMINISTRATION

In contrast to the administration of the Orthodox Church, that of the imperial bureaucracy was, by the late twelfth century, no longer functioning as planned. Positions in public service were frequently bought, sold, and transferred through dowries and legacies. The wealthiest provincial families competed for posts in the central administration that guaranteed a place in the court hierarchy, while the less well-to-do sought sinecures at the local level. Although the sale of public appointments was traditional, twelfth-century practice failed notably to ensure the participation of suitable candidates. This undoubtedly contributed to the feebleness of the administration.[66]

Civilian officials were nonetheless responsible for the basic running of Hellas and Peloponnesos. The governor (*praitôr*) was appointed from Constantinople in the same way as the *doukes* of Asia Minor, normally for a three-year period. Many, however, did not take up the post; they simply directed provincial administration from the capital, becoming in effect absentee governors. This development drastically weakened the contact between capital and province, and increased the autonomy of local subaltern agents. Most of the twelfth-century governors of Hellas and Peloponnesos were drawn from established government circles of the capital. Kônstantinos Choirosphaktès, Basileios Xèros, and Epiphanios Kamatètros also had local connections, but their families were based at Constantinople and their relatives held important functions beyond the provincial boundaries. Others were recruited from the judiciary, for example, Serblias and Tripsychos.[67] Of the eighteen governors, thirteen were quite clearly from a civilian background. Three held the post of *megas doux* conterminously, while the remaining two may have been associated with this office. But the great majority was not in any way connected with the highest naval authority.

Despite the nominal authority of the *megas doux*, there can be no doubt of the *praitôr*'s extraordinarily wide powers. He controlled the entire area "from Tempe to Sparta" and governed in just the same way as a *doux kai anagrapheus* of Asian themes.[68] During the eleventh century the commuting of services and concomitant decline of provincial troops meant that most local administrative work was reduced to its financial aspects, which could be covered by tax farmers.[69] To facilitate the collection of new taxes that replaced such former services as the provision of horses for the imperial post and supplies of food for local garrisons, numerous fiscal agents were sent from Constantinople or recruited on the spot. This slow process permitted a concentration of economic affairs in the hands of the governor. From his residence in Thebes he controlled all aspects of taxation, the judiciary, the local economy, and provincial defense (now rather limited). It was within his effective power to raise or lower the rate of tax levies, to exercise his right to personal services and transportation, and to ignore ecclesiastical privileges. In addition, it was also possible for him to effect real improvements in provincial life, but these are rarely noted.[70]

This extensive authority can be illustrated by the program of reform drawn up during the brief reign of Andronikos I to correct abuses in provincial government. First, and most significantly, governors were to be selected on their merits and suitability. Second, they were to be adequately paid. These two provisions constituted a major change from the normal practice of appointing favored friends to unsalaried posts—the candidate earned his income in whatever way he could—or of permitting governorships to be sold to the highest bidder.[71] Thus in Hellas and Peloponnesos, special new measures were taken: a new tax register (κατάστιχον) based on an up-to-date survey of provincial landholdings and tax records was made. But when the governor issued an order (ὁρισμός) authorizing its use, the bureaucrats at Constantinople refused to validate it. So taxes continued to be assessed at the previous incorrect rate. Another reform was sabotaged, this time by local chicanery. A general remission of outstanding taxes (ἐκκοπή) had been issued at the accession of Alexios II, probably by Andronikos acting as regent. While Euripos and Corinth apparently benefited from this event, Athens was excluded. So Choniates felt that his parishioners were being singled out for rough treatment, both in the province and at the capital.[72] His analysis of the situation is instructive: he accuses Choumnos, *chartoularios* of one of the Constantinopolitan bureaus, of deliberately wrecking the reform by refusing to validate the new *katastichon*. In addition, Choniates characterizes this attitude as typical of a *praktôr*, thereby suggesting that it was those officials who were the real villains of provincial affairs.[73] Any improvements that might be made at the local level were without legal standing until authorized by Constantinople. But Athens had friends neither at home nor at the center of government. The first two governors appointed by Andronikos, Nikèphoros Prosouch and Dèmètrios Drimys, were nonetheless able to effect some improvements. Difficulties increased when Drimys preferred to remain at the capital rather than to serve a second term of office, thus abandoning the administration to junior agents, *praktores* and *anagrapheis*, who ran things according to their own interests.[74] Later the situation deteriorated yet further when an *antipraitôr*, an interim or substitute governor, was sent out from the capital. This official brought nothing but destruction to the province, levying irregular taxation three times in one year.[75] The metropolitan begged a friend at Constantinople to ensure that a proper governor be sent, hoping to revive the administration of Prosouch and Drimys. Such were the miseries of misgovernment that the period of Andronikos's rule seemed virtually halcyon by comparison, despite that emperor's brief and unpopular reign.

His successors, Isaac II and Alexios III, did nothing to check the decline in provincial administration.[76] Two governors of this period, 1185 to 1203, are known: Nikolaos Tripsychos, *prôtonotarios* of one of the departments of the central administration, and Kônstantinos Maurikas, possibly *praitôr* in 1198; other *praitores* remain anonymous.[77] At the beginning of the period Tripsychos was awaited with great anticipation. Choniates was unable to greet him personally, as one of his nephews had recently been wounded by pirates (an indication of the decline in local defense). The new governor had a suitable training, and swiftly rose in the judicial administration at Constantinople to become *dikaiodotès* and *megas logariastès tôn sekretôn* by 1196. Unfortunately there is no account of his presumably brief stay in Hellas and Peloponnesos.

By 1198 the situation in Athens had become so desperate that the metropolitan submitted a Memorandum (Ὑπομνηστικὸν) to Alexios III on the irregularities and abuses perpetrated by governors. At the same time he also informed several friends at the capital in very bitter terms, urging them to intervene.[78] Not only were provincial inhabitants subjected to excessive taxation and demands for all kinds of services, but, in addition, the governor had flaunted the chrysobull that protected Athens from his devastating visits. Under the guise of worshipping at the church of the Theotokos, he had stripped the city of supplies, requisitioned the domestic animals, and refused to leave until special money gifts were made. Governmental response to the metropolitan's outrage probably took the form of an official visit by the *logothetès*, Basileios Kamatèros, the emperor's brother-in-law.[79] Michael was gratified that such an influential public figure from the capital should see at first hand the plight of the Athenians, but apart from the speech of welcome nothing is recorded about the visit.

Other local officials continued to cause the metropolitan grave problems. From repeated though more muted complaints, and from the spread of revolts against central authority in the Argolis, Sparta, and Thessaly, it is evident that by the close of the century provincial government had seriously disintegrated. Where there was no firm control, independent forces were taking over. Such movements as those led by Sgouros, Chrysos, and Chamaretos were common in the Asian provinces of the empire as well.[80] Constantinople's complete failure to maintain imperial administration in Hellas and Peloponnesos through its governors was finally illustrated by the crusaders' easy advance into Greece. From Thessalonike to Lakedaimonia the sole organized opposition was offered by groups of individuals and by city communities with defensible fortifications.[81] There was no trace of either provincial militia or of naval forces under the *praitôr*'s control.

LOCAL GOVERNMENT OFFICIALS

The chief function of twelfth-century provincial officials was to ensure the collection of taxes; they were also expected to keep order and to provide continuity of imperial control. Some were nominated like the governor from Constantinople: for example, the *anagrapheus* held a three-year term of office; others were chosen by the governor, and junior clerks were probably recruited in the province to serve on a more permanent basis.[82] Tenth-century provincial financial administration was altered both as a result of changes in the central bureaucracy effected by Alexios I and by the growth of civilian power in the provinces. While some posts disappeared altogether, others were combined in a simplified titulature, but functions remained almost unchanged.[83]

The *praktôr*. Of the many fiscal agents the *praktôr* gradually became the most powerful, taking over responsibility for assessing and organizing the collection of regular taxes, the land tax (ἀκρόστιχον), and irregular services (ἐπήρειαι).[84] The development of this office occurred at a time when all landowners, military, civilian, and ecclesiastical, were trying to extend their possessions and to obtain tax exemptions for them. Disputes over boundaries, over the services of dependent peasantry attached to landed estates, over the use of water mills and pastures, became extremely common. In all these matters the local *praktôr* often had a key role, one which is well illustrated in Michael Choniates's letters. This official had control over the establishment of taxes in central Greece and was thus in a position to perpetuate an unfair distribution which favored the wealthy. With this authority consecutive *praktores* rated Attica more highly than neighboring regions, and failed to apply the new *katastichon* which would have corrected such abuses.[85] The *praktorikè energeia* was also responsible for many typical acts of rapaciousness and greed condemned by Michael Choniates.[86] From Athens he identified these officials as "destroyers of the poor," and singled out the exorbitant demands of Tessarakontapèchys, *praktôr* in 1182, as particularly evil.[87] The prominence of the post is confirmed by the titles of a provincial governor, *doux kai praktôr* of Thessalonike, who presided over a dispute between some soldiers and the monastery of Lavra.[88]

The *anagrapheus.* Closely connected with the *praktores,* the *anagrapheus* assumed the duty of land measurement and assessment, which was the basis of regular taxation, and in particular the calculation of *epibolè,* which established the rate of taxation on scattered, uncultivated, and partially exempt lands.[89] As measuring techniques were notoriously inefficient, whatever method was used, these officials were often accused of cheating. They were also in charge of the provincial register, which gave them opportunities to favor their friends, for example, in the registration of tax exemptions.[90] Michael Choniates records one striking example of this activity. The entire village of Orapos, an estate and a church that formed part of the ἀθηναϊκὴ ἐπίσκεψις, was registered in the *praktika* of Thebes. The officials responsible for this attempt to impoverish Athens were the *anagrapheus* Geôrgios Kolymbas, and his assistant (σύντροφος), Sergios Nomikopoulos.[91] From other accusations leveled against Kolymbas—failure to protect the isthmus inhabitants against pirates, and corruption in public courts of justice—it appears that he may have been acting as governor. The combination of titles, *praitôr kai anagrapheus,* is recorded elsewhere; it clearly indicates even wider powers.[92] But perhaps Choniates was just pouring out his anger and despair over the state of public disorders at agents whom he already suspected.

The titles of *anagrapheus* and *apographeus* were generally interchangeable in twelfth-century terminology, certainly for the governors of the Asia Minor themes.[93] Michael Choniates, however, lists the two posts separately and suggests that the *apographeus* was in charge of the special contributions paid toward naval defense (συνδοσίαι). As these payments were assessed in relation to the wealth of each region, the official probably worked under the orders of the *praktôr*.[94] Another subordinate officer, the *exisôtès* (ἐξισωτής), was normally attached to the *anagrapheus*.[95] Choniates accuses both Kolymbas and Nomikopoulos of behaving as any typical *exisôtès*, indicating that perhaps the latter held this title.[96] The function of the *exisôtès* was assimilated to that of *anagrapheus/apographeus* in the thirteenth century, when the terms *apographè* and *exisôsis* were both commonly used for land measurement.

The *logariastès*. In the governor's residence at Thebes, the *praitôr* tried to emulate, with reduced resources, the pomp and ceremony of the emperor's entourage. Whenever he traveled he was accompanied by an εἰσκομιδή of followers, among whom were a *logariastès*, *prôtobestiarios*, and *prôtokentarchos*. On occasion this group was so large that Michael Choniates likens it to an army. It was preceded by a smaller group of officials called *hypodochatores*, whose task was to prepare board and lodging for the rest.[97] The duty of providing hospitality was most resented by provincial inhabitants.

Provincial *logariastai* (or *logistai*) were originally minor officials who assisted in the financial work of the *praktôr*. By the twelfth century the post had developed into that of chief adviser to the governor, particularly on financial matters. Governors normally selected their own *logariastai*; for example, the duke of Crete chose Michael Chrysobergès.[98] In Hellas and Peloponnesos one *logariastès*, Basileios Pikridès, was a sophisticated man to whom Michael Choniates could describe the lack of culture in Attica and the region's barbarian dialect. Like others holding this position, Pikridès probably issued documents confirming privileges, authorizing land sales, and ensuring the validity of grants, but nothing specific about his role is revealed by the metropolitan.[99]

The *prôtokentarchos*. This official commanded the provincial troops at the governor's disposition. As the size of military contingents had been greatly reduced throughout the empire by the late twelfth century, and as Hellas and Peloponnesos had to provide chiefly naval services, this military strength was very small. It may have constituted more of a bodyguard than a troop division; certainly there is no indication that the *prôtokentarchos* took part in direct military operations, for example, against pirate attacks or against Sgouros's advance into central Greece. On one occasion Choniates complained of the rough treatment one of his ecclesiastics received from this official.[100] Possibly the *prôtokentarchos* was connected with the δρούγγοι, small detachments appointed to guard strategic mountain passes probably on the northern frontier of Hellas that bordered on the insurgent Bulgars. These military bases were often maintained by forced recruitment, for which the governor's chief military adviser might well have been responsible.[101]

The *prôtobestiarios*. This title is normally associated with the emperor's wardrobe; it represents a position of great importance, one usually reserved for trusted friends, relatives, and eunuchs.[102] There is no evidence that provincial governors generally had an equivalent official on their staff. For this reason, it has been suggested that the reading should be corrected to πρωτοβεστιαρίτης, a title that becomes common in the empire of Nicaea and the Despotate of Epiros, mainly in association with financial matters.[103] Unfortunately, there is no indication of the duties of this official in the *praitôr*'s entourage, but the post should be considered in connection with another of Michael's complaints: "In addition to all these, the demand for a new revision of taxes made by the βεστιαρίτης his most terrifying and threatening assistant."[104] This seems to reflect the work of an agent sent by Constantinople to increase taxation from the province by taking new measurements. Normally such revisions would be made on the spot by the *praktôr* and *anagrapheus*. But this was probably a special arrangement that would correspond quite well with the known activities of twelfth-century provincial *bestiaritai*. They were attached to the public section of the treasury (ἔξω βεστιάριον) and held military as well as financial responsibilities. Andronikos Batatzès, for example, was the *bestiaritès* in charge of drawing up a *praktikon* for Lavra in 1181, to clarify the position of its dependent peasantry.[105] During the thirteenth century, this position became more exclusively financial.

The *hypodochator* (ὑποδοχάτωρ). As Choniates describes the governor's visit to Athens, the hypocrisy angers him even more than the illegality. While the governor and all his party prayed, "the *hypodochatores* came seeking out the wealthiest citizens, collecting food for men and for beasts; taking whole flocks of sheep and fowl, all the produce of the sea, and wine and gold to the value of all our vines."[106] And they demanded προσκυνητίκια, gifts of respect, and insisted that they be paid in gold.[107] This was all nominally legal and due to the governor and officials, except that Athens was specifically protected from such unsolicited visits. In addition, the *hypodochatores* grossly abused the customary duty of providing draught animals for transport by demanding that their owners buy them back.[108] This official's title is derived from ὑποδοχή, a term used in association with the maintenance and lodging of provincial troops. It is frequently mentioned with διατροφή and διατριβή, among irregular taxes and *epèreiai* in tax exemption charters.[109] It must have been one of the worst impositions for provincial inhabitants.

Officials involved in the actual collection of taxes made up the largest group in the local power structure. Some were known by the name of the tax they levied, for example, *zeugologountes*; others by more general terms, *dasmologoi, phorologountess, synergountes,* and so on. To the metropolitan these officials, sent out from the capital every year, appeared to be more numerous than the frogs sent to plague Egypt.[110] He does not, however, give any indication of how many there were, how they were appointed to the province, or how they perpetrated their extortions.

The *kapnologountes* among these officials were responsible for the *kapnologion,* thirteenth-century name for the καπνικόν (hearth tax). In the same way, *zeugologountes* must have collected the *zeugologion,* a tax on haulage animals. As these two basic charges were usually calculated and collected together, the officials probably went round together—they may have simply adopted the name of the particular tax.[111] It is not clear what proportion of the population of Hellas and Peloponnesos was liable for these taxes. A law of 1144 exempted clergy from the *zeugologion,* and many ecclesiastical institutions did not pay the *kapnikon/kapnologiou.*[112] But most peasant families probably had to pay; they were rated according to the number and kind of animals they possessed.[113]

A different set of officials took charge of naval taxes, which consisted of a regular basic tax (βάρος πλοὸς or πλώϊμον), and contributions (συνδοσίαι) destined for ship building, maintenance, equipment, arms, and procurement of local naval forces. Both taxes were established by official surveys, such as the *apographè* made on the order of Iôannès Doukas, *logothetès tou dromou.*[114] But they could also be levied at any time as an irregular tax for specific campaigns, *epèreia tou stolou,* a provision that was greatly abused by maritime tax collectors, πλωϊμολόγοι, κατεργοκτίσται, and ναυτολόγοι. Choniates records that in one year three separate naval contributions were demanded: one for ship building (κτίσις κατέργων); one on the occasion of Steiriônès's visit to Athens; and a third levied in the name of Sgouros and the *praitôr.*[115] The official survey also listed the number of sailors to be provided by Athens. If personal service was not required, another money payment would certainly have been added. According to the metropolitan, maritime taxes were especially heavy in the *horion* of

Athens, in comparison with Thebes and Euripos, and the tax agents often demanded more than the rate settled for contributions.[116]

In conclusion, the *praktôr* was the most powerful local official after the governor, who often preferred to stay in the capital rather than take up a provincial appointment. Once established in the official residence, the *praitôr* had almost unrestricted authority and was free of supervision; so, in turn, were the *antipraitôr*, *praktôr*, or *anagrapheus* when acting as governor. Local inhabitants could resist this authority by armed force, and there is evidence of such resistance; otherwise their only means of redress was to appeal to Constantinople—a common practice but not very effective. The decline of central administrative control in the provinces was left unchecked and the development of independent forces thereby encouraged. These might be organized by breakaway officials from the capital—for example, Michael Komnènos Doukas, *phorologos* of Mylassa and Melanoudion; Isaac Komnènos in Cyprus; and the Gabras family in Trebizond—or by local landowners such as Sgouros, Chamaretos, and Chalkoutzès.[117] The latter owned property in the provinces where they were sometimes identified as θεματικοὶ καὶ κτηματικοὶ ἄρχοντες. While they aspired to imperial honors, they were not entirely at home in Constantinopolitan society. In contrast to the all-powerful *dynatoi*, these provincial families represented lesser landowners, who sent many of their numbers into the local administration. Of the agents named by Michael Choniates, the *praktôr* Tessarakontapèchys can be identified with one of these. Others such as Rendakios, Pothos, Pardos, and Leobachos had a strong influence over regional developments.[118] It was possibly from the ranks of these families that the καστρηνοί (city dwellers) and the βοιωταρχοῦντες (Boiotian leaders) were drawn—anonymous groups who were powerful enough to resist the provincial governor and the metropolitan.[119] They were typical of local landowners all over the empire whose generally independent attitude brought them into conflict with the capital. Toward the end of the twelfth century they did not hesitate, when they saw an opportunity, to improve their personal fortunes at the expense of the central administration.

MILITARY ADMINISTRATION

The *megas doux* had supreme authority in Hellas and Peloponnesos, but the practical effects of his control were very slight. By the end of the twelfth century, instead of manifesting itself as a living embodiment, this most powerful post appears only to have cast a distant shadow over provincial life. High titles from the capital stood in inverse proportion to actual influence over developments in the provinces.

The origin of the post of *megas doux* lay in two revolts of 1092, when the commanders of important naval bases on Cyprus and Crete rebelled. Their alleged purpose was to protest against excessive taxation, but they may also have taken advantage of the Emir of Smyrna's activity in the Aegean; they may even have supported him.[120] As Alexios I realized the threat posed to his already precarious military situation, he sent a large sea and land force against the emir. His brother-in-law, Iôannès Doukas, was recalled from Dyrrachion to command this expedition as *megas doux tou stolou*.[121] In the course of the campaign, several Aegean islands were retaken, and from this base Doukas was able to put down the mutiny on Crete. Leaving a garrison there, he sailed on to Cyprus, where forces were landed and the rebel leader captured.[122]

In his concern to prevent a repetition of these revolts, Alexios seems to have undertaken a systematic overhaul of naval organization. The new post of *megas doux* assumed total responsibility for levying troops, ships' crews, and equipment in all naval areas, and for maritime defense throughout the empire.[123] To the strategically sensitive bases, the Adriatic coast, Cyprus, and Crete, the *megas doux* appointed his own trusted men, for example, Iôannès Helladikos, κατεπάνω Κρήτης καὶ οἰκεῖος ἄνθρωπος of the supreme commander, Philokalès.[124] Often relatives of the emperor held these crucial positions, but this custom reflects the development of "familial" government favored by the Komnènoi.[125] In addition to reliable military officials, naval regions also had civilian administrators appointed from the capital; this civilian government was, however, thoroughly subordinated to naval priorities. The system can be illustrated by the situation of ca. 1094: Iôannès Doukas left Eumathios Philokalès on Cyprus as *stratopedarchès*, and he appointed Michael Karantènos *doux* of Crete. Simultaneously, one Kalliparios was sent to Cyprus as *kritès kai exisôtès*, a civil and judicial figure who doubtless had his counterpart on Crete.[126] The *megas doux* also controlled several subaltern naval commanders (θαλασσοκράτορες and δούκες), such as Kônstantinos Dalassènos, who led a successful mission to remove the Emir of Smyrna. Lesser officials ran the administration of the *megas doux* from the capital.[127]

In Hellas and Peloponnesos (and this was important to east/west communication but not to the most sensitive coastlands of the empire) the *megas doux* did not appoint a similar naval commander on a regular basis. Although it would have been logical to revise the whole structure uniformly, there is no direct evidence that governors of the province were normally appointed in the same way as other "men" of the *megas doux*. Rather, they corresponded to civilian governors of the eleventh century, supervising provincial law courts, tax offices, and so on (see earlier). Given the relative unimportance of the area, both in naval matters and in administrative status, this anomaly is not surprising.[128] It was very probably generated by financial considerations: if Constantinople had to appoint a civilian governor anyway, then there was no need to pay another man. Unlike the key islands or the vital Adriatic coast, Hellas and Peloponnesos rarely attracted officials who were making a professional career in the administration.[129]

So the weakness of Greek naval forces in relation to other maritime areas is understandable. But the degree of disorganization was revealed only in the Norman raid of 1147. Monemvasia proved the sole port capable of self-defense—which it may well have owed to its extraordinary site—and the Normans were allowed to advance inland to Thebes and to sack Corinth, despite the existence of a military garrison at Acrocorinth.[130] Thus, in the first half of the twelfth century, provincial forces could be utterly ineffective. The central administration responded with the appointment of Stephanos Kontostephanos as *megas doux*, sent to relieve Corfù in 1148/49.[131] But there is no indication that he or his successors were concerned about improving the situation in central Greece.

Clear evidence is lacking on the composition of naval and military forces assigned to the province after Alexios's reforms. The organization had its origins in the thematic military formations of the Middle Byzantine period. The fleets of Hellas and Peloponnesos were composed of sailors holding a *pleustikè strateia*; they were inscribed on naval lists corresponding to military ones as *apotetagmenoi plôimoi*.[132] During the eleventh century, reorganization of fighting forces and commutation of personal service to a money payment meant an increase in overall taxation. But in the *horion* of Athens, in addition to heavy naval taxes, sailors still had to be provided. As the naval bureau's abuses were well known, the monastery of Lavra was careful to stipulate that its sailors should not be pressed into public service, even if the empire might be in the greatest danger.[133]

Following the reforms of Alexios I, the system can be reconstructed as follows: a local naval squadron was attached to each significant port in the maritime provinces. It patrolled coastal waters and defended the area. These ports were the bases for military and naval operations in the surrounding region, which became subdivisions of the province known as κατεπανίκια or ὅρια. They were administered by officials, κατεπάνω, δούξ, or ἄρχων, appointed from Constantinople with wide-ranging powers over all maritime activity—transport, commercial events involving foreigners, and so on. They may also have supervised the collection of naval taxes.[134] There is no evidence that a whole flotilla of special boats and crews was constantly maintained. Probably local captains and sailors were enlisted for specific services when necessary, but it is difficult to tell how such units operated in practice.[135]

Beginning with the reign of John II (1118–43), money raised from all regular naval taxation was diverted to the capital rather than remaining in the provinces. Local defense as well as the entire naval apparatus declined. This development may well indicate a turning point, for the *archontes* seem to disappear in the late twelfth century. The administrative division of the province into *horia* survived, but its purpose and main role were obliterated.[136] Officials such as *plôimologoi* and *nautologoi* continued nonetheless to collect taxes. In times of crisis, imagined or real, men were conscripted into active service. Toward the end of the twelfth century, a special fleet was to be equipped for the purpose of destroying Gafforio, a Genoese pirate, whose activities were hampering Byzantine shipping in the Aegean. On the orders of the *megas doux*, Steiriônès was sent to central Greece to levy additional taxation to cover expenses. Not only did the local population furnish supplies and money to outfit the boats, but men were impressed into service as oarsmen and sailors. And although Gafforio was eventually defeated, Michael complained that Attica still suffered pirate raids.[137]

Nor was service confined to the navy. Small inland garrisons, often connected by mountain passes, required "volunteers." The process of forced recruitment of men to maintain these garrisons—an echo of the complaints about naval duty demanded of some Athenians'—is recorded by Euthymios of Neopatras. As soon as a farmer had been sent off to join the garrison, his lands were expropriated by the official responsible for his departure.[138] Thus, governors and junior staff could arrange their own personal gain at the expense of those unfortunates. Illegal occupation of peasant holdings was apparently common in the lawless atmosphere of twelfth-century Greece. Choniates accused the *kastrènoi*, more powerful Athenians with influence in local government circles, of driving farmers off the land, only to occupy but not to cultivate it. As a result, impoverished peasants were "blown over the countryside like leaves in the wind," and everyone suffered the waste of fallow lands.[139]

These developments produced a paradoxical situation: the population paid heavy maritime taxes that should have been used to maintain the squadron based in each *horion*, but in practice there was a total lack of naval defense. After the departure of the *archôn*, local seamen who owned boats, *nauklèroi*, probably reverted to transporting goods and persons from port to port; fishermen went back to their fishing; and pirates continued to harass coastal settlements without opposition. A Monemvasiot boat sailed between its home port and Athens, while pirate activity from Makri (Makronisi), a small island off Attica, persisted about as regularly.[140]

This process of decline in regional forces was symptomatic of a much broader and disruptive development in twelfth-century Byzantine administration. Naval policy during the reign of Alexios I was directed specifically toward the control over trade routes between Constantinople and the Mediterranean, and the destruction of hostile forces in Byzantine waters. In this, the Byzantines were assisted by the Venetians, who agreed to provide naval support for the empire in exchange for trading concessions.[141] Those holding the post of *megas doux* took an active part in the planning and execution of naval operations. They commanded Venetian flotillas and drew upon local forces where possible, but the imperial fleet based in Constantinople was the chief fighting force. On their orders, subordinate naval commanders led expeditions probably with smaller squadrons outfitted in the capital.[142]

John II, however, abandoned his father's policy and tried to repudiate the Venetian treaty. Venice retaliated with an effective punitive naval raid in which several Aegean islands were devastated. In 1126, therefore, the treaty was renegotiated and the old arrangements rather shakily restored.[143] The Italian Republic extended its trading position within the empire and pledged naval protection. John II seems to have considered this promise adequate to cover all local maritime defense, for he approved a proposal by Iôannès Poutzès, a financial minister, to withdraw regular naval taxation from the provinces to the capital.[144] From this time on, *archontes* in the *horia* and regional fleets gradually disappeared. Simultaneously, the post of *megas doux* and the whole naval bureau at Constantinople were reduced to largely financial concerns. Some provincial naval activity continued, especially in the waters of Crete and the Adriatic, and ports such as Monemvasia survived as bases. But after the reign of Manuel I (1143–80), *megaloi doukes* commanded few and often unreliable foreign forces, indigenous regional fleets were no longer maintained, and naval operations took place with very low morale. Dependence upon Venice, which failed conspicuously to check the success of Norman and other Italian ships in Byzantine waters, and neglect of native shipping destroyed the Byzantine navy.[145]

In this situation, top military and naval officials were not much concerned with the strategic defense of the empire; they accepted their posts as sinecures, honorary titles to be bought.[146] While the *megas doux* could have taken an interest in the efficiency of local government and regional forces, his main activity was to ensure the collection of taxes destined officially for naval upkeep. This primary economic concern developed through the overfiscalization of the central administration—following Poutzès's example, all bureaus sought to increase their revenues from the provinces. Such actions did nothing to restore any semblance of vigor to the ailing Byzantine military machine.

The official structure of government is reflected, nonetheless, in the titles adopted by *megaloi doukes* during the twelfth century. Eumathios Philokalès, who governed Cyprus for many years before he was promoted to *megas doux*, took the title of *praitôr* between 1112 and 1118. Alexios Komnènos Bryennios appears to have spent some time in the area and was known as *anthypatos*, though it is doubtful whether his role was as great as Michael Choniates claimed.[147] Last, *megas doux* Stryphnos paid a visit to Athens also as *anthypatos*. A measure of his attitude toward the province can be gauged from Michael's letter promising him the customary gifts, *antidoseis*.[148] In addition, several officers of the *megas doux* were associated with Hellas and Peloponnesos: Leôn Nikeritès, a brilliant commander, held the post of governor (*stratègos*) in Peloponnesos for a time, and also the title of *anthypatos*. In the 1160s Alexios Kontostephanos was appointed to the province as the subordinate of his brother Andronikos, *megas doux*.[149] Garrison commanders should also be considered together with these junior officials, although the method of their appointment is not clear. At the time of the Norman raid, Nikèphoros Chaiouphès was in charge of the strong defenses of Acrocorinth. Despite his failure to protect the population of Corinth, he appears to have had a long career under Manuel.[150] Another force stationed in Peloponnesos marched to the relief of Thessalonike in 1185 under the command of Iôannès Maurozômès, a member of an important local family.[151] Finally, Bardas, an ἀρχιτελώνης, was responsible for ordering the enforced military service of poor peasants.[152] As such, he was probably one of the governor's men who worked together with the *prôtokentarchos*.

To sum up the military situation in Hellas and Peloponnesos, it is clear that the new system established by Alexios I was never as firmly implanted in Greece as in other regions. It was seriously undermined by the policies of John II, who removed naval *archontes* from the provinces by cutting off their resources. While small military detachments continued to guard important castles, usually at strategic inland sites, the forces making up local fleets gradually disintegrated. Naval authority remained officially the most powerful in the province, but the *megas doux* had very little direct influence or concern. In the final years of Byzantine rule in central Greece, *megas doux* Stryphnos provides an archetypal example of the degeneration of the plans of Alexios I.

CONCLUSION

Eleventh- and twelfth-century reforms in Byzantine administration shattered the relationship between province and capital. The centralization of military control and fiscalization of services and dues, previously performed in person or paid in kind, produced great hostility to Constantinople in the themes. Taxation drained the provinces of resources without providing any of the services (among others, local defense, upkeep of roads, bridges, and government buildings) that were basic to the most minimal administration. These developments changed the attitude of provincial inhabitants. Constantinople was no longer seen as the source of concerned paternalistic government; the benefits of living under Byzantine rule as "Rômaioi," once an index of civilization, had gone. The capital had developed a parasitic relationship with the provinces.

As economic affairs worsened at the center, the local government of Hellas and Peloponnesos developed a competitive aspect—all sectors of the administration attempted to collect their own taxation from the same regional population. Interaction between administrators became hostile when they tried to capture the limited resources available for themselves. The *megas doux* was usually present only through his officials, who persisted in levying taxes destined supposedly for local defense. On rare occasions he might make a personal visit to receive the customary gifts due to the supreme authority in the province, that is, his concern was basically mercenary. Similarly, the civilian governor who was more often on the spot aimed to get his full share of supplies and services. Given the fact that the position did not carry a fixed salary, it is hardly surprising that governors often spent only a short period in the province, taking advantage of whatever benefits could be obtained.

In contrast to military and civilian authorities, ecclesiastical administrators had less incentive to impose financial hardships on their parishioners. They naturally guarded their rights to the *kanonikon* and tried to enforce the rents due on ecclesiastical properties in the region. Such ecclesiastical taxation, however, constituted a tiny fraction of the total sum expected from local inhabitants.

This decline in provincial administration, which was common to all parts of the empire, illustrates various differences between the three sectors. On the recruitment and suitability of administrators, it is clear that metropolitans were, on the whole, cultivated men, educated and trained at the capital in the highest clerical circles. Many were not prepared for provincial life, but most accepted its privations as part of the job. To a certain extent their training motivated them to the task of working and preaching in a largely illiterate community, and they recognized the value of such work. Governors, of course, were also experienced officials, and those from the central administration were often well qualified to run provincial government. Many, however, left the capital most unwillingly, while some, Iôannès Hagiotheodôritès, for example, were simply exiled. This was not particular to the period. For centuries all officials accustomed to life in Constantinople usually found provincial duty tedious, an experience to be avoided if possible. But in the context of twelfth-century bureaucracy, a rather different and contradictory situation arose. On the one hand, officials were even more reluctant to leave the capital. On the other, they went to the provinces to recoup and to increase funds used to purchase the position. Provincial administration was thus reduced to a form of investment expected to yield as much as or more than other forms. Such corruption was hardly an example of impartial and just administration for junior agents who were often left in control. As for *megaloi doukes*, their qualifications for the post came to depend more on a close relationship with the emperor than on any particular skill. Not all of them were as bad commanders as Stryphnos, but very few had any concept of the potential of provincial fleets or tried to do anything about them.

When it came to maintaining some continuity of provincial government, ecclesiastics were again in a better position than other officials. Twelfth-century metropolitans of Athens assisted at church synods at Constantinople, but they normally resided on the Acropolis and were concerned for their see. Michael Choniates appears to have left the area only once in a twenty-year period. Another factor contributing to the continuity of metropolitan administration lay in the employment of local deacons and monks on the staff usually for long periods. The civilian governors, by contrast, changed all too rapidly and were often absent, to judge by the number of stand-in officials recorded. The coming and going of such figures resulted in more disruption than traditional administration. Subordinate agents working in the provincial government did preserve a minimal continuity, but as this would have existed at the lowest level only, it cannot have constituted a strong influence. While officials of the *megas doux* made very regular appearances in the province, at least once a year according to Choniates, their activity was certainly not a positive factor in naval administration. Frequent changes in the post of *megas doux* and its preoccupations with affairs beyond the theme of Hellas and Peloponnesos almost ruled out continuity in this sector.

As imperial control in central Greece became progressively weaker, local landowners began to take matters into their own hands, albeit in a small way. Numerous individuals and groups, often anonymous, resisted all forms of established authority and tried to create their own independent territories. The activity of Leôn Sgouros provides an outstanding example, and one of the most developed, in that he recruited an army and sought to gain entry into court circles, both by the assumption of titles and through marriage. Lesser *archontes* in Boiotia united to prevent the governor from visiting Euripos, doubtless on another of his raiding expeditions. Similar actions by Manuel Kammytzkès further north in Thessaly, and by Leôn Chamaretos in the region of Sparta, indicate that this was a general and widespread reaction to the decline in provincial government. Independence from the arbitrary demands of official administrators was the common aim. In Hellas and Peloponnesos no distinction was made between representatives of the *megas doux* and other tax collectors, as by now all these officials had the same concern. There was absolutely no respect for the highest authority in the province.

In this situation the church gained a new position in provincial society. When the civilian administration proved incapable, it was the metropolitans who had to deal with both foreign and indigenous threats. Michael Choniates's organized resistance to Leôn Sgouros was merely one instance of this phenomenon that can be traced throughout the empire. Although the church had no physical strength in the form of armed soldiers, several successful defenses against military attacks were mounted by churchmen with the help of local inhabitants. Even when forced into exile the Orthodox Church could run a shadow administration, but it was naturally incapable of replacing imperial government. Its strength grew from the fact that the church represented all that was most advanced in the culture of Constantinople—education, use of written documents, and enduring Christian ideals that benefited the local population. The performance of services necessary to Orthodox life, baptism, marriage, burial, and celebration of the liturgy, gave metropolitans in the disorders of the late twelfth century effective authority in provincial society. Despite its military and juridical impotence, for the inhabitants of outlying regions the church stood for the stability of imperial government which was so rapidly disintegrating.

This breakdown of administrative structures in Hellas and Peloponnesos was by no means exceptional; on the contrary, it was typical of a general decline. At the end of the twelfth century Byzantine provincial government was in reality a series of agents competing for the wealth of the theme. Of the three sectors, the ecclesiastical, through its charitable and educational work, played a more beneficial role than the civilian or military. And in the face of separatist movements and local revolts, it displayed more strength and courage than either of them.

NOTES

1. *M. Ch.*, I and II (Michael Choniates in the text). Cf. the critical notes by P. N. Papageorgiou, Ἐπίκρισις τῆς ἐκδόσεως τοῦ Μιχαὴλ Ἀκομινάτου (Athens, 1883). **Update** See now the new edition by Ph. Kolovou, *Michael Choniates: symvole ste melete tou viou kai tou ergou tou: to Corpus ton epistolon* (Athens, 1999); M. Angold, *Church and Society in Byzantium under the Comneni 1081–1261* (Cambridge, UK, 1995), 197–212; P. Speck, "A Byzantine Depiction of Ancient Athens," in his volume of essays, *Understanding Byzantium*, ed. S. Takács (Aldershot, UK, 2003), 29–32; A. Kaldellis, *Hellenism in Byzantium* (Cambridge, UK, 2007), 318–34; idem, *The Christian Parthenon: Classicism and Pilgrimage in Byzantine Athens* (Cambridge, UK, 2009), 145–65; Ch. Bouras, *Vyzantine Athena 10os–12os ai. Mouseio Benaki, 60 Paratema* (Athens, 2010), 263–68; and T. Shawcross, "The Lost Generation (ca.1204–ca.1222): Political Allegiance and Local Interests under the Impact of the Fourth Crusade," in J. Herrin and G. Saint-Guillain, eds., *Identities and Allegiances in the Eastern Mediterranean after 1204* (Aldershot, UK, 2011), 9–45.

2. J. Darrouzès, *Georges et Dèmètrios Tornikès. Lettres et Discours* (Paris, 1970), 124–25, letter 9; R. Browning, "Unpublished Correspondence between Michael Italicus, Archbishop of Philippopolis, and Theodore Prodromos," *Byzantinobulgarica* 1 (1962), 279–97.

3. Benjamin of Tudela, *Itinerary*, ed. and trans. M. N. Adler (London, 1907), 10; N. Svoronos, "Recherches sur le cadastre byzantin et la fiscalité aux XIe et XIIe siècles: Le cadastre de Thèbes," *BCH* 83 (1959), 36, 53, 71, 73–75; A. Lombardo and R. Morozzo della Rocca, *Documenti del commercio veneziano nei secoli XI– XIII* (Turin, 1940), nos. 233–35, 239, 273–75, 353, 403; *N. Ch.*, 99–101, 608–9. It is most unfortunate that no records of provincial administration in Thebes survive. **Update** Leonora Neville, *Authority in Byzantine Provincial Society, 950–1100* (Cambridge, UK, 2004), and "Organic Local Government and Village Authority," in *Authority in Byzantium*, ed. P. Armstrong (Aldershot, UK, forthcoming, 2013)

4. *M. Ch.*, II, 11–12, 26–27, 42, 69; G. Stadtmüller, "Michael Choniates, Metropolit von Athen (ca. 1183–ca. 1222)," *OC* 33 (1934), 125–325; K. Setton, "Athens in the Later Twelfth Century," *Speculum*, 19 (1944), 179–207; idem,

"A Note on Michael Choniates, Archbishop of Athens (1182– 1204)," ibid., 21 (1946), 234–36.

5. Hélène Glykatzi-Ahrweiler, "Recherches sur l'administration de l'empire byzantin aux IXe–XIe siècles," *BCH* 84 (1960), 76. Unification of provinces was not unusual at this time; farther north, Strymon was joined to Boleron and Thessalonike.

6. These titles are recorded on his seal; see A. Bon, *Le Péloponnèse byzantin jusqu'en 1204* (Paris, 1952), 200f., no. 53. **Update** The *Prospography of the Byzantine World* (*PBW*), a database of persons named in written Byzantine sources as well as on seals, is an invaluable new tool now available online at http://www .pbw.kcl.ac.uk/. All references here to persons, their seals, and offices should be updated by consulting the *PBW*. See also E. Limousin, "L'administration byzantin du Péloponnèse (X–XII siècles)," in *Le Péloponnèse: archéologie et histoire: Actes de la Rencontre internationale de l'Orient, mai 1998*, ed. J. Renard (Rennes, 1999), 295–311.

7. A. Bon, *Le Péloponnèse byzantin*, 200, no. 52; cf. Michael Attaliota, *Historia*, Bonn ed. (1853), 182; G. G. Litavrin, *Sovety i rasskazy Kekavmena* (Moscow, 1972), 266; Michael Psellos, *Epistulae*, ed. K. Sathas, Μεσαιωνικὴ Βιβλιοθήκη, 5 (1876), 344; cf. Psellos, *Scripta minora*, ed. E. Kurtz and F. Drexl, II (Milan, 1941), letter 8, addressed to the same Nikèphoros, *sebastophoros*; Johannes Zonaras, *Epitome Historiarum*, ed. L. Dindorf, IV (Leipzig, 1871), 219. **Update** See also the second edition of G. Litavrin's study of Kekaumenos (St. Petersburg, 2003).

8. On the post of *megas doux*, see R. Guilland, *Recherches sur les institutions byzantines* (Berlin/Amsterdam, 1967), I, 542–62; Hélène Ahrweiler, *Byzance et la Mer* (Paris, 1966), 275–77; A. Hohlweg, *Beiträge zur Verwaltungsgeschichte des oströmischen Reiches unter den Komnenen*, Miscellanea Byzantina Monacensia, 1 (Munich, 1965), 134–57; N. Oikonomidès, "Les institutions, l'évolution de l'organisation administrative de l'empire byzantin au XIe siècle," paper delivered at the "Table ronde sur le onzième siècle," Paris, 1973. I am most grateful to Professor Oikonomidès for allowing me to consult his paper and for many helpful references. **Update** Professor Oikonomidès's paper was published in *TM*, 6 (1976), 125–52.

9. *M. Ch.*, I, 145, 177, 315, 338, and passim; N. Bănescu, "La signification des titres de πραίτωρ et de προνοητής à Byzance aux XIe et XIIe siècles," *Miscellanea Giovanni Mercati*, III (Vatican City, 1946), 387–98; Guilland, *Recherches sur les institutions*, II, 68–79.

10. When Michael Choniates recalled the fact that Alexios Komnènos held the title of *anthypatos*, he referred to his position as *megas doux*. It was in this capacity that Alexios governed Hellas and Peloponnesos. On the new hierarchy, see Hohlweg, *Verwaltungsgeschichte*, 34–40. **Update** P. Magdalino, *The Empire of Manuel I Komnenos 1143–1180* (Cambridge, UK, 1993); E. Malamut, *Alexis Ier Comnène* (Paris, 2007).

11. This can be only in roughly chronological order, given the nature of some of the evidence. **Update** Seals continue to provide significant new material for such lists of officials, see *PBW*.

12. N. *Ch.*, 83–84, 254–57, 284, 800. On Patriarch Sergios's participation in the defense of Constantinople, see F. Barišić, "Le siège de Constantinople par les Avares et les Slaves en 626," *B* 24 (1954), 378–89. **Update** J. Howard-Johnston,

Witnesses to a World Crisis: Historians and Histories of the Middle East in the Seventh Century (Oxford, 2010); Angold devotes Part III of *Church and Society in Byzantium* to "The Bishop and Local Society," 139–262.

13. The *Ordo ecclesiasticus* of Isaac II (1189) most accurately reflects these positions; see H. Gelzer, *Analecta byzantina* (Jena, 1892), I, 4.

14. These are recorded in the *Notitia* partially published by H. Gelzer as *Notitia* V, from Athens, cod. gr. 1371, in *Ungedruckte und ungenügend veröffentlichte Texte der Notitiae episcopatuum*, AbhBayer, Philos.-Philol. Kl., 21 (1901), 584. The two new suffragans are clearly visible on fol. 390r of the MS. For a detailed examination of this *Notitia*, see my study "The Ecclesiastical Organization of Central Greece at the Time of Michael Choniates," reprinted as chapter 4 of this volume.

15. *PL*, 215, cols. 1559–62; V. Laurent, "L'érection de la Métropole d'Athènes et le statut ecclésiastique de l'Illyricum au VIIIe siècle," *EtByz* 1 (1943), 58–78.

16. See note 2 earlier.

17. *M. Ch.*, II, 131, 210–11, 311; PL, 215, cols. 1559–62; cf. E. Herman, "The Secular Church," *Cambridge Medieval History*, vol. 4, pt. 2 (Cambridge, UK, 1967), 118–25.

18. *M. Ch.*, I, 308; II, 71, 107; F. Dölger, *Regesten der Kaiserurkunden des oströmischen Reiches* (Munich/Berlin, 1924–60) (hereafter, Dölger, *Regesten*), no. 1541.

19. lbid., nos. 1285–88, 1541–46; P. Lemerle, "Trois actes du despote d'Epire Michel II concernant Corfou connus en traduction latine," Προσφορὰ εἰς Σ. Π. Κυριακίδην (= Ἑλληνικά, suppl. 4 [1953]), 405–26, esp. 424; G. Brătianu, *Privilèges et franchises municipales dans l'Empire byzantin* (Bucharest, 1936), 104–14.

20. E. Herman, "Appunti sul diritto metropolitano della chiesa bizantina," *OCP* 13 (1947), 522–50; cf. *M. Ch.*, II, 75.

21. J. Darrouzès, *Recherches sur les Ὀφφίκια de l'église byzantine* (Paris, 1970). This study has made several basic revisions to the older work of L. Clugnet, "Les offices et les dignités ecclésiastiques dans l'Eglise grecque," *ROChr* 3 (1898), 142–50, 260–64, 452–57; ibid., 4 (1899), 116–28.

22. Twelfth-century patriarchs elected from the *archontes* included Nikètas Mountanès, Basileios Kamatèros, and George Xiphilinos. On the significance of the group, see V. Tiftixoglu, "Gruppenbildungen innerhalb des Konstantinopolitanischen Klerus während der Komnenenzeit," *BZ*, 62 (1969), 25–72, esp. 33–36, 53–60.

23. J. Darrouzès, "Obit de deux Métropolites d'Athènes, Léon Xéros et Georges Bourtzès, d'après les inscriptions du Parthénon," *REB* 20 (1962), 190–96; and "Notice sur Grégoire Antiochos (1160 à 1196)," ibid., 79–80.

24. On this training, see *M. Ch.*, I, 347–49; II, 8–10, 67. Altogether, six letters to Eustathios, six to Patriarch Theodosios, two to Xiphilinos, and seven to Autoreianos are preserved.

25. A. Frantz, "From Paganism to Christianity in the Temples of Athens," *DOP* 19 (1968), 185–206; A. D. Norre, "Studies in the History of the Parthenon" (Diss., Los Angeles, 1966), 1–43. **Update** Kaldellis, *Hellenism in Byzantium*, 173–87; and *The Christian Parthenon*, 81–91.

26. On the Parthenon inscriptions, see A. K. Orlandos and L. Branouses, Τὰ Χαράγματα τοῦ Παρθενῶνος (Athens, 1973), nos. 56, 60, 277; for those on the

Propylaia, Antonin, *O drevnih' hristrianskih' nadpisjah' v' Afinah'* (St. Peters-burg, 1874), 33, no. 4; 35, no. 8.

27. Ibid., 28, no. 29: Leontios died in 1078; Iôannès Blachernitès held office from 1068/69 to 1086.

28. On the disagreement between the Pleuritès brothers, see Darrouzès, *Georges et Dèmètrios Tornikès* (note 2 earlier), 126, no. 9; cf. *M. Ch.*, II, 290–91.

29. The Athenian officials are recorded in *M. Ch.*, II, 30, 32, 138, 243–44, 290, 313, 318. On the division of the staff into groups or *pentades*, see Dar-rouzès, *Offikia*, 100–101. The five main *archontes*, called *exôkatakoiloi*, under-took the work of the patriarchate and provided a secretariat for the Holy Synod, the supreme authority of the church; see S. Vailhé, "Le droit d'appel en Orient et le Synode de Constantinople," *ÉO*, 20 (1921), 129–46; J. Hajjar, "Le Synode permanent dans l'Eglise byzantine des origines au XIe siècle," *OCA*, 164 (1962); V. Tiftixoglu, "Gruppenbildungen," 57; Darrouzès, *Offikia*, 334–36.

30. *M. Ch.*, I, 310; II, 284, 285, 314.

31. *EM* I, 51–52. For the clergy of the Metropolitan of Smyrna, cf. Hélène Ahrweiler, "La région de Smyrne entre les deux occupations turques, 1081–1317," *TM*, 1 (1965), 102–4, 118–21.

32. The posts of *chartophylax*, *prôtekdikos*, and *hypomnèmatographos* are mentioned only after 1205. **Update** See Shawcross, as earlier.

33. *M . Ch.*, II, 138; cf., Ahrweiler, "Smyrne," 111 n. 177, on the epithet *megas*.

34. *Charagmata*, nos. 169, 188, 219, 221.

35. *M. Ch.*, II, 30–34; Darrouzès, *Offikia*, 310–14.

36. Darrouzès, *Offikia*, 312–18; *M. Ch.*, I, 103–4, 325; II, 27.

37. *M. Ch.*, II, 290–91.

38. *Charagmata*, nos. 38, 64, 87, 172, 192, 213, and so on.

39. *M. Ch.*, II, 243–44. The first occasion on which George is addressed as *hypomnèmatographos* occurs later: ibid., II, 284.

40. On the importance of the *chartophylax* and his assistants, see Darrouzès, *Offikia*, 334–53; V. Tiftixoglu, "Gruppenbildungen innerhalb" (note 22 earlier), 56 ff. One Theodègios, father of Philippos, metropolitan in the tenth century, held the position; see *Charagmata*, no. 61.

41. *M. Ch.*, II, 206, 242. On the metropolitan's library, see S. Lampros, Περὶ τῆς βιβλιοθήκης τοῦ Μητροπολίτου Ἀθηνῶν Μιχαὴλ Ἀκομινάτου, in Ἀθηναῖον, 6 (1877/78), 354–67. Copyists were certainly available, for Athens was the home of Kônstantinos Tarsitès, scribe of a MS dated 1129, and copying went on in the monastery of Hosios Meletios; see M. Vogel and V. Garthausen, *Die griechischen Schreiber des Mittelalters und der Renaissance* (Leipzig, 1909), 28, 242, 251.

42. On the *Synodikon*, see V. Laurent, "La liste épiscopale de la Métropole d'Athènes, d'après le Synodicon d'une de ses églises suffragantes," *Mémorial L. Petit* (Bucharest, 1948). Choniates's role is suggested: ibid., 276 n. 3.

43. The creation of a rival ecclesiastical organization forced Choniates into self-imposed exile on the island of Kea, one of his suffragan sees. Although the Latin clergy were instructed to be tolerant and only one bishop in central Greece accepted the leadership of Bérard, the first Latin archbishop of Athens, Greek monasteries were put under considerable pressure; see R. L. Wolff, "The Orga-nization of the Latin Patriarchate of Constantinople, 1204–1261: Social and

Administrative Consequences of the Latin Conquest," *Traditio*, 6 (1948), 33–60; and the letters of Innocent III, *PL* 215, cols. 959, 1030–31, 1141–66. Update J. Herrin and G. Saint-Guillain, eds. *Identities and Allegiances in the Eastern Mediterranean after 1204* (Aldershot, UK, 2011).

44. M. *Ch.*, II, 257, 285–89, 311–13, 314–18, 334; cf. Stadtmüller, "Michael Choniates," 204–5; Wolff, "The Organization of the Latin Patriarchate," 40; V. G. Vasil'evskij, "Epirotica saeculi XIII, izʻ perepiski Ioanna Navpaktskago," *VizVrem*, 3 (1896), nos. 5, 6, 9–13, 248–52, 254–63.

45. M. *Ch.*, II, 337, 350.

46. Ibid., II, 313.

47. Darrouzès, *Offikia*, 323–32. In the Great Church there was a particular spot where this tribunal met, and a shrine reserved for murderers: N. *Ch.*, 446.

48. See, for example, Nikolaos *presbyteros*, *prôtekdikos*, and *nomikos* of the bishop of Hierissos in 1071: *Actes de Lavra. Première partie des origines à 1204*, ed. P. Lemerle et al., *Archives de l'Athos*, V (Paris, 1970), no. 35. Update Many similar junior officials are recorded in the later volumes in this series, *Archives de l'Athos*.

49. See note 40 earlier.

50. M. *Ch.*, II, 284; cf. The *hypomnèmatographos* of the metropolitan of Thessalonike: *Actes de Lavra,* I, no. 64. Provincial *hieromnèmones* are known in the area: ibid., nos. 22, 47; *Actes de Xéropotamou*, ed. J. Bompaire, Archives de l'Athos, III (Paris. 1963), no. 7; and a *logothetès*: MM, VI, 99.

51. M. *Ch.*, I, 310; cf. II, 125, where the *mystikos*'s agent, *hypodrèstèr*, is connected with further depredations. Stadmüller, " Michael Choniates," 296–97, corrects "dephendarios" to "repherendarios," but identifies the official as one attached to Athens. The *mystikos* was one of the most influential figures in the imperial chancellery; see R. Guilland, "Le mystique," *REB*, 26 (1968), 279–96; Dölger, *Regesten*, no. 1550. There is no suggestion that provincial *mystikoi* ever existed. The activity of these officials in Attica may be related to the appearance of the emperor's brothers-in-law, particularly Stryphnos: M. *Ch.*, II, 98–100, 125.

52. *Charagmata*, nos. 78, 129, 186, 191, 229 (*chartoularioi*); 170, 192 (*prôtopsaltai*); 60, 141, 146 (*domestikoi*); 102 (*deutereuôn*), 184 (*kouratôr*); cf. M. *Ch.*, II, 137.

53. Antonin, *O drevnih' hristrianskih' nadpisjah' v' Afinah'* (note 26 earlier), 35, no. 12; cf. 36, no. 17.

54. *Charagmata*, nos. 14, 132, 199, 42, 43, 17, 19; Antonin, O *drevnih' hristrianskih' nadpisjah' v' Afinah'*, 35–36.

55. V. Laurent, "Nicolas Kalommalos et l'église des SS. Théodore à Athènes," Ἑλληνικά, 7 (1934), 72–82; K. Konstantopoulos, Ἐπιγραφὴ ἐκ τοῦ ναοῦ τοῦ ἁγίου Ἰωάννου Μαγκούτη, inἘπ.Ἑτ. Βυζ. Σπ., 8 (1931), 247. Update Shawcross, as earlier, app., 38–45.

56. M. *Ch.*, II, 36, cf. 136–37. Nikolaos may possibly have been related to Èsaias, the holy man who lived near Monemvasia.

57. Ibid., II, 96, 98, 100, 106, 109, 237; the title of respect "entimôtatos" was always used for Thomas. The metropolitan of Thebes also had a secretary: ibid., II, 199–200. Other *grammatikoi* of Athens included George the *presbyteros* (see *Charagmata*, no. 54) and Leontios (see note 27 earlier).

58. *M. Ch.*, II, 26–30; *EM*, I, no. 34; cf. V. Grumel, *Les regestes des actes du patriarcat de Constantinople*, I, fasc., 3 (Paris, 1947), no. 1164. Michael had to call a local synod in Euboia, where he delivered a long sermon and settled the problem; see *M. Ch.*, I, 180–86.

59. *M. Ch.*, II, 137, 170.

60. Ibid., II, 281–82, 330–32, 332–33, and so on.

61. Ibid., II, 119–20 (mention of the bishop of Daulia and monastic communities in his see), 128,198, 205–6, 207–10, 295, 308, and so on. One stray letter to Epiphanios, bishop of Gardikion and Peristera, suffragan sees of Larissa, makes a specific request for the help of workmen not available in Athens; it has no ecclesiastical purpose: ibid., II, 69.

62. Ibid., II, 148–49, 155–57, 272–73, 313–14 (monastery of Hosios Meletios); 247–48 (monastery of the Philosophers); 252–57, 261–63 (monastery of the Confessors); 311–13 (Kaisareianè); and many others.

63. Ibid., II, 221–34, and many other letters to these three, Euthymios Tornikès, Nikolaos Pistophilos, and Manuel Beriboès.

64. Michael wrote frequently to Nikolaos Kalodoukès and Geôrgios Kallistos, his doctors; for example, ibid., II, 147, 201; to local friends such as Manuel Yalas, Iôannès Kalokairos, and Dèmètrios Makrembolitès, see ibid., II, 244, 249, 275; and to wives and widows of friends, ibid., II, 332–33, 338.

65. *N. Ch.*, 800–802. **Update** On Sgouros, see Photeine Vlachopoulou, *Leon Sgouros: o vios kai e politeia tou archonta tes voreioanatolikes Peloponnesou stis arches tou 13e aiona* (Thessalonike, 2002).

66. Ibid., 584, 598–600, 637–39; Dölger, *Regesten*, no. 1165; P. Lemerle, "'Roga' et rente d'état," *REB*, 25 (1967), 97–100. **Update** L. Neville, *Authority in Byzantine Provincial Society, 950–1100* (Cambridge, UK, 2004), 39, 47–50, 53–65.

67. On these governors, see Table 3.1, notes 15, 22, 16, 20, and the following.

68. *M. Ch.*, I, 177.

69. P. Lemerle, "Recherches sur le régime agraire à Byzance: la terre militaire à l'époque des Comnènes," *CahCM*, 2 (1959), 265–81. **Update** On the fiscalization of military services, see John Haldon, *Warfare, State and Society in the Byzantine World* (London, 1999), 124–28.

70. *M. Ch.*, I, 307–11; II, 54, 65–66, 81–84, 106–7. Among the governor's personal services there was a special tax, πραιτωρικὴ ἐπήρεια: ibid., I, 308. He also controlled the minting of coinage at a local mint that was established, probably at Thebes, in the course of the twelfth century; see M. F. Hendy, *Coinage and Money in the Byzantine Empire 1081–1261* (Washington, DC, 1969), DOS XII, 128–30.

71. *N. Ch.*, 426; C. M. Brand, *Byzantium Confronts the West, 1180–1204* (Cambridge, MA, 1968), 61–66.

72. *M. Ch.*, II, 48, 54. It was customary for emperors to grant a general remission of outstanding taxes at the outset of their reign. Individuals could also gain a specific, smaller exemption; see *Epistoliers byzantins du Xe siècle*, ed. J. Darrouzès (Paris, 1960), 377, no. 47.

73. This official should probably be identified with Theodôros Choumnos, who was active in the imperial chancellery at this time; cf. *Actes de Lavra*, I, no. 66 (1184); J. Verpeaux, "Note prosopographique sur la famille Choumnos," *BS*

20 (1959), 252–54. In a previous letter, Michael mentioned the same Choumnos as a very powerful person who might be able to help: *M. Ch.*, II, 43.

74. Nikèphoros Prosouch was welcomed by Michael with a long speech. He appears to have been an efficient governor; see *ibid.*, I, 142–49; II, 54, 66. He may be the same Nikèphoros Prosouch who was ambassador and adviser to Manuel I at the time of the Third Crusade; see Joannes Cinnamos, *Epitome, CSHB* (Bonn, 1836), 33–35, 51; *N. Ch.*, 71, 88. In this case he would have been an old man in 1182. Despite this gap of nearly forty years, Lampros supported the identification: *M. Ch.*, II, 455; cf. Bon, *Le Péloponnèse* (note 6 earlier), 201, no. 54. Drimys was obviously a younger man making a legal career. Michael addressed him as *dikastès* and *prôtoasèkrètis*: *M. Ch.*, I, 157–79; II, 66, 81–84. In 1186 he held the post of *kritès tou bèlou*; see *MM*, VI, 121.

75. *M. Ch.*, II, 65–66; the *antipraitôr* had the same role as a *hypodoux* in twelfth-century Thessalonike, or a thirteenth-century *antidoux*; see Eustathios of Thessalonikè, *De simulatione, PG*, 136, col. 376; Ahrweiler, "Smyrne," 161, 163. They all served as substitutes before the arrival of nominated officials; cf. the *hypopraktôr* mentioned by Eustathios, *De simulatione, PG*, 136, col. 376.

76. *N. Ch.*, 584, 599, 639–40. Nikètas's accusation that the Aggeloi were totally unconcerned about the public good and interested only in accumulating taxes is borne out by his brother, who condemns the policy of draining the provinces of wealth: *M. Ch.*, II, 83.

77. See table 3.1, notes 28, 29. The metropolitan addressed Tripsychos as *hypertimos*, not an exclusively ecclesiastical title, and as *megalyperochos prôtonotarios*: ibid., II, 67–68; cf. *Actes de Lavra*, I, nos. 67, 68. His position as *praitôr* is also recorded on his seal; see N. Bees, "Zur Sigillographie der byzantinischen Themen Hellas und Peloponnesos," *VizVrem*, 21 (1914), 205–6.

78. *M. Ch.*, I, 307–11; but see the new edition and commentary by Stadtmüller, "Michael Choniates," 286–305. The accompanying letters went to Dèmètrios Tornikès, the Belissariôtai, Theodôros Eirènikos, and Stryphnos: *M. Ch.*, II, 96, 98–101, 102–4, 105–7.

79. Ibid., I, 312–23. On Basileios Kamatèros, see R. Guilland, "Les logothètes," *REB*, 29 (1971), 62–63. Michael had written to him on his return from exile after the death of Andronikos in 1185 (*M. Ch.*, II, 62–64), but as with so many officials at the capital it is difficult to tell whether Michael knew him personally. In this case there may well have been a personal friendship dating from the days of Michael's training in Constantinople. Nikètas addressed three letters to the same Basileios; see J.-L. van Dieten, *Nicetae Choniatae orations et epistulae* (Berlin/New York, 1972), 202–3, 209–11, 216–17.

80. See J. Hoffmann, *Rudimente von Territorialstaaten im byzantinischen Reich (1071–1210)*, Miscellanea Byzantina Monacensia, 17 (Munich, 1974), 47–60, 90–96.

81. Local *archontes*, such as Sgouros, Chalkoutzès, Doxapatrès, and Chamaretos, and walled cities like Larissa and Acrocorinth were able to resist the crusaders, but many in fact welcomed the Latins as a relief from Byzantine rule; see J. Longnon, *L'Empire latin de Constantinople et la principauté de Morée* (Paris, 1949), 69–75. **Update** Michael Kordoses, *Southern Greece under the Franks, 1204–61* (Ioannina, 1987); Peter Lock, *The Franks in the Aegean, 1204–1500* (London, 1995).

82. Ahrweiler, "Recherches sur l'administration" (note 5 earlier), 68–69, 71–72, 75. *Anagrapheis* in the province of Strymon, Boleron, and Thessalonike appear to have served slightly less than the three-year term in the eleventh and twelfth centuries; see *Actes de Lavra*, I, 220–22.

83. An ideal account of this system is given in a tenth-century document; see F. Dölger, *Beiträge zur byzantinischen Finanzverwaltung, besonders des 10. und 11. Jahrhunderts* (Leipzig/Berlin, 1927; repr. Hildesheim, 1960). In the twelfth century the title of *prôtonotarios* was reserved for heads of the chief departments of central administration; those of *epoptès* and *exisôtès* were generally combined with the office of *anagrapheus*, judicial and recording functions of the old *dioikètès* and *chartoularios* passed to the governor. On the reorganization, see E. Stein, "Untersuchungen zur spätbyzantinischen Verfassungs- und Wirtschaftsgeschichte," *Mitt IÖG*, 2 (1923–25), 33–34; Dölger, *Finanzverwaltung*, 15, 17–19; N. Oikonomidès, *Fiscalité et exemption fiscale à Byzance, IXe–XIe siècles* (Athens, 1996).

84. *M. Ch.*, I, 307, 310; II, 66, 96, 99, 106f.; *Kekaumenos* (note 7 earlier), 152, 296; Zepos, *Jus*, I, 363f.; Dölger, *Finanzverwaltung*, 71–73; Ahrweiler, "Recherches sur l'administration," 88, 90.

85. *M. Ch.*, I, 307–8; II, 54. **Update** On the gradual switch from registration in *katasticha* to *praktika*, see Neville, *Authority in Byzantine Provincial Society*, 48–50, 62–65; and the evidence of a partially surviving *praktikon* from the region of Athens, E. Granstem, Igor Medvedev, and D. Papachryssanthou, "Fragment d'un praktikon de la région d'Athènes (avant 1204)," *REB*, 34 (1976), 5–44.

86. Ibid., I, 308; II, 42, 48, 54. Cf. the excessive *epèreiai* levied by *praktores* and their harassment of rich monastic communities: *Actes de Lavra*, I, no. 43; *MM*, VI, 55–57, 57–58; *PG*, 126, col. 316A. On one occasion, the entire rural population of the theme of Nikopolis revolted against its *praktôr*, Iôannès Koutzomytès; see Georgius Cedrenus, *Synopsis historiarum*, Bonn ed. (1838–39), II, 529.

87. *M. Ch.*, I, 146; II, 48. In his editorial comments Lampros indicates a marginal note in the Laurentianus MS that identifies Tessarakontapèchys: ibid., II, 457. He should not be confused with Geôrgios Tessarakontapèchys, correspondent and friend of the metropolitan; see ibid., II, 16, 17, 23, 43–46.

88. *Actes de Lavra*, I, no. 64; cf. D. Polemis, *The Doukai* (London, 1968), 76, no. 30.

89. Several documents refer precisely to this control over *epibolè* (ἐπιβολή): see *Actes de Lavra*, I, nos. 50, 52; cf. N. Svoronos, "L'épibolè à l'époque des Comnènes," *TM*, 3 (1968), 375–95; E. Schilbach, *Byzantinische Metrologie* (Munich, 1970), 248–63. On the establishment of a land register (*praktikon*), see C. Astruc, "Un document inédit de 1165 sur l'évêché thessalien de Stagoi," *BCH*, 83 (1959), 213–15. **Update** See the fragmentary document that may record the lands of a monastery close to Athens, published by Grandstrem, Medvedev, and Papachryssanthou, as earlier.

90. *M. Ch.*, I, 307; II, 66. Cf. PG, 126; col. 448C; Schilbach, *Byzantinische Metrologie*, 244–48.

91. *M. Ch.*, II, 129–31. On the use of *episkepsis* as estate, see Dölger, *Finanzverwaltung*, 41, 151; there were imperial and personal as well as ecclesiastical estates: *MM*, VI, 131; *Actes de Xéropotamou*, no. 8. Lampros's identification of

Geôrgios Kolymbas with Sergios Kolybas, an imperial secretary and *prôtonotarios* active in 1192, is merely hypothetical; see M. *Ch.*, II, 599; F. Dölger, *Byzantinische Diplomatik* (Ettal, 1956), 31.

92. *Actes d'Esphigmenou*, ed. J. Lefort, Archives de l'Athos, VI (Paris, 1973), no. 5; Bănescu, "La signification des titres" (note 9 earlier), 392.

93. *MM*, VI, 317, 324, 325; N. *Ch.*, 526.

94. M. *Ch.*, I, 308, 310 (*apographè*); cf. the verbal participle, ἀπογραφέντες, II, 107. Ibid., I, 310; II, 105, 107 (*synodosiai*). The term *apographè* is used exclusively for the calculation of the *syndosiai* rate, which had been made at the orders of Iôannes Doukas.

95. See, for example, Kônstantinos Hagioeuphèmitès, *bestarchès* and *exisôtès* of the *anagrapheus* of Thessalonike in 1104: *Actes de Lavra*, I, no. 56.

96. M. *Ch.*, II, 131.

97. Ibid., I, 309; II, 106–7.

98. *MM*, IV, 317; VI, 125–27; *Actes de Lavra*, I, nos. 45 and 64; Ahrweiler, "Recherches sur l'administration" (note 5 earlier), 41, 72; Dölger, *Finanzverwaltung*, 118; R. Guilland, "Etudes sur l'histoire administrative de l'Empire byzantin. Le logariaste, le megas logariaste," *JÖB*, 17 (1969), 101–13.

99. M. *Ch.*, II, 87. In ca. 1198 Michael condemned the *praitôr's logariastès* as one of the many officials who descended on Athens: ibid., I, 309.

100. Ibid., II, 119.

101. Ibid., I, 311; *EM*, I, 49–50; cf. Stadtmüller, "Michael Choniates," 301–3; Ahrweiler, *La Mer* (note 8 earlier), 278–79. Choniates associates the destruction of the *drouggoi* with the increase in fallow land as part of the same process of decline, suggesting that a certain amount of cultivation was carried out in the mountainous garrisons.

102. Guilland, *Recherches sur les institutions* (note 8 earlier), I, 216–36.

103. This correction was proposed by Lampros, M. *Ch.*, II, 516. On the post, see R. Guilland, "Le Protovestiarite," *RSBN* N.S. 4 (1967), 3–10; A. Papadopoulos-Kerameus, Ἰωάννης Ἀπόκαυκος καὶ Νικήτας Χωνιάτης, in Τεσσαρακονταετηρίς (Athens, 1909), 379; *MM*, IV, 232–33; VI, 181–89, 199–201; Ahrweiler, "Smyrne," 161, 164–65, 177–78; but cf. M. Angold, *A Byzantine Government in Exile: Government and Society under the Laskarids of Nicaea (1204–1261)* (Oxford, 1974), 204–7, 233–35, 253, 256, 268.

104. M. *Ch.*, II, 107.

105. *Actes de Lavra*, I, no. 65. On the important division of the Treasury into two parts and the work of *bestiaritai*, see Oikonomidès, paper cited in note 8.

106. M. *Ch.*, I, 309; cf. II, 106.

107. Ibid., I, 309; cf. II, 106. *Proskynètikia* were often denoted by other terms, such as *kephalatikion, kaniskion*, and *misthos*; see *MM*, V, 142–43; VI, 47, 121–22. Michael also uses *antidosis* in the same sense: M. *Ch.*, II, 100. All were gifts to which provincial officials were entitled and often consisted of provisions; for example, see the contents of a *kaniskion* (literally, basket) due to a judge: one loaf, one fowl, one *modion* of wheat, and half a measure of wine: *Actes d'Esphigmenou*, no. 5.

108. On this *aggareia tôn hypozygiôn*, see M. *Ch.*, I, 309; II, 107.

109. *MM*, V, 137, 144; VI, 47. Cf. Stadtmüller, "Michael Choniates," 293–94.

110. *M. Ch.*, II, 105; cf. I, 307; II, 83, 106; *Life of Hosios Meletios*, ed. V. Vasil'evskij, *Pravoslavnyj Palestinskij Sbornik*," 17 (1886), 49. In the singular, these terms might refer to an individual tax collector of some importance; see *N. Ch.*, 342, (*dasmalogos*), 700 (*phorologos*); Hélène Ahrweiler, "L'Administration militaire de la Crète byzantine," *B*, 31 (1961), 227.

111. *M. Ch.*, II, 106; *MM*, V, 83; VI, 7; *PG*, 126, cols. 515D, 536A; Dölger, *Finanzverwaltung*, 51, 53; Ahrweiler, "Smyrne," 125–27. On the exemption accorded to certain monasteries, see Zepos, *Jus*, III, 447, 453; *Actes de Lavra*, I, nos. 38, 44.

112. *JusGR*, III, 432.

113. The method of assessment is illustrated in the *praktikon* of Andronikos Doukas: *MM*, VI, 4–15.

114. On Iôannès Doukas, see Guilland, "Les logothètes" (note 79 earlier), 44–45, 63–65; and, most recently, A. P. Kazhdan, *Le parole e le idée*, 9 (1969), 242–47, and P. Karlin-Hayter, *B* 42 (1972), 259–65, 300–301. Contributions for a very wide range of ancillary services might be demanded; see, for example, Ahrweiler, *La Mer*, 212.

115. *M. Ch.*, I, 307–8; II, 105, 106–7.

116. Ibid., I, 308, 310; cf. H. Antoniadis-Bibicou, *Etudes d'histoire maritime de Byzance* (Paris, 1966), 41–43.

117. *N. Ch.*, 700–701, 376–79, 443–44, 483–84, 547; M. Ch., II, 277–78, 279–80; cf. Hoffmann, *Rudimente von Territorialstaaten.*

118. The Rendakios and Tessarakontapèchys families of central Greece had been related to imperial dynasties in the ninth and tenth centuries, but failed to maintain good relations with the Komnènoi; see Cedrenus, *Synopsis historiarum* (note 86 earlier), II, 297–98, 548; Constantimo Porfirogenito, *De thematibus*, ed. A. Pertusi (Vatican City, 1952), 91; Antonin, *O drevnih' hristrianskih' nadpisjah' v' Afinah'* (note 26 earlier), 23–25, no. 17; Svoronos, "Le cadastre de Thèbes" (note 3 earlier), 11, 13–14, 18; Bees, "Zur Sigillographie" (note 77 earlier), 199–200.

119. *M. Ch.*, I, 311, 315–16; D. Jacoby, "Les archontes grecs et la féodalité en Morée franque," *TM*, 2 (1967), 427–28.

120. Ahrweiler, *La Mer*, 184–86.

121. Anna Comnène, *Alexiade*, ed. and trans. B. Leib (Paris, 1937–45), III, 158–62.

122. Ibid., III, 162–64; *Life of Meletios*, 27.

123. On the general reorganization, see Ahrweiler, *La Mer*, 197–99; Oikonomidès, paper cited in note 8. The regions that thus became specifically naval had held a similar status in previous military administration; see N. Oikonomidès, *Les listes de préséance byzantines des IXe et Xe siècles* (Paris, 1972), 265. **Update** Malamut, *Alexis Ier Comnène*, 116–19, on Ioannes Doukas and Eumathios Philokales, as examples of supreme military and naval leaders; T. C. Lounghis, *Byzantium in the Eastern Mediterranean: Safeguarding East Roman Identity (407–1204)* (Nicosia, 2010), 168–74.

124. *MM*, VI, 96–97. Lounghis, *Byzantium in the East Mediterranean*, 33–34.

125. Hohlweg, *Verwaltungsgeschichte* (note 8 earlier), 15–34; J. Verpeaux, "Les oikeioi. Notes d'histoire institutionelle et sociale," *REB*, 23 (1965), 89–99. **Update** Magdalino, *Empire of Manuel I Komnenos*, 180–91.

126. *Alexiade*, III, 169; H. Grégoire, *Recueil des inscriptions grecques chré-tiennes de l'Asie Mineure*, fasc. 1 (Paris, 1922), no. 2268; cf. L. Robert, "Sur Didymes à l'époque byzantine," *Hellenica*, 11–12 (1960), 495–96; and on the date, see Ahrweiler, "L'Administration militaire de la Crète byzantine" (note 110 earlier), 225–26.

127. *Alexiade*, III, 160, 164; Ahrweiler, *La Mer*, 209–10; Hohlweg, *Verwal-tungsgeschichte*, 146–57, correctly stresses that *megaloi doukes* were often responsible for military and land operations as well as naval. Often other *thal-lassokratores* and *doukes tou stolou* commanded sections of a force, while the *megas doux* remained in overall control. Lounghis, as earlier.

128. Ahrweiler, *La Mer*, 208–9, 275–77; Oikonomidès, paper cited in note 8.

129. On these promotion channels, see esp. V. Laurent, "Andronikos Synad-enos, ou la carrière d'un haut fonctionnaire byzantin au XIIe siècle," *REB* 20 (1962), 210–14.

130. Cinnamos, *Epitome* (note 74 earlier), 96–101; *N. Ch.*, 96–102; cf. the analysis in Ahrweiler, *La Mer*, 241–43.

131. Cinnamos, *Epitome*, 97; *N. Ch.*, 103–5. **Update** Magdalino, *Empire of Manuel I Komnenos*, 137–40, emphasizes the ineffectiveness of naval protection.

132. Ahrweiler, *La Mer*, app. 1, 401; Antoniadis-Bibicou, *Etudes d'histoire maritime* (note 116 earlier), 39–46, app. 2, 138–40, on the recruitment of sailors, ἐκβολὴ πλωΐμων.

133. *Kekaumenos* (note 7 earlier), 294–96, on the *pleustikoi archontes*; *Actes de Lavra*, I, no. 55.

134. This activity is illustrated by the archon of Athens, ἀθηνάρχος, known from the *Life of Meletios*, 32–33, that is, before 1105; cf. Ahrweiler, *La Mer*, 210, 223–25, 277–78.

135. Although there is evidence of provincial ships participating in Byzantine naval campaigns during the twelfth century, the efficient upkeep of all local forces can not be assumed.

136. The existence of these *horia* is confirmed in several treaties and in the *Parti-tio regni Graeci (Partitio Romaniae)* drawn up by the crusaders in 1204; see *TT*, I, 264–67, 469–92; but there is no evidence of appropriate *archontes*. There were five *horia* in Greece at the end of the twelfth century: Larissa, Thebes-Euripos, Athens, Patras-Methone, and Corinth-Argos-Nauplion; and several *episkepseis*, such as Megara. In other parts of the empire these units were known as *katepanikia* and *chartoularata*. **Update** Magdalino, *Empire of Manuel I Komnenos*, 234–35.

137. *M. Ch.*, I, 310; II, 107, 122, 125, 129. Cf. Ahrweiler, *La Mer*, 277, 289–91.

138. *EM*, I, 73–74. Bardas, the *architelônès*, was in charge of this operation.

139. *M. Ch.*, I, 311; II, 99, 124–25.

140. Ibid., II, 99, 129, 137, 238. **Update** Magdalino points out that Venice was not permitted to trade in Monemvasia, suggesting the independent naval and trading capacity of the city, *Empire of Manuel I Komnenos*, 148–50; H. A. Kal-ligas, *Byzantine Monemvasia: The Sources* (Monemvasia, 1990), 1–70; R.-J. Lilie, *Handel und Politik zwischen dem byzantinischen Reich und den italienischen Kommunen, Venedig, Pisa und Genua* . . . (1081–1204) (Munich, 1984), 47–49.

141. Dölger, *Regesten*, no. 1081; Ahrweiler, *La Mer*, 180–82. **Update** Lilie, as earlier, 613–43.

142. Ahrweiler, *La Mer*, 186–87, 192–97.

143. Ibid., 229–33; Dölger, *Regesten*, no. 1304.

144. *N. Ch.*, 54–56; *Synopsis Chronikè*, ed. K. Sathas, Μεσαιωνικὴ Βιβλιοθήκη, 7 (1897), 220–22; Lemerle, "Recherches sur le régime agraire" (note 69 *earlier*), 275. Poutzès has been blamed for causing the decline of the Byzantine navy, but the worst effects of his measure were felt in the provinces, where naval *archontes* were left without funds for the upkeep of local forces.

145. The imperial fleet of Constantinople sustained some fighting capacity, but it was a weak successor to the tenth-century fleet. On this decline and on the consequences of dependence on Venice, see Judith Herrin, "The Collapse of the Byzantine Empire in the Twelfth Century: A Study of a Medieval Economy," *University of Birmingham Historical Journal*, 12 (1970), 190–93, 199, 202, reprinted as chapter 5 of this volume. **Update** Magdalino, *Empire of Manuel I Komnenos*, 233–35, 257–58; Lounghis, as earlier.

146. See, for example, Stryphnos's sale of naval materials: *N. Ch.*, 716. **Update** Neville, *Authority in Byzantine Provincial Society*, 34–38, on the contrast between the title and function of offices.

147. See table 3.1, notes 6 and 10.

148. *M. Ch.*, II, 98–100. It appears that Stryphnos had demanded these payments even though he was not in the province nor doing anything for it.

149. See table 3.1, notes 17 and 24.

150. *N. Ch.*, 101; Cinnamos, *Epitome* (note 74 earlier), 248–49, 262–63, 265; Dölger, *Regesten*, no. 1464. During Manuel's campaign in Dalmatia, Nikèphoros Chalouphès was left in command of recently conquered territory in a sensitive area, but he was taken prisoner and had to be ransomed from the Hungarians.

151. Eustathios of Thessalonikè, *La Espugnazione di Tessalonica*, ed. S. Kyriakidès (Palermo, 1961), 88. Among other members of the family, Theodôros Maurozômès, a naval commander under Andronikos Kontostephanos, is mentioned in connection with the local flotilla of Euboia: *N. Ch.*, 208, cf. 234, 827–28, 842. **Update** J. R. Melville Jones, *The Capture of Thessaloniki*, a translation with introduction and commentary, *Byzantina Australiensia* 8 (Canberra, 1988).

152. *EM*, I, 49–50.

4

THE ECCLESIASTICAL ORGANIZATION OF CENTRAL GREECE AT THE TIME OF MICHAEL CHONIATES

NEW EVIDENCE FROM THE *CODEX ATHENIENSIS 1371*

❧

This short article took me into the archives of the National Library of Greece in the 1970s, where an important manuscript contained a list of bishops not fully published in the basic editions by H. Gelzer and G. Parthey. During my investigations of the number of bishoprics in central Greece, a hint in Choniates's letters alerted me to the possibility that the older editors of the *Notitiae episcopatuum*, or lists of bishops compiled in Constantinople during the Byzantine centuries, might have overlooked some material. It was a considerable delight to discover that the Athenian manuscript confirmed this hunch.

At that time the library was located in central Athens and there did not seem to be very many visitors. I would like to thank the Director and curators who afforded me every assistance in the study of the document and made my visits there so enjoyable. The study of the *Notitiae* has now been greatly advanced by the work of Père Darrouzès, whose edition published in 1981 has clarified many of the problems of dating, which are now being put to most productive use by scholars like Constantin Zuckerman. My small contribution to this field of study was to establish that additional bishoprics existed in quite insignificant provincial towns in central Greece, where they upheld the traditions of Byzantine cult and administration under the direction of their metropolitan, Michael Choniates. In combination with the large number of small village churches constructed in the twelfth century, these new bishoprics suggest a growing population that required additional pastoral care. But in the absence of any of the traditional records of births, deaths, and marriages available to western medieval historians, the problem of calculating specific Byzantine populations remains particularly difficult.

IN THIS BRIEF CHAPTER I discuss the state of the church in Central Greece at the time when Michael Choniates was Metropolitan of Athens (1182–1205). In particular, I examine episcopal organization as it is reflected in the *Codex Atheniensis 1371*. This manuscript contains a *Notitia episcopatuum* (list of metropolitans and bishops subject to the patriarchate of Constantinople), which has not so far received sufficient attention.

To establish the ecclesiastical sees in Central Greece at the end of the twelfth century, it is necessary to distinguish between several *Notitiae*, which present confused and often contradictory evidence. Their reliability can be tested in a variety of ways, most obviously by the criterion of external confirmation, generally from other sources (episcopal seals, patriarchal records, and so on). In addition, the criterion of internal coherence and consistency should also be exercised. From the evidence of one particular *Notitia*, it is often assumed that the metropolitan of Athens controlled a total of ten suffragan bishops from the late tenth century to the end of the twelfth without change.[1] But during this period most other metropolitan sees, Corinth, Patras, Neopatras, Larissa, and Thebes, increased in size, some quite dramatically. Therefore, a short review of the material on which this assumption is based is not out of place.

The *Notitiae* that have been employed are as follows:

1. The τάξις of metropolitan sees issued by Isaac II in 1189. This is a most valuable document, securely dated, but it is not helpful for the suffragan bishops that are not included.[2]
2. The *Notitia* no. 10 in Parthey's edition, which appears to reflect a date later than 1189. It has been more closely dated by a subsequent editor to the early thirteenth century (pre-1216 at least) and is often taken as a record of the situation in about 1205.[3]
3. The *Notitia* drawn up by Neilos Doxapatris, the Sicilian monk, in 1142/43 for King Roger II. This has the advantage of a secure date, even if its author was rather poorly informed.[4]
4. *Notitia* no. 5 in the collection published by Gelzer and dated by him to the reign of Manuel I (1143–1180). This date has since been restricted to the middle years of the reign, at least before 1166. The *Notitia* is preserved in the *Codex Atheniensis 1371*.[5]

At first glance it is Parthey's *Notitia* no. 10 that appears to offer the best chance of reconstructing the episcopacy of Central Greece in the late twelfth century. It is known from several MSS that all follow the traditional hierarchy of metropolitan sees. Athens, ranked 28th in the list, is accorded the normal ten suffragans: Εὐρίπου, Διαυλείας,

Κορωνείας, Ἄνδρου, Ὠρείου, Σκύρου, Καρύστου, Πορθμοῦ, Αὐλῶνος, Σύρας. But at 50th place, Neopatras, a relatively recent foundation, is suddenly endowed with five suffragan sees, instead of its single suffragan, Μαρμαριτζῶν. These new sees are in fact the suffragans of Mitylene, which precedes Neopatras at the 49th position. The metropolitan see of Euchaïta, which follows Neopatras at 51st place, is also involved in this confusion; it is given the see of Μαρμαριτζῶν in addition to its customary four. This is an error that can occur so easily that there would be no point in mentioning it, except for the fact that it is not limited to Parthey no. 10. A similar muddle occurs at this point in Parthey's *Notitia* no. 3. It is similar (not identical) but so close that I don't think we can overlook the possibility of a major corruption common to both lists.[6] So Parthey no. 10 is not a completely reliable guide to the situation in Central Greece. And even if the suffragans are correctly rearranged, they do not provide evidence of any change from the late tenth-century *Notitiae*.

The second twelfth-century list is the *Notitia* of Neilos Doxapatris dated to 1142/43. While there is no doubt that it is an incomplete record, it merits attention. For in this list there are eleven suffragan sees under Athens, the new one being the combined island bishopric of Κέως and Θερμῶν. This is one of the few provincial sees recorded in quite a different source: the seal of Thomas, bishop of Kea, which is to be attributed to the eleventh or twelfth century.[7] So in this respect the evidence of Neilos is well confirmed. At the controversial point in the Parthey tradition, however, Neilos fails by omitting the metropolitan see of Euchaïta completely. He attributes six suffragans to Mitylene (one more than usual), four to Neopatras (three more than usual), and three entirely new sees to Thebes (none identified by name). Although some of this information will be confirmed by the *Codex Atheniensis 1371*, as we shall see, the *Notitia* of Neilos is clearly too partial and ignores too many well-established metropolitan sees to be used except with the greatest caution.[8] This leaves Gelzer's *Notitia* no. 5, with which we are directly concerned.[9] It was only published in part because Gelzer found the first 49 entries almost identical to earlier lists. He observed, nonetheless, that there were a few changes, without noticing that they were of great relevance to the situation in Central Greece. As far as the suffragans of Mitylene, Neopatras, and Euchaïta are concerned, the *Codex 1371* returns to the correct order and attributes the right sees to each metropolitan. Mitylene has the five known bishoprics and one new one (Ἱερᾶς); Neopatras has its usual Μαρμαριτζῶν plus two new ones (Βελᾶς and Ἀγιᾶς); Euchaïta has the normal four.[10] This *Notitia*, therefore, corrects the errors and confusions found in Parthey's no. 3 and no. 10. It also places the newly created sees below the established suffragans, following the rule of seniority. So at this particular point we seem to have a more accurate record than that preserved in the Parthey tradition.

Additional information in the *Codex 1371* noticed by Gelzer includes the metropolitan see of Thebes at 59th position, with a total of five entirely new suffragans. In 62nd place the diocese of Greater Russia appears with its eleven sees.[11] After the Russian entry there is a list of 24 metropolitans without suffragans, some of them new, others known from previous lists. The fact that these metropolitans are confirmed by the 1189 τάξις of Isaac II, which follows the same order, provides further proof that we are dealing with a reliable document.

It is among the first 49 metropolitan sees not published by Gelzer that we find several important changes. The most striking innovation is that Athens, at its usual position 28th in rank, has twelve suffragans—the normal ten, plus two new ones: no. 11 ὁ Μουντινιτῆς, and no. 12 ὁ Μεγάρων.[12] Patras also has an addition to its five sees, no. 6 ὁ Μορεοῦς, which is known from a seal of its bishop, Θεόδωρος.[13] The twelfth Athenian suffragan, Μεγάρων, can be confirmed in a similar fashion, for it is recorded in Pope Innocent III's letter as one of the bishoprics subordinated to Athens. This may also be true of the eleventh suffragan, Μουντινιτῆς, which could have formed part of the Latin bishopric of Thermopylae.[14] But Μουντινιτῆς poses something of a problem, for the eleventh position ought properly to be filled by the see of Κέως and Θερμιῶν, recorded in that place by Neilos. I must point out that before I had seen the *Codex 1371* this is exactly what I assumed. But on looking at the manuscript here in Athens, it is perfectly clear that the name of this bishopric is ὁ Μουντινιτῆς. This is a site in the mountains behind Thermopylae, known as Boudonitsa during the Latin occupation, today as Μενδενίτσα. It is somewhat far-flung for the diocese of Athens, but it lies no farther north than Ὠρείου, one of the Euboian bishoprics that were always subject to Athens. So I do not see any reason to doubt the evidence of the *Codex 1371*, which we have found to be quite reliable in other respects. And I think that the strange situation in which two suffragans seem to compete for the eleventh position under Athens can be understood if we consider the conditions that prevailed in Central Greece toward the end of the twelfth century.

But first, let me summarize what the *Codex Atheniensis 1371* records about the ecclesiastical organization of this region. From this document, dated to the 1160s, we learn that Athens had twelve, not ten, suffragans; Patras had six (not five); Neopatras had three (not one), and Thebes had five new suffragans. This means that at least ten new bishoprics had been created in Central Greece since the time of the Emperor John Tzimiskes. The ephemeral see of Κέως καὶ Θερμιῶν, which certainly must have existed, for it too is known to Pope Innocent III as a suffragan of Athens, may constitute an eleventh creation. From this it is evident that the metropolitan see of Athens shared fully in the growth of the episcopacy during the eleventh and twelfth centuries. How should this increase be interpreted? Within the context of provincial society in Central Greece, I suggest that these new bishoprics were created to meet an immediate need—an expanding Orthodox population, which required additional ecclesiastical staff.

Although it is impossible to measure an increase in population by any quantitative method, given the paucity of records relating to this region in the eleventh and twelfth centuries, there are several factors that may confirm this hypothesis:

1. Population movement. In his study of the Cadastre of Thebes, Professor Svoronos identified a large number of Byzantine families with names more familiar to Sicily and Southern Italy than mainland Greece.[15] He observed that in the course of the eleventh century, as Byzantine control over the Italian provinces was progressively weakened and finally destroyed, many of these families settled in Central Greece. There was no sudden influx of refugees, but over the years many small groups established themselves in and around Thebes, undoubtedly adding to the Orthodox population.

2. Building evidence. It is extremely hazardous to deduce anything about population changes from the number of buildings constructed in any area at anyone time. And the evidence of ecclesiastical construction is even more difficult to handle, given that churches may be built as private foundations, family and funerary chapels, rather than as parish churches. Nonetheless, the concentration of church building in Central Greece in the eleventh and twelfth centuries is so striking that I think it may be taken as a factor.[16] Despite the small size of many Middle Byzantine churches in the area, and despite the fact that their function is not always clear, the great number that are clearly datable to this period may well reflect a growth in population.

3. Economic factors. Many years ago Father Laurent put forward the thesis that it was the mulberry that brought a new dimension to the economy of Western Elis.[17] And recently the significance of mulberry cultivation in Italy has been more closely documented and underlined

by Professor Guillou.[18] Now, in view of the prominent position held by Thebes in twelfth-century Byzantine silk production, it is not perhaps unreasonable to suppose that the mulberry crop of Central Greece was of great importance to the region. Unfortunately we have only the barest hints as to the organization of all stages of silk production, from the planting of mulberry groves right through to the finished silk fabric, but several independent sources testify to the quality of Theban products. Benjamin of Tudela mentions the role of Jewish weavers and embroiderers in the finishing of silk made in Thebes, and at the end of the twelfth century these silks were specifically requested in a treaty made by Alexios III.[19] While we have no direct evidence that the population of Thebes and its environs expanded from the eleventh century onward, the existence of a thriving silk industry and the increase in suffragan bishoprics attached to the metropolitan see of Thebes would appear to support a theory of growth rather than decline.

In fact, this series of seemingly unrelated phenomena, a concentration of church building particularly in the eleventh century, the arrival of refugees from Italy (possibly even from areas where mulberry cultivation was highly developed), the development of silk production on a fairly large scale, and the steady growth of the episcopacy, all suggest an expanding population and a vigorous economy. That this hypothesis is in no way confirmed by the major literary source of the period, the writings of Michael Choniates, poses less of a contradiction than may be imagined.[20] For Choniates, who was writing from his library on the Acropolis, was comparing twelfth-century Athens either with the sophisticated and cosmopolitan existence contemporary in Constantinople, or with the past grandeur of classical Athens. He was certainly not familiar with the situation in Thebes, nor did he (as far as I know) profit from a tax on mulberry cultivation. Despite his somewhat gloomy account, Central Greece was possibly witnessing a relatively prosperous period. I would like to suggest that in the eleventh and twelfth centuries the region experienced a developing economy and an expanding population, of which the *Codex Atheniensis 1371* provides indirect evidence.

NOTES

1. V. Laurent, *Le Corpus des sceaux de l'Empire byzantin*, vol. 1, *L'Église* (Paris, 1963), 437.

2. On the *Ordo ecclesiasticus* of Isaac II, see H. Gelzer, *Analecta byzantina* (Jena, 1892).

3. G. Parthey, *Hieroclis Synecdemus et notitiae graeca episcopatuum* (Berlin, 1866); cf. the other MSS published by C. Fink, *Zeitschrift der Savigny-Stiftung*, 50 (1930) Kanon-Abt. 19; V. Beneševič, *Studi bizantini*, 2 (1927).

4. Parthey, *Hieroclis Synecdemus*, 265–308; cf. V. Laurent, "L'oeuvre géographique du moine sicilien Nil Doxapatris," *Echos d'Orient* 36 (1937), 5–30. Update See the new edition by J. Darrouzès, *Notitiae episcopatuum ecclesiae Constantinopolitanae* (Paris, 1981).

5. H. Gelzer, *Ungedruckte und ungenügend veröffentlichte Texte der Notitiae episcopatuum*, AbhBayerPhilos.-Philol. Kl., 21 (1901), 585–89; cf. A. Poppe, "L'organisation diocésaine de la Russie aux XIe–XIIe siècles," *B* 40 (1970), 165–217, esp. 171f. Update Michael Angold, *Church and Society in Byzantium under the Comneni 1081–1261* (Cambridge, UK, 1995), 140–45, on the problems raised by the *Notitiae*.

6. In Parthey no. 3 Larissa is given an incredible list of 28 suffragan sees; this is corrected in Parthey no. 10 to the normal ten, indicating that it is not a direct copy; see Parthey, *Hieroclis Synecdemus,* 120f., 127.

7. V. Laurent, *Le Corpus des sceaux de l'Empire byzantin*, vol. 2, *L'Église* (Paris, 1965), 427f. (no. 1595). Update This seal together with many others are now searchable through the *PBW*.

8. Laurent, "L'oeuvre géographique . . ." 24–30, records that the MS, *Vat. gr. 1578*, is severely interpolated.

9. Athens, National Library, *Codex 1371*, fols. 389–391.

10. Ibid., fol. 391r.

11. This part of the Notitia must have been composed before 1166, when the bishopric of Novgorod was promoted to the rank of πρωτόθρονος, see A. Poppe, "L'organization diocésaine . . . ," 171f.

12. Athens, National Library, *Codex 1371*, fol. 390v.

13. Ibid., fol. 390v; cf. V. Laurent, "L'évêche de Morée (Moréas) au Péloponnèse," *REB* 20 (1962), 181–99; and *Corpus des sceaux*, vol. 1, 492f. (no. 656).

14. *PL*, 215, col. 1560C; cf. J. Koder, "Der Schutzbrief des Papstes Innozenz III für die Kirche Athens," communication delivered at the Fifteenth International Congress of Byzantine Studies (Athens, 1976). Update The continued existence of the see is confirmed by fifteenth-century records; see Guillaume Saint-Guillain, "La carrière d'un prélat unioniste au milieu du XVe siècle et l'établissement du culture grec à Venise," *Thesaurismata* 39/40 (2009/10), 91–110.

15. N. Svoronos, "Recherches sur le cadastre byzantin et la fiscalité aux XIe et XIIe siècles: Le cadastre de Thèbes," *BCH* 83 (1959), 68–71.

16. Several little-known Middle Byzantine churches were presented at the Congress; see for example the communications of Ch. Bouras, "Twelfth and Thirteenth Century Variations of the Domed-Octagon plan," and L. Bouras, "Architectural Sculptures of the 12th and the Early 13th Century in Greece." Update See now Charalambos Bouras, *Byzantine and Post-Byzantine Architecture in Greece* (Athens, 2006), and *Vyzantine Athena 10os–12os ai. Mouseio Benaki, 60 Paratema* (Athens, 2010).

17. Laurent, "L'évêche de Morée," *REB* 20 (1962), 188.

18. A. Guillou, "Production and Profits in the Byzantine Province of Italy (Tenth to Eleventh Centuries): An Expanding Society," *DOP* 28 (1974), 89–109, esp. 92–95.

19. Benjamin of Tudela, *Itinerary*, ed. and trans. M. N. Adler (London, 1907), 10; Nicetas Choniates, *Historiae* (Bonn, 1835), 608f.

20. Μιχαὴλ Ἀκομινάτου τοῦ Χωνιάτου τὰ σωζόμενα, ed. S. Lampros, 2 vols. (Athens, 1878–80); cf. J. Herrin, "Realities of Byzantine Provincial Government: Hellas and Peloponnesos, 1180–1204," *DOP* 29 (1975), 253–84, reprinted as chapter 3 of this volume.

5

THE COLLAPSE OF THE BYZANTINE
EMPIRE IN THE TWELFTH CENTURY

A STUDY OF A MEDIEVAL ECONOMY

ℰℐ

The origins of this study lie at Birmingham in the late 1960s, when the University published its own historical journal. At the urging of the Committee for Byzantine Studies, which under its dynamic chairman, Ellis Waterhouse, was planning the creation of a Center devoted to Byzantine and Modern Greek Studies, Anthony Bryer was invited to edit part 2 of the twelfth volume in the series. Staff and graduate students alike were pressed into service with the result that the *Historical Journal* for 1971 contains a good range of articles on medieval and modern topics. Mine is a first foray into the deep waters of Byzantine economic history, which at the time had precious few records to use. (The situation is much improved by the publication of the monastic archives of Mount Athos and the three-volume *Economic History of Byzantium*, edited by Angeliki Laiou.) It was generally agreed that the loss of much territory in Asia Minor to the Seljuks was compensated by investment in the western (European) provinces, but the methods used by Constantinople to extract additional resources from this area remained unclear.

From my reading of Michael Choniates's correspondence and a study of the published records of Italian merchants trading in Hellas and Peloponnesos, I had come to the distinct conclusion that in the twelfth century the Queen City was exploiting the provinces. Constantinopolitan officials were demanding additional taxes, while Italian shippers were exporting the region's olives, oil, wheat, and cloth to western ports. The metropolis was not supporting the provincial economy or investing in it but was draining it of resources. This interpretation was probably rather one-sided; my analysis of the way the medieval economy worked was not sufficiently sophisticated, nor was my reading wide enough to realize the potential benefits of Italian trading arrangements, for example. It did, however, draw attention to source material that had not been used systematically.

More recent studies of the twelfth century have corrected my view of the exploiting imperial center, showing that Constantinopolitan control was failing in other parts of the empire. External pressures from both the Seljuks and the Bulgars created constant demands for frontier defense that required additional mercenary support for local military forces, and the hire of such foreign troops was both expensive and unreliable. In addition, all twelfth-century emperors were obliged to extend the privileges granted to Italian trading powers in order to sustain the international market of Constantinople, which meant reduced income from customs' excise and tax on merchandise passing through it. There was a systemic weakness to the Byzantine economy as a whole, which is not covered in this study of Hellas and Peloponnesos but should be borne in mind.

IN MANY RESPECTS the Byzantine state machinery of the tenth to twelfth centuries was extremely sophisticated; it directed a systematic foreign policy and maintained a developed network of diplomatic relations with neighboring powers; it controlled the minting and circulation of a stable gold currency, and it ran a complex bureaucratic administration. Important social controls also existed, in the form of a hierarchy of honorific titles and positions attached to the imperial court, and in the regulations governing the wearing of certain robes and silks of different colors and the carrying of certain arms and insignia to which the great Byzantine families aspired. But its economic organization was primitive. It was very different, of course, from contemporaneous feudal organizations in the West; complicated in contrast to their simplicity; but nonetheless underdeveloped in comparison with the other departments of the Byzantine state. The relative backwardness of the economic organization did not mean that it was any less centralized or regulated than other departments. On the contrary, an elaborate and inflexible machinery was devised to bring all aspects of industrial and commercial activity under state management. But in the course of centuries this restrictive regulation came to jeopardize all economic activity, with very serious consequences for the empire.[1]

The purpose of this chapter is to examine the fiscal and commercial aspects of the economic organization of a provincial area of the Byzantine Empire under the Angeloi, 1185–1204, and to suggest a possible explanation for the collapse of 1204. For the conquest and sack of Constantinople by the Fourth Crusade constitutes a collapse and disappearance of the empire, and the establishment of a Latin Empire, however feeble, on Byzantine territory constitutes a definite break with the former Byzantine organization. In 1185 Isaac II Angelos inherited an organization already weakened by the extravagance of Manuel I Komnenos and by the chaotic period of his successors, Alexios II and Andronikos I (1180–85), but under the Angeloi it finally collapsed. The process as it developed in these twenty years in Central Greece can be documented from the evidence of Michael Choniates, Metropolitan of Athens, 1182–1205, and from Italian commercial contracts relating to trade in the area. But it can only be understood against an analysis of the established Byzantine organization.

The Byzantine Empire would have been conquered many centuries before 1204, but for two important factors: the efficiency of tax collection and the organization of imperial defense. The first provided a regular source of income, from direct taxes levied per head of population, on land, houses and farming equipment, and from indirect taxation on commercial sales and transportation. This was supplemented by revenue from state lands and imperial estates. It paid for the administration, court expenses, state industries, the professional army (*tagmata*), embassies, gifts and peace treaties—the chief outgoing expenses.

Imperial defense, apart from the *tagmata* of professional soldiers normally stationed in the capital, was organized locally. Each province (*thema*) supplied and maintained its own force, the theme army, either by direct provision of arms and supplies, or by an equivalent money payment. The efficiency of this force as a military organ is open to question, but the way it was run, at almost no cost to the central administration apart from the inscription of those families who held military land, guaranteed a permanent standing army in every province of the empire at very little expense.[2]

But if anything prevented the smooth running of these two factors, there were repercussions through all the departments of the state machinery. The great military expansion of the tenth century strained the resources of both the army and the treasury, but it was not until the second quarter of the eleventh century that they began to fail. After the death of Basil II in 1025, when the central administration became incapable of enforcing the collection of taxes, and when imperial armies were conclusively defeated, the basis of the Byzantine organization was destroyed, the administration could no longer function. The situation was considerably worsened by the Byzantine defeat at Mantzikert in 1071, which permitted the Seljuk Turks to occupy the central provinces of Asia Minor. As well as the dangerous advance of the Turks, this defeat resulted in a loss of manpower, taxes, and produce, which had to be made good by the rest of the empire—the European provinces. But in the ten years following the battle of Mantzikert, little was done to adapt Byzantine organization to the new conditions. The state machinery ceased to have any control over the provinces, tax farming became widespread, and imperial authority was frequently abused. The self-sufficiency of the economic organization was destroyed, and the empire got heavily into debt.[3]

In these circumstances it was the great achievement of Alexios I Komnenos to reconstruct the Byzantine administration. He stabilized the eastern frontier and reimposed imperial provincial government. He reorganized the theme armies but relied chiefly on the *tagmata* of professional soldiers and hired mercenaries in his campaigns against the Turks. He succeeded in reestablishing the empire as the major power in the Eastern Mediterranean. But the internal weakness of the Byzantine organization was not resolved. The decline of the theme armies was never reversed, and militarily the empire became more and more dependent on mercenary forces, often Latin.

The characteristic features of Alexios's highly centralized organization were its dependence on naval strength and its chronic shortage of money. The Byzantine navy of the tenth century had been one of the glories of the empire. The role it played in the recapture of Crete and Cyprus from the Arabs revealed its superiority over Arabic shipping, the chief rival in the Eastern Mediterranean. But during the decline of imperial power in the eleventh century, the navy was ignored, and at the accession of Alexios in 1081 local coastal defense was almost negligible. When 150 Norman ships set sail from Southern Italy for Avlona, on the west coast of Epiros, Alexios had only a few boats at his disposal and they did not constitute a force that could attack the Normans. That role fell to Venice, now the strongest maritime power in the Adriatic. And as it was absolutely necessary to combat the Normans by land and sea, Alexios appealed to Venice for assistance.[4] The Venetian and Byzantine fleets had often cooperated in campaigns against their mutual enemy, the Arabs of Sicily and North Africa, and the two powers were already linked by treaties that clearly delineated the relationship between the empire and its vassal. This was not altered by the agreement of 1082, concluded during the Norman war, but the position of Venetian merchants in the empire was considerably changed. The doge and the Venetian Senate might still be the servants (*douloi*) of the emperor, but nonetheless they were able to fix the price of their naval aid. Alexios was so anxious to secure their naval support that he issued no instructions as to the terms of the agreement, except that they should not be injurious to the empire. The extensive privileges and trading concessions that were finally agreed, had, in fact, unforeseen and deleterious effects on all Byzantine economic activity, although they were not immediately injurious. In this respect the 1082 chrysobull marks a turning point not only in Byzantino-Venetian relations but also in the imperial state machinery.[5]

Both Alexios and his grandson Manuel I were aware of the empire's need of a strong naval force and undertook the construction and arming of important fleets. Manuel was undoubtedly influenced by the failure of his father's policy: John II attempted to curtail Venetian privileges, while at the same time refusing to spend maritime taxes on the upkeep of the fleet. The result was Venetian attacks on several Aegean and Ionian islands and the occupation of Chios and Rhodes. In 1126 John was forced to confirm Alexios's chrysobull. The same privileges were confirmed by Manuel at the beginning of his reign (1147), but he was determined to end the dependence of the empire on Venetian shipping.[6] He made agreements with both Pisa and Genoa to prevent the Venetians from establishing a monopoly of large-scale trade in the empire, and then proceeded to play one republic off against the others. Next, he built a new imperial fleet, which was sent aggressively to the Adriatic, and finally he decided to break the agreement of 1147. In 1171 Venetians resident in the empire were suddenly arrested and all their property seized. In the following decade Venetian trade with the empire was minimal, and over twenty years later individual merchants who had suffered losses were still claiming compensation.[7] Manuel's extravagant foreign policy may have had short-term successes, but in the long run it severely damaged the Byzantine organization. On his death in 1180 the empire was still without a well-organized naval force; the treasury was depleted; the Venetians were hostile, and both Pisan and Genoese merchants were established in privileged trading positions. Goods still passed through the empire in Italian ships.

The foundation of Italian trading communities in Constantinople and in the main commercial centers of the empire brought certain benefits to those places, not least the presence of a wealthy population demanding food and other necessities. They constituted a sector of society that could have supported heavy taxation, but instead their installation was based on those privileges conceded by Alexios I in 1082, which included exemption from the 10 percent tax levied on the transport and sale of goods (*kommerkion*).[8] This had been done because Alexios had no other way of rewarding the Venetians for their services during the Norman war. He was able to raise an army only by a confiscation of ecclesiastical property from the Constantinopolitan churches, and with the private funds of his supporters. Payment for the original naval aid in various privileges for the doge and the patriarch of Grado, and in the right to trade freely in all parts of the empire except the Black Sea, entailed most dangerous consequences.

First, it guaranteed the Venetians a privileged position in Mediterranean trade. From their bases in the empire they consolidated their contacts in Syria, Palestine, and Egypt, making trading agreements with the Latin and Arab rulers in the East, and setting up a complete network of specifically Venetian trade routes. Although they remained dependent on these rulers to honor their agreements, their access to such a variety of highly valuable goods, especially pepper and other spices, gave them a position of great power. Second, it gave them a crucial role in Byzantine defense, which in fact increased imperial dependence on Venetian shipping. Although the Venetian naval force was to be under the control of the Byzantine *megas doux*, supreme naval commander, when it joined the Byzantine fleet, its sailors were to be paid by the empire, and it could act autonomously before and after the particular services requested. Toward the end of the twelfth century the Venetians cannot have failed to notice the virtual absence of any Byzantine navy on these occasions. Third, this sort of service gave them an insight into the internal organization of the Byzantine state and its weaknesses—one that they soon exploited. When they observed the ineffectiveness of the Byzantine fleet, they made attacks on the islands and coastlands that rapidly developed into regular raiding activity. By the last quarter of the century there were Genoese, Pisan, and "Longobard" pirates, as well as Venetian, in all parts of the Aegean. Fourth, and perhaps most important, the arrival of privileged Venetian merchants had the effect of stifling the development of a Byzantine merchant fleet and mercantile class. Wherever they installed themselves, the Italians monopolized commercial activity at all levels. Although they bought and sold goods manufactured by Greeks, to and from Greeks, it was in Italian ships manned by Italian sailors that these goods were transported. In this way the Italians captured the internal Byzantine trade, as well as developing and expanding the profitable East/West trade.

Thus by the end of the twelfth century the relationship between the empire and the Italian Republics, especially Venice, had been reversed: instead of granting privileges to a vassal, the Byzantine economic organization was hampered by a built-in foreign power, which had destroyed its delicate balance. The Italian merchants held a key economic role, which the indigenous merchants and the population of Constantinople appreciated fully. They very often served as ambassadors of the Byzantine state to the West, and almost invariably provided the ships that transported embassies.[9] In return they received honors and property. It is hardly surprising that the local population should have resented their wealth and influence, for at the time when the Italians were consolidating their positions, the Byzantine administration was imposing its most extreme demands on all those who could not claim exemption from taxes.

The second characteristic of the organization reconstructed by Alexios I was its constant shortage of money. Because the first need in 1081 was for ready money to pay an army, Alexios's administrative reforms were designed to bring in taxation. The provincial administration was completely revised in this attempt to ensure a steady income.[10] Officials who combined the civil and military powers replaced the old purely military governors of themes. Tax collection had been made more difficult by the fact that successive debasements of the gold coinage in the eleventh century had rendered the 1081 *nomisma* one-third of the fineness of the *nomisma* of 1034, although it retained the same weight. So taxes were reckoned at the rate of so many old *nomismata*, now used as a money of account, and then payment would be made in the equivalent new debased coinage, *trachea nomismata*. As this system did not facilitate the collection of taxes, Alexios undertook a deliberate debasement and reform of the coinage, probably in 1092. This was followed by the establishment of a uniform rate of taxation, with clear instructions as to the relative values of the new coins and as to the method of levying taxes—the *Nea Logarike* (1108/9).[11] Finally, a new hierarchy of court positions was created for the supporters of the Komnenos faction. In this way the machinery of tax collection was successfully reconstructed, but it could not supply adequate funds to cover the greatly increased expenditure. New sources of wealth had to be found. The church and all Byzantine ecclesiastical institutions were richly endowed by Orthodox from all levels of society. The families of rich landowners had accumulated wealth. Certain public servants and military families had extensive resources gained through imperial favor and reward. But Alexios had been placed on the throne with the support and influence of these sectors, whose interests had to be protected. So there was no hope of raising any revenue from them, although they could have supported heavy taxation. In fact, throughout the twelfth century, despite repeated financial crises, institutions and individuals were able to demand exemptions from taxation, which diverted formerly state revenue into private hands. This is particularly clear in the case of monastic property, which was enormously expanded in the course of the century.[12]

These exemptions resemble the grants of privileges for Venice, in that they constituted a method of paying or rewarding the beneficiary that privatized a section of state revenue. This could take two forms: either the beneficiary received exemption from a specific tax, as the Venetians were exempt from the *kommerkion*,[13] or he received the right to collect all the taxes and dues from a certain area previously paid to the state. For monasteries this right was invariably accompanied by a guarantee that no state officials would enter their lands to levy the normal taxes. This privilege was granted in perpetuity and was almost always extended to cover later acquisitions, so that monastic institutions were able to develop their resources most fully. In 1196 the monastery of Lavra had to defend itself against the charge that it was dealing in illegal wine trade, in boats exempt from the normal boat tax but reserved to the use of the monastery only. Similarly the monastery of St. John on Patmos had a small fleet for which it did not pay this tax.[14] Few individuals had such privileges. The beneficiary of a grant in *pronoia* received an estate, a village, or some other property, with everything in it, peasants, houses, animals, and so on, for his own use. The taxes due from the area would be paid direct to him, instead of to the state officials. But these grants were always conditional and could be rescinded by the emperor at any time. After the defense of Larissa against the Normans in 1083 Alexios I gave his general, Leon Kephalas, the village of Chospiane in *pronoia*, and later he added Mesolimna, which had previously been given in *pronoia* to two Frankish knights. However, after Kephalas's death, his heirs managed to secure the same lands for their own use. Under Manuel I, grants in *pronoia* became more common, but it was not until the reign of Michael Palaiologos (1261–85) that the institution became generally hereditary. Manuel particularly favored Latins in this way—for example, Baldovino Guercio, who held in *pronoia* a palace in Constantinople for twenty years. It was eventually taken away from him by Alexios III Angelos during the 1198/99 campaign against Genoese merchants in the empire.[15]

The inevitable result of this practice of granting exemptions, coupled with the rapid development of Italian trade within the empire, was that in 1185 the Angeloi inherited an economic organization crippled by nonproductive sectors and drained by foreign merchants.[16] As the need for money was as pressing as ever, Isaac II turned to the only remaining source of wealth: the already overtaxed peasantry. This was not a choice, nor was an offensive planned against the peasants. It was simply that apart from confiscations and exactions from those who had supported the late Emperor Andronikos I Komnenos, there were no riches to tap. It is doubtful whether extra taxation ever got back to the treasury, given the disarray of provincial administration. This had deteriorated, despite the short-lived reforms of Andronikos I, to a state in which there was almost no provincial government. Theme governors often preferred to live in the capital and visited their provinces only to collect their salaries. After these visits, which usually took the form of armed raids, the local officials were left to their own devices, without any form of central control. In these circumstances provincial administration became a long series of abuses, which are repeatedly cited by Michael Choniates, Metropolitan of Athens from 1182 until its capture by the Franks in 1205.[17] Although his evidence refers specifically to what was happening in Central Greece, it reflects a decline of imperial control which was general and it shows how desperately the Angeloi were trying to make ends meet. Michael Choniates's complaints can be listed:

1. The *praktor*'s unfair application of a tax exemption (*ekkope*) accorded by Alexios II.
2. Incorrect division of the *akrostichon*, the total sum of taxes to be raised by the theme.
3. The levy of maritime taxes, *ploimoi*, three times in one year by three different officials, the governor (*praîtor*), Leon Sgouros, and Steiriones, and,
4. at a higher rate than that stipulated in the *apographe* of the *logothetes*, Ioannes Doukas.
5. Frequent and inaccurate measurement of Athenian land, and,
6. its subsequent assessment at a higher rate than that applied in neighboring Theban lands (that is, at a rate of fewer *modia* per *nomisma*) so that the Athenians paid more taxes than the Thebans.
7. Excessive *epereiai* (taxes to cover the expense of visits of state officials) demanded by the *energountai* of the governor.
8. The abusive use of the corvée of providing animals, *angaria ton hypozygion*.
9. Repeated demands for *proskynitikia*, presents of respect given to visiting officials.[18]

In addition to these particular fiscal abuses Michael often mentions the numerous depredations of local officials and their corrupt practices. The last three complaints listed concern the duty of provincial towns to entertain officials. These much-hated visits were the ruin of poorer places, such as Athens, and it is not surprising that the richer population of Thebes should have refused to accept the governor and his staff on at least one occasion.[19] But when the official party arrived at Athens on the pretext of coming to worship in the famous church of the Mother of God (the Parthenon), the Athenians could not or dared not refuse hospitality.

The first six complaints reveal the partiality of local fiscal agents; when they were not favoring the rich at the expense of the poor, they favored the Thebans at the expense of the Athenians. In these activities certain Constantinopolitan officials: a *bestiarites*, a *referendarios*, and a *mystikos*, seem to be implicated.[20] Certainly they were doing nothing to correct local abuses. The central administration either could not or would not exert control—one suspects that the former is most likely. Imperial orders (*prostagmata*) were openly flaunted, and to be effective local privileges had to be claimed by a show of force.[21] Those with no means of riposte, inevitably the poor, suffered the heaviest tax burdens, while the rich managed to enforce their claims to tax immunity.

This pattern of tax exploitation was not something peculiar to Central Greece at the end of the twelfth century. Provincial taxation was probably always collected with some sort of pressure, but not always with the same disregard for imperial orders. In 1104 Demetrios Kamateros was ordered to produce double the normal tax provided by Macedonia. When he failed he lost the job, which was bought by one Nikephoros Artabasdos. The following year Nikephoros's agents (*praktores*) managed to double the tax return, but not by demanding extra contributions from the monasteries and other important institutions (*prosopa*). On the contrary, these continued to pay the normal tax and the extra burden was imposed on the peasantry, who could least afford it.[22] This typifies the reconstructed administration of the Komnenoi, which failed completely to utilize the richest sectors of society. Michael confirms that the Angeloi perpetuated this practice, because they could find no alternative, and that the rich continued to avoid taxation. He claims, moreover, that any provincial fiscal agent (*praktor*) would act in the same way as the Athenian one: that he would always favor the rich.[23] From a passage in a letter to Demetrios Drimys, a former governor of Hellas and the Peloponnese, it is clear that Michael understood and deplored the workings of the Byzantine state machinery:

> What do you (in Constantinople) lack? Not the wheat-bearing plains of Macedonia, Thrace and Thessaly, which are farmed by us; nor the wine of Euboia, Ptelion, Chios and Rhodes, pressed by us; nor the fine garments woven by our Theban and Corinthian fingers; nor all our wealth, which flows, as many rivers flow into one sea, to the Queen City.[24]

This manner of expropriation of all provincial wealth to the capital was consolidated by the Angeloi in their attempt to maintain their support in Constantinople, and it quite understandably provoked hostility between the provincial population and Constantinopolitan officials. Michael's brother, the historian Niketas Choniates, witnessed a similarly hostile reaction in Selymbria, when he arrived there from occupied Constantinople in 1204. But on this occasion the peasants were laughing, delighted to see grand city families reduced by their flight to such conditions.[25]

There was one further factor that impoverished the Byzantine provinces in the twelfth century, and that was the Italian penetration of local markets and export centers. In this respect Greece, which was not considered a particularly prosperous area by the Byzantines, was no exception. In every commercial center Venetian, Pisan, and Genoese merchants established themselves and organized the export of Greek products.[26] Thessalonike was undoubtedly the most important of these centers, because of its huge annual fair, but smaller places, such as Thebes and Lakedaimonia, and ports like Corinth, Halmyros, Coron, and Modon are more often mentioned in Italian documents. In these centers the Italians found few Byzantine merchants with the resources to organize trading on a large scale, and so they were able to build up and control the export market. There must have been local Greek artisans, weavers, potters, glass-blowers, carpenters, and wheelwrights, among other craftsmen. The excavations of the medieval agorai of Athens and Corinth have revealed the existence of extensive local production,[27] and Michael mentions such craftsmen in his letters. Once he requested the Bishop of Gardikion and Peristera to send him men who can make carts, because he cannot get one made in Athens.[28] There must also have been some local transporters who brought olives and oil, grapes, wool, flax and grain, among the natural products, to the markets. The concentration of large quantities of goods for export in the few export centers, would have been unlikely if left to the individual peasant. And, finally, there was probably a group of Greek merchants who sold the finished products to the Italian exporters. But when it came to organizing the transport of these goods, either overland or by sea, to foreign markets or to other markets within the empire, the Italians seem to have established almost a total monopoly. In the flourishing port of Halmyros, on the Gulf of Volos, they were very active. By 1112 Venetians were trading there, and in 1171 twenty of their ships fled the port to avoid arrest. The Pisans also had an extensive quarter at Halmyros, including two churches and storehouses and wharves for storing and embarking goods. Genoese merchants also called regularly at the port, where one of their ships was burned by the Venetians in 1171. Of the twenty-one sailors mentioned in a series of Venetian documents concerning trade in Almyros, sixteen have obviously Italian names, two are "Longobards" from Southern Italy and Sicily, and three are surnamed Greco. These three present the sole indication that local sailors were participating in the transport of Greek products overseas.[29] The documents from Thebes, Corinth, Lakedaimonia, and Modon reveal the same closed circle of Italian merchants competing for the local trade.

At the local level the Italians obviously brought money to the producers of oil, dried fruits, cloth, and the celebrated silk. They were dealing in large quantities and they disposed of large sums of money—34 *miliaresia* of oil, costing 1,000 *hyperpera*, changed hands in one sale of 1201.[30] But it is unlikely that the Greek producers were able to improve local conditions with this money. All Byzantine merchants had to pay the full 10 percent tax both on the transport and on the sale of goods, while the Italians had a total or partial exemption. The Greeks also had to meet increased costs for production on a larger scale, and additional and arbitrary taxation. The results of this inequitable competition plus extremely high expenses effectively prevented them from expanding their economic activity. Only those centers that had already established a certain degree of autonomy and independence from imperial control, such as Theban silk manufacture and the port of Monemvasia, seem to have been immune to repressive state measures. Michael corresponded with a holy man of Monemvasia through a Greek sailor, Katzaris, who occasionally brought his boat to Athens.[31] Like the Aegean islands and the seabound monasteries, Monemvasia could not survive without some naval force, but coastal sailing at this time was chiefly the preserve of pirates of all nationalities.

For the empire as a whole the effects of Italian commercial practice were generally deleterious. Economically the loss of the *kommerkion* was very harmful, as can be shown by the fact that no other republic than Venice managed to obtain the right to duty-free trading. Both Pisa and Genoa made several attempts to get further reductions, but both were forced to pay 4 percent of the tax. And all the Italian merchants, even Venetian, were often harassed by the *kommerkiarioi*, agents responsible for its collection, who demanded double payment or confiscated cargo.[32] Socially, the establishment of splendid foreign quarters in Constantinople infuriated the native merchants and local populace, and provoked several serious anti-Western attacks.[33] After the violent campaigns of 1171 and 1183 it seemed possible that Andronikos I would be able to prevent a return of the Italian stranglehold on Byzantine trade, but once again naval assistance against the Normans was necessary, and he was forced to allow the Venetians to regain their privileged position. The continuing

lack of a Byzantine navy meant that the ships of one republic were always needed, and by the 1190s the choice was usually determined by the
one whose representatives had recently committed the most outrageous
acts of piracy. In 1196/97 Alexios III Angelos had to hire Pisan ships
under the command of Giovanni Steirione, a Calabrian pirate, to check
the activities of Gafforio, a Genoese merchant turned to piracy.[34] When
they were not quarreling among themselves—the republics were almost
constantly at war during the twelfth century—they were attacking the
Greek littoral. Michael Choniates provides evidence of numerous raids
by pirates, some Longobard, others unidentified. They may have been
Greek islanders who like the Cretans had the means to join in the unrestricted looting.[35] Meanwhile the Athenians paid their maritime taxes to
three different authorities, but none of them could provide protection.
The central administration had completely collapsed, abandoning them
to the merciless pressures of official and unofficial taxation and endemic
piracy. Niketas Choniates described the disorders prevalent at the time of
the Latin invasion of Greece as follows:

> Money was stolen, young children kidnapped, people were slaughtered and
> put to flight, and there were a thousand other terrible things like this, of
> which the worst was the activity of the tyrants among the suffering Romans,
> and above all the activity of Leon Sgouros.[36]

He continues with an account of Sgouros's spectacular career as a local
tyrant in the Argolid, ending with the murder of Nikolaos, the metropolitan thrown off the rocks at Nauplion.

This complete failure of provincial government reflected the disintegration of the whole administrative machinery set up by Alexios I Komnenos. The process was accelerated by the presence of a foreign element
introduced in a new permanent form in 1082. This became autonomous
and uncontrollable in the course of the twelfth century, and finally took
over a vital role. By the last decade, the Angeloi were so dependent on
Italian shipping that they allowed its activities to determine their foreign
policy. The role of the Venetian navy in the capture of Constantinople
in 1204 highlighted the special strengths of the most important Western republic, as well as the obvious weaknesses of the empire. Not that
Venice alone was responsible for the diversion of the Fourth Crusade;
the interests of the Normans, who had already launched a major attack
against the empire in 1185, and of the other crusaders, were strong. But
the Venetians had interests that were immediately put at stake by the failure of Alexios IV to fulfill his part of the agreement that had restored him

to the imperial throne. When they found themselves in a position to take for the Venetian Republic what it had held at the pleasure of Alexios III and his successors, they could not resist. In fact, the only surprising thing about the conquest of 1204 is that it had not happened before.

NOTES

1. These regulations are listed in two important texts: *The Rhodian Sea Law* and *The Book of the Eparch*. The former is edited by W. Ashburner (Oxford, 1909), and the latter is to be found in the French edition by J. Nicole (Geneva, 1893; London, 1970) and in English editions by A.E.R. Boak, in *Journal of Economic and Business History*, I (1929), 547–619; and by E. H. Freshfield, *Roman Law in the Later Roman Empire* (Cambridge, UK, 1938). On the guilds, see B. Mendl, "Les corporations byzantins," in *BS* XX (1961), 302–19; S. Vryonis, "Byzantine Demokratia and the Guilds in the Eleventh Century," in *DOP* XVII (1963), 287–314. **Update** A fundamental guide to the Byzantine economy is *The Economic History of Byzantium: From the Seventh through the Fifteenth Century*, ed. Angeliki Laiou, 3 vols. (Washington, DC, 2002), available online at http://www.doaks.org/publications/doaks-online-publications/byzantine-studies/the-economic-history-of-byzantium with many specialist contributions (hereafter *EcHB*). On the Rhodian sea law, see A. Laiou, "Exchange and Trade, Seventh to Twelfth Centuries," 705–13. On the Book of the Eparch, see Johannes Koder, ed., *Das Eparchenbuch Leons des Weisen*, CFHB, vol. 33 (Vienna, 1991), with useful commentary.

2. P. Lemerle, "Esquisse pour une histoire agraire de Byzance: les sources et les problèmes," in *Revue Historique* CCXIX (1958), 32–74, 254–84, and CCXX (1958), 43–94; G. Ostrogorsky, *Pour l'histoire de la féodalité byzantine* (Brussels, 1954). **Update** On Byzantine military forces, see J. Haldon, *Warfare, State and Society in the Byzantine World* (London, 1999).

3. C. Neumann, "La situation mondiale de l'empire byzantin avant les croisades," *Revue de l'Orient Latin* X (1903–4), 65–171; N. Svoronos, "Société et organisation intérieure dans l'empire byzantin au XI siècle: Les principaux problèmes," *Thirteenth International Congress of Byzantine Studies* (Oxford, 1967), Main Paper XII, 373–89; S. Vryonis, "Byzantium: The Social Basis of Decline in the Eleventh century," *GRBS* II (1959), 157–75; H. Antoniadis-Bibicou, "Problèmes d'histoire économique de Byzance au XI siècle: démographie, salaires et prix," *BS* XXVIII (1967), 255–61. **Update** There is a vast bibliography on the eleventh-century decline; see for example, *The Empire in Crisis (?): Byzantium in the 11th Century (1025–1081)*, ed. V. Vlyssidou (Athens, 2003); M. Angold, *The Byzantine Empire 1025–1204: A Political History*, 2nd ed., (London, 1997); A. Harvey, "The Middle Byzantine Economy: Growth or Stagnation?," *BMGS* 19 (1995), 243–61; A. Laiou, "Exchange and Trade, Seventh to Twelfth Centuries," in *EcHB*, 736–46.

4. H. Ahrweiler, *Byzance et la Mer. La marine de guerre, la politique et les institutions maritimes de Byzance aux VII–XV siècles* (Paris, 1965); Anna Comnène, *Alexiade*, I, 56. **Update** R.-J. Lilie, *Handel und Politik zwischen dem*

byzantinischen Reich und den italienischen Kommunen, Venedig, Pisa und Genua . . . (1081–1204) (Munich, 1984).

5. The text of the chrysobull is published in *TT, Urkunden* I, 43–54; and the grant of honors and pensions to the Doge and patriarch of Grado is published as a separate chrysobull, ibid., 54–55. See the analysis by F. Dölger, *Regesten* I, no. 1081. In both cases the agreement is dated May 1082. On this question and the redating to 1084, see E. Frances, "Alexis Comnène et les privilèges octroyés à Venice," in *BS* XXIX (1968), 17–23. Update The treaties have been reedited by M. Pozza and G. Ravegnani, *I tratti con Bisanzio, 992–1198* (Venice, 1993); see also D. M. Nicol, *Byzantium and Venice: A Study in Diplomatic and Cultural Relations* (Cambridge, UK, 1988), 57–58; and Lilie, *Handel und Politik,* as earlier, 8–16. All confirm the date of 1082. Subsequent attempts to assign the chrysobull to 1092 have not won great support; see the helpful survey by Michael Angold, "The Venetian Chronicles and Archives as Sources for the History of Byzantium and the Crusades (992–1204)," in *Byzantines and Crusaders in Non-Greek Sources, 1025–1204,* ed. Mary Whitby, *Proceedings of the British Academy* 132 (Oxford, 2007), 59–94.

6. For the chrysobull of John II, see *TT, Urkunden* I, 96–98, (= Dölger, *Regesten*, II, no. 1304). On the decline of the navy during his reign, see Ahrweiler, *La Mer*, 230–33. For Manuel I's agreements with Venice, see *TT, Urkunden* I, 109–13, 113–24 (= Dölger, *Regesten*, II, no. 1365). Update P. Magdalino, *The Empire of Manuel I Komnenos, 1143–1180* (Cambridge, UK, 1993), 45, 53–54.

7. In July 1193 Frugerio Senatore da Equilo put in a claim for 55 *hyperpera*, which he had invested in a company formed in November 1170 in Thebes. Cf. A. Lombardo and R. Morozzo della Rocca, *Documenti del commercio veneziano nei secoli XI–XIII* (Turin, 1940), I, no. 418.

8. On the installation of the Italians, see W. Heyd, *Histoire du commerce du Levant au Moyen Age* (Leipzig, 1885; Amsterdam, 1967), I, 190–264; C. Manfroni, "Le relazioni fra Genova, l'Imperio bizantino e I Turchi," in *Atti della Società ligure di storie patria,* XXVIII (1896–98), 575–858; G. Bratianu, *Recherches sur le commerce génois dans la Mer Noire au XIII siècle* (Paris, 1929), 15–155; F. Thiriet, *La Romanie vénitienne au Moyen Age: Le développement et l'exploitation du domaine colonial vénitien (XII–XV siècles)* (Paris, 1959), 29–63; S. Borsari, "Il commercio veneziano nell'Imperio bizantino nel XII secolo," in *Rivista storica italiana* LXXVI (1964), 982–1011. On the Byzantine customs, see H. Antoniadis-Bibicou, *Recherches sur douanes à Byzance* (Paris, 1963). Update Lilie, *Handel und Politik*; A Laiou, "Exchange and Trade," *EcHB,* 751–54, 759; D. Jacoby, "Italian Privileges and Trade in Byzantium before the Fourth Crusade: A Reconsideration," *Annuario de estudios medievales* 24 (1994), 349–68.

9. For example, Jacob the Pisan was a member of the embassy sent to Frederick Barbarossa in 1189; another Pisan, Pipino, was sent to Cyprus in 1192 aboard a "Longobard" ship. In 1179 a Genoese merchant, Baldovino Guercio, provided the ships that carried Princess Agnes from France to Constantinople to marry the young Alexios Komnenos, the future Emperor Alexios II. It was a Venetian ship that transported Saladin's envoys and Byzantine merchants back from Alexandria to the capital. On the increasing use of Latin mercenaries, see L. Halphen, "Le rôle des 'Latins' dans l'histoire intérieure de Constantinople à la fin du XII siècle,"

in *Mélanges C. Diehl* (Paris, 1930), I, 141–45, reprinted in L. Halphen, *A travers l'histoire du Moyen Age* (Paris, 1950), 343–49.

10. H. Ahrweiler, *Recherches sur l'administration de l'Empire byzantin aux IX–XI siècles* (Athens/Paris 1960) and *BCH* LXXXIV (1960), 67–78; F. Chalandon, *Essai sur le règne d'Alexis Ier Comnène (1081–1118)* (Paris, 1900; New York. n.d.), 277–320.

11. N. Svoronos, "Recherches sur le cadastre byzantin et le fiscalité aux XI et XII siècles: Le Cadastre de Thèbes," *BCH* LXXXIII (1959), 1–145; M. Hendy, *Coinage and Money in the Byzantine Empire, 1081–1261* (Washington, DC 1969), 39–65, 71–102. **Update** C. Morrisson, "La Logarikè: réforme monétaire et réforme fiscale sous Alexis Ier Comnène," *TM* 7 (1979), 419–64; N. Oikonomides, *Fiscalité et exemption fiscale à Byzance IXe –XIe s.* (Athens, 1996).

12. Apart from one desperate expropriation of ecclesiastical treasure in 1081/2, Alexios respected church property and forbade its alienation; cf. Dölger, *Regesten*, I, no. 1085. On the growth of monastic estates, see P. Charanis, "Monastic Properties and the State," *DOP* IV (1948), 51–119; N. Svoronos, "Les privilèges de l'Église à l'époque des Comnènes: Un rescrit inédit de Manuel Ier Comnène," in *TM* I (1965), 325–91.

13. The *kommerkion* was by no means the only tax that the Venetians were excused, but it was probably the most severe. Their exemption also covered all the taxes normally paid by merchants: "xilocami, limenatici, poriatici, caniskii, exafolleos, archontichii et aliorum tributorum causa eorum que debent negociari," *TT, Urkunden* I, 53.

14. P. Lemerle, "Notes sur l'administration byzantine à la veille de la IVe Croisade d'après deux documents inédits de Lavra," *REB* XIX (1961), 258–72. On the privileges of Patmos accorded by Alexios I in 1088, see *MM*, VI, 47–50. But these did not include total exemption from the *dekateia* and *kommerkion*, which was added in 1186 by Isaac II; see ibid. VI, 119. On these maritime exemptions, see the important additional note by N. Svoronos, in *TM* I (1965), 384–85.

15. On the development of grants in *pronoia*, see G. Ostrogorsky, *Pour l'histoire de la féodalité*. The privileges of Leon Kephalas are recorded in the *Actes de Lavra*, ed. G. Rouillard and P. Collomp (Paris 1937), I, nos. 41 (1086), 38 (1084), and 42 (1089). On the date of no. 38, cf. Dölger, *Regesten*, II, no. 1134, which places the grant in April 1087. On the position of Guercio, see A. Sanguineti and G. Bertolotto, "Nuova serie di documenti sulle relazioni di Genova coll'Imperio bizantino," in *Atti della Società ligure di storia patria*, XXVIII (1896–98), 406–8, 454–64, 471. **Update** On Baldovino Guercio, see G. W. Day, *Genoa's Response to Byzantium, 1155–1204: Commercial Expansion and Factionalism in a Medieval City* (Urbana/Chicago, 1988); Magdalino, *The Empire of Manuel I Komnenos*, 101–2.

16. On the Angeloi, see F. Cognasso, "Un imperatore bizantino della decadenza: Isacco II Angelo," *Bessarione* XXXI (1915), 29–60, 247–89; C. Brand, *Byzantium Confronts the West* (Cambridge, MA, 1968). **Update** Angold, *The Byzantine Empire, 1025–1204*.

17. Michael Choniates's letters and speeches are published in *Michael Akominatou tou Choniatou Ta Sozomena*, ed. S. Lampros (Athens, 1879–80; Groningen 1968). There is a new edition of the famous *Hypomnestikon* addressed to

Alexios III Angelos in G. Stadtmüller, "Michael Choniates," 282–305. **Update** See the new edition by Ph. Kolovou, *Michael Choniates: symvole ste melete tou viou kai tou ergou tou: to Corpus ton epistolon* (Athens, 1999).

18. *M. Ch.*; for (1), see II, 54 and 66; (2) II, 107; I, 310; (3) I, 308; II, 106; (4) I, 310; (5) I, 307; (6) II, 66; (7) I, 307; II, 106; (8) I, 310; II, 107; (9) I, 309; II, 106.

19. *M. Ch.*, I, 316.

20. The *bestiarities* demanded a new tax contribution (*M. Ch.*, II, 107), and the *repherendarios* and *mystikos* were plundering the Athenians (*M. Ch.*, I, 310). On the correction of *dephendarios* in the text of Lampros to *repherendarios*, see G. Stadtmüller, "Michael Choniates," 295–97.

21. *M. Ch.*, II, 107. These *prostagmata* obviously concerned the collection of maritime taxes, of which Michael complains so frequently.

22. *JusGR*, III, 393. It was on the basis of these experiences that Alexios I established the *Nea Logarike*.

23. *M. Ch.*, II, 54.

24. *M. Ch.*, II, 83.

25. *N. Ch.*, 785. **Update** See the translation by H. Magoulias, *O City of Byzantium* (Detroit, 1984).

26. In addition to the collection of Venetian documents in Lombardo and Morozzo della Rocca, *Documenti*, see A. Lombardo and R. Morozzo della Rocca, *Nuovi documenti del commercio veneto dei secoli XI–XIII* (Venice, 1953). G. Müller, *Documenti sulle relazioni delle città toscane coll'Oriente cristiano e coi Turchi fino all'anno MDXXXI* (Florence, 1879), contains the chief Pisan documents. For the Genoese, see Sanguineti and Bertolotto, "Nuova serie di documenti."

27. The results of the excavations at Corinth are published by the American School of Classical Studies (Cambridge, MA, 1929 onward). On the trades identified in the Agora at Corinth, see K. Davidson, "A Medieval Glass Factory at Corinth," *American Journal of Archaeology* XLIV (1940), 297–327; K. Davidson, *Corinth XII, The Minor Objects* (Princeton, 1952); C. H. Morgan II, *Corinth XI, The Byzantine Pottery* (Cambridge, MA, 1942). On the excavations in the Athenian agora, see A. Frantz, "Digenis Akritas: A Byzantine Epic and Its Illustrators," *B* XV (1940–41), 87–91; A. Frantz, "Medieval Byzantine Pottery in Athens," *Hesperia* VII (1938), 429–67. **Update** The case studies in the *EcHB* by Aspasia Louvi-Kizi (Thebes), Maria Kazanaki-Lappa (Athens), and G.D.R. Sanders (Corinth) have greatly expanded knowledge of the twelfth-century economy of these centers.

28. *M. Ch.*, II, 69. Shortly after his arrival in Athens in 1182, Michael wrote to several friends complaining of the lack of craftsmen and tools (for example, he could not find a cutler, a smith, and a pair of bellows, *M. Ch.*, II, 12). He asked for farming implements and a copy of Virgil's "Georgics" to be sent and eventually became very attached to the primitive conditions in Attica. Kazanaki-Lappa (as earlier), 645, notes the late twelfth-century decline but gives no sufficiently clear reason for it.

29. The names of these *naucleri* are found in Lombardo and Morozzo della Rocca, *Documenti*, nos. 33, 56, 65, 113, 191, 214–15, and 221 and 223, 222, 236, 313, 336, 380, 381, 392, 400, 417, 426, and 451, which are dated from 1111 to 1200. This brief survey cannot possibly prove anything about the role of

native merchants in local trade, but it suggests that they were not much involved in sea transport.

30. Lombardo and Morozzo della Rocca, *Documenti*, no. 456. The Venetian Leonardo Simitecolo bought 34 miliaresia of oil from three Pisan merchants in Modon. The sale was recorded for them by the bishop, who drew up a "simioma greca," the most official act possible, for the two parties. Most exports of oil were of smaller quantities; 5 1/4 *miliaresia* (no. 358); unless merchants were acting together in a group, like the eleven Venetians who claimed to have lost 105 *miliaresia* in Lakedaimonia in 1171 (nos. 316 and 320).

31. In the twelfth century Theban silks were famous in the East Mediterranean, but their production is a completely unknown subject. It is not unreasonable to suppose that the manufacture of such a prized material brought a certain wealth to the city. Certainly the Thebans, unlike the Athenians, were able to enforce their exemption from payment of maritime taxes, and to ward off the impending visit of a governor (see *M. Ch.*, II, 107, and I, 316). Similarly the site and the fortifications of Monemvasia gave it a particular strength. In 1147 it was able to drive off an attack by the Norman fleet, which went on to sack Corinth and Thebes. It had always been an important naval base, but at the end of the twelfth century it was controlled by families rather than by official provincial agents. Representatives of these families surrendered the town to the Franks after a three-year siege in 1248; cf. *The Chronicle of the Morea*, ed. Kalonaros (Athens, 1940), lines 2946–47. On the Monemvasiot ship, see M. Ch., II, 137. **Update** The studies by David Jacoby have established significant evidence for the silk production in central Greece; see "Silk in Western Byzantium before the Fourth Crusade," *BZ* 85 (1992), 425–500, which is borne out by the excavation of dyeing vats in Thebes; see A. Louvi-Kizi, *EcHB*, 631–38.

32. The Pisan embassy of 1198 and the Genoese of 1201 both tried to get a reduction of the tariff, cf. Müller, *Documenti sulle relazioni*, 68–73, and Sanguineti and Bertolotto, "Nuova serie di documenti," 469–99. Although there is a marked decline in the twelfth century in the number of *kommerkiarioi* known from seals (see H. Antoniadis-Bibicou, *Les Douanes*, 225–38), those of Constantinople, Crete, and Adrianople were extremely active (see Sanguineti and Bertolotto, "Nuova serie di documenti," 399–401). It was an arbitrary demand for extra taxation, levied by the *megas doux* Michael Stryphnos, which caused the Genoese merchant, Gafforio, to turn to piracy (cf. *N. Ch.*, 637).

33. The wealth of the three foreign quarters and of individual merchants can be gauged by the following documents: (1) the instructions given to Grimaldi, Genoese ambassador in 1174, which included a list of property confiscated or destroyed in 1171 and for which compensation was claimed (Sanguineti and Bertolotto, "Nuova serie di documenti," 368–405); (2) a similar list drawn up for the Pisans in 1199, by Bernardo Cenami, who was responsible for the administration of Pisan possessions in the empire (Müller, *Documenti sulle relazioni*, 75–79); (3) the Venetian chrysobull of 1198, which lists all the centers in the empire where the republic had interests (*TT, Urkunden*, I, 273–76; = Dölger, *Regesten*, no. 1647); and (4) the evidence of the size, population, and numerous buildings of the Venetian quarter in H. F. Brown, "The Venetians and the Venetian Quarter in Constantinople to the Close of the Twelfth Century," *JHS* XL (1920), 68–88.

Update C. Maltezou, "Il quartiere veneziano di Costantinopoli (scali marittimi)," *Thesaurismata* 15 (1978), 30–61; and "Venetian *Habitores*, *Burgenses* and Merchants in Constantinople and Its Hinterland (Twelfth–Thirteenth Centuries)," in C. Mango and G. Dagron, *Constantinople and Its Hinterland* (Aldershot, UK, 1993), 233–41; D. Jacoby, "The Venetian Quarter of Constantinople from 1082 to 1261: Topographical Considerations," in *Novum Millennium: Studies on Byzantine History and Culture Dedicated to Paul Speck*, ed. Claudia Sode and Sarolta Takács (Aldershot, UK, 2001), 153–70; C. Otten-Froux, "Identities and Allegiances: The Perspective of Genoa and Pisa," in *Identities and Allegiances in the Eastern Mediterranean after 1204*, ed. J. Herrin and G. Saint-Guillain (Farnham, UK, 2011), 245–63, with interesting data about Genoese and Pisan properties in the Byzantine capital before as well as after the Fourth Crusade.

34. *N. Ch.*, 636–37. When Pisan and Genoese pirates joined forces under Guglielmo Grasso and captured two important embassies, Isaac II had no means of riposte except the demand for compensation from the republics and the threat of confiscation of their property; see Müller, *Documenti sulle relazioni*, 66–67, and Sanguineti and Bertolotto, "Nuova serie di documenti," 448–51.

35. The effects of rivalry between the Italians were often felt in Greek waters and ports; for example, in 1193 Venetian shipping was delayed because of Pisan attacks (Lombardo and Morozzo della Rocca, *Documenti*, no. 417), and in the 1171–72 campaign of Venice against the empire, a Genoese boat was burned at Halmyros, because the Genoese supported Manuel I (Sanguineti and Bertolotto, "Nuova serie di documenti," 371 and 388). On the "Longobard" pirates, see *M. Ch.*, I, 315; and the eighth *katechesis* published by S. Lampros in the appendix of his translation of F. Gregorovius, *Geschichte der Stadt Athen—Historia tes poleos Athenon* (Athens, 1904), II, 703. In the letters of Michael Choniates there are numerous references to unidentified pirates and their raids; see for example *M. Ch.*, II, 42–43, 68, 75, 98, 107. Cretan pirates were known to attack Italian merchant ships; see Sanguineti and Bertolotto, "Nuova serie di documenti," 474.

36. *N. Ch.*, 841.

6

BYZANTINE KYTHERA

eᴏ

From 1963–70 George W. Huxley and J. Nicholas Coldstream excavated and studied a Minoan site on the island of Kythera, off the southeast tip of the Peloponnese. They were interested in tracing the impact of the destruction of Knossos beyond Crete, and in the upper levels they found some Byzantine potsherds. In true British School style, they realized that they would have to publish them and invited me to join a study season. This instance of the riches of archaeological material was an appropriate reminder of the potential buried in the earth, which continues to expand in the most unexpected way (see the Theodosian harbor excavations in Istanbul or those currently undertaken in the Crimea). At the time (1970), few scholars were aware of Kythera's past, despite its magnificent monuments, its rich archive of documents in many languages, and its obvious connections with broader Byzantine culture. The following short account must be read as something of a pioneering effort to plot "a guide to Kythera in the Byzantine period," written in the late 1960s when I walked all over the island, in an attempt to identify settlements and trace connections. It was a delightful, informal style of exploration, which has since been extended by others in more systematic investigations. In addition to the central fortified settlement at Kastro, Kythera contains a large number of medieval churches, some with fresco decoration and sculpted fragments. At Palaiochora, it preserves a deserted medieval village that formed a refuge for local people until it was pillaged by Hayreddin Barbarossa. Its local holy man, St. Theodore, was commemorated in a "Life" that records his own activities and building works. Like so many saints, generally unknown, he promoted the Byzantine faith and cared for the island's inhabitants in traditional ways. Combining this record and the few stray references in other sources with the buildings still standing, I was able to construct a brief history of medieval Kythera.

Today several teams of archaeologists are actively working to excavate and document the island's many sites, notably the Kythera Island Project (KIP, see www.ucl.ac.uk/kip/index.php), and the Australian Paliochora-Kythera survey, which has produced *Paliochora on Kythera* by G. E Ince and Andrew Ballantyne (British Archaeological Reports, International

Series, 1704, Oxford, 2007). The Hellenic Institute of Marine Archaeology conducts underwater excavation of a wreck off the coast of Kythera, while the Hellenic Education and Research Center provides training programs for archaeology students. Population studies have established profiles of the island's families, and Manolis Chatzedakes and Ioanna Bitha's full survey of the island's churches has produced the most detailed study to date in both Greek and English editions (*Corpus of the Byzantine Wall-Paintings of Greece. The Island of Kythera*, Athens, 2003). This ongoing work has increased our knowledge of the island's development beyond all bounds. Chrysa Maltezou's many contributions to the study of Kythera in the Venetian period are particularly notable: *Ta Kythera ton kairo pou kyriarchousan oi Venetoi* (Venice, 2008); and Chrysa Maltezou and Maria Koumanoudi, eds., *Venezia e Cerigo: atti del simposio internazionale*, Venezia, 6–7 dicembre 2002 (Venice, 2003).

During the early Christian and Byzantine era, the island of Kythera maintained the same close connection to the mainland that had existed from the time of the Argive–Spartan rivalry. The introduction of Christianity in the fourth century AD was allegedly due to Hosia Elesse, and its tenth-century revival was almost certainly the responsibility of Hosios Theodoros, who like Hosia Elesse came from the Peloponnese. Following these "saintly" people, settlers came from the mainland to repopulate Kythera after its devastation or abandonment. At first the inhabitants of Laconia used the island as a hunting ground, but later they settled permanently.[1] Natives of Crete also came to live, predominantly in the south, where a different accent is still noticeable, but they formed only a small proportion of the population until the fourteenth century. Before 1205 ties between the island and the mainland were much more important than those with Crete.

This connection is reflected in the political and commercial relations of Kythera. It was a part of the same eparchy, later *thema*, as the Peloponnese, and even after the fall of Constantinople in 1453 the island and the hinterland around Monemvasia remained areas of Greek domination and resistance to the Venetians and Frankish crusaders. From the twelfth century the Eudaimonoioannis family of Monemvasia controlled Kythera, and their influence was increased after the flight of all Orthodox clergy and many leading *archontes* from Monemvasia in 1248, when it was captured by William Villehardouin. When the three fortresses of Monemvasia, Mistras, and the Grand Maine were ceded to the Emperor Michael Palaiologos in 1262, the whole area, including Kythera, became a base for the reconquest of the Morea.[2]

But the island had passed into the control of the Venetian Republic after the Fourth Crusade of 1204–5. This influence was nominal only, until 1363, when Kythera became a colony ruled over by a Venetian governor. Despite this status the Greek citadel of Palaiochora, the city of Hagios Demetrios, remained a major center of Orthodoxy until its capture by the Ottoman admiral, Barbarossa, in 1537. Throughout its recorded history Kythera was tied to the mainland by commercial interests. From the tenth century onward it was connected with the growing economic centers of Lakedaimonia (ancient Sparta) and Monemvasia, which exported local produce such as wine, oil, pottery, dyes, and finished cloth. The Venetians reinforced these trading contacts through their markets in the Peloponnese and on Crete, and under their influence Kytherian trade expanded.

In the area around Kastri, which is the site under particular consideration, it is impossible to document the whole history from the fourth century to the sixteenth. It was probably not occupied continuously. But by looking at the development of the island one can formulate a guide to Kythera in the Byzantine period.

THE LATE ROMAN PERIOD:
FOURTH TO SEVENTH CENTURIES

In contrast with other islands such as the Cyclades or the western Ionian group, Kythera remained relatively obscure in this period. It was part of the tenth eparchy, Achaia, according to the *Synekdemos* of Hierokles, and belonged to the ecclesiastical province of Illyricum, which was dependent on Rome rather than Constantinople until the mid-eighth century.[3] Unlike Rhodes, Naxos, Lesbos, Tenos, Skiathos, Karpathos, and other islands, it was not the seat of a bishopric. The suggestion that it had a bishopric in 662 and under the eighth-century iconoclast emperors[4] may be due either to a confusion with the seat of Chytron in Cyprus, which was an autocephalous province,[5] or to reliance on the so-called *Notitia* of Leo III the Isaurian.[6] This has been proved to be a list of cities on the pattern of the *Synekdemos*, not a list of episcopal sees. But the lives of the patron saints and the early church building that survives record the existence of Christians in Kythera.

The island was known to geographers and travelers. It is mentioned in the *Geography* of Ptolemy, the *Geography* of the Anonymous of Ravenna, the *Tabula Peutingeriana*, as well as the *Synekdemos*. The *Peutingeriana*

Table of Itineraries provides interesting information about Kythera in the mid-fourth century. Route 79 in the Balkan peninsula section, running from Dyrrachium to Cape Malea, shows an extension from Boiai to *Cytera*, twenty-five *milia passuum* by sea.[7] The editor remarks that it is difficult to see any point in such a long journey, but the additional trip by sea to a landing place near Kastri certainly suggests that there was some purpose. Possibly the nearby temple of Aphrodite was still an attraction, even in the fourth century. The Emperor Theodosius (379–95) and his successor, Arcadius (395–408), tried to stamp out pagan worship, but without much success.[8] Perhaps the purple-fishing and dye-manufacture, which gave rise to the name Phoinikous, was still undertaken. Most probably the settlement at Kastri, inhabited and perhaps fortified, was known as a safe harbor site. A stray find of a coin of Constantius II (348–61) (ω 355 in the original publication) confirms that there were visitors to this part of the island at the time.

The area around Kastri was still occupied in the sixth and seventh centuries, though it is impossible to prove continuous settlement from the fourth onward. Finds include coins of Justin II (565–78), Maurice (582–602), and Heraclius, as well as sherds of pottery that date from the sixth and early seventh centuries (Deposits υ, φ and χ). The fortification on Kastri cannot be closely dated but almost certainly existed by the time of Justinian. Much of the southern and western outer wall has now fallen into the sea, but on the north side one can distinguish definite corner towers, one round and one square in plan, and a solid stone and tile wall linking them (figures 6.1 and 6.2). This was the building drawn by Cyriac of Ancona when he visited Kythera in 1437. There are three churches in the area that date from this period before the mid-seventh century abandonment of Kastri.[9] Close to the fort of Kastri is the church of Hagios Panteleimon (figures 6.3 and 6.4); on the Palaiokastro mountain, the double-apsed church of Hagioi Kosmas and Damianos (figures 6.5 to 6.9);[10] and farther away on the mountain above Avlemon, the church, later a monastery, of Hagios Georgios tou Bounou. In the last a mosaic floor, the work of a local artist, depicting secular subjects such as animals and hunters, testifies to the wealth of the area (figures 6.10–12). It is unlikely that this floor dates from a period before the seventh century, as no earlier occupation is known hereabouts, but the late Georgios Soteriou suggested that it was not laid for the existing church.[11] On the construction and materials of Hagioi Kosmas and Damianos, see appendix A by Hugh Plommer; and on Hagios Panteleimon, appendix C by A.H.S. Megaw, in the original publication. Another church built in this period is

Figure 6.1. Round tower at Kastri.

Figure 6.2. Rectangular tower at Kastri.

Figure 6.3. Hagios Panteleimon from west.

Figure 6.4. Hagios Panteleimon: apse.

Figure 6.5. Hagios Kosmas, from narthex.

Figure 6.6. Hagios Kosmas, view toward apses.

Figure 6.7. Hagios Kosmas, archaic Doric capital.

Figure 6.8. Hagios Kosmas, archaic Doric capital.

Figure 6.9. Hagioi Kosmas and Damianos: apses.

Figure 6.10. Hagios Georgios, mosaic: hunter.

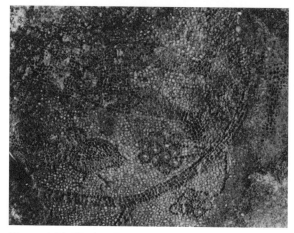
Figure 6.11. Hagios Georgios, mosaic: birds.

Figure 6.12. Hagios Georgios mosaic: panther.

the chapel of Saints Sergius and Bacchus founded by the holy Theodore when he arrived in Kythera in the mid-tenth century. It was probably incorporated in the monastery built on the same site.

Apart from the geographers no Byzantine sources mention Kythera in the years AD 300 to 700. Recent research into Peloponnesian life before the Slav invasions of the late sixth and seventh centuries has revealed that its social and ecclesiastical organization was quite highly developed, and the same may be true of Kythera.[12] It is rather surprising that the island is not mentioned at all in connection with these incursions, as many inhabitants of Greece fled abroad and to the islands to avoid the barbarians, who not only took over the mainland but also sailed to many islands and occupied them. By the mid-seventh century the late Roman settlement had been abandoned; it was obviously no longer safe from attacks by Slav or Arab pirates. At this time the mainland inhabitants either retired into the mountains, the Taygetos range and the east coast area, building themselves strong fortifications, or fled to the islands, Sicily and Southern Italy.[13] The Kytherians may have done the same, or they may have been captured and removed by one of the sea-borne Slav attacks against "the islands and Hellas and even the Cyclades and the whole of Achaia."[14] In 623 the Slavs sailed to Crete.[15] But it is possible that Kythera was raided by Arabs also. In 648/49 Cyprus was attacked by them; two years later Crete, and in 655 Crete again and Cos. From the late seventh century there were Arab bases in Crete and in other Aegean centers from which raids became common.[16] In the resulting insecurity few island settlements survived unless, like Rhodes, they were well fortified; Rhodes castle withstood a total devastation of the island in 807.[17] The Arabs in the Southern Aegean and the Slavs coming from the north constituted a double danger, and when united the two became a highly difficult enemy. When Patras was besieged by a combined force of Arabs and Slavs, it was saved only by the miraculous intervention of the patron saint Andrew.[18] In 768/69 the emperor had to give the Slavs pieces of silk to ransom Orthodox prisoners of war, removed from their homes in the northern islands of Imbros, Tenedos and Samothrace.[19] And twenty years later Theophilos, the Byzantine *strategos* of the Kibyrrheot *thema*, was captured and martyred by Arabs from Cyprus.[20]

It is most likely, therefore, that Kythera was for a time abandoned. It does not seem to have been settled by either Slav or Arab pirates for any lengthy period; at least no trace of such an occupation survives, and by the tenth century it was used as a hunting ground by the mainland inhabitants.

THE MIDDLE BYZANTINE PERIOD: MID-TENTH CENTURY TO 1205

Following the triumphant expedition of Stravrakios to central and southern Greece in 783, Byzantine authority was gradually reimposed, but the position of Kythera remained precarious owing to the proximity of Arab-occupied Crete. There was probably no permanent settlement on Kythera until after the reconquest of Crete by Nikephoros Phokas in 961. Hosios Theodoros, who is supposed to have arrived "in the time of the Emperor Romanos" (probably Romanos II, 959–63), met no one in the island. According to the saint's *Life*, Theodoros and his companion, Antonios, went from Monemvasia to seek solitude, but the diet of nothing but carobs and herbs forced Antonios, an elderly monk, to return. Theodoros lived for several years in the center of the island, where he found a small church dedicated to Saints Sergius and Bacchus. Outside this church his body was discovered by hunters who came from the mainland. When they returned to Laconia with this news, the *Despotes* of Sparta ordered that the body should be buried and a shrine constructed on the spot. So the monastery of Hosios Theodoros (figure 6.13), near Logothetianika, was built and the island was gradually repopulated.[21]

It is necessary to distinguish fact from fiction in this account, but unfortunately evidence is scarce. Certainly the reconquest of Crete and the destruction of the Arab fleet were preconditions of safety on Kythera, and

Figure 6.13. Hosios Theodoros, Logothetianika.

it may have been only after 961 that huntsmen cared to venture out to the island. But the reoccupation must have taken many years, and it is hardly surprising that there is no evidence of settlement until the eleventh and twelfth centuries. As for the alleged support of the "Despot of Sparta," this may have been an important factor in the repopulation, as most of the settlers were to come from Laconia. But no such official title is recorded for any ruler of medieval Lakedaimonia. *Despotes* is probably a glorified name for the *archon*, the local governor who was responsible to the *strategos* of the Peloponnese. From the early ninth to the twelfth century Laconia formed part of this *thema*, governed by the *strategos* from Corinth, and later incorporated with the *thema* of Hellas, that is, central Greece. In the tenth-century *Life* of St. Nikon, patron saint of Lakedaimonia, there is no mention of a *despotes* or any other rival power to that of the *strategos*.[22] It is only at the end of the twelfth century, in a period when imperial authority began to decline in the provinces, that we find an independent power in Laconia, the family of Leon Chamaretos, who ruled the plain of Sparta like a tyrant.[23] So the repopulation of Kythera may have been encouraged by the local *archon* of Lakedaimonia. Later, settlers were to come from Crete, but not until Byzantine authority had been reestablished there in the eleventh century. The Laconians must have recommended the cultivation of olive and vine, which flourish in Kythera, as carobs were reputedly the only food of Hosios Theodoros.[24] The expanding and increasingly important commercial towns of Monemvasia, Korone, Methone, and Lakedaimonia probably found it profitable to maintain contact, exporting their cloth and taking from Kythera excess olives for pressing.[25] The island must have shared in the prosperity of southern Greece in the eleventh and twelfth centuries, for the churches built in this period are richly decorated. The monastery of Hosios Theodoros was founded by Laconians on the order of the *despotes*, presumably in the tenth century. The church of Hagios Demetrios at Pourko (figures 6.14 and 6.15) can be dated by an inscription to the year 1100, and the *Spelaion* of Hagia Sophia near Mylopotamos, is decorated by eleventh- and twelfth-century paintings.[26] The churches of Hagios Nikon, Potamos; Hagios Blasios, Phriligkianika; Hagios Andreas, Leibadi; Hagios Petros, Areoi; and Hagios Nikolaos, Moligkates, near Mylopotamos, were probably built before the island passed under Venetian control (figures 6.16–6.19).

In the twelfth century the area around Metata came under the control of Georgios Pachys, a powerful if unofficial governor related to the Eudaimonoioannis family of Monemvasia.[27] Metata probably replaced Kastri, as it was a safer settlement in the mountains, not so exposed to the sea, and it is possible that pots were brought from Metata to Kastri and left there (Deposit ψ). Most of the pottery is rough green-and-brown glazed ware, but some pieces are more elaborate and have parallels in the pottery of Lakedaimonia (ψ I). It is quite likely that the Kytherians used to import special dishes and pots from the mainland. They must have continued to use the landing at Kastri, but it is impossible to tell whether the site was permanently occupied. Connections with Monemvasia grew increasingly strong in the Middle Byzantine period until the twelfth century, when the Eudaimonoioannis family came to regard the island as their own property. This development, which is paralleled in other parts of the empire, probably took place earlier here than elsewhere, because southern Greece was so far distant from the capital and also because there were three extremely powerful families in Monemvasia. Together with the Mamonades and the Sophianoi, the Eudaimonoioannides controlled the city and its valuable trading activity, and withstood siege by the Normans in 1147.[28] (In 1248, however, after a three-year siege by the Franks and Venetians, they were starved into surrender.) During the twelfth century their merchant fleet sailed round the coasts of the Peloponnese and put into the port of Athens.[29] This naval power provided direct access to Kythera and must have facilitated the Eudaimonoioannis domination. By the end of the twelfth century Monemvasiot influence over Kythera had completely removed any trace of Spartan control, and it was to continue long into the following centuries.

In the Middle Byzantine period the episcopal status of Kythera is problematic. As S. Binon pointed out in his article on the metropolitan see of

Figure 6.14. Hagios Demetrios at Pourko, from southwest.

Figure 6.15. Hagios Demetrios at Pourko, from southeast.

Figure 6.16. Hagios Blasios.

Figure 6.17. Hagios Petros, at Areoi near Mylopotamos.

Figure 6.18. Mylopotamos: walls of Kastro.

Figure 6.19. Hagios Andreas, Leivadhi (Leibadi).

Monemvasia,[30] Kythera does appear as a suffragan bishopric of Corinth in the *Codex Athenensis 1372*, fol. 486v, which was published in part by Gelzer as *Notitia III*, and dated by him to the reign of John Tzimiskes, 969–72.[31] But Gelzer did not publish the suffragan bishoprics and made no comment on the inclusion of Kythera.[32] In the first list of the *Nea Taktika*, published as Gelzer's *Notitia II* (pre-940), and part of Parthey's *Notitia 3* (eleventh century), the suffragan bishoprics of Corinth are always the same seven: Damala, Argos, Monemvasia, Kephalonia, Zakynthos, Zemaina, and Maina.[33]

There was no change in this list until the arrival of the Franks: see the twelfth-century lists, *Codex Atheniensis 1371*, partly published by Gelzer as *Notitia V* and by Parthey, *Notitia 10*.[34] The stray mention of Kythera in the tenth-century list is not retained in later ones. It is unwise to accept the tenth-century list on other grounds as well: in the 970s Kythera was barely repopulated. It could hardly have had sufficient souls to merit a bishop before the eleventh century at the earliest. Also, the list is part of a manuscript written in 1779 for Dorotheos, Archbishop of Trebizond. It must have been copied from an earlier one that attributed to Corinth an eighth suffragan see of Kythera. But it is highly improbable that Kythera was the site of an episcopal see in the tenth century. The first occasion when such an honor might have been accorded was at the elevation of Monemvasia to metropolitan status soon after the recapture of Constantinople and the return of Monemvasia to the empire.[35] The site was favored by Palaiologan emperors in many ways, and it was perhaps the most important military stronghold in the Morea.[36] It was promoted from 98th position in the metropolitan hierarchy to 34th, 13th and 10th in about twenty years, and during this period it was given four suffragan sees: Maina, formerly under Corinth; Elous, formerly under Patras; and two new ones, Reontos and Kythouria (Kythera). These are confirmed in the *Chrysobullon* of 1301, which also adds three more, Korone, Methone, and Zemaina.[37] This reflects the reorganization of the Greek Church in the Peloponnese necessitated by the Frankish occupation of Patras and Corinth, the two oldest metropolitan sees. All their suffragan bishoprics were either transferred to Monemvasia or became autocephalous archbishoprics, with the exception of Bolaina, Amykleion, and Damala. The disappearance of these three was compensated by the creation of two new sees, Reontos and Kythouria (Kythera). Despite the Frankish occupation of the Morea, the Orthodox church succeeded in maintaining its authority, and the emergence of two new bishoprics in the south is an indication of the growing Greek strength of this area.

The Venetian Domination, 1205–1537

Although Kythera is not mentioned in the Partition Treaty of 1204, which divided the Byzantine Empire between the Venetians, the Franks, and the pilgrims of the Fourth Crusade, it was included among those parts of the Peloponnese that were allotted to the Republic. Because of its trading activity, Venice was particularly interested in the ports of mainland Greece and of the islands: Corfù, Korone, and Methone, for example, which served as trading stations on the way to Crete and Cyprus. In 1205 Nikolaos Eudaimonoioannis was ruling Kythera. Two years later Marco Veniero was appointed Marquis of Cerigo (the Italian name for the island) by the Republic, but he was also given lands in Crete, where he preferred to live.[38] He may have sent officials to his possession, but the Eudaimonoioannis family continued to rule. In 1238 the two families were united by a judicious marriage between Nikolaos's daughter and Marco's son, Bartolomeo. Kythera was given to the couple by Nikolaos as part of his daughter's dowry.[39] The fall of Monemvasia to the Franks strengthened the Eudaimonoioannis influence, which was maintained by Palaiologan emperors. When a Venetian envoy visited Kythera in 1275 he found a Greek official, Paulus Savastos, in control. He was "homine domini Imperatoris et capitaneus dicti loci Cedrigi," and a member of the Monoioannis family (another name for the Eudaimonoioannis).[40] Veniero rule in Kythera was further disrupted in the 1280s by the activities of Licario, Grand Duke of the Byzantine fleet.[41] So throughout the thirteenth century Kythera was not much affected by nominal Venetian control.

But after 1309, when another marriage alliance gave the Venieri greater power over Kythera, the island was divided up in a feudal fashion.[42] The four grandsons of Bartolomeo established twenty-four *carati* (lots) and took six each. The whole island was thus assigned to one of the brothers, except the area around Palaiopolis (Kastri) and lands below Kapsali. These parts were held communally by all four, "forsè come la più bella parte che potea esser nell'isola."[43] This is the contemporary description of the region of *Paiopoli* [sic]. In the twenty-four *carati* the inhabitants were reduced to the status of serfs, called *parichi*, and were bound to the land and to the authority of the Venieri in all important matters.[44] The *Memorie* states bluntly that their condition was "si può dire di captività."[45] During this period the Venieri ignored the prosperity of the island and used it purely as a base for piracy in the Aegean, especially against Catalan ships. At the same time they failed to prevent the establishment of a group of Turkish pirates on Kythera, and a contingent of a hundred soldiers had to be sent from Crete to assist Nicolo Veniero in dislodging them.[46] Crete also had to supply wheat for the Kytherian population. Relations between the Republic and the Venieri, already worsened by the latter's continued piracy against allies of Venice and their lack of co-operation during the war with Genoa, deteriorated yet further in 1354, when the brothers demanded a license to export 2,000 staia of wheat per annum to Kythera. The Senate granted a license for half the amount. From this time onward the Cretan branch of the Veniero family became a recognized center of opposition to Venetian rule.[47]

The Cretan uprising of 1363, in which close relations of the Venieri played a prominent part, resulted in the Republic's victory and much more direct control over Aegean possessions. The four brothers in Kythera were removed from their positions, and the island became a Venetian colony administered by a governor called *castellano*.[48] The strategic importance of Kythera as a staging post between the Peloponnese and Candia, capital of Crete, and its wealth of natural resources were recognized and developed by the Republic.[49] The defense system was taken in hand. Kapsali (figures 6.20 to 6.23), Mylopotamos (figures 6.18 and 6.24), and the spectacular site of Palaiochora, the Greek city of Hagios Demetrios, were fortified (figures 6.25 to 6.30). With funds sent from Crete, the two main harbors of Kapsali (figure 6.23) and Hagios Nikolaos (Avlemon) were strengthened, and there was a project, never fulfilled, to build a castle on the mountain overlooking Avlemon, where the monastery of Hagios Georgios stands.[50]

Despite direct Venetian rule during the fourteenth and fifteenth centuries, neither the prosperity nor the Orthodoxy of the Greek inhabitants appear to have declined. Kythera became the seat of a bishopric, first mentioned in the 1301 *Chrysobullon* for Monemvasia, and many churches were built and decorated.[51] The Venetians did not interfere with the Orthodox clergy, and Hagios Demetrios, which may have been founded by the Eudaimonoioannis family before 1205, remained a Greek citadel. It almost certainly replaced the settlement at Kastri as the most important site on the east coast of the island, although Avlemon also became an important center. The position of Palaiochora, only two kilometers but invisible from the sea, on a crag in the middle of a deep ravine, gave it preeminence (figures 6.28, 6.30, and 6.31). The city reputedly held 7,000 people or more in 1537 when it was destroyed by a Turkish fleet under Barbarossa.[52] The Bishop of Kythera probably resided at Palaiochora, but the actual church of Hagios Demetrios has not been identified.[53] By the second half of the fourteenth century the island appeared to be under the ecclesiastical control of a *protopapas*, rather than a bishop.[54] (*Protopapas*

Figure 6.20. Chora, Kastro: general view.

Figure 6.21. Chora, Kastro: Archeion.

Figure 6.23. Kapsali harbor.

Figure 6.24. Mylopotamos: gate of Kastro.

Figure 6.25. Palaiochora: Hagia Barbara.

Figure 6.26. Palaiochora: Hagios Antonios.

Figure 6.27. Palaiochora: Unidentified church.

Figure 6.28. Palaiochora: Hagios Antonios.

Figure 6.29. The gorge at Palaiochora.

Figure 6.30. Palaiochora: building at summit.

Figure 6.31. Palaiochora, from west.

is the usual title for an episcopal deputy: for example, the *protopapas* of Athens carried out the commands of the Metropolitan in exile, during the Frankish occupation.[55]) But this situation did not prevail for long, and Kythera remained a stronghold of Byzantine Orthodoxy long after the fall of Constantinople in 1453.

The Turks did not succeed in capturing Kythera when they gained control of mainland Greece, and so the island, together with the Venetian ports of Korone, Methone, and Monemvasia, continued to be an outpost of the Republic, now even more important than before in the struggle between Venice and the Turks. But it never recovered from the devastation of Barbarossa's attack in 1537. Governors made repeated requests for families to be resettled in formerly fertile parts of the island, which became poor and barren due to lack of regular cultivation, but these passed unheeded.[56] When Monemvasia was handed over to the Turks in 1540, its inhabitants were offered homes on Kythera. But they demanded to be rehoused in more prosperous parts of the Republic, and many were eventually settled in Crete, Cyprus, and the Ionian islands.[57] So Kythera declined although it remained one of the last centers of Byzantium in the East. In 1540 the Bishop of Kythera inherited the exclusive right of ordaining the Greek clergy of Crete.[58] And at the end of the sixteenth century, long after the political and strategic decline of the island, Bishop Maximos Margounios was famous as a Greek scholar, theologian, poet, and letter writer.[59]

ADDENDUM

On Hosios Theodoros, see the most recent edition of the *Life* by N. A. Oikonomides, Ὁ βίος τοῦ ἁγίου Θεοδώρου Κυθήρων, in Πρακτικά, Τρίτον Πανιόνιον Συνέδριον, ἀνάτυπον (Athens, 1967). On Barbarossa's activity in the Mediterranean, see F. Braudel, *La Méditerranée et le monde méditerranéen à l'époque de Philippe II* (2nd ed., Paris, 1966), I, 106; II, 181.

NOTES

1. *Life of Hosios Theodoros*, K. Doukakkes, *Megas Synaxaristes*, 5 (Athens, 1889–96), 21–13.
2. *The Chronicle of Morea*, ed. P. Kalonaros (Athens, 1940), 183, lines 4329–31.
3. The *Notitia* of Basil of Ialimbana, ed. H. Gelzer, *Georgii Cyprii Descriptio Orbis Romani* (Leipzig, 1890), 27.

4. Kasimates, *Ἀπὸ τὴν πάλαια καὶ συγχρόνη Κυθηραϊκὴ* (Athens, 1957), 38–39. I have been unable to find the two articles by Alvanakes in *Kytheraike Epeteris* (1909 and 1912–13), which deal with the early church organization of Kythera.

5. J. Hackett, *A History of the Orthodox Church of Cyprus* (London, 1901), 13–33; and *Mansi*, VII, 160; VIII, 300; XIII, 388. The Cypriot bishopric is called *Chytrennus*, Χύθρων, or Κύθρων, and the site is known to geographers as Κύθροι or Χύτροι: Georgius of Cyprus, ed. Gelzer, as in note 3, 56; and Stephanus of Byzantium, *Ethnica*, ed. Meineke, 698, 9. This confusion is more noticeable in the *Anonymous of Ravenna*, ed. Parthey and Pinder (Berlin, 1860). For the Cypriot site he gives *Cythara* (393, 10) and for the island, *Cyrise* (395, 15), which the editors identify as "Cerigo, antiquis Cythera."

6. It was first published by C. de Boor, *Zeitschrift für Kirchengeschichte*, 12 (1891) 303–22, and 519–43; 14 (1894) 573–99. But L. Duchesne established the nature of the MS, *Mélanges d'histoire et d'archéologie de l'École française de Rome*, 15 (1895) 375–85, and this is confirmed by A. Bon, *Le Péloponnèse byzantin jusqu'en 1204* (Paris, 1951), 22–24.

7. *Tabula Peutingeriana*, ed. K. Miller, *Itineraria Romana* (Stuttgart, 1916), 569.

8. *Cod. Theod.*, XVI, 1, 2. The edict of February 27, 380, established Christianity as the state religion of the Byzantine Empire.

9. For an informative survey of the churches on the island, see Lazarides, *AD* 20 (1965), BI, 183–99. Important restoration work has been undertaken, which is reported in *AD* 21 (1966), BI, 22–25; 22 (1967), BI, 17f., and 204f. The article by the late Georgios Soteriou, who visited Kythera in 1916, is also of great value: *Kytheraike Epitheoresis* 1 (1923), 313–22. I am greatly indebted to Miss Alison Frantz and A.H.S. Megaw for their advice.

10. The double-apsed churches in Kythera provide important evidence of this rare architectural form: P. Vokotopoulos, in *Charisterion eis Anastasion Orlandon* 4 (Athens, 1968), 66–74.

11. Soteriou, *Kytheraike Epitheoresis*, 314.

12. The book of A. Bon cited earlier (note 6) and the work of N. Drandakis, Βυζαντιναί Τοιχογραφίαι τῆς Μέσα Μάνης (Athens, 1964), have done much to fill in the shadowy history of Southern Greece.

13. *Chronicle of Monemvasia*, ed. P. Lemerle, *REB* 21 (1963), 10, lines 39–50; P. Schreiner, "La Fondation de Monemvasie en 582/3," *TM* 4 (1970) 471–76.

14. Miracula Sancti Demetrii, *PG*, 116, col. 1325.

15. *Libri Chalipharum*, ed. J.P.N. Land, *Anecdota Syriaca* 1 (1862), 115.

16. Orations of Saint Andrew of Crete, *PG*, 97, col. 1168; G. Miles, "Byzantium and the Arabs: Relations in Crete and the Aegean Area," *DOP* 18 (1964) 1–31.

17. *Theophanes*, 1, 483; Mango and Scott, 633.

18. Constantine Porphyrogenitus, *De Administrando Imperio*, ed. Moravcsik and Jenkins, 1 (Budapest, 1949), ch. 49, 228–32; 11 (London, 1962), 182–85. **Update** N. Oikonomides, "St Andrew, Joseph the Hymnographer and the Slavs of Patras," in *ΛΕΙΜΩΝ: Studies Presented to L. Rydén on His Sixty–fifth Birthday*, ed. J. O Rosenqvist (Uppsala, 1996), 71–78.

19. *Nikephoros*, 76; Mango, 612–13.

20. *Theophanes*, I, 465; Mango and Scott, 639.

21. In the *Bibliographie des Acolouthies grecques*, by L. Petit (Subsidia Hagiographica 16, Brussels, 1926), 278f., three editions of the *Akolouthia* of Hosios Theodoros are listed: those of Venice, 1747; Smyrna, 1841; and Athens, 1899. In 1961 a new edition was prepared by the Metropolitan of Kythera. All these editions are based on two surviving manuscripts, both of the fifteenth century: F. Halkin, *Bibliotheca Hagiographica Graeca,* 3, suppl., 74. The *Life* of Holy Theodore in Doukakkes, *Megas Synaxaristes,* 213 (see note 1 earlier) reproduces the *Synaxarion* of the Athens edition (1899), which was also printed in the Smyrna one of 1841. I have been unable to trace either of these. The basic story of the *Life* is also found in a later Italian document, *L'Antique Memorie dell'Isola di Cerigo,* edited by Sathas in *Documents rélatives à l'histoire de la Grèce médiévale,* 6 (1885) 299–311, but with slightly different details. The Metropolitan Meletios discusses some of these variations and the date of the *Life* in his edition, 22. See addendum.

22. *Life of Hagios Nikon,* ed. Lampros, *Neos Hellenomnemon,* 3 (1906) 129–222. **Update** *The Life of Saint Nikon: Text Translation and Commentary,* Denis F. Sullivan (Brookline MA, 1987).

23. *N. Ch.,* ed. I. Bekker (Bonn, 1835), 841. **Update** Two seals of Leon Chamateros are recorded; see *PBW,* nos. 20199 and 20200.

24. Sathas, *Documents relatives,* "herbe et carobe selvadeghe," 300.

25. *Documenti del Commercio Veneziano nel secoli XI–XIII,* ed. Morozzo della Rocca and Lombardo (Turin, 1940), 135, 229–30. F. Thiriet, *La Romanie vénitienne au moyen âge* (Paris, 1959), 47, 48. As early as the tenth century Italian merchants began to frequent Lakedaimonia: *Life* of Hagios Nikon, *Neos Hellenomnemon,* 215.

26. Xyngopoulos, *Ninth Congress of Byzantine Studies* (Thessalonike, 1955), 1, 178–83. **Update** See now M. Chatzedakes and I. Bitha, *Corpus of the Byzantine Wall-Paintings of Greece: The Island of Kythera* (Athens, 2003).

27. Sathas, *Documents rélatives,* 301–2; apparently the *despotes* ordered Zorzi Pacchi da Malvasia to be *Gastaldo;* Eudaimonoioannis, however, remained *assoluto padrone et signore.* For all late Byzantine families, the *Prosopographisches Lexikon der Palaiologenzeit,* ed. F. Trapp et al. (Vienna, 1976–96), is an indispensable aid.

28. *N. Ch.,* ed. I. Bekker (Bonn, 1835), 97–98. *The Chronicle of Morea,* 123, lines 2946–49, mentions these families, whose members held influential positions in the Byzantine administration of the Morea throughout the fourteenth and fifteenth centuries.

29. *M. Ch.,* II, 137.

30. *ÉO,* 37 (1938), 274–311.

31. "Ungedruckte und ungenügend veröffentlichte Texte der Notitiae episcopatuum," *Abh. der philos.-philol. Cl. der König. Bayer. Akad. der Wissenschaften,* Band 21 (Munich, 1901), 574.

32. Examination of the manuscript shows that all the suffragan bishoprics were copied out at the same time; Kythera is not a later addition.

33. Parthey, *Hieroclis Synecdemus et notitiae graecae episcopatuum* (Berlin, 1866), 117; Gelzer, *Georgii Cyprii,* 556. **Update** I. Bitha, "Ta Vyzantina Kythera mesa apo tis martyries ton ekklesion kai ton toichographion," *9th International Panionian Congress, Zakynthos, September 1997, Praktika,* vol. 4 (Athens, 2004),

565–78, at 567 cites the deaths of Bishop Theoktistos of Kythera in 1110 and of Neilos, monk and so-called bishop in 1122, recorded in Parisinus graecus 1581 f. 35, as an indication that Kythera was already a bishopric under Corinth.

34. Parthey, *Hieroclis Synecdemus*, 215; Gelzer, *Georgii Cyprii*, 585–86.

35. Binon, *ÉO*, 37 (1938), 274–311. **Update** Promotion to episcopal status in the eleventh century does appear to be confirmed by seals; see two attributed to a bishop Nikolaos, *episkopos Monembasas*, or *Monobias* at Dumbarton Oaks (*PBW* under Nikolaos, nos. 21067 and 21068).

36. *MM*, 5, 154–55, 161–65, 165–68.

37. Binon, *ÉO*, 37 (1938), 274–311; D. Zakythinos, *Le Despotat grec de Morée*, II (Athens, 1953) 273–77. This MS of the Byzantine Museum, Athens, no. 3570, is the original *Chrysobullon*. The *Codex Atheniensis 1462*, dated 1293, published in *MM* 5, 155–61, has been identified as a later forgery by Binon, *ÉO*, 289–93.

38. Cheilas, "Chronikon monasterii S. Theodori," ed. K. Hopf, *Chroniques Gréco-Romanes inédites ou peu connues* (Berlin, 1873), 346. At the same time the Viaro family was given the island of Antikythera (Cerigotto). **Update** C. Maltezou, "Le familie degli Eudaimonioiannis e Venier a Cerigo dal XII al XIV secolo. Problemi di cronologia et prosopografia," *Rivista di studi bizantini e slavi* 2 (1982), 208–10; M. Angold, "The Latin Empire of Constantinople, 1204–1261: Marriage Strategies," in J. Herrin and G. Saint-Guillain, eds., *Identities and Allegiances in the East Mediterranean after 1204* (Farnham, 2011), 47–67, esp. 60.

39. Sathas, *Documents rélatives*, 302.

40. *TT*, *Urkunden*, 3, 181. *Savastos* may be a corruption of the Byzantine title Σεβαστός.

41. W. Miller, *The Latins in the Levant* (London, 1909), 141, 564.

42. Marino Sanudo Torsello, *Istoria del Regno di Romania*, in Hopf, *Chroniques Gréco-Romanes*, 127.

43. Sathas, *Documents relatives*, 302.

44. Sathas, ibid.. The Italian *paricho*, "che vuol dire servo particolare," obviously corresponds to the Greek πάροικος, but it is not clear whether the duties and status of Greek peasants in the Byzantine Empire and those under the Venetians were the same. Cf. D. Jacoby, *La Féodalité en Grèce Médiévale. Les "Assises de Romanie": Sources, Application et Diffusion* (Paris, 1971).

45. Sathas, ibid.

46. Thiriet, *La Romanie vénitienne*, 251, n. 3.

47. *Ibid.*, 275–76. Thiriet, *Régistes des Délibérations du Sénat de Venise concernant la Romanie* (1958) 1, 75, no. 20.

48. Miller, *The Latins in the Levant*, 565; Sathas, *Documents rélatives*, 303. The Republic took over eleven of the twenty-four *carati* of land.

49. The reports of later governors make this clear; see "Relatio viri nobilis Joanis Superantii Reversi proviso Cytherici," of 1545, in Sathas, *Documents relatives*, 286–89.

50. Ibid., 288. The port of Kapsali was "habile a salvar X o XII gallie." H. Noiret, *Documents inédits pour servir à l'histoire de la domination vénitienne en Crete de 1380 à 1485* (Paris, 1892), 93, 94.

51. Miller, *JHS* 27 (1907), 232, suggested that natives of Kythera were responsible for building the church of the *Panayia Myrtidiotissa*, one of their patron saints,

at Monemvasia. The church of Hagios Nikolaos, next door to the monastery of Hagios Georgios tou Bounou, is also dedicated to the Panayia Myrtidiotissa. **Update** H. Kalligas, *Byzantine Monemvasia: The Sources* (Monemvasia, 1990).

52. Sathas, *Documents rélatives*, 289; Miller, *JHS*, 507 and 567. In the same year the acropolis of Aegina was attacked and Palaiochora fell. Six thousand women and children were taken off as slaves. See addendum.

53. A reference (*AD* 21 [1966], BI 24) by persons engaged in restoration of churches at Palaiochora to a church of Hagios Demetrios suggests that the building may now have been identified. Bitha, *Corpus des églises*, 97–101, 316, proposes a possible identification of the church, but see note 33 earlier.

54. Cheilas, "Chronikon monasterii S. Theodori," 348f.

55. *MM*, 2, 259.

56. Sathas, *Documents relatives*, "Relatio of Joanis," 287, 289, and the "Relatio" of another provisor, Maphio Baffo. Ibid., 289–95.

57. Miller, *JHS* 27 (1907), 240.

58. *MM*, 2, 139.

59. Miller, *The Latins in the Levant*, 568. D. Geanakoplos, *Byzantine East and Latin West* (Oxford, 1966) 165–93. **Update** As several scholars have pointed out, Margounios never resided in Kythera, as the island rejected him as too pro-Western. He remained titular bishop but lived in Venice, where he devoted himself to these non-episcopal duties.

METROPOLIS

7

BYZANTIUM

THE PALACE AND THE CITY

❧

An invitation to participate in a conference on the role of the sovereign in East and West prompted the first version of this study in French (published in the Belgian periodical *Byzantion* 41, 1991). The editors, Jean-Marie Sansterre and Alain Dierkens, organized a series of events devoted to the study of Byzantium in a comparative perspective, so I was particularly glad to contribute. By contrasting the imperial system with other medieval styles of government, the specificity of each becomes much clearer. My interest in the role of the Great Palace within the city of Constantinople grew out of a seminar on the *Parastaseis syntomoi chronikai* (*Brief Historical Notes*) directed by Alan and Averil Cameron. The exciting process of working on this anonymous text that survives in only one eleventh-century manuscript sparked a greater attention to its contribution to the study of medieval Constantinople, which was disputed. This encouraged me to focus on the imperial center, the court of Constantinople, and its departments of government that ruled the empire, moving my attention from margins to the metropolis.

Constantine's foundation of a new capital on the site of ancient Byzantion gave rise to a series of epithets for the metropolis: the Queen City, or ruling city, *basileuontas polis*, as it became known, or simply "the city." These reflected the emperor's intention that his city should replace Old Rome; its destiny was to rule the Roman world. While it took some time for Constantinople to grow into this role, by the sixth century when Justinian rebuilt the center dominated by the great church of Holy Wisdom (Hagia Sophia), the founder's ambition was clearly being realized. And despite a later decline, the roots of this ruling identity were so deeply embedded that no other city could challenge it. Constantinople and the Great Palace within it remained unrivalled until the early thirteenth century.

In this chapter I explore some of the relations between the imperial court within the palace and the local population who proudly called themselves "Byzantines," reflecting their claim to have lived in the ancient Greek colony of Byzantion. As the original inhabitants of the city they cultivated a special affinity with the ruling family in power, being closest to the palace and thus in a position to congratulate the emperor on the birth of a son or to criticize his ministers. In spite of very limited access, they found ways to make their views known. When an urban mob marched toward the palace, those inside condemned the *demokratia* (rule by the *demos*, crowd, sometimes a group of Hippodrome fans known by their colors, Green or Blue). Such a term had no place in a well-ordered empire where monarchy authorized by divine approval had attained an all-powerful, if not god-like power. Yet the population could, in certain circumstances, have influence, and rulers who ignored popular feeling within the ruling city could lose their office. On such occasions the people confronted the emperor in the Hippodrome, which always remained the site of potential discord as well as shared exhilaration—both were equally devoted to the races.

IN THE EAST ROMAN EMPIRE the words "palace" and "city" generally had only one meaning—the Great Palace of the emperors in the city of Constantine, inaugurated in 330 AD and named Constantinople after him. Although it took many years for this dominance to take hold, by the Middle Ages there were no rivals and no equivalents in the West. The imperial capital contained the largest concentration of population in the medieval world (though a few Asian cities were larger, and during the tenth century Baghdad would overtake it). But this ruling city, the Queen City, was far larger than any city of medieval Europe. Even in the twelfth century, the crusaders who were familiar with Paris, Rome, Lyons, were astonished by the area within the walls, as well as the wealth of Constantinople. A city *sans pareille*, it sustained urban traditions and incorporated and elaborated ancient histories and myths. Heir to a Greek world stretching back over a thousand years, though it developed from a small Greek colony rather than a famous city like Athens or Ephesos, it was also called New Rome from the fourth century.

This name, New Rome, indicates Constantine's determination to create a rival, even a replacement, for Old Rome in the West. New Rome was said to have followed the older model, however, being built on seven hills with fourteen districts; and the palace of the emperors was based on the Palatine overlooking the Circus Maximus, where rulers presided over the races, entertainment, victory parades, and so on. In Constantinople the plan of Old Rome was adapted to new terrain, with public buildings, state monuments, and grand squares, all decorated with ancient statuary, and linked by avenues bordered by colonnades and defended by a great land wall formed of three lines of fortification.[1] After the Nika riot of

January 532, Justinian I cleared the central area and rebuilt in appropriately grander style, with the massive doomed church of Holy Wisdom replacing an earlier basilica, new public buildings like the Senate House, and additional cisterns to increase water supplies. Under his patronage New Rome flourished, while Old Rome on the Tiber never recovered from several devastating sacks in the fifth and sixth centuries.

Constantinople was the only imperial foundation that survived the decline of the urban traditions of Antiquity.[2] And even Constantinople experienced a catastrophic reduction in its population after the attacks of pestilence, which continued from the sixth into the eighth century. This decline can be gauged from the fact that the city survived the destruction of the aqueduct in 626 by besieging Avar forces, and managed with reduced water storage capacity until 766 when Constantine V repaired the structure.[3] The restoration suggests that a growing population required larger supplies, and the emperor now found the means to rebuild and protect the long impressive aqueduct that carried water nearly 250 kilometers from the Belgrade forest into the city.

From this point on the city began to witness an expansion. For a variety of reasons, merchants, clerics, intellectuals, adventurers, and all those who believed the stories of streets paved with gold came to look for work in the Queen City. The striking case of the future emperor Basil I in the ninth century must be one of the many instances, which remain unrecorded because they did not document the career of a new ruler.[4] The city's healing shrines had always generated pilgrims hoping for a miraculous cure, and as the city's collection of relics and wonder-working icons grew, so did the number of visitors. Some provincial families sent their children to Constantinople, intending boys to acquire a better education and hoping that castrated boys and young girls could find work in the imperial court, as eunuchs and ladies-in-waiting. In these ways Constantinople retained and deepened its position as metropolis of the Christian universe and attracted people from the four corners of the world.

Even during the darkest times, the idea of urban life always remained dominant. In Constantinople the Roman ideology of "bread and circuses" was adapted to medieval life.[5] The emperor provided not only what was necessary for life, but also for the pleasures of the city: circus entertainments, public baths, the pomp and largess of the court in numerous processions and rituals outside the palace. The Hippodrome still served as the place where the people gathered to celebrate a military triumph or the anniversary of the foundation of the city with horse and chariot races, so warmly appreciated. Even more important, however, was the role of the

Hippodrome as the site where emperor and people met: before the opening of the games and races, the people acclaimed him and the emperor blessed them. And these ritual exchanges demonstrate the structural relations between the palace and the city, which persisted throughout the middle Byzantine period.[6]

The presence of the people (*laos* or *demos* without a more specific name) was organized by the Prefect of the City (*eparchos tes poleos*) on official occasions, when they exercised their traditional role in imperial government: the acclamation of a new ruler.[7] This ancient Roman right continued into the medieval period and might sometimes lead to unexpected consequences, when, for example, an urban crowd demanded to see the Empress Zoe, who had been illegally confined to a monastery by her consort Michael VI, or when they marched off to liberate her sister, Empress Theodora.[8] The people were invited to go and meet all important visitors to the city, like Pope Constantine I when he traveled from Rome and was received at the seventh mile from the city, or the fiancée of Leo IV who arrived by sea from Athens.[9] Sometimes the Prefect summoned them to the Forum of Constantine, to hear the news of the day.[10] Military updates from the war zone might be announced together with instructions for the city's defense. If a serious invasion was threatened, the population was expected to buy in sufficient food supplies for up to three years, or to leave the city at once.[11] On other occasions, revelations of corruption by imperial officials, rumors of cowardice among military leaders or abuse of the rights of young emperors might rouse the inhabitants to more spontaneous and aggressive actions. Traditional reactions and resistance to injustice remained strong, now within the framework of a medieval and Christian civilization.

In this ancient city the pagan past left many traces. Nearly all the monuments were decorated with statues of the gods or pre-Christian emperors, and also with antique symbols such as tripods, Gorgon heads from Ephesos, or the great bronze horses installed at the entrance to the Hippodrome (now at the church of San Marco, Venice).[12] In the West there was no comparable sense of an earlier pagan civilization, except possibly in Rome.[13] Most western cities suffered a much more profound break between Antiquity and the Middle Ages and had lost their lived experience of urban customs. In Constantinople this was not the case, though its inhabitants were often uncertain about the individuals or stories commemorated in the antique statues or where they came from. They continued to be aware of them, partly because no one doubted that some had a certain force; they could even cause earthquakes.[14] Others in the region of the Xerolophos, which was dominated by pagan statues, simply inspired prophecies, sacrifice, and astronomy.[15] The emperor regularly made a procession there.

In Constantinople "the palace" refers to the "Great Palace,"[16] even though there were many other palaces in the city and suburban region. Late Antique villas, known by the names of their founders (the Palace of Macrina or the Palace of Placidia, for example) were used for particular functions, such as the accommodation of the papal envoy, *apocrisiarius*, to the imperial court, or of distinguished visitors. On the European shore of the Bosphorus, the palace in the region of St. Mamas had its private hippodrome, where the emperors could take part in horse races.[17] In the palace of Hiereia, situated on the Asiatic shore of the Sea of Marmara, Constantine V presided over the council of 754, which identified itself as the Seventh Ecumenical gathering. Toward the end of the eighth century, Empress Irene built herself a new palace called the Eleutherios, in central Constantinople that served as her private residence and where she also installed charitable institutions.[18]

None of these palaces rivalled the Great Palace, which also served as the center of government. It extended over a vast area covering the site of the ancient citadel where the first inhabitants of Byzantion, as the city was called in the fifth century BC, had built their most important temple. The surrounding area descended to the Golden Horn in the north, to the shore of the Bosphorus in the east and the Marmara in the south. At the summit of the hill, which still offers magnificent views over the sea and the city, the Great Palace abutted the land around the churches of St. Sophia and St. Irene, dedicated to Wisdom and Peace, which had replaced the pagan altars. Farther to the west, the palace was contiguous with the Hippodrome, and the emperor could ascend to the imperial box (*kathisma*) in order to preside at the games without leaving his residence.

This palace was anything but a single construction, since it was composed of numerous buildings erected at different times. These were started by Emperor Septimius Severus in the second century, enlarged by Constantine, who did not however live there, and then extended and embellished by nearly all his successors, who generally resided at Constantinople. The Great Palace thus became an enormous agglomeration of structures, which fulfilled the functions of the imperial court, of the seat of government with quarters for the most important officials, of imperial receptions and ecclesiastical ceremonies; it also contained private houses with gardens, baths, and fountains for the imperial family and relations, imperial workshops, and soldiers' barracks. Within the palace several large reception halls, dining rooms, courtyards, churches, baths, kitchens, vegetable gardens, orchards, and buildings devoted to public administration were all linked by corridors, colonnades, and secret passages.

Unfortunately, very little of all this remains. Archaeology has preserved some fragments of a large mosaic pavement, which give an idea of the rich decoration and favorite imperial themes: scenes of hunting and fighting wild beasts, gladiatorial combat, and agricultural life.[19] Delightful images of children at play contrast with violent and bloody attacks by lions, tigers, and boars on weaker animals. Sections of palatial architecture survive on the sea of Marmara, identified as the "House of Justinian" and the "Palace of Boukoleon," because it contained a colossal statue of a lion and a bull. From the descriptions of many new buildings, for example the New Church (*Nea*) constructed by Basil I,[20] we get an impression of an abundance of gold everywhere. In addition, the reception halls decorated in mosaic and colored marbles were hung with silk tapestries, and silver entrance doors were so impressive that they deeply influenced many palaces built in the West. This influence was not limited to the interior. From the outside the walls of the palace erected by Justinian II made it look like a fortress. Its modern equivalent is the Kremlin of Moscow, a direct descendant of the Great Palace.

These walls protected the imperial court from the curious crowds of city dwellers. But they were marked by many doorways, which varied according to their function: the *Chalke,* called the Bronze House, through which the entire Senate could enter, and the guard troops who protected the emperor, should be contrasted with the more private entrances open only to chosen individuals who could pass from the world of the court to the city.[21] Although they were closely guarded, these doors might also be opened by imperial servants in order to allow people who were not supposed to enter the palace to get in, usually for treacherous purposes.[22] In 820 the small Elephantine gate, regularly used by priests coming into the palace to mount the night vigil before the Sunday liturgy, was used by the assassins of Leo V.[23] The walled citadel of the Great Palace therefore could be breached, often by usurpers determined on a change of ruler. While it was generally believed that the emperor who controlled the city would also rule the empire, it may also be the case that without control of the Great Palace, it was almost impossible to rule in Byzantium. Ambitious usurpers always made a point of gaining access to the palace in order to assert imperial authority.

In order to analyze the mutual relations of palace and city in Byzantium, it's necessary to trace the coming and going between the two, in other words, to examine the occasions when the emperor had contact with his people. The *Book of Ceremonies* has preserved a rich collection of accounts of imperial rituals, but it is especially concerned with what ought to take place, that is, it is prescriptive.[24] To discover more about what actually happened, we have to consult the historians who describe occasions when the protocol was not followed. Inevitably this evidence is usually anecdotal and refers to events later treated as embarrassing moments, ceremonial failures, when the carefully ordered procedure was not observed. They are often more informative than the dry descriptions of what should happen. And the contrast between the two reflects the underlying problem of interpretation: which record is more reliable or gives a more accurate account? Where it's possible to compare and contrast, the meaning of such events for contemporary observers as well as later writers may become clearer. But usually there are gaps left in our knowledge between court protocol and "mistakes" that occurred when detailed plans were not followed. They constitute one of the great pleasures as well as anxieties of historical research.

In addition, there are stories about monuments of the city that circulated among the citizens before being written down toward the end of the tenth century and later. Their authors are called patriographers, that is, people who wrote the history of their *patria*, the city of Constantinople.[25] They record what was well known to those who were largely illiterate rather than educated. Of course, there is a lot of fantasy in their accounts, which often attempt to explain the names of particular buildings in connection with events long past, but they preserve a rather special interest and help us to understand the mutual relations between the emperor and his people, between the palace and the city, the great and the small. Since they nearly always fall into the anecdotal category and can often be shown to be far-fetched or just incorrect, it is the argument and the information indirectly preserved than often proves very revealing.

While the emperor could always go out of his palace, the inhabitants of Constantinople were not normally permitted to go in at any old time. So most movement involves emperors or empresses, suitably accompanied, leaving the palace to go into the city. But there are circumstances when a few representatives of the population do penetrate the palace wall. They fall into four groups: members of the Blues and the Greens, so called after the colors they wore as groups responsible for public entertainment in the Hippodrome (sometimes known as circus factions or *demoi*); members of trading corporations or visiting merchants; members of the local guard or particularly selected military officers; and groups of the poor, orphans, or old people, who were singled out for imperial philanthropy at Easter. In the tenth century, the emperor left the palace on the Thursday before Easter (Maundy Thursday) to distribute alms in the charitable institutions of the city, an act that inspired many imitations among later rulers. But later, in the twelfth century perhaps, the ceremony was reversed. Instead of going out, the emperor received twelve old people chosen from among the poor of the city inside his palace; he washed their right feet and invited them to dine with him.[26] In this way a symbolic presence of unprivileged people is recorded inside the palace.

Among the groups who can enter the palace, the Blues and Greens had always filled important functions in association with the emperor: in the circus they acclaim him when he presides at the games, races, and spectacles that they organize. Under the direction of the prefect of the city, who assures the protection of the ruler outside the palace, they accompany him in the city with ritual acclamations. They also direct the acclamations that greet the emperor who has won a military victory, who celebrates his birthday or the birthday of the city.[27] Because of the ceremonial functions that derive from these activities, they are often invited to enter the palace with the city's choirs, where they entertain the guests at banquets by playing their organs and dancing.[28] This proximity gives the factions a very critical position in the relations of the emperor with his people. They form a well-established link between the court and the city population normally excluded from the palace, and as a result they can take on the function of the people's messenger.

In particular, the duty of acclaiming the emperor both in the palace and when he goes out into the city permits the factions the possibility of denouncing or criticizing him, or simply manifesting the anger of the city's inhabitants against him. This most often takes place in the Hippodrome, where the factions control what happens and can direct the feelings of the crowd of spectators. And during the ritual exchanges, the factions might always launch a new slogan.[29] They adjust the traditional acclamations and adapt then to new situations, for example, when they acclaim Leo III like his predecessor Leo the Great, comparing both of them to Constantine I.[30] Moreover, the circus people who provided entertainments between the races, had a tradition of telling the emperor the truth, even when he didn't want to hear it. Under Theophilos, the mimes (*paigniotai*) took over a rite connected with the celebration of the city's foundation on May 11, which they adapted to attract the emperor's attention to an injustice suffered by a widow.[31] And since they had the right to approach the imperial box from the arena, the emperor could hear their appeal. In this way the people, represented by the mimes, could discuss issues with their ruler, and not only in the prescribed fashion.

This means that the regular acclamations could always serve new ends, quite different from the intended ones: they could in effect reverse the imperial order, mock the ruler, and even demand his death. Between the eighth and tenth centuries this happened very rarely, but the possibility always existed and rulers were probably aware of it every time that they went into the city.

Apart from the representatives of the factions, people could be admitted to the palace in their capacity as soldiers, members of the city guard, the imperial guard, or troops of professional fighters. Some belonged to the *tagmata* of the city, a well-equipped corps that constituted the strongest arm of iconoclast rulers, but others were simple recruits from the provinces, for instance, the soldiers of the Armeniakon army who accompanied their leader Leo into the capital in 717, or the sailors who supported the naval commander Romanos Lekapenos when he made his bid for power. In the medieval period military forces could play a decisive role, especially at Byzantium where succession to the throne was open to talent. Among the twenty rulers who held supreme Byzantine power between 717 and 1025, eight—Leo III, Nikephoros I, Leo V, Michael II, Basil I, Romanos I, Nikephoros II, and John I—usurped the throne. Only two of them, the first Nikephoros and the first Basil were connected with the palace and were pushed toward the throne by rivalries engendered at the court. All the others installed themselves in the palace by military force, either after decisions taken far from the city in the huge provinces called themes (*themata*), or after surprising victories that recommended them as suitable leaders for the supreme power. The latter all came into the city with their personal guard, which they introduced to the palace.

The relations of emperors with the mixed forces that made up the Byzantine army were crucial. During the decades of iconoclasm, the soldiers of the *tagmata* continued to defend the memory of Constantine V, their hero, long after his death.[32] Their enthusiasm may have depended more on their victorious campaigns against the Arabs than on their iconoclasm, but the two aspects are intimately linked. On the other hand, some women in the city maintained the proscribed veneration of icons, even when they knew the risks involved.[33] In the final analysis, the military preserved the dynasty of Leo III like so many others, but during the reigns of his grandson and great grandson the weight of popular opinion in favor of icons gained influence. During the dispute over iconoclasm divisions both within the palace and in the city render the mutual relations between palace and city even more complex.

After the end of iconoclasm in 843, the factions are mentioned less and less and instead the merchants of Constantinople begin to take a larger place in public life. Naturally there were always merchants in the city but the organization of their professional groups is rather unclear before the edict of Leo the Wise, known under the title of the *Book of the Prefect (Eparchikon Biblion)*.[34] This incomplete text includes information about some groups of workers who produce necessities for the city—food provisions, bread, meat, fish, soap, candles, and so on. They also have to supply the Great Palace, but they don't go into it except in unusual circumstances. It's different for those who work with precious materials, for instance, gold- and silversmiths, jewelers and perfumers, and several different sorts of silk workers. Those who spin, weave, finish, and decorate the luxury cloth, which was highly sought after throughout the medieval world, are privileged specialists, who can be ordered into the palace at any hour.[35]

The city also needed leather workers, who were considered superior to tanners, and craftsmen such as distinct groups of carpenters, locksmiths, decorators, marble workers, who assisted with building works in the palace. Among these specialists, mosaic workers were experts in an art almost unknown elsewhere, and the palace employed them as if they were a very valuable export. Thus in about 965 Caliph al-Hakam of Cordoba asked Nikephoros Phokas to send him an expert who knew how to assemble mosaic cubes on a vault in order to decorate the Great Mosque. As a result, the celebrated mosaics of the mihrab of Cordoba, bordered by a line of typically Byzantine polychrome ceramic tiles, were put up under the direction of a worker from Constantinople.[36]

While the city produced the luxurious objects so deeply appreciated in the Western world, the most important workshops of Constantinople were found inside the palace itself, where gifts destined for foreign powers and the imperial vestments, such as the robes and insignia of consecration, were made. The palace was thus a center of production, with its imperial workers, some of whom were slaves who worked for the state under the close supervision of controllers. As regards the production of silk, the imperial workshop identified and dated some of its products with woven inscriptions: "Under Basil and Constantine, the Christ-loving emperors," that is, between 976 and 1025.[37] Sometimes even the names of the officials in charge of the work were also woven into the silk.[38] From the middle of the tenth century, under Constantine VII, several products of imperial workshops are preserved, for example, a reliquary of the True Cross now at Limbourg, enameled and covered with precious stones and pearls mounted in filigree, which is identified as a work commissioned by this emperor and his son Romanos.[39]

Many workers, especially those who knew the industrial secrets of this prestigious art, lived in the palace, and their situation was more like that of slaves than free men. They did not form part of the coming and going between the palace and the city. But others took part in this movement, for example, when the palace needed additional workers, like the silver- and goldsmiths who replaced a golden dinner service, which was presented to the Russian princess Olga during her stay in Constantinople. Constantine VII also patronized more modest artisans, professional workers who were invited into the palace to encourage the production of sumptuary arts, for instance, the enamel and ivory specialists, and scribes and painters who illuminated luxury manuscripts.[40] His attention to detail and the care he took is evident in the illustrated manuscripts sent to the Caliph in Spain: the emperor chose the history of Orosios in Latin and a medical text of Dioskorides as presents that were both useful and beautiful.[41] Before undertaking work commissioned by patrons in the city, these workers had to contribute to imperial production. At the court's demand, they broke through the frontier between the two separate worlds. Like the prefect of the city, the controllers of production and their officials also entered the palace from time to time to guarantee the quality of the objects produced there.

Thus in the relations of the palace with the city there were three important groups of people who could enter its doors: circus factions, soldiers, and merchants. But by the tenth century their relative importance had changed: the *demoi* symbolized the traditions of the past, while the merchants represented the future (soldiers constituted a more permanent feature). For the factions the loss of some political power was partly compensated by their entrance into the palace for numerous ceremonial events and rituals, at which their presence became essential. Their changed status must be understood in the context of a much larger transformation that created a medieval state out of the eastern half of the Roman Empire. Constantinople always remained the carrier of an imperial ideology, incorporated in the Great Palace, where the concentration of power isolated the metropolis from other cities. But the process of transformation involved the inclusion of Christianity within the empire and the elevation of the bishop of Constantinople to the head of a patriarchate. Under this Christian impact some aspects of even the emperor's power were diminished.[42] So it's not only a question of a decline of the factions; a wider process of development affects most elements of imperial government.

When we now examine the circumstances in which the emperor left the palace, two must be distinguished: the first involves journeys established by imperial protocol, for fixed ceremonies, and the second, unplanned visits to the city. The formal processions can be qualified as liturgical or secular. The observance of the great liturgical feasts of the church and also saints' days, take the emperor and the court out of the palace. These must be considered separately from occasions when the emperor went to St. Sophia using his personal entrance, without leaving the palace, even though he was generally accompanied by the factions and palace guards. For the great feasts such as Easter, Whitsun[43] (celebrated at St. Sophia) or feasts like the Dormition of the Virgin (which is held at the church of Blachernai), protocol prescribes the procession that accompanies the emperor. Easter Monday is celebrated by a day-long parade to the Forum of Constantine, and on to the churches of the Virgin Diaconissa, St. Polyeuktos, the Holy Apostles, St. Christopher, and St. Euphemia, and then back to the palace.[44] On the feast of the Ascension, there are thirteen receptions organized by the factions on the return from St. Kallinikos, near the Xerolophos.[45] These liturgies are concentrated between the feasts of Easter and Whitsun, a joyous period in the liturgical year. The emperor participates with the patriarch, the clergy, choirs, and all the ecclesiastical hierarchy. As we have seen, at Easter the ceremony in which he is personally involved takes place within the palace, where he serves a symbolic number of the city's poor.

The people's participation in these liturgical processions was often required, for instance, on the Tuesday of Easter when the emperor left the palace to go to the Hippodrome, where he was greeted by all the people (τὰ δε πλήθη τῶν 'οχλῶν) before attending a service at the church of St. Sergios. Later he dined in a *triklinos* below the galleries there, and finally returned by the same route to the Hippodrome.[46] Or again, during the major procession which took place on the Wednesday of the Mesopentekoste (mid-Whitsun), with a procession to the church of St. Mokios, on foot and mounted, which stopped on seventeen occasions for receptions by the factions.[47] Local people knew what to expect on such occasions and would not miss an opportunity to collect the coins that might be distributed. For the baptism of an imperial child, the *Book of Ceremonies* prescribed a procession of the emperor and empress from the Great Palace to the cathedral of St. Sophia. But in 720 when young prince

Constantine was due to be christened, his father Leo III left the Empress Maria to take part in the procession on her own. She duly dispensed the distribution of coin, which traditionally accompanied a christening, to the people who must certainly have participated in her procession with cheers of delight.[48]

There were also times when the emperor had to go into the city for nonreligious reasons, for instance to examine the *Horrea*, the granaries that held stocks for the city. For this event, he rode in the imperial carriage, accompanied by the prefect of the city, left the Hippodrome, and crossed the city in order to reach the place situated on the Golden Horn, which was called the Strategion, where the granaries were situated.[49] A similar journey took place at the time of the grape harvest, when the emperor crossed over the Bosphorus to Hiereia.[50] Even less official activity, such as the emperor's attendance at spectacles given in the private Hippodrome of St. Mamas, were organized according to protocol.[51] The population gathered to witness these outings in hope of some distribution of largess.

During official processions, the emperor was usually accompanied by the factions, as well as his imperial guard and members of the senate. These ceremonies were fixed in advance and the people participated in them under the direction of the prefect. But at other times the processions could take place without rehearsal, as for example in 784, when Empress Irene and her son left the city to make a tour of Thrace, accompanied by musicians and of course armed troops.[52] Irene also adapted the ceremony laid down for Easter Monday, in order to cross the city in a chariot pulled by four white horses from which she threw gold coins into the street as emperors were expected to do.[53]

In contrast to these officials journeys, some emperors chose to walk around the city's streets incognito. Theophilos wanted to hear what people said about him, as Harun al-Rashid was also reported to have done at an earlier time. But Theophilos also established a regular procession on horseback, entirely official, during which anyone could come and ask him for justice.[54] His son, Michael III, however, liked to ride out with a few companions and accost the city's inhabitants, as an unusual story reports.[55] Later in the ninth or early tenth century, Leo VI is alleged to have tested the security of Constantinople by wandering around the city at night. When guards arrested him and forced him to spend the night in the police cells, he rewarded their behavior.[56] The *Patria* also reveal occasions when emperors, empresses, and their children visited the city. The wife of Leo III, for instance, incorrectly identified as Anna, rode to the celebrated church of the Virgin at Blachernai in an advanced stage of pregnancy and was forced to give birth in the house of a local citizen. This house was later transformed into a monastery dedicated to Haste (*Spoude*), because the empress didn't have time to get back to the palace.[57] In another more credible case, Theodora, wife of Emperor Theophilos, used to send her children to visit their grandmother in a monastery, where the old lady instructed her granddaughters on the subject of the veneration of icons, and this at a time when the emperor was persecuting the iconophiles![58] The imperial family also liked to take their children for picnics on the banks of the Bosphorus.[59]

In Byzantium it was quite common to see an imperial procession in the streets of the city, and people remembered the dates of fixed ceremonies and gathered to collect coins, or handouts of free wine, bread, and clothing that were sometimes added. Some may have recognized the emperor and knew how to approach him, sometimes with the help of a leader of the factions, though the prison warder who locked up Emperor Leo VI when he was found wandering through the streets at night said that he had no idea who he was.[60] While Liutprand characterized the ceremony in which Nikephoros II Phokas participated as a miserable affair, for the local population it was yet another chance to witness the emperor in their streets, symbolizing the critical link between palace and city. His exposure to praise, insults, or jeers did not lead to attempts on his life, which would have been prevented by the palace guards in attendance, and in effect the corridors of the palace proved much more dangerous than the streets of the city.

Novel ceremonies could provoke threatening behavior, perhaps because many people had to be informed of the emperor's movements and sought to take advantage. In 713 Philippikos decided to leave the Great Palace to make contact with some important people of the city, perhaps to assure himself of their support. They met in a public space, the famous Baths of Zeuxippos, where they dined together to the sound of organs probably provided by the factions and other musicians to divert them between the courses. For such a banquet with representatives of the best families of the city, there may have been a protocol to be followed, but it's not recorded.[61] After the dinner Philippikos returned to the palace to rest and everyone else went home to sleep off the results of the feast. But later the same day, soldiers of Thrace, commanded by their general and the count of Opsikion, a region situated opposite Constantinople, rushed into the city, got into the palace, seized and blinded him in a room near the Hippodrome controlled by the Green faction. And the following day, the *laos*, the people including the army, came together to the Great Church, and the *protoasekretis* Artemios was crowned emperor with the more imperial name of Anastasios.[62] The announcement of the ceremonial dinner had allowed disaffected troops to liaise with the Greens and civilians led by Artemios, the chief secretary, in order to plot the overthrow of Philippikos.

The eunuchs in charge of court ceremonial must have decided that this type of outing might give rise to similar plots, and it seems to have remained unique. But on later occasions ceremonies could be adapted to novel circumstances, or simply improved. In the mid-tenth century, for instance, after many military defeats, the Byzantine army captured the cousin of an Arab emir and Constantine VII celebrated this event as a triumph. But instead of the prescribed ceremony in the Hippodrome, the emperor invented a new one, centered on the ancient rite of humiliation, the *calcatio*, in which he put his foot on the neck of the enemy.[63] This ceremony began in the church of St. Sophia, from where the emperor and the patriarch processed, in two separate groups, to the Forum of Constantine. There, the Arab prisoners were waiting for them with their lances and standards, which had been exposed as booty. After chanting the victory ode, all the generals and military officers responsible led the Arab captive to the feet of the emperor and the *calcatio* took place, accompanied by many chants, forty "Kyrie eleisons" and a prayer from the patriarch. Finally, the prisoners were taken away and the acclamations connected with a real triumph were chanted; then Constantine took off his ceremonial *loros* and rode back to the palace on horseback.

In this new ritual the population of the city and the factions played only a very restricted role: the two *demotai* took their places among many other officers in order to chant the acclamations to the ruler. Their members, and the people in general, took part only as spectators, and any danger of unplanned enthusiasm was prevented. But the ceremony reveals that imperial court ritual was not frozen: it could be adapted to new circumstances with innovative forms. Under the direction of a ruler like Constantine VII, who recorded the official ceremonies, it could serve new ends.[64] Between these two examples of the early eighth and mid-tenth century, however, relations between the emperor and his people, the palace and the city, seem to have changed. From a fairly close cohabitation they had been elevated to a more ritualized distance, not only to avoid the obvious dangers, but also to enhance the imperial mystery even more. This development has often been described as a retreat within the palace, which removed the emperor from the city; an almost total demise of the games, which took him away from the Hippodrome, that is, the disappearance of the emperor behind the walls of the Great Palace, where he participated in ceremonies more as an imperial statue.

This impression, which is derived from the *Book of Ceremonies*, doesn't take into consideration the continuity of Constantinople's urban traditions. During the eighth, ninth, and tenth centuries, it's true, there are fewer occasions when the role of the people isn't carefully regulated; the ceremonies of the Great Palace tend to leave very little to chance. Ruler and people continue to meet but usually in situations that are much better planned than before. But the ways of their meeting always existed. Factions continued to acclaim the ruler; craftsmen who worked in the palace were always going to and fro; city merchants went in to translate what foreign ambassadors reported; and servants of the emperor could always open a door to rebellious soldiers. At the end of the day, the structure of relations between palace and city ensured that the people of the city continued to interest themselves in everything that happened inside the palace, among the emperors. Their expressions of praise and affection also insisted on imperial responses, although restricted by court ceremonial, and these responses led to exchanges, which characterized the relations between the people and the ruler, the city and the palace at Byzantium.

Notes

1. G. Dagron, *Naissance d'une capitale: Constantinople et ses institutions de 330 à 451* (Paris, 1974).

2. **Update** See among the many studies, J.H.W.G. Liebeschuetz, *The Decline and Fall of the Roman City* (Oxford/New York, 2001); Claudia Rapp, "The Christianization of the Idea of the Polis in Early Byzantium," *Proceedings of the 22nd International Congress of Byzantine Studies* (Sofia, 2011), vol. 1, Plenary Papers, 263–84 (with helpful bibliographies).

3. *Theophanes*, I, AM 6258, 440; Eng. trans. by Cyril Mango and Roger Scott, 608. **Update** Paul Magdalino, *Constantinople médiévale: études sur l'évolution des structures urbaines* (Paris, 1996).

4. Theophanes Continuatus, ed. I. Bekker (Bonn, 1838), paras. 7, 9, 12–15, 223–25, 230–32.

5. **Update** Judith Herrin, "From Bread and Circuses to Soup and Salvation: The Origins of Christian Philanthropy," chapter 13 in this volume.

6. Alan Cameron, *Circus Factions* (London, 1976), app. C, "A Circus Dialogue," 318–33. **Update** Gilbert Dagron, *L'Hippodrome de Constantinople: Jeux, peuple et politique* (Paris, 2011), esp. 13–25.

7. For example, in 713, the people (*laos*) acclaimed Artemios with the imperial name of Anastasios, Theophanes, AM 6205, 383; Mango and Scott, 533; or

in 867 when Basil was acclaimed by *tou ochlou tou astikou*, the crowd of the city, Theophanes Continuatus, paras. 28, 255.

8. Psellos, *Chronographia*, ed. E Reynaud (Paris, 1926–28), bk. 5, 34–38; Eng. trans., E.R.A. Sewter, *Fourteen Byzantine Rulers* (Harmonsworth, 1979), 142–44, 151. **Update** Dimitris Krallis, "'Democratic' Action in Eleventh-Century Byzantium: Michael Attaleiates' 'Republicanism' in Context," *Viator* 40, no. 2 (Fall 2009), 35–53.

9. *LP*, 3, I, 390; *Theophanes*, AM 6261, I, 444; Mango and Scott, 613.

10. Known as the father of the city, *pater poleos*, according to the Book of Ceremonies, where his role of cleaning and decorating the streets of the city before the emperor visits the Great Church is laid down in the very first chapter, *Constantine VII, De cerimoniis aulae byzantinae*, ed. J. J. Reiske, 2 vols. (Bonn, 1929–30), ch. 1. On his wide judicial powers and responsibilites, see F. Uspenskii, "Konstantinopolskii Eparkh," *Izvestiya of the Russian Archaeological Institute of Constantinople* 4 (1899), 79–104; J. B. Bury, *The Imperial Administrative System in the Ninth Century*, British Academy Supplemental Papers, I (London, 1911), 169–73, an edition of the *Kleterologion* of Philotheos, now updated by N. Oikonomidès, *Les listes de préséance byzantines des IXe et Xe siècles*, (Paris, 1972); R. Guilland, "Etudes sur l'histoire administrative de l'Empire byzantine, I. L'Eparque de la ville," *BS* 51 (1980), 17–32, 145–65. His economic role is revealed by the *Book of the Eparch*; see note 34. **Update** J. Koder, *Das Eparchenbuch Leons des Weisen*, CFHB, vol. 33 (Vienna, 1991).

11. *Theophanes*, AM 6206, I, 384; Mango-Scott, 534

12. *Constantinople in the Early Eighth Century: The "Parastaseis syntomoi chronikai,"* eds. Averil Cameron and Judith Herrin (Leiden, 1984), Columbia Studies in the Classical Tradition, X; available online at google books; *Parastaseis*, chs. 69, 78, 84; and Cameron and Herrin, 150, 158, 160.

13. **Update** C. Wickham, *The Inheritance of Rome: A History of Europe from 400 to 1000* (London, 2009), 255–56, 277–78.

14. G. Dagron, *Constantinople imaginaire: Etudes sur le recueil des Patria* (Paris, 1984); G. Dagron and J. Paramelle, "Un texte patriographique, le "récit merveilleux, très beau et profitable sur la colonne de Xérolophos, *Vindob. Suppl. Gr. 172*, fols. 43v–63v," *TM* 7 (1979), 491–523.

15. John of Ephesus, *Ecclesiatical History*, VI, 23, ed. and trans. E. W. Brooks, 2 vols. (Paris/Louvain, 1935–36), CSCO, Scriptores Syri, series III, vol. 3, I, 323, and II, 245; *Parastaseis*, ch. 20, and Cameron and Herrin, 82.

16. Known particularly from the excavations of 1935–38 and 1951–54; see *The Great Palace of the Byzantine Emperors: First Report*, ed. G. Brett, W. J. Macaulay, R.B.K. Stevenson (London, 1947); *Second Report*, ed. D. Talbot Rice (Edinburgh, 1958); J. Ebersolt, *Le grand palais de Constantinople et le Livre des Cérémonies* (Paris, 1910); H. Hunger, "Der Kaiserpalast zu Konstantinopel. Seine Funktionen in der byzantinischen Aussen- und Innenpolitik," *JÖB* 36 (1986), 1–11.

17. R. Janin, *Constantinople Byzantine: Développement urbain et répertoire topographique*, 2nd ed. (Paris, 1964), 141, 148–50, 473–74, 498–99.

18. *Theophanes*, AM 6283, 6295, I, 467, 476, 478; Mango and Scott, 641, 655, 656. **Update** On these structures, see J. Herrin, "Political Power and

Christian Faith: The Case of Irene (Regent 780–90, Emperor 797–802)," chapter 8 in *Unrivalled Influence: Women and Empire in Byzantium*.

19. See note 12 earlier and J. Trilling, "The Soul of the Empire: Style and Meaning in the Mosaic Pavement of the Byzantine Imperial Palace in Constantinople," *DOP* 43 (1989), 27–72, with bibliography. The new Mosaics Museum in Istanbul has covered over the largest area and moved other pieces onto its walls.

20. Theophanes Continuatus, paras. 76, 83–86, 319, 325–29.

21. C. Mango, *The Brazen House* (Copenhagen, 1959), Arkaeolokiskkunsthistoriske Meddelelser, Bind 4, no. 4.

22. In 802 the officers who supported Nikephoros against Empress Irene persuaded the guards of the Chalke to let them enter by this door; Theophanes, AM 6295, I, 476; Mango and Scott, 655.

23. Joseph Genesios, *Regnum Libri*, Quattuor I, 20, ed. A. Lesmüller-Werner and I. Thurn (Berlin, 1978), CFHB 14; *On the Reigns of the Emperors*, trans. Anthony Kaldellis (Canberra, 1998), *Byzantina Australiensia* 11, 21–22.

24. See note 10 earlier. The first 83 chapters of book I have been re-edited with a French translation and commentary by A. Vogt, 2 vols. (Paris, 1967).

25. *Parastaseis syntomoi chronikai* (see note 12) and *Scriptores Originum Constantinopolitanarum,* ed. T. Preger, 2 fasc. (Leipzig 1901–6); Albrecht Berger, *Untersuchungen zu den Patria Konstantinupoleos,* Ποικίλα βυζαντινά 8 (Bonn, 1988).

26. *DC,* ed. Reiske, I, ch. 12, 89–90; ed. Vogt, I, 12; cf. Pseudo-Kodinos, *Traité des Offices,* ed. J. Verpeaux (Paris, 1966), 228–29; P.-F. Beatrice, *La lavanda dei piedi* (Rome, 1983), Ephemerides Liturgicae–Subsidia 28, 204–5.

27. Dagron, *L'Hippodrome,* 183–84, 230–58.

28. Cameron, *Factions,* 244–70. 297–308; R. Guilland, "Etudes sur l'Hippodrome de Byzance. Les factions au Xe siècle," *BS* 30 (1969), 1–17. **Update** Dagron, *L'Hippodrome,* 285–87, on the organ; cf. J. Herrin, "Constantinople, Rome, and the Franks in the Seventh and Eighth Centuries," chapter 11 in this volume.

29. Dagron, *L'Hippodrome,* 20–22; cf. ibid., 206–7, on the factions' seating arrangements, and note 27 earlier.

30. *Parastaseis,* ch. 3; Cameron and Herrin, ch. 58; Dagron, *Constantinople imaginaire,* 178–80, 186–89, provides an excellent analysis of the mechanism of adaptation.

31. *Patria,* III, 28, ed. Preger, 223–25; Dagron, *Constantinople imaginaire,* 167–68; and *L'Hippodrome,* 22.

32. W. E. Kaegi, "The Byzantine Armies and Iconoclasm," *BS* 27 (1966), 48–70; J. Herrin, *The Formation of Christendom* (Oxford/Princeton, 1987), 360–68. **Update** L. Brubaker and J. Haldon, *Byzantium in the Iconoclast Era, ca. 680–850: A History* (Cambridge, UK, 2011), 740–43.

33. *Life of St Stephen the Younger,* ed. and Fr. trans. M.-F. Auzépy, paras 56–57; Auzépy, "La destruction de l'icône du Christ de la Chalcé par Léon III: Propagande ou réalité?" *B* 60 (1990), 445–92, where the author shows how unlikely the story is. This however, does not reduce the significance attributed by the sources to the presence of women in the attack" see J. Herrin, "Women and the Faith in Icons in Early Christianity," chapter 3 in *Unrivalled Influence: Women and Empire in Byzantium*.

34. See the edition of J. Nicole with Fr. trans.; and the Eng. trans. of E. Freshfield to the edition of I. Dujčev, *To eparchikon biblion* (London, 1970); M. Ya. Siusiumov, *Vizantiiskaya kniga eparcha* (Moscow, 1962), esp. 191–96; Koder, *Das Eparchenbuch Leons des Weisen*.

35. R. Lopez, "Silk Industry in the Byzantine Empire," *Speculum* 20 (1945), 1–42; A. Guillou, "Production and Profits in the Byzantine Province of Italy (Tenth to Eleventh Centuries): An Expanding Society," *DOP* 40 (1986), 33–53. **Update** A. Muthesius, "Silken Diplomacy," in J. Shepard and S. Franklin, eds., *Byzantine Diplomacy* (Aldershot, UK, 1992), 237–48.

36. G. Marçais, "Sur les Mosaïques de la Grande Mosquée de Cordoue," *Studies in Islamic Art and Architecture in honour of Professor K.A.C. Creswell* (Cairo, 1965), 147–56.

37. See the catalogue of the exhibition, *Splendeur de Byzance*, Musées royaux d'Art et d'Histoire (Brussels, 1982), 216–17.

38. For example, on the elephant silk preserved in the Treasury of the Cathedral of Aix-la-Chapelle: "Under Epimachos, *primikerios* . . . and Petros *archon tou Zeuxippou*," H. Schmitz-Clieve-Lepie, *Der Aachener Domschatz* (Aix-la-Chapelle, 1986), 23. **Update** This inscription is illustrated in Muthesius, "Silken Diplomacy," 243.

39. The reliquary was mounted in its box by Basil, *proedros*, in about 964/5, Marvin Ross, "Basil the Proedros, Patron of the Arts," *Archaeology* 11 (1958), 271–75; W. G. Brokaar, "Basil Lekapenus," *Studia bizantina e neoellenica Neerlandica* 3 (1972), 199–234.

40. Theophanes Continuatus, paras. 22–24, 452–55; see also the ivories of Constantine VII himself, or of Romanos and Eudokia, probably his son and with his first wife, *Splendeur de Byzance*, 98.

41. R. Jenkins, *Byzantium: The Imperial Centuries 610–1071* (London, 1966), 265–66. **Update** See John Lowden, "The Luxury Book as Diplomatic Gift," in *Byzantine Diplomacy*, 249–60; Anthony Cutler, "Significant Gifts: Patterns of Exchange in Late Antique, Byzantine and Early Islamic Diplomacy," *Journal of Medieval and Early Modern Studies*, 38, no. 1 (2008), 79–101.

42. Herrin, *The Formation of Christendom*, 303–6.

43. *DC*, I, ch. 9, 58–71; ed. Vogt, I, 9.

44. Ibid., ed. Reiske, I, ch. 10, 71–86; ed. Vogt, I, 10.

45. Ibid., ed. Reiske, I, ch. 8, 54–58; ed. Vogt, I, 8.

46. Ibid., ed. Reiske, I, ch. 11, 86–89; ed. Vogt, I, 20.

47. Ibid., ed. Reiske, I, ch. 17, 98–108; ed. Vogt, I, 26.

48. *Theophanes*, AM 6211, I, 400; Mango and Scott, 551–52; cf. J. Herrin, "Political Power and Christian Faith in Byzantium: The Case of Irene (Regent 780–90, Emperor 797–802)," chapter 8 in *Unrivalled Influence: Women and Empire in Byzantium*.

49. *DC*, ed. Reiske, II, ch. 51, 699–701. I thank Eugenia Bolognese Recchi-Franceschini for her help in identifying these imperial trips.

50. Ibid., I, ch. 78, 373–75.

51. Ibid., I, app., 493.

52. *Theophanes*, AM 6276, I, 457; Mango and Scott, 631.

53. Ibid., AM 6291, I, 474; Mango and Scott, 651. The event is characterized by Treadgold, *The Byzantine Revival 780–842* (Stanford, 1988), 114, as "grand but rather silly." But on this day the emperor usually made a procession to the Holy Apostles (see note 38 earlier), from which he returned by the principal road, the *Mese*, to the Great Palace. In 799 Irene followed this protocol, although she was accompanied by four patricians who each held the reins of one of her horses.

54. Leo Grammatikos, *Chronographia*, ed. I. Bekker (Bonn, 1842), 217–18; W. Treadgold, *The Byzantine Revival*, 266–67, 271–72, 327.

55. Michael III and the poor woman who was coming from the bath; Theophanes Continuatus, para 37, 199.

56. Liutprand, *The Embassy to Constantinople and Other Writings*, trans. F. A. Wright (London, 1930; repr. 1993), bk. I, ch. 11, 12–15.

57. *Patria*, III, 107, ed. Preger, 251; Dagron, *Constantinople imaginaire*, 317. Like many stories in the patriographic accounts, this note tries to give an etymological sense to names poorly understood, by making often ridiculous associations: here *spoude*, haste, in place of its other meaning, *zealous*.

58. Symeon Logothetes, *Chronographia*, ed. I Bekker (Bonn. 1838), 628–29; Theophanes Continuatus, 90–91 (who muddles Euphrosyne with Theoktiste, Theodora's mother); Genesios, 4.2, 72, merely notes that Theodora and her mother, the *patrikia*, and brothers, the *patrikioi*, had sustained icon veneration.

59. Theophanes Continuatus, para. 15, 233–34.

60. **Update** Liutprand, *The Embassy*, as earlier, 13–14: the jailer said, "How could I know him? (the emperor) ... I have gazed at a distance once or twice when he has appeared in public, but I could not get close and it seemed to me that I was looking at a wonder of nature rather than at a human being." Skylitzes records a moral tale in which the widow of a soldier claimed justice from Emperor Theophilos while he was on his regular visit to Blachernae, John Skylitzes, *Synopsis historion*, ed. I. Thurn (Berlin/New York 1973), 54–55; Eng. trans. John Wortley, John Skylitzes, *A Synopsis of Byzantine History 811–1057* (Cambridge, UK, 2010), 56–57.

61. At the end of the ninth century the list, *kleterologion*, which recorded the seating order of the guests (edited by Bury and Oikonomidès; see note 10 earlier), doesn't provide any information for this sort of meeting.

62. *Theophanes*, AM 6205, I, 383; Mango and Scott, 533. Nikephoros, *Breviarium historicum*, 48, ed. and trans. C. Mango (Washington, DC, 1990), *CFHB*, 13, Dumbarton Oaks Texts X, 114–17. **Update** J. Herrin, "Philippikos and the Greens," chapter 8 in this volume.

63. M. McCormick, *Eternal Victory* (Cambridge, UK, 1986), 159–60.

64. Averil Cameron, "The Construction of Court Ritual: The Byzantine 'Book of Ceremonies,'" in *Rituals of Royalty*, ed. D. Cannadine and S. Price (Cambridge, UK, 1987), 106–36.

8

PHILIPPIKOS AND THE GREENS

ఌ

Paul Speck was a distinguished Byzantinist in the tradition of Hans-Georg Beck. When I first went to the Institut für Byzantinistik und neu-griechische Philologie in Munich, he was teaching palaeography and questioning established views through his studies of the iambic verses of Theodoros Stoudites and the Imperial University of Constantinople (showing that it never existed). I found his contrarian attitude and ironic nature very persuasive and was deeply indebted to his challenging of assumptions, as well as his hospitality while I looked for a place to stay. Although I found it difficult to accept his argument about the existence of two parallel texts of the *Chronographia of Theophanes*, which dominated his later research, we always kept in touch and it was an honor to contribute to his festschrift, where this article first appeared in 2001. It is reprinted by permission of the publishers from "Philippikos and the Greens," in *Novum Millennium*, ed. Claudia Sode and Sarolta Takács (Farnham: Ashgate, 2001), 137–46, © 2001. Paul subsequently wrote to thank me for the article, pointing out that the inexplicable gap in the text of the *Chronographia*, to which I drew attention, was probably one of those holes in the transmission that he was intent on identifying.

The role of the circus factions, Greens and Blues, in making and unmaking emperors had been established by earlier writers, but this episode involving the Greens in 713 had been generally ignored or dismissed as insignificant. I hope this chapter demonstrates beyond doubt that some members of the Green faction had political ambitions and skills. With their help, soldiers from the nearby military units of Opsikion and Thrace were able to get rid of Philippikos and impose a civilian official, Artemios the secretary, as emperor. So the Greens could still play a critical role in the political development of Byzantium. And clearly Artemios may have been the prime mover behind it all, in that he did not share Philippikos's dedication to Monotheletism, but was "pious and orthodox."

EVER SINCE THE PUBLICATION of Alan Cameron's book on the circus factions, it has been agreed that the Blues and Greens played a much less political role after the tumultuous reigns of Maurice and Phokas.[1]

Herakleios (610–41) diverted their energies into the far more manageable and benign roles of court entertainment: music and dancing, which had already been expanded in the sixth century. Together with the choirs of the major city churches, they were invited to bring their organs into the palace to provide musical entertainment.[2] Members of the factions were instructed to perform dances at important banquets, presumably wearing their official livery and holding their own ceremonial weapons. In this way their official tasks were expanded. Even in the period of most rapid turnover of rulers (695–717), Cameron asserts that the factions only participated in the acclamation of emperors and coronation ceremonial after the fighting was over. While soldiers attached to a particular *thema*, regional forces, plotted their coups d'état, raised their candidates on shields, and then marched on the capital to impose a new ruler, the role of the factions remained the traditional one of acclaiming him with appropriate slogans.[3]

Nonetheless, this development did not curtail the significance of the factions as a force in the cities of Late Antiquity; indeed, their importance in providing a group identity for their members and supporters may have become more pronounced in the turbulent period of the late seventh and early eighth centuries. The Greens and Blues existed as organized groups in most large centers and performed an important ceremonial role through local acclamations of the emperor. Recent discoveries at Gortyna, Crete, suggest that the well-known acclamations for Herakleios, his first wife and son, commemorated a stop-over in the Cretan port en route from Carthage to Constantinople in 610, and the new emperor's later patronage of a vast basilica, rebuilt after 618.[4] These provincial factions were quite likely to sustain interest in political changes in Constantinople, although there is less reference to their acclamations of emperors of the period.[5] In the capital itself the emperor's official movements were always followed with cheers and faction support, and the most essential function of the factions remained his imperial acclamation at the all-important moment of inauguration.

Turning now to the events of 711, which ended the second reign of Justinian II, a similar combination of factors connected with the political ambitions of the *themata* can be observed. They inaugurate an unstable succession of emperors, four in the next six years. Philippikos is typical of these men, one of the ephemeral rulers of the early eighth century who usurp the throne, pass through the corridors of the Great Palace ever so briefly, and are removed from the imperial stage by sudden death or deposition—leaving the empire even more disorganized and weaker than before. Two are military leaders connected with a specific *thema* whose troops pursue and promote their own ambitions; the other two are civilians selected by groups of soldiers. And a curious feature is that these rebellions are often presented in the sources as the outcome of prophesies by aged hermits, holy monks, and astronomers, who cloak the conspiracies in a sort of respectability—claiming in effect, "this was destined to happen."[6] As a result of these revolts, the fairly regular succession of the Herakleian dynasty, which managed to impose its sons through four generations from 641 to 695, finally came to an end in 711.

Philippikos was originally called Bardanes and came from Persarmenia. His father, Nikephoros, held patrician rank, which suggests that the family had been successfully incorporated into Byzantine society. He had made a military career, and his ambitions were sustained by a prophesy that he would one day become emperor. Under Apsimar-Tiberios, Bardanes's imperial hopes were revealed to the emperor in a dream: he saw Bardanes with an eagle shading his head, and therefore had him cudgeled and tonsured and exiled to Kephalonia off the west coast of Greece in 702/3.[7] Bardanes was recalled by Justinian II during his second reign (705–11) and later exiled again, this time being forced to accompany a naval expedition to Cherson led by Stephanos Asmiktos and Helias, the *spatharios*, who was to be installed as governor of the ill-fated city. They had instructions to make sure that Bardanes remained in internal exile in the Black Sea port, but he escaped from Cherson and fled to the Chazars.[8] Justinian II exercised a vengeful policy against the inhabitants of Cherson, because of their treatment of him during his own exile there (695–705); he therefore ordered Stephanos to kill every man, woman, and child in the city. When the commander failed to do so and spared the lives of some children, intending for them to be enslaved, the emperor sent him back with a second naval attack, which was shipwrecked.[9] Since Justinian continued to persist in his determination to annihilate the entire population of the region, and organized another massive naval force under Mauros, the leaders of Cherson decided to counter the situation by planning a coup.[10] They recalled Bardanes from the Chazars and proclaimed him emperor with the more suitably Greek name Philippikos. After a brief flurry of fighting outside Cherson, Mauros and his forces joined the revolt. Under the leadership of the recently exiled general and with Khazar allies, they then set sail for the capital.[11]

Philippikos therefore had important supporters and in particular a powerful naval base from which to attack the capital by sea. Justinian II got wind of this plot of course and called up his Bulgar allies under Tervel, whom he had honored in a monument in the capital.[12] But he made the mistake of leaving the city and marching up to the Black Sea coast to investigate what Bardanes/Philippikos was planning. From the village of Gingilissos he saw the fleet from Cherson sailing down to Constantinople and had to race back on foot.[13] Due to Justinian's unpopularity, Philippikos was welcomed into the city; there was little opposition to a change of emperor. Helias the *spatharios* was sent to persuade troops from the Opsikion and Thrakesion forces to go over to Philippikos. As they deserted Justinian, Helias leaped forward and beheaded him. Philippikos sent the severed head through the western parts of the empire to Rome as proof that Justinian really was dead.[14] Finally, he ordered officials to dispose of Justinian's young son, Tiberios, and over the protests of his grandmother, he was slaughtered like a lamb. All other supporters of the Herakleian dynasty were rounded up and killed.[15] In these unsavory circumstances Philippikos became emperor.

Like his predecessors Leontios (emperor 695–98) and Apsimar (who ruled as Tiberios, 698–705), Bardanes had also been told by Paul, an elderly monk and astronomer at the monastery of Kallistratos, that he too would one day be emperor. But unlike the others, he was also given instructions to ensure that his rule would be mighty and long: he was to reinstate the Monothelete belief in the one will and energy of Christ, a belief condemned as heretical by the Sixth Ecumenical Council in 681/82. The new emperor therefore proceeded to anathematize the council and commemorate the heroes of Monothelete belief.[16] While this change was accepted in Byzantium, it provoked a forceful reaction in Rome, where the rejection of Philippikos, his images, coin, and orders, is matched by relief at his rapid overthrow and the accession of an orthodox emperor, Anastasios.[17] For the authorities in Rome, Philippikos's brief reign was dominated by his resumption of a heresy already condemned by a universal Christian council. Even farther west, the *Chronicle of 754* merely recorded that Philippikos ruled for a year and a quarter amid civil war, a fairly accurate description.[18] In nearly all the Greek sources, however, his reign is marked by another incident: the celebration in 713 of the foundation of Constantinople. And with affection and respect I offer an analysis of this event to a master of the close scrutiny of ceremonial celebrations.

Like all emperors, regardless of their lack of preparation for the role and unfamiliarity with imperial ceremonial, Philippikos celebrated the birthday of the city on May 11, which had become the major feast of Constantinople, always marked by special games and races. This celebration was one of the fixed points in the annual calendar; it had become a public holiday, marking the dedication of the city by Constantine I in 330. Whatever their origins, all emperors understood that they had to finance races in the Hippodrome to win and sustain the loyalty of the population. They duly instructed the circus factions to organize sporting events plus the *entr'acte* entertainments that were an essential part of the show. So a certain amount of activity relating to Hippodrome life was encouraged, and the Blues and the Greens were still in control of this vital aspect of public entertainment.

Philippikos made no change in the annual commemorative arrangements, but in 713 he decided to hold additional celebrations that took place in the Baths of Zeuxippos. There are several accounts of this event by Byzantine authors and they differ: a brief note by the deacon Agathon, a contemporary who wrote shortly after the event; an entry by Nikephoros the patriarch, which lacks one key element; and a more circumstantial account by Theophanes the Confessor. There are also echoes of the event in some Latin sources of the period: the *Liber Pontificalis*, and *Chronicon Altinate*. Clearly there was some lack of clarity in the sources that were reused by the chroniclers.[19]

Nonetheless the basic story is clear enough: on 11 May 713 Philippikos celebrated the city's birthday with the customary races in the Hippodrome. Theophanes adds, the Greens won. Although Malalas claims that the procession of the city *tyche* and its reception by the emperor continued into the sixth century, Paul Speck has cast doubt on this.[20] Horse and chariot racing, interspersed with other sporting events; displays of dancing, acrobatics, and gymnastics; and musical intermissions remained the core of public entertainment. In addition the emperor decided to ride over to the Baths of Zeuxippos, which lay to the north of the Hippodrome, accompanied by great pomp and music; the organs were played.[21] By the eighth century these baths were perhaps the only monument still used for their original purpose and also decorated with antique statuary. The original collection of works of art had burned in the fire of 532 during the Nika riot. But Philippikos had added his own image, a *stele ek chromaton*, probably a colored relief, to the replacement decoration installed by Justin II and later rulers. So the Zeuxippos still combined the function of the bath with that of an art collection.[22] After bathing Philippikos entertained the oldest and most distinguished families of the city with a great banquet in the baths.[23] Both the public site and the circumstances of this celebratory feast are unusual, perhaps unique. It is not clear exactly what is meant by "citizens of ancient lineage," *politon archaiogenon*.[24] Presumably those who could prove that they had been established in Constantinople from its foundation, senators appointed by Constantine I and his sons, those who had lived for generations in the city, patronized its institutions, and founded its famous churches. Philippikos, as far as is known, was not allied with these circles.[25] As a military commander of Armenian descent, he may have needed their support. After the banquet they all retired to sleep off the huge amount of food and drink they had consumed.

Whether this was intended to mark the victory of the Greens in the races on May 11, or to bind the most distinguished families of the city into a closer alliance with the emperor, it seems that the announcement of the new celebration had been made in advance: it was to take place on the Saturday before Pentecost, that is, on June 3. The three-week gap between May 11, the regular holiday with races, and the new celebration allowed time for the participants to get ready, but was clearly put to a different purpose by some of the thematic military forces and members of the factions. In the previous year the Bulgars had raided across Thrace and right up to the walls of Constantinople, causing serious damage to suburban settlements. To prevent any repetition of this danger, troops from the Opsikion *thema* had been transferred to Thrace to join the Thracian soldiers in the defense of the European approaches to the capital.[26]

At this point, on Saturday, June 3, a plot that had surely been hatched in the previous three weeks, was put into operation. Knowing that the emperor would be celebrating in such style, George Bouraphos, count of the Opsikion troops, which had been transferred from Asia Minor to Thrace, acting in concert with a patrician, Theodore Myakios (Myakes), sent a few soldiers into the city. They were led by the *protostrator* of the Opsikion, named Rouphos, who suddenly entered the city through the Golden Gate and rushed into the palace, where he found the emperor sleeping. He woke him up and dragged him out to the *ornatorion* of the Greens in the Hippodrome. There Philippikos was blinded and that is the last mention of him in the chronicles of Theophanes and Nikephoros. The date of his death is noted in two later texts as January 20, which if correct suggests that he survived a minimum of seven months after the blinding.[27] This is perhaps why the year of his death is frequently given as 714.[28] The *Necrologium* adds that Philippikos died at Dalmatoi (*sic*) and was buried there, which is probably modeled on the fact that other deposed emperors were sent to the monastery of Dalmatou, for example, Justinian II in 695, Leontios in 698.[29] The place had perhaps become associated with this particular function as a suitable prison for emperors. The *Necrologium* may have assumed that the blinded Philippikos also retired to the same monastery.

However, in 713 there was no public announcement of what had happened on the Saturday before Pentecost, until the following day, June 4, when the entire population of the city gathered in the church of Holy Wisdom to celebrate the feast. There a new emperor was acclaimed. He was Artemios, previously secretary (*grammateus*) to Philippikos; Nikephoros adds this is the post which the Italians call *asekretis*.[30] Agathon has greater detail, his original name was Philartemios; he was *eusebes* and *orthodoxos* (in contrast to Philippikos), and formerly numbered among the *schole* of the *asekretion*. He was proclaimed (*anagoreutheis*) with the more imperial name of Anastasios, "by the common vote and scrutiny of the holy senate, and all the listed hierarchs and the Christ-loving soldiers stationed in the city, and all the political people [*demos*]."[31] Clearly, for such a ceremony to be successfully carried through, there had to be a certain amount of preparation. Not only the new imperial candidate, the patriarch, some members of the senate, and possibly some of the bishops and soldiers stationed in the city had to be forewarned and their cooperation prepared. But most essentially, the factions had to be instructed what to shout, as they led the acclamations. This aspect of the coup d'état is ignored in all the sources, of course. Agathon continues his account with a description of the replacement of the icons of Sergios and the other heretics, by the image of the Sixth Ecumenical Council, which was restored to the Milion; he does not mention the celebration of May 11.

So this immediately introduces the problem: what is the connection between the commemoration of the foundation of Constantinople and the rebellion that is presented as the next event by both Theophanes and Nikeplioros? If the coup occurred on June 3, and Artemios was proclaimed emperor on Whit Sunday, 4 June 713, twenty-four days had elapsed since the birthday races.[32] There is no doubt, however, that the coup against Philippikos was planned to coincide with major celebrations at the Zeuxippos. Theophanes is clear about the purpose of this innovation: the oldest and most ancient lineages were invited to dine with the emperor at the Zeuxippos. The link between the coup and the banquet is ignored by both Nikephoros and Agathon.

This was a coup with a difference. True, it was led by crack troops of the Opsikion forces, so it conforms to the regular style of military revolts of the times. And Kaegi has a clear analysis of the reasons for its success: "timing and access to the capital, not sheer quantities of troops or resources, were the key elements."[33] He also emphasizes that it was the transfer of Asiatic troops of the Opsikion to European Thrace, where they would defend the capital against the Bulgars, that caused the downfall of

Philippikos.[34] In fact, the numbers of troops involved in the coup of 713 appear to have been very small indeed—though the fact that they were backed by the Opsikion theme commander left no doubt as to the serious purpose of the coup.

This rebellion also took advantage of a special event that everyone knew would occupy all the most important people in Constantinople. After the grand banquet, as the cooks, servers, entertainers, and organists were tidying up and the rest of the guests took their siesta like the emperor, a small body of conspirators might be able to find a way into the palace. Normally, such illegal entry required the connivance of allies on the inside, since the Great Palace was a walled kremlin guarded by loyal troops. On this occasion no traitors are mentioned, but (Phil)Artemios, the imperial secretary, may have been involved. The only clue as to the efficiency and success of the coup lies in the strange word *ornatorion*, which obviously brings the Greens into the plot.[35]

This Latin word is supposed to derive from the *urna* from which the factions drew lots to decide in which lane a chariot or horse would start the race. The urn, which is depicted according to the Kugelspiel carving in Berlin as a narrow-necked amphora mounted on two horizontal sticks, was filled with four balls representing the four original colors of the factions. These were shaken around by three turns and the first ball to fall out determined which faction would take the most favored position at the start of the races. The faction officials then established which track each competitor would run in.[36] The *orna* was kept in the room named *ornatorion* after it.[37] The term is known both in the singular and the plural from references in the chapters devoted to horse races in the *Book of Ceremonies*, suggesting that each faction had its own.[38]

In his commentary Vogt points out that these rooms appear to be situated above the race track, probably in the building that surmounted the starting gates, *carceres*.[39] From there the *orna* was sometimes taken to the *stama*, where the process of selection took place, and then was sealed by the eparch of the city to prevent any tampering.[40] Guilland further suggests that the words *ornatorion* and *armatourion* appear synonymous, and must designate those rooms where the factions kept their *orna* and *arma*. Both served as changing rooms where costumes and equipment were stored. In a lengthy analysis of the long narrow structure over the *carceres* of the Hippodrome, topped by the quadriga tower, which displayed the four bronze horses later removed to Venice, Guilland suggests that the Greens' dressing rooms were to the left of the quadriga tower while the Blues had theirs to the right. Access to the upper gallery would have been by internal staircases. Both rooms had windows looking out over the arena and could thus be used as observation posts. After the Latin conquest of Constantinople when the Hippodrome was used for jousts, passes d'armes, and tournaments, people watched the displays from the windows that pierced the upper stories of the *carceres*, precisely where the *ornatoria* had been situated.

Both Vogt and Guilland comment on the blinding of Philippikos but fail to locate the precise site of the *ornatoria* of the Greens. Guilland has mistakenly assumed that the emperor was seized in the Zeuxippos baths, whereas the chronicler makes it quite clear that he had returned to the *palation*, which can only mean the Great Palace.[41] Nonetheless, it is evident that the *ornatorion* of the Greens must have been located within the Hippodrome complex, and thus not far from the palace.

A further clue as to the function of the *ornatoria* may come from the Latin term *ornator*, which can mean dresser, person who dresses; this has all the right connotations to have added to the meaning of the word and its association with faction equipment. While the factions stabled their horses near the Dihippion and elsewhere in the city,[42] their dressing rooms must have been nearer to hand. In a more general way, *ornatoria* and *armatouria* probably also served the same purpose as the *paraskeuas*,[43] places where fiction members got changed into their livery, stored their extra chariot axles, reins, whips, and all the kit used for racing and entertainment.

Anyway, in 713 it was to the *ornatorion* of the Greens that Philippikos was taken to be blinded. Rouphos performed the gruesome deed, and he was the only one involved in this conspiracy who was not punished for his act of *lèse-majesté*. The others, Theodore Myakios, the patrician, and George Bouraphos, the Count of Opsikion, were later blinded by Anastasios and exiled to Thessalonike.[44] Yet for the plot to succeed, they must have established relations with someone in the Green faction who had access to the *ornatorion*; otherwise Rouphos would not have known where to take Philippikos.

So on this occasion it is not possible to insist that the factions had no role whatsoever in the downfall and replacement of Philippikos. At least some of the Greens must have been a party to the coup. They provided the safe place where the emperor could be taken and held incognito after the blinding. It was vital that no one in the palace broke the news before the following morning. They may also have participated in the choice of (Phil)Artemios as emperor; obviously they had to proclaim him correctly with his new name at the feast of Pentecost the following day. There is no further evidence of their political activity in the early eighth century. But the races continued to be given, the Blues and Greens continued to provide public entertainment, and the Hippodrome remained the one site in the city where the emperor confronted the citizens. Long into the medieval period ceremonial greetings shouted by the people might be changed, perhaps at the insistence of the factions, so that the emperor would hear demands that he correct public scandals, distribute more grain, or punish his wicked advisers. The factions were not just ornamental parts of palace ceremonial, nor were they mere cyphers of court decisions; they might participate in more strictly political events also. While they continued to orchestrate the public entertainment considered such a vital part of Byzantine life, their access to the Hippodrome, their semi-private facilities, and their political allegiance could be exploited by outside forces. So it is precisely the involvement of the factions in fundamental imperial festivities that permits them to reassert a previous, more political role.[45]

NOTES

1. Alan Cameron, *Circus Factions: Blues and Greens at Rome and Byzantium* (Oxford, 1976).

2. *Parasteseis syntomoi chronikai*, § 36, in *Scriptores Originum Constantino-politanarum*, ed. T. Preger, vol. I (Leipzig 1901); Averil Cameron and J. Herrin, *Constantinople in the Early Eighth Century: The Parastaseis Syntomoi Chronikai* (Leiden, 1984), 96; Cameron, *Circus Factions*, 249–58; J. Herrin, "Constantinople, Rome, and the Franks in the Seventh and Eighth Centuries," chapter 11 in this volume. The factions had a silver organ, and the imperial one was of gold; see N. Maliaras, *Die Orgel im byzantinischen Hofzeremoniell des 9. und des 10. Jahrhunderts. Eine Quellenuntersuchung* (Munich, 1991), 221–29, 252–56. **Update** G. Dagron, *L'hippodrome de Constantinople: Jeux, people et politique* (Paris, 2011), 285–87.

3. Cameron, *Circus Factions*, 261.

4. *Inscriptiones Creticae*, ed. M. Guarducci, Rome, 1950, IV, no. 512, 414f., dated 612. These may not have been pronounced by the factions of Gortyna, but the Greens certainly existed there; see no. 513, ibid., 415. On the basilica, see A. di Vito, *Atti della Scuola, Annuario della Scuola archeologica di Atene*, 68–69 (1990–91), 481–486, and ibid. 70–71 (1992–93), 461–67.

5. C. Roueché, *Performers and Partisans at Aphrodisias in the Roman and Late Roman Periods* (London, 1993), 143–47, 153–56. In 695 Leontios was acclaimed by the Blues, in 698 Apsimaros-Tiberios by the Greens, and both these ceremonial acclamations occurred after their successful military coups; see Cameron, *Circus Factions*, 261f., 267f.

6. This is the cover for Leontios, Apsimaros-Tiberios, Philippikos, and Leo III among others. **Update** P. Magdalino, *L'Orthodoxie des astrologues* (Paris, 2006),

esp. 23–32, on the survival of astronomical calculations in the seventh and eighth centuries.

7. *Theophanes*, AM 6194, I, 372; *The Chronicle of Theophanes Confessor: Byzantine and Near Eastern History, AD 284–813*, translated with introduction and commentary by C. Mango and R. Scott, with assistance of G. Greatrex (Oxford, 1997), 519; Nikephoros Patriarch of Constantinople, *Short History*, text, translation, and commentary by C. Mango (Washington, DC, 1998), ch. 45, 108; Agathon, *Epilogos*, in *Concilium universale Constantinopolitanum tertium*, ed. R. Riedinger, Acta Conciliorum Oecumenicorum, ser. II vol. 2/2 (Berlin, 1992), 899.

8. *Theophanes*, AM 6203, I, 378–379; *Nikephoros*, ch. 45, 110.

9. *Theophanes*, AM 6203, I, 377.29–378.3, 11–16; *Nikephoros*, ch. 45, 13–16, 24–32, 108 (on Stephens's failure).

10. *Theophanes*, AM 6203, I, 379.17–22; *Nikephoros*, ch. 45, 56–60, 110; W. E. Kaegi, *Military Unrest, 471–843* (Amsterdam, 1981), 189.

11. *Theophanes*, AM 6203, I, 379. 26–380.3; *Nikephoros*, ch. 45, 51–67, 110; Kaegi, *Military Unrest*, 190.

12. *Parasteseis* § 37, Cameron-Herrin, *Constantinople*, 98.6–9; *Nikephoros*, ch. 45, 72–73, 110.

13. *Nikephoros*, ch. 45, 77–80, 110–112; *Theophanes*, AM 6203, I, 380.5; Kaegi, *Military Unrest*, 190, supposes that Justinian anticipated an attack at Sinope.

14. *Theophanes*, AM 6203, I, 380.30–381.6; *Nikephoros*, ch. 45, 84–92, 112; Kaegi, *Military Unrest*, 190f.

15. *Theophanes*, AM 6203, I, 380.10–15; *Nikephoros*, ch. 45, 92–103, 112.

16. *Theophanes*, AM 6203, I, 381.6–20; 382.10–21; *Nikephoros*, ch. 46, 112; Agathon, *Epilogos*, 890.

17. *LP*, I, 90; Constantine (708–715); Eng. trans., R. Davis, *The Book of Pontiffs* (Liverpool, 1989), 91f.

18. I. E. López Pereira, ed., *La Crónica mozárabe de 754: édición crítica y traducción* (Zaragoza, 1980), 60; Eng. trans. K. Baxter Wolf, *Conquerors and Chroniclers of Early Medieval Spain* (Liverpool, 1990), 135.

19. Speck has shown that *Nikephoros* and *Theophanes* share a common source; see *Das geteilte Dossier. Beobachtungen zu den Nachrichten über die Regierung des Kaisers Herakleios und seiner Söhne bei Theophanes und Nikephoros* (Ποικίλα Βυζαντινά 9) (Bonn, 1988), 203f.

20. Malalas, *Chronographia*, ed. L. Dindorf (Bonn, 1831), 320–22; P. Speck, "Urbs, quam Deo donavimus. Konstantins des Großen Konzept für Konstantinopel," *Boreas* 18 (1995), 143–73, esp. 170.

21. *Theophanes*, AM 62205, I, 383.5–7; *Nikephoros*, ch. 48, 1–2, 114.

22. *Parasteseis* § 82, Cameron–Herrin, *Constantinople*, 160, and commentary, 272f.; A. Berger, *Das Bad in der byzantinischen Zeit* (Munich, 1982), 109, 145–47; S. Guberti Bassett, "Historiae Custos: Sculpture and Tradition in the Baths of Zeuxippos," *American Journal of Archaeology* 100 (1996), 491–506.

23. Kaegi, *Military Unrest*, 191, incorrectly states that Philippikos was planning to dine with them when he was overthrown, but the fullest account given by Theophanes indicates that the banqueting had taken place and everyone had gone home for their siesta, *en to mesymbrizein*.

24. There is a list of such expressions in P. Yannopoulos, *La société profane dans l'Empire byzantin des 7e, 8e, 9e siècles* (Louvain, 1975), 14–21; cf. the more helpful analysis by P. Magdalino, "Byzantine Snobbery," in M. Angold, ed., *The Byzantine Aristocracy* (Oxford, 1984), 62–65.

25. For a different interpretation, see B. Anderson, "Classified Knowledge: The Epistemology of Statuary in the Parastaseis Syntomoi Chronikai," *BMGS 35* (2011), 1–19.

26. *Theophanes*, AM 6204, I, 382.22–30; *Nikephoros*, ch. 47, 114.

27. Philip Grierson, "The Tombs and Obits of the Byzantine Emperors (337–1042)," *DOP 16* (1962), hereafter *Necrologium*, 18 and 33. **Update** M. Angold, "The Byzantine Political Process at Crisis Point," in P. Stephenson, ed., *The Byzantine World* (London/New York, 2010) 5–21, esp. 12–13 on this coup d'état but without sufficient attention to the role of the Greens.

28. See G. V. Sumner, "Philippicus, Anastasius II and Theodosius III," *GRBS* 17 (1976), 287–294.

29. *Necrologium*, 52, n. 123, quoting R. Janin, *Constantinople byzantin*, (Paris, 1950), 87.

30. *Theophanes*, AM 6205, I, 383.17–19; *Nikephoros*, ch. 48, 15–20, 114–116.

31. Agathon, *Epilogos*, 900, 16–18, with the expression *tou politikou demou pantos*, which does not necessarily mean the factions, but in this context implies that those normally responsible for acclaiming a new emperor, who would have to have some warning as to the name chosen, were given instructions in advance of the rest of the population.

32. V. Grumel, *La Chronologie* (Paris, 1958), 248. In 713 Easter fell on April 16 and thus Pentecost seven weeks later on June 4. The birthday races were held on Tuesday, May 11, leaving three and a half weeks to prepare for the banquet. Since Agathon confirms that the event occurred in year 11 of the indiction, there can be little doubt about the year, 712/3. For the ingenious theory that Theophanes was in fact referring to the Mesopentekostes, see Maliaras, *Orgel*, 257–60, where the hypothesis is rejected because the mid-Pentecost feast must fall on a Wednesday.

33. Kaegi, *Military Unrest*, 203.

34. Ibid., 213.

35. The term occurs only in Theophanes' more detailed account, AM, 6205, I, 383.16; see also Mango and Scott, 534, n. 6.

36. *DC*, I, 69, 71 (vol. I, 312.15–313.18); cf. A. Vogt, ed., *Le Livre des Cérémonies*, 2 vols. (Paris, 1935–39), vol. 2, 131–134, 158, 163. In *DC*, I, 72, this process is repeated using the term *kylistras* rather than *orna*. **Update** Dagron, *L'hippodrome* (as in note 2) 129–30.

37. Alan Cameron, *Porphyrius the Charioteer* (Oxford, 1973), 63 and plate 15.

38. *DC*, I, 69 (vol. I, 312–20), with ref. at 312.5 (commentary, vol. II, 318–19); *DC*, I, 71 (vol. I, 352, 14). **Update** Dagron, *L'hippodrome*, 80.

39. Vogt, *Commentaire*, vol. 2, 131, 134, 158, 163.

40. *DC*, I, 72 (vol. I, 360.18 and 364.2–5).

41. R. Guilland, *Études de topographie de Constantinople byzantin* (Berlin, 1969), 386–88.

42. *Scriptores Originum Constantinopolitanarum*, 2 vols., ed. Th. Preger, II (Leipzig, 1907), 185; A. Berger, *Untersuchungen zu den Patria Konstantinupoleos* (Ποικιλία Βυζαντινά 8) (Bonn, 1988), 315.

43. *DC*, I, 72 (vol. I, 363.17 and 20).

44. *Theophanes*, AM 6205, I, 383.19–21; *Nikephoros*, ch. 48, 20–22, 116, and note correcting Myakyos to Myakes, 206. W. Treadgold, "Seven Byzantine Revolutions and the Chronology of Theophanes," *GRBS* 31 (1990), 203–26, claims Rouphos was also blinded (218).

45. As Cameron suggested for the reign of Constantine V, *Circus factions*, 302–4.

9

PHILIPPIKOS "THE GENTLE"

☙

The Byzantine Emperor Philippikos reigned for less than two years from June 711 to May 713, but in that short time he became closely associated with a fascinating text, the *Parastaseis syntomoi chronikai*, often mentioned in this volume.[1] It was my good fortune to hold a Senior Research Fellowship at the Warburg Institute in London when Professors Alan and Averil Cameron decided to study this text, prompted by its records of the circus factions. Alan was then preparing his book on the Greens and the Blues and wanted to pursue these references, which he included in *Circus Factions*.[2] In an effort to tie up some of the loose ends, I offered this short contribution in Averil's honor, as a tribute to the friend and scholar who inspired our work then and who continues to generate and promote so much stimulating research.

It was prompted by the use of a most unusual term, "praos," associated with Christ in the Gospels, which was applied to the eighth-century emperor Philippikos. His successful usurpation was accompanied by a determination to return the Byzantine church to the observance of Monotheletism, a doctrine promoting the one will of Christ that had been condemned at the Sixth Ecumenical Council in 680/81. So a term of great honor was granted to a ruler considered a heretic. While the change was apparently provoked by a prophesy, other reasons lay behind it. And since I had spent quite some time on the switches in definitions of Orthodoxy between 553 and 711, I was curious to investigate this step back to an unorthodox interpretation.

The whole business of changing the definition of correct belief must have been challenging for contemporaries. In contrast to the first 300 years of Christianity, when biblical texts were not fixed, local practices often varied from place to place and theological interpretations were by no means uniform, the definitions agreed at ecumenical councils were intended for the whole of Christendom. Yet even these fully authorized statements of belief might be challenged, as Philippikos did when he removed the images relating to the Sixth Ecumenical Council of 681/82 and restored those of his Monothelete heroes. This symbolic act preceded his decision to return the church of Constantinople to what he considered to be the correct faith, by dismissing the patriarch who was replaced by a Monothelete supporter and holding a council to reestablish this belief.

Through these mechanisms the change of doctrine would have been made plain to the people of the capital, patriarchal or imperial messengers would have taken the news to the provinces and to Ravenna and Rome in the West. Philippikos took all these steps to ensure that his favored belief was restored, but it was not popular and played a part in his downfall (see "Philippikos and the Greens," chapter 8 in this volume). Changing the established faith remained very difficult, as the iconoclasts were to discover later in the eighth century.

In THE SUMMER OF 695 Justinian II suffered the fate of many young rulers in Byzantium. After provoking considerable opposition to his arbitrary decisions, the emperor was taken prisoner by troops loyal to Leontios, general of the Anatolikon theme. He was publicly humiliated in the Hippodrome, mutilated in such a way that made it unlikely he could ever rule again, and then exiled to the Crimea. As is well known, the slitting of his nose and tongue did not deter him, and Justinian returned to power in 705 with the help of Khazar and Bulgar allies. Together with his new wife, the daughter of the Khazar khagan renamed Theodora, and his young son Tiberios, Justinian intended to consolidate the dynasty of Herakleios and to punish all those who had caused his first exile. His second reign (705–11) was dominated by a fervent desire for revenge, which eventually provoked another revolt. This time Bardanes (Vardan) challenged the emperor, taking command of a naval force in the port of Cherson and sailing across the Black Sea to the capital in an effort to seize power.

Recent research has drawn attention to the unusual qualities of this military leader.[3] Bardanes was of Armenian descent and came from a family well established in Constantinople. During the 660s his father Nikephoros held the position of πατρίκιος and was entrusted by Constans II with military campaigns. Bardanes followed his father into the military and cherished imperial ambitions. These are cited as the reason why Tiberios II exiled him to Kephalonia in 702/3. He seems to have been recalled by Justinian II during his second reign but was then sent away again to the Crimea. The coup d'état of 711 was planned with the help of Khazar troops who acclaimed Bardanes as emperor in Cherson. He adopted the new name Philippikos, not a familiar imperial name like Constantine, but one less obviously Armenian. Nichanian suggests that the family had a connection with Emperor Maurice, whose son-in-law Philippikos is the most prominent bearer of this unusual name.[4]

Like many other military rulers who aspired to the Byzantine throne, often promoted by their troops, Philippikos failed to establish his own power securely. But in this unruly period of coups d'état, assassination, and blinding, he is more than a name—for he was highly educated and appears to have encouraged a group of Constantinopolitan scholars who were trying to record the city's ancient pagan monuments. He also had a coherent, if unpopular ecclesiastical policy: to restore the Monothelete definition of Christ's one will. Because of his theological views, he is condemned as a heretic and worse in most Greek sources of the period. But Eastern sources preserve a different account and show a contrasting profile of the emperor. Can these be reconciled? And if so, what does the combination add to our knowledge of Philippikos?

Agathon, a deacon of the Great Church at the time of the Sixth Ecumenical Council (680/81), sets the tone for all later assessments of the emperor. He was responsible for making the six authorized copies of the acts of 680/81, which condemned Monotheletism as heretical, one for each of the patriarchs, and knew that Philippikos had ordered the one held in the patriarchal library in Constantinople to be burned. So after the latter's overthrow Agathon replaced the destroyed copy and added an appendix to explain why he had to do this.[5] In the *Epilogos* he reports that after the victory over Justinian II in 711, the new emperor was so committed to the policy of reviving Monotheletism that he refused even to enter the city before the Sixth Ecumenical Council was overturned. He demanded that the image of the council erected by Constantine IV between the Fourth and Sixth *Scholai* in the vestibule of the imperial palace should be removed, and that the names of Patriarch Sergios, Pope Honorius, and their followers, all condemned in 680/81, should be proclaimed in the sacred diptychs of the holy churches and that their images should be set up again.[6] Later he also removed the image of the Sixth Council at the Milion, leaving only the previous five, and commissioned a double portrait of himself with Patriarch Sergios in its place. In this magisterial way he commemorated the return to the doctrine devised by Herakleios to win back the Monophysite churches into communion with Constantinople.[7]

Agathon says that Philippikos had been instructed in this κακοδιδασκαλία, that is the Monothelete belief, from his childhood by abbot Stephanos, who was himself a disciple of Makarios.[8] Makarios was the Monothelete Patriarch of Antioch who had refused to accept the Sixth Council and Stephanos served as his deacon. Both had been exiled to Rome in 681.[9] He then describes how Philippikos had the official copy of the Sixth Council burned and persecuted pious and orthodox men, exiling some, especially those whom he could not bring round to his way of thinking.[10] Agathon continues:

> After two years . . . divine justice intervened and he was overthrown because of all that he had done very often, and other persons who served him, with total shamelessness in the pious monasteries of women, his unlawful machinations [ἀθεμίτους ἐγχειρήσεις] and indecent behaviour [αἰσχρουργίας]. In addition, most importantly he had made an untold dispersal and diminution of the monies collected and stored in the imperial palace by Justinian.[11]

So here Agathon adds charges of immoral activity with female monastics and wasteful dissipation of imperial treasure to the emperor's heresy. Whether the unlawful machinations relate to illegal confiscations of wealth or indecent conduct with dedicated nuns, the text combines sexual and financial misdemeanors in a telling fashion. What decided the emperor's fate, however, was quite independent of these charges: it was his refusal to pay the Onugur Bulgars the agreed tribute, which provoked them to raid Thrace, devastating the entire region and advancing up to the walls of the capital. This serious inroad prompted the army stationed in Thrace to revolt against Philippikos, who was removed from power and replaced by Anastasios.[12]

Nikephoros and Theophanes, who both wrote over a century after the death of Philippikos, follow Agathon in characterizing the emperor as a wicked heretic. They add details about the synod held in the capital to authorize the return to Monotheletism: Patriarch Kyros was exiled to the Chora monastery, and in his place Philippikos installed his friend and co-heretic, John. Germanos of Kyzikos, Andreas of Crete, and Elpidios and Antiochos, officials of the Great Church, and others participated, as well as Nikolaos, the quaestor and eparch of the city.[13] Despite Theophanes's strident condemnation of this "pseudo-synod," there is evidence that the Sixth Ecumenical Council had not been accepted in many parts of the East. Supporters of the Chalcedonian definitions of 451 found that the decrees of 680/81, associated with the name of Maximos Confessor, did not conform with the earlier council and refused to accept them.[14] The Maronites were equally hostile.[15] There was therefore a groundswell of concern in Syria and Palestine, which might have welcomed Philippikos's Monothelete compromise. Clearly, leading bishops and officials supported it, though later Germanos and Andreas would say that they only did so under duress.

The attempt to restore the Monothelete definition of Christ's wills and natures is nonetheless characterized on several occasions as one of the evil deeds that helped to bring the Roman state into confusion.[16] Theophanes attributes this policy to a heretical monk from the monastery of Kallistratos, who predicted that Philippikos would become emperor if he overturned the "wicked" Sixth Council.[17] In other respects he follows Agathon's account quite closely, emphasizing that the emperor was also an adulterer (μοιχός),[18] which seems to echo Agathon's charge of "unlawful machinations and indecent behavior." Possibly Philippikos tried to impose the Monothelete definitions on nuns in the monasteries of the capital rather than assaulting them. But in traditional fashion the chronographer links heresy with sexual depravity in general:

> He lived a carefree life in the palace where he had found an abundance of money and splendid belongings that for many years had been collected by his predecessors as a result of confiscations and under various pretexts, especially by the aforesaid Justinian, and these he dissipated at random without taking any trouble. And whereas in his discourse he appeared to be eloquent and prudent, he was proved by his actions to be in every way incompetent, living as he did in an unseemly and incapable manner. He was also a heretic and an adulterer. He drove out of the Church the patriarch Kyros and appointed his accomplice and fellow-heretic John.[19]

In addition to condemning his heresy, Theophanes continues with the emperor's military failures. While the Arabs made repeated raids in Asia Minor, capturing Amaseia, Mistheia, and many other forts, the Bulgars devastated all of Thrace and advanced as far as the city walls, causing havoc. Philippikos also ordered all the Armenians to leave the empire, which resulted in their going over to the Arabs, who settled them in Melitene.[20]

Nikephoros is briefer but describes the emperor's behavior in clearly derogatory terms, ἀσέμνως and ῥαθύμως.[21] Like Theophanes he reports that Philippikos sent the head of Justinian II to Rome so that people in the West would know that he was really dead.[22] Although this was appreciated in Ravenna, which had suffered particularly from Justinian's policy of revenge, when Philippikos's religious policy became known in the West the reaction was immediate and extreme. The *Liber pontificalis* records that to show Rome's dedication to the six ecumenical councils, the pope ordered that no one should acknowledge Philippikos's image, not even on his coinage.[23] In this contemporary source, written shortly after the death of Pope Constantine, who had traveled to the East to negotiate with Justinian II over the canons of the council in Trullo, Rome's loyalty to that agreement is made clear. It also constitutes a reliable measure of how the revival of Monotheletism was perceived in the West.

In marked contrast to this emphasis on heresy, an Eastern source more closely dated to the reign of Philippikos describes the emperor in a more positive fashion:

> Philippikos was well educated, having both impressive learning and rhetorical skill and being thoroughly acquainted with the traditional academic curriculum in profane studies. He commanded that all Armenians be expelled from his empire; these exiles sought asylum with the Arabs who settled them in Melitene and on its borders. The following year the Romans deposed Philippikos and gouged out his eyes.[24]

This passage brings together a previously unrecorded appreciation of the emperor's thorough education with his treatment of the Armenians, which is listed by Theophanes as part of his failed foreign policy.[25] Under Philippikos the empire was attacked on both eastern and western fronts, and the Bulgar invasion proved fatal to his rule. In Armenia he inherited an uneasy situation. The existence of two factions, pro-Byzantine and pro-Arab, coupled with a serious religious split between the majority Monophysite clergy and minority pro-Chalcedonian, created great instability, which had been exploited by Justinian II. When increased Arab pressure, accompanied by massacres of the Christian populations, forced many groups of Armenians to flee, Justinian settled Smbat Bagratuni and his naxarars and followers at Poti on the Black Sea coast in 705. Six years later Smbat decided to return to Armenia at the invitation of the Caliph, pillaging the city of Poti and removing all its church treasure.[26]

This defection of sections of the Armenian aristocracy to the Caliphate may have provoked Philippikos's decision to expel all remaining Armenians from Byzantium.[27] He presumably wanted to strengthen Byzantine relations with the pro-Constantinopolitan faction in Armenia. And if this Chalcedonian party in Armenia also clung to the definitions of 451, then his renewal of Monotheletism might have been welcomed there. His reasons for ordering the expulsion of all Armenians from Byzantium should probably be related to this religious policy.

It seems, however, to have failed, as it pushed the pro-Arab party in Armenia into closer relations with the Caliphate and gave it greater prominence. In religious terms, the Monophysite Armenian church retaliated against Byzantium at the Council of Mantzikert in 725/26, when it united with the Syrian church and expelled all Chalcedonians from its territory.[28] This realized the danger that Philippikos had been trying to prevent through his policy of moderate Monophysite and Monothelete compromise. Between 711 and 713, however, he was unable to prevent regular military raiding across the eastern borders of Byzantium. The Arabs continued to cross over, possibly with the assistance of the Armenians newly settled as their allies in Melitene. In 711/12 Maslama captured Amaseia and many other forts; Abas took many captives from Pisidian Antioch in 712/13, and Maslama returned to devastate Galatia the following year. These raids presaged the major combined land and sea attack on Constantinople which took place in 717.

By then, of course, Philippikos was dead. It is, however, interesting to trace the stories of his learning and culture that circulated in Constantinople not so long after. They are preserved in the *Parastaseis* in three chapters: 28, 37, and 82. The first is the marvelous story of Theodore and Himerios the χαρτουλάριος and their investigation of statues in the Kynegion, which was apparently commissioned by a certain Philokalos. This area to the north of the Great Palace on the acropolis of Byzantion contained an ancient amphitheater decorated with many statues. By the seventh century it was used for political executions and had become a ruin. In this deserted place, as Himerios identified a statue of Maximian, the builder of the Kynegion, it fell and killed him. Theodore, who witnessed the accident, was so terrified that he dragged the body of Himerios away to the ditch "where they throw the convicts" and then ran off to seek asylum in the Great Church.

When the spectacular death of Himerios the *chartoularios* became known, the dead man's relatives and the "friends of the emperor" came to inspect the scene where the statue had fallen. Theodore had to swear under oath that it was the statue of Maximian that had killed Himerios. John "the philosopher" then claimed that in the writings of Demosthenes he had read "'that a man of rank would be killed by a statue [ζώδιον].' And he told this at once to the Emperor Philippikos and was commanded to bury the statue in that place; which indeed was done, for it was impossible to destroy it."[29] Theodore's own account of the accident, written in the first person to clear himself of blame, concludes with a warning to Philokalos to be careful when examining pagan statues.

From this vignette of self-styled philosophers investigating ancient statues, we learn that Philippikos had friends who were interested in pre-Christian pagan monuments. He also knew how to destroy their powers, for if the statue could not be broken up it had to be buried. So he ordered the group to dig a pit and bury it, to prevent it from causing any more harm. The *Patria*, a later and often less accurate collection of similar stories about the monuments of Constantinople, records that Philippikos also destroyed two out of a group of four statues from the Sophian harbor because they had inscriptions that foretold the future, γράμματα περὶ τῶν μελλόντων.[30] This was a monument of four statues on columns, representing Justin II and his wife Sophia, after whom the harbor was named, with her niece Arabia and Narses the general. This group is not known to the authors of the *Parastaseis*, although in the catalogue of women they record a slightly different group representing Sophia, Arabia, and Helena at the Milion. They make no mention of inscriptions attached to these gilded statues.[31] Both the early and later patriographic texts, however, associate Philippikos with the sort of work that Himerios and Theodore were doing—identifying statues from written sources, by reading the inscriptions on their bases and trying to interpret unfamiliar groups of statuary, sometimes identified as "spectacles" (θεάματα).

The second reference to Philippikos in the *Parastaseis* occurs in chapter 37: "On the golden roofed basilica," where Justinian II set up a statue of himself and his Bulgar and Khazar allies. The text continues: "after the defeat of Tiberius Apsimaros, when Philippikos also was censured in that part of the golden-roofed Basilica,"[32] as if to indicate the date. The incident must therefore relate to the very poorly documented period between his recall from exile in Kephalonia and his second exile to Cherson during the second reign of Justinian II (705–11). Clearly, the emperor had erected statues of his supporters who assisted his return to power at the Basilika, thus adding a commemorative group to one of the major monuments in the city. He also passed sentence on Philippikos in the same place (perhaps the censure that resulted in exile to the Crimea). The compilers of the *Parastaseis* are not interested in what provoked this judgment; their concern is with the imperial statues that they wanted to identify. So the text cannot help to elucidate Philippikos's history, but at least it records that he was publicly chastised at an important site decorated with statues of Justinian II.

However, by far the most significant echo of the eastern sources occurs in chapter 82, which is devoted to the imperial image that Philippikos erected in the Baths of Zeuxippos. This famous passage, much quoted out of context, refers to a colored portrait of the emperor (στήλη ἐκ χρωμάτων), which artists praised highly because it captured a genuine likeness of the emperor.[33] Whether it was a panel painting, a mosaic, a colored relief, or (most improbable) a colored statue, is not clear. But this particular image was reported to bear a very close likeness to Philippikos himself. And since the *Parastaseis* was written by compilers who knew about the emperor's "friends" and who suggest that Philippikos was interested in their research activities, they may indeed have been in a position to judge.

In erecting his own portrait, Philippikos was also following imperial tradition, indeed he was competing with his predecessor Justinian II, who had recently erected group statues at the Golden Basilica. The choice of the Baths of Zeuxippos is also significant in that this complex had been something of a museum of ancient statuary.[34] Although much was destroyed in the fires lit during the Nika riot in 532, Philippikos added his own image to what remained of the collection, making a claim to be as good as all the other rulers displayed there. As is well known, Philippikos also used the site for a major banquet held in honor of all the senators and high-ranking officials on the Saturday before Whit Sunday in May 713. The celebration was to prove his downfall, as opponents got wind of the proposed festivities and decided to use the afternoon siesta period for their revolt, which ended the short reign of Philippikos.[35]

It is clear that Philippikos had a sense of propaganda and used visual means to achieve it. Not only in the case of his own image but also in the group portrait of Monothelete heroes and his own portrait with Patriarch Sergios erected at the Milion, he reinforced the new doctrinal definition on a prominent landmark in the center of the city. Similarly he systematically removed images of the Sixth Ecumenical Council and replaced them by Monothelete leaders, Patriarchs Sergios, Pyrrhos, Paul, Peter, John, and Pope Honorius. As soon as he had been blinded, his successor Anastasios reversed the process.[36] Religious orthodoxy was again restored to the Milion. These changes cannot be called iconoclasm, although destructive, since images of one set of church leaders were replaced by others. But the process reflects a heightened awareness of the power of images, their use in political and ecclesiastical policy, especially in a city dominated by visual messages in statue, fresco, and mosaic form.[37] It was to become one of the hallmarks of the eighth century, when images and epigrams on the Chalke Gate of the Palace denoting the beliefs of the current ruler were frequently changed.

But the most curious feature of this passage in *Parastaseis* chapter 82 is the epithet given to Philippikos: he was πρᾷος, "gentle," and was deceived through ignorance. This seems to be an attempt to excuse his shortcomings or to blame his errors on bad advice. It is tempting to see in this an echo of Abbot Stephanos's influence, or the story that his rule had been predicted by the monk at Kallistratos, on condition of reversing the Sixth Council. But πρᾷος is a most interesting term. In early Christian and

Byzantine texts it is used repeatedly of Christ, who described himself as gentle and humble of heart, and recommended these qualities to the disciples.[38] In the Sermon on the Mount Christ also applies it to those who are meek and shall inherit the earth.[39] Because of this injunction to be gentle, the first text is much quoted in Greek patristic writings, sermons, commentaries, and prayers.[40] It is applied to Old Testament prophets, Moses and David, early Christian martyrs, and holymen like St. Antony. While Eusebius quotes the Gospel text in a proverbial sense, he also applies the term to the pagan Maxentius, who tried to win over the Christians by seeming to be more gentle. Sozomen also recognizes that Julian demonstrated the same virtue in his benevolence toward Christians, while Theophylact Simocatta applies it to the Sasanian ruler Chosroes. In the preface to his *Ecclesiastical History*, Sozomen applies it as an imperial attribute to Theodosius, who imitated the heavenly king. Gregory of Nazianzos recommends the quality of gentleness as a remedy for anger. Thanks to the *Thesaurus Linguae Graecae* these multiple uses of πρᾷος and its overwhelmingly positive connotations can be fully documented.[41]

The fact that "gentle and humble of heart" was so widely quoted in Byzantium points up the contrast between its use in the *Parastaseis* and later accounts of Philippikos. Nikephoros and Theophanes nowhere use the term πρᾷος of their own ninth-century secular contemporaries, and would not have dreamed of applying it to the heretical Armenian ruler. So when the compilers of the *Parastaseis* combine a Christ-like quality of gentleness with Eastern traditions about the emperor's learning and culture, they present him in a very favorable light. It seems inconceivable that they were unaware of the widespread use of the Gospel quotation and its entirely complimentary use. Rather, they seem to wish to stress that any errors committed by Philippikos arose from ignorance, or were the result of his naïve trust in Monothelete advisers. Perhaps they intend to contrast his errors with those of Justinian II, who punished all those who had opposed him in a vindictive fashion.

Further, since the text does not connect this characteristic of Philippikos with the Monothelete synod of 712, it may be referring to other errors or acts committed out of ignorance: the emperor's policy toward the Armenians, his military errors, possibly the immorality alleged by Agathon and Theophanes. But the implication remains that Philippikos was gentle and humble, in the sense recommended by Christ as appropriate for all good Christians. In addition, the compilers seem to be drawing on Syriac traditions of the emperor's excellent education in rhetoric and secular learning, to which Theophanes alludes in a rather back-handed fashion: "in his discourse he appeared to be eloquent and prudent."[42] The Eastern tradition is unaware of the charge of adultery or immorality made against Philippikos or suppresses it.

This alternative opinion also provides a glimpse of Constantinopolitan educational facilities in the last quarter of the seventh century, when Philippikos acquired a complete training in profane, that is, secular wisdom, at what was obviously considered a high level. Abbot Stephanos also instructed him in the correct, imperially sponsored theology. Even after its condemnation in 680/81 Monotheletism was cherished in the Kallistratos monastery in the capital, where a certain monk persuaded Philippikos that he would have a long and successful rule if he reversed the Sixth Ecumenical Council. Whether or not this prediction was actually responsible for his commitment to Monotheletism, he probably had reason to believe that Christians beyond the empire might welcome the change. Far from being yet another inadequate nonentity promoted by his troops, Philippikos was a well-educated military officer with a clear program of theological reform.

Finally, the *Parastaseis* also document Philippikos's interest in the work of local "philosophers," who tried to identify ancient statues in Constantinople and to understand their powers. However inadequate their research, they were dedicated to recording the early history of Byzantion, its pre-Christian monuments, and the collection of ancient statuary made by previous rulers to decorate the city. With his good education in the ancient Greek aspects of the academic curriculum and his mastery of rhetoric, Philippikos was well equipped to follow and support their efforts. These were criticized when proximity to and study of pagan works of art had fatal results, such as the unforeseen death of Himerios. Nonetheless, when the concerns of the compilers of the *Parastaseis* are taken together with the Eastern sources, they create a fuller picture of a "gentle" Philippikos, even if his reign, partly because it was so brief, still remains obscure.[43]

ADDENDUM

In December 2006 Dr. Tim Greenwood gave a fascinating paper at King's College London in which he drew attention to a long-published but little read text in Armenian, which makes sense of Philippikos's determination to restore Monotheletism. He cited this text, virulently hostile to the Sixth Ecumenical Council, which continued to circulate after that Council's condemnation of the Monothelete doctrine. As noted earlier, Philippikos must have received a thorough education in Monothelete theology and was known for his learning. So it seems very likely that he would have been aware of this continuing strand of Armenian opposition to the Orthodoxy prevailing after 681. I would like to thank Dr. Greenwood most warmly for discussing this text with me and look forward greatly to his forthcoming publication of it. **Update** It has now appeared; see "New Light from the East: Chronography and Ecclesiastical History through a Late Seventh Century Armenian Source," *Journal of Early Christian Studies* 16 (2008), 197–254, esp. 244–54 on the marked Monothelete tradition in Armenia displayed by this text, which was written between September 686 and 689/90.

NOTES

1. Averil Cameron and Judith Herrin, eds., *Constantinople in the Early Eighth Century: The Parastaseis Syntomoi Chronikai*, Columbia Studies in the Classical Tradition 10 (Leiden, 1984), 19 (hereafter *Parastaseis*).

2. *Circus factions: Blues and Greens at Rome and Byzantium* (Oxford, 1976).

3. Basic bibliography in J. R. Martindale, ed., *Prosopography of the Byzantine Empire I (641–867)* (Aldershot, UK, 2001), CD-ROM, s.v. Philippikos I; in F. Winkelmann et al., eds., *Prosopographie der mittelbyzantinischen Zeit 1.3 (641–867)* (Berlin/New York, 2000), no. 6150; F. Winkelmann, *Der monenergetisch-monotheletische Streit*, Berliner Byzantinistische Studien 6 (Berlin, 2001), esp. 253–55; J. Herrin, "Philippikos and the Greens," chapter 8 in this volume; M. Nichanian, "Aristocratie et pouvoir impérial à Byzance VIIe–IXe siècle" (Doctorat de l'Université de Paris 4, sous la direction de J.-C. Cheynet), to be published in Monographies du Centre de recherche d'histoire et civilisation de Byzance. **Update** M. Angold, "The Byzantine Political Process at Crisis Point" in P. Stephenson, ed., *The Byzantine World* (London/New York, 2010) 5–21, draws attention to the importance of this turning point, 12–13.

4. Nichanian, "Aristocratie et pouvoir impérial," chapter on "Complots et révoltes."

5. Agathon, Deacon and Chartophylax of the Great Church, *Epilogos*, in R. Riedinger, ed., *Concilium universale Constantinopolitanum tertium*, ACO, ser. 2, vol. 2.2 (Berlin, 1992), 898–901. Also in *Mansi*, 12 (repr. Graz, 1960–61), cols. 189–90. Winkelmann, *Der monenergetisch-monotheletische Streit*, 187.

6. Agathon, *Epilogos*, 898, lines 17–124; C. Mango, *The Art of the Byzantine Empire, 312–1453: Sources and Documents* (Englewood Cliffs, NJ, 1972), 141.

7. Agathon, *Epilogos*, 900, lines 31–35; Mango, Art, 141; Winkelmann, *Der monenergetisch-monotheletische Streit*, passim, with full bibliography.

8. Agathon, *Epilogos*, 899, lines 14–16; Winkelmann, *Der monenergetisch-monotheletische Streit*, 231–34.

9. Winkelmann, *Der monenergetisch-monotheletische Streit*, 263–67; J. Herrin, *The Formation of Christendom* (Princeton, 1989), 275–78, 287. Makarios was allowed to return briefly under Philippikos's renewed Monothelete regime.

10. Agathon, *Epilogos*, 899, lines 25–31.

11. Ibid., 899, line 32–900, line 4.

12. Ibid., 900, lines 6–12.

13. *Theophanes*, AM 6203, 6204, I, 381–82; AM 6209, I, 395; Nikephoros Patriarch of Constantinople, *Short History*, text, translation, and commentary by C. Mango (Washington, DC, 1998), ch. 48.

14. S. Brock, "Two Sets of Monothelete Questions to the Maximianists," in his *Studies in Syriac Christianity* (London, 1992), no. 15; and "An Early Syriac Life of Maximos the Confessor," ibid., no. 12, draws attention to the active opposition of the Chalcedonians in Syria and Palestine.

15. A. Palmer, *The Seventh Century in West Syrian Chronicles*, TTH 15 (Liverpool, 1993), 29, 89.

16. *Theophanes*, AM 6209, I, 395 line 7; C. Mango and R. Scott, trans., *The Chronicle of Theophanes* (Oxford, 1997), 544–45.

17. *Theophanes*, AM 6203, I, 381, lines 7–13.

18. Ibid., I, 381, line 30.

19. Mango and Scott, *The Chronicle of Theophanes*, 530.

20. *Theophanes*, AM 6204, I, 382.

21. Nikephoros, *Short History*, ch. 45.

22. Ibid., ch. 45; *Theophanes*, AM 6203, I, 381, lines 5–6.

23. L. Duchesne, ed., *LP*, 1 (Paris, 1955), 90; Eng. trans., R. Davis, *The Book of Pontiffs*, 1, TTH 6 (Liverpool, 1989), 91.

24. Ps-Dionysios, paragraph 148, as restored by Palmer, *The Seventh Century*, 209–10. Michael the Syrian and the Chronicle of 1234 also praise his learning following the Syriac tradition.

25. *Theophanes*, AM 6204, I, 382.

26. J. Laurent, *L'Arménie entre Byzance et l'Islam* (rev. ed. by M. Canard; Lisbon, 1980), 236–37, 245.

27. J. F. Haldon, *Byzantium in the Seventh Century: The Transformation of a Culture* (Cambridge, UK, 1990), 321–22.

28. Palmer, *The Seventh Century*, 210, n. 527; Haldon, *Byzantium*, 322.

29. *Parastaseis*, ch. 90. On Philippios and statuary, see B. Anderson, "Classified Knowledge: The Epistemology of Statuary in the Parastaseis Syntomoi Chronikai," *BMGS* 35 (2011) 1–19.

30. Theodorus Preger, ed., *Scriptores Originum Constantinopolitanarum, Patria* 3.37 (fasc. alter; Leipzig, 1907), 230.

31. *Parastaseis*, ch. 35, 94. The compilers do not mention statues at the harbor of Sophia.

32. Ibid., ch. 98.

33. Ibid., 160; Mango, *Art*, 133.

34. S. Bassett, *The Urban Image of Late Antique Constantinople* (Cambridge, 2004), 25–28, 50–58, 160–85.

35. Herrin, "Philippikos and the Greens" (chapter 8 in this volume).

36. J. Herrin, "Blinding in Byzantium," in C. Scholz and G. Makris, eds., Πολύπλευρος νοῦς. *Miscellanea für Peter Schreiner zum seinem 60. Geburtstag*, Byzantinisches Archiv 19 (Leipzig, 2000), 56–68.

37. G. Dagron, *Constantinople imaginaire; études sur le recueil des "Patria,"* (Paris, 1984), 133–36, 143–46; and *Emperor and Priest: The Imperial Office in Byzantium* (Cambridge, UK, 2003), 183–85.

38. Matt. 11.29.

39. Matt. 5.5.

40. With the help of the *Thesaurus Linguae Graecae*, it is now possible to survey the many uses of πρᾷος in a wide range of ancient and Byzantine texts. My warm thanks to Professor Charlotte Roueché for encouraging me to exploit this most useful tool.

41. http://www.tlg.uci.edu. At last count there were 845 entries for πρᾷος and additional texts are being searched and entered.

42. *Theophanes*, AM 6203, I, 381.

43. Winkelmann, *Der monoenergetisch-monotheletische Streit*, 255, observes that it is hard to say more about Philippikos, but neither the *Prosopography of the Byzantine Empire* nor the *Prosopographie der mittelbyzantinischen Zeit* takes account of the references in the *Parastaseis*.

10

THE HISTORICAL CONTEXT
OF ICONOCLAST REFORM

In 1975 Bryer and I decided to devote the Spring Symposium at Birmingham to the topic of iconoclasm—the subject was not then as popular as it is now. The *Proceedings* were the first to be published in the Symposia series now in its fifteenth volume. It is still regularly downloaded as an ebook, partly because it has such an interesting range of papers, especially Ihor Ševčenko's very novel analysis of the *Lives of Saints* written during the second phase of iconoclasm. My own contribution—reprinted with kind permission of the Centre for Byzantine, Ottoman and Modern Greek Studies, University of Birmingham—was short and simple, but it has been borne out by more recent research. As many historians have pointed out, the dynasty of Leo III did not give its name to a century or more of Byzantine history, as Basil "the Macedonian" or Alexios Komnenos did; instead his reign inaugurates iconoclasm, and the Iconoclast era continues to identify the eighth century. Yet Leo III achieved a great deal more than the ban on icon veneration.

This was the point of my article, accompanied by a graph (see figure 10.1) designed to show in visual terms how significant his long reign must have been in comparison with the short-lived emperors who preceded it. To put an end to the rapid turnover of rulers was itself important; it permitted other factors to gain traction in the unstable world of annual Arab invasions of Asia Minor. Eventually Leo and his son Constantine also put an end to these repeated incursions, as well as driving back the Bulgars behind the Balkan frontier. Military initiatives, a new legal code, the restoration of Constantinople's water supply, and a firm dynastic control resulted in nearly a century of rule by this military family from Northern Syria (which is why I sometimes referred to it as the Syrian dynasty).

The pendulum has now swung so far in this direction that iconoclasm has been displaced as the major achievement of these emperors. Yet to minimize the debate over icons and the appropriate veneration to be given to them is to neglect the much wider ramifications of Byzantine questioning. Both in Rome and Milan, north of the Alps in Francia and even in Spain and Anglo-Saxon England, echoes of the quarrel were heard and resulted in writings for and against Byzantine positions. So it's useful to recall what Leo III had initiated in 730 (rather than the traditional date of 726, when he began to speak against the icons, according to his detractors), and to bear in mind that only traces of the official propaganda that must have been produced at the time have survived. In this respect the icon venerators proved themselves as destructive as the original icon breakers.

THE EARLY EIGHTH CENTURY was a time when the Byzantine Empire was in danger of total collapse. From 695 to 717 internal conflicts threatened to divide the empire, while Muslim forces seemed poised ready to capture Constantinople itself. This troubled period is therefore crucial to an analysis of Byzantium during the first outbreak of iconoclasm.

The first reign of Justinian II, the last ruling member of the Heraclian dynasty, ended in a palace coup of 695, which established a usurper, Leontios, as emperor.[1] This event was the first of many similar upheavals that followed with all too regular repetition, making nonsense of the tradition of a Byzantine imperial family. In twenty-two years no less than six candidates claimed the throne in rapid succession.[2] Only one, the unfortunate Justinian II, had truly imperial credentials (and even these were debased by a slit nose, a deformity imposed in 695 precisely with the intention of preventing such a return to power). While there was no guarantee of sound government in imperial blood—Justinian's second reign, devoted almost exclusively to revenge, is a clear example—few of the five other emperors of the period were in any way competent.[3] Three were military, candidates pushed by their own troops who also disposed of them at will. The other two, civilians, were pawns set up and directed by forces beyond their control.

None was able to establish himself as a true emperor. Leontios, Tiberios II, Philippikos, Anastasios II, and Theodosios III are all rulers without a history. Their names are hardly known, except to collectors of their coins. They reigned on average for a little more than three years each, a figure that should be compared to the average reigns of sixth- and seventh-century rulers: seventeen and twenty years, respectively (see Figure 10.1).

During the second reign of Justinian II (705–11), the rule of his father and grandfather was within living memory—a traditional sequence of ordered government, in which son succeeded father, that constituted the apex of the essentially conservative Byzantine system. Within this established framework usurpers could sometimes find a place, provided that they were infrequent and managed to found a new dynasty. The emperors Justin I and Heraclius both fell into this category. They were accepted and praised exactly because they installed their own families in the given

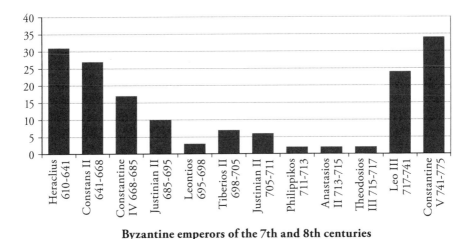

Byzantine emperors of the 7th and 8th centuries

Figure 10.1. Graph illustrating length of reign. Drawing J. Dowling.

manner. A rebellious military officer who aspired to the imperial insignia and thereafter maintained Byzantine prestige abroad and peace at home, would gradually become the legitimate emperor of his time. On the other hand, those candidates who did not impose themselves, could expect only the treatment accorded to failures—revolt, counter-coup, death or mutilation and exile, imposed as often as not, by erstwhile supporters.

In sharp distinction to the relative stability of the Heraclian dynasty, the "decades of anarchy" provided little but confusion. In a situation where there was no settled government at Constantinople, and no respect for the offspring of past emperors, any general could chance his luck. Thus, the commander of the Anatolikon *thema* (Leontios); a *drouggarios* of the fleet (Tiberios), and an ambitious Armenian noble, with naval and Opsikion troop support, (Philippikos) seized the throne.[4] But only Tiberios survived more than three years. After the deposition of Philippikos, military forces installed first Anastasios and then Theodosios, for two years each. And during the latter's reign (715–17), there was virtual civil war as Anastasios refused to accept his demotion and Leo (later Leo III) never recognized Theodosios' authority.[5] In these circumstances continuity in imperial administration was negligible; changes in nominal emperors caused disorder and instability, not only in the capital but also in the provinces. It was hardly surprising that in the face of such disarray, the Arab Caliphate decided to strike at the heart of Byzantium in a final effort to make Constantinople the Muslim world capital.

Such an enterprise had been attempted in the course of the seventh century. But conditions were now much more favorable to an Arab victory.[6] From their capital at Damascus successive caliphs had extended their control over much of the southeast Mediterranean. In 698 Carthage had been captured, despite an initially successful defense by Byzantine sea forces. A by-product of this momentous event was the revolt that removed Leontios from office and installed Apsimar, the naval commander, as Emperor Tiberios II.[7] Arab power continued to advance west from Carthage, taking Ceuta, the last Byzantine outpost in North Africa, in 711. From this springboard Spain and Western Europe were immediately threatened, while simultaneously sea-borne raids in the east Mediterranean seriously damaged Byzantine bases in the Aegean and on the coasts of Africa Minor.[8] Byzantine control over outlying regions of the empire, particularly Italy, was inevitably weakened by this hostile encirclement.

Soldier emperors were in part a response to these widespread threats. But for a period of over twenty years not one was capable of checking the disintegration of imperial authority. Fortunately for Byzantium, Leo III was to succeed where others had failed. He gained the throne in the same way as many of his immediate predecessors: by challenging an incumbent, winning control of the capital, and getting himself proclaimed by the people and crowned by the patriarch. Like most military candidates, he was supported by his own troops, soldiers of the Anatolikon *thema* army, together with those of the Armeniakon, which was commanded by his ally and future son-in-law, Artavasdos.[9] There was nothing uncharacteristic in all this, or in his background. Those who aimed at the purple often came from distant provinces, and adopted a more regal and Byzantine name in order to get on in the ranks.[10] They usually had little formal education and had to give evidence of their personal commitment to the orthodoxy of the time. In Leo's case all these factors can be observed. His family originated in Northern Syria and later moved to Thrace: he abandoned his baptismal name of Konon, and made the usual claims to Orthodox belief.[11] By a stroke of good luck and ingenuity, he won the patronage of Justinian II (if a somewhat legendary account preserves some historical basis), and between 711 and 717 he was promoted to become commander (*stratègos*) of the large Anatolikon *thema*.[12] During his career, as he witnessed the demise of three emperors, he obviously began to consider the question of his own qualifications. This is suggested not only by the fact that he refused to serve the Emperor Theodosios III, but also by the latter's apparent willingness for him to take over in 717.[13] Thus in March of that year he was acclaimed and crowned like so many other soldier emperors. But in contrast, both his immediate and more long-term actions suggested that he would prove to be very different from the two-year rulers. As well as confirmed military skills, he had a clear idea of traditional imperial government and was determined to secure the empire and his own rule for posterity.

In the effort to understand the phenomenon of iconoclasm, nonreligious aspects of eighth-century iconoclast rule have often been overlooked. Both Leo III and Constantine V have been portrayed as megalomaniacs, determined to reform the Eastern Church, rather than as outstanding and efficient administrators. Without discounting the momentous development in religious practice instituted by the iconoclasts, it is necessary to examine their primary tasks in political administration. A glance at the Figure 10.1 reveals that they were successful in one thing—the restoration of traditional Byzantine government, judged by a return to the sixth-century pattern of long reigns and hereditary succession. The Syrian dynasty established by Leo averaged eighteen years per reign, a respectable figure to be held up to those of the Justinianic and Heraclian centuries. After the immense disruption of the period 695–717, this clear and continuous family rule takes on a special significance.

Only a few months after Leo's coronation the long-awaited threat of a major attack on Constantinople materialized in the form of a large Arab fleet, which had successfully sailed through Byzantine defenses in the Aegean and was fast approaching the Dardanelles. News of this threat had already persuaded Anastasios II to repair the fortifications of the capital and to build ships, weapons, and ballistic machines, but even so, imminent warfare and so close at hand constituted a serious challenge.[14] Leo dealt with it by a judicious combination of military and diplomatic activity—highly combustible "Greek fire" was very effectively used against the Arab navy, while Bulgarian forces were drawn in to harrass part of the army encamped in Thrace. In addition, the twelve-month-old defense was greatly assisted by a very hard winter. As the Muslims were not familiar with snow, and as they did not usually campaign during winter months, cold, hunger, and disease took an abnormally high toll on those outside the city walls.[15]

The final withdrawal of Arab forces in August 718, plus the fortuitous destruction of many Arab ships by storm, established the new emperor with a certain authority. Leo used this victory and the ensuing peace treaty, which gave Byzantium a break from annual campaigning, to consolidate his position further.[16] He dealt promptly with a rival emperor who had been proclaimed in Sicily. As soon as the *stratègos* of the island had learned that Constantinople was besieged, he decided to promote his own candidate, one Basileios Onomagoulos, who adopted the imperial name of Tiberios. But these plans were effectively nullified by Leo's forces under the patrician Paul, who became general of Sicily. Thereafter Byzantine control of both Sicily and Italy was strengthened by a new census, intended to increase taxation as well as to record population.[17] Similarly, when Leo got wind of a conspiracy between the ex-emperor Anastasios II, a group of exiles in Thessalonike and the Bulgar Khan, he acted rapidly, and ruthlessly.[18] Constantine V was later to display the same single-minded attitude to any challenge to his own position as emperor. Both recognized that the ability to crush rivals was an essential part of their staying power.[19]

From the first years of his reign Leo appears to have conceived a substantial reform of military forces, designed to maximise their effectiveness. Immediately after the siege of 717–18 he turned his attention to the organization of Byzantine naval resources, which had failed to check either the preparatory activity, or the final Muslim attack on Constantinople. The previous supreme naval command, the post of *stratègos tôn karabisianôn*, was abolished.[20] An entirely new military organ assumed responsibility for maritime affairs, the Kibyrreot *thema*, based on the southwest coast of Asia Minor. It was formed from the coastal territory formerly part of the Anatolikon *thema*, and it was comparable in every way except its size to the other Asian ones. The institution of this type of military administration in a specifically maritime area provided the region with a powerful and local naval weapon. Its troops were inherited in part from an earlier force commanded by a *drouggarios*, which had been subordinated to the general of the *Karabisianoi*, and additional sailors were recruited from among Mardaïtes settled in Pamphilia and round Attaleia. As *thema* forces, both men and ships were maintained, supplied, and equipped by that area. Thus, a sensitive coastland received an organized naval defense, while from its base the new regular Kibyrreot fleet could oversee the movement of Arab shipping.[21]

In disbanding the older maritime formations, Leo doubtless wished to prevent a repetition of those successful revolts sparked off by the *Karabisianoi*, and to limit direct access to the capital that a disgruntled fleet offered to rival emperors. The imperial fleet, based at Constantinople, was therefore transformed and brought under closer control.[22] But the reorganization was also motivated by the need to create a permanent naval strike-force in all strategic parts of the empire. The great innovation of Leo, and Constantine after him, was to extend seventh-century administration to Byzantine waters. The *thema tôn Kibyrraiôtôn* was the first attempt to meet such a need. It was followed by the creation of naval themes on Crete (by 767) and in the Aegean (by 843), with subordinate detachments stationed in the Dodecanese and the Cyclades. In conjunction with these sea-borne forces, the European provinces of the empire were given mixed troops, both naval and territorial, which provided additional maritime defense. In the course of the eighth century the successes of these forces, for example, off the coast of Cyprus in 747, when a Syrian fleet was almost entirely destroyed, confirmed the significance attributed by Leo and Constantine to naval strength.[23]

In the same way it was Leo's aim to consolidate Byzantine land armies. From his experience in the Anatolikon *thema*, he knew both the strengths of the established administrative system, and also the competitive and separatist tendencies so often displayed by provincial troops. His own career illustrated what a stepping stone to higher aspirations the post of *stratègos* might constitute. These factors demanded a reform that would limit the power of individual generals without weakening the *thema* system. Leo achieved this by reducing the size of the Anatolikon *thema*, the first and most prestigious. It gave up a large part of its western region to the Thrakesion, and its southern coastland to the Kibyrreot. Later, Constantine V followed this example, dividing the Opsikion to form a central Anatolian *thema*, called the Boukellarion.[24] In this instance the past history of Opsikion troops backing imperial rivals and imposing their own candidates, most recently Artavasdos, may well have been decisive. Although it was almost impossible to break the loyalty of provincial soldiers to their own commanders, a powerful factor in the process of uniting the armed forces was the sustained military success of Leo and Constantine. Through their victorious campaigns against both the Arabs and Bulgars, they gradually won a respect from *thema* troops that balanced that accorded to *stratègoi*. Both emperors also paid great attention to the elite garrison troops of Constantinople, organized in three *tagmata*. Their loyalty became in time one of the major forces of iconoclasm.[25]

Early in his reign Leo III indicated his determination to secure the hereditary succession of his family, by the coronation of his infant son, Constantine, as co-emperor.[26] This event of 720 was reflected in imperial coinage, in the issue of a new type of gold *solidus* (*nomisma*), which carried a portrait of the young emperor on the reverse.[27] This replaced the traditional reverse with the cross potent, which had been used throughout the seventh century with a few exceptions. The second imperial portrait thus can be interpreted as an iconoclast measure designed to remove a representation of the cross from coinage. But the change was certainly introduced for purely dynastic reasons. It was traditional for emperors to signal their heirs as co-emperors on imperial coinage; in this way Justinian II displayed his son, Tiberios, on the reverse of gold coins struck during his second reign.[28] Also, there was no question of removing the cross potent from the coinage altogether. With the introduction of a new gold coin type in 720, this image was transferred to the obverse of the *miliarèsion*, a new silver coin struck for the first time on the same occasion.[29] Far from banning the use of the cross, the Iconoclasts gave it great prominence. The image of the cross replaced the icon of Christ on the Chalke Gate of the imperial palace, and it was given special significance in iconoclast church decoration.[30] Leo's new gold coin proclaimed his son as co-emperor and celebrated this fact in normal Byzantine fashion, which could be immediately appreciated. This coin type, with two full imperial portraits, continued to be used throughout the eighth century, and after 843 it was still employed on occasions. Even the iconophile Empress Eirene did not alter it. When she reigned alone (797–802) she merely put her own portrait on both sides, as if to emphasize her sole authority.[31]

Once the succession had been established, and while military reforms were being put into effect, Leo ordered legal experts, including the *quaestor*, consuls, and patricians, to draw up a handbook of basic law.[32] They were instructed to prepare a short compilation in Greek, the spoken language of Byzantium, rather than Latin, the legal language, which was hardly understood. The emperor intended it to provide a convenient manual for provincial judges. At the same time he made strenuous efforts to reform the judiciary, so that both the body of law and all its agents would be set on a sounder footing. All officials involved in the administration of justice were to be salaried and were forbidden to accept gifts. Judges were exhorted to bring all criminals, even the powerful and the rich, to justice. At the same time the Code stated emphatically that Christian clemency should be exercised.[33] The *Ekloga* (Selections) combined a simplified version of the *Corpus Juris Civilis* of Justinian I, with various customary rulings of the church on questions of marriage, inheritance, and property. The latter introduced not only considerable Christian influence but also specific alteration from traditional Roman law in domestic matters. Hardly any new legislation was incorporated in the *Ekloga*— instead the handbook set out the most straightforward guidelines by which to provide justice. In the same way as other short legal codes, the Farmers' Law of Justinian II, the "naval" and "military" laws, the *Ekloga* was designed to help resolve practical problems, such as matters relating to unpaid dowries, repayment of loans, or compensation for the loss of a guard dog.[34] Leo III realized that this was very necessary in an Empire where there had been so little central control for many years, and where even established law was not generally understood; the introduction to the *Ekloga* draws attention to this quite specifically.[35] While he does not appear to have been a great legislator, Leo clearly recognized the importance of making old laws available in comprehensible form—laws that are neither codified nor accessible cannot be efficiently applied.

Throughout his reign Leo was concerned to restore the traditional institutions of Byzantium, and its now much-shaken claim to military invincibility. Both he and his son devoted their considerable tactical skills to the planning and execution of annual campaigns, in an attempt to consolidate the empire's reduced frontiers—an attempt that was largely successful.[36] After an earthquake in 740, and again after the 747 epidemic of plague in Constantinople, both emperors insisted upon rebuilding and repopulating the city. This desire to strengthen the capital may well reflect a distrust of provincial loyalties, but it also corresponds to the normal wish of emperors to leave their own mark on the Queen City.[37] Through their efforts to make imperial administration effective and fair, to maintain basic food supplies when economic life was seriously disrupted by both internal and external factors, and to encourage market activity by monetary reforms, they tried to bring order and greater prosperity to the provinces.[38] Little of this, however, is directly acknowledged by the uniformly biased sources of the period, which prefer to condemn both Leo and Constantine as "Saracen-minded," a "Pharaoh" and a "second Midas."[39]

This then constituted the historical setting in which the ideological controversy over the use of icons was argued. These two aspects of Byzantium in the eighth century should not be treated in isolation, as they were of course closely connected and interdependent. The degree to which religious, economic, military, and political factors combined can be illustrated by an incident that took place during the iconophile lull of the early ninth century. Rebellious soldiers, recently dismissed from service in the central garrisons, broke into the tomb of Constantine V and called for a resumption of iconoclasm in order to defeat the Bulgars.[40] Victorious military campaigns and iconoclast theology had become inextricably entwined, however confusedly, with the activities of Leo and Constantine. This popular association centered particularly on the person of Constantine, whom the soldiers exhorted to rise up and lead them into battle again.

But the relationship between political events and religious movements was not fixed and static throughout the period of iconoclasm; it varied from one decade to another. It is precisely the structure of this interdependence that requires further research. Such an investigation, however, is beyond the scope of this chapter, which has simply noted the efforts of Leo and Constantine to end a political crisis that nearly brought down the Byzantine Empire. For it was during the "decades of anarchy" that the continued existence of Byzantium came into question. The accumulated effects of so many short, uncertain, and ineffectual reigns were multiplied by the constant threat of Muslim domination. It is necessary, therefore, to draw attention to Leo and Constantine's major achievement—the restoration of imperial authority that prevented the empire's demise. The methods by which this restoration was accomplished were developed by Leo in the first decade of his reign (717–26), a highly significant period, and one in which no question of theology, or of any religious nature, was accorded primary importance. Later these matters did assume a primary importance. This in turn was dependent upon the reestablishment of Byzantine authority. For without Leo and Constantine's principally political and military success, there would have been no iconoclast controversy as we know it.

NOTES

1. *Theophanes*, AM 6187, I, 368–69; *The Chronicle of Theophanes Confessor: Byzantine and Near Eastern History, AD 284–813*, translated with introduction and commentary by C. Mango and R. Scott, with assistance of G. Greatrex (Oxford 1997), 514–15; Nikephoros Patriarch of Constantinople, *Short History*, text, translation, and commentary by C. Mango (Washington, DC, 1998), chs. 37–39. The publication by C. Head, *Justinian II of Byzantium* (Madison, WI, 1972), adds little to Bury's excellent treatment; see J. B. Bury, *A History of the Later Roman Empire from Arcadius to Irene* (London/New York, 1889), II, 327–30. **Update** M. Angold, "The Byzantine Political Process at Crisis Point," in P. Stephenson, ed., *The Byzantine World* (London/New York, 2011), 5–21, stresses the critical danger of this period and confirms the importance of iconoclast reform.

2. From 695 to 717 the six emperors were Leontios (695–98); Tiberios II (698–705); Justinian II, second reign (705–11); Philippikos (711–13); Anastasios II (713–15), and Theodosios III (715–17). **Update** Among the many recent studies of these emperors, see W. Treadgold, "Seven Byzantine Revolutions and the Chronology of Theophanes," *GRBS* 31 (1990), 203–26; L. Brubaker and J. Haldon, *Byzantium in the Iconoclast Era ca. 680–850: A History* (Cambridge, UK, 2011), 70–75.

3. On the second reign of Justinian II, see *Theophanes*, AM 6197, I, 374–81; *Nikephoros*, chs. 41–48.

4. On Leontios, see note 1 earlier; on Apsimar/Tiberios, see *Theophanes*, AM 6190, I, 370–71; *Nikephoros*, 41; and on Philippikos, see *Theophanes*, AM 6203, 379–81; *Nikephoros*, chs. 45–46; J. Herrin, "Philippikos and the Greens," "Philippikos 'the Gentle,'" chapters 8 and 9 in this volume.

5. On Anastasios, see *Nikephoros*, chs. 49–52, and *Theophanes*, AM 6205–6207, I, 383–86; on Theodosios, *Nikephoros*, ch. 50–52, and *Theophanes*, AM 6207–8, I, 385–90. For the veiled references to a state of near civil war, *Theophanes*, AM 6207, I, 386, and AM 6209, I, 395.

6. P. K. Hitti, *A History of the Arabs* (London, 1956), 206–23. The attack had been planned since 714; see *Theophanes*, AM 6202, I, 383–84; *Nikephoros*, chs. 49–50; M. Canard, "Les expéditions des Arabes contre Constantinople dans l'histoire et dans la légende," *JA* 208 (1926), 80. **Update** R.-J. Lilie, *Die byzantinische Reaktion auf die Ausbreitung der Araber* (Munich, 1976).

7. On the revolt of Apsimar, see note 3 earlier, and H. Ahrweiler, *Byzance et la mer* (Paris, 1966), 50.

8. The establishment of a naval base at Tunis (704) extended Muslim naval power into the west Mediterranean, while Arab pirates, attested in many provincial waters, made highly destructive attacks, such as the expedition of 715 to Lycia, which stripped the region of cyprus wood for ship building; see *Theophanes*, AM 6207, I, 385; *Nikephoros*, ch. 50. **Update** T. C. Lounghis, *Byzantium in the Eastern Mediterranean: Safeguarding East Roman Identity (407–1204)* (Nicosia, 2010), 8–11, 45–46.

9. *Theophanes*, AM 6208–9, I, 390–91; *Nikephoros*, ch. 52; W. Kaegi, "The Byzantine Armies and Iconoclasm," *BS* 27 (1966), 51. Artavasdos later married Anna, Leo's daughter; see *Theophanes*, AM 6207, I, 386, and AM 6209, I, 395.

10. Bardanes, who ruled as Philippikos, was Armenian; Leontios was from Isauria; Apsimar, the original name of Tiberios II, suggests a Slav origin; and Artemios changed his name to rule as Anastasios II. These double names are preserved in the chapter titles of a ninth-century chronicle; see Georgius Monachus, *Chronicon*, ed. C. de Boor, 2 vols. (Leipzig, 1904), II, 732, 734, 735.

11. Leo's origins are discussed at length by S. Gero, *Byzantine Iconoclasm during the Reign of Leo III with Particular Reference to the Oriental Sources* (Louvain, 1973), 1–24.

12. *Theophanes*, AM 6209, I, 391. He is named *strategos ton Anatolikon* at AM 6207 and 6208, I, 386–87.

13. *Theophanes*, AM 6209, I, 395; *Nikephoros*, ch. 52. In the course of his career he may well have acted in complicity with Arab forces; see for example, the strange account of his meeting with the general Maslama, *Theophanes*, AM 6208, I, 387–91; Arab sources record similar dealings, see Gero, *Byzantine Iconoclasm*, 32–33.

14. *Theophanes*, AM 6206, I, 383–84; *Nikephoros*, chs. 49–50.

15. *Theophanes*, AM 6209, I, 395–99; *Nikephoros*, ch. 53–55; R. Guilland, "L'expédition de Maslama contre Constantinople (717–718)," *Études Byzantines* (Paris, 1959), 109–33; M. Canard, "Les expéditions des Arabes" (note 6 earlier), 80–94. On the siege, see also Gero, *Byzantine Iconoclasm*, 36–43; F. Gabrieli, "L'eroe omàyyade Maslamah ibn 'Abd al-Malik," *Academia dei Lincei*, 346, Rendiconti morali, 150, serie 8, vol. 5, fasc.1–2, 22–39, esp. 25–32. Both Ahrweiler,

Byzance et la mer, 30, 441 (app. IV), and Gero, *Byzantine Iconoclasm*, 172–80 (app. 3), have drawn attention to an anonymous account of the siege, published by S. Lampros, *Historika Meletèmata* (Athens, 1884) (in Greek), 142–44; cf. the verses attributed to Theodosios *grammatikos*, which may also refer to this event, ibid., 129–32. **Update** L. Brubaker and J. Haldon, *Byzantium in the Iconoclast Era (ca. 680-850): The Sources: An Annotated Survey* (Aldershot, 2001).

16. In this Leo was assisted by increasing divisions within the Muslim world. During the second quarter of the eighth century, the Umayyad Caliphate was severely weakened by internal disagreements, which led finally to the Abbasid coup of 750 and the establishment of a new capital at Baghdad. On this shift in the East, see P. K. Hitti, *A History of the Arabs*, 279–96.

17. *Theophanes*, AM 6210, I, 398–99; *Nikephoros*, chs. 54–55; *LP*, I, 403. **Update** V. Prigent, "Les empereurs isauriens et la confiscation des patrimoines pontificaux d'Italie du sud," *MEFR*, Moyen Age, 116 (2004), 557–94; C. Zuckerman, "Learning from the Enemy and More: Studies in 'Dark Centuries' Byzantium," *Millennium* 2 (2005), 78–135.

18. On the conspiracy, see *Theophanes*, AM 6211, I, 400–401; *Nikephoros*, ch. 57; cf. the ingenious theory of H. Ahrweiler, *Byzance et la mer* (note 6 earlier), 26–31, which depends upon the dating of a crucial passage in the *Miracula Sancti Demetrii*, PG, 116, col. 1368ff.

19. The civil war brought about by Artavasdos, Constantine's brother-in-law, was the single, most serious challenge to the emperor; see *Theophanes*, AM 6233–35, I, 414–20; *Nikephoros*, chs. 64–66; A. Lombard, *Constantin V, Empereur des Romains* (Paris, 1902), 23–30. **Update** Prigent (as earlier), 743–45; Zuckerman (as earlier), 92–94.

20. On the dissolution of the *Karabisianoi*, see H. Antoniadis-Bibicou, *Études d'histoire maritime de Byzance* (Paris, 1966), 63–87; H. Ahrweiler, *Byzance et la mer*, 22–35. **Update** Zuckerman (as earlier), 107–22, on the financing of the fleets; Lounghis (as earlier n 8), 77–78, 189–90, on the strategy of the fleets.

21. On the Kibyrreot formation, see A. Pertusi, *Costantino Porfirogenito De Thematibus* (Vatican, 1952), 149–53; on the previous *drouggarios* (Apsimar), see notes 3 and 20 earlier.

22. Leontios, Apsimar/Tiberios, and Philippikos all owed their successful revolts to naval power. On the imperial fleet, manned by mercenaries, see H. Antoniadis-Bibicou, *Études d'histoire maritime*, 86–87; cf. H. Ahrweiler, *Byzance et la mer*, 44, 69. **Update** Lounghis (as earlier) 50, 193.

23. On the creation of naval *themata*, see H. Ahrweiler, *Byzance et la mer*, 50–52; H. Antoniadis-Bibicou, *Études d'histoire maritime*, 88–89; N. Oikonomidès, *Les listes de préséance byzantines des IXe et Xe siècles* (Paris, 1972), 45–47, 49, 53, 352–53. While the *drouggarios* of the Dodecanese remained a subordinate of the Kibyrreot *stratègos*, by 889 the equivalent officer attached to the Cyclades was promoted to become the first *strategos* of Samos, a new naval *thema*; see H. Ahrweiler, *Byzance et la mer*, 80–81. **Update** Zuckerman (as earlier), 124–25, cf. Lounghis (as earlier), 135–40; L. Brubaker and J. Haldon, *Byzantium in the Iconoclast Era (c.680–850): A History* (Cambridge, 2011), 583–84, 729–30.

24. On the creation of these *themata*, see A. Pertusi, *Costantino Porfirogenito* (note 21 earlier), 124–26, 133–36; cf. H. Antoniadis-Bibicou, *Études d'histoire*

maritime (note 20 earlier), 68–70, 75–77. **Update** On the underlying changes behind this reorganization, and criticism of the origins of the *themata*, see Brubaker and Haldon, *A History*, 739–64.

25. On the loyalty of *thema* forces and Constantine's campaign to reform the *tagmata*, see Kaegi, "The Byzantine Armies" 50–51, 53, 56, 61.

26. *Theophanes*, AM 6211, I, 400; *Nikephoros*, chs. 56, 58.

27. On the new gold coin, see P. Grierson, *DOC*, III, part 1 (Washington, DC, 1973), 227, and plate 1, type 3 onward; C. Morrisson, *Catalogue des monnaies byzantines de la Bibliothèque Nationale* (Paris, 1970), II, 450–53, and plate LXVI, type A/02 onward. The coronation was also marked by a new series of copper coins, on which Constantine was portrayed, and by an entirely new silver coin, see note 29.

28. In place of the cross potent on the reverse, Constans II had previously portrayed first his two sons between a long cross on a small globus and then all three sons; see P. Grierson, *DOC*, II, part 2 (Washington, DC, 1968), plate XXIV, type 28; plate XXV, type 40. Justinian II's revolutionary new coin had the emperor holding the cross potent on the reverse; see J. Breckenridge, *The Numismatic Iconography of Justinian II* (New York, 1959), plate 1, nos. 5–10. For the coins of his second reign with co-emperor Tiberios, see P. Grierson, *DOC*, II, part 2, 644–46, plate XLIII, types 2, 4, 6, 7. There are large reproductions of this type in C. Head, *Justinian II of Byzantium*, 114, 121.

29. On the silver reform introduced in 720, see P. Grierson, *DOC*, III, part 1, plates II and III, type 22 onward; C. Morrisson, *Catalogue des monnaies byzantines*, II, 450–52. This silver *miliarèsion* was the first Byzantine coin to employ a Greek term "basileus."

30. On the Chalke cross, see Mango, *The Brazen House: A Study of the Vestibule of the Imperial Palace of Constantinople*, Arkeol.–Kunst. Meddelelsev . . . Bind 4, nr 4 (Copenhagen, 1959), 118–19; cf. P. Speck, "Symmeikta. Die ikonoklastischen Jamben an der Chalke," *Hellènika* 27 (1974), 376–80. On the mosaic cross put up in the church of Saint Eirene, see W. S. George, *The Church of Saint Eirene at Constantinople* (Oxford, 1921), 47–54, pl. 17.

31. On the gold coins of Eirene, see P. Grierson, *DOC*, III, part 1, 347–48, plate XV. The same type was used in the ninth century by Basil I: see idem, *DOC*, III, part 2 (Washington, DC, 1973), pl. XXX, types 3–6.

32. For the text of the *Ekloga*, see C. Zachariae von Ligenthal, *Collectio Librorum Juris Graeco-Romani Ineditorum* (Leipzig, 1852), 9–52; Zepos, *JusGR*, II (Athens, 1931; repr. Aalen, 1962), 11–62; E. A. Freshfield, *A Manual of Roman Law: The Ecloga* (Cambridge, UK, 1926; Eng. trans.). The Code was issued in March 726; see Gero, *Leo III*, 48, n. 1. **Update** The new edition of the *Ekloge* by L. Burgmann argues persuasively for its issue in 741; see *Das Gesetzbuch Leons III und Konstantinos V* (Frankfurt, 1983), 10–12.

33. Zepos, *JusGR*, II, 13–14 (instructions); 14–17 (reform of judicial practice). Christian influence is evident throughout the introduction; see esp. 12. Cf. T. E. Gregory, "The Ekloga of Leo III and the Concept of 'Philanthropia,'" *Byzantina* 7 (1975), 267–87.

34. For the three codes, see Zepos, *JusGR*, II, 67–103. The military and naval laws are not securely dated, but in character and objective they are close to the

Ekloga. On specific problems, see ibid. 27–28 (*Ekloga*, title 3 on dowries); 39–42 (*Ekloga*, title 10, on securities); and 69–70 (Farmers' Law, titles 45 and 65, on guard dogs).

35. Ibid. II, 13, 16; cf. G. Ostrogorsky, "Über der vermeintliche Reformtätigkeit der Isaurier," *BZ* 30 (1929/30), 394–400, which overlooks the fact that seventh-century emperors had not continued the legal work of Justinian, and does not draw sufficient attention to the influence of the *Ekloga* on Slavic, Latin, and even Arabic law; see Gero, *Leo III*, 50, n. 4.

36. The victory at Akroïnon in 740 was a turning point in the struggle against the Arabs; see *Theophanes*, AM 6231, I, 411; on subsequent campaigns, *Theophanes*, AM 6247, I, 429; AM 6250, I, 430; AM 6254, I, 432–33; AM 6256, I, 436; AM 6257, I, 437; AM 6263, I, 446; AM 6265, I, 446–47; *Nikephoros*, chs. 67, 70, 73, 76, 79. **Update** Angold, n. 1, draws attention to these major military achievements, frequently overlooked. Cf. Zuckerman, as earlier, 134, stressing the relative stability of eighth-century iconoclast rule.

37. On the earthquake, see *Theophanes*, AM 6232, I, 412; *Nikephoros*, 63; and on other building activity, *Theophanes*, AM 6232, I, 412; AM 6258, I, 440. Cf. also accounts of Constantine V's redecoration of the Blachernai church, *Life of Saint Stephen the Younger*, PG, 100, cols. 1120–21. **Update** Brubaker and Haldon, *Byzantium in the Iconoclast Era*, 212–18.

38. During Constantine's reign the price of grain was particularly cheap; see *Theophanes*, AM 6259, I, 443; *Nikephoros*, 76. This fact was remembered in the ninth century; see PG, 100, cols. 492–93. Leo and Constantine's efforts to maintain economic activity must be seen in the context of a marked decline in towns and markets. This shrinkage is probably reflected in the gradual disappearance of smaller coin denominations. Leo took steps to simplify imperial coinage, which had always been issued in a bewildering complexity of types and ceremonial pieces. By the end of the eighth century only the gold *nomisma*, silver *miliarèsion*, and copper *follis* were struck, not the half and quarter *follis* normally used as small change, nor the fractional gold coins.

39. *Theophanes*, AM 6218, I, 405; AM 6224, I, 410; AM 6238, I, 423; AM 6259, I, 443; *Nikephoros*, ch. 85.

40. *Theophanes*, AM 6305, I, 501; Alexander, *Nikephoros*, 111–25; A. Lombard, *Constantin V*, 20–21; cf. another aspect of this legend, N. Adontz, "Les légendes de Maurice et de Constantin V," *Annuaire de l'institut de philologie et d'histoire orientales et slaves* 2 (1934), 9–11.

11

CONSTANTINOPLE, ROME, AND THE FRANKS IN THE SEVENTH AND EIGHTH CENTURIES

✌

During the long period of research that lay behind *The Formation of Christendom* (published 1987), I became aware of the shift in European diplomacy that proved critical to Western-Byzantine relations: successive bishops of Rome abandoned their traditional alliance with Constantinople and turned instead to the Franks. The move was initiated by an unprecedented journey over the Alps made in 753 by Pope Stephen II, who was greeted at Langres by the eleven-year-old son of King Pepin, Charles (later known as Charles the Great, Carolus magnus, Charlemagne) and escorted to Ponthion. At Jonathan Shepard's suggestion I explored this development for the 24th Spring Symposium, published in *Byzantine Diplomacy* (1992).

Since 731 bishops of Rome had condemned the iconoclast policy adopted in the Eastern capital, which led to more increasingly bitter correspondence between Old Rome and New. Religious antagonism then led to the decision to involve the major force north of the Alps in the defense of Rome, which was increasingly threatened by the Lombards, established in northern Italy.

To counter this break with tradition, Emperor Constantine V sought to win over the Franks to a more considered position. Several embassies armed with more and more extravagant gifts arrived to persuade Pippin and later Charles into an alliance with Byzantium that would be sealed by a marriage. But Pope Stephen's initiative, which included the anointing of Pippin, his wife, and children, bound the Frankish king into a commitment to support the pope and to return lands recently conquered by the Lombards to Rome.

My interest in this period of dense diplomatic activity was spurred by the mention of an organ, a gift quite unfamiliar in the West though much used in Byzantium. Indeed a later poet would take the Frankish ownership of such an instrument as evidence of their overall superiority. It suggests that Constantinople was making a special effort to impress the Franks and construct a better relationship, but this failed. Pippin and his son remained in close contact with the bishops of Rome. In this way they upset the East/West diplomacy by substituting a new North/South axis between Italy and Francia. The paradox is that in the long term Charlemagne approved a policy much closer to Byzantine iconoclasm and the spiritual worship adopted in the Eastern capital, while the popes remained attached to icon veneration.

AT THE BEGINNING of the seventh century relations between Constantinople and Rome followed the model established under Constantine I, when the Roman empire dominated the entire Mediterranean world. Despite the demise of the Western half, the two capitals continued to communicate in fourth-century style. But since there was now only one emperor ruling in the East, he was represented in the West by an exarch based at Ravenna, while in Rome the bishop took over more and more responsibility for the ancient capital. But no exarch or bishop doubted the reality of imperial power and authority. In communication with Constantinople popes addressed their secular overlords as most pious, *piissimi imperatores*, and looked to them for protection and support. Their relationship may be illustrated by a negotiation that was resolved in 607. When Emperor Phokas allowed Old Rome to claim ecclesiastical primacy over New Rome (Constantinople), the exarch raised a column in the forum, topped by the imperial ruler's statue. This was a thoroughly traditional way to honor an emperor.

By the mid-eighth century relations between Constantinople and Rome had been transformed. Instead of being praised, emperors are condemned as *nefandissimi, perversi, odibiles*, most wicked, evil, and hateful.[1] And in contrast popes now address the Frankish ruler as *spiritalis compater*, "spiritual co-father," referring to the relationship established between Pope Stephen II and Pippin III, by which the bishop of Rome became godfather to the children of the Frankish king.[2] This was an institutional as well as spiritual bond that remained an important feature of later Frankish-papal relations. It symbolizes the substitution of Frankish for Byzantine secular rule in Rome as a remarkable measure of the upheaval in European diplomacy and politics that had occurred. One of the difficulties of investigating this process of change is that the sources for Byzantine history at the critical point in the mid-eighth century are notoriously sparse. In particular, the reign of Constantine V, who ruled from 741 to 775, right through the period of the break with Rome, is documented almost entirely by writers who hated him and his policies. So he has had a bad press, which is hard to overcome.[3] Nonetheless, his diplomatic reactions to the shift in Rome's orientation are better preserved in some Western sources than they are in Byzantine ones. And from these we learn of the stupendous gift of an organ, sent by Constantine to King Pippin in 757, as well as proposals for a hitherto unprecedented marriage alliance. These initiatives, it will be argued, reflect Constantinople's seriousness in its dealings with the novel circumstances of the eighth century.

In an effort to explain such a decisive change, I will first examine contacts between Constantinople and Rome, which provided a structure for other fields of diplomacy, and second, relations within the triangle created by the Franks' entry as a significant power in international relations. Finally, I will return to the organ and other diplomatic gifts exchanged during this period. Throughout, one must stress, it is very difficult to distinguish foreign policy from diplomacy, and diplomacy from intrigue. The dissemination of bad news, threats of invasion, especially in the key area of southern Italy, which was of immediate concern to all three powers, seems to have been another Byzantine gift to the medieval world.[4]

For much of the sixth and seventh centuries, relations between Constantinople and Rome took place against a background of almost continual warfare. The eastern empire was under threat from either Persian or Arab attack, while the area around Rome, a Byzantine duchy under overall authority of the exarch of Ravenna, suffered increasing insecurity as the Lombards pressed south from northern Italy. As a result of these military conflicts, both of the parties concerned suffered drastic changes. The empire shrank to a fraction of its fourth-century size (geographical change), while the Byzantine duchy of Rome gradually became the core of the papal state in central Italy (change of identity). Despite these developments, the structural subordination of Old Rome to New Rome continued to carry great weight even as political reality made it untenable.

By "structural subordination," I mean Constantinople's determination to replace Rome as the center and capital of both the empire and the Christian universe (*oikoumene*). With Justinian's treatment of Rome after the Gothic war, novel forms of eastern primacy were imposed, for instance, in ecclesiastical politics: witness the kidnap of Pope Vigilius and the pressure on him to sign the decrees of the Fifth Council. Byzantium thus revealed its determination to make Rome an obedient province and its leading representative, the bishop, a loyal subject, who would help to keep Italy and Sicily, with its valuable supplies of grain, secure for Constantinople.

The results of this imperial hegemony are revealed in traditional Roman protocol: bishops of Rome said prayers for the ruling emperor, honored his portrait both in public images and on coinage minted in Rome, dated documents from his assumption of the consulship or imperial rule.[5] In the absence of any other official, responsibility for observing these honors fell to the bishop, although the exarch would help with such an expensive one as a column. Imperial coins were minted in Rome as in all other centers of the empire, but the church of Rome also entered the names of rulers and patriarchs of Constantinople in its diptychs and mentioned them in its liturgy. The imperial presence was clearly felt and was visible in images of the ruling emperor that constantly reminded the Romans of their overlord on the Bosphorus.

The systematic subordination of Old Rome to New Rome was then realized through a diplomatic arrangement. A series of papal *apocrisiarii* were appointed to form a regular Roman representation in the eastern capital; these legates lived at their official residence in the Placidia palace in Constantinople and took part in the ceremonial of the imperial court. For example, they attended ceremonies at the Great Palace to mark imperial marriages, baptisms, and deaths; they participated in theological debates and witnessed important trials. As the pope's representatives in the East, they took precedence at ecumenical councils of the church and signed the acts before anyone else. Roman legates to Constantinople are documented from the 530s to the early eighth century, and Gregory, later Pope Gregory the Great, is a typical example of these ecclesiastical diplomats.[6]

The post of *apocrisiarius* was the most prestigious one open to Roman deacons, who gained useful experience at the Eastern court and capital. Of those who held it, nearly half went on to be elected as bishop of Rome. Their knowledge of diplomacy and imperial court procedure was very useful in the West, with its now reduced level of international contacts. But the structure was also important for Constantinople, in that it brought a regular series of the most brilliant clerics from Rome to the East, where they were exposed to imperial traditions. Thus prepared, they were considered suitable candidates for the leadership of the church of Rome, to which they brought some understanding of Byzantine court and administrative methods. Concern that they should support official Eastern positions is evident from the treatment accorded to Pope Martin I's legates, who were persecuted together with their superior.

But the lasting significance of this diplomatic arrangement becomes clearer from its employment by Roman pontiffs in their relationship with the Franks, with whom they tried to re-create a similar institutional link. In the circumstances of a mobile Frankish court, whose procedures were unfamiliar to Rome, the parallel could not be precise, and Roman deacons were not employed for the task. But by appointing apostolic legates from among clerics who had experience of ecclesiastical matters in Francia, successive popes hoped to create the same sort of connection. They also used this conduit to press for increasing Roman influence and Roman-inspired reforms in the Frankish church.

This switch from Constantinople to Francia must have occurred between 714, when Pope Constantine's *apocrisiarius*, Michael, assisted at the translation of Germanus to the patriarchate of Constantinople, and ca.746, when Pope Zacharias established Boniface as his personal representative in Francia.[7] Between these dates, of course, Eastern iconoclasm provoked a schism between Constantinople and Rome, and Emperor Leo III arbitrarily removed the ecclesiastical diocese of East Illyricum from Western control, two occasions on which popes might have recalled their legates. No contemporary evidence concerning Illyricum survives, but Roman dismay at the rumors of harsh persecution of iconophiles and great bonfires of Christian images is very clear from the *Life* of Pope Gregory II.[8] Either this pontiff or his successor, Gregory III, would have had good reason to sever the established links with the East.

But it was, in fact, the next pope, Zacharias, who took the step of appointing an apostolic legate in Francia. Zacharias, who was of Greek origin, had to deal with Lombard threats to both Rome and Ravenna, the last outpost of Byzantium in the West. While he negotiated skillfully to curb Lombard ambitions in central Italy, his efforts to prevent the capture of Ravenna were in vain. Constantinople sent no military assistance, and King Aistulf's successful siege of 751 brought to an end Byzantine authority in Italy. So Zacharias was forced to look elsewhere for protection from the Lombards, and turned to the Franks. The pope's decision to appoint a legate to the Frankish court must be seen against this political and military backdrop, although the nomination of Boniface preceded the crisis of 751. Whether the choice of Boniface was made more as a result of the Anglo-Saxon's missionary zeal than of his concern for the faith of the Franks, he certainly appreciated the honor. Boniface first identified himself as a legate of the Roman church, *legatus Romanae ecclesiae*, in a letter to Eadburga, abbess of Thanet, dated ca. 742–46.[9] And when archiepiscopal duties weighed too heavily, Boniface declared himself ready to continue in his capacity as apostolic legate.[10] Pope Zacharias responded that he should maintain both functions if possible, naming Boniface *legatus et missus ... sedis apostolicae.*

The practice was continued by Pope Stephen II, who named Chrode-gang of Metz as apostolic legate.[11] And although the line was often bro-ken, the notion of appointing a Roman representative in Francia became rooted during the ninth century in a regular position attached to the court at Aachen. In this way Rome's old structural connection with the Eastern Empire was diverted and gradually transferred to the Western power of the Franks. It thus represents the replacement of Byzantium by the king-dom of the Franks as the secular protector of the bishops of Rome.

Back in the seventh century, however, Constantinople had no diffi-culty in imposing its imperial hegemony on Rome. The tradition was well established and neither party appears to have contemplated any change. A concrete awareness of this subordination was manifested after Constans II had moved his court to Syracuse and in 663 decided to visit Rome. In ceremonies devised by Pope Vitalian to look as impressive as possible, he was received as emperor and master of the city. These in-volved the emperor's welcome by the bishop and the clergy at the sixth mile outside the walls; probably many of the local people accompanied his entry into Rome, where he visited the major churches and laid a gold silk *pallium* on the altar of St. Peter's.[12]

Similar honors were reciprocated when Pope Constantine I traveled to the East in 710 to meet Justinian II: the pontiff was acclaimed by Byzantine officials in Naples, Sicily, and the Aegean before receiving an official welcome outside Constantinople. At the seventh mile beyond the walls he was greeted by the emperor's son Tiberios, by the whole senate, all the patricians, the patriarch, clergy, and people and thence ceremoni-ally escorted into the city where he lodged at the Placidia palace with his legates.[13] In this way the traditional relationship was preserved in appar-ently unchanging forms.

One factor that was constantly changing, however, was the medium of communication between the two parties. Physical communication had always been a slow process, depending on the season. But letters and in-structions passed back and forth with considerable regularity. By the end of the sixth century when Constantinople had abandoned Latin and used only Greek as the language of diplomacy, it was the medium of commu-nication that became more awkward. Knowledge of Greek was already rare in the West during the pontificate of Gregory the Great. Later, as the Arabs advanced through the east Mediterranean, an influx of monks like Maximus Confessor temporarily increased the number of inhabit-ants of Rome who spoke Greek as their first language. They dominated Roman councils held in the seventh and early centuries, where Greek was the medium of discussion, to the inconvenience and discomfort of some

Latin-speaking participants.[14] But this improvement was not permanent, and from the middle of the eighth century most popes were recruited in Rome from a purely Latin-speaking background. Without skilful translation mutual incomprehension became only too evident, as at the time of the Seventh Ecumenical Council.[15]

During the seventh century traditional ties were strained in two distinct ways, in addition to the danger of incorrect translations: the first was theological and concerned the energy and will of Christ. The eastern adoption of Monotheletism, the doctrine of one-will, caused Martin, with expert assistance from eastern monks including Maximus Confessor, to establish the unorthodox nature of the one-will belief.[16] In response, Constantinople ordered the arrest and removal of the pope. His trial and humiliation in the Eastern capital, followed by exile to the Crimea, revealed that the empire would not tolerate ecclesiastical division.[17]

The persecution of Pope Martin and his legates, as well as Maximus Confessor and other opponents of Monotheletism represents the nadir of East-West relations, but it was rapidly effaced in official imperial circles by the successful conclusion of the Sixth Ecumenical Council in 681. After the condemnation of Monotheletism, the pope's legate, John of Portus, celebrated mass in St. Sophia in the presence of the entire court, emperor, and patriarch.[18] The Latin rite, unfamiliar to the Greeks, was rarely used in Constantinople. Close relations were then symbolized by a special gift from Constantinople: under Pope Benedict II (684–85), Constantine IV sent locks of hair from his sons Justinian and Heraclius to the clergy and army of Rome.[19] As well as designating the city's protection of the emperor's heirs, it was supposed to mark Rome's acceptance of them as future rulers.

So the theological difference appeared resolved. But the second issue, which rumbled on continuously, concerned arguments over taxation and Rome's military needs. In particular the growing severity of attacks by Lombards based in northern Italy revealed the exarch of Ravenna's inability or unwillingness to help. Gregory the Great had complained of the same problem in the late sixth century and nothing had been done to relieve the weakness of Rome. This was partly due to increasing regionalism throughout Italy, which produced in Ravenna, as in many other regions of Italy, a sense of local identity in opposition to Constantinople. Rome's weakness was also a fault of its geographical isolation from Ravenna, a factor the Lombards successfully exploited. So at the death of Justinian II in 711, Rome and Ravenna had grounds for serious disagreement with Constantinople: heavy taxation and inadequate military protection against the Lombards. To these Emperor Leo III then added a third: a new ecclesiastical policy toward religious images.

I have argued elsewhere that Byzantine iconoclasm had much less to do with Western opposition to Constantinople than with imperial taxes, a perennial complaint.[20] Under Leo III a new tax survey (*census*), designed to impose higher demands, provoked armed opposition to the empire quite independently of policy over images.[21] Nonetheless, the rumors of iconoclast persecution and destruction did nothing to endear the Romans to the emperor. In 731 normal relations were ended when Gregory III summoned a Roman council to condemn iconoclasm.[22] This was the event that appears to have prompted Leo III to remove the ecclesiastical diocese of East Illyricum from Rome's control. By placing it under the patriarchate of Constantinople, he added considerable fiscal and natural resources to the empire, notably the grain produced in Sicily.

In the absence of contemporary references, it is impossible to say whether Pope Gregory III used either the 731 council or the subsequent transfer of East Illyricum as grounds for withdrawing his legates from Constantinople. But it is clear that the schism provoked by Byzantine iconoclasm did not encourage the maintenance of close diplomatic contacts.

As a result of these antagonisms, the half century from ca. 730 to ca. 780 witnessed the gradual separation of Rome from its old alliance with Constantinople. The process was propelled by the fall of Ravenna to the Lombards in 751, and news of the council of Hiereia held 754, which identified itself as the Seventh Ecumenical gathering of the church.

This council consolidated Constantine V's iconoclast control in the East, while estranging the West. But, as is well known, it was the prospect of unrelenting Lombard pressure that forced Pope Stephen II to seek alternative military help—not from the Byzantines, who had so often failed to come to Rome's rescue and now only sent embassies to demand the return of Ravenna and *reipublicae loca*, but from the northern Franks. This quite novel development, which coincides with preparations for the iconoclast council, marks the end of the old alliance and a reorganization of Rome's position in the West. Once the pope had crossed the Alps and been welcomed by Pippin, East-West diplomacy became a triangular affair.

This fundamental change inaugurated a period in which the Franks played a decisive role. Of course, they had been very important in the west long before the mid-eighth century, and had sent embassies to the Eastern capital from the late sixth. But the extent of mutual awareness in the early eighth century is hard to gauge. The Franks' famous victory over the Arabs in 733, recorded by Bede in Anglo-Saxon England, was not known in Byzantium. While certain Frankish chronicles of the period employ an imperial dating pattern, it is no longer used by the end of the century. The *Chronicon Moissiacense*, for instance, abandons Eastern imperial dating with Emperor Anastasios II in 715 and later adopts the regnal year of Charlemagne. In this respect they share the Roman ambivalence over traditional dating systems.

On the other hand, there can be no doubt that in 751 both Pope Stephen II and Pippin recognized the political authority of the emperor in Constantinople. Whether Pippin had announced his assumption of royal authority to the emperor as well as to the pope is unclear. Quite possibly, he felt this would be a circumspect move.[23] But there is no evidence that Constantine V took cognizance of enhanced Frankish power before 755. Even if spies had reported on Pippin's growing influence, this could hardly have prepared Constantinople for the change that made the alliance between the Frankish kings and Roman bishops the most important one in the Christian world. And Constantine was preoccupied by other matters, military and theological.

By the papal consecration of 754 Pippin's authority was greatly enhanced, and the two parties were united in the spiritual bond of *compaternitas*, by which Stephen received Pippin's sons Carloman and Charles as his spiritual sons.[24] From the mid-eighth century Rome sent its ambassadors to the Frankish court, wherever it might be—the kings moved from one estate to another—and the Franks sent ambassadors to Rome, where they were impressed by the ceremonial and processions of a more elaborate court, based largely on Constantinople. Gifts were exchanged, including Roman liturgical books, and Roman chant was gradually adopted.[25]

Pope Stephen II's visit also had practical results: in 755 and again in the following year Pippin completed his part of the agreement by campaigning against the Lombards in Italy. Some of the welcome consequences of the alliance were that it authorized Frankish plunder and looting of fertile lands in Italy, although Pippin did not succeed in persuading the Frankish nobility of this potential immediately. At the 754 Easter assembly voices may have been raised against a trans-Alpine campaign. Nonetheless, once the precedent had been established, the Franks crossed the Alps again in 773 and 781 to defend the pope; Charles conquered Pavia and renewed the bond of spiritual *compaternitas* in Rome.

As soon as Constantinople realized that Rome was getting military help from the Franks, it made a desperate attempt to woo the previously ignored Frankish kings. And here foreign policy and diplomacy are impossible to disentangle. In 756 Constantinople sent an embassy to Pippin, which was reciprocated; and while it was on the way back it crossed another one from the east.[26] Clearly, after a period of negligible diplomacy, several embassies were sent with impressive gifts, that included, according to Frankish chronicles, one quite extraordinary object, an organ: *venit organus in Franciam,*[27] something "not previously seen in Francia," according to the later chronicle.[28] More significant still, a proposal of marriage between the Byzantine prince and future emperor Leo and Pippin's daughter, Gisela, followed in a determined diplomatic campaign to subvert the Frankish-papal agreement. Meanwhile Rome was studiously ignored for not taking the imperial line on icons.

If this sequence is correct, these two diplomatic initiatives represent a most unusual step for Byzantium. First, the organ was not merely a most extravagant and exotic gift, of the sort Constantinople liked to impress upon less civilized allies; it was also a symbol of ancient royalty, not previously shared with any Western power. Second, the proposal of marriage offered an even more intimate link, one previously extended only to the Khazars, whose military assistance had been necessary to Justinian II. The Franks were thus promised inclusion in the so-called Byzantine family of kings, and again this was the first time such a proposal had ever been made. It constituted a departure from imperial tradition, an unprecedented effort to win over the Franks.

Now in the tenth century, as is well known, Emperor Constantine VII justifies marriages with the Franks in his treatise, *De administrando imperio*: the Franks, he says, are the only foreign people that the Romans (that is, Byzantines) intermarry with; this was specifically permitted by Constantine I, "because he himself drew his origin from those parts . . . [and] because of the fame of those lands and the nobility of those tribes."[29] However, in the eighth century there is no evidence that this argument was used, and the proposal of marriage cut little ice with Pippin, who could see that within the Byzantine family of kings he would always remain very much a junior son-in-law. In contrast, his position in the West had been elevated by the alliance with Rome. In particular he had a spiritual link with the bishop of Rome, who had become a different "father" to the Franks. As godfather to Pippin's children, the pope had forged a bond with them both of greater meaning than anything the East could offer.

For a decade Constantine V persisted until his legates learned at the synod of Gentilly (767) that the Franks supported the Roman iconophile position over icons.[30] Thereafter, Bulgarian ambitions and the Lombard principalities of southern Italy demanded Byzantine attention, rather than Rome or Francia. In effect, Constantinople had been isolated by the

Frankish-Roman axis, which reduced the international scope and influence of Byzantine diplomacy. This remained so while iconoclasm prevailed in the East; in Rome the doctrine was again denounced as heretical by Stephen III and Frankish bishops in 769.[31]

The isolation of Constantinople was broken only after the death of Leo IV, when Irene assumed responsibility for her young son Constantine and reopened contact with the Franks. In 781 she resumed the matter of a marriage alliance, suggesting a match between Constantine and Charles's daughter Rotrud. The seriousness of this alliance can be gauged by the fact that the agreement progressed from the written negotiations of a betrothal to an exchange of portraits. A Greek tutor was dispatched to prepare the Frankish princess for her future role as Byzantine empress.[32]

But by then Rome had witnessed a major change under several pro-Frankish bishops. Charles had twice been hailed in the old imperial capital as the savior of both Christianity and the papal state in central Italy, while the vigor of Frankish power made a sad contrast to Byzantine weakness. Even though Irene in 785 also proposed the restoration of icon veneration, welcomed by Hadrian as meaning a return to church unity, the pope felt his territory threatened by a possible Byzantine invasion. Disputes over Benevento in the south and Istria in the north prevented any real improvement in relations between Old and New Rome.

Growing independence from the East and increasing Frankish influence in Rome was symbolized by changes in chancellery practice in four areas: in the method of dating and the language employed, in official prayers, and in the coinage. After the election of Hadrian the imperial method of dating (last attested in 772) was abandoned and dating by pontifical reign was introduced. By the end of the century Pope Leo III would date documents by the year of his own reign and from the accession of Charles, a change that further emphasized the departure from the imperial system. Similarly, the chancellery gave up any effort at maintaining Greek. Zacharias, who had the *Dialogues* of Gregory the Great translated into Greek, was the last pontiff with such expertise. Thereafter the series of entirely Western popes had no knowledge of the language of imperial diplomacy.

Growing Frankish influence in Rome was also registered in the prayers said for Pippin and his family and all subsequent Frankish kings. Since the schism had effectively removed the names of Eastern rulers and patriarchs from Roman Prayers between 731 and 787, this commemoration of the Franks appeared as something of a replacement. An even clearer indication of papal independence is found in the coins minted in Rome during the eighth century. Thanks to a recently found hoard of Roman silver, a similar process of distancing Rome from Constantinople can be traced. Rome had traditionally preserved the right to mint official Byzantine coins that commemorated the ruling emperor. By the middle of the eighth century it was the sole city in the West that produced such coins.[33] Although Pope Sergius in the late seventh century had added his own initial to imperial silver, coins struck in Rome continued to recognize the emperor reigning in Constantinople until Hadrian's pontificate. He was the first bishop of Rome to issue a silver coin identified by his own name only. This departure from century-old practice, which had itself been a symptom of past subordination to the East, marked the culmination of a long process of separation.[34]

Whether Constantinople was aware of these developments is unclear. In 790, however, Irene brusquely broke off the Frankish engagement, whether because Charles's formidable power altered his suitability as an imperial father-in-law, or because of Frankish threats to Byzantine Sicily or disputes over Benevento in southern Italy. Constantine VI had allegedly fallen in love with Rotrud via the *lauraton*, the official portrait received as an engagement gift and is said to have wept at the decision. Instead, he was married to Maria of Amnia, chosen in one of the fixed Byzantine beauty contests,[35] and the attempt to win Frankish support was abandoned.

After the brief reign of Constantine alone (790–97), few embassies went from East to West until about 798, when Irene announced her sole rulership to Charles and requested the return of Byzantine prisoners-of-war, who had been captured in southern Italy. This was agreed.[36] One Western source, which may well be a forgery, records another Byzantine mission that came to offer Charles the position of emperor in Constantinople, a proposal not known in the East for obvious reasons.[37] Shortly after this, however, Byzantine sources record a marriage proposal that Irene is said to have received from Charles.[38] If such a proposal really was made, it was certainly a grander attempt to unite the Byzantines and Franks, more important than any previous one. But was it serious? And who initiated it? Historians are divided because the sources are equivocal.

In any case the proposal came to nothing: Irene was overthrown by a palace coup in 802 before she had made a considered reaction to the imperial coronation and the proposal of Charles. This was left to her successor, Nikephoros I, who procrastinated as long as possible, so that in turn his son-in-law Michael I had to settle it. In 812 he conceded the Greek title *basileus* to Charles, who was acclaimed in the Greek *laudes*.[39]

In one respect Byzantine diplomacy in this period concludes on a profoundly negative note: in performing the imperial coronation of Charles in 800 Pope Leo III extended the ritual of Pope Stephen II and his successors, deepening both the ceremonial recognition of supreme secular authority in the west and the necessity of sacral power, that bestowed only by papal unction. For the Franks this represented a triumph, though it proved not to be a lasting one. For the bishop of Rome and his successors, on the other hand, it meant a strategic role in Western politics that became more lasting with time, not less. For Byzantium, therefore, this conclusion of the Frankish-papal alliance was not merely an offensive usurpation; it also set a precedent, recognizing a Western Empire with an imperial ruler, where Byzantium saw none. Later East-West relations remained stalled on the precise significance to be accorded to the rite of 800.[40]

Finally, we must consider some of the diplomatic gifts exchanged during this period. Traditionally, Eastern emperors offered Roman bishops gifts at their accession when *synodica* were exchanged, when they visited Rome or sent important embassies. Such sumptuous gifts might include precious liturgical objects, such as the silver cross presented by Justin II and Sophia, or silks, like the *pallium auro textilem* laid by Constans II on the altar of St. Peter's during his visit to Rome, or the gold Gospel book, richly decorated with gems and sent in the name of the same emperor to mark the beginning of Vitalian's pontificate.[41]

But with the dispatch of an organ to Pippin in 757, the Eastern Empire opened a new stage in diplomacy, which reflects its appreciation of the new Frankish alliance with the papacy. The organ was a quintessentially royal instrument, "an integral part of imperial pomp, its sound in some way symbolic of the magesty of power."[42] In Byzantium organs were used in court receptions primarily for secular ceremonies, not in church.[43] A typical occasion occurred in May 713, when the emperor Philippikos went to dine in the Zeuxippos baths after the races held to celebrate the city's foundation accompanied by organs.[44] Later in the eighth century, Irene and Constantine VI made a victory tour of Thrace with organs and musical instruments.[45] These were the imperial circumstances that demanded organs, complicated instruments that made a great noise to herald the approach or departure of mighty rulers. In Constantinople they were usually played by the Blues and Greens, whose silver organs accompanied most events in the Hippodrome, imperial processions, and other events.[46]

The use of organs in the Great Palace is even better documented in the reign of Theophilos (829–41), who built two very large golden organs, inlaid with precious stones, and one with sixty bronze pipes. He also had a golden plane tree filled with singing birds, whose twittering was operated by the same mechanism.[47] Such organs and mechanical toys were powered by compressed air produced by bellows. Ancient hydraulic models do not seem to have continued in use beyond Late Antiquity, although the principle of the hydraulis remained known from manuscripts.[48] Such was their fame that Byzantine bellows organs were copied abroad; Theophilos's contemporary, the Abbasid caliph al-Mamun (813–33), had a Greek organ (*urghan rumi*) in his palace. It had a reputation for producing music that was beautiful enough to induce death.[49] The association of both organs and other automata with royalty was inherited from the ancient Near East, and was shared by many centers of power. In the thirteenth century Arab models reached China via the Mongol Empire, and Queen Elizabeth I chose a complex sixteenth-century automaton that functioned like an organ as a suitable gift for the sultan.[50]

Byzantine organs were also employed in a military context, where they functioned as siren alarms with a capacity to sound over a considerable distance. Such sirens were used to encourage the troops, to inform people of danger, and perhaps to frighten the enemy.[51] Only a small adaptation was required to convert the siren alarm to a more musical organ possibly with four tones, such as might have been played in the Great Palace. But all these machines were probably produced by a state workshop for court and army alike.[52]

There is no evidence that Roman organs had survived in the West; they seem to have fallen into oblivion with the decline of the empire, certainly well before the eighth century. The idea of organs as musical instruments is recorded in poetry, for example, in the *De metris* by Aldhelm of Malmesbury, or the *Ritmo Milanese*, which associates the singing of organs with the regular modulation of the psalms.[53] But there is no evidence of their actual existence or use. Nor were military siren alarms known. So in 757 Constantine V's gift was quite an innovation and caused a stir. This may be the organ that features in an obscure Arabic text as an instrument that the author had personally assembled for the king of the Franks. It is described as the "great organ nicknamed the Capacious Mouth with the Loud Voice"![54] The text is, however, unclear in the extreme and experts are divided on its interpretation.

If the Byzantine organ survived the mobile court life of the next forty years it would probably have been established at Aachen in the new Carolingian capital, to fulfill a function very similar to that of Byzantine organs. But the fate of Constantine's gift is unclear; it gets confused with other later organs, recorded under Charlemagne and his son, Louis the Pious. The first, recorded by Notker the Stammerer, is described as a diplomatic gift from Emperor Michael I to Charlemagne in 812.[55] But as no contemporary sources mention this Byzantine organ, Notker appears to have mistaken it for the 757 one, or for a mechanical water clock sent by the Arabs. His long circumstantial description has caused many difficulties, not least because if it refers to the eighth-century gift, then Pippin's organ was not only a most elaborate instrument but had been reassembled at Aachen where it was functioning most splendidly in the early ninth century.

The sources for Louis the Pious's instrument relate how in 826 a Venetian priest called George constructed a hydraulic organ for the emperor.[56] An otherwise unknown technician endowed the palace of Aachen with this symbol of royal power, thus depriving the Greeks of their pride, which had swelled inordinately at their control of the instrument![57] This must be the organ fully described by Ermold Nigellus, one of Louis's court poets.[58] Ermold adds that since the Greeks have now lost their principal claim to glory, perhaps those who owned the organs before should bow themselves to the Frankish yoke. Clearly, the organ was appreciated; Louis liked to have it played whenever he entered or left the palace. That is, sixty years after 757, Pippin's grandson knew a lot about the instrument so intimately connected with imperial ceremonial.

In sending such a gift, therefore, Constantine V demonstrated both Byzantine recognition of Pippin as a powerful figure in the West and concern to win him away from the alliance with Rome. The suggestion that it also represented approval of Pippin's rule, after his 751 usurpation of Merovingian authority, seems more dubious.[59] In Rome, of course, this issue had been discussed and Pope Zacharias had given his approval. No such discussion took place in the East, where Rome's novel orientation toward the Franks came as a surprise. Nonetheless, the rapid diplomatic reaction by Constantinople and the choice of an organ as the principal gift in 757 illustrate Byzantine ability to open new initiatives. And even if Constantine V was in the long run unsuccessful, he had the desired effect of impressing Frankish rulers with Byzantine mastery of everything that pertains to a great power, the sophisticated, unusual and incredibly extravagant—"majesty." In this respect, the embassy of 757 set a trend that would be followed in Byzantine diplomacy for many centuries to come.

NOTES

1. Examples taken from the *Codex Carolinus*, MGH, Epistulae III, letter 32.
2. See J. Herrin, *The Formation of Christendom* (Princeton/Oxford, 1987), 374–75, and, on the bond of *compaternitas*, see the following.

3. S. Gero, *Byzantine Iconoclasm during the Reign of Constantine V* (Louvain, 1977).

4. For a useful overview of diplomacy in this period, see F. L. Ganshof, *Histoire des relations internationales*, I, *Le Moyen Age* (Paris, 1958; 2nd ed.), 36–54. **Update** M. McCormick, "Byzantium and the Early Medieval West: Problems and Opportunities," *Europa medievale e mondo bizantino: contatti effetivi e possiblità di studi comparati*, ed. G. Arnaldi and G. Cavallo (Rome, 1997), 1–17; S. Lampakis, M. Leontsini, T. Lounghis, and V. Vlysidou, *Byzantine Diplomacy: A Seminar*, trans. N. Russell (Athens, 2007).

5. J. Deér, "Die Vorrechte des Kaisers in Rom (772–800)," *Schweizer Beiträge zur Allgemeinen Geschichte* 15 (1957), 5–63; Herrin, *Christendom*, 413–14.

6. J. Richards, *The Popes and the Papacy in the Early Middle Ages 476–754* (London, 1979), 293–95 (an incomplete list); cf. Herrin, *Christendom*, 157–61.

7. Michael, the papal legate, is documented in a Byzantine source, *Theophanes*, AM 6207, I, 385; for Boniface, see *Briefe des Bonifatius*, ed. R. Rau (Darmstadt, 1968), ep. 202. See the English translation of the letters of Boniface, E. Emerton (New York, 1973), reissued with a new introduction by T.F.X. Noble (New York, 2000).

8. *LP*, I, 409. **Update** See now the suggestion that the transfer had already occurred by 692, when the Council in Trullo records a reordered hierarchy of bishops, with those from East Illyricum previously attached to Rome now integrated into the patriarchate of Constantinople; Heinz Ohme, *Concilium Quinisextum* (Turnhout, 2006), 28.

9. See note 7 earlier.

10. See *Briefe des Bonifatius*, ed. Rau, ep. 80, 268.

11. *LP*, I, 456. **Update** M. A. Claussen, *The Reform of the Frankish Church: Chrodegang of Metz and the* Regula canonicorum *in the Eighth Century* (Cambridge, UK 2004), 27–28, 267–69.

12. *LP*, I, 343.

13. Ibid., I, 390.

14. For example, Wilfrid; see *The Life of Bishop Wilfrid by Eddius Stephanus*, ed. B. Colgrave (Cambridge, UK, 1927), ch. 53; see also W. Berschin, *Griechisch-lateinisches Mittelalter: von Hieronymus zu Nikolaus von Kues* (Bern, 1980), 114–16.

15. The entire council was bedeviled by inaccurate and in some cases intentionally incorrect translations. Pope Hadrian's letter to the emperors had been abridged and rendered acceptable to eastern expectations, while from a very poor translation of the acts, Pope Hadrian formed an inaccurate impression of the council's proceedings. Neither position was correctly represented; cf. Berschin, *Mittelalter*, 137–38. **Update** L. Wallach, *Diplomatic Studies in Latin and Greek Documents from the Carolingian Age* (Ithaca, NY, 1977); E. Lamberz, "Studien zur Überlieferung des Akten des VII. Ökumenischen Konzils: Der Brief Hadrians I. an Konstantin VI. und Irene (JE2448)," *Deutsches Archiv für Erfoschung des Mittelatlers* 53, no. 1 (1997), 1–43; idem, "'Falsata Graecorum more?' Die griechische Version der Briefe Papst Hadrians I. in den Akten des VII. Ökumenischen Konzils," in *Novum Millennium: Studies on Byzantine History and Culture Dedicated to Paul Speck*, ed. C. Sode and S. Takács (Aldershot, UK,

2001), 213–39; B. Neil, *Seventh Century Popes and Martyrs: The Political Hagiography of Anastasius Bibliothecarius*, Studia Antiqua Australiensia II (Turnhout, 2006), 68–71.

16. *LP*, I, 336–38.

17. Ibid., I, 338. **Update** The account written by Pope Martin in four letters is edited and translated by Neil, *Seventh Century Popes and Martyrs*, 93–121, 162–265; see also the conference papers, *Martino I Papa (649–53) e il suo Tempo* (Spoleto, 1992), esp. Ambrogio M. Piazzoni, "Arresto, condanna, esilio e morte di Martino I," 187–210.

18. Ibid., I, 354.

19. Ibid., I, 363.

20. Herrin, *Christendom*, 329–43.

21. *LP*, I, 403. **Update** V. Prigent, "Les empereurs isauriens et la confiscation des patrimoines pontificaux d'Italie du sud," *MEFR*, Moyen Age, 116 (2004), 557–94; C. Zuckerman, "Learning from the Enemy and More: Studies in 'Dark Centuries' Byzantium," *Millennium* 2 (2005), 78–135.

22. Ibid., I, 416. **Update** L. Brubaker and J. Haldon, *Byzantium in the Iconoclast Era ca. 680–850: A History* (Cambridge, UK, 2011), 84–86. Cf. Sebastian Scholz, *Politik—Selbstverständnis–Selbstdarstellung. Die Päpste in karolingischer und ottonischer Zeit* (Stuttgart, 2006); Zuckerman (as earlier) on dating systems, 88–90. On the removal of East Illyricum from Roman to Constantinopolitan control, see also Ohme, n. 8.

23. On the likelihood that numerous exchanges of embassies are unrecorded in early medieval sources, see Evangelos Chrysos, "Byzantine Diplomacy, AD 300–800: Means and Ends," in *Byzantine Diplomacy*, ed. J. Shepard and S. Franklin, (Aldershot, UK, 1992), esp. 31–33. **Update** M. McCormick, "Pippin III, the Embassy of Caliph al Mansur and the Mediterrean World," *Der Dynastiewechsel von 751. Vorgeschichte, Legitimationsstrategien und Erinnerung*, ed. M. Becher and J. Jarnut (Münster, 2004), 221–441; and "From One Center of Power to Another: Comparing Byzantine and Carolingian Ambassadors," in *Places of Power—Orte der Herrrschaft—Lieux de pouvoir*, ed. C. Ehlers (Göttingen, 2007), 45–72.

24. A. Angenendt, *Kaiserherrschaft und Königstaufe* (Berlin/New York, 1984), 103, 155–63; and "Das geistliche Bündnis der Päpste mit den Karolingern," *Historisches Jahrbuch* 100 (1980), 1–94. Pippin's daughter, Gisela, was also brought into the special relationship when Pope Paul accepted her as his goddaughter.

25. Herrin, *Christendom*, 376–77.

26. Fredegarius Continuatus, s.a. 751, reports: "in the meantime, for the sake of good relations and since it was in the national interest, Pippin sent a mission to the Emperor Constantine." Later the author confesses that "what happened then is unknown to me": *The Fourth Book of the Chronicle of Fredegar with Its Continuations*, ed. and trans. J. M. Wallace-Hadrill (London/New York, 1960), para. 40, 109; cf. *Annales Laurissenses*, s.a. 749, 755; *Annales of Einhard*, s.a. 749, 755, *MGH Scriptores* in folio vol. I, Hannover, 1826, 136–37, 138–39. **Update** M. McCormick, "Diplomacy and the Carolingian Encounter with Byzantium down to the Accession of Charles the Bald," *Eriugena: East and West*, Papers of the Eighth International Symposium of the Society for the Promotion

of Eriugenean Studies (Notre Dame, 1994), 15–48; and "Textes, images et iconoclasme dans le cadre des relations entre Byzance et l'Occident carolingien," *Testo e immagine nell'alto medioevo*, XLI Settimana di studio del Centro italiano di studi sull'alto medioevo (Spoleto, 1994), 95–162.

27. *Annales Laureshamenses*, s.a. 757, *MGH Scriptores* I, (as earlier) 28; cf. *Annales Alamannici*, s.a. 757, *venit organa in Franciam*. **Update** G. Dagron, *L'hippodrome de Constantinople: Jeux, people et politique* (Paris, 2011), 285–87; T.F.X. Noble, *Images, Iconoclasm, and the Carolingians* (Philadelphia, 2009), 354, on the early ninth century comments of Ermoldus Nigellus, implying that with the organ supreme power had also passed from Byzantium to Aachen.

28. *Annales Mettenses*, s.a. 757, *MGH Scriptores* I, 333. See also A. Muthesius, "Silken Diplomacy," in Shepard and Franklin, *Byzantine Diplomacy*, 244.

29. Constantine Porphyrogenitus, *De administrando imperio*, ed. and trans. Gy. Moravcsik and R.J.H. Jenkins, vol. 1 (Budapest, 1949), ch. 13, 70–73; vol. 2 *Commentary*, ed. R.J.H. Jenkins (Washington, DC, 1967), 63, 67; see also R. Macrides, "Dynastic Marriages and Political Kinship," in Shepard and Franklin, *Byzantine Diplomacy*, 263–80. **Update** J. Shepard, "A Marriage Too Far? Maria Lekapena and Peter of Bulgaria," in *The Empress Theophano*, ed. A. Davids (Cambridge, UK, 1995), 121–49.

30. T. C. Lounghis, *Les ambassades byzantines en Occident depuis la fondation des états barbares jusqu'aux Croisades* (Athens, 1980), 152. **Update** McCormick, "Textes, images et iconoclasme," in note 26 earlier, stresses that the sending of a eunuch on such a diplomatic journey signifies an intention to educate the Carolingian princess in Greek and Byzantine customs; and "Pippin III, the Embassy of Caliph al Mansur, and the Mediterranean World," as in note 23.

31. Herrin, *Christendom*, 392–95.

32. *Theophanes*, AM 6274, I, 455; Lounghis, 153. *The Chronicle of Theophanes Confessor: Byzantine and Near Eastern History, AD 284–813*, translated with introduction and commentary by C. Mango and R. Scott, with assistance of G. Greatrex (Oxford, 1997), 628.

33. M. O'Hara, "A Find of Byzantine Silver from the Mint of Rome for the Period AD 641–752," *Revue suisse de numismatique* 64 (1985), 105–56.

34. C. Morrisson and J.-N. Barraudon, "La trouvaille de monnaies d'argent byzantines de Rome, (VII–VIII siècles): analyse et chronologie," *Revue numismatique*, ser. 6, 30 (1988), 149–65, esp. 164–65.

35. *Theophanes*, AM 6281, I, 463.

36. Lounghis, 156–57.

37. H. Loewe, "Ein Kölner Notiz zum Kaisertum Karls des Grossen," *Rheinische Vierteljahrsblätter* 14 (1949), 7–34.

38. *Theophanes*, AM 6293, and 6294, I, 475–76 (two mentions of the proposal).

39. *Annal. Fuldens.*, s.a. 812, *MGH Scriptores* I, 355; Herrin, *Formation*, 466.

40. W. Ohnsorge, *Das Zweikaiserproblem im früheren Mittelalter* (Hildesheim, 1947); idem, "Das abendländische Kaisertum," in *Reallexikon der Byzantinistik* (Amsterdam, 1969) I, 126–69, repr. in Ohnsorge's *Ost-Rom und der Westen* (Darmstadt, 1983), 1–36.

41. *LP*, I, 343.

42. J. Perrot, *The Organ from Its Invention in the Hellenistic Period to the End of the Thirteenth Century* (London, 1971), 171. **Update** See note 27 earlier.

43. Perrot, 169–83; P. Williams, *A New History of the Organ* (London, 1980), 29–30.

44. *Theophanes*, AM 6205, I, 383.

45. Ibid., AM 6276, I, 457.

46. Constantine VII Porphyrogennitos, *De Cerimoniis aulae byzantinae*, 2 vols, ed. J. J. Reiske (Bonn, 1829–30), I.69, 318; 70, 344; A. Vogt, ed. *Le Livre des Cérémonies*, 2 vols. (Paris, 1935–39) II, 125, 146. In the second reference, the imperial organ is mentioned.

47. Pseudo-Symeon, in Theophanes Continuatus, *Chronographia*, ed. I. Bekker (Bonn, 1838), 627; Michael Glycas, *Annales*, ed. I. Bekker (Bonn, 1836), 537.

48. Williams, *New History*, 22–28; Perrot, *The Organ*, 171.

49. H.G. Farmer, *The Organ of the Ancients from Eastern Sources* (London, 1931), 67–68.

50. Williams, *New History*, 31. Dr. M. Kunt's (unpublished) paper on "Ottoman Diplomacy" revealed the fate of this very organ: because of its iconic decoration it was destroyed.

51. Farmer, *Organ of the Ancients*, 128, 137.

52. P. Hardouin, "De l'orgue de Pépin à l'orgue médiévale," *Revue de musicologie* 52 (1966), 23–35.

53. Aldhelm, *De metris*, para. 135, in *Aldhelmi Opera Omnia, MGH AA* XV, 189; *Versus de Verona . . .* , ed. G. B. Pighi (Bologna, 1960), 146.43.

54. This is the so-called Muristos text; see Farmer, *Organ of the Ancients*, 128–35; cf. Hardouin, "De l'orgue de Pépin," 23–28.

55. Notker the Stammerer, *Taten Kaiser Karls des Grossen* II, 7, ed. H. F. Haefele (Berlin, 1962), 58.

56. In this respect it is similar to the Muristos text.

57. Perrot, *The Organ*, 213.

58. Ermold Nigellus, *In honorem Hludowici . . . carmen*, ed. E. Faral (Paris, 1932), 192.2520–3. **Update** Noble, as in note 27 earlier.

59. "Le symbole concret de la reconnaissance de son usurpation du pouvoir des Merovingiens": Hardouin, "L'orgue de Pépin," 23. **Update** See Becker and Jarnut, as in note 23 earlier.

12

THE PENTARCHY

THEORY AND REALITY IN THE NINTH CENTURY

ભ

In *The Formation of Christendom* I traced the development of a division that gradually separated the West from the East. With linguistic and geopolitical roots that were exacerbated by the rise of Islam, it also reflected an imbalance as conversion brought more Christians into the Western churches, while their numbers declined in the East. The impact of these changes on the government of the universal church was profound. From an early date Christians had accepted that their leaders would meet in councils to resolve disputes and issue laws. To the apostolic foundations of Rome, Antioch, and Alexandria, Constantinople, the New Rome, was added because Constantine had moved his capital there, and Jerusalem became the fifth see in honor of Christ's ministry there. Theodosius I insisted on the promotion of Constantinople at what became known as the Second Ecumenical Council held in the capital in 381; and Jerusalem was joined at the Fourth, held at Chalcedon in 451. The bishops of these five sees were honored with the title patriarch, and the rule of five, in Greek *pentarchia*, was later recognized as the governing structure of Christian government. All five patriarchs or their representatives had to be present for a council and its decrees to be truly universal: the dogmatic statements and laws issued were intended for all Christians everywhere. Since Constantine I had summoned the first such council to Nicaea in 325, emperors of Constantinople insisted on their right to order the bishops to gather and to preside over their meetings. This secular control sat uncomfortably beside the determination of bishops to deal with issues of ecclesiastical interpretation and legal definition.

By 650 AD the three eastern patriarchates of Antioch, Alexandria, and Jerusalem had been overrun by the Arabs and brought under Muslim rule, with many defections to the new faith. For nearly another century Old and New Rome remained independent as the pentarchy was weakened by Muslim dominance. By the late eighth century, some Christians in the West also claimed that Rome did not always represent their views adequately.

But the see of St. Peter maintained its status and began to function as a court of appeal when judicial problems were brought to its court. From Rome decisions were sent throughout the West with a binding character close to that of decrees of universal councils.

The problem addressed in this chapter was the replacement of the rule of five by a distinct authority vested in the bishop of Rome by virtue of his Petrine tradition. In the ninth century the conversion of the Bulgars provoked a new conflict between East and West that inevitably brought the pentarchy into question. Although Constantinople eventually won the contest for the soul of Bulgaria, Rome established a new, broader authority on the basis of papal acts now known to be forgeries (the Pseudo-Isidorian Decrees). Christian unity and church government was deeply shaken. Yet today as the Catholic and Orthodox churches seek ways of overcoming an ancient division, the traditions of the pentarchy seem once again to be relevant.

The annual meetings of the Centre for the Study of the early Middle Ages in the medieval, hilltop, walled city of Spoleto have become a major source of new research in European history, and provide wide-ranging guides to the general topic selected. When that topic was Eastern and Western Christianities, it provided a suitable venue for a more detailed analysis of the importance of the pentarchy in Eastern Christianity.

IN 1986 PROFESSOR PERI delivered a magisterial lecture here at Spoleto on the pentarchy, which established a new base for further research.[1] As he defined it, the pentarchy formalized the existence of a hierarchy of five major sees: Rome, Constantinople, Alexandria, Antioch, and Jerusalem, which assumed collective responsibility for the united direction of the entire church within the confines of the empire. The pentarchy had three manifestations: institutional, canonical, and theological, which developed in the course of the fourth and fifth centuries. They received visible force when representatives of the ancient centers of Christianity met to define correct belief and practice, as well as methods of imposing it by disciplinary canons. The first gathering at Nicaea, summoned by the emperor Constantine I in 325, set a pattern, which grew into an exclusive system manifested at the Fourth Ecumenical Council at Chalcedon in 451. Although bishops of Rome remained unhappy at the equal status claimed by Constantinople (by canon 3 of the council of Constantinople, confirmed by canon 28 of Chalcedon), the Eastern capital sustained its elevation, since it was now the seat of imperial government. By the seventh century the pentarchy of five great sees claimed to share extraordinary powers as equals, though Rome always commanded most honor as the see of St. Peter.

Following on from Peri's analysis of what made the pentarchy an intellectual force as well as a theory of ecclesiastical government, I shall examine the fate of both its theory and reality from the point at which he ended, from the 640s until the 880s. This period links the Arab conquests of the Near East, which left the three Eastern patriarchs under Muslim control, with the Eighth Ecumenical Council, the last gathering of Christian leaders to give itself that title. During this period the Eastern patriarchs begin to adopt Arabic as their liturgical language— a change that reflects the permanent Muslim occupation of the Near East and its increasing distance from both Constantinople and Rome. Although representatives of the ancient sees of Alexandria, Antioch, and Jerusalem participated in the councils of 869/70 and 879/80, I will argue that these gatherings marked the end of the pentarchy in its early Christian form.

There are three phases to this development. The first reflects a continuing physical reality as representatives of the five sees continued to meet in council to legislate for the entire body of Christians. The second is marked by the growth of appeals to the other four patriarchs against official iconoclasm in Constantinople. And in the final phase of rivalry between Old Rome and New Rome, Petrine claims to primacy for the first time challenge a renewed theory of the pentarchy. I will concentrate on this phase in which two great intellectuals of the ninth century, Pope Nicholas I and Patriarch Photios, developed quite different theories of ecclesiastical authority.

THE FIRST PHASE, 640–90

During the first phase, the weakness of Christian communities within the Eastern patriarchates that remained loyal to Constantinople became apparent. The impact of the definitions of the Council of Chalcedon only increased with time, as a Monophysite hierarchy of bishops created a rival church leadership.[2] In these Monophysite churches the liturgy was celebrated in vernacular languages, Syriac, Armenian, Georgian, or Coptic, marking a clear distinction from Constantinople. This factor helped to define them as "national" churches in the East, in contrast to the concept of a universal Christendom under five patriarchs. Since their beliefs had been condemned as heretical in 451, they held their own synods and legislated for their communities. Their use of languages other than the three sacred ones of scripture, Hebrew, Greek, and Latin, also separated them from Christians in the West, for whom Latin was the only medium of both the liturgy and private prayers.

In contrast, those in the East Mediterranean who accepted the Council of Chalcedon and Pope Leo I's Tomus, which formed the basis for the definition of the two natures in one person of Christ, remained outnumbered and isolated. Deprived of imperial law, which had previously provided a means of imposing ecclesiastical definitions, they survived, but with difficulty. Arab domination reduced the ease of communication between the imperial churches and Constantinople and occasionally led to persecution. Some monastic communities abandoned their original sites and sought refuge in Old and New Rome; others remained in the East, where the celebrated monastery on Mount Sinai may have inspired them through its successful adaptation to an unfavorable environment. They maintained contact through personal links and the monastic practice of *xeniteia*, which can be observed in the travels of Sophronios, Maximos Confessor, and later Gregory Dekapolites.[3]

All this disruption inevitably affected the functioning of the pentarchy as an institution whose duty was to define dogma and set regulations for all Christians. Yet the first ecumenical councils to meet after the loss of so much imperial territory to the Arabs seem to have followed the traditional pattern quite effectively. When Constantine IV summoned all the Orthodox to assemble in 680, the five patriarchs participated in person or via their representatives and decreed the Monothelete belief to be heretical.[4] A decade later Justinian II ordered the bishops to return in order to issue regulations intended to make binding the decisions of the Fifth and Sixth Ecumenical Councils, hence its title, Quinisextus. This in itself reflects the standing of the pentarchy as a legislative body. Although the lists of bishops who attended present difficulties and gaps are left for the signatures of quite a number of leading ones, including Rome, Thessalonike, Herakleia, Sardinia, and Ravenna, the four eastern patriarchs were present in person and Rome was represented by Basileios, bishop of Gortyna in Crete, who "held the place of the whole synod of the church of Rome," not a title he had used in 680/81.[5] While the ecumenical nature of the council is not in doubt, the range of rulings illustrates the growth of different practices in different regions: days of fasting, clerical celibacy, the wording of certain prayers, and the condition of Christian bishops who had been forced from their sees by "barbarian incursions" (that is, Muslim occupation).[6]

Clearly, Arab domination of the three eastern patriarchs restricted their capacity to represent the Christians still living in the Holy Places and threatened the unity of the pentarchy. While this military pressure was not fully appreciated in the West, in the course of the eighth century the Lombard capture of Ravenna and advance on Rome would bring a comparable anxiety, which was only resolved by Pope Stephen II's appeal to the Franks to intervene.[7] From 751 onward Byzantine failure to provide adequate military protection for Rome led to a profound shift in international allegiance. Through the alliance forged between Stephen II and Pepin, successive bishops of Rome were able to call on Frankish military power to protect Rome. This move coincided with a split within the church over the policy of iconoclasm, enshrined at the Council of Hiereia in 754. The Byzantine doctrine was condemned at the Lateran Synod, summoned by Pope Stephen III in Rome fifteen years later. In this way the political issue of the military defense of Rome was linked to a theological one. Constantinople's failure to protect the Western patriarchate, coupled with its unorthodox attitude to ecclesiastical art, reduced its standing. Inevitably, this weakened the reality of the pentarchy as an institution.

THE SECOND PHASE, 787–843

During the second phase of this process the participation of the three Eastern patriarchs in ecumenical councils was a critical factor. Their presence became a touchstone for the vitality of the pentarchy. Already in the 780s when Empress Irene and her newly installed patriarch, Tarasios, decided to summon such a council to restore the veneration of icons, Rome and Constantinople were conspicuously the only two centers capable of providing a team of theologians and experts.[8] Two monks were pressed into service as nominees of the Eastern patriarchs, John and Thomas, but Alexandria. Antioch, and Jerusalem later insisted that they had not been properly represented.[9] John presented the official analysis of iconoclasm, which was duly condemned by all. New Rome, however, failed to translate all the references to the primacy of Old Rome in Pope Hadrian's letters to the emperors and patriarch. Although the council's decisions met with papal approval, this issue continued to rankle with Rome.

Prolonged Arab occupation of the Holy Places of Christianity is often held responsible for the decline of the pentarchy. But the issue is more complicated. Muslim rule demanded a different strategy of survival in each of the eastern patriarchates, and this must have played a role in their growing distance from the pentarchy as the ruling body of Christendom. Jerusalem, for example, remained the center of the world, represented by the circular shrine of the Holy Sepulchre, the *omphalos*, to which numerous pilgrims traveled in search of relics and blessings.[10] In comparison, few Western pilgrims made the extra effort to visit Antioch or Alexandria. Both cities remained centers for trade in products from the Near East, such as spices, jewels, silks, and incense, which continued to be in demand in Europe. But once trading with the "infidel" had been condemned by the imperial authorities, only the most intrepid merchants persisted. In 829 Venetians removed the relics of St. Mark from the cathedral church of Alexandria, and dedicated their growing city at the head of the Adriatic to the saint, whose symbol, the lion, became the sign of his protection.[11] Any memory of the Christian shrines and martyrs of Alexandria and Antioch was cherished only by local Christian pilgrims. This relative neglect of the Arab-occupied patriarchates of Antioch and Alexandria was emphasized at the end of the eighth century, when Charles, king of the Franks, sent an embassy via Jerusalem to make contact with Caliph Harun al Rashid in 797.[12] The patriarch of Jerusalem met with the Westerners, perhaps to solicit financial assistance and to secure greater protection for Christian pilgrims to the Holy Places. This contact was deepened by an exchange of letters between Alcuin and Patriarch George. As a result Charles's envoy Zacharias was sent to Jerusalem and at the end of 800 he returned to Rome carrying keys to the churches and the city, as well as the patriarchal banner.[13] Accompanied by two monks, one Latin, one Greek, Zacharias could confirm that Christians in Jerusalem were anxious to extend relations with the West, not via the pope but through secular contacts.

EAST-WEST DIVISIONS OVER THE *FILIOQUE*

Carolingian interest in Jerusalem resulted in the sending of Benedictine monks to establish monasteries in the Holy City with facilities for pilgrims. This was the medium through which the creed with the additional *filioque* clause, as recited in Francia, became known in the East. It was this addition that provoked opposition from Greek monks of St. Sabas and strong disagreement on Christmas Day 808.[14] Patriarch Thomas of Jerusalem and the Western monks appealed to Pope Leo III, who reported the issue to Charles. As a result Frankish theologians investigated testimonies to support the additional clause, which was debated at Rome in 809.[15] While Pope Leo III did not tolerate any change to the wording of the creed, and commissioned silver shields containing the traditional text in Greek and Latin for the doors of St. Peter's, the Roman discussion gave greater prominence to the *filioque*.[16]

The addition, "and from the Son," in relation to the procession of the Holy Spirit was to become the most serious difference between Christians in East and West during the Middle Ages, but in these early stages it was used only in parts of Western Europe. Since the clause represented a change from the wording agreed at the Council of Chalcedon, Rome, Constantinople, and the Eastern patriarchs were all united in their opposition to it. Here is a rare occasion when the pentarchy spoke with one voice. Yet even though it opposed the clause, the pentarchy had no mechanism for imposing its collective will; it could only realize its strength in ecumenical councils. And the emperor who normally took responsibility for arranging such meetings was not made aware of the problems caused by the *filioque*.

Debate over the clause continued, however, and is alleged to be the reason for the arrival of Michael the *synkellos* and his two disciples, the brothers Theodore and Theophanes, in Constantinople during the reign of Michael I Rhangabe (811–13).[17] The saint's *Life* states that they were on their way to Rome to inform Pope Leo III of the trouble engendered by the *filioque* in Jerusalem. Auzépy has correctly observed that this cannot be the case.[18] If the three monks from Jerusalem were supposed to report to the pope, they did not take the direct sea route to Rome, nor did they go on to Rome from Constantinople, nor did they discuss the *filioque* issue. She has suggested that they were in fact refugees from Jerusalem, from the pro-Roman policy of Patriarch Thomas and disturbances that followed the death of Caliph Harun al Rashid in March 809. During a turbulent period of civil war from 809–14, the churches in Jerusalem and the ancient monasteries of St. Chariton, St. Kyriakos, and St. Sabas and the *koinovias* of Euthymios and Theodosios were devastated. Flight from the threat of further Arab attacks on the Holy Sites swelled the numbers of Palestinian refugees in the capital, who exercised an important influence and also renewed imperial links with Jerusalem.[19]

Rather than discussing the *filioque* issue, however, the Palestinian monks were caught in the "moicheian" schism, which dated back nearly twenty years and still divided the church of Constantinople.[20] Ever since Constantine VI had divorced his first wife and married another in 795, monks based at the monastery of Stoudios in Constantinople had opposed the patriarch for tolerating the "adultery."[21] They called it adultery because the emperor could not justify sending his first wife into a nunnery, and while she lived the second marriage was illegal and adulterous. After many debates, in 809 Patriarch Nikephoros settled the issue at a synod, which banished the monks from the Stoudios and from the city. Their abbot, Theodore, wrote to Pope Leo III and the abbot of the Greek monastery of St. Sabas at Rome to protest against this decision.[22]

The *Pentakoryphos Soma* of the Church

This appeal to Orthodox communities beyond the empire reflects the pentarchic structure of the universal church, the *pentakoryphos soma* of the church, as Theodore calls it.[23] In this formulation he documents the understanding of Constantinople and the Eastern patriarchs. But in contrast, his letters to popes Leo III and Paschal I use quite forceful terms for apostolic and Petrine authority. He addresses the pope as "angelic, most honored and apostolic father of fathers"; "our first apostolic head of the universal church"; "divinely appointed shepherd of the lambs of Christ, our ecumenical lord, master and apostolic pope, he who holds the keys of heaven."[24] More significant, however, is his appeal to the bishop of Rome to hold a council in order to correct the innovation (*kainotomia*) adopted in Constantinople.[25] In the first case, he wishes to draw the pope into his dispute with Patriarch Nikephoros over the moicheian controversy and the *oikonomos* Joseph (who had been vindicated in 809); in the second, he wants Roman support against the resumption of iconoclasm and his ill-treatment at the hands of the iconoclast authorities, Patriarch Antonios and Emperor Leo V. Although he accepts the five-headed body of the church, when he needs support for his battles with the patriarch of Constantinople, he calls on Rome's power to override decisions taken in Constantinople. His emphasis on Rome's power to intervene suggests an authority that lies outside the shared power of the pentarchy, for it implies that the Western patriarch has superior juridical power over the other patriarchs.[26]

The Council of Sardica in 343 had established by canons 3, 4, and 5 that dissatisfied clerics might in certain circumstances appeal to Rome.[27] And on the basis of these regulations bishops had often submitted their cases to papal judgment. On a few occasions appeals were also made from one patriarchate to another (for example, in 643 when the church of Cyprus appealed to Rome over Monotheletism).[28] So there were precedents for those in the East to appeal to the authority of Rome, which were then used by Theodore. His appeal of 809 was repeated in stronger tones in letters to Pope Paschal I, relating to the resumption of iconoclasm by Leo V.[29] When these were unanswered, Theodore proposed in 823 that the emperor should send representatives of both parties (iconoclast and iconophile) to the first see (*protothronos*) Rome, so that a guarantee of the faith could be given (*to asphales tes pisteos*).[30] The claim that Rome is specially qualified to give such a guarantee implies its superior authority which can overrule other patriarchs.

In addition to these letters to Rome, Theodore also wrote to the Eastern patriarchs and to the lavras of St. Sabas and St. Chariton in Palestine informing them of the resumption of iconoclasm.[31] These letters may have had one indirect result, of generating greater concern about events in the capital. Although the Arab occupation disrupted contact between the oriental patriarchs with Constantinople and Rome, and prevented them from contributing equally to the ancient principles of the pentarchy, the three Eastern leaders were in regular communication. In 836 the celebration of Easter provided an occasion for such a meeting. The patriarch of Antioch took his entire clergy for the feast and the Alexandrian sent his representatives to participate in a council, which produced an appeal to Emperor Theophilos to abandon iconoclasm and persecution.[32] It survives in two versions, one much longer than the other. This *Letter of the Three Patriarchs* opens with a restatement of belief as defined by previous councils, definitions, and creeds. Its iconophile stance is clear from the miracles performed by icons, used to justify their position in the church.[33] Neither version of the *Letter* itself mentions the pentarchy explicitly, nor Rome as one of the centers of Christian power. The oriental patriarchs identify the emperor as the authority responsible for iconoclasm and beg him to desist from persecution. They treat it purely as an Eastern affair.

Nonetheless, the second period of iconoclasm forces a breach in the principle of the pentarchy that is difficult to mend after 843. The central issue is one of jurisdiction. Theodore's appeals to Rome had called on successive popes to call synods to condemn decisions taken in Constantinople. He also proposed that iconophile and iconoclast representatives should submit their arguments to a papal judgment. These become defining features of the third phase of the process, when the two leading sees of Christendom challenge each other's authority. Constantinople and Rome now form two centers of power in evident rivalry and despite restatements of the role of the pentarchy it is evident that only these two count. Naturally, the first uses the theory of a five-headed body, while the second relies increasingly on Petrine supremacy.

THE THIRD PHASE: THE PENTARCHY
IN THE MID-NINTH CENTURY

It is one thing for an individual monk to appeal to the bishop of Rome, quite another for one of the five patriarchs to impose an independent judgement on another. But this is what happened around the middle of the ninth century as Pope Leo IV first questioned the election of Patriarch Ignatios in 847 and then refused to accept his deposition of Gregory Asbestas, archbishop of Syracuse, and two followers.[34] These three bishops then appealed to Rome, citing the canons of Sardica.[35] The quarrel permitted Leo IV to claim that no bishop should be deposed without the approval of Rome.[36] He and his successor, Benedict III, insisted that Gregory's case should be judged in Rome.[37] The conflict was still unresolved in 856 when a change of government in Constantinople brought about the deposition of Ignatios. Photios was imposed in his place and was consecrated by none other than Gregory Asbestas, still suspended from his episcopal functions.[38] Rome was unlikely to react favorably to these developments.

The third phase of the development of the pentarchy thus opened with the elevation of Photios to the patriarchate from lay status in 857, and was marked by increasing rivalry between Old Rome and New Rome. In the West the primacy of St. Peter, which had been inherited by his successors as bishops of Rome, was now constantly emphasized. In contrast, the pentarchy of five patriarchs who shared supreme authority was considered decisive in the East. An additional difference and source of potential discord may be observed in the two leaders: while Nicholas had been brought up within the papal court with impeccable clerical qualifications, Photios was a scholar of exceptionally broad learning who had followed a civil service and diplomatic career.[39] Nicholas disapproved of the patriarch's rapid promotion through the clerical ranks and sent legates to investigate it. Later he also refused to ratify the anathematization of Ignatios pronounced in 861 at a council called by Photios to condemn iconoclasm. He described Photios's appointment as "an invasion of the see held by Ignatios."[40] Although Rome and Constantinople were now united in opposition to iconoclasm, the dispute over the patriarchal throne provoked serious differences. Two years later in 863 Nicholas held a synod to condemn Photios, Gregory Asbestas, and their supporters, as well as iconoclasm.[41] This set the scene for the most dangerous disagreement between the two leading sees of the pentarchy, and effectively ruined the theory of a five-headed government of Christendom.

East Illyricum

Further disagreements added to the already inflamed situation. The first concerned a long-standing quarrel between Old Rome and New Rome over the status of the diocese of East Illyricum, which had been removed from papal control by Emperor Leo III at the onset of iconoclasm, probably early in the 730s.[42] Nicholas raised the issue in his letter of 25 September 860, demanding at the end that the diocese of East Illyricum should be returned to papal control.[43] To this, Photios responded that he could not do anything about Illyricum, which lay within the emperor's authority.[44] The issue of Illyricum was raised at this point because Bulgaria, a territory roughly corresponding to the ancient diocese, had recently come under the leadership of Khan Boris, who appeared to be interested in Christianity. Both Rome and Constantinople wanted to direct the process of conversion in order to ensure the dominance of its own church in the area.

In this battle for the soul of Bulgaria, Photios made considerable progress. In 864 Khan Boris was baptized with Emperor Michael standing as his godfather; the brothers Constantine-Cyril and Methodios had already begun to devise an alphabet in which the Slavic language spoken in Bulgaria could be written. They planned to translate the Gospels into this new written vernacular to facilitate the conversion of the Bulgars according to Eastern traditions, which permitted translations of the Bible. Their skills had initially been put to use in Moravia, where King Rastislav asked for help in the conversion of his people. After some success there the brothers traveled to Rome via Venice, where their use of the vernacular was attacked. In the West, only the three sacred languages, Hebrew, Greek, and Latin, were permitted for liturgical use. By devising and preparing a Slavonic version of Scripture Constantine-Cyril and Methodios were bound to cause conflict, although later popes approved of their policy.[45]

In Bulgaria, however, Khan Boris was dissatisfied by Constantinople's decision not to allow Bulgaria an independent patriarch and turned instead to Rome. Pope Nicholas I welcomed this change and immediately dispatched bishops to take over the process of conversion, instructing the Bulgarians in the Latin liturgy.[46] As a result, late in 866, the Byzantine missionaries were ordered to leave Bulgaria. It was the arrival of these Greek refugees in Constantinople, with the news that some Western missionaries were instructing the Bulgarians to recite the creed with the added *filioque* clause, that provoked Photios most particularly. He wrote a treatise against the incorrect addition, which was sent to the Eastern patriarchs in his encyclical letter of 867.[47] To the serious divisions between Constantinople and the West was thus added another more critical theological argument.

WESTERN PROBLEMS

Further disputes within the Frankish church, where Pope Nicholas intervened as dramatically as in Constantinople, raised issues that were also known to Photios. Hincmar of Rheims was at the center of these quarrels. After a long disagreement with Rothad, bishop of Soissons, over a priest, he eventually deposed the bishop and appointed an alternative candidate to the see of Soissons. From prison Rothad appealed to Pope Nicholas, citing the canons of Sardica, and after much obstruction by Hincmar, took his case to Rome in 864. Pope Nicholas reviewed the evidence and then reinstated him as bishop of Soissons.[48] In his argument the pope quoted from the Pseudo-Isidorian Decretals, a collection of allegedly papal documents, which became known in Rome at this time; they claimed supreme authority for the bishop of Rome in such matters (*majora negotia*). The pope had jurisdiction over the whole church, *judicia totius ecclesiae*. Hincmar refused to accept the decision to restore Rothad and noted that Nicholas had restored the bishop "not according to the rules, but according to an arbitrary and overbearing decision"; "by his own power alone."[49]

The second more public disagreement arose over Emperor Lothar's determination to divorce his wife and marry his concubine. In 863 a council at Metz approved of this solution and sent its emissaries, Gunther of Cologne and Theutgaud of Trier, to Rome to inform the pope. Hincmar, however, condemned the decision. Nicholas then investigated the legitimacy of the divorce and deposed the two senior ecclesiastics, Gunther and Theutgaud, for supporting Emperor Lothar's wish.[50] This did nothing to resolve the problem and incensed many of the bishops who had participated at Metz. Like Photios in the East, they insisted on having control in their own dioceses, and opposed the broader conception of papal authority, upheld in Rome. The patriarch was informed of their situation, which must have seemed similar to his own.[51]

ROMAN CLAIMS

So both in Constantinople and in northern Europe bishops protested against what they perceived as illegitimate papal intervention in the internal affairs of their churches. Nicholas, however, found additional justification for his superior authority in canon 9 of the council of Chalcedon (451). This is devoted to the procedure for judging complaints made by a suffragan bishop against the metropolitan of the province, which should be heard by the *exarchos* of the diocese or the patriarch of Constantinople.[52] In the mid-fifth century each diocese appears to have had an exarch, who retained this supreme legal power. But a century later at the time of Justinian all legal authority had been concentrated in the hands of the patriarch. Nicholas, however, noticed that the Greek words *exarchos tes dioikeseos* for "exarch of the diocese" were rendered in the translation of the canons by the Latin *primas*. This term *primas* fitted with all the other echoes of the primacy of St. Peter, which had passed to his successors as the leader of the church. Nicholas considered that the right to judge such matters surely belonged to Rome rather than Constantinople, although the original text was in no way connected with Rome, and indeed enhanced the authority of Constantinople.[53] However, since the ruling related to appeals, Nicholas was prepared to interpret it as an additional support for his position as the leading patriarch of Christendom. It was now used to enhance the papal right to judge all other clerics, including metropolitans and patriarchs.

In his letter to Charles the Bald, which ordered the reinstatement of Rothad as bishop of Soissons, Nicholas used the same justification. He cited the ancient right of bishops to appeal to Rome, if they were dissatisfied with a local judgement, and quoted the ninth canon of Chalcedon in support of his intervention in the Frankish church.[54] Over the centuries clerics in the West had appealed to Rome for clarification of canonical issues and no one doubted the superior authority of the pope when he issued a particular ruling. These decisions constituted the base of Rome's collection of decretals, based on individual cases and providing precedent for later judgements.[55] Within the West, these were respected and regularly used to settle quarrels between clerics. Indeed, without the existence of a developed practice of appeal to Rome and the issue of authentic papal decretals to settle such appeals, the fabrication of an inauthentic collection would never have succeeded. Yet at the same time, Hincmar raised issues that reflected the growing independence among groups of bishops. This would lead to accusations that popes could not intervene in the internal affairs of particular dioceses, and also that Rome did not adequately represent all the Christian communities of the West.

Such judicial practices, however, were not well known in the East, nor did they apply to the church of Constantinople, which had its own mechanisms for regulating disputes and issued its own judgments.[56] The growth of separate legal traditions contributed to a growing division between East and West, which came to a head in the 860s. Constantinople and Rome had different ways of resolving disputes, although these were not supposed to have any impact on the theory of the pentarchy. But at the point where one patriarch claimed the right to intervene in matters internal to another, the equal authority of each leader of the pentarchy was put in question. Photios and Nicholas each tried to extend his power beyond the established field of his own church, and as a result the theory of shared power enshrined in the pentarchy was rendered irrelevant.

When these diverse elements are analyzed together, it is clear that the central issue confronting the pentarchy was one of jurisdiction. Normally, each patriarch had supreme judicial power within his own patriarchate. But at the very beginning of this final phase, pope Leo IV's claim (made in the early 850s) that the condemnation of any bishop in any church should be referred to Rome, as the first patriarch, leader of all the priests, extended the supreme judicial powers of Rome throughout Christianity. If the papacy could sustain this claim, then its standing in the pentarchy was not merely a seniority based on honor but also on the power to adjudicate across the entire realm of Christendom.

THE CONVERSION OF BULGARIA

This can be seen in the dispute over Bulgaria. After the baptism of Boris-Michael in 864 each patriarch sent instructions to the new Christian leader. Patriarch Photios's long letter outlined the theory of correct belief by reference to the ecumenical councils of the church.[57] This attributes the highest authority overall to the representatives of the five patriarchs meeting in council. In contrast, Pope Nicholas's *Responsa*, which were answers to questions posed by Boris-Michael, dismissed the idea of the pentarchy as the ruling authority of the church, downgrading Constantinople's status because it lacked an apostolic foundation and was not mentioned at the First Ecumenical Council of Nicaea.[58] When asked by Boris which were the true patriarchs, Nicholas replied that only those sees founded by an apostle: Rome, Alexandria, and Antioch. Alexandria therefore ranked second after Rome. Constantinople's rank was entirely dependent on the fact that it was called New Rome. Because of Christ's instruction to Peter, Rome had a supreme authority over and above the other patriarchal sees and would of course ordain the archbishop of Bulgaria. Since Boris-Michael had asked about certain Greek customs, the *Responsa* can be read as critical of the Greek missionaries. However, Nicholas was faced with specific points raised by the new convert and answered them without laying down a full statement of the faith.[59] The contrast between the two patriarchs was quite clear nonetheless: for Constantinople the pentarchy was fundamental, for Rome it was almost insignificant.

The combination of these factors heightened tension between Old Rome and New Rome. The Eastern Church refused to accept papal claims to adjudicate issues relating to the elevation of two successive patriarchs of Constantinople, and insisted on its own right to depose bishops; it was scandalized by papal attitudes to the pentarchy in the teaching laid down for the fledgling Bulgarian church, and by Frankish teaching of an incorrect wording of the creed. From the point of view of the papacy, incorrect procedures in elections to the patriarchal see of Constantinople, illegal deposition of bishops (whether in the Eastern or the Frankish Church), and a manifest tendency to bend to the secular authority were grounds for intervention, based on the canons of Sardica and Chalcedon.

MUTUAL CONDEMNATION

Early in 863 a Roman council summoned by Nicholas condemned Photios and his supporters.[60] Emperor Michael III's reply to this development is lost but it can be reconstituted from Nicholas's next and most famous letter, dated 28 September 865, to the emperor.[61] The pope criticizes Michael's unbrotherly accusations and defends the apostolic authority of Rome based on its Petrine foundation. The ninth canon of Chalcedon is cited to prove that *exarchos dioeceseos* refers to the Roman pontiff and therefore Nicholas has supreme authority to judge any delinquent bishop. He invites Ignatios and Photios to come to Rome, where their dispute can be settled. When no official response was received, Nicholas sent his largest courier to the East: eight long letters dated 13 November 866 are addressed to the emperor, his mother, his wife, his uncle; to Ignatios, Photios, the bishops, and a senator. All stressed the illegal promotion of Photios, his invasion of the church of Constantinople, his illegal consecration by Gregory of Syracuse, and urged the restoration of Ignatios to the patriarchal throne. In the face of this extreme pressure, Photios composed a long encyclical letter to the Eastern patriarchs in which he prepared them for a council to be held in Constantinople to respond to the situation.[62] This letter includes a defense of the procession of the Holy Spirit, criticizing the Western missionaries in Bulgaria who taught a dual procession from the Father and the Son (*filioque*); it urged the Easterners to accept the Seventh Ecumenical Council (Nicaea 787), and informed them that he had received complaints about the bishop of Rome from the West.

Since no record survives of the 867 council, which condemned Nicholas and deposed him from his see, it is very difficult to establish what actually happened.[63] It can be argued that Photios made a personal attack on Nicholas motivated as much by his anger at the assumed powers of Rome as by the implicit attack on the pentarchy. But papal interference in what the patriarch considered internal matters of his own church was probably a primary motive. The assembled bishops identified their council as ecumenical and sent envoys to Francia and Rome to inform Louis II and Pope Nicholas of their decisions. They were overtaken by events: in the night of 23–24 September, 867, Michael III was murdered and Basil I proclaimed as sole emperor. One of the first acts of the new ruler was to depose Photios and restore Ignatios to his see. The envoys were recalled. Nicholas himself died (13 November 867) after writing to secure the support of the Frankish bishops in his quarrel with Photios but before issuing any conclusive statement.[64] Nonetheless the idea that an Eastern council could depose a Rome bishop was totally unacceptable in the West. Nicholas's successor, Hadrian II, responded to the act in like fashion two years later by anathematizing Photios, and ordered the acts of the council of 867 to be burned in public.[65]

THE EIGHTH ECUMENICAL COUNCIL

At the Eighth Ecumenical Council held in Constantinople from October 869 to March 870, the issue of the pentarchy was raised in an acute form: previous councils had not been truly representative and this one had to be correct.[66] This is recognized in an unusual fashion by Anastasius, who translated the acts into Latin.[67] He prefaced the document with a statement on the importance of the five patriarchal sees, likened to the five senses, of which sight is the most significant. Sight is thus reserved to Rome. But all the senses are necessary to the body, and remain in contact with each other through the body, a neat simile for the leadership of the universal church, but a symptom of its virtual reality.[68] The pentarchy was now a metaphor for Christian unity rather than a decision-making organization. In the eighth session the issue of properly authorized representation was discussed and monks who had allegedly spoken for the Eastern patriarchs at previous gatherings were interrogated. These supposed legates were forced to admit that they had participated as individuals without the authorization of their patriarchs. Several claimed not to have signed the acts, with the implication that their signatures had been interpolated. These records of the Photian councils of 861 and 867 were ceremoniously condemned to the flames.[69]

In the ninth session of the council, which reconvened only in February 870 after a long delay, the vicar of Michael, Patriarch of Alexandria, was admitted and his credentials approved.[70] This was followed by the scrutiny and condemnation of other patriarchal representatives who were all dismissed as unofficial. In self-defense they said that they had been forced into action by Photios. Henceforth, only representatives of the patriarchs who arrived with letters of authorization were to be recognized. In this way, the pentarchy would be protected. Elias of Jerusalem closed the session by giving thanks to God for permitting the patriarchs to reunite, but this could not reconstitute a pentarchic quality to the council of 869/70.[71]

The issue of the pentarchy was also related to the condemnation of iconoclasm, which had been urgently pursued by Photios. When Theodoros Krithinos, an inveterate iconoclast, was summoned to appear, Baanes, the *patrikios*, an imperial official, gave a disquisition on the pentarchy as the foundation of the church. He assured Theodoros that since all five patriarchs were united in the condemnation of iconoclasm, he too should give it up. This is a fine statement of the theory of the pentarchy. Two supporters of iconoclasm were persuaded to make a public renunciation (Niketas and Theophanes), and the unrepentant Theodoros was condemned again.[72] The eighteen anathemas decreed by the council of Rome and those against the iconoclasts and Photios himself were repeated.[73] In this way the authority of the five patriarchs was employed to ensure that iconoclasm could never be revived. The acts were signed by 103 bishops.[74]

Three days after the conclusion of the council Emperor Basil arranged a further session, held to receive a delegation from the Khan of Bulgaria. Boris-Michael sent his relative Peter to ask the representatives of the patriarchs to determine the alliance of his church. The papal legates, who included two previous missionaries in Bulgaria, responded immediately that the church of Bulgaria was subject to Rome. But the representatives of the Eastern patriarchs supported the claims of Constantinople, reminding the Bulgarians that the first missionaries in their country had been Greek. Over the protests of the papal party that only the bishop of Rome could decide such an issue, the council in a move clearly planned by Basil assumed responsibility for the decision: the church of Bulgaria was to be subject to Constantinople.[75] Boris-Michael had seized on the opportunity of a universal council to appeal to all five authorities, and the Eastern patriarchs supported his wish to reject the authority of Rome. The issue of Illyricum was thus settled: Rome would never win back the territory removed by Leo III.

With these two appeals to the authority of the pentarchy, its theoretical and real powers were manifested. The agreement of all five patriarchs in the denunciation of heresy and the establishment of correct belief was essential in the struggle over icons. But in reality the presence of the emperor and his officials could influence decisions—as the Roman legates found when they objected to Boris-Michael's request. Despite their insistence on taking the issue to Rome for a formal decision, they were overruled. Pope Hadrian II, however, could never accept a decision, even if made by a universal council, that gave Bulgaria to the East. In this way the Eighth Ecumenical Council witnessed the last moment of reality for the pentarchy. An institution born in the early Christian period had survived partly through the determination of the Eastern patriarchs to participate. In 869/70 they had managed to exercise an influence greater than normal. But whatever the theory of the pentarchy, its claim to constitute the supreme government of the church was now seriously reduced.

Its final ruin was accomplished in 879 when a further ecumenical council was summoned by Basil I to reverse the decisions of 869/70.[76] By a quirk of fate, Ignatios had died in office in 877 and Photios had resumed the position of patriarch, so he was now in a position to restore his reputation. Once again representatives of the Eastern patriarchs and of Rome came to Constantinople to expunge the memory of the previous gathering. As before, it was necessary to claim that Michael of Alexandria's representative at the Council of 869/70 had not been properly authorized but had illegally assumed the role. In order to remove every shred of the ecumenical authority of the previous council, the credentials of previous representatives had to be shown to be false. In addition, Pope John VIII sent instructions that Photios should apologize to the council, which he refused to do, considering that such an action was inimical to the standing of a patriarch. The papal letters were therefore altered before they were read to the assembled bishops. Photios managed to secure the assent of the Roman legates and, the council of 879/80 was duly proclaimed the Eighth Ecumenical gathering, in place of its predecessor. The previous records with the record of Photios's own condemnation were burned. This was approved by all present, including the papal legates. But the destructive actions that were necessary to secure this agreement reduced the pentarchy to the position of rubber-stamping decisions taken in Constantinople.

Even this conflagration of past ecumenical decisions could not remove the record of Pope Nicholas's insistence on Petrine supremacy, by which he had set his own judgment above those of the other leaders. Rome's claim to a higher power of jurisdiction extended from matters directly concerned with the propagation of the true faith (such as the conversion of the Bulgars) to issues internal to other churches. Neither Photios nor Hincmar had been convinced of the validity of these claims, but by the end of the ninth century the ideal of shared authority and conciliar power was so damaged that it could never reassert itself.

CONCLUSION

Over a two-hundred-year period, the pentarchy had lost both vitality and force. The geography of Christendom had been violently altered, as Muslim occupation restricted the three Eastern patriarchs, while missionary work extended the regions subordinate to Rome. A linguistic development created further distance as continuing Muslim occupation of the three patriarchates encouraged the use of Arabic, which eventually replaced Coptic, Syriac, and Greek as the language of Christian worship.[77] This very basic division between the Eastern churches and the church in Western Europe is frequently overlooked. But the use of vernaculars in numerous churches of the East, reflecting their historic development, contrasts with the obligation to worship in Latin imposed on all Christians in the West. And it is striking that this development coincides with the period of heightened tension between Constantinople and Rome.[78] The shift to Arabic is another indication of the break-up of the pentarchy and reflects a growing separation of Alexandria, Antioch, and Jerusalem from the other two centers of Christendom.

Meanwhile missionary activity in the West was enhancing the position of Rome as well as increasing the numbers of Christians loyal to its bishop. The decline of the authority of the pentarchy is not only a question of numbers, but Western expansion must be contrasted with the shrinking of Christian communities in the East. The conversion of Anglo-Saxon England, Denmark and large areas of central Europe had expanded Christendom far beyond the geography of the five ancient patriarchates and had unbalanced the original conception of the pentarchy. As the papacy received increasing testimony of devotion to St. Peter, in the form of pilgrimage as well as judicial appeals to his successors, it was encouraged to undertake a larger role. Against this background, the emergence of rival claims by Old and New Rome took on new force under the personal rivalry between Nicholas and Photios, whose incompatible versions of the pentarchy spelt its end.

The principle of a five-headed body meeting in council to represent all Christians was confronted by Rome's insistence on its preeminent authority as the heir of St. Peter to whom Christ had entrusted the church. Petrine supremacy had been given additional authority by the forgery of spurious decretals. Photios, Hincmar, and other Western bishops experienced this in an acute form as Nicholas accumulated additional grounds for his interventions. The pope's desire to summon a council to settle the problems caused by Gunther, Theutgaud, and Ignatios, all deposed bishops, suggest that he considered the issues comparable.[79] Nicholas certainly stressed the capacity of the see of St. Peter to adjudicate in such matters wherever they might arise. But by lowering the status of a patriarch of Constantinople to that of one of the leading archbishops of the West, he willfully neglected the leading position of the Eastern capital and its role in the pentarchy. For centuries New Rome had played a decisive part in the definition of Orthodoxy, hosting ecumenical councils, which established disciplinary regulations for all Christians. From its earliest days the patriarchate of Constantinople had also settled the succession of its bishops with no interference from outside. For both Ignatios and Photios, Pope Nicholas's claim to decide which candidate should hold the see was quite unacceptable.

Constantinople had its own Eastern traditions, which were not comparable to those of Rome. Among these it clung to the theory of the pentarchy that sustained its position. There was, therefore, a structural reason for the Eastern determination to project the ideal of Christian unity embodied in the pentarchy. But as continued Arab occupation weakened the material base of pentarchic government, even its idealistic manifestations became empty. Constantinople was left with an antique theory, a shadowy trace of a once-powerful pentarchic structure, which no longer corresponded to ninth-century realities. Yet long after the five sees could reasonably manage all aspects of ecclesiastical government and discipline Constantinople insisted on the ancient Christian authority of the pentarchy.

In this effort to sustain an outdated institution, the Eastern capital ignored the serious damage inflicted on the ideal of shared authority by the reversals of the ecumenical councils. The pentarchy had become too closely linked with the tradition of universal meetings of Christians, summoned by the emperor and held in the East frequently under the direction of the patriarch of Constantinople. This was no longer acceptable to Rome and the Christians of the West. In addition, after Basil I no emperor sought to use the principle of shared conciliar authority to adjudicate ecclesiastical matters in the East. The five patriarchs moved away from any attempt to forge dogmatic or disciplinary canons for the entire body of believers, and instead each proceeded to take decisions based on its own needs. After the council of 879/80 the old ideal of universal Christian government declined together with the institution of the pentarchy. The five-headed body of the church could never again assert itself as a reality.

The theory lived on in the East, where Petrine supremacy in its most developed form was never accepted. In the West, however, Pope Nicholas I and his successors had strengthened the basis for Rome's claims to an overriding authority, which developed into an alternative way of ruling Christendom. This division between the Christians of East and West, intensified by the quarrel between Photios and Nicholas, put an end to the reality of the pentarchy in its original early Christian form. In this long history what is most striking is that the pentarchy should have survived until the ninth century, 200 years after the conquest of the Near East by the Arabs. This surely reflects the earliest aspirations for Christian unity, which had become traditional in the early Middle Ages through the system of government perpetuated by ecumenical councils. After many centuries, when Rome and Constantinople took their separate ways, the same desire for unity persists and drives many of the efforts to reunite the churches today.

NOTES

1. V. Peri, "La pentarchia: istituzione ecclesiale (IV–VII sec.) e teoria canonico-teologica," in *Bisanzio, Roma e l'Italia nell'Alto Medievo, Settimane di studio del Centro italiano sull'alto medievo,* XXXIV, (Spoleto, 1987), 209–311, with excellent bibliography.

2. See B. Flusin, "Eglises chalcédoniennes et Eglises monophysites en Syrie et en Palestine à l'arrivée des Arabes," in *Cristianità d'Occidente e Cristianità d'"Oriente (secoli VI–XI), Settimane di Studio,* LI, (Spoleto, 2004), 667–705; and also W.H.C. Frend, *The Rise of the Monophysite Movement* (Cambridge, UK, 1972).

3. See E. Malamut, "Les itinéraires sacrés de Grégoire le Decapolite," in *Cristianità d'Occidente e Cristianità d'Oriente,* 1191–1220.

4. The list of signatories at the final session reflects the universal representation achieved at this meeting: John of Porto, Abundatius of Tempsa, and John of Reggio sign as legates of Pope Agatho; patriarchs of Constantinople and Antioch sign in person; Alexandria and Jerusalem through a *presbyteros kai topoteretes; Mansi,* 11, coll. 687–93; *ACO,* II, 752–65.

5. *Mansi,* 11, coll. 988–1005 (all the bishops), coll. 987–89 (Basileios). A precedent for nominating a leading bishop of Illyricum to represent the pope was made in 451, when Pope Leo I appointed Ioulianos of Kos, to sign the acts on behalf of the apostolic throne of Rome, in addition to his three official representatives. But by 692 the island of Kos, together with Rhodes and Cyprus, had been threatened by naval raids and was no longer able to send a bishop to the council. See also H. Ohme, *Das Concilium Quinisextum und seine Bischofliste. Studien zum Konstantinopeler Konzil von 692* (Berlin/New York, 1990); but cf. N. Dura, "The Ecumenicity of the Council in Trullo," in *The Council in Trullo Revisited,* ed. G. Nedungatt and M. Featherstone, *Kanonika* 6 (1995), 229–62,

esp. 241–44. **Update** H. Ohme, *Concilium Quinisextum übersetzt und eingeleitet* (a new Greek edition with German translation) (Turnhout, 2006), stresses the unofficial position of Basileios of Gortyna, who assumed the post of legate of the Roman see without papal authority, 26–28.

6. These bishops are instructed to return to their sees as soon as possible. Clerics are advised to maintain the faith and orthodox practices as well as possible, but not necessarily to separate from their wives (a measure that is imposed only on those elevated to the episcopacy), c. 30, cf. C. G. Pitsakis, "Clergé marié et célibat dans la législation du Concile in Trullo: le point de vue orientale," *Kanonika*, 6 (1995), 263–306; see also V. Peri, "Le Chiese nell'Impero et le Chiese "tra i barbari"—La territorialità ecclesiale nella riforma canonica trullana," ibid., 199–213.

7. See J. Herrin, *The Formation of Christendom* (Princeton/London, 1987), 344–89; and "Constantinople, Rome, and the Franks in the Seventh and Eighth Centuries," chapter 11 in this volume; Peri, *La pentarchia* (as in note 1 earlier), 236–37, shows how this weakened the pentarchy.

8. Later the Carolingian theologians demonstrated in the *Libri Carolini* that they could formulate an independent theology in response to the definitions of Nicaea.

9. *Theophanes*, AM 6277, I, 460–61, records that the Byzantine ambassadors brought John, previously *synkellos* of the patriarch of Antioch, and Thomas, from Alexandria (he later became archbishop of Thessalonike); cf. C. Mango and R. Scott, *The Chronicle of Theophanes Confessor* (Oxford, 1997), 634. Similarly, the Carolingians were later to claim that Rome could not represent all western Christians. See Peri (note 1 earlier) 284–85, on the role of the pentarchy at the council of 787 as a guarantee of orthodoxy. **Update** H. Ohme, *Concilium Quinisextum, übersetzt und eingeleitet*, 28–30.

10. Following Jerome, *Commentarium in Hiezechielem*, II, 5.5/6, ed. F. Glorie, CCSL 75 (Turnhout, 1964), 56.70; J. J. Wilkinson, *Jerusalem Pilgrims before the Crusades* (Warminster, 1977).

11. M. McCormick, *Origins of the European Economy: Communications and Commerce, AD 300–900* (Cambridge, MA, 2001), 238–40.

12. A. Grabois, "Charlemagne, Rome et Jerusalem," in *Revue belge de Philologie et d'Histoire*, 59 (1981), 792–809; Alcuin's letter to Patriarch George, *MGH Epistolae*, IV = *Epistolae Karolini Aevi*, II (Berlin, 1895), no. 210, 350–51. M. Borgolte, "Papst Leo III, Karl der Grosse und die Filioque-Streit von Jerusalem," in *Byzantina* 10 (1980), 401–7; V. Peri, "Il filioque nel magistero di Adriano I e di Leone III," in *Rivista di storia della chiesa italiana*, 41 (1987), 5–25.

13. *Annales Regni Francorum*, a. 799, 800; *Annales Lauriessenses*, a. 799, 800; both in *MGH Scriptores*, in folio vol. I (Hannover, 1826), 186–80; the Jerusalem legates arrived in Rome on December 23; Grabois (as earlier), 805–8.

14. Herrin, *The Formation of Christendom*, 463; M. B. Cunningham, *The Life of Michael the Synkellos*, text, trans., and comm. (Belfast, 1991), Belfast Byzantine Texts and Translations 1, para. 6, 54–59. Michael himself wrote a letter to monks about the clause, *Life of Michael*, para. 6, 56–57.

15. *MGH Concilia Aevi Karoli*, II, part 1, *Notitia de colloquio Romano*, 240–44.

16. *Vita Leonis papae*, para. 84; L. Duchesne, *LP*, II, 26; Eng. trans., R. Davis, *The Lives of the Eighth Century Popes* (Liverpool, 1992), 219 (hereafter Davis).

17. *Life of Michael the Synkellos*, para. 6, 58–59; M.-F. Auzépy, "De la Palestine à Constantinople (VIIIe–IXe siècles): Etienne le Sabaïte et Jean Damascène," in *TM*, 12 (1994), 183–218.

18. Auzépy, as earlier, 209–11.

19. *Theophanes*, AM 6305, I, 499, notes the flight of many monks, laymen, and Christians from Palestine and Syria first to Cyprus then on to Constantinople, but M.-F. Auzépy, "Les Sabaïtes et l'Iconoclasme," in *The Sabaite Heritage in the Orthodox Church from the Fifth Century to the Present*, ed. J. Patrich *Orientalia Lovaninsia Analecta*, 98 (Louvain, 2001), 305–14, believes this is exaggerated.

20. There is no evidence that the *filioque* issue was considered significant in the capital at the time for the obvious reasons that the text of the creed had been fixed at Chalcedon and could not be changed.

21. On the moicheian schism, see E. Patlagean, "Les Stoudites, l'empereur et Rome: figure byzantine d'un monachisme réformateur," in *Bisanzio, Roma e l'Italia nell'Alto Medioevo*, esp. 438–39; P. Speck, *Kaiser Konstantin VI. Die Legitimation einer fremdem und der Versuch einer eigenen Herrschaft*, 2 vols. (Munich, 1978), I, 251–59, 262–69; D. Afinogenov, "Κωνσταντινούπολις ἔχει ἐπίσκοπος. The Rise of the Patriarchal Power in Bizantium from Nicaea II to Epanagoga. Part I," in *Erytheia*, 15 (1994), 45–65, esp. 52–63. **Update** P. Hatlie, *The Monks and Monasteries of Constantinople, ca. 350–ca. 850* (Cambridge, UK, 2007), 368–73.

22. *Theodori Studitae Epistulae*, ed. G. Fatouros, 2 vols. (Berlin/New York, 1992), nos. 33 and 34, I, 91–94, and 94–99, and the following letter no. 35 to Basileos abbot and archimandrite in Rome, I, 99–101. The title of archimandrite implies that Basil controlled other Greek monasteries in Rome; see Auzépy, *Les Sabaïtes et l'Iconoclasme*, 305–14.

23. *Pentakoryphos soma* of the church, *Epistulae*, ed. Fatouros, in the *katechesis*, letter no. 406.27, and to Naukratios, letter no. 407.21–22: vol. II, 563 and 565; and no. 478.63–66: vol. II, 695–98 to Leo the *sakellarios*, where Rome has the first place, Constantinople the second, and the five together have responsibility for decisions regarding the divine dogmas. Theodore complains that Emperor Leo V has severed this church (in Byzantium) from the other four.

24. Some of the titles and epithets used of the papacy in letters to Pope Leo III, ed. Fatouros, nos. 33 and 34, I, 91–99, cf. nos. 271, 272 to Pope Paschal, II, 399–403, sent in the name of five iconophile abbots: "the most divine head of all heads," "our first apostolic head of the universal church," "who holds Keys of the empire of heaven"; cf. Patlagean, *Les Stoudites*, 441–42; P. Hatlie, "Theodore of Stoudios, Pope Leo III and the Joseph Affair (808–812): New Light on an Obscure Negotiation," *OCP* 61, no. 2 (1995), 407–23, stressing Theodore's terminology of eminence and accolades; Hatlie, *Monks and Monasteries* (as earlier); cf. J. Gouillard, "L'Église d'Orient et la primauté romaine au temps de l'iconoclasme," in *Istina*, 21 (1976), 25–54. **Update** E. Morini, "Roma nella Pentarchiam," *Roma fra Oriente e Occidente*, XLIX, *Settimana di Studio* (Spoleto, 2002), 833–939.

25. Innovation, against the Byzantine devotion to tradition, was generally viewed in a very negative light, for example, in letter no. 33 to Pope Leo III: νύν καινοτομία ἐν τῇ καθ᾽ ἡμᾶς ἐκκλεσία I, 91.11.

26. Although Theodore stresses the importance of the pentarchy for the maintenance of true dogma and discipline, his reaction to being exiled by the

patriarch of Constantinople is to appeal to Petrine authority. But as Thomas Pratsch shows, *Theodoros Studites* (Berlin, 1997), 313–14, there was no one else to whom he could appeal, and this does not mean that he supported the primacy of the Roman see.

27. P. P. Ioannou, "Discipline générale antique," I, 2, *Les canons des synodes particuliers* (Rome, 1962), 162–63, cf. canons 4 and 5, 163–65.

28. Herrin, *The Formation of Christendom*, 251, 254; the appeal by Sergios of Cyprus to Pope Theodore, read at the Lateran Council of 649, *Mansi*, 10, coll. 913–16, cf. *ACO*, series secunda, vol. 1, *Concilium Lateranense a. 649 celebratum*, ed. R. Riedinger (Berlin, 1984), 60–65.

29. Letters to Pope Pascal of 817, ed. Fatouros, nos. 271, 272: II, 399–403. Cf. no. 273: II, 403–5, dated 818.

30. Ed. Fatouros, letter no. 478.90–91 to Leo *sakellarios*, II, 695–98, suggesting that representatives from each side should go to Rome, where the security of the faith can be maintained. Letter no. 271.47–49 to Pope Paschal, II, 399–401: it is most important to condemn the anathematized (that is, the heretical iconoclasts) by a synod.

31. Ed. Fatouros, letters to eastern patriarchs (Christopher of Alexandria and Thomas of Jerusalem) and the abbots of St. Sabas and St. Chariton in Palestine, nos. 275–78, II, 406–18, all written in 818.

32. *The Letter of the Three Patriarchs to Emperor Theophilos and Related Texts*, ed. J. Munitiz, J. Chrysostomides, E. Harvalia-Crook, Ch. Dendrinos (Camberley, 1997); P. O'Connell, "The Ecclesiology of St Nicephorus . . . ," *OCA* 194 (Rome, 1972), 35–36, notes that the text "shows no anti-Roman spirit."

33. *The Letter*, sections 6f, and the long section 7.1–15, the core of the argument, which had a long life; see E. Harvalia-Crook, "A Witness to the Later Tradition of the Florilegium of the Letter of the Three Patriarchs (BHG 1386): An Anonymous Collection of Icon Stories (Hierosolymitanus S. Sabas gr. 105)," in *Porphyrogenita. Essays on the History and Literature of Byzantium and the Latin East*, ed. Ch. Dendrinos, E. Harvalia-Crook, J. Harris, and J. Herrin (Aldershot, UK, 2003), 345–68.

34. It was of course unfortunate that Gregory represented Syracuse, a see in the disputed diocese of East Illyricum, claimed by the papacy but officially under the authority of Constantinople; D. Stiernon, *Constantinople IV. Histoire des Conciles Oecuméniques*, vol. 5 (Paris, 1967), 20 (hereafter Stiernon).

35. P. Karlin-Hayter, "Gregory of Syracuse, Ignatios and Photios," in *Iconoclasm*, ed. A. Bryer and J. Herrin (Birmingham, 1977), 141–45. Pope Leo IV's refusal to accept the deposition of Gregory Asbestas by Ignatios, *MGH Epistulae V = Epistolae Karolini Aevi III* (Berlin, 1898), letter no. 9, 589, in which he claims that the deposition of bishops should in no way be done in the absence of papal legates and letters, and "sine conscientia nostra congregatis."

36. Gregory's recent appeal to Rome strengthened Pope Leo IV's claim to judge bishops everywhere, made in the letter cited earlier, note 35.

37. Pope Benedict III repeated the same claim, and summoned Ignatios to appear in his court to decide the position of Gregory Asbestas, Spring 858; see the references in Pope Nicholas's letter, *MGH Epistolae VI = Epistolae Karolini Aevi IV* (Berlin, 1925), no. 90, to Michael III, 488–512, esp. 500.5–7; and no. 91

to the metropolitans and bishops of Constantinople, 512–33, confirming that he would not accept the deposition of the three bishops by Ignatios, and including the *capitula* against Photios passed at the Roman council, 519–22.

38. The coup d'état of 856 brought Michael III's uncle Bardas to the head of the government in place of Theoktistos, and removed Empress Theodora from her position as regent; see J. Herrin, *Women in Purple: Rulers of Medieval Byzantium* (London, 2001), 226–27. Ignatios was replaced by Photios, who was promoted through all the clerical ranks in a week. This rapid promotion was later criticized by Rome; see H. Chadwick, *East and West: The Making of a Rift in Christendom* (Oxford, 2003), 94–102, 125–33; D. S. White, *Patriarch Photios of Constantinople* (Brookline, MA, 1981), 15–37.

39. *LP*, II, 151–67; Davis, 205–47, W. Ullmann, *The Growth of Papal Government in the Middle Ages*, 3rd ed. (London, 1970), 190–209. There is no "Life" of Photios, but he was included as a saint in the *Synaxarion ecclesiae Constantinopolitanae. Propylaeum ad Acta sanctorum Novembris*, ed. H. Delehaye (Brussels, 1902), 448.19–23. He was the author of numerous works; see C. Gallagher, *Church Law and Church Order in Rome and Byzantium* (Aldershot, UK, 2002), 80–84, and L. Canfora, earlier.

40. Nicholas's first actions: letters 82 and 83 dated 25 September 860 sent to Michael II and to Photios, with a delegation, *Epistolae VI*, 433–39, 440; trans. Stiernon, 249–53, 253–54. Cf. the two letters nos. 85 and 86 of 18 March 862, to Michael III and Photios, which are already much more hostile, and refuse to ratify the synod of 861 held in Constantinople to depose Ignatios: *Epistolae VI*, 443–46, partial French trans. in Stiernon, 258–61.

41. Accounts of the Roman synod held in July–August 863 to condemn Photios, Gregory Asbestas, and their supporters are found in Pope Nicholas's letter no. 88 to Emperor Michael III, in *Epistolae VI*, 454–87; Mansi, XV, coll. 178–86; for the *libellus* of the council, see *Mansi*, XVI, coll. 293E–302B; *MGH Concilia Aevi Karoli IV*, 138–46, with the sources.

42. *Theophanes*, AM 6224, 6232, I, 410, 413, mentions taxation imposed on the people of Sicily, Calabria, and Italy, and the loss of papal patrimonies that may be related to the transfer of East Illyricum to Constantinople, cf. F. Dölger, *Regesten der Kaiserurkunden des oströmischen Reiches*, vol. 1, teil 1 (Munich/Berlin, 1924), no. 301. **Update** H. Ohme considers that the transfer may have been effected much earlier; see *Das Concilium Quinisextum* (as earlier), 208–28; and *Concilium Quinisextum* (as earlier), 28–30; see also chapter 11 in this volume.

43. Letter no. 82 of 25 September 860 to Michael III, *MGH Epistolae VI*, 433–39; Photios is condemned, 434.29–435.5; Illyricum is reclaimed, 438.25–31, 439.2–11.

44. In his letter to the Pope Nicholas of 861, ed. I. Valettas, Φωτίου Ἁγιωτάτου Πατριάρχου Κωνσταντινουπόλεως (London, 1864), no. 3 (incomplete); *Photii patriarchae Constantinoplitani Epistulae et Amphilochia*, ed. B. Laourdas and L. G. Westerink, vol. III (Leipzig, 1983), 123–38; cf. V. Grumel and J. Darrouzès, *Les regestes des actes du Patriarchat de Constantinople. I. Les actes des Patriarches*, rev. ed. (Paris, 1989), no. 472.

45. Photios was very closely involved in the conversion of several Slavic peoples, the Rus, the Khazars, and the Bulgars; see F. Dvornik, "Photios, Nicolas I

and Hadrian II." *BS* 34 (1973), 33–50, esp. 46 (repr. in *Photian and Byzantine Ecclesiastical Studies*, London, 1974). Cf. V. Peri, "L' ingresso degli Slavi nella cristianità altomedievale europea," in *Roma fra Oriente e Occidente, Settimane di studio del Centro italiano sull'alto medioevo* XLIX, (Spoleto, 2001), 401–53: see also Gallagher (as in note 39), 88–89, 91–94.

46. *LP*, II, 164–65; Davis, 226–31. **Update** V. Gjuzelev, "The Adoption of Christianity in Bulgaria," in *Medieval Bulgaria* (Villach, 1988), 115–203.

47. Photios, letter to the eastern patriarchs, ed. Valettas, no. 4; ed. B. Laourdas and L. G. Westerink, vol. I (Leipzig, 1983), no. 2, 40–53.

48. Nicholas wrote four letters about the reinstatement of Rothad, *Epistolae VI*, nos. 58–71; see esp. no. 69 to Charles the Bald, ibid., 384–88, and no. 70 to the bishops of Gaul, 392–400, with many references to the Pseudo-Isidorian decretals; H. Fuhrmann, *Einfluss und Verbrietung des pseudoisidorischen Fälschungen*, *MGH Schriften* 24, 3 vols. (Stuttgart, 1972–74); Ullmann, *Papal Government*, 180–84; Pseudo-Isidore "was to become the pantheon of all papal prerogatives," 181; Gallagher (note 39 earlier), 49–55. **Update** B.Neil, *Seventh-Century Popes and Martyrs: The Political Hagiography of Anastasius Bibliothecarius*, Studia Antiqua Australiensia (Brepols, 2006), 7.

49. Cf. *Les Annales de Saint Bertin*, ed. F. Grat, J. Vielliard, and S. Clemencet (Paris, 1964), anno 865 (hereafter *Annales de Saint Bertin*), 119; Eng. trans. J. L. Nelson, *The Annals of St-Bertin: Ninth Centuries Histories*, vol. 1 (Manchester, 1991), 123–24 (hereafter Nelson).

50. Hincmar's opposition to the divorce is clear from his treatise, *de Divortio Lotharii Regis et Theutbergae reginae*, ed. L. Bohringer, *MGH Concilia* IV, I, suppl. (Hannover, 1992); Nicholas's letter is reproduced in the *Annales de Saint Bertin*, anno 863, 99–103; Nelson, 107–10. See also S. Airlie, "Private Bodies and the Body Politic in the Divorce Case of Lothar II," in *Past and Present*, 161 (1998), 3–38; K. Heidecker, "Why Should Bishops Be Involved in Marital Affairs? Hincmar of Rheims on the Divorce of King Lothar II (855–869)," in *The Community, the Family and the Saint: Patterns of Power in Early Medieval Europe*, ed. J. Hill and M. Swan (Turnhout, 1998), esp. 233.

51. See the appeal of bishops Theutgaud of Trier and Gunther of Cologne, against their deposition by Pope Nicholas, which was circulated to bishops in the West as well as Photios, claiming that Pope Nicholas was trying to make himself emperor of the whole world, quoted in the *Annales of Saint Bertin*, anno 864, 107; Nelson, 113). Photios mentioned the letter in his encyclical to the eastern patriarchs: ἀπὸ τῶν τῆς Ἰταλίας μερῶν συννοδική τις ἐπιστολὴ πρὸς ἡμᾶς ἀναπεφοίτηκεν, ed. Laourdas and Westerink, vol. I (Leipzig, 1983), 40–53, lines 322–323. J. B. Bury, *A History of the Eastern Roman Empire from the Fall of Irene to the Accession of Basil I* (London, 1912), 201–3, connects this with an elaborate plot by Photios to get rid of Nicholas by persuading Louis to drive him out of Rome, cf. Photios's letter to the Frankish rulers (Grumel-Darrouzès, *Les actes*, no. 499).

52. Joannou, *Discipline générale antique* cit., I, 1, *Les canons des conciles oecuméniques*, 76–77 (with the original Latin translation by Dionysios exiguous, *primatem dioceseos*, 77.12).

53. See his letters nos. 68–71, as in note 49 earlier. On canon 9 of Chalcedon, he says in the letter to Charles the Bald: "est multo magis apud Romuleam urbem

quam apud Constantinopolitanam esse penitus observandum," 385.18–25; cf. 392.32–393.10.

54. Nicholas's letter no. 69, *Epistolae VI*, 384–88.

55. Ullmann, *Papal Government*, 12, 169–78, 185, 208.

56. See Grumel-Darrouzès, *Les actes des patriarches de Constantinople* (as in note 44 earlier); Gallagher (note 39), 60–63.

57. Photios, ed. Valettas, no. 6; letter 1, ed. Laourdas and Westerink, vol. I, 2–39; translation in D. Stratoudaki White and J. R. Berrigan Jr., *The Patriarch and the Prince* (Brookline, MA, 1982). **Update** Gjuzelev, as earlier.

58. *Responsa* of Pope Nicholas, *Epistolae VI*, no. 99, 568–600; also in *Mansi*, XVI, coll. 978–1016. Chapters 92 and 93 are devoted to the pentarchy, *Epistolae VI*, 596–97; *Mansi*, cols. 1011D–1012C.

59. G. Dennis, "The 'Anti-Greek' Character of the 'Responsa ad Bulgaros' of Nicholas I?," *OCP* 34 (1958), 165–74.

60. The acts of the Council of 863 do not survive; they are recapitulated in Nicholas's letter to the archbishops, bishops, and metropolitans of Constantinople, which includes the anathemas pronounced in 6 capitula, *Epistolae VI*, no. 91, 512–33 (see earlier, note 41).

61. *Epistolae VI*, no. 88, 454–87; Ignatios and Photios ordered to Rome, 481.15.

62. Photios letter to the eastern patriarchs, as in note 51 earlier; Valettas, no. 4; Laourdas and Westerink, vol. I, no. 2, 40–53.

63. Nothing authentic survives from the council of 867. Stiernon, 64–66, 302, reconstructs the timetable as follows: April–June, first meeting with encyclical letter to the eastern patriarchs for their support in the condemnation of Nicholas; August–September, formal condemnation of Nicholas in Constantinople. Cf. Grumel-Darrouzès, *Les actes des patriarches de Constantinople*, vol. 1, no. 482.

64. Pope Nicholas to the Frankish bishops and Hincmar in Oct 867, one of his last letters, *Epistolae VI*, no. 100, 601–9.

65. *Mansi*, XVI, coll. 129–30, col. 133; and coll. 372–82, anathema and condemnation of Photios, Gregory Asbestas, and all those ordained by Photios; cf. *LP*, II., 179 on the autodafé of the acts of 867; Eng. trans. Davis, 275. Hadrian's letter to Ignatios, instructing him to place the acts of the Roman council of 869 in his records, *Mansi*, XVI, coll. 50–53. Hadrian's letter to Basil I, Mansi, XVI, coll. 2–24, cf. *Epistolae VI*, 2, 755–58. **Update** J. Herrin, "Book Burning as Purification in Early Byzantium," chapter 16 in this volume.

66. Acts in *Mansi*, XVI, coll. 209–550; canons in Joannou, *Discipline générale antique* I, 1, 293–341; detailed commentary in Stiernon, 87–165, with Fr. trans. of canons, 278–99. Cf. a long account in *LP*, II, 180–85; Davis, 275–82.

67. Anastasius's Latin translation in Mansi, XVI, coll. 1–208. **Update** Neil, *Seventh-Century Popes and Martyrs*, 67–68.

68. Anastasius on the pentarchy, *Mansi*, XVI, col. 7C–D; Dvornik, *Byzantium and the Roman Primacy*, 104–5.

69. *Mansi*, XVI, eighth session, coll. 136D–137D, coll. 384D–385C (confessions of the eastern delegates); coll. 135–36, coll. 381E–384C (with burning of the offensive documents).

70. Ibid., ninth session, held on 12 February 870 after a long pause: Michael of Alexandria's letter to Basil I (coll. 145–47); he was represented by his archdeacon, the monk. Joseph, with complaints about difficulties caused by the Arab occupation: *Mansi*, XVI, coll. 143–57, coll. 389–98.

71. Ibid., col. 397C, Elias gives thanks that after so many years the patriarchal heads had united with each other.

72. Ibid., coll. 139–41, coll. 388A–389B, questioning of Theodore Krithinos and the three other iconoclasts.

73. Ibid., coll. 142–43, col. 389, anathema of iconoclasm.

74. Ibid., coll. 135–36, col. 383A–C, on burning; coll. 188–96, signatures; coll. 196–200, *epistola encyclica*; coll. 409–10, a brief notice that all had signed the five copies; cf. Stiernon, 154–57 on the numbers and manner of signing.

75. *Mansi*, XVI, coll. 11–12 (Anastasius's claim that the interpreter was unable to cope); *Epistolae VII*, 294, *LP*, II, 182–84; Davis, 282–85; Dvornik, *The Photian Schism*, 152–54. Pope Hadrian had confirmed Nicholas's choice of missionaries, who left Rome shortly after his inauguration in 867, *LP*, II, 175; Davis, 264–65. **Update** Neil, as earlier.

76. *Mansi*, XVII, coll. 373–524, a full record of the seven sessions; Stiernon, 184–95.

77. S. H. Griffith, *The Monks of Palestine and the Growth of Christian Literature in Arabic, The Muslim World*, 78 (1988), 1–28, repr. in his *Arabic Christianity in the Monasteries of Ninth-Century Palestine* (Aldershot, UK, 1992).

78. Ibid., 22–28, with special emphasis on the Christian Arabic writers Theodore Abu Qurra and the anonymous author of the *Summa Theologiae Arabica*.

79. As reported by Hincmar in the *Annales of Saint Bertin*, anno 864, 115; Nelson, 120.

13

FROM BREAD AND CIRCUSES TO SOUP AND SALVATION

THE ORIGINS OF BYZANTINE CHARITY

✧

In 1984/85 when the Shelby Cullom Davis Center at Princeton University devoted its seminar to problems of charity and welfare, I was fortunate to participate as a Visiting Fellow. For six months I experienced the incredibly stimulating weekly seminar run by Lawrence Stone on Friday mornings in a deep basement room in Firestone Library, followed by a grand lunch. To my surprise, this was the only physical manifestation of the Center, apart from the office of its wonderful secretary, Joan Daviduk. The Fellows could meet informally whenever they wished, but there was no room labeled the Davis Center. Yet the cross-fertilization of different disciplines and approaches it encouraged, the research it generated, and the publications it produced rank high among the impressive achievements of Princeton's star-spangled History Department.

My interest in charity was stimulated by an apparent failure of historians to focus on material aspects of the transformation from Late Antiquity to the medieval period, a relatively new field at the time. Each week the text to be discussed at the seminar would be circulated in advance; the author would introduce it very briefly, since all the participants would have read it, and two hours would be devoted to discussion. Lawrence was a bit skeptical about my paper on medieval Byzantine charity and started his questioning with some taxing issues: the precise evidence for rural philanthropy exercised by monasteries, the exaggerated claims of ecclesiastical welfare in general, the origin of the hospital, and so on. But the lively debate that followed was very helpful to my analysis and fed into the shorter paper "Ideals of Charity, Realities of Welfare," chapter 14 in this volume, which recapitulates some material and looks forward into the medieval period.

This paper circulated in typescript for many years and I regularly received inquiries about where it would be published. After devoting my energies to *The Formation of Christendom*, other books, teaching and supervising graduate students, I'm delighted to publish it here for the first time. But I must point out that it was written in 1985 before the discussion launched by Peter Brown of the episcopal "invention of the poor." While it's clear that much evidence for Christian concerns about the poor derives from sermons by bishops, urging their congregations to assist those less well-off, many stray references to poor relief, help for the sick, aged, mad, and simply unfortunate, suggest that Christians did practice a more wide-ranging charity than their contemporaries. Julian's veiled admiration, "Look how they love each other," and accusations of improper behavior based on the Christian exchange of the kiss of peace imply a determination to include rather than restrict fellowship. Another provocative suggestion that Constantine I embraced Christianity because he thought the church would look after the poor is also too large for debate. Both ideas require detailed analysis, not possible here, which can be initiated using the additional bibliography.

Another limitation of the piece is that it was written before the publication of the *Oxford Dictionary of Byzantium*, 3 vols. (Oxford, 1999), a major undertaking edited by Alexander Kazhdan. Most of the notes (for instance, on prisons) would benefit from an additional reference to this indispensable work. Alexander had insisted that my own contribution to the *Dictionary* should focus on topics connected with the family rather than charity.

Finally, Peter Brown's new study, *Through the Eye of A Needle* (Princeton, 2012), which deepens his study, *Poverty and Leadership in the Later Roman Empire* (Hanover, NH, 2002), will undoubtedly alter and enrich this whole area of study. In an entirely fresh manner, he explores the central theme of wealth and how the church of the poor came to terms with it. His book sets a new agenda for work on early Christian charity.

THE REPLACEMENT OF pagan by Christian "welfare" in the early centuries AD was a long process that formed part of the transition from the ancient to the medieval world. Although imperial structures of government survived in the Eastern part of the Mediterranean, in those areas subsequently designated by the term "Byzantine," they were nonetheless completely transformed. For during this crucial period the established social and economic organization of the empire suffered an almost total breakdown, from which the Eastern half based on Constantinople emerged within new parameters. The example of philanthropy permits a clear demonstration of this process—the emergence of a Christian Roman Empire. My title has been chosen as a crude paradigm of this change: bread and circuses was not the sum of Roman imperial welfare, any more than the Christian variety was restricted to soup and salvation. But these phrases are symptomatic of more than the transformation of eating habits that accompanied the collapse of the traditional provisioning of city. A fundamental shift can also be traced in the services provided by each system.

Bread was a staple of ancient diet. Its role in daily eating patterns may be symbolized by the dole distributed to citizens of the empire's urban centers. Bread was the chosen accompaniment to the basic commodities of Roman diet—meat, fish and fish paste, cheese, oil, wine, and fruits. The organization of grain supplies to meet this central role, from production of the seed, its purchase, transport, storage, and baking into free loaves, was a dominant factor in the commerce of ancient Rome.[1] In New Rome/Constantinople also, the import of sufficient quantities of grain demanded an annual fleet from the wheat fields of North Africa and Egypt. Every major city council had to secure a regular supply, adequate to meet its needs, and when the harvests failed and famine or other disasters brought refugees to the cities seeking relief, it was the officials responsible for bread supplies who faced the crowds of hungry and angry poor. While bread continued to be a staple food in medieval times, after the Persian and Arab conquests of the Roman granaries of the southern Mediterranean shores very different qualities of bread were consumed and probably in smaller quantities.[2] The dominance of bread in everyday eating gave way to a variety of alternatives, though people seem to have wanted bread—especially good-quality wheat bread.

Among other changes soup assumed a larger role in daily consumption. It had always been a form of welfare, being easy to produce, not dependent on imported ingredients or elaborate machinery. Soup required only water and vegetables, which were usually available locally, and a large pot and heat for cooking. The skill of the baker and sophisticated equipment of his trade did not apply to boiling vegetables: anyone could make soup. The soup kitchens attached to churches, such as those established by John Chrysostomos at Antioch, represent a reduction of culinary skills and organizational capacities, as well as a degeneration of eating habits. While perfectly healthy, in fact probably healthier than traditional Roman fare, boiled vegetables constituted an inferior diet. In the hierarchy of foods, so closely related to status, soup occupied a lowly position.[3] It was a subsistence food rather than an elaborate one dependent on a complex process. Of course, bread continued to be baked and eaten, baking did not become a skill of the past, but it did not remain the established form of "welfare."

Whether the corresponding changes in charitable services followed the same pattern of decline is another matter. But the shift from circuses to salvation is very evident. In place of the free entertainment intimately connected with the celebration of traditional pagan and imperial rites offered by emperors, the wealthiest notable and city senators, the Christians invited active participation in liturgies conducive to individual salvation. People who looked for an equivalent excitement and pleasure in Christian "entertainment," may have found it in the funeral banquets and celebrations held in memory of the martyrs rather than in regular Sunday services. Church leaders also provided joyous occasions comparable to pagan ones. The feast given by Bishop Porphyrios for the population of Gaza at the dedication of his new church lasted for the entire week of Easter, in exactly the same fashion as a pagan consecration.[4] But while the formula of not sparing any expense may be identical in both cases, the motives of both donor and beneficiary were very different. In distinction to the pagan, who used the occasion for an ostentatious display of wealth, seeking higher status and greater patriotic and civic honor through benevolence, the Christian stressed the desire for future salvation, forgiveness of sins, and life everlasting in the world to come. Recipients also participated in Christian services with an aim and purpose lacking from municipal spectacles, whether wild beast shows, gladiatorial combats, torture of criminal and Christian martyrs, exhibitions of dancing girls, or chariot racing.

Incidentally, although Christian authorities condemned circuses as cruel and futile spectacles, which diverted from the love of God, the torture and decapitation of criminals in public was justified as a necessary charity.[5] And throughout Byzantine history the humiliation and mutilation of rebels, heretics, enemies, and those who had offended the authorities continued to be a popular spectacle held in the Hippodrome. There was particular enthusiasm among the crowds when the individual was of imperial status or was held responsible for excessive taxation. Salvation obviously involved a different form of entertainment because it was concerned with the future, which no one doubted, after death. As imperial traditions dwindled and Christian faith spread throughout Late Antique society, services devoted to salvation assumed a very significant place.

So much for my title, now for the substantive problem of charity. This is a project conceived in a comparative framework to try and identify specific elements that were peculiar to Byzantium, or more developed there than in other medieval societies. It is, therefore, a very preliminary investigation into what is an ongoing and wide-ranging problem. It's useful to begin with what Christians meant by charity, so the way the term is used in the New Testament provides a starting point. For those familiar with the version of the Bible Authorized by King James, St. Paul's great hymn to charity (I Corinthians 13) established it as the key virtue: "Faith, hope, and charity, but the greatest of these is charity." All the connotations of giving, sharing, and doing good to others appear to be lauded in this famous passage. Charity is the first translation of the Latin Vulgate, *caritas*, which is related to the noun *carus*, dear. But caritas is here a rendering of the Greek *agape*, which is the term for love.[6] Paul is here praising Christian love and is using *agape* in a particular way that is avoided by pagan Greek authors of the early centuries AD for this very reason. The prime duty of Christians is to love one another (as Christ instructs, John 15.17). And not only each other, but also strangers and enemies, too.

This commandment represents a universal application of Mosaic law: "Thou shalt love thy neighbor as thyself." There are no exceptions to this duty, for by loving all men a Christian develops the capacity to love God, which is the highest duty of all. To understand the original sense of Paul's chapter, we should therefore substitute the word love for charity:

> Though I speak with the tongues of men and of angels and have not *love*, I am become as sounding brass or a tinkling cymbal And though I have the gift of prophecy and understand all mysteries and all knowledge; and though I have all faith, so that I could remove mountains, and have not *love*, I am nothing. And though I bestow all my goods to feed the poor; and though I give my body to be burned [a reference to martyrdom] and have not *love*, it profiteth my nothing."

This last verse raises the question whether charity, as we generally understand it, is mentioned at all in the New Testament. To bestow all one's goods to feed the poor must rate as an act of charity by most standards. But Paul is so concerned to stress the importance of love that he condemns this as a worthless act if it is done without love. This qualification should serve as a reminder that Christianity, like all great ideological systems, can contain contradictory positions. Its message is not presented in a series of clear injunctions but wrapped in sheets of allegorical and symbolic instances, capable of very different interpretations. The fact that these may conflict produces a great ductility, itself a tribute to the lasting appeal of Christian belief and its strengths. Christ's teaching was not easily understood, either by the chosen twelve or by later followers, and the meaning of some parables is still hotly debated today. We should not, therefore, expect a straightforward statement on charity, but must examine the activities of the early Christian communities as they struggled to come to terms with the complexities of the Word. And we must

remember that this continued to pose a problem for Christians throughout the medieval period. Prayers, hymns, and stories based on the Gospel
narratives were read out at every church service, a constant reminder of
Christ's original rejection of the world, his espousal of poverty and praise
for the poor, meek, and humble.

Since all their activity was a preparation for the end of this world
and for their eternal life in the world to come, it is hardly surprising
that Christ's followers paid little attention to a structure of charity. Their
urgent duty had been laid down bluntly in the instruction: "Sell all thou
hast and give to the poor"[7]—an act of charity perhaps designed to free
the donor of his worldly ties more than to benefit those in need. But this
second aspect of giving away money and possessions was emphasized in
frequent references to good works and simply doing good. The obligation
to alleviate suffering, hunger, thirst, pain, and distress was closely linked
to the blessed condition of the poor, amongst whom are numbered the
merciful.[8] This quality of mercy is perhaps the closest equivalent to our
sense of charity in the New Testament. Demonstrating a generous mercy
toward those in need was a natural way of doing good, assumed as part
of a Christian's life. In the very first recorded instance of public preaching, the Sermon on the Mount, Christ distinguished the proper form of
charity from those practiced by the leaders of the Jewish community:
Give alms in secret, without show. Pray in secret, not in public out aloud.
Fast in secret, rather than making your fasting conspicuous. Lay up treasures in heaven not on earth, where moth and rust corrupt and thieves
can break in and steal. Ignore all daily needs, for God will provide. Do
good and your righteousness will be recognized, for "by their fruits ye
shall know them."[9]

The apocalyptic nature of Christ's teaching produces an abstract sense
of ethical behavior and ignores all practical matters of daily existence.
The simple injunction: "Ask and it shall be given to you; seek and ye shall
find; knock and it shall be opened unto you,"[10] is associated with a form
of prayer, the short version of the Lord's prayer that includes the verse,
"Give us this day our daily bread."[11] Although this request alludes to the
bread of the world to come, the everlasting life promised to repentant
believers, it represents the same carefree attitude to the necessities of this
life. Christ also assumed that no Christian would give his son a stone if
he asked for bread.[12] Thus sharing and giving characterize the merciful
daily activity of the community, which remains committed above all to
the passing of this world and a better existence in the next. In Christ's emphasis on Divine Providence and the greater significance of the bread of

tomorrow lies a total rejection of the careful Roman planning, transport, storage, and baking that lay behind the bread dole. The same attitude pervades those incidents in the Gospel stories when 5,000 people can be miraculously fed from five loaves and two fishes.[13] Christianity is symbolized by this boundless giving and sharing that will take care of all needs.

There is, therefore, no particular charitable activity that is distinct from the supreme duty to love, for love would accomplish all that was necessary to Christian perfection. In the writings of St. Paul an additional stress is placed on faith; faith alone would justify the Christians.[14] Good works had no value unless they were motivated by love and were generally subsumed into the normal pattern of daily existence rather than singled out. At Paul's initiative, however, one of the first wide-scale practices of Christian charity was instituted: the collection for Jerusalem. In this effort to support "the poor among the saints in Jerusalem," Paul asked those who could manage to save a little to put it aside each week for the Mother Church.[15] The project appears to have come to a disastrous end, in that the arrival of considerable funds, escorted by Paul and members of the Gentile community in Macedonia and Greece, provoked a split in the largely Judeo-Christian group at Jerusalem. The result: Paul's arrest, trial, appeal to Caesar, and journey to Rome, where he was martyred. By the year 70 AD the Christians of Jerusalem suffered with much of the larger Jewish population in the Roman determination to impose imperial rule, and there is no subsequent reference to monetary support for them. The Christian group in Jerusalem disappeared. The organization of mutual self-help and financial support beyond the confines of one local community was set back, though the idea of taking a weekly collection for those in need became rooted in Christian practice by the second century.[16]

In the development of a specifically Christian charity, however, it is the doctrine of good works that assumes a more permanent place in Christian vocabulary. The Epistle of James spells this out in no uncertain manner: "Be ye doers of the word and not hearers only" (James, 1.22). "Faith, if it hath no works, is dead, being alone" (2.17); "By works a man is justified, and not by faith alone" (2.24). "Pure religions and undefiled before God and the Father is this. To visit the fatherless and widows in their affliction and to keep himself unspotted from the world" (1.27).[17] The classic act of charity—care of orphans and widows—is here related to personal perfection, as the two major aims of a Christian. By combining a dissociation from the world with a merciful attention to those with most immediate worldly needs, one can do good without losing sight of the hereafter. These contradictory currents would find their most lasting expression in monastic charitable institutions of the medieval world. But it is important to note that they drew on a tradition that was already removed from the other-worldly concerns of Apostolic times.

Christianity therefore, presented a series of highly contrasting attitudes toward the problems of daily existence before the *Parousia* or Second Coming. The exaltation of poverty and the needs of the church; the universal duty to give and the worthiness of recipients;[18] the obligation to give with love and the need for good works;[19] and debate over the best use of resources, for instance in Mary's extravagant consumption of precious ointment for the anointment of Christ.[20] As Peter Brown has so eloquently described it, the *lithomania* (passion for stone) of many church leaders frequently resulted in buildings,[21] though there was never a shortage of opponents who condemned the use of gold and silver and urged that finely decorated hangings and altar cloths should be used as shrouds for the poor.[22] The fact that these fundamental problems continued to be discussed with such passion is a remarkable testimony to the variety within Christian ideology and some sophistication in the arguments. In reading the texts it is impossible not to notice a persistent tension and anxiety that can be seen in the parable of the rich man and the camel's inability to pass through the eye of a needle.

In the development of Byzantine charity three stages may be traced: the first, from Apostolic times to the ending of imperial persecution (313); the second, from the endowments of Constantine I, the first Christian emperor, to those of Justinian (527–65); and a third, from the Christian patronage of Justin II (565–78) to that of Herakleios (610–41), a transitional phase in which the basic components of a medieval system become evident. I will then look forward to single out features that characterise Byzantine charity in its most developed medieval form.

In the earliest period groups of Christians, small in the first century AD but growing continuously, tried to live their lives in accordance with what they knew of Christ's teaching. The self-definition of these groups took place against a backdrop of the high point of Roman imperialism, under the shadow of an apparently omnipotent pagan administration. Although at first indifferent to the Christians, imperial officials could not ignore the spread of a faith which claimed a moral superiority and universal character. Conversely, despite Christ's order to render to Caesar what is Caesar's, the Christians could not continue to participate in emperor-worship, animal sacrifice, augury and associated pagan rituals.

In these circumstances the communities developed a theory and practice of charity that set them apart in the Roman world. They elevated poverty to an exalted position and singled out the poor—very broadly defined as all those in need (*deomenoi*)—as particularly deserving.[23] Through the efforts of early Christian writers, especially Sts. Clement of Alexandria (died about 215) and Cyprian of Carthage (died 258), the rich were not inevitably condemned because of their wealth.[24] A concept of social justice that created greater equality between rich and poor would also permit those with inherited fortunes to renounce luxury, avarice, and extravagant display of wealth by acts of generosity, which redistributed it to those in need. The correct use of riches would enable the wealthy to become poor in spirit. If they were truly repentant they would then be able to enter the kingdom of heaven. Wealth, like all otherworldly things, was a gift of God to be used in imitation of God rather than for personal satisfaction.[25]

In practice, this compromise meant that the Christian communities were able to offer a radically different conception of charity from that used by pagan benefactors and civic authorities.[26] In place of the distribution of foodstuffs, free bread, clothing. and coin, to the registered citizens of Roman cities—generally male freeholders, not those in need—Christians developed the duty to assist the weak, sick, poor, and humble, those singled out by Christ in the Sermon on the Mount. Households were instructed to look after travelers, strangers, beggars, and the destitute, and the elders, presbyters and bishops of every community were expected to take particular care of the fatherless; those taken captive, imprisoned, or condemned to hard labor; victims of shipwreck or other natural disasters.[27] All who had fallen on hard times and could no longer support themselves, especially poor unmarried women and prostitutes, were to be helped. This radical shift in focus made charity an instrument of real assistance to a new constituency.

Among additional services the obligation to provide Christian burial to all believers led to the growth of special graveyards maintained by the community. Inhumation represented a departure from ancient traditions of mummification or burning the dead on a funeral pyre. Although the catacombs outside Rome are justly famous, many other Mediterranean cities had similar burial grounds where the dead were commemorated with annual services and banquets. These created an opportunity to celebrate at tombs. During periods of imperial persecution the Roman authorities made a point of burning the bodies of martyrs to prevent their supporters from creating special tombs, marking their sacrifice, which could become Christian shrines. In 356 St. Antony made his two companions swear to bury him in an unidentified grave in the desert, to spare him the humiliation of traditional mummification, which would have preserved his body as a focus of devotion.[28]

Although it is difficult to evaluate the efficiency of Christian charity in the early period, pagan as well as Christian authors commented on an entirely new spirit amongst the faithful and attributed it to their brotherly love.[29] The involvement of widows in visiting and nursing the sick; the use of Christian funds to redeem prisoners; the provision of shrouds for the poor and a concern for the outcast of society, those who suffered from leprosy or madness, seem to have been notable features of this novel Christian practice. Mutual self-help and support among Christian households was extended to care for victims of persecution.[30] Under the most severe pressures many gave in, handed over their Christian Scriptures and again took part in pagan rituals (emperor worship was the key element). As lapsed Christians there was considerable disagreement about their status within the community, but they were usually readmitted.[31] Some groups emerged from persecution strengthened, taking pride in their local heroes and celebrating their resistance to imperial pressure in additional services of commemoration.

Before the time of his own martyrdom in 258 Cyprian had already established a hierarchy of honor among Christians, reserving the purple crown for those who died for the faith, in contrast to the white crown bestowed on those who did good works.[32] All could aspire to the latter but only a few could gain the former. Similarly it had become evident that the commitment to total poverty in imitation of Christ was reserved to a few, who abandoned the civilized world for a precarious existence in the wilderness.[33] Their struggle against all forms of temptation, as the athletes of God, was an individual one, which could not be realized by all Christians. Instead, the majority of believers brought their offerings to Sunday services and gave or bequeathed their wealth to the church for use among the poor.[34]

Those chosen as bishops were often members of the intellectual élite who considered it appropriate to dispose of their worldly goods and establish funds dedicated to charitable purposes before assuming the post. By redistributing their wealth they sought to remedy the inequality of rich and poor. And they must have had some success if the claim that 1,500 widows and other poor people were supported by the church of Rome in the mid-third century is correct.[35] Since impoverished women had no place in the city's list of those eligible for free bread it was a completely new category of poor who were assisted by the church. In what was still a minority group in the polytheistic Roman world, the

Christians were developing different objectives and novel methods of delivering charity.

In the second period in this process, from the early fourth to the mid-sixth century, Christian efforts toward poor relief were institutionalized under imperial patronage. Constantine I's decision to guarantee freedom from persecution by the so-called Edict of Milan (313) revolutionized the position of the Christians. Like other sects they could now celebrate their faith openly and could develop a public ritual appropriate to their belief. The physical presence of Christianity in late Roman society was altered almost overnight by the emperor's support. In the ancient capital itself the Lateran Palace was transferred from imperial ownership to the church of Rome and became the residence of the bishop.[36] Additional endowments, not only at Rome but in many other important centers, exemplified this initiative and established a pattern and scale of giving which Christians could follow and improve on. Finally, Constantine reformed the legal mechanism for making gifts, which facilitated the accumulation of wealth by Christian institutions.[37]

In the city of Constantine, Constantinople, also called New Rome, which was refounded in 330 AD, the emperor endowed monuments considered essential to an imperial metropolis: a much expanded Hippodrome; an oval-shaped Forum; numerous stoas, baths, foundations, and colonnaded streets, all decorated with ancient statuary removed from other cities, and enclosed within new city walls. He set aside funds to establish free bread for the citizens (free male inhabitants) and constructed homes for the aged and the poor. But he was also the first emperor to build churches and to erect crosses, which guaranteed an overt Christian presence in the city.[38] His son Constantius II completed the original Hagia Sophia, which was dedicated in 360 with gifts of golden and silver liturgical plate, gold-threaded altar cloths, and curtains. The emperor made donations to all the clergy, the order of virgins and widows, the hospices, including beggars, orphans, and prisoners, and also established the leprosarium of St. Zotikos.[39]

The inauguration ceremonies that celebrated the foundation of Constantinople confirmed this mixture of traditional and novel:[40] the emperor's statue (a reused pagan one, possibly of Apollo) was escorted into the new Forum, raised on a column, and acclaimed by all the people. Christian priests accompanied the procession and organized the chanting of "Kyrie eleison" (Lord have mercy) at important moments. Another imperial statue holding a small statue of the Tyche of the city (a symbol of good fortune) was carried in procession to the Hippodrome, where it too was acclaimed. Again, priests provided their own blessing for the new city and prayed for its heavenly protection: "O Lord, set it on a favorable course for boundless ages." A festival lasting forty days was declared; the emperor distributed gifts of corn, paid for chariot racing in the Hippodrome, and instituted the birthday celebrations as an annual event.[41] Later writers, both pagan and Christian, record the event in their own terms, suggesting that memories of the inauguration were mixed; but as Constantinople grew in importance both tried to claim predominance and responsibility.

In one particular respect Constantine recognized the importance of Christian observance in his new capital: officials of the church of St. Sophia (Holy Wisdom, later known as the Great Church) were put in charge of burials. The task of providing graves and burying the dead was a public service performed by a corporation (*philiakon*). The emperor's innovation lay in the assignment of state taxes from 950 workshops in the city, paid directly to the church which supervised the service.[42] Giving the Christian authorities responsibility for burial was highly significant. In the late fifth or early sixth century the arrangement was confirmed by Emperor Anastasios, who added funds including the taxes of a further 150 shops, to make it a free service. These shops were exempt from all other public taxes and duties relating to city maintenance, an exemption which different institutions often sought obtain by fraud and corruption.[43] Free burial was further expanded by Justinian, who also specified how the administrators of the great Church were to divide the monies and stipulated that they had to pay interest if the funds were not handed over by the correct date. The system was also extended to major hospitals in the capital. In Ephesos clerics attached to the church of the Virgin were responsible for a similar system.[44]

This was perhaps the first example of imperial and ecclesiastical cooperation in charitable activities, an arrangement that was to become more and more common as Christian influence increased. In addition to the customary charities provided, quite separately, by city councils, individual patrons and churches, emperors instituted a new form of public beneficence: permanent institutions for those in need financed by imperial funds and administered by the Christian hierarchy of bishops. Financial support came initially from state taxes, as in the case of burial and other public services of Constantinople; it might also be derived from landed estates and property belonging to pagan temples that were confiscated, or from rents or revenues on state and imperial properties. Further funding came from the private treasuries of the emperor and empress, and their personal family wealth.[45] In the middle of the fifth century Empress Pulcheria and her husband Marcian were responsible for many charitable endowments, one of which was based on confiscated pagan property: a temple on the ancient acropolis of Constantinople was converted to a hostel, the *xenon* of Marcian.[46] While many temples were turned into churches and their endowments transferred to Christian control, all the property devoted to the cults of the ancient gods was subject to imperial confiscation and the traditional resources of the pagans were gradually reduced. In 529 Justinian ordered the closure of the Platonic Academy in Athens, and the last teachers left for Persia.[47]

This transformation in the economic and social conditions of the Christian communities demanded a reconsideration of the basic problems raised by Christ's exaltation of poverty. In place of a daily preparation for the Second Coming, Christians found that measures for their survival in the present were now supported by the Caesars. Instead of being outsiders, they gradually became incorporated as worthy members of imperial society.[48] The response of the Cappadocian Fathers of the fourth century, St. Basil, bishop of Caesarea, his brother St. Gregory of Nyssa, and friend St. Gregory of Nazianzos, stressed the necessity of social justice and equality among Christians, while establishing permanent institutions of charity that were open to all. In their writings they elaborated the theory, which was put into effect in their charitable activity.[49] Basil in particular, combined a literary skill, evident in his numerous sermons as well as his version of the Byzantine liturgy, with a determination to provide for the sick and needy. He and his brother Gregory and sister Macrina had already decided to devote their inheritance to monasteries, in which they lived, a common procedure among devout Christians.[50] In about 372, however, Basil set up a large philanthropic institution outside Caesarea that became known as the New City. It included a hospital and a special refuge for lepers, apparently funded by his appeals to rich local landowners.[51] From an ad hoc and quite inadequate arrangement of care for those with disabling and infectious diseases, a regular and systematic service was created, staffed by doctors and monks from Basil's religious foundations. Since Caesarea lay at the intersection of several major routes across Asia Minor, a hospice for travelers was also provided; there was a house for the poor (*ptocheion*), and probably other residential quarters for old people, orphans, and abandoned children or destitute women— these being the categories of people most frequently in need.[52]

Unfortunately it is extremely difficult to document these institutions and the precise mechanisms whereby they functioned. While Basil's contemporaries extolled his New City, no records relating to its foundation have survived. This brings us to a fundamental problem for all students of Byzantine social history, namely, the lack of archival material, which would provide evidence of the aims, methods of funding, intended scope, and administration of particular philanthropic institutions. Foundation charters survive from later periods.[53] From the fourth to sixth centuries legal provisions state what should be the case and often give detailed accounts of imperial intention. Hagiographic records and inscriptions provide useful but generally limited information. So we are often dependent on stray references in a variety of written sources, and rarely learn anything specific about the actual practice of charity, the numbers fed and clothed, by whom and on what occasions. For Basil's famous establishment our information is largely derived from his Funeral Oration pronounced by Gregory of Nazianzos and the Encomium by Gregory of Nyssa.[54] These rhetorical panegyrics tend to exaggerate the brilliance of the founder at the expense of detailed evidence. The New City was probably financed from funds accumulated by the church of Caesarea as well as from Basil's personal resources; but it is impossible to tell what proportion may have been donated by the laity.

While these new public forms of Christian charity spread rapidly to other cities in the fourth century, the Roman bread and circuses tradition was maintained. City councils also continued to provide facilities for their inhabitants, such as clean water supplies, baths and hostels, as well as repairing roads, bridges, and city walls. Individual senators added their own grand donations for specific ceremonies, whether racing in the Hippodrome or theatrical shows, and frequently constructed public utilities and monuments for their own glory, or simply erected statues of themselves as benefactors.[55] A continuous flow of inscriptions reveals no let-up in this tradition in the East Mediterranean through the fifth century, but it is matched by the steady growth of churches, silver altar vessels, silk curtains, and other furniture often labeled with the names of the donors.[56] The two systems of charity competed for the loyalty of citizens, and the fundamental difference between them may be symbolized by John Chrysostomos's stress on the category of the deserving poor of Antioch and their complete absence from the writings of his contemporary Libanius.[57]

The results of Christian charity became particularly visible in centers of Christian pilgrimage, such as Jerusalem, for instance, where Constantine I created imperial foundations, beginning with his lavish building over the Holy Sepulchre. His mother, Helena, was also active in Jerusalem, as was Eudokia, the wife of Theodosios II, who founded an old people's home (*gerokomeion*), several poor houses (*ptocheia*) and hospices for travelers (*xenodocheia*), as well as a special hospital for up to 400 epileptics.[58] In the following century at the request of St. Sabas, Justinian provided medical care for the poor in the form of two *xenodocheia*, next to the church of the Virgin. One of these was later expanded to 200 beds, financed by an annual revenue of 1,850 gold coins. It was presumably run by the monks of St. Sabas monastery, who also maintained the numerous *xenodocheia* established by the saint, two at Jericho, four at or near his monastery outside Jerusalem, and another inside the city.[59] These monastic institutions were independent, self-governing bodies.

Most charitable foundations in Jerusalem, however, were supervised by the bishop, who took responsibility for the city's pilgrim hostels and medical centers, which included one specifically for the blind (*typhlokomeion*) in which local women nursed.[60] This duty was such a heavy burden that in 536 the church of the Holy Sepulchre appealed to Justinian to exempt it from the law prohibiting the sale of church property. The community wanted to sell certain buildings in order to increase its revenue (presumably to finance services in the hospital). In reply the emperor ruled that the Holy Sepulchre could sell houses as long as the price so realized was equivalent to fifty years' rent. Those who purchased would gain full rights to the buildings but were obliged to bequeath them to the church at their death.[61] The principle that ecclesiastical property could not be alienated was thus maintained.

Figures for the endowments of these imperial foundations are rare: at Antioch Justinian's *xenodocheion* had an annual revenue of 4,000 gold coins.[62] But usually the sources refer simply to a plentiful income or generous funding, which might include clothing for the inmates.[63] In cities charitable houses competed with municipal services and private benefactions; in the countryside they were often attached to particular shrines. At Pythia, in western Asia Minor, hot springs provided a natural cure to which Justinian added a hospital and a church.[64] Churches with miracle-working relics or icons, such as those at Germia or Sozopolis, also attracted pilgrims, so hostels and hospitals were often built there. But there is less evidence of imperial patronage at rural sites where local monasteries and bishops provided more aid for the destitute. Monastic definitions of charitable activity were profoundly influential in Byzantium.[65]

In the countryside rural monasteries appear to have been the focus of local charities, *diakoniai*, devoted to the poor.[66] In the fifth century John Cassian observed the participation of lay groups, who arranged for produce to be brought to Egyptian monasteries, where it was distributed. Most well-endowed establishments provided food and shelter, maintained some form of medical care, and also looked after the aged. *Gerokomeia* were often founded for elderly monks when they could no longer participate in the regular monastic routine. The laity might assist in running these homes and in serving in hospitals. But most of the evidence for lay involvement in charitable work comes from cities, where groups called *spoudaioi* (zealous Christians) or *philoponoi* (those who take pains, who love caring) were dedicated to good works.[67] Men and women were admitted and donated money to these celibate organizations of Christian charity, some of which observed a quasi-monastic discipline. They met in the evening and cared for the destitute, washing the sick and preparing the dead for burial. These appear to have been common tasks undertaken by *philoponiai* in Antioch and *diakoniai* in Constantinople. In Jerusalem the *spoudaioi* were closely associated with the church of the Anastasis (Resurrection) and performed similar tasks.[68] Everywhere the washing of sick people was considered particularly suitable for such people, which created a firm association with baths. The task combined Christ's example in washing the feet of the Apostles (which later became an imperial ritual) with ecclesiastical distrust of the pagan culture intimately linked to bathing. An alternative form of cleanliness was regularly urged on Christians and is evident in the *diakoniai* set up in Rome in the late seventh century.[69] Not only was abundant water supplied and soap distributed free at Christmas and Easter, but pilgrims using these hostels were ordered to wash as a condition of receiving free food. Since this Western institution derived from the East, the association of washing with charity may be similarly connected with practices in the major cities of the Eastern Mediterranean.

In Egypt, where *philoponoi* are well documented from the fourth century onward, they gained an established place in the local church and participated in all ecclesiastical rituals.[70] They may also have been attached to the estates of great landowners, performing the same sort of tasks among the destitute who sought assistance from rich lay patrons in the countryside. Papyri illustrate the integration of lay workers into the staff of a bishop or magnate.[71] Like all ancillary helpers, the women who looked after widows, artisans responsible for construction work, those who rowed the administrator's boats, carried his correspondence and looked after his flocks, they benefited from annual distributions of wine. Although these *philoponoi* appear as beneficiaries of rural employment, most seem to have been recruited in large cities among the wealthy.

In times of famine the hungry poor always congregated in cities, where there was a greater likelihood of finding food. At such times the soup kitchens of the churches and tables of produce set up outside monasteries could draw on institutional reserves as well as additional contributions from lay groups.

While this form of lay charity was often associated with episcopal institutions, a separate form of Christian charity flourished in the private homes converted to religious foundations by individual patrons. In addition to creating a privileged retirement for the patron, the property and revenue was inalienable and was used for donations to the poor on set occasions.[72] Pious foundations such as these were often exempt from public services, but still had to pay the regular land tax. They were usually placed under the control of the local bishop, who would make sure that they continued to fulfill the founder's intentions. The fact that few can be traced for a long period suggests that some had only a brief existence.[73] This hypothesis is perhaps confirmed by the laws forbidding the foundation of churches or charitable institutions without sufficient funds, and urging the repair and maintenance of existing ones.[74] While personal foundations accounted for a good many charitable institutions, it was probably imperial support that guaranteed their survival for centuries, as suggested by the case of the hospital (*xenodocheion*) of Samson.[75] The combination of private and public funding provided the most successful and lasting model for Byzantine charity.[76]

An innovation in imperial and episcopal cooperation during this second period concerns the use of charitable institutions for disciplinary purposes. The most striking example is the practice of confining prostitutes and heretics to monasteries, in order to force them to reform their ways. According to Procopius Empress Theodora converted a palace to a monastery, called *Metanoia* (Repentance), with room for 500 inmates, and every woman who accepted her proposal to enter it also received a gift of money.[77] Throughout the history of Byzantium there were repeated efforts to prevent prostitution, and monasteries of repentance existed in several centers, attending to the more usual tasks of poor relief as well as reform. Some had prisons, presumably used for disciplinary purposes.[78] Offenders of any importance were generally confined in imperial palaces used as prisons. During Pope Martin I's trial in Constantinople, however, he was imprisoned with ordinary criminals. The overtly political nature of his crime—refusal to endorse the imperial definition of Orthodox belief—meant that he stood trial on nonreligious charges and was treated as a secular criminal.[79]

All churches traditionally provided asylum to those seeking a refuge from arbitrary power or injustice, and this role was extended to one of the most important orphanages in the capital, dedicated to St. Paul. Those who feared bankruptcy might seek and obtain refuge there, illustrating the numerous functions served by charitable institutions.[80] This orphanage was also used to accommodate important people visiting the capital on official business, as is clear from one patriarch's determination not to permit a rival monastic leader to stay there.[81] Since there was often an overlap in the categories of the poor, as the elderly also needed medical attention, for instance, institutions may well have provided more than the service implied by its title: *nosokomeion* and *xenodocheion* often appear interchangeable.

Thanks to Procopius's record of the construction work undertaken by Justinian, we can guess that by the mid-sixth century imperial and ecclesiastical patronage had far outstripped that of city councils. In contrast to the concerns of municipalities whose corn dole and other forms of assistance had always been organized on a local basis, Christian charity was committed to a universal application, both urban and rural. It also created a system of redistribution to those in need whatever their origin. When he first went to Constantinople from Antioch, John Chrysostomos deplored the lack of medical care for people visiting the city. So he provided church funds to endow hostels where they could stay and be looked after without paying.[82] Similarly Empress Pulcheria set aside land in Constantinople for *xenotaphia*, cemeteries for foreigners, strangers, and visitors, who might not have had a proper burial otherwise.[83] The medical saint, Artemios, attracted people from distant parts of the Mediterranean world, even one from Gaul in the early seventh century. The poor were also directed to his tomb in Constantinople when doctors either failed to cure them or demanded too high a fee, for the saint granted his services free of charge.[84] And he sent female patients on to the shrine of St. Febronia, who looked after women.

During the third period of the development of Byzantine charity, these universal features of Christian practice finally supplanted the ancient traditions of bread and circuses for local citizens. But at the same time, they were restricted by economic recession, political failure and the very reduced circumstances of the seventh century, from which the medieval empire gradually emerged. This is the culmination of a long process of transformation, evident throughout the empire and brilliantly documented by Patlagean in her study of poverty.[85] Here I shall concentrate on the situation in the capital, where the symbolic shift from bread and circuses to soup and salvation is particularly striking. During the reign of Herakleios (610–41) the Roman tradition of bread distribution came to an end in Constantinople. The decisive break occurred at a time of increasing external threat to the empire, first from the Sasanian Persians, then from the Arabs, which coincided with a depletion of imperial resources, both financial and military. Herakleios gained the throne partly by withholding the grain fleet that sailed every year from Africa to Constantinople to supply the city's needs.[86] He therefore understood the significance of the tradition. Yet he was unable to maintain it in the face of a six-year-long invasion by the Persians, who captured major cities like Antioch and Caesarea, and made it clear that they would advance to the capital.

Since the reign of Justin II (565–78) citizens who were entitled to receive bread had been obliged to pay four gold coins per annum for the privilege, so the distributions were no longer free.[87] In the yearly years of Herakleios's reign they were charged three bronze coins for each loaf (or paid a tax of three gold coins per annum). But the official in charge of the bread system, John, nicknamed "the Earthquake," tried to charge people eight bronze coins.[88] Palace guards and citizens marched to the Great Church to protest, interrupting the services, and Patriarch Sergios only resolved the matter by having the official arrested and putting the city prefect in charge of bread distributions at the old price. But a few years later, in 618, the disruption of corn supplies by the Persian military occupation of Egypt led to the definitive end of the system. No fleet sailed from Alexandria carrying the wheat grown on the banks of the Nile to Constantinople, and alternative supplies had to be found. There was no longer any semblance of a provision of free or even cheap bread. Yet the citizens appeared to adjust to the change, presumably because other ecclesiastical forms of charity provided adequate substitutes.

In place of the ancient tradition of free bread distributions, which he could no longer afford, Herakleios was forced to rely on the resources of the church, the wealthiest institution in Constantinople. He negotiated with Patriarch Sergios for financial support, which included the loan of liturgical silver vessels belonging to the Great Church, and confirmed the privileges of the four churches under patriarchal control.[89] When he left the capital for what developed into a six-year campaign against the Persians (622–28), he established Sergios and Bonos, a military leader, as regents for his young son, and put them in charge of the empire. Their successful defense of the city against a combined Persian and Avar siege in 626, achieved by both military and spiritual weapons, confirmed the vital role that ecclesiastical leaders could play. It effectively signed the alliance of church and state that became a dominant feature of the medieval empire.[90] This is the point at which some historians identify the Byzantine church as the empire's "Department of Social Welfare,"[91] a phrase that emphasizes the extremely significant role the church played in imperial administration, but does not take account of the private charitable activity of individuals.

Herakleios developed the alliance by extending patriarchal control over charitable organs within the capital: one of the major establishments devoted to the care of orphans, named after its founder Zotikos, was handed over to the patriarchate. It already had a reputation for training the orphans to sing, as well as an association with a leprosarium.[92] A large number of institutions to take care of the poor and needy were founded by patriarchs and administered by patriarchal officials, nearly always deacons of the Great Church; their existence is sometimes signaled by the promotion of such a figure to the patriarchate. Sergios himself had been *ptochotrophos,* in charge of a poorhouse at a place called Phrixou and Phialou before 610.[93] Similarly, Patriarch Peter elected in 654, had previously served for twelve years as director of the *gerokomeion* (home for the aged) of St. Clement's; Thomas II had run a poorhouse and an old people's home; and John V had served as *gerokomos* of the Dexiokrates home.[94] While the practice of choosing patriarchs from among the staff of these charitable institutions was by no means novel, there is quite a striking increase during the seventh century, which also seems to imply their growth and expansion.

Alongside urban institutions for the poor, destitute, homeless, sick, and handicapped, who sought assistance in the cities, rural monasteries and shrines associated with healing relics or icons provided relief, which is documented in the lives of saints. When municipal assistance failed, local people turned increasingly to the church, whether in urban or country settings, where ascetic settlements and informal monastic retreats were known to receive pilgrims, travelers, and people suffering from illnesses. The shift was not sudden but came to a head in the late sixth and seventh centuries under the pressures of a profound internal transformation of society and repeated external threats. A revolution in gift giving, which had transferred private wealth from the municipal to the ecclesiastical sphere meant that Christian authorities were both expected and able to perform social tasks previously associated with secular, civic corporations.

In the field of public health, for instance, the churches took over not only burial services but also the provision of baths. For despite deep opposition to the ancient tradition of bathing for purely pleasurable purposes, cleanliness was considered close to godliness even in early Christian times. Only the isolated hermits who made a point of never washing, never cutting their hair, and generally mortifying the body, avoided the use of water and soap. Bishops maintained the water supplies and baths of their cities as a public necessity, while insisting on the strict separation of the sexes and the functional value of bathing.[95] As city councils found it impossible to maintain public entertainment and theaters, colissea and hippodromes were abandoned or converted to other uses, the church expanded its public liturgies, developing new rituals, ceremonies, and festivals that demanded popular participation. In general the church avoided supporting forms of public entertainment associated with pre-Christian times, and condemned women dancing, bears used to foretell the future, and actors wearing masks to perform the ancient tragedies.[96]

In one respect, however it was unable to curb the ancient tradition of circuses. While wild beast fights and gladiatorial combats gave way to spectacles such as the display of unusual animals and objects brought by foreign embassies, or captured in distant military campaigns, horse racing was never abolished at Constantinople.[97] The Byzantine passion for particular charioteers and their horses was satisfied by imperially funded racing, which gave way in the twelfth century to the imported Western sport of jousting, at which the emperor Manuel excelled. Ecclesiastical authorities continued to condemn such vain entertainments and forbade clerics from participating in them. But these regulations were clearly ignored, for at the end of the seventh century the council of 692 established that priests who attended weddings had to leave the festivities when these transferred to the Hippodrome.[98]

While Byzantine clerics benefited from increased influence, the alliance forged by Herakleios and Sergios also institutionalized increasing secular interference in the church. The promotion of John of Cyprus to the patriarchate of Alexandria in 610 was an instance of direct imperial intervention, in this case extremely successful, for John brought his own personal wealth to the already rich capital of the Egyptian church and created an unparalleled philanthropic system.[99] Even allowing for the exaggeration of his hagiographers, John's humanitarian concern for the poor was unusual. Before he arrived in Alexandria to be enthroned as patriarch he ordered officials to seek out all those in need. As a result of this investigation, 7,500 were enrolled as beneficiaries of patriarchal charity. In addition to the construction of numerous institutions for the sick, seven maternity hospitals each with forty beds were provided, and special officers were sent out to find and carry in those who required medical attention.[100] But the promotion of laymen to the highest ecclesiastical positions often provoked dissent within the church, even schism, for instance in the cases of Tarasios in the eighth century or Photios in the ninth. Monastic opposition to such secular promotion may have sprung from a greater commitment to ecclesiastical discipline and a rigorous application of canon law. It could, however, be generated by factionalism within the church. And when the opposition came from Rome, the Eastern irregularity served as an additional factor in a growing estrangement of the churches of Constantinople and the West.

The effective replacement of ancient philanthropy by Christian charity was complete by the seventh century and was sanctioned by the state-church alliance forged by Herakleios. Although there is a sense in which the form of imperial largesse (symbolized by bread and circuses) was replaced by a different but also imperial form (soup and salvation, supported and often financed by Christian rulers), the medium of Christian institutions used to administer charity implied an enormous change. And although these institutions were brought into an imperial alliance under certain secular constraints, they retained the memory of their previous independence and could draw on early Christian ideals. During the seventh century those ideals received a most forthright treatment by Maximos the Confessor, whose *Four Centuries on Charity* confirm the New Testament doctrine of love and the universal duty to do good.[101] The compromise worked out in the early Christian period was thus reformulated in ascetic terms, which proved very influential not only in Byzantium but also in the West.

Once the empire had adjusted to the challenge of Islam, Christian charity became enshrined not only in imperial and church foundations but also in those set up by individuals, whose contribution to the social welfare of Byzantium was by no means negligible. In the charters by which rich founders set out their intentions, the need to do good, to be charitable and merciful is constantly evoked.[102] These donors clearly also had selfish motives, in that they hoped that by endowing charitable institutions they would gain salvation. The redemption of sins, not only for oneself but also for one's parents or children, was an abiding desire among even modest benefactors.[103] Their buildings often appear to have had a transitory existence. As in the early period a lasting success was sometimes reserved to those institutions that acquired imperial support in addition to individual benefactions. The monasteries of Mount Athos, for example, secured a permanent hold on the peninsula through the endowments not only of Byzantine but also Serbian, Georgian, and Russian rulers.

The best documented and most visible forms of charity remained those associated with the imperial court and the patriarchate of Constantinople. Following the example of the *spoudaioi* and *philoponoi*, emperors and patriarchs ceremonially washed the feet of the poor, visited the sick in hospitals, and distributed gifts of money, clothing, and food. Public rituals in the capital seem to have concentrated around the major church festivals, especially Easter. During Lent those in need gathered in the city to receive special donations, clearly related to the climate as well as the period of fasting, and on the Thursday before Easter were given money.[104] On Easter Sunday there were special distributions and Patriarch Tarasios personally visited the Old Royal House to attend to its inmates.[105] In the tenth century on the Wednesday after Easter orphans were brought to the imperial palace to be given purses of money. They were also remembered in public charities bestowed at the feast of the Presentation in the Temple.[106] While the number thus assisted was symbolic, the regularity of the ceremonies meant the poor could at least try to take advantage of them. Since there is some evidence that provincial bishops emulated patriarchal practice, the poor might also seek help from their local ecclesiastics. But in the countryside monasteries probably provided better services.

Since new evidence for Byzantine charity is so sparse, it is a pleasure to conclude by citing a quite recently discovered document, which indicates the survival of lay associations devoted to charitable purposes. Unlike seventh-century *spoudaioi* and other lay groups that existed later at Constantinople,[107] this association was founded in central Greece far away from such traditions and 400 years later. Its function was to care for a particular icon that was transported from one center to another to raise money for charity.[108] The icon represented the Virgin of Naupaktos (*Naupaktiotissa*). Both women and men were members of the group, although it seems most unlikely that they actually participated in transporting the icon. Nor is it certain that they led a celibate life. But their effort to do good through an association with charitable aims serves as a reminder of the enduring qualities of early Christian examples, from which Byzantine charity drew its strengths.

NOTES

1. E. Tengstrom, *Bread for the People: Studies of the Corn Supply of Rome during the Late Empire* (Stockholm, 1974); G. Rickman, *The Corn Supply of Ancient Rome* (Oxford, 1980). **Update** Peter Garnsey, *Food and Society in Classical Antiquity* (Cambridge, UK, 1999); D. P. Brothwell, *Food in Antiquity*, 2nd

ed. (Baltimore/London, 1998); Mary Douglas, *Food and Culture: A Reader* (New York, 1997); Wendy Mayer and Silke Trzciouka, ed., *Feast, Fast or Famine: Food and Drink in Byzantium* (Canberra, 2005).

2. Andrew Watson's very interesting article, "The Arab Agricultural Revolution and Its Diffusion, 700–1100," *Journal of Economic History* 34, no. 1 (1974), 8–35, suggests what changes must have occurred in the East; also J. A. Raftis, ed., *Pathways to Medieval Peasants* (Toronto, 1981).

3. E. Patlagean, *Pauvrété économique et pauvrété sociale à Byzance 4e–7e siècles* (Paris, 1977), 36–44, esp. table 1, p. 38; P. Brown, Response to R. M. Grant, *The Problems of Miraculous Feedings in the Graeco-Roman World*, The Center for Hermeneutical Studies, colloquy 42 (Berkeley, 1982), 19. **Update** Claude Levi-Strauss, *Le cru et le cuit* (Paris, 1964); *The Raw and the Cooked*, Eng. trans. (New York, 1969; London, 1986); Jack Goody, *Cooking, Cuisine and Class: A Comparative Sociology* (Cambridge, UK, 1982).

4. P. Vehne, *Le Pain et le Cirque* (Paris, 1976), 51–52; Eng. trans. *Bread and Circuses* (London, 1990).

5. Veyne, *Le Pain et le Cirque*, 63.

6. Article, *Charité*, in *Dictionnaire de Spiritualité* (Paris, 1953), vol. II, cols. 507–69 (J. Farges and M. Viller).

7. Matthew 19.21, cf. Mark 10.21; Luke 18.22 (and 12. 33).

8. *Eleemones*, Matthew 5.7; cf. Luke 6.36, "Be ye therefore merciful," *oiktirmones*.

9. Matthew 6.1–7 (paraphrased); 7. 20.

10. Matthew 7.7; Luke 11.9.

11. Matthew 6.9–13; Luke, 11. 2–4; J. Jeremias, *The Prayers of Jesus* (London, 1976).

12. Luke, 11.11. One of the most striking aspects of daily life as recorded in the Gospels is the preoccupation with bread, evident in many different contexts. This consistent anxiety gives added significance to the contrast recorded in John 6, between the Old Testament manna from heaven and the true bread: "For the bread of God is he which cometh down from heaven and giveth life unto the world" (6.33). Christ says repeatedly, "I am the bread of life" (6.35, 48, 51) and then spells out the symbolic meaning of Eucharist (6.53–58).

13. Grant, *Miraculous Feedings* (as in note 3 earlier).

14. See Romans 5.1–2, for example.

15. R. Batey, *Jesus and the Poor* (New York, 1972), 51–67; W. A. Meeks, *The First Urban Christians* (New York/London, 1983), 65–66, 110.

16. The descriptions by Justin (*First Apology* 67.6) and Tertullian (*Apology* 39.5–7) reveal that the Christian communities of both Rome and Carthage collected voluntary donations, either every week or once a month, and used them to relieve all kinds of suffering, cf. M. Hengel, *Property and Riches in the Early Church* (Philadelphia, 1974), 67–68.

17. On the disputed authority of the Epistle of James, see the *Cambridge History of the Bible*, ed. P. R. Ackroyd and C. F. Evans, vol. I, *From the Beginnings to Jerome* (Cambridge, UK, 1970), 303, 305. It nonetheless became part of the New Testament canon and was very widely quoted as an authoritative statement on the necessity of good works.

18. II Thessalonians 3.10–12 provided a clear justification for excluding the idle: "If any should not work, neither should he eat."

19. Charity had to be a voluntary act done with love, not grudgingly or under compulsion, "for God loveth a cheerful giver." Yet good works were essential for salvation, II Corinthians 9.7.

20. When Judas claimed that it would have been better to sell the ointment and distribute the money to the poor, Christ supported her action as one of extreme faith and devotion, John 12.3–8.

21. P. Brown, "Art and Society in Late Antiquity," in K. Weitzmann, ed., *The Age of Spirituality* (New York/Princeton, 1980), 17–27.

22. Epiphanius of Cyprus, Letter to Emperor Theodosius, ed. G. Ostrogorsky, *Studien zur Geschichte des byzantinischen Bilderstreites* (Breslau, 1929), 67–75; trans. in C. Mango, *Art of the Byzantine Empire 312–1453, Sources and Documents* (Englewood Cliffs, NJ, 1972), 41–42, and discussed by many later authors now summarized by Leslie Brubaker and John Haldon, *Byzantium in the Iconoclast Era ca. 680–850: A History* (Cambridge, UK, 2011), 46–47; cf. Epiphanius's letter to John of Jerusalem, also in Mango, *Art of the Byzantine Empire*, 42–43.

23. Patlagean, *Pauvrété*, 25–35, esp. 28.

24. Clement's treatise, *The Rich Man's Salvation* and Cyprian's *On Good Works and Almsgiving* are the two most important texts. **Update** L. W. Countryman, *The Rich Christian in the Church of the Early Empire: Contradictions and Accommodations* (New York/Toronto 1980), 47–68, 183–207.

25. Hengel, *Property and Riches*, 60–83.

26. A. R. Hands, *Charities and Social Aid in Greece and Rome* (Ithaca, 1968), 62–88; J. Leipoldt, *Die soziale Gedanke in der altchristliche Kirche* (Leipzig, 1952); Veyne, *Le Pain et le Cirque*, 44–50.

27. P. Brown, *Poverty and Leadership in the Later Roman Empire* (Hanover, NH, 2009); C. Rapp, *Holy Bishops in Late Antiquity* (Berkeley, 2005), 223–34.

28. *Life of Antony*, ch. 91, in Migne, *PG*, 26, col. 972; cf. R. C. Gregg, *Athanasius' Life of Antony* (London, 1980), 97.

29. Hengel, *Property and Riches*, 42–46, 67–68. **Update** D. Kyrtatas, *The Social Structure of the Early Christian Communities* (London, 1987); Michael Philip Penn, *Kissing Christians: Ritual and Community in the Late Ancient Church* (Philadelphia, 2005).

30. Meeks, *The First Urban Christians*, 29–31, 74–75.

31. Eusebius, *Ecclesiastical History* VI, 43, on the debate; cf. VI, 42, 6 on the readmission of *lapsi*, categorically opposed by Novatian; see R. E. Gregory, "Novationism: A Rigorist Sect in the Christian Roman Empire," *Byzantine Studies/Etudes byzantines* 2, no. 1 (1975), 1–18.

32. Cyprian, *De opere et eleemosynis*, ch. 28, ed. M. Simonetti (Turnhout, 1976), 72, lines 556–57.

33. P. Brown, *The Making of Late Antiquity* (Cambridge, MA/London, 1978), 81–101; A. Vööbus, *A History of Asceticism in the Syrian Orient*, 2 vols. (Louvain, 1958–60). **Update** Daniel Caner, *Wandering, Begging Monks: Spiritual Authority and the Promotion of Monasticism in Late Antiquity* (Berkeley, 2002).

34. Their weekly offerings included the bread and wine blessed for Eucharistic use; see G. Galavaris, *Bread and the Liturgy* (Madison/London, 1970), 42–43.

Only later was special Eucharistic bread baked in separate bakeries. **Update** Béatrice Caseau, "Sancto sanctis. Normes et gestes de la communion entre Antiquité et Moyen Age," in N. Bériou, B. Caseau, and D. Rigaux, eds., *Pratiques de l'eucharistie dans les églises d'Orient et d'Occident (Antiquité et Moyen Age)*, 2 vols. (Paris, 2009), I, 371–420.

35. Eusebius, *Ecclesiastical History* VI, 43, 11–12. **Update** See the studies of Jens-Uwe Krause, *Witwen und Waisen im Römischen Reich*, vol. IV, also in French, "Le prise en charge des veuves par l'église dans l'antiquité tardive," in C. Lepelley, ed., *La fin de la cité antique et le début de la cité médiévale: de la fin du IIIe siècle à l'avènement de Charlemagne* (Bari, 1996), 115–26.

36. Leaving aside the vexed question of Constantine's motivation, for the changes in Rome, see R. Krautheimer, *Rome: Profile of a City 312–1308* (Princeton, 1980). *LP*, I, 34–35. **Update** J. Curran, *Pagan City and Christian Capital: Rome in the Fourth Century* (Oxford, 2000).

37. D. Simon, *Konstantinisches Kaiserrecht* (Frankfurt-am-Main, 1977); Patlagean, *Pauvreté*, 195–96.

38. G. Dagron, *Naissance d'une capitale* (Paris, 1974); and "Le christianisme dans la ville," *DOP* 31 (1977), 3–25. **Update** Rapp, *Holy Bishops*, 235–39, on Constantine's promotion of Christian bishops; J.H.W.G. Liebeschuetz, *The Decline and Fall of the Roman City* (Oxford, 2001); C. Lepelley, *La fin de la cité antique*, as earlier.

39. For a detailed description, see *Chronikon Paschale*, ed. L. Dindorf, 2 vols. (Bonn, 1832), I, 543–45; Eng. trans. *Chronicon Paschale 284–628 AD*, Michael Whitby and Mary Whitby (Liverpool, 1989), 34–35; R. Janin, *Constantinople byzantine*, 2nd ed. (Paris, 1964); D. J. Constantelos, *Byzantine Philanthropy and Social Welfare* (New Brunswick, NJ, 1968).

40. For a discussion of the sources and conflicting interpretations of them, see Averil Cameron and J. Herrin, *Constantinople in the Early Eighth Century: The Parastaseis Syntomoi Chronikai* (Leiden, 1984), 35–37, 242–43. *Parasteseis syntomoi chronikai*, § 36, in *Scriptores Originum Constantinopolitanarum*, ed. T. Preger, vol. I (Leipzig, 1901).

41. This combination of pagan and Christian elements is very clearly preserved in the *Parasteseis syntomoi chronikai*, in *Scriptores originum Constantinopolitanarum*, ed. T. Preger, vol. I (Leipzig, 1901); chs. 5, 38, 53, 56, and 68a.

42. Patlagean, *Pauvreté*, 68–69, 193.

43. *Ibid.*, 172–73. 363.

44. M. Kaplan, *Les propriétés de la couronne et de l'église dans l'empire byzantin (V–VI siècles)* (Paris, 1976), 57–58, 623–23, discussing Justinian's novels 43 and 59.

45. On the different categories of private wealth, see Kaplan, 10–16.

46. *Patria Constantinopoleos*, ed. Th. Preger (Leipzig, 1901–7), III, 234; cf. *Theophanes* I, 106, on Pulcheria's philanthropy.

47. Alan Cameron, "The Last Days of the Academy at Athens," *Proceedings of the Cambridge Philological Society* 195, N.S. 15 (1969). **Update** Joëlle Beaucamp, "Le philosophe et le joueur. La date de la 'fermeture de l'Ecole d'Athènes,'" in *Mélanges Gilbert Dagron*, TM 14 (2002), 21–35, with copious bibliography.

48. Rapp, *Holy Bishops*, as earlier, 213–19, 223–34, and 274–89 on the bishop as the new urban functionary.

49. See for instance, Gregory of Nyssa, *De pauperibus amandis. Orationes II*, ed. A. van Heck (Leiden, 1964); Basil of Caesarea, *Homélies sur la richesse*, ed. Y. Courtonne (Paris, 1935). **Update** S. R. Holman, *The Hungry Are Dying: Beggars and Bishops in Roman Cappadocia* (Oxford, 2001); Raymond Van Dam, *Friends and Families in Late Roman Cappadocia* (Philadelphia, 2003); Rapp, *Holy Bishops*, esp. 113, 213–14, 225, 241; Dionysios Stathakopoulos, "Prêcher les émotions incarnées. Évêques, mendiants et leurs publics dans l'Antiquité tardive," in *La Chair des Émotions*, ed. D. Boquet, P. Nagy, and L. Moulinier-Brogi, *Médiévales* 61 (2011), with useful bibliography.

50. Their decision to embrace the monastic life is documented in Gregory of Nyssa's *Life of Macrina*, ed. P. Maravel (Paris, 1971), chs. 7, 21 (pp. 164, 174–80), where much of the initiative is attributed to Macrina and her mother, who set up a house monastery for local women. **Update** Eng. trans. in Joan M. Petersen, *A Letter of Gregory, Bishop of Nyssa, on the Life of Saint Macrina* (Kalamazoo, 1996); Susanna Elm, *Virgins of God. The Making of Asceticism in Late Antiquity* (Oxford, 1994); Van Dam, *Friends and Families*, 99–113.

51. Sozomenos, *Ecclesiastical History* VI, 39.9; Life of Gregory of Nazianzos, in Migne, *PG*, 35, col. 273; Gregory of Nazianzos, *Discours funèbres*, ed. F. Boulenger (Paris, 1908), 188; Stathakopoulos, art. cited earlier.

52. Constantelos, *Byzantine Philanthropy*, 154–55; S. Giet, *Les idées et l'action sociale de Saint Basile* (Paris, 1941).

53. For the *Lives* of monastic founders and the *Rules* later written down to describe monastic routine, see for instance the biographies by Cyril of Scythopolis, ed. E. Schwartz (Leipzig, 1939) and the *Typos* of the Great Lavra on Mount Athos, ed. A. Dmitrievsky, *Opisanie Liturgicheskikh Rukopisei* (Kiev, 1895), vol. 1, 222–24, cf. E. Kurtz, *BZ* 3 (1894). **Update** Most of the monastic rules are now available online at http://www.doaks.org/publications/doaks_online_publications/typ000.html. *Byzantine Monastic Foundation Documents: A Complete Translation of the Surviving Founder's Typika and Testaments*, ed. John Thomas and Angela Constantinides Hero, 5 vols. (Washington, DC, 2000); see also P. Hatlie, *The Monks and Monasteries of Constantinople, ca. 350–850* (Cambridge, UK, 2007).

54. Gregory of Nazianzos, *Discours funèbres*; Gregory of Nyssa, *Encomium on his brother St Basil*, ed. J. A. Stein (Washington, DC, 1928). **Update** See now the study with excellent translations of particular sermons by Holman, *The Hungry Are Dying* (as earlier), 183–206.

55. In ancient Byzantium, the Emperor Severus was associated with many public buildings, which subsequently became known by other names—the baths of Zeuxippos, for example. After 330 many individuals gave their names to monuments: the three sons of Constantine I were supposedly commemorated in a triple statue symbolizing their affection, which provided the name of the Philadelphion; Aetius and Aspar were both held responsible for building cisterns; Harmentius, Viglentius, Eleutherius, and Anthemius all gave their names to different regions of the city; see Cameron and Herrin, *Constantinople in the Early Eighth Century*, as earlier.

56. K. Weitzmann, *The Age of Spirituality*, for photos. **Update** Susan A. Boyd and Marlia Mundell Mango, eds., *Ecclesiastical Silverplate in Sixth-Century Byzantium* (Washington, DC, 1993).

57. As noted by Stathakopoulos, "Prêcher les émotions," n. 13; Hands, *Charities and Social Aid*, 89–115; cf. the detailed study of Oxyrhynchos by J. M. Carrié, "Les distributions alimentaires dans les cités de l'empire romain tardif," *MEFR* 87 (1975), 995–1101. **Update** I. Sandwell, *Religious Identity in Late Antiquity: Greeks, Jews and Christians in Antioch* (Cambridge, UK, 2007); and B. Leyerle, "John Chrysostom on Almsgiving and the Use of Money," *Harvard Theological Review* 47 (1994), 29–47.

58. Eusebius, *De Vita Constantini*, III, 25–44 (on Constantine and Helena); Cyril of Scythopolis, *Life of Euthemius*, ch. 35, and *Life of John Hesychastes*, both ed. E. Schwartz (Leipzig, 1939), 53, 204 (for Eudokia). For the hospital for the treatment of epilepsy, see Constantelos, *Byzantine Philanthropy*, 263

59. Cyril of Scythopolis, Life of Sabas, chs. 72–73, ed. Schwartz, 174–78, esp. 178 on Justinian; cf. ch. 32, 117–18 on Sabas. The regulation governing Sabas's monastery emphasized its duty to care for those in need; see the *Typos*, ed. Dmitrievsky, vol. I, 222–24. **Update** See the new edition in *Byzantine Monastic Foundation Documents*, note 53 earlier; Joseph Patrich, *Sabas, Leader of Palestinian Monasticism*, Dumbarton Oaks Studies 32 (Washington, DC, 1995).

60. Constantelos, *Byzantine Philanthropy*, 275–76.

61. The arrangement is recorded in Justinian's novel 40; see Kaplan, *Les Propriétés*, 55–56.

62. Malalas, *Chronographia*, ed. L. Dindorf (Bonn, 1831), 452 (on the income); Procopius, *On Buildings*, II, 10, ed. J. Haury (Leipzig, 1964), 80.

63. Procopius, *On Buildings*, II, 10 (as earlier) on a large sum bestowed on the church of the Virgin at Antioch.

64. Ibid., III, 156. Empress Theodora made a trip to the hot springs with 4,000 attendants; see *Ioannis Malalae Chronographia*, ed. Ioannes Thurn (Berlin, 2000), bk. 18.25; *The Chronicle of John Malalas*, trans. Elizabeth Jeffreys, Michael Jeffreys, and Roger Scott (Melbourne, 1986), 256.

65. The *Life of St. Theodore of Sykéôn*, ed. A.-J. Festugière (Brussels, 1970), provides numerous instances of monastic charity, pilgrimages to isolated shrines, and long journeys by people seeking cures in the largely rural context of Galatia; see for example, the saint's pilgrimage to Mousge and Sozopolis, chs. 71, 105–9; the healing of children from Ephesos, ch. 110; the miraculous provision of grain for public distribution by the monastery on Palm Sunday, ch. 104. On the importance of monastic philanthropy, see Constantelos, *Byzantine Philanthropy*, 88–110, Patlagean, *Pauvreté*, 194–95.

66. Article, *Confréries*, in *Dictionnaire d'"Archéologie chrétienne et de liturgie* (Paris, 1907–53), vol. III (H. Leclercq).

67. E. Wipszycka, "Les confréries dans la vie religieuse de l'Egypte chrétienne," *Proceedings of the XIIth International Congress of Papyrology* (Toronto, 1970), 511–25. **Update** Peregrine Horden, "The Confraternities in Byzantium," in *Voluntary Religion*, ed. W. J. Sheils and Diana Wood (Oxford, 1986), 25–45.

68. Patlagean, *Pauvreté*, 192–93; P. Petrides, "Le monastère des Spoudaei à Jérusalem et les Spoudaei à Constantinople," *ÉO* 4 (1901), 255–31; and "Spoudaei

et Philopones," ibid. 7 (1904), 431–33. **Update** Paul Magdalino, "Church, Bath and *Diaconia* in Medieval Constantinople," in Rosemary Morris, ed., *Church and People in Byzantium* (Birmingham, 1990) 165–88.

69. H.-I. Marrou, "L'origine orientale des diaconies romaines," *Mélanges de l'école française de Rome*, 57 (1940), 95–142; cf. *LP*, I, 364; **Update** Anna Maria Giuntella, "Gli spazi dell'assistenza e della meditazione," *Roma nell'Alto Medioevo*, XLVIII, *Settimana di Studio* (Spoleto, 2001), 639–91, esp. 670–91; P. Brown, *Poverty and Leadership in the Later Roman Empire* (Hanover, CT, 2002); and now his defining new study of Christian welfare in the early medieval West, *Through the Eye of the Needle* (Princeton, 2012).

70. S. Vailhé, "Les Philopones d'Oxyrhynque au IVe siècle," *ÉO* 14 (1911), 227–28.

71. Wipszycka, "Les confréries," as earlier.

72. The conversion of an already existing structure into a Christian institution was probably the simplest method of creating a foundation, and had been practiced since the fourth century; see for instance the family monasteries established at Rome, R. Lorenz, "Die Anfange des abendländischen Mönchtums im 4. Jahrhubert," *Zeitschrift für Kirchengeschichte* 77 (1966), 1–61; and the example of St. Macrina cited earlier.

73. On the status of pious foundations, see Kaplan, *Les propriétés*, 17–21. Monasteries for women seem to have been especially vulnerable to collapse. Justinian's novel 131 reaffirmed the exemption from public services except road and bridge maintenance, *hodostrosias* and *gephyron*, ibid., 73.

74. This is discussed in Justinian's novel 67; see Kaplan, *Les propriétés*, 64–65, but is constantly referred to in other enactments concerning ecclesiastical property.

75. On the hospital of Samson, see Constantelos, *Byzantine Philanthropy*, 191–95; F. Halkin, "Saint Samson le Xénodoque de Constantinople (VIe siècle)," *Rivista di Studi bizantini et neoellenici*, 14–16 (1977–79), 5–17. **Update** T. Miller, *The Birth of the Hospital in the Byzantine Empire* (Baltimore/London 1985), 80–83.

76. E. Patlagean, "La pauvreté à Byzance au VI siècle et la legislation de Justinien: aux origins d'un modèle politique," in *Etudes sur l'histoire de la pauvreté*, ed. M. Mollat, 2 vols. (Paris, 1974), I, 59–81. **Update** P. Sarris, *Economy and Society in the Age of Justinian* (Cambridge, UK, 2006).

77. Procopius, *On Buildings*, I, 9 (ed. Haury, 35–37); cf. his *Secret History*, XVII, 5–6, describing the women's successful attempt to escape. See also Judith Herrin, "In Search of Byzantine Women: Three Avenues of Approach," chapter 2 in *Unrivalled Influence: Women and Empire in Byzantium*.

78. E. Wipszycka, *Les resources et les activités économiques des églises en Egypte du IVe au VIIIe siècle* (Brussels, 1972), 117, on the monastic prison at Oxyrhynchos.

79. Pope Martin's two letters to Theodore Spoudaios, nos. XIV and XV, as well as the later accounts of his sufferings, probably by Theodore but published as letters nos. XVI and XVII, all document the political character of his trial and the imperial prisons in which he was held; see Migne, *PL*, 878, 197–204; see also *Mansi*, X, 849–64. **Update** Eng. trans. by Bronwen Neil, *Seventh-Century Popes*

and Martyrs: The Political Hagiography of Anastasius Bibliothecarius, Studia Antiqua Australiensia (Turnhout, 2006), 166–83.

80. Constantelos, *Byzantine Philanthropy,* 243–47; Janin, *La géographie ecclésiastique,* 580–81. **Update** Timothy S. Miller, *The Orphans of Byzantium: Child Welfare in the Christian Empire* (Washington, DC, 2003).

81. Cyril of Scythopolis, *Life of Sabas,* ch. 87 (Schwartz, 194–95). **Update** T. S. Miller, *The Birth of the Hospital in the Byzantine Empire* (Baltimore/London, 1997), 130–32; and *The Orphans of Byzantium: Child Welfare in the Christian Empire* (Washington, DC, 2003), 200–202, on the *diakonia* of Eugenios.

82. Palladios, *Life of John Chrysostomos,* ch. 6, ed. R. P. Coleman-Norton (Cambridge, UK, 1928)..

83. *Theophanes,* I, 106. Empress Eirene did the same in the eighth century; see *Patria Constantinopoleos,* III, 246. **Update** Judith Herrin, "Political Power and Christian Faith: The Case of Irene (Regent 780–90, Emperor 797–802," chapter 8 in *Unrivalled Influence: Women and Empire in Byzantium.*

84. *Miracula Sancti Artemii,* in A. Papadopoulos-Kerameus, *Varia graeca sacra* (St. Petersburg, 1902). **Update** Now reprinted with an Eng. trans. by J. W. Nesbitt and V. Crisafulli, *The Miracles of St Artemios* (Leiden/New York, 1997).

85. This is the fundamental investigation of Byzantine poverty, to which I am greatly indebted, as my frequent references to Patlagean, *Pauvreté,* make clear.

86. *Chronikon Paschale,* ed. L. Dindorf (Bonn, 1832), 699; Whitby and Whitby, 149, on the rebellion; cf. *Theophanes,* AM 6100, I, 295–6; Mango and Scott, 424.

87. Patlagean, *Pauvreté,* 186–87.

88. *Chronikon Paschale,* 715–16, but note the suspension of the bread dole earlier, 711; Whitby and Whitby, 168–89 (and 164), possibly entered under the year 626 by mistake. K. Ericsson, "Revising a Date in the Chronikon Paschale," *JÖB* 17 (1968), 17–28, suggests that the year should be 615.

89. *Theophanes,* AM 6111–13, I, 302–3; Herakleios, novel 1, *JusGR,* I, 27–30.

90. *Theophanes,* AM 6113, I, 303, on the regency; *Chronikon Pashcale,* 716–26, on the Persian campaign; F. Barisic, "Le siège de Constantinople par les Avares et les Slaves en 626," *B* 24 (1954), 371–95. **Update** B. I. Pentcheva, "The Supernatural Protector of Constantinople: The Virgin and Her Icons in the Tradition of the Avar Siege," *BMGS* 26 (2002), 2–41; J. Howard–Johnston, *Witnesses to a World Crisis: Historians and Histories of the Middle East in the Seventh Century* (Oxford, UK, 2010).

91. C. Mango, *Byzantium, the Empire of New Rome* (London, 1980), 36.

92. See his novel 3, *JusGR,* I, 33–36; Miller, *The Orphans of Byzantium,* as earlier, 52–61.

93. *Chronikon Paschale,* 699; Whitby and Whitby, 149; J. van Dieten, *Geschichte der Patriarchen von Sergios I bis Johannes VI (610–715)* (Amsterdam, 1972), 1.

94. Van Dieten, as earlier, 106, 117, 121.

95. Patlagean, *Pauvreté,* 197, 208; *Mansi,* XI, 931–88, canons of the Council in Trullo held in 691/2, which include regulations on clerical use of the baths: canon 9 (not bathing with Jews), canon 75 (not bathing with women). **Update** Magdalino, "Church, Bath and *Diaconia,*" as earlier; A. Berger, *Das Bad in den*

byzantinischen Zeit (Munich, 1982); Herrin, "'Femina Byzantina': The Council in Trullo on Women," chapter 5 in *Unrivalled Influence: Women in Empire in Byzantium*.

96. John of Ephesos was very scathing about a bishop who wanted to restore a hippodrome at Antioch: "building a church for Satan," *Ecclesiastical History* III, 27–34; cf. canons of the Council in Trullo against popular forms of entertainment, in *Mansi*, XI; P. P. Joannou, *Discipline générale antique*, 2 vols. (Grottaferrata, 1962), I, 1 (Greek, Latin, and Fr. trans.); G. Nedungatt and M. Featherstone, *The Council in Trullo Revisited, Kanonika* 6 (1995), 45–185 (Greek, Latin, and Eng. trans.).

97. Alan Cameron, *Circus Factions* (Oxford, 1976), on the continuation of racing; John of Biclar, *Chronikon*, ed. T. Mommsen, *MGH Auctores antiquissimi*, vol. XI (Berlin, 1898), 214, lines 7–16 describes a triumph in the capital in which 24 elephants participated, and comments on the unusual sight of a giraffe.

98. The Council in Trullo issued 102 canons of great interest for the social historian, including canon 24 prohibiting clerical participation in hippodrome racing. **Update** Eng. trans. by G. Nedungatt and J. Featherstone, as earlier; new edition with German trans. by H. Ohme, *Concilium Quinisextum übersetzt und eingeleitet* (Turnhout, 2006); and Herrin, "The Council in Trullo on Women," as earlier.

99. Leontios of Neapolis, *Vie de Syméon le Fou et Vie de Jean de Chypre*, ed. A.-J. Festugière (Paris, 1974), 260–63.

100. Leontios, as earlier, ch. 1, 444–45 (8–9 in the edition by Gelzer; 325, ch. 7, in the anonymous life, ed. Delehaye, 22); cf. Mango, *Byzantium*, 37–38.

101. A. Cerea-Gastaldo, *Massimo Confessore Capitoli sulla carità* (Rome, 1963), cf. P. Sherwood, *St Maximus the Confessor, the Four Centuries on Charity* (London, 1955). **Update** Andrew Louth, *Maximus the Confessor* (New York/London, 1996); D. Bathrellos, *The Byzantine Christ: Person, Nature and Will in the Christology of Saint Maximus the Confessor* (Oxford, 2004); Neil, *Seventh Century Popes and Martyrs*, on Maximus and the translations into Latin, 72–79, 82–91, 99–105.

102. In the introduction to his charter for a poorhouse and a monastery, Michael Attaleiates records his desire to realize a good work, which will be pleasing to God; despite his great sins, he does not despair of being saved and dedicates part of his wealth to God in gratitude; see P. Gautier, "Le Diataxis de Michel Attaliate," *REB* 39 (1981), 5–143, esp. 21–25. He also mentions that at the death of his first wife he distributed all her wealth to the poor, 19. **Update** See the new edition of the diataxis in *Byzantine Foundation Documents*, as earlier; Dimitris Krallis, *Michael Attaleiates and the Politics of Imperial Decline in Eleventh Century Byzantium* (Tempe, AZ, 2012).

103. See for example the small inheritance that the widow Domna bequeaths to the church for the redemption of her sons; F. Trinchera, ed., *Syllabus graecarum membranarum* (Naples, 1865), no. 46 (1063).

104. This is the model for the British monarchy's tradition of handing out purses of money on Maundy Thursday, usually to the Chelsea pensioners.

105. Constantelos, *Byzantine Philanthropy*, 76; Tarasios also served meals in the city following a tradition that may go back to the early eighth century; see Cameron and Herrin, *Constantinople in the Early Eighth Century*, 220.

106. Constantine Porphyrogenitus, *Le Livre de Cérémonies*, ed. A. Vogt (Paris, 1935–39), I, ch. 21, 82; ed. J. J. Reiske (Bonn, 1822), I, ch. 12, 89–90.

107. In the 660s a group attached to the Anastasis church of Constantinople appear to have continued the traditions of the *spoudaioi*, but more as a confraternity of devout Christians. Subjected to imperial persecution (as heretics) and condemned to exile in remote regions, they sustained each other through correspondence and even personal visits; see R. Devreesse, "La lettre d'Anastase l'Apocrisiaire sur la mort de S. Maxime et de ses compagnons d'exile," *AB* 73 (1955), 5–16. **Update** Bronwen Neil, *Seventh-Century Popes and Martyrs*, 128–33, esp. 129, n. 13, pointing out that the church of the Anastasis in Jerusalem also had a confraternity of *spoudaioi* attached to it.

108. J. Nesbitt and J. Wiita, "A Confraternity of the Comnenian Era," *BZ* 68 (1975), 360–84. **Update** L. Neville, *Authority in Byzantine Provincial Society, 950–1100* (Cambridge, UK, 2004); G. Prinzing, "The Authority of the Church in Uneasy Times: The Example of Demetrios Chomatenos, Archbishop of Ohrid, in the State of Epiros 1216–1236," in Pamela Armstrong, ed., *Authority in Byzantiium* (Farnham, forthcoming, 2013), records another group without any defining charitable function, though it may also have maintained an icon of the Virgin.

14

IDEALS OF CHARITY, REALITIES OF WELFARE

THE PHILANTHROPIC ACTIVITY OF THE BYZANTINE CHURCH

❧

This chapter developed out of my interest in Byzantine charity and welfare nurtured at Princeton University in 1985. It reuses some introductory material from that period and then explores the systems in use in the medieval period. At the Byzantine Spring Symposium of 1988 held at Manchester University, Rosemary Morris arranged the program, and I remember the event as one of the most successful meetings inaugurated at Birmingham with *Iconoclasm*, which continue to be held annually in different venues. The volume was published in 1990 as *Church and People in Byzantium* and remains a very handy introduction to a wide range of activities associated with the Byzantine church. My chapter in it is reprinted here with kind permission of the Centre for Byzantine, Ottoman and Modern Greek Studies, University of Birmingham.

It was clear that bishops were expected to take a major role in the administration of ecclesiastical charity, and many were recruited from the charitable institutions of the capital city (poorhouses, old age homes, orphanages, and so on). In addition, a parallel system of similar facilities developed in many monasteries, thus providing care for elderly monks as well as local people who were occasionally allowed to use the bathhouse or the hospital. Since most of these institutions were founded by individuals, often imperial, the practice of charity was also largely secular, and can be traced in the wills of generals and civilian officials, as well as women.

I was surprised to discover how many charitable acts and donations could be documented at all levels of society, from the freeing of slaves, who were often endowed with property, money, and possessions, to the provision of shelter and medical care for pilgrims visiting healing shrines. Of course such generosity was always linked to the hope of prayers for the soul of the donor, as the Last Judgment remained a constant reminder of the eternal world of heaven. But even if the motivation behind Byzantine charity was personal and selfish, the results remained to assist the living when old age, leprosy, blindness, or other disasters rendered them dependent on institutional care.

ALTHOUGH MODERN SCHOLARS sometimes doubt the extent of early Christian charity, claims made by late second-century apologists, particularly Justin Martyr and Tertullian, which are clearly confirmed by hostile, pagan witnesses, should alert us to the new religion's innovations in philanthropic activity.[1] The dispossessed, the downtrodden, and all those who were destitute, sick, and unable to help themselves, were singled out for compassion and alms (*eleemosyne*). Christ's identification, and elevation, of these unfortunates as persons most worthy and deserving of good works (*kala erga*) gave his followers unmistakable instructions. For the first time adherents of a particular belief were to show solidarity with those in need, whatever their origins. Thus, prostitutes, lepers, political enemies, aged slaves, shipwrecked sailors, those committed to the mines or taken prisoner by bandits, among others, were to be comforted. And people in these categories could expect to receive attention, as proper recipients of Christian charity. During the early centuries AD there is ample evidence of concern for these new categories, as well as those more traditionally cared for by Jewish philanthropy, orphans and widows, for example. In addition, the followers of Jesus generally offered each other hospitality, took care of the sick, and made sure that burial according to Christian rite was not denied to any believer. What is more, this concern for the poor, the meek, and the humble, who had been so graphically listed in Christ's Sermon on the Mount, can occasionally be given a numerical value. The figures available only provide the barest indication, yet the fact that in the mid-third century Bishop Cornelius of Rome supported 1,500 widows and needy people, as well as maintaining a large clergy, provides some idea of the scope of such assistance. Since women and the nonresident poor, who did not own property in Rome, were specifically excluded from the city's bread dole, it is clear that the church was directing its aid to a new constituency.[2] While ecclesiastical philanthropy grew and changed over centuries, the earliest Christian experience remained an important model, frequently reasserted in an effort to imitate the direct charitable activity of Christ and the Apostles.

In extremely simplified form, the two outstanding features of this duty to assist those in need were summed up by Jesus' instructions to his followers to love one another and to sell all they had and give to the poor. The subject of the first, love, involves a Greek word, *agape*, which

Christian authors were to make exclusively theirs in the early centuries AD.[3] This duty to love one another extended to strangers and enemies, too, it was a universal application of the Mosaic law, "Thou shalt love thy neighbor as thyself." No exceptions were admitted, for by loving all people a Christian would develop the capacity to love God, which was the highest duty of all. In their practice of *agape*, every stranger had to be welcomed, since each was a potential representation of Christ.

The subject of the second, charity, is very closely related. For in the Latin Vulgate translation of the New Testament, *agape* is rendered by *caritas*, charity.[4] In the famous passage in I. Corinthians, 13: "Faith, hope and charity, these three; but the greatest of these is charity," St. Paul is in fact praising love above all other virtues. Of course, love and charity were intimately connected in the mutual-aid structure of the first recorded Christian communities, which were characterized by a voluntary adoption of poverty. Their charity was to be marked by an indiscriminate care for the immediate needs of all in trouble, combined with a lack of attention to future needs. All these ideals of Christian philanthropy find an echo in later Byzantine practice, although the structures that developed in the fourth and fifth centuries implied a permanency little appreciated in Apostolic times, when Christians expected the *Parousia*, Second Coming, very soon.

In this brief chapter I shall examine two aspects of the development of Byzantine charitable institutions: the mechanisms by which welfare was administered, and the underlying theory of good works.[5] First, the mechanisms. From the fourth century onward, when official state protection permitted the open accumulation of ecclesiastical wealth, church leaders began to establish lists of people in need, whom the Christian community had to assist. St. John Chrysostom in Antioch provides evidence of 3,000 widows and virgins recorded on a *katalogos*, and an unspecified number of men who are inscribed, *engegrammenon*, on separate lists.[6] All these are fed daily. In addition, a host of captives in prison, sick in hospital, mutilated, ship-wrecked, fearful, and healthy people traveling through Antioch depend on church resources. Many come regularly to the door to be fed: others wait for help to come to them. Among these in need, John singles out those women who weep, mourn and lament, or who are merely frightened. Finally, the needs of all the clergy who serve are met from church resources.[7]

During the late fourth and early fifth century, Bishop Porphyrios of Gaza also drew up a register of those in need, and each received 6 obols a week, a sum increased during the forty days of Lent to 10. This arrangement was made permanent in his will, which set aside special funds for the purpose.[8] Although not all bishops could endow similar systems of charitable distributions, the notion of keeping a record of the poor in cities seems to have been adopted. In the early seventh century John the Almsgiver ordered officials to identify and record all the poor of Alexandria prior to his arrival as bishop, and 7,500 were inscribed.[9] The principle of registration may imply some form of discrimination—who was worthy? who was sick?—but Leontios of Neapolis, who described John's philanthropy in great detail, was at pains to stress his immense generosity. In addition to his own private, family wealth, the church of Alexandria was perhaps the richest of all. John was certainly well placed to assist those who fled from Jerusalem when it was sacked by the Persians in 614, and to finance the rebuilding of churches in the Holy City. But his philanthropic capacity was exceptional rather than the norm.

In the more straightened circumstances of the late eighth century, Patriarch Tarasios of Constantinople still employed a register of the poor: all those whose names were written in his papyrus record got a monthly payment in silver.[10] It is, however, impossible to ascertain how many were recorded, how they were selected, if they were, and how many were not caught in this charitable net. Some of the poor also benefited from the patriarch's distribution of warm clothing and blankets in the winter and his gifts of corn. At Nicaea, Bishop Theophylact established a similar system of welfare, which was maintained by his successors.[11] But since the ranks of the urban poor were frequently swelled by famine, disease, and enemy activity in the provinces, it seems unlikely that this episcopal philanthropy could satisfy all those in distress.

Christian charity was also administered through institutions devoted to the assistance of the very old and very young, the poor, blind, sick, and so on, who gave their names to specific refuges: *ierokomeion, brephotropheion, ptocheion*, and the like. A great number of hostels, *xenones*, appear to have provided shelter for travelers, pilgrims and occasionally those suffering from particular diseases, or just old age.[12] All these institutions were usually attached to an episcopal church or monastery; they were staffed by clerics, monks, deaconesses, and pious lay people; they were supported by donations from the faithful, ecclesiastical revenues, and income from properties, urban and rural. This structure was designed to redistribute part of the resources of the wealthy to the needs of the poor; it employed the mechanism of voluntary assistance by the rich to those unable to help themselves. Such a rationalization of Christian resources permitted the well-to-do to act as true followers of Christ and justified their wealth.

Throughout the Greek East charity always remained heavily dependent on lay initiative, on the personal decision of individuals, couples,
and sometimes whole families, to adopt poverty. When this was accompanied by entry into a Christian community, the wealthy could rid
themselves of personal riches without sacrificing their security—a future,
however humble, was assured. This desire for voluntary poverty motivated great numbers of Christians, for instance, Melania and other rich
widows who became benefactors in Jerusalem, and on a more modest
scale, St. Elizabeth of Herakleia.[13] Her *Life* embraces all the well-known
stages of Christian philanthropy: when her parents died, Elizabeth freed
all her slaves, sold all her inheritance, and distributed her wealth to the
poor. She then went to join her aunt in a nunnery in Constantinople,
where she later became abbess. By the same system many church leaders
were also recruited, bishops like St. John Chrysostom or Epiphanios of
Salamis, who both maintained a humble life-style and denounced luxury
within the church. Yet paradoxically, this mechanism of transference
meant that when the rich abandoned their worldly goods, the church
acquired problems provoked by such wealth. Conflicts over the correct
priorities for ecclesiastical expenditure were inevitable. When Epiphanios
protested at the use of extravagantly embroidered silk curtains, and said
that they would be better used as shrouds for the poor, he drew attention
to a running sore in Byzantine religious life.[14]

While bishops dealt more with the problems of the urban poor, frequently destitute and completely dependent on charity, monks often
found hospitality their main task, particularly if they could provide shelter for those traveling between cities. Pilgrims making the journey south
from Jerusalem to Mount Sinai discovered a well-worn route of monastic
halts, where they could refresh their mounts and themselves, until they
reached the desert. There, at Elusa, they had to prepare for five to six days
through uninhabited regions without a resting place. Eventually, however, the monks of Sinai would welcome them with fruit, fresh water, and
hospitality.[15] In the countryside in times of famine monasteries frequently
distributed additional supplies of grain; at major festivals they always
provided food, and sometimes clothing, to local inhabitants as well as
travelers. No uniform system of rural charity emerged, however, because
the capacity of each monastery and ecclesiastical diocese varied according
to its resources. The wide range of episcopal incomes and expenses meant
that a major see like Caesarea could construct a host of buildings devoted
to needy people, while a smaller bishopric in rural Asia Minor might rely
on the donations of local peasants and pilgrims to relieve poverty. And at

this "New City," established by St. Basil in the late fourth century, family wealth as well as the resources of other rich landowners was responsible for the establishment of a *leprosarion*, hostels, old people's homes, and other institutions for the poor.[16] The theory of social justice and equality among Christians elaborated by the Cappadocian Fathers could be put into effect in their charitable foundations partly because of special circumstances that did not pertain in other regions of the empire.

The provision of hospitals provides a case in point. From the fourth century onward the church took the lead in establishing institutions where the sick could be cared for. While these tried to provide adequate medical care, individual doctors were frequently responsible for hospitals, for instance, Samson, who set up his practice in Constantinople in the fifth century. His foundation was taken over and expanded by imperial funds to become one of the most famous in the capital, famous also because it survived for centuries.[17] Similarly, through imperial patronage, St. Sabas was able to establish hospitals in Jerusalem.[18] And in seventh-century Constantia, on Cyprus, a rich layman, Philentolos, was responsible for building the hospital, not the archbishop.[19] In Oxyrhynchos, on the other hand, hospitals and hostels for travelers were often constructed and maintained by the church and administered by clerical officials.[20] So while the church made medical provision one of its priorities, and Christians devoted themselves to washing and nursing those who were ill, even with infectious diseases like leprosy, medical services were by no means a Christian preserve. In this field as in so many others, secular imperial intervention could be decisive.

For besides these instances of episcopal and monastic charity, imperial assistance played a crucial role in the development of Byzantine charity. On numerous occasions it is the additional income from the imperial treasury, or from public funds sanctioned by emperors, that secures the survival of ecclesiastical institutions for the poor. From an early date appeals to imperial generosity, like that by Bishop Porphyrios, indicate the significance of state funding. Not only did the Empress Eudoxia finance the replacement of the pagan temple of Zeus Marnas at Gaza by a grand Christian church, but she also provided a hostel where visitors could stay free of charge for three days.[21] Similarly, through the generosity of Empress Pulcheria, strangers who died in the Byzantine capital could receive a proper burial in her *xenotapheia*.[22] The reign of Justinian, as Patlagean has shown, is vital to an understanding of church/state relations in the administration of charity.[23] At this point, the poor are recognized as a legal category worthy of assistance, which is often entrusted to ecclesiastical bodies.

A combination of private initiative, clerical foundation, and imperial finance reveals the close alliance that persisted throughout the history of the Byzantine Empire. Although the church has been characterized as "the department of state responsible for social welfare,"[24] this does not do justice to the independent aspects of ecclesiastical philanthropy. It would be more accurate to say that the relationship between church and state was based on imperial recognition of the value of ecclesiastical organs of charity, which it supported with additional privileges and duties. The same pattern of autonomous initiative safeguarded by imperial protection is reaffirmed by nearly all the major monasteries of Byzantium. In a great many cases monastic communities or their founders, appealed to emperors to confirm their landholding by granting exemption from public taxation, a normal privilege for pious institutions.[25]

Over the centuries the development of Byzantine charity is accompanied by a shift from largely episcopal to more monastic forms, with a concomitant increase in discrimination against certain types of poor. The process is part of the transition from Late Antiquity to the medieval world, a process marked by the reduction of resources, the decline of ancient cities and the growing importance of monasticism in Byzantine society. In specific instances the Christian principle of assisting all the needy had already been tempered in practice by a reluctance to support scroungers. The abuse of hospitality by visitors staying more than two nights at Christian shelters is noted in the Teaching of the Apostles, the *Didache*, possibly as early as 100 AD. True Christians would not stay longer. While the early communities in the desert of Nitria gave pilgrims a better diet than their own and broke their vows of silence to receive travelers with humanity, they decided to put the visitors to work after a week's holiday.[26]

This practical notion passed into Byzantine tradition and was revived, to cite one example, in the eleventh century at the monastery of Mount Galesion, near Ephesos. St. Lazaros had established himself here close to the main highway that led north from Ephesos, and the *xenon* of the monastery was frequented by travelers who occasionally abused the monk's hospitality. After one particular incident, the *xenodochos* in charge of the hostel imposed the three-day rule, but he was in turn accused of mistreating the visitors. The abbot, forced to intervene, removed the restriction on hospitality, and took the opportunity to stress the monastery's customary duty to receive all and especially to care for the sick.[27] In any debate over this fundamental aspect of Byzantine charity, several authorities could be cited. In the opinion of St. Maximos Confessor unlimited giving was essential, while St. Cyril Phileotes continued to oppose aid for the able bodied or lazy, because they thereby deprived those in genuine need.

Subsequent developments in the administration of charity tended to a symbolic, exemplary philanthropy, rather than generalized efforts to assist. This was frequently liturgified, as donations to the poor became related to church festivals and the commemoration of monastic founders. Easter had always been such an occasion. But in the eleventh century Michael Attaleiates ordered that on the anniversary of his death, twelve old men in need, mutilated or infirm, should each be given one gold coin, *nomisma*, and six *annuarioi modioi* of corn at his monastery in Raidestos. On this occasion six *trachea nomismata* and a loaf made of six *modioi* (of grain) were also to be distributed to the poor.[28] The anniversary of the death of a benefactor, Patriarch Nikephoros of Antioch, was to be marked by the distribution of two *nomismata* to each of the monks for the necessary liturgical services, and three gold coins to the poor. While six needy people were fed at the refectory table every day, and a further eighteen, widows and old men, were to be supported, Attaleiates implied that he wished his own monks to represent the poor, to take the place of those who were most worthy of charity.[29]

Throughout the empire this private and individual charity coexisted with the ideal of anonymous giving, not for self-aggrandisement but out of real concern or love. The unknown "lover of Christ" (*philochristos*), who established a burial ground for the *xenon* of the Evergetis monastery in Constantinople, paid serious attention to the needs of travelers, who were otherwise well served by this famous institution. It provided for the hungry to be nourished with both food and spiritual care; supplied clothing and shoes when necessary; and arranged for the monks to sing *epitaphia* at the death of any stranger, who would then be buried in the special cemetery.[30] Similarly, humble donors supported the wandering ascetic, John Xenos, when he wanted to construct shrines.[31] These anonymous *philochristoi*, committed to charity with no immediate recognition, provide a clue to the continuing force behind Byzantine support for the poor—it grew out of, and in turn reinforced the theory of good works. Good works, always considered useful if not necessary for salvation, were a determining factor in the Byzantine practice of philanthropy.

The fundamental ambiguity over the role of good works in salvation was evident in New Testament times and has vexed Christians ever since.[32] In its most extreme form the contrast is between St. Paul's doctrine of "justification by faith alone," and the Epistle of St. James, which draws on Jewish practice and stresses the need for visible proof of faith in the form of good works: "Faith, if it hath not works, is dead, being alone. . . . By works a man is justified, and not by faith alone." These positions are partly resolved by the gift of grace, which unlike good works is essential to salvation. Christians must therefore strive for God's grace, and in this struggle good works are a practice ordained by God and instilled in men as a proper pattern of Christian behavior (Ephesians 2.8–10). Once good works are understood as a result, rather than a condition of salvation, the emphasis on motivation can take its rightful place. As Paul said and many others repeated after him, actions as charitable as bestowing all one's goods to feed the poor, if done without love, are worthless.

In a series of sermons on these and other New Testament texts, the Church Fathers did not completely succeed in correlating grace and good works. They did not investigate the preordained pattern of good works, which led St. Augustine to emphasise predestination, the determining force that antedates any human effort to do good. This Western doctrine of man's utter dependence on God for that grace that is necessary for salvation may be contrasted with the Eastern theology developed by St. Maximos Confessor on the basis of Chalcedonian Christology. Against both the Monophysite view of human nature, which was basically pessimistic, and the Augustinian doctrine of predestination, Maximos argued that: "The Christ who is known in two natures is able to be the model for our freedom and individuality," as Chadwick puts it.[33] This dual nature permits a positive interpretation of the created world and humanity, including the human capacity to love. In this respect Maximos reinforced the New Testament identification of love/charity as the supreme Christian virtue, elevated to a ruling position in his great work, *The Four Centuries on Charity*.[34] This text is a crucial one in the development of the Byzantine theory of philanthropy. It provides the clearest statement of the importance of joyful, selfless giving and altruistic service to those in need, and emphasizes the value of boundless giving as an indication of Christian love.[35]

Since Maximos also devoted much time to the relative strengths of other Christian virtues, establishing the significance of restraint/temperance (*sophrosyne*), for instance, his considered view of love set it apart and above all others. In this way, the gift of material benefits and goods was reduced to a mere external sign of charity, to be contrasted with the infinitely superior inward expression of love which directed true charity.[36] Those who delayed their charitable activity, by establishing that commemorative liturgies or distributions to the poor should be made after their death, or who waited for their relatives to provide these services, were similarly taken to task. Maximos restated in forceful terms the original Pauline doctrine:

> Though I speak with the tongues of men and angels and have not *love*, I am becoming a sounding brass, or a tinkling cymbal. And though I have the gift of prophecy, and understand all mysteries and all knowledge; and though I have all faith, so that I could remove mountains, and have not *love*, I am nothing. And though I bestow all my goods to feed the poor; and though I give my body to be burned and have not *love*, it profiteth me nothing.

While this emphatic claim is echoed in many later Byzantine theologians, the notion that good works and alms giving (*eupragiai*) were part of the Christian duty to love remained engrained. St. John of Damascus, for instance, quoted St. Gregory of Nazianzos on the value of doing good, *eupoiein*: "Nothing is more honorable or philanthropic than to be merciful and do good, because nothing is more desirable to God."[37] Patriarch Germanos of Constantinople stressed that good works (*agathoergias*) are necessary for salvation and reminded his flock that the servants of God have revealed themselves through their good works and pious deeds.[38] But good works alone, or giving in expectation of reward, was never sufficient. A fascinating episode recorded in seventh-century Cyprus will serve to make the point. Philentolos was that rich benefactor mentioned earlier, who provided funds to build a hospital in Constantia.[39] He devoted considerable resources to relieve poverty but persisted in the sin of fornication. At his death the bishops of Cyprus debated his fate and could not agree whether his good works would secure his entrance to Paradise. In a dramatic vision, an old holyman called Kaioumos discovered the answer. He reported that he had seen Philentolos with an angel, who asked: "Have I not warned you many times, telling you to cease from fornication? If through your alms-giving you are freed from Geenna (Hell), through your failure to cease from fornication, you are deprived of the joy of Paradise." And at Philentolos's protests that he had given alms and counted on being saved, even if he sinned, the angel repeated that the sins of the flesh were like a continual sacrifice to the Devil, which encouraged even greater fornication. Philentolos was lucky to be spared the fires of eternal Hell, but he would remain forever deprived of the kingdom of heaven. "God is light," the angel concluded, "and he who is deprived of light finds himself in perpetual darkness."

In a sense Philentolos got off lightly, for the darkness of Limbo was preferable to the tortures of Hell that awaited most obstinate sinners. The Byzantines knew that their fate in the hereafter depended on their observance of biblical law; they had to desist from sinning and lead a godly life in imitation of the saints, embodying the Christian duty to love one another. In all this, good works helped.[40] And to the end, the theory of good works provided a major stimulus to the practice of all Byzantine philanthropy.

NOTES

1. *The Apologies of Justin the Martyr*, ed. A.W.F. Blunt (Cambridge, UK, 1911); Tertullian, *Apologeticum*, in *Opera*, ed. E. Dekkers (Turnhout, 1954), I, esp. c. 39, 85–171. For background information in general, see L. W. Countryman, *The Rich Christian in the Church of the Early Empire: Contradictions and Accommodations* (New York/Toronto, 1980), esp. 103–30; M. Hengel, *Property and Riches in the Early Church* (Philadelphia, 1974); D.J. Constantelos, *Byzantine Philanthropy and Social Welfare*, 2nd. ed. (New Brunswick, NJ, 1987).

2. Eusebius, *Hist. Eccles.*, vol. II, vi, 43, ii, 618; G. E. Rickman, *The Corn Supply of Ancient Rome* (Oxford, 1980), 161, 172–73, 183–84, 210–11, stresses that women were not generally admitted to the imperial system, which completely lacked any sense of altruism or poor relief. **Update** See, for example, the attention paid to lepers and the provision of leprosaria, Dionysios Stathakopoulos, "Prêcher les émotions incarnées. Évêques, mendiants et leurs publics dans l'Antiquité tardive," in *La Chair des Émotions*, ed. D. Boquet, P. Nagy, and L. Moulinier-Brogi, *Médiévales* 61 (2011), with useful bibliography.

3. See article *Agape: New Catholic Encyclopedia*, I, 193–94 (C. Bernas), with previous bibliography.

4. Article, *Charité*, *Dictionnaire de Spiritualité*, II, cols. 507–68 (J. Farges and M. Viller).

5. I shall omit private expressions of Christian charity such as those organized by *philoponoi*, which are studied by Paul Magdalino, "Church, Bath and *Diakonia*," in *Church and People in Byzantium*, ed. R. Morris, Centre for Byzantine Studies, University of Birmingham (Birmingham, 1990), 165–88.

6. John Chrysostom, *Homilia in Matthaeum*, LXXVI, PG, 57, col. 630; *Hom. in epist. primam ad Corinth.*, XXII, col. 179.

7. As earlier, *Hom. in epist. primam ad Corinth.*, col. 180.

8. Mark the Deacon, *Vie de Porphyre, évêque de Gaze*, ed. H. Grégoire and M.-A. Kugener (Paris, 1930), 72–73. **Update** *Life of Porphyry, Bishop of Gaza, by Mark the Deacon*, trans. with notes by G. F. Hill (London, 1913).

9. Leontios of Neapolis, *Leben des heiligen Iohannes*, ed. H. Gelzer (Freiburg im Breisgau/Leipzig, 1893), c. 2, 8–9; trans. A. J. Festugière (Paris, 1974), 444–45; H. Delehaye, "Une vie inédite de S. Jean l'Aumonier," *AB* 45 (1927), c. 7, 22 (trans. Festugière, 325); cf. C. Mango, *Byzantium: The Empire of the New Rome* (London, 1980, repr. 1994), 37–38. **Update** Eng. trans. by Elizabeth Dawes, *Three Byzantine Saints: Contemporary Biographies* (Oxford, 1948), and Kenneth Urwin, *Life of the Saint John the Almsgiver* (London, 1980).

10. Ignatios the Deacon, *Vita S. Tarasii*, PG 402. **Update** *The Life of Patriarch Tarasios by Ignatios the Deacon*, intro., ed., trans., and comm. by Stephanos Efthymiadis (Aldershot, UK, 1998).

11. A. Vogt, "S. Théophylacte de Nicomédie," *AB* 50 (1932), c. 8, 75.

12. For example, the monastery of Mt. Tabor had special quarters for its oldest monks called the *ierokomeion*; see R. Thomson, "An Armenian pilgrim on Mt Tabor," *JTS* 18 (1967), 27–33, esp. 32; Constantelos, *Byzantine Philanthropy*, 152–276. **Update** T. S. Miller, *The Birth of the Hospital in the Byzantine Empire* (Baltimore/London, 1985).

13. F. Halkin, "St. Elisabeth d'Heraclée, abbesse à Constantinople," *AB* 91 (1973), 249–64. **Update** Alice-Mary Talbot, ed., *Holy Women of Byzantium: Ten Saints' Lives in English Translation* (Washington, DC, 1996), 117–36.

14. Letter to John of Aelia (Jerusalem); see G. Ostrogorsky, *Studien zur Geschichte des byzantinischen Bilderstreites* (Breslau, 1929; repr. Amsterdam, 1964), 73–75; Eng. trans. in C. Mango, *The Art of the Byzantine Empire, 312–1453: Sources and Documents* (Englewood Cliffs, NJ, 1972, repr. 1986), 42. Epiphanios was cited by the iconoclasts as a supporter; the *Libri Carolini* by Charlemagne refer to the same text in a translation made by Jerome.

15. See, for example, the Piacenza pilgrim's description of the *xenodocheion* of St. George on the edge of the desert, *Itineraria*, ed. P. Geyer (Turnhout, 1965), cc. 35–36, 146–47, and Egeria's reception by the monks of Mt. Sinai, John Wilkinson, *Egeria's Travels to the Holy Land* (London, 1971, repr. 1981), 93–98. **Update** Jennifer L. Hevelone-Harper, *Disciples of the Desert: Monks, Laity and Spiritual Authority in Sixth Century Gaza* (Baltimore, 2005).

16. Sozomen, *Hist. Eccles.*, VI, 34, 9, 291; Gregory Nazianzos, *Oratio XLIII. In laudem Basilii Magni*, *PG*, 36, cols. 493–605, esp. cols. 577–80; Eng. trans. in L. P. McCauley, *Funerary Orations by S. Gregory Nazianzen and S. Ambrose* (Washington, DC, 1968), 80–81; *Vita S. Gregorii Theologi*, *PG*, 35, col. 273; cf. S. Giet, *Les idées et l'action sociale de Saint Basile* (Paris, 1941). **Update** Philip Rousseau, *Basil of Caesarea* (Berkeley/Oxford, 1994); Raymond Van Dam, *Families and Friends in Late Roman Cappadocia* (Philadelphia, 2003).

17. F. Halkin, "S. Samson le Xénodoque de Constantinople (VIe siècle), *RSBN* 4, no. 16 (1977/79), 5–17.

18. E. Schwartz, *Kyrillos von Skythopolis* (Leipzig, 1939), c. 72, 175. **Update** Miller, as earlier.

19. F. Halkin, "La vision de Kaioumos et le sort éternel de Philentolos Olympiou," *AnalBoll*, 63 (1945), 56–64. **Update** Jane Baun, *Tales from Another Byzantium* (Cambridge, UK, 2007), 123, sets this tale in its correct context.

20. E. Wipszycka, *Les ressources et les activités économiques des églises en Egypte du IVe au VIIIe siècle* (Brussels, 1972), 117–19; cf. *The Oxyrhynchus Papyri*, XVI, ed. B. P. Grenfell, A. S. Hunt, and H. I. Bell (London, 1924), no. 1898 (hospital of Abba Elias).

21. *Vie de Porphyre*, (see note 8, earlier), paras. 53 (44); 75–79 (59–63); 83–84 (65–66); 92–93 (71–72).

22. *Theophanes*, 106.

23. E. Patlagean, "La pauvreté à Byzance et la législation de Justinien: aux origines d'un modèle politique," in *Études sur l'histoire de la pauvreté*, ed. M. Mollat, 2 vols. (Paris, 1974), I, 59–81.

24. Mango, *Byzantium*, as earlier 36.

25. See, for example, the account by John Xenos of his journey to the capital to gain an imperial *chrysobullon* that confirmed the independence of his many

foundations; H. Delehaye, *Deux typica byzantins de l'époque des Paléologues* (Brussels, 1921), 194.

26. *La doctrine des Douze Apôtres (Didache)*, ed. and trans. W. Rordorf and A. Tuilier (Paris, 1978), XII, 1–5, 188; *The Lausiac History of Palladius*, ed. C. Butler (Cambridge, UK, 1904), II, c. 7, 25–26. A similar limit of seven days (or three, if there were crowds of poor or pilgrims) was established at the lavra of St. Sabbas; A. Dmitrievsky, *Opisanie Liturgicheskikh Rykopisei*, 3 vols. (Kiev, 1985–1901, Petrograd, 1917), I, 224; repr. by Kurtz, *BZ* 3 (1894), 170.

27. Gregory, *Life of St Lazaros*, cols. 552–53. **Update** *Life of Lazaros of Mt Galesion: An Eleventh Century Pillar Saint*, intro., trans., and notes by Richard P. H. Greenfield (Washington, DC, 1999).

28. P. Gautier, "La Diataxis de Michel Attaliate," *REB* 39 (1981), 5–143, esp. 49, 136–39. **Update** *Byzantine Monastic Foundation Documents: A Complete Translation of the Surviving Founder's Typika and Testaments*, ed. John Thomas and Angela Constantinides Hero (Washington, DC, 2000), and available online at http://www.doaks.org/publications/doaks_online_publications/typ000.html.

29. *Diataxis of Attaliates*, 99, ll.1329–33; 47, ll.496–505, the six who dined with the monks also received four *folleis* (copper coins) each. In addition, there was provision for a regular Sunday distribution of bread at the monastic gate.

30. Dmitrievsky, *Opisanie*, I, c. 38, 649–50. **Update** Also translated in *Byzantine Monastic Foundation Documents*, as earlier, and studied in the Evergetis Project volumes, ed. Margaret Mullett (Belfast, 1994).

31. Delehaye, *Deux typica byzantins* (as earlier), 193, 19 (*oi delothentes choritai*); 193, 25; 194, 4; 195, 2, 4, 19. **Update** Also translated in *Byzantine Monastic Foundation Documents*, as earlier.

32. On the Jewish background and the Christian theory of good works, see Countryman, *The Rich Christian* (see note 1), 107–30; Constantelos, *Byzantine Philanthropy*, 20–25.

33. H. Chadwick, *The Early Church* (Harmondsworth, 1967), 211.

34. Maximos Confessor, *Capita de caritate*, PG, 90, cols. 960–1080; new edition and translation, A. Ceresa-Gastaldo, *Massimo Confessore, Capitoli sulla Carità* (Rome, 1963); see P. Sherwood, *The Four Centuries on Charity* (Westminster, MD/London, 1955); G. C. Berthold, *Maximus Confessor: The 400 Chapters on Love* (London, 1985), 35–87.

35. He is very strict about the correct interpretation of alms giving and good works, stressing that the motive is all-important; see, for instance, *Four Centuries*, I, 24; II, 35.

36. *Four Centuries*, I, 45; III, 1, 3, 11; IV, 44.

37. John of Damascus, *Sacra Parallela*, PG, 95, VIII, *de eleemosyna*, 1456–73.

38. Patriarch Germanos, *Epistola . . . ad Joannem episcopum Synadensem*, PG, 98, 159 D; *Epistola . . . ad Thomam episcopum Claudiopoleos*, PG, 98, 173 A; see V. Grumel, "Homélie de S. Germain sur la délivrance de Constantinople," *REB* 16 (1958), 188–205, esp. para. 25 (199).

39. F. Halkin, "La vision de Kaioumos," see note 20 earlier.

40. For instance, Patriarch Euthymios recommended "alms giving and good deeds, freeing debtors and prisoners" to Leo VI; see *Vita Euthymii Patriarchae CP*, c. X; ed. and trans. P. Karlin-Hayter (Brussels, 1970), 63.

15

Mathematical Mysteries in Byzantium

The Transmission of Fermat's Last Theorem

తో

Mathematics was never my strong suit so nothing had prepared me for this area of research. But in 1993 when Andrew Wiles offered a lecture for the layperson on his solution to Fermat's last theorem, I was determined to get into the crowded auditorium at Princeton University. It was too complicated, as I recall, but spell-binding in its complexity. I hadn't realized that mathematics is a universal language shared by specialists around the world, who talk to each other in theorems about theorems. Wiles demonstrated this in his emphasis on the significance of the Japanese and German contributions to his long search for a solution.

His lecture also made me wonder how Fermat had become aware of the work of Diophantos, an Alexandrian scholar of the third century AD, and this started my quest to trace its transmission. Much research had been devoted to the routes taken by ancient Greek scientific texts in their journey to the medieval West—via Baghdad, Alexandria, Spain, and Sicily. The contributions of Latin scholars who went to Catalonia to learn Arabic, for instance, to translate the workings of the astrolabe, were much better known than mathematical texts. So when Meg Alexiou and Panagiotis Roilos invited me to participate in a conference titled "Reading Byzantium Backward" at Harvard University, I decided to look into the Late Antique and medieval history of Diophantos. Identifying the pathways from the Göttingen Prize won by Wiles back to the writings of the Alexandrian mathematician proved a stimulating way to contribute to this challenging event. The detours I was forced to make into unknown territory, especially the Arabic translations of Greek mathematics, gave me great pleasure and formed a critical stage in the journey. In addition to this additional route via Baghdad, it also confirmed the vital role of Byzantium in the preservation of ancient Greek culture, which it passed on to the West enriched with commentaries. Without Byzantium there would be no Europe as we know it.

I could not have reached the final conclusion without the resources of the Warburg Library in London, where this paper was expanded for publication in the journal, *Dialogos. Hellenic Studies Review* 6 (1999).

WHEN IN 1993 Andrew Wiles claimed to have found a general solution to Fermat's last theorem, the announcement indicated a breakthrough in a problem that had fascinated mathematicians for over 350 years.[1] International interest was expressed, since Japanese, French, German, and American mathematicians among many others had worked on this problem in number theory, and the Göttingen Academy of Sciences had offered a substantial prize for the first successful solution. Fermat's last theorem claims that "the equation $xn + yn = zn$ has no nontrivial solutions when n is greater than 2."[2] And ever since Fermat first propounded it in the Latin notation of the time, and claimed in a famous marginal note: "I have found a truly marvellous demonstration of this," mathematicians have been trying to confirm what he indicated. The story of their endeavors is now well known, and Wiles's publication, which fills an entire number of *Annals of Mathematics* and draws extensively on Japanese and German theories for particular stages of the solution, has been accepted. He has collected the prize, once a large sum of money but now much reduced by nearly a century of inflation.[3]

Less familiar than the account of this long effort is the history of the text that provoked Fermat's last theorem. The seventeenth-century scholar Pierre de Fermat was a lawyer by profession and an amateur mathematician and physicist. He worked in relative isolation and formulated several original concepts in addition to the celebrated "last theorem."[4] One of his sources was the *Arithmetika*, a collection of number problems written by Diophantus, a mathematician who appears to have flourished in Alexandria in the third century AD. This text was famous throughout the Middle Ages and was closely studied by both Greeks and Arabs. In Byzantium Diophantus was read, copied, and commented on by generations of intellectuals, among them scholars who occupy a strategic position in the transmission of ancient Greek culture to the modern world. His work was translated into Arabic in the early ninth century. It was, however, through the Greek text translated into Latin that Fermat became familiar with the mathematical problems of Diophantus, and in particular the one at book II, 8, which encouraged the formulation of his own last theorem.

Since its history from Fermat's time onward is now so well documented, in this chapter I will examine the means by which Diophantus was preserved for about 1,400 years. Why, when so many important works of ancient Greek literature and science disappeared, were these number puzzles preserved? They are not of much practical use, being essentially abstract problems, yet they seem to have met a certain need, or stimulated a curiosity that remained fairly constant from the period of Late Antiquity up to the Renaissance and beyond. Their survival suggests a mathematical and philosophical culture that positively encouraged the text; an articulate awareness of the value of mental calculation, however remote from everyday matters. The medieval context in which so many technical skills, such as building, and silk weaving, were passed on from generation to generation by word of mouth, may also have favored an oral tradition of playing with numbers. It is important to remember that there were no Indian numerals at the time; numbers were represented by letters of the Greek alphabet. Since all the calculations are written out in word form, preserved texts of Diophantus have a very literary feel and look. For whatever reason, it is striking that in Byzantium the mathematical problems of Diophantus not only survived but flourished.

The *Arithmetika* originally had thirteen books, of which ten are preserved; Diophantus also wrote a treatise on polygonal numbers, and several other books on mathematics now lost.[5] His major work is an anomaly, rather unusual by Greek standards, being devoted to an investigation of five kinds (εἴδη) of numbers that share the same attributes: for example, squares, cubes, squares of squares, cubes of cubes. He introduced the sign sigma, ς, as a number that shares none of the properties but has an indeterminate multitude of numbers. This is called "the number," ὁ ἀριθμός. In any problem, ς equals the number whose determination is necessary to the solution.[6]

Within a unified notational system, the problems discussed by Diophantus are quite self-contained; each begins: "To find . . ." or "To divide . . ." a number or numbers that have specific properties. The techniques were rooted in concrete problems, such as the solution of awkward or difficult divisions of inheritance between a number of heirs, which are documented in Babylonia and Egypt. But by the third century AD these numbering-off techniques had become abstracted so that they could be applied to different problems, and the abstraction had begun to reveal the method lying behind such solutions. In turn the abstract method had become an object of interest. Diophantus did not establish a mathematical investigation of the techniques used in his solutions, nor did he enunciate a developed system of the number theory underlying his procedure. His solutions frequently take off from an intelligent guess, which is worked around with great ingenuity to produce a proof. It has been said that while he matches Euclidean geometry in rigor, Diophantus's proofs fail to convince us of their validity; there is a sense of frustration at their lack of explicit generality.[7] He is usually satisfied with a single answer to his problems rather than a complete solution, and it has recently been shown that no general algorithm for Diophantine problems exist. Readers have to go beyond his mathematics to uncover the real workings of these intricate proofs, identified from the Renaissance on as "the mysteries" of Diophantus.[8]

We know next to nothing of this author, whose skills are recorded in an epigram inscribed on his tomb, composed by an anonymous Greek.[9] It records the phases of his life in an arithmetical riddle that runs as follows:

> God granted him to be a boy for the sixth part of his life, and, adding a twelfth part to this, He clothed his cheeks with down. He lit the light of wedlock after a seventh part, and five years after his marriage He granted him a son. Alas! late-born wretched child; after attaining the measure of half his father's life, chill Fate took him. After consoling his grief by this science of numbers for four years, he ended his life.

The answer to the puzzle is 84: for he was a boy for fourteen years, a youth for seven, that is, he became an adult at twenty-one years, at thirty-three he married, at thirty-eight he had a son born to him who died at the age of forty-two, and he survived him by four years, dying at the age of 84: $38 + 42 + 4 = 84$! This is typical of the arithmetical epigrams and riddles so popular in Byzantium.[10] Indeed, the transmission of Diophantus in Greek is associated with a collection of thirty-eight of very similar character.[11] Possibly both number problems and riddles were learned as elements of mental arithmetic, since they are easily memorized and may be preserved by oral tradition. It is clear, however, that in his day, Diophantus was considered very distinguished. Anatolios of Alexandria admired him as "the most erudite," and when he brought together the most essential parts of mathematical science then known, he dedicated them to his friend Diophantus.[12]

A century or so later, the philosopher and mathematician Hypatia, one of the few female professors of Late Antiquity, studied the works of Diophantus and Ptolemy, which she expounded in public lectures at Alexandria. She wrote commentaries on both these authors, including at least the first six books of the *Arithmetika*; this may be why they have survived in Greek. Her father, Theon, a famous teacher, had trained her to continue the established education of young men of the day in the traditional style, and from a recent study of Ptolemy's *Almagest*, it is clear that they worked together. Theon deferred to her scholia in his introduction to book III.[13] Although so little of Hypatia's own writings has survived, her elevated position in Alexandrian society is well documented in the correspondence of Synesius of Cyrene, who greatly admired her. Her commitment to Neoplatonist philosophy involved a life of celibacy and scholarship, which is commemorated in an epigram.[14] Hypatia is better known for the manner of her death than her life: she was the distinguished teacher lynched by irate Christian monks in the great riot of 415, which pitted supporters of Patriarch Cyril against the Prefect Orestes and other non-Christian groups.[15]

Yet the riot did not quench enthusiasm for Diophantus, who continued to be studied in Christian Byzantium. Testimonia of his works have been mapped by Tannery, and include a curious reference in the *Life* of St. John of Damascus, who is said to have studied Diophantus, together with his adopted brother Kosmas the Hymnographer, in late seventh-century Palestine.[16] As Cyril Mango has shown, however, the Late Antique traditions of a basic education, including the quadrivium of mathematics, appear to have lived on longer in Palestine than in other parts of the Byzantine world.[17] The suggestion that young men in the 680s and 690s, destined for ecclesiastical careers, could have studied Pythagoras, Diophantus, Euclid, and music is remarkable. Their own writings reveal a solid background knowledge of ancient scholarship, for example Kosmas's commentary on the mythical elements in Gregory of Nyssa. Another allusion to Diophantus in medieval Byzantium occurs in Ignatius the deacon's *Life* of Tarasius, patriarch of Constantinople from 784 to 806. There is, however, no suggestion that either Tarasius or Ignatius studied his theorems.[18]

In his recent study of Diophantus, André Allard has clarified the medieval transmission of the Greek text, positing an archetype now lost that may fill the same role as intermediaries hypothesized by previous editors.[19] From this text two families descend, both represented by manuscripts of the thirteenth century. One is based on a copy from which a manuscript now in Madrid was made;[20] the other consists of a copy made by Maximus Planudes himself, who worked on the text in the 1290s. Only a few folios of his autograph are now preserved in Milan.[21] The first version was known to the famous Renaissance teacher of Greek, Constantine Laskaris, who left his copy to the Cathedral Chapter of Messina, the Sicilian city, in which he lived and taught.[22] From there it passed to Madrid like so many important Byzantine manuscripts now preserved in Spain, such as the illustrated Skylitzes, and the Middle Byzantine Taktikon of 971–75 in the Escorial. This library also preserves a copy of Michael Psellus's letters; in a long one on mathematics, he mentions his own copy of the *Arithmetika* of Diophantus.[23] The second version, with the Planudean commentaries is represented by two important texts in the Vatican library, to which I will return.

In parallel with the medieval Greek transmission, the Arabs were also busy studying Diophantus, whose writings they translated.[24] From a recent discovery in the Isfahan library, it has been established that they had access to a fuller version of the *Arithmetika*.[25] Four previously unknown books must have been placed between books III and IV as preserved in the Greek tradition. The Arabic translation appears to have been made in the early ninth century, during the rule of Caliph al-Mamun (813–33), which was a particularly important period in the development of this branch of mathematics. It is at this moment that Arab scholars coined the term "algebra," which was used to describe the theorems of Diophantus and others. It occurs for the first time in the title of al-Khwarizmi's *Book of the calculation of the Algebra and the Al-muqabala,* written under the patronage of al-Mamun.[26] The popularity of Diophantine theorems in the tenth and eleventh centuries is evident from the quarrels that arose between three philosophers, al-Khujandi, al-Khazin, and Abu Ga'far, who were all trying to demonstrate a proof of one theorem to the third power.[27]

For both Arabs and Greeks the appeal of Diophantus seems to have derived from his number theory, which often coincided with the medieval fascination with number magic. It may also be connected with the popularity of epigrams and collections of arithmetical riddles and puzzles, much beloved by peoples ancient and medieval, Christian and Muslim.[28] In the early seventh century when the Armenian scholar Ananias of Shirak was searching for instruction in advanced mathematics, he may well have used a Greek collection in the compilation of his Armenian one, devised "for retelling at feasts."[29] The fact that he includes riddles with contemporary references to Constantinople, for instance, in the puzzle to calculate the number of pounds of gold distributed to the clergy of the cathedral church of St. Sophia, suggests familiarity with topical problems transmitted in Greek.[30] Not only are these puzzles curious brain-teasers; they can easily be memorized and transmitted orally with no reference to a written text. This is obviously an important aspect of the long history of recreational mathematics.

From the Caliphate of Baghdad, Muslim scholars translated and mastered ancient Greek science, making their own very significant contributions to mathematics, as if in competition with the medieval Greeks. The process may be illustrated by a story, probably apocryphal, recorded in the ninth century during the reigns of Caliph al-Mamun and the Emperor Theophilos, when a Byzantine student was taken prisoner by the Arabs and found himself in a Baghdad jail.[31] To entertain his fellow prisoners he expounded theorems and number puzzles. When this fact was observed, he was summoned to the Caliph, who asked him to demonstrate his knowledge. It transpired that the Arab mathematicians had translated the works of Euclid, but could not prove his theorems. The Greek prisoner was ordered back to Byzantium to persuade his teacher to visit Baghdad. But when Theophilos heard of the proposal, he instead appointed the said teacher to give lessons at the church of the Forty Martyrs in Constantinople.

This expert was Leo the Mathematician, also called the Philosopher, whose life and education remain rather obscure, since the teacher from whom he acquired most of his knowledge is described as "a wise man" who lived on Andros.[32] In the mountains of the same Aegean island, Leo found books that he studied and took with him when he returned to the capital. According to Theophanes Continuatus, Leo followed the ancient principle of seeking a learned man and studying with him, in order to overcome the lack of advanced training in mathematics and philosophy in Constantinople. Having learned all that his teacher could impart, he then went off in search of manuscripts, and eventually set up as private teacher in Constantinople.[33]

Once the emperor realized what an important scholar Leo was, paid employment followed in a school established at the church of the Forty Martyrs. There is no suggestion that this position involved an official church post, but Leo was soon ordained, for in 840 Theophilos appointed him to the archbishopric of Thessalonike, a very senior ecclesiastical position. There he remained for three years while the iconoclast policies of the emperor were in force. If we may conclude that Leo was considered a reliable opponent of the iconophile veneration of images, he would have been a colleague of the iconoclast Patriarch, John the Grammarian, also a scholar of advanced skills.[34] After the restoration of the images, he must have left his ecclesiastical position and seems to have returned to teaching. In 863 the acting head of government, Bardas, made him head of the Magnaura school, where he held the title "chief of the philosophers" and taught both philosophy and the quadrivium of mathematics, assisted by

Theodore (his pupil) who taught geometry, Theodegios, for astronomy, and Kometas, for grammar. Arethas, a younger scholar and bibliophile, heard Leo lecture on Euclid, and incorporated Leo's commentary into his commissioned copy of the *Elements*.

Leo's importance in the preservation of ancient Greek mathematics rests on his role in the production of manuscripts that form a vital link in the line of descent from Antiquity. Because this can be demonstrated in the case of several key texts, it seems quite reasonable to associate him with the transmission of Diophantus. But first let us survey the surviving manuscripts, for instance, the copy of Euclid's *Elements*, made by Stephanos, *klerikos* in AD 888, which was commissioned by Arethas.[35] It contains Leo's *hypomnema scholikon*, a commentary in the form of a scholion, on definition 5 of Book VI, which Arethas had heard expounded by Leo.[36] A very early minuscule text of Ptolemy, *Syntaxis*, dated to the ninth century is also preserved, Vaticanus graecus 1594, which contains a marginal note: "the book of Leo, the excellent astronomer."[37] While the note has been shown to be a much later addition, there is no reason to dissociate this manuscript from Leo and his circle. A similar tribute closes a version of the works of Archimedes. Two later copies preserve the invocation: "May you prosper, Leo the geometer, may you live many years, much the dearest to the Muses."[38] From this it seems likely that Leo was responsible for having the text of Archimedes copied.

In connection with the transmission of Archimedes, an additional aspect of Leo's importance derives from the fact that many of the manuscripts had to be transcribed from uncial into the novel minuscule script of the ninth century. This new cursive script was developed during the theological controversy over icons and facilitated quicker writing. But for the copying of ancient texts, a complete process of transliteration was required, and it seems clear that Leo took a major role in organizing the method of conversion. The dangers inherent in this activity may be documented by the famous codex of Giorgio Valla (ca. 1430–99), now in Paris, which has a long colophon describing the transcription, "made from a very old ... exemplar, which exhibited a very great, even immeasurable lack of clarity because of mistakes." Paul Lemerle suggested that some of these errors were the result of copying a text in uncial script into minuscule during the period of transliteration from one letter form to the other, which took place under Leo's direction.[39] Leo's scholarship also forms the basis of the incomplete Archimedes compiled by Isidore, which formed the archetype (lost in the sixteenth century) for a twelfth-century copy that passed through the Norman kings' library in Sicily and on to the Vatican. There it was used by William of Moerbeke in his translation of Archimedes into Latin.

Given his position as the leading philosopher and mathematician in ninth-century Byzantium, Leo should probably be connected with the lost version of Diophantus posited by Tannery and Heath.[40] The suggestion that the *Arithmetika* must have been copied in the eighth or ninth century and that this copy served as the model for the thirteenth-century version preserved in Madrid ignores the dearth of evidence for any mathematical innovation in the eighth. In the ninth, however, when renewed interest generated by Leo was encouraged by the schools set up by Theophilos and Bardas, an obvious context emerges. Leo's interests may also be reflected in copies of Apollonios *On Conics*, which served as the prototype for two copies made in the tenth and twelfth centuries, both now in the Vatican library; of Theon of Alexandria on astronomy, bound with a treatise on geometry by Proklos of Xanthos, and a treatise on mechanics by Kyrinos and Markellos. The combination of this copying and transliterating activity with Leo's teaching also generated manuscripts on astronomy, a short treatise, and further interpretations of Archimedes.

In addition, Leo is associated with several literary manuscripts: he owned copies of Porphyry, for which he composed a distich (*AP*, IX, 214), and Achilles Tatius's *Leucippe and Clitophon*, on which he probably composed another (*AP*, IX, 203). This literary interest is the link to another of Leo's activities, namely, the writing and arranging of epigrams in a *sylloge* (collection). He not only produced his own, autobiographical verse full of Homeric allusions, in which he identifies himself as a Hellene (*AP*, XV, 12), he also made contributions to book IX of the *Greek Anthology*. Many of these epigrams are transmitted in series which suggests that they were taken from a Late Antique anthology possibly by Leo himself.[41]

Writing epigrams was an activity shared by Leo's contemporaries, including his student and rival, Constantine the Sicilian, who contributed to book XV of the *Greek Anthology*. In an important manuscript, the *Barberinianus graecus 310*, Leo, Constantine, and Theophanes (another contemporary) are also bracketed together as ninth-century *grammatikoi*, who all wrote anacreontics. At a gap in Book XV, the scribe J brings the three together, referring to Leo as the Hellene and the other two as *makarioi* (recently deceased). This occurs in his *sylloge* of epigrams more contemporary than ancient, including some by Michael the Chartophylax, who played a major role in the transmission of the *Anthology*.[42]

Given Leo's mathematical interests, might he also have copied the arithmetical epigrams that form a large part of book XIV of the *Greek Anthology*? This collection goes back to Metrodoros, an author who flourished at the turn of the sixth century, and provides epigrams 116 to 146, which are very close to the numbering-off tradition of Diophantus. The same book also contains the thirty-eight found in Diophantus's manuscript, beginning with the group attributed to Socrates, *AP*, XIV, 1, which follows the established style of a mathematical riddle or number game.

As an example of this type of epigram, I cite XIV, 3:

> Cypris thus addressed Love who was looking downcast: "How, my child, hath sorrow fallen upon thee?" And he answered: "The Muses stole and divided among themselves, in different proportions, the apples I was bringing from Helicon, snatching them from my bosom. Clio got the fifth part, and Euterpe the twelfth, but divine Thalia the eighth. Melpomene carried off the twentieth part, and Terpsichore the fourth and Erato the seventh. Polymnia robbed me of thirty apples and Urania of a hundred and twenty, and Calliope went off with a load of three hundred apples. So I came to thee with lighter hands, bringing these fifty apples that the goddesses left me."

Solution: 3,360.[43]

The same problem is addressed in several more devoted to apples (XIV, 117–99), while 120 is a division of walnuts from a tree (cf. 138). The epitaph of Diophantus himself is preserved here (126); an identical structure describes a certain Demochares (127); and 139 is a mathematical problem about the measurement of time, based on a sun-dial, addressed to Diodorus, the great glory of dial-makers. The combination of arithmetical epigrams and the epitaph of Diophantus in this form perhaps points to another slight connection between Leo and the author of the *Arithmetika*.

Leo's name is also attached, incorrectly, to a fragment of an epic poem on the Arethusa source of Sicily, dating from the Roman period (IX, 579). Nestor of Laranda may be the author of this whole series devoted to rivers, springs, sources, and so on, and the attribution to Leo derives from his authorship of the preceding epigram, 578. Similarly, other epigrams are attributed to Leo (for example, IX, 361), although in the *Sylloge Euphemiana*, dating from the reign of Leo VI (886–913), the poem is accurately described as anonymous. Such suppositions reflect the fame of Leo as a composer of verses as well as a mathematician and philosopher.

I have emphasized the contribution of Leo to the development of mathematical as well as literary traditions in Byzantium not only because he seems the person most likely to have commissioned a ninth-century copy of Diophantus, but also because he embodies the wide range of skills associated with the study of philosophy in medieval times. All the works of the ancients were important to these scholars, who made no distinction between the need to use metre correctly and to work out scientific problems accurately. To the Byzantines Leo was famous as both a mathematician and a philosopher. He has justly been called "the first example in Byzantium of a truly "Renaissance man,"[44] a polymath with a passion for all things ancient. His heritage was not lost in Byzantium, although it is difficult to trace the study of Diophantus through the medieval period. Many of the gaps in the written record may be filled by oral transmission. Writing between 808 and 969 John Patriarch of Jerusalem (or his Arabic source) believed that the seventh-century saint John of Damascus had studied Diophantus together with Euclid and Ptolemy. The compilers of the *Suda* also knew of the importance of Diophantus in the tradition of number theory and recorded the commentaries made to the first six books by Hypatia (quoting from the *Life* of Isidore by Damascius).[45] And in 1007/8 the *Quadrivium* of higher learning was revised in Byzantium, indicating persistent concern to ensure the study of the "mathematical quartet," although Diophantine equations did not feature in it.[46] In the mid-eleventh century, Michael Psellus owned a copy of the *Arithmetika* and wrote a long letter about mathematics.

Between this mention of Diophantus and the intensive study of his works by the Late Byzantine authors George Pachymeres and Maximus Planudes there is another breach in our knowledge, although considerable progress was made in Byzantine mathematics, including the introduction of Indian (Arabic) numerals and Indian (Oriental) methods of calculation. Toward the end of the thirteenth century Pachymeres made a partial paraphrase[47] of Diophantus's *Arithmetika* and incorporated it into his introduction to the *quadrivium*.[48] But Planudes produced a systematic commentary on the first book and part of the second.[49] According to Nigel Wilson he "manages to set out some of the problems in a form which is easier to understand than that of the original and not much harder than that which they might assume in modern notation."[50] At II, 8, there is the remarkable scholion: "May your soul, o Diophantus, rest with Satan on account of the difficulty of your other theorems and particularly of the present theorem," which is perhaps a consequence of this editorial work of Planudes. So the mysteries of Diophantus were still unyielding. But the same scholion in the Madrid manuscript has been authoritatively attributed by Wilson to a later hand, that of the polymath, John Chortasmenus.

Nonetheless, to reach this level of mastery over the text, Maximus Planudes took pains to collate his own copy of Diophantus against another which he wanted to borrow from Manuel Bryennius (letter 33), and yet another which he lent to Theodore Mouzalon, the grand logothete.[51] Planudes's autograph of the edition and commentary of Diophantus, written in 1292–93, survives in only ten folios now in Milan.[52] But it is only one of the many manuscripts produced at the Chora monastery in Constantinople, where Planudes had access to an excellent library. There he also devoted expert attention to ancient geographers, studying both Ptolemy and Strabo: his enthusiasm at finding a text of Ptolemy is celebrated in hexameter verses that accompany his careful edition of 1295–96 (Vaticanus graecus 177).[53] A later copy of Ptolemy is found in the same manuscript as Diophantus, together with an astronomical work by Theodosius, confirming Planudes's wide range of scientific interests. His autograph corrections to parts of Strabo's geography are preserved in a Paris text (Parisinus graecus 1393), which includes later Classical authors, such as Pausanias. These justly celebrated manuscripts demonstrate the erudition of Late Byzantine humanists including Nikolaos Artabasdos Rhabdas and Demetrios Kydones, who mentions his own study of Diophantus and Euclidean geometry in letter 347.[54] There is no sense of division between literary and scientific subjects in their enthusiasm. Rather, they cherished the wisdom of the ancients and sought by all possible means to preserve and perpetuate it.

Thus Maximus Planudes was also responsible for reorganizing and editing the *Greek Anthology* from a fuller version than that preserved in surviving manuscripts. From this he was able to restore 388 epigrams missing from the second half of book IX, which today forms book XVI, the so-called Planudean appendix. While none of them take the form of arithmetical riddles, Planudes rescued a vast number of verses dedicated to statues, as well as reproducing epigrams from the monuments in the Hippodrome of Constantinople.[55] In this activity, he makes the same connection between the epigram and arithmetic as Leo before him. But when it came to ancient culture, his real love was reserved for Plutarch, whose *Moralia* he copied in his own hand, because he greatly liked the man.[56] As a monk of the Chora monastery, Planudes bears witness not only to its resources for research but also to the far-ranging intellectual curiosity of late Byzantine scholars.

This tradition was maintained throughout the fourteenth and fifteenth centuries, influencing those Byzantines who emigrated to the West to teach Greek and promote the study of ancient texts. Within the

Constantinopolitan circle John Chortasmenus played a distinguished role. A product of the patriarchal chancellery in Constantinople, he wrote iambic verses and epigrams, a *Life* of Constantine and Helena, prolegomena to the *Logic* of Aristotle, orations and numerous letters, among other works. His collection of manuscripts reveals a very deliberate bibliophile, who copied astronomical texts for his own use and was responsible for the rebinding of the famous sixth-century herbal by Dioskorides dedicated to Juliana Anicia.[57] He too studied Diophantus and is now recognized as the author of the despairing scholion in the margin at book II, 8.[58] As the teacher of Bessarion he probably had an impact on the young scholar from Trebizond, who in turn became an avid collector of Greek manuscripts. Certainly he imparted to the man whose library became so famous a sense of the interconnected relationship between mathematical, philosophical, and literary studies, which had characterized Byzantine scholarship since the teaching of Hypatia in Late Antiquity. Bessarion, as is well known, followed an ecclesiastical career, converted to Western Catholicism, and was made a cardinal in 1439. But he wrote prolifically on many topics, not only theological, and his interest in scientific and philosophical works is amply demonstrated by his collection, which was bequeathed to the Republic of Venice.[59]

Among these manuscripts is one important copy of Planudes's edition of Diophantus, which was to play a crucial role in the transition from East to West. It was brought to Italy by Bessarion and is now *Codex 308* of the Marciana library.[60] In 1464 the Renaissance scholar Regiomontanus, who served as secretary to the cardinal, knew that it contained only six books and not the promised thirteen, but reported: "it is really most wonderful and most difficult. ... I should like to translate it into Latin, for the knowledge of Greek which I have acquired while staying with my most reverend master Bessarion would suffice for this."[61] At about this time, 1463–64, in a public lecture, an *Oratio* given at Padua, he observed: "No one has yet translated from the Greek into Latin the fine thirteen Books of Diophantus, in which the very flower of the whole of Arithmetic lies hid, the *ars rei et census* (the art of the thing and the power) which today they call by the Arabic name of 'Algebra.'"[62] While this "hidden" character was perhaps enhanced by the riddle-like form of transmission, its very difficulty and obscurity served to confirm the mysterious quality of Diophantus's work.

Thus, only a decade after the fall of Constantinople to the Turks one manuscript of Diophantus had been identified and one Western scholar was anxious to translate it into Latin. Another copy was already recorded in the Vatican catalogue of Greek manuscripts, Vaticanus graecus 304, which entered the papal library with Pope Nicholas V (1447–55) before 1453.[63] It lacks the Planudean commentaries, so must represent the Madrid family, and also contains the Tables of Theon of Alexandria. Two other copies of Diophantus came to the Vatican in the course of the sixteenth century, one made from Bessarion's Venice manuscript.[64]

But no use was made of this work until the mid-sixteenth century, when algebra became a new classical subject. Among scholars responsible for this endeavor, Francisco Maurolico, the son of Greek refugees from Constantinople, spread an interest in number theory through his study of arithmetic in two books published in 1575 after his death.[65] More influential was the work of Raphael Bombelli, who attempted to theorize the discipline using the *Arithmetika* of Diophantus, which he intended to translate. Together with a colleague, he prepared a Latin version of several books, but this was never published.[66] Instead, Bombelli incorporated all the first four books and some of the fifth (148 problems in all) into his own *Algebra* (published in 1572) without distinguishing the reasoning of Diophantus from his own. Thus Diophantus got no credit and his text remained unknown.

At about the same time, however, more useful contributions to the transmission of Diophantus were made by professional scribes, who copied his work for patrons. The most important of these is the famous Giovanni of Otranto, who signed his copies using the Latin form, Ioannes Honorius Hydruntinus.[67] From 1535–56 he served as Greek scribe and restorer of manuscripts in the Vatican Library, and was responsible for copying a large number of scientific works, including Diophantus. Realizing that in two Vatican manuscripts he had different traditions of the *Arithmetika*, he collated *Vaticanus graecus 304* of the Madrid family, and *Vaticanus graecus 200*, a copy of Bessarion's copy of Planudes's edition, to form a composite more complete than either. This piece of editorial sophistication combined the earlier tradition represented by Madrid with the late thirteenth-century edition and commentary. Giovanni was a prolific copier; in some manuscripts he used his daughter as an assistant; and together they produced many texts of mathematics, the *Conics* of Apollonios, Nikomachos, Ptolemy, Euclid, and a large number of early Christian writings. His Diophantus was taken to France, where in the 1570s François Viète read it (*Parisinus graecus 2379*).[68]

By a similar process of sensitive editing, Andreas Dudicius Sbardellatus, a scholar active in Poland, commissioned a Venetian scribe to make a composite copy of two later versions (*Ambrosianus A91* and *Guelferbytanus*

Gudianus 1), which is now *Reginensis 128*.[69] This is the text from which the first Latin translation of Diophantus was made in 1571–75 by Wilhelm Holzmann, who called himself Xylander, "wood man" in Greek.[70] It had been carefully prepared, yet Xylander complained of enormous difficulties in the very corrupt text. More mysteries, then, which may have been especially discomforting to a scholar who prided himself on his skill at editing Plutarch, Stephanos, and Strabo. His Latin translation was published in 1575 and dedicated to Prince Ludwig of Wittenberg: the mysteries of Diophantus were beginning to yield.

Xylander also planned to publish the Greek text, and his edition is preserved, apparently prepared for printing, in another manuscript, *Palatinus graecus 391*. But the first Greek edition only appeared much later, in 1621; it was made by the French scholar Bachet de Méziriac using *Parisinus graecus 2379*, the composite Greek copy put together by Giovanni of Otranto.[71] Bachet included the Latin translation of Xylander, corrected and improved in ways that were intended to enhance his own contribution and downplay that of Xylander. He also consulted Bombelli's translation, which he found better than Xylander's in some cases.

It was this same edition of the Greek that was republished with Fermat's notes by his son in 1670.[72] The notes had been taken from Fermat's copy of Bachet's edition of Diophantus, now lost, in the margins of which he had noted at book II, 8: "On the other hand it is impossible to separate a cube into two cubes or a biquadrate into two biquadrates, or generally any power except a square into two powers with the same exponent. I have discovered a truly marvellous proof of this, which however the margin is not large enough to contain."[73] He thus formulated the theorem that became known as Fermat's last theorem and that Andrew Wiles has now solved. Whether Fermat thought he had a general proof, or a proof that the theorem was not correct to the third and fourth power, is not entirely clear. But ever since his claim, mathematicians have been trying to demonstrate that the proposition has no nontrivial solutions. In 1753 Euler reported to Goldbach that he had proved Fermat's theorem to the third and fourth powers, but could not find a method to prove the fifth, which seemed to require a different technique.[74] That was achieved by Legendre and Dirichlet before 1825, yet any hope of finding a general solution seemed remote at the beginning of the twentieth century, when Paul Wolfskehl established a very handsome prize at the Göttingen Academy of Sciences.[75]

The study of Diophantus in modern times is now well-known and brilliantly chronicled in Simon Singh's recent study. However, Fermat would never have learned of the problem but for the patient work of scholars who for over a millennium kept these mathematical puzzles alive. And it was in Byzantium, a part of the medieval world that cherished the memory of all things Greek, that the mysteries of Diophantus were preserved, embellished, developed, and enjoyed by many generations of amateur mathematicians like Fermat. Much less evidence and detail of their work survives than the documentation for problem solving in the Renaissance and later eras. But I hope that this article has shown how crucial their concern was for the modern understanding of ancient Greek mathematics.

It used to be said that the fall of Constantinople to the Turks provided an important stimulus to the Renaissance.[76] But this claim has been so much debunked that it has been rendered impotent. So there is a certain satisfaction in observing that the transmission of Diophantus to the modern world in its original language occurred through the medium of a manuscript brought to Italy by the infamous Cardinal Bessarion, an apostate from Byzantine Orthodoxy. Through his collection of Greek manuscripts, given to Venice, the West acquired what became the core of the Marciana library. Among them, his own manuscript of Diophantus was in turn copied several times; collated with an earlier version by a particularly intelligent scribe, Giovanni of Otranto, in the mid-sixteenth century; and edited in Paris by a humanist scholar Bachet de Méziriac, with input from Holzmann (Xylander), who made the first Latin translation. There is, thus, a direct link back to Byzantium, where intellectuals, such as Leo the Mathematician (a humanist before his time), and monks such as Maximus Planudes not only copied and studied the mysteries of Diophantus, but also wrote commentaries that tried to make sense of them. Their work highlights a continuous thread of fascination with ancient mathematics otherwise represented by orally preserved riddles and epigrams of number theory passed on from generation to generation in ways that remain largely hidden.

The association of mathematical riddles with collections of epigrams, such as those in the *Greek Anthology*, is common to many cultures. Recreational brain teasers were popular not only in medieval Byzantium, but also in ancient China, India, Egypt, and even in seventeenth-century France, where Bachet, the editor of Diophantus, made his own collection.[77] Here is an example: "If you multiply 5525, a number composed of six squares . . . into 1073, a number composed twice . . . the produce is 5929325, a number composed (and this is marvellous) twenty four times from two squares"—and he gives the sides. This is precisely the type of mental exercise that the Byzantines used to enjoy, a game with numbers that can be transmitted without writing. Because of the similarity between such problems and the equations of Diophantus, we can imagine the oral channels of communication that kept his number theories alive between Late Antiquity and the Renaissance. And for the written forms, it is perhaps the abiding curiosity about the properties of numbers that accounts for the perseverance with which generations of Byzantine scholars struggled with the mysteries of Diophantus.

NOTES

1. I am most grateful to Professor Wiles for conversations about this paper and about the way in which mathematicians have evaluated proof over the centuries. For coverage of the discovery, see G. Kolata, "Andrew Wiles: A Math Whiz Battles 350-Year-Old Puzzle," in *Math Horizons* (Winter 1993), 8–11. I particularly thank George Baloglou for sending me a copy of this item. The recent publication by S. Singh, *Fermat's Last Theorem* (London, 1997), gives copious details.

2. Kolata, "Wiles," 8; A. Baker, *A Concise Introduction to the Theory of Numbers* (Cambridge, UK, 1984), 200.

3. Singh, *Fermat*, 116, 135–37, 143–46, with extraordinary detail on the prize of 100,000 Marks established in 1908 by Paul Wolfskehl and administered by the Göttingen Academy of Sciences. In the course of investigating its history I have been introduced to a whole new world of recreational mathematics and complex number riddles, which would have remained unexplored but for the coincidence of the solution announced by Wiles and the interest of colleagues at Princeton University associated with the Program in the History of Science and the Program in Hellenic Studies. Without their help and guidance it would have been impossible for me to pursue the mysteries of Diophantus through the Byzantine era. I would also like to acknowledge the assistance of many friends and students for questioning my presentations and improving my understanding of the issues: Meg Alexiou, Panagiotis Roilos, and Greg Nagy, who invited me to a Harvard seminar in May 1995; Dominic Rathbone and members of the KCL graduate seminar; Robert Thompson and members of the Oxford Byzantine Seminar; Simon Pembroke and an ICS seminar; and Pat Easterling and Michael Reeve and members of a Cambridge manuscript group. To Nigel Wilson, Giles Constable, and Anthony Barnett, my warmest thanks for critical advice.

4. On Pierre de Fermat, I am greatly indebted to Mike Mahony, whose study, *Pierre de Fermat* (new ed., Princeton, 1993) has been a revelation of the culture of seventeenth-century mathematics. On his other theorems and concepts, such as Fermat primes, an optimization theory (Steiner's problem) and the principle of least time (physics), see also Baker, *Introduction*; Singh, *Fermat*, 37–47, 60–72.

5. Diophantus is an exceptionally difficult author of algebraic problems; see N. G. Wilson, *Scholars of Byzantium*, rev. ed. (London, 1996), 42. On Diophantus's contribution to the history of mathematics, see T. L. Heath, *A History of Greek Mathematics*, 2 vols. (Oxford, 1921), II, 448–517; and on his significance in Byzantium, A. P. Kazhdan et al., *ODB*, 3 vols. (Oxford, 1991), II, 1313–14.

6. For all that follows on Diophantus and the way his work was read in the Renaissance, see the outstanding study by J. S. Morse, "The Reception of Diophantus' Arithmetic in the Renaissance" (PhD Diss., Princeton, 1981); also T. H. Heath, *Diophantus of Alexandria: A Study of the History of Greek Algebra*, 2nd ed. (Cambridge, UK, 1910; repr. New York, 1964), 32–37.

7. For explication of Diophantus's procedure, I am most grateful to Michael Mahony; see also the thesis by Morse, which was written under his supervision, "Reception," 9–11.

8. Morse, "Reception," 15.

9. *The Greek Anthology*, book XIV, no, 126, trans. W. R. Paton, 5 vols. (London/New York, 1969; repr. Cambridge, MA, 1993), 5, 92–94; see also Heath, *History*, II, 441–43.

10. The next one in the same collection of Metrodoros concerns Demochares and follows exactly the same pattern, book XIV, 127; Paton, vol. 5, 94.

11. See the critical edition of Diophantus by P. Tannery, *Diophanti Alexandrini Opera omnia*, 2 vols. (Leipzig, 1895), II, 43–72; the discussion of Metrodoros in Heath, *History*, II, 442–43; Alan Cameron, "Michael Psellus and the Date of the Palatine Anthology," *GRBS* 11 (1960), 339–50.

12. See the useful article by Kurt Vogel in *The Dictionary of Scientific Biography* (New York, 1971), IV, 110–19.

13. Alan Cameron, "Isidore of Miletus and Hypatia on the Editing of Mathematical Texts," *GRBS* 31 (1990), 103–27; Maria Dzielska, *Hypatia of Alexandria* (Eng. trans. Cambridge, MA, 1996), 70–72; M. E. Waithe, ed., *A History of Women Philosophers* (Dortrecht/Boston/Lancaster, 1987), vol. 1, 175, notes that Tannery spotted Hypatia's use of the sexagesimal fraction in working out solutions, which was also observed by Rome in his edition of the commentary on book III of Ptolemy's *Almagest*; see A. Rome, *Commentaires de Pappus et de Théon d'Alexandrie sur l'Almageste*, vol. III, Studi e Testi, 106 (Rome, 1943), cxvi–cxxi. Waithe suggests that this seems to be particular to her and may identify her own contribution, *Women Philosophers*, 1, 176–92. For a more detailed analysis of her method, with clear translations and commentary, see now W. R. Knorr, *Textual Studies in Ancient and Medieval Geometry* (Boston/Basel/Berlin, 1989), 753–804. **Update** Michael A. B. Deakin, "Hypatia and Her Mathematics," *American Mathematical Journal* 101 (March 1990), 234–43, stresses her original contribution as a teacher; see also Silvia Ronchey, *Ipazia. La vera storia* (Milan, 2010), 150 (and 261–65, with notes critical of Waithe, and recent bibliography).

14. *AP*, IX, 400, which is not about a Christian virgin, *pace* Alan Cameron, *The Greek Anthology from Meleager to Planudes* (Oxford, 1993), 323–25. See Marc Lauxtermann, "The Byzantine Epigram in the Ninth and Tenth Centuries," (PhD Diss., Amsterdam, 1994), 243, n. 131. See also the testimony of Synesius on Hypatia's brilliance as a teacher analyzed by Dzielska, *Hypatia*, 28–55, 58–65.

15. On the death of Hypatia, see Socrates, *Ecclesiastical History*, VII, 13–15; Sarolta Takács, "The Magic of Isis Replaced," *Poikila Byzantina* 13 (Bonn, 1994), 491–507; J. Rougé, "La Politique de Cyrille d'Alexandrie et le Meutre d'Hypatie," *Cristianesimo nella storia* 11 (1990), 485–504. **Update** Ronchey, as earlier, 57–67, 217–22.

16. Tannery, *Diophanti*, II, 36; see now B. Flusin, "De l'arabe au grec, puis au géorgien: une Vie de S. Jean Damascène," in *Traduction et traducteurs au Moyen-Age* (Paris, 1989), 51–61. The Greek *Life*, based on the Arabic, was written by Patriarch John VII of Jerusalem (951–64).

17. C. Mango, "Greek Culture in Palestine after the Arab Conquest," in G. Cavallo et al., eds., *Scritture, libri e testi nella aree provinciali de Bisanzio* (Spoleto, 1991), 149–60.

18. S. Efthymiades, *The Life of Patriarch Tarasios by Ignatios the Deacon* (Aldershot, UK, 1998), 95.

19. André Allard, "La tradition du texte grec des Arithmétiques de Diophante d'Alexandrie," *Revue d'Histoire des Textes* 12/13 (1982/3), 57–137; and "Les Scholies aux Arithmétiques de Diophante d'Alexandrie dans le Matritensis Bib. Nat. 4678, et les Vaticani gr. 191 et 304," *B* 53 (1983), 664–760. Cf. Heath, *Diophantus of Alexandria*, 14–15. Following the link posited by P. Tannery, *Diophanti*, II, xviii, Heath suggested that this important copy must have been made in the eighth or ninth century.

20. This is *Matritensis Bib. Nat. 4678* (previously 48); see G. de André, *Catalogo de los Códices Griegos de la Biblioteca Nacional* (Madrid, 1987), cos. 128, 227–28. It entered the library in 1712.

21. Allard, "*L'Ambrosianus Et. 157 Sup.*, un manuscrit autographe de Maxime Planude," *Scriptorium*, 33 (1979), 219–34; see also Wilson, *Scholars of Byzantium*, 233.

22. See Morse, "Reception," 189–91; Allard, "Les Scholies," 667.

23. See Tannery, *Diophanti*, II, 37–42.

24. Heath, 19, citing the author Ibn al-Nadim, *The Fihrist of al-Nadim: A Tenth Century Survey of Muslim Culture*, ed. and trans. Bayard Dodge (New York, 1970), ch. VII, 2: 642, 668. The translator of Diophantus is named as Qusta ibn Luqa in ch. VIII, 3: 695. Cf. J. Stroyls, "Survey of the Arab Contributions to the Theory of Numbers," in *Proceedings of the First International Symposium for the History of Arab Science*, vol. 2 (Aleppo, 1978), 173–79.

25. See R. Rashed, "Les travaux perdus de Diophante," *Revue d'Histoire des Sciences* 27 (1974), 97–122; and 28 (1975), 3–30. The same author has now published an Arabic translation of the four previously unknown books from a mid-ninth century translation of Diophantus's work (Cairo, 1980); cf. J. Sesiano, *Books IV to VII of Diophantus' Arithmetica in the Arabic Translation Attributed to Qusta ibn Luqa* (New York, 1982). The recent Budé edition also by R. Rashed provides a French translation; see Diophante, *Les Arithmétiques*, vols. 3 and 4 (Paris, 1984). They must have been placed between books III and IV in the original Greek.

26. On al-Khwarizmi, see R. Rashed, "L'idée de l'algèbre chez al-Khwarizmi," and "La nouvelle analyze diophantienne: l'exemple d'al-Khazin," both reprinted in *Entre Arithmétique et Algèbre* (Paris, 1984), 17–29, 195–225.

27. Rashed, "Nouvelle analyze," 220–25.

28. On the Chinese and Indian contributions to recreational mathematics, in which medieval Christians and Arabs also delighted, see H. Hermelink, "Arab Recreational Mathematics as a Mirror of Age-Old Cultural Relations between Eastern and Western Civilizations," in *Proceedings of the First International Symposium for the History of Arab Science*, vol. 2 (Aleppo, 1978), 44–52; J. Sesiano,

"Arabische Mathematik im 8.–10. Jh." in *Science in Western and Eastern Civilization in Carolingian Times*, ed. P. L. Butzer and D. Lohrmann (Basel, 1993), 399–442, esp. 436–42 on magic squares.

29. Kurt Vogel, "Byzantine Science," in *Cambridge Medieval History*, rev. ed., vol. IV, part II (Cambridge, UK, 1966), 268. Ananias's 24 riddles in Armenian have been translated into Russian, by I. Orbeli (Petrograd, 1918), and into German, by P. S. Kokian, "Des Anania von Schirak Arithmetische Aufgaben," *Zeitschrift für die österreichischen Gymnasien*, 69 (1919–20), 112–17. Two examples are published in French translation by J. P. Mahé, "Quadrivium et cursus d'études au VIIe siècle en Arménie et dans le monde byzantin," *TM*, 10 (1987), 159–206, esp.195–96. For assistance in tracking down the German version I would like to thank Dr. Jochen Twele for his expertise and persistence. **Update** Tim Greenwood, "A Reassessment of the Life and Mathematical Problems of Anania Shirakac'i," *Revue des études arméniennes* 33 (2011), 131–86.

30. Ananias of Shirak, no. 4, Kokian, *Anania von Schirak*, 114; Herakleios, *Novel* 1, which established the permitted number of clergy attached to the church of St. Sophia, *JusGR*, I, 27–30; cf. the new edition with full commentary by J. Konidares, "Die Novellen des Kaisers Herakleios," *Fontes Minores*, 5 (1982), 33–106. **Update** See now Greenwood, "A Reassessment," as earlier.

31. Theophanes Continuatus, IV, 29, 185–90; Paul Lemerle, *Byzantine Humanism*, trans. Helen Lindsay and Ann Moffatt, *Byzantina Australiensia* 3 (Canberra, 1986), 174–78. This testimony is variously interpreted: for two opposing views, see P. Speck, "Byzantium: Cultural Suicide?" in *Byzantium in the Ninth Century: Dead or Alive?*, ed. L. Brubaker (Aldershot, UK, 1998), 73–84, esp. 81; and P. Magdalino, "The Road to Baghdad in the Thought-world of Ninth Century Byzantium," in ibid., 195–214.

32. Vogel, "Byzantine Science," 265; see also his article, "Byzanz, ein Mittler—auch in der Mathematik—zwischen Ost und West," in *Beiträge zur Geschichte der Arithmetik* (Munich, 1978), 35–53.

33. On Leo's education, see Lemerle, *Humanism*, 171–75. Of course this information is probably pure invention. For an ingenious new interpretation of the reference to Andros, see C. Angelidi, "Le séjour de Léon le Mathématicien à Andros: réalité ou confusion?," in Εὐψυχία. *Mélanges offerts à Hélène Ahrweiler* (Paris, 1998), 1–7. The source of the ancient texts studied by Leo remains unknown, but on his reputation, see Kurt Vogel: "Without him [Leo] the revival of mathematical studies in the West based on Greek texts is well nigh inconceivable," "Byzantine Science," 265.

34. According to Theophanes Continuatus, John was actually a relative of Leo, an assertion that may be intended to tar both scholars with the same iconoclast brush. **Update** It is accepted by Brubaker and Haldon, *Byzantium in the Iconoclast Era*, 404, and by Paul Magdalino, *L'Orthodoxie des astrologues* (Paris, 2006), 62, who also makes a serious assessment of scientific hellenism and iconoclasm, with useful comments on Leo the Mathematician, 11, 62–63, 65–68.

35. It is *D'Orville 301* in the Bodleian library, Oxford; see E. M. Thompson, *An Introduction to Greek and Latin Palaeography* (Oxford, 1912), 221–23 and pl. 53; E. Gamillscheg and D. Harlfinger, *Die Repertorium der griechischen Kopisten*, teil 1 A, (Vienna, 1981), no. 365, 183.

36. K. Vogel, "Buchstabezchnung und Indische Ziffern in Byzanz," in *Akten des XI Internationalen Byzantinisten-Kongresses*, ed. F. Dölger and H.-G. Beck, (Munich, 1960), 660–64.

37. As claimed by Lemerle, *Humanism*, 196, but see now the important note by N. G. Wilson, "Three Byzantine Scribes," *GRBS* 14 (1973), 223, in which he shows that the scholion is by a later hand and may not refer to Leo the Mathematician.

38. Lemerle, *Humanism*, 196.

39. Ibid., 196–97.

40. See earlier, note 18, Heath, *Diophantus*, 15. As Kurt Vogel aptly noted, it is much more likely that a copy of Diophantus would have been made at Leo's instigation between ca. 830–70 than in the previous century; see "Byzanz, ein Mittler . . . ," esp. 37–38.

41. The epigrams have been reedited by L. G. Westerink, "Leo the Philosopher: Job and Other Poems," *Illinois Classical Studies* 11 (1986), 193–222; cf. B. Baldwin, "The Epigrams of Leo the Philosopher," *BMGS* 14 (1990), 1– 17. Lauxtermann, *Epigram*, has demonstrated the importance of Leo's role in the transmission, 244–48. See also V. Katsaros, "Leo the Mathematician: His Literary Presence in Byzantium during the Ninth Century," in *Science in Eastern and Western Civilization*, 383–98. **Update** Leo also commissioned a copy of the Palladas Sylloge, a collection of epigrams, to which he added many written by himself; see Marc D. Lauxtermann, *Byzantine Poetry from Pisides to Geometres: Texts and Contexts*, vol. 1 (Vienna, 2003), 100–101.

42. Lauxtermman, *Epigram*, 247–48. **Update** See now Lauxtermann, *Byzantine Poetry*, 101–7.

43. Paton, vol. 5, 28.

44. Lemerle, *Humanism*, 171. **Update** Lauxtermann, *Byzantine Poetry*, 106–7, emphasizes the importance of Leo's enthusiasm for classical literature and observes that after his death "the legacy of Hellenism has to be christianized in order to become acceptable." Anthony Kaldellis, *Hellenism in Byzantium* (Canbridge, UK, 2007), 182–83, links the opposition to hellenism more clearly to the church and traces Christian hostility to ancient philosophy through to George Gemistos Plethon.

45. *Suidae Lexikon*, ed. A. Adler (Leipzig, 1935), para. 4, 644–66.

46. For the sources employed in this *Quadrivium*, see the note by A. Diller, *Isis* 36 (1946), 132.

47. Edited by Tannery, *Diophanti*, II, 78–122; it occurs in his main work, the Quadrivium, possibly written between 1285 and 1292; see Allard, "Les Scholies," 670–72; C. Constantinides, *Higher Education in Byzantium in the Thirteenth and Early Fourteenth Centuries* (Nicosia, 1982), 62–63.

48. Wilson, *Scholars of Byzantium*, 241 (an autograph is preserved in the Vatican Library).

49. Tannery, II, 125–60. **Update** Magdalino, *L'Orthodoxie des astrologues*, 140–41.

50. Wilson, *Scholars of Byzantium*, 232–33.

51. On the editorial work of Planudes and his efforts to obtain additional copies of Diophantus, see Allard, "Les Scholies," 669–71; Constantinides, *Higher Education*, 71–74; Robert Browning, "Recentiores non deteriores," *Bulletin of*

the Institute of Classical Studies, 11 (1960), 11–21, repr. in his *Studies on Byzantine History, Literature and Education* (London, 1977).

52. On these folios, which were discovered by Tannery, see Allard, "L'*Ambrosianus Et. 157 Sup.*," 219–34.

53. Wilson, *Scholars of Byzantium*, 234; I. Ševčenko, "Theodore Metochites, the Chora and the Intellectual Trends of His Time," in *The Kariye Djami*, ed. P. A. Underwood, vol. 4 (Princeton, 1975), 19–91, esp. 24, 37, 42, 44. Cf. Constantinides, *Higher Education*, 66–89. **Update** Magdalino, 141–61, on Metochites and the importance of the Chora monastery library in fourteenth-century Constantinople, and 147–52 on Planudes.

54. R. J. Loenertz, *Demetrius Cydones, Correspondence*, vol. II, *Studi e Testi* 208 (Vatican, 1960), 287. I thank Professor Anne Tihon for pointing out the significance of this reference to Diophantus.

55. Cameron, *The Greek Anthology*, 75–77, 317–20, app. I and II, 345–53. **Update** Lauxtermann, *Byzantine Poetry*, 115–16 (on Planudes' sources), 153.

56. Wilson, *Scholars of Byzantium*, 235–36.

57. Kazhdan, *ODB*, 1, 431–32.

58. Tannery, *Diophanti*, II, 260, noted that the scholion was made by a second hand; Wilson, *Scholars of Byzantium*, 233, and esp. add. 279.

59. His collection consisted of 482 Greek manuscripts and 264 in Latin; see L. Labowsky, *Bessarion's Library and the Biblioteca Marciana* (Rome, 1979).

60. See Morse, "Reception," 190–91; Allard, "Les Scholies," 665, dates this manuscript to the thirteenth century, but most authorities assign it to the early fifteenth century.

61. Morse, "Reception," 61–62; Heath, *Diophantus*, 20.

62. Heath, ibid.

63. See Allard, "Les Scholies," 668.

64. These are *Vaticanus graecus 191*, acquired from the collection of thirty Greek MSS previously owned by Cardinal Isidore of Kiev, after his death in 1463; see R. Devreesse, *Le fond de la Bibliothèque Vaticane des origines à Paul V* (Città del Vaticano, 1965), 42; and *Vaticanus graecus 200*, a copy of Bessarion's Venice manuscript, which is recorded in the inventory of 1481, ibid., 93. Manuscripts of Diophantus were frequently lent by the Vatican; *Vaticanus graecus 304* in 1522, *Vaticanus graecus 191* in 1518, 1522, and 1531; the Marciana library also lent its copy in 1545–56, see P. L. Rose, *The Italian Renaissance of Mathematics* (Geneva, 1975), 38, 46.

65. See Jean Cassinet, "The First Arithmetic Book of Francisco Maurolico . . . A Step toward a Theory of Numbers," in *Mathematics from Manuscript to Print, 1300–1600*, ed. C. Hay (Oxford, 1988), 162–80.

66. Heath, *Diophantus*, 21–22; Morse, "Reception," ch. iii.

67. Heath, *Diophantus*, 16; Morse, "Reception," 193; M. Gardthausen and K. Vogel, *Die griechischen Schreiber des Mittelalters und der Renaissance* (Leipzig, 1909; repr. 1966), 181–84, lists over 50 manuscripts made by Giovanni. See now the corrected list in E. Gamillscheg and D. Harlfinger, eds., *Repertorium der griechischen Kopisten, 800–1600*, Teil 2 A Frankenreich (Vienna, 1989), no. 232, 99–100; and esp. the study by B. Rainò, *Giovanni Onorio da Maglie. Trascrittore di codici greci* (Bari, 1972).

68. On this important manuscript, see H. Omont, *Inventaire sommaire des manuscrits grecs de la Bibliothèque nationale*, 4 vols. (Paris, 1886–93), II, 249. On the contribution of Viète, see G. J. Whitrow, "Why Did Mathematics Begin to Take Off in the Sixteenth Century?," in *Mathematics*, ed. C. Hay, 264–70, esp. 269–70.

69. Morse, "Reception," 193–94.

70. Heath, *Diophantus*, 22–26; Morse, "Reception," 194–212.

71. Heath, *Diophantus*, 26–28.

72. Heath, *Diophantus*, 28–29; Singh, *Fermat*, 64–66.

73. Heath, *Diophantus*, 144–45.

74. Singh, *Fermat*, 79–98.

75. See earlier, note 3; Wiles has received $50,000, all that is left of the original prize money.

76. Singh, *Fermat*, 60, repeats the claim that 1453 was "the vital turning point for Western mathematics," but ignores both the immense contribution of medieval Arab scholars to the development of the science, and even more crucially for Diophantus, the editorial investment and pedagogic use of his writings by generations of Byzantines. N. G. Wilson, *From Byzantium to Italy: Greek Studies in the Renaissance* (London, 1992), 162, rightly stresses the damage caused by the sack of 1204 and emphasizes that late Byzantine scholars conserved all the ancient texts that survived this much greater disaster. For a more balanced view of the impact of Greek manuscripts in the West after 1453, see L. Jardine, *Worldly Goods* (London, 1996), 57–64.

77. Singh, *Fermat*, 61–62; cf. Morse, "Reception," 259–60, quoting Bachet's *Pleasant and Delectable Problems Which Are Solved by Means of Numbers* (Lyon, 1612), which she characterizes as "almost the first in the genre of recreational mathematics."

16

BOOK BURNING AS PURIFICATION
IN EARLY BYZANTIUM

ɛ⁄ɔ

In January 1989 a group of Muslims set fire to *The Satanic Verses*, Salman Rushdie's novel that had won the Whitbread Award in the previous year. Their wrath at his references to Muhammad and Islam received official backing when the Ayatollah Khomeini issued a law, fatwa, instructing devout believers to kill the author. He went into hiding, though Anthony Barnett and I kept in touch with him, and he occasionally came to dinner with his armed guard. The importance of the topic was immediately confirmed by a stray reference to the burning of heretical books in the canons of the Council in Trullo. Since the existence of medieval palimpsests indicate the regular reuse of parchment, from which the original text has been washed or scraped off, why did the church insist on the total destruction of some manuscripts by burning? In an effort to understand the role of burning I found many curious references, and Daniel Hadas subsequently sent me a lot more for which I would like to thank him.

Selecting a topic worthy of Peter Brown was bound to be problematic—his omniscience, linguistic brilliance, and endless curiosity has led him through many obscure texts written in Late Antiquity. From our marvelously exciting cooperation at Princeton, I knew that he would know about the ramifications of book production and destruction, the evaluation and condemnation of theological interpretations, and the efforts of church leaders to guide their followers in a correct understanding and practice of Christian faith. The burning of heretical texts would not be unfamiliar, but I hoped that my treatment of it would intrigue him. It appeared in the volume titled *Transformations of Late Antiquity: Essays for Peter Brown*, edited by Philip Rousseau and Manolis Papoutsakis (Farnham, 2009).

IN THESE DAYS of instantaneous television transmission of images of warfare, natural disasters, and catastrophic accidents, fire is usually associated with destruction—forest fires, bombed cities, oil wells blazing. Burning is also a chosen method of displaying contempt, for instance, in setting fire to enemy flags or hated books. Even before the Ayatollah's fatwa condemned it, Salman Rushdie's *The Satanic Verses* was torched in Bradford. This served a symbolic purpose, as it reduced to ash words considered offensive to the Prophet and deterred Muslims from reading it for themselves. Similarly, in late fifteenth-century Florence, Savonarola had persuaded local people to burn, in a bonfire of vanities, pornographic images, pagan books, copies of the *Decameron* of Boccaccio, and the works of Ovid. During the *Reconquista* of Spain and the Reformation, many collections of books were committed to the flames, particularly vernacular translations of Scripture. And in the twentieth century, book burning gained a notorious publicity as the Nazis condemned all writings they considered un-German. These practices have engendered a modern horror of book burning as one of the worst sorts of vandalism.[1]

The other use of fire is beneficial: fire as purification. In his analysis of the role of fire in history, Johan Goudsblom stresses its ritual associations with sacrifice and the well-being of cities.[2] Rome was protected by a sacred fire, which virgins selected for the role kept constantly burning in the Temple of Vesta. Among the secular uses of fire, he points to the development of lighthouses, and the significance of cremation rather than burial. In the world of ancient Greece, the public cremation of dead heroes became the only way of honoring men like Patroclus and Hector. The system passed into the Roman world to mark the transition of the semi-divine rulers to the divine world, as eagles or peacocks accompanied their souls heavenward.

Although book burning appears to be entirely destructive, the ancients seem to have considered it a form of purification, designed to protect readers and listeners from inaccurate or downright misleading material. Texts that might inspire developments dangerous to the state were regularly condemned to destruction by fire in a public ritual. Protagoras's *Peri theôn*, for instance, which doubted the existence of the gods, was burned in the Agora of Athens in the late fifth century BC.[3] Such efforts reflect the power of the written word, manifested both in ritual acclamation of beneficial writings and the removal and obliteration of those tending to mislead or corrupt. Given the generally tolerant attitude of the ancient Greeks, this type of destruction is more likely to have been understood as a preventative measure than as censorship.

Yet the burning of books obliterates written forms of wisdom. And in the case of papyri and manuscripts, copied by hand, the knowledge had been accumulated by such labor-intensive means that to us its loss is even more shocking. The destruction of the library of Alexandria, variously attributed to "barbarians," who could not appreciate the contents, or "fanatical Christian monks" hostile to ancient wisdom, is frequently held up as an example of growing intolerance. Both of these stereotypes are of no help in attributing responsibility for the disappearance of the library, but the loss of so much accumulated learning still causes particular regret among "educated people."[4]

In his seminal novel *Fahrenheit 451*, Ray Bradbury, and following him the filmmaker François Truffaut, played on this sense of outrage—depicting a future in which books were banned. In the face of systematic destruction, a community of intellectuals committed works of literature to memory, so that each could preserve one text. Individuals became known by the title of the book that they knew by heart, to overcome the bookless dystopia. In most modern cases of book burning, the act is usually justified by an authority that is determined to suppress thought, the content of the book. The destruction is imposed by censorship. But it is important not to project our modern notion of censorship back into the early centuries AD.

There is, however, an intimate connection between destruction, burning and purification, and this is the topic that I wish to explore in an effort to honor Peter Brown, teacher of wisdom, and promoter of boundless curiosity about the ancient world. Whenever I think of Peter, I recall his appreciation of Handel's *Xerxes*, which opens with the magnificent aria, "Ombra mai fu," as Xerxes addresses his favorite tree: "Never was there such a tree." Peter is one of those great trees with deep roots and huge leafy branches that cast a welcome shadow over so many of us.

❧

In the ancient world, fire was the chosen means of destruction for four reasons: it was deemed irreparable; it had a purifying effect, which removed any polluting or blasphemous aspects; it fulfilled a magical role, in that it symbolized the destruction of the author; and it provided a public expression of civic condemnation.[5] The process may be illustrated by the ritual employed in the first century AD when Alexander of Abonouteichos, a disciple of Apollonios of Tyana, tried to destroy the writings of Epicurus. He collected fig tree wood, a cleansing and purifying agent, made a fire on the market place, and burned the *kyriai doxai* of Epicurus in public; he then scattered the ashes over the sea with a magical curse formula to ensure total obliteration.[6] Such acts of deliberate destruction account for the loss of a large proportion of ancient literature, including all the works of Epicurus. It is amazing how much written material survived. Knowledge of Epicurus's thought could not be entirely removed, of course, because many knew his writings and could quote his ideas even without having a copy of them. Memory regularly preserves what fire can destroy.

Magical texts were regularly condemned to be burned, but the failure of such policies is all too clear from their repetition. After several earlier attempts by Roman authorities to curb the practice of predicting future events, Augustus took more vigorous steps: in 12 BC he made a great bonfire of 2,000 oracular and prophetic scrolls, sparing only the Sibylline Books. Burning was gradually extended from such writings to any work considered insulting to the new monarchical order. This political use of book burning marked a progression from toleration to censorship as Augustus interpreted insults and criticism of his rule as treason.[7] In the spate of trials that followed the famine of AD 6–8 and culminated in the condemnation of Aulus Cremutius Cordus, individual authors were punished by exile and their writings were burned to remove all trace of the offensive words. This notion of literary treason provoked strong resistance. At the trial of Labienus, Cassius Severus pointed out how ineffective the destruction would be, since he knew Labienus's condemned works by heart. And for this courageous support, he too was sent off to Crete and spent the remaining twenty-five years of his life in miserable exile.[8]

The Roman imperial policy of destroying books by fire continued to be applied to individuals and groups considered treasonous. After the war of Bar Kokhba (AD 135–38), Torah scrolls were burned (together with rabbis) to punish the Jews. But since they also knew their scripture by heart, they could replace their holy books.[9] Under Roman rule, they (exceptionally) were excused the otherwise obligatory act of making sacrifice to the emperors. When the Christians emerged as a more identifiable new sect, rather than an offshoot of Judaism, and in turn refused to perform the required actions, the rulers of the empire reacted more firmly. In his famous letter to Pliny, Trajan makes it clear that the law must be applied (that is, Christians who refused to honor the emperor in the normal way were to be condemned), while urging his governor not to seek them out and not to rely on potentially corrupt informants. In their turn, the Christians tried to reduce the practice of ancient magic by persuading those who owned magical books to destroy them. After preaching in the synagogue at Ephesus, St. Paul converted both Jews and Greeks, who brought their books of "curious arts" and burned them in public to demonstrate their new belief.[10]

The political use of destruction by burning was also applied to slanderous charges in anonymous pamphlets and gossip posted in *libelli famosi*.[11] The *Theodosian Code* orders that *libelli* with anonymous accusations were to be torn down and burned unless their authors identified themselves and brought the accusations to a court in person. This procedure repeated what was already common practice, namely that such notices posted in public could not be used as evidence in a court of law. They were most often directed against public figures—for example, those made against Jovian when he returned from Persia in AD 363: "You came back from the war. You should have come to grief there!"[12]

Emperors used fire to ensure the removal of legislation when it was repealed—for example, copies of the much hated *chrysargyron*, a tax abolished by Anastasios (AD 491–518). He ordered all tax lists relating to it to be collected up in all parts of the empire and burned. Then the ashes were to be scattered at sea, a clear indication of the magical formula employed to guarantee the disappearance of the text.[13] Emperors sanctioned official destruction by fire of works that might endanger the empire, both books and their authors. In AD 370, when Emperor Valens accused numerous high-ranking Antiochene dignitaries of treason and subjected them to trials, torture, and execution, his agents went round collecting innumerable books allegedly of magic arts and burned them publicly. The philosopher Simonides, who resisted every attempt to force him to name those involved in the plot, was burned alive. Maximos of Ephesos was taken to that city to be beheaded, while many others were killed.[14]

Burning of magical and astrological texts had a long history and persisted for centuries. It is attested in the late fifth-century *Life* of Severus, later Monophysite Patriarch of Antioch, with long accounts of how the pagan magicians were unmasked, their books burned, and they themselves converted to Christianity. One magician was discovered when he gave his book to a scribe to be copied, and the scribe turned out to be a Christian! To check that other magicians were no longer clinging to old ways, the Christians made them eat meat with them—because real magicians don't eat meat, they think it is impure. Another group of magicians were vagabonds who came to Berytus promising to discover treasure by Persian magic arts. Chrysaorios, a magus, was taken in by them and agreed to participate in necromancy at night in an isolated temple with the help of silver objects, including a silver censer from a Christian church. An earthquake unleashed by divine power interrupted it all and they fled. The same Chrysaorios later tried to send his magic books to Berytus on a rented boat, with his books of law, his silver possessions, and his children with their mother, his concubine. Despite the ship's master taking astrological advice, his vessel went down and all were drowned.[15]

It was, however, in the field of religious beliefs that book burning was to have such a momentous future. In about AD 297, Diocletian directed the anti-Semitic precedent against the Manichaeans, and their books were burned as a foreign import from Persia.[16] Soon after, he used the same measure against Christians in the first edict of AD 303 ordering churches to be destroyed and scriptures burned.[17] For ten years the laws were applied—not always systematically, as the West appears to have suffered less; but many copies of Christian writings as well as church silver plate used in the eucharist were destroyed. In AD 313, when the emperors Licinius and Constantine met in Milan, they agreed that the Christians were not so dangerous after all, and the Edict "of Milan," issued by Licinius as the senior emperor when he returned to Bithynia, suspended the persecution. In this he followed the example of Galerius on his deathbed, who had relaxed the laws against Christians on condition that they prayed to their god for the safety of the emperors and the state.

Since Peter Brown has done so much to deepen our understanding of the first Christian centuries, it seems superfluous to rehearse the developments that followed. But it is important to note how quickly those who had recently been persecuted turned the same weapons against their own enemies: these were the enemies within the church who had to be exposed and condemned.[18] At the Council of Nicaea in AD 325, the full power of the empire was directed against the writings of Arius. The official church, meeting in a universal gathering under Constantine's commanding presence, debated the theology of Arius, found it incorrect, and condemned it as harmful: his *Thalia* was prohibited and copies were systematically burned.[19] At the same time, *libelli* written by Christian bishops against each other were ceremoniously burned to put an end to squabbles that dishonored the community. Once enshrined in imperial legislation, the church also directed official anti-Arian policy against all unofficial interpretations of Christian scripture, thus bringing military and secular forces into the church. This paved the way for increased violence and created a new model of religious intolerance.

As W. F. Adeney wrote in the 1921 *Encyclopaedia of Religion and Ethics*, all monotheistic revelations tend to be intolerant of any deviation from the true religion. He added: "Greater intolerance has been found in Christian actions than among any other people. . . . Christianity is necessarily intellectually intolerant . . . it claims to be a universal religion . . . is essentially aggressive . . . with positive missionary work and moral earnestness, in extreme cases degenerating into fanaticism."[20] This traditional view is borne out by the increasingly intolerant attitude of all Christian groups to alternative interpretations of Scripture.[21] When the Arian clergy regained imperial favor, for instance, they took revenge on their oppressors and are reported to have burnt the images of their Christian rivals.[22]

The intimate link between the identification of heresy and the order to destroy it by fire created a fixed association, which emperors fostered in their role of secular guardians of the Christian faith. In AD 398, Arcadius ordered that the books of the Eunomians be burned.[23] Theodosius II later ordered the burning of all the works of Porphyry and other enemies of Christ, which might bring people into danger. The unorthodox books of Nestorius were particularly singled out for condemnation.[24] In AD 455, Marcian added the dogmas of Apollinarius and Eutyches.[25] Book burning is therefore found in the context of rival Christian groups attempting to impose "correct" belief by building bonfires of the "godless writings" of their opponents.

As religious persecution became more general throughout the area of the ancient Near East, the followers of the old gods, Jews, Manichaeans, and Christians of all types suffered, and not always at the hands of the civil authorities. In the fourth century, Christians in North Africa and Constantinople showed no reluctance in setting fire to the books (and occasionally the persons) of their Donatist or Arian opponents, while those in Alexandria were responsible for some of the greatest acts of Christian aggression: the lynching of the mathematician and philosopher Hypatia in AD 415 and, before that, the burning of the Serapeum (which housed part of the library of Alexandria) in AD 391.[26] While responsibility for the loss of the library is much disputed, Christian hostility to ancient temples and statues of the gods is very clear.[27] Did this new level of violent destruction by Christian forces account for the report attributed to the fifth-century Neoplatonic philosopher, Proclus, who said he would be content to see all literature destroyed except Plato's *Timaeus* and the Chaldaean Oracles?[28]

The determination to destroy writings believed to be incorrect presupposes that both parties attributed the same decisive power to books. To protect and preserve their holy writings and especially important documents, an ancient practice of burying them continued to be used. Thanks to the dry sands of Egypt, one of the most beautiful texts of the *Iliad* book 2, written on a second-century AD papyrus roll, was recovered. It was not uncommon for texts to be buried with their owners; other tombs contained both books 1 and 2 of the *Iliad*. In the same way, the codices recovered at Nag Hammadi preserved a library of Gnostic writings that might otherwise have been burned.[29] Other burials, for example, to hide the works of Aristotle from eager manuscript collectors, nearly destroyed the entire corpus.[30]

Hiding books may have preserved a few texts, but, like other hoards buried in times of danger, many must have been permanently lost—for instance, the Book of Psalms dug up on 20 July 2006 from Fadden More in north Tipperary "with part of a fine leather pouch in which the book was kept originally. . . . The investigation results suggest the owner concealed the book deliberately, perhaps with a view to its later recovery."[31] Like coin hoards, collections of valuable gold and silver, such as the David plates or the Sevso treasure, books were buried as the only way of preserving them. But like so many treasures, they were often not recovered until modern times.

Throughout the fourth and fifth centuries, as Christianity struggled to define its theology more closely, every official condemnation was followed by ritual destruction. From the late fifth century onward bishops of Rome tried to prevent the spread of Mani's teachings by burning Manichaean books in the center of Rome at Santa Maria Maggiore.[32] Later, under Symmachus (AD 498–514), the Manichaeans were sent into exile, and all their images and books were destroyed outside the doors of the Constantinian basilica in the Forum.[33] And again under Hormisdas (AD 514–23), when adherents of the banned faith were discovered, the pope tried them with blows and investigations, sent them into exile, and burned their books.[34] This public destruction of heretical writings, performed in the heart of the city, became the bishop of Rome's traditional method of designating and destroying heretical writings and continued long into the medieval period. In AD 649, the Lateran Synod ordered the burning of all condemned Monothelete texts, and the Sixth Ecumenical Council in 680/81 repeated the procedure in Constantinople.[35] The efficacy of burning was similarly appreciated in Persia, where fire had both a purifying and destructive quality and the Zoroastrians persecuted Christians and Manichaeans alike; in AD 528, followers of Mani were slaughtered and all their holy writings were burned in public.[36]

By the sixth century AD, the gradual integration of Christian ideals and legal regulations with imperial law gave the Christians heightened powers. Emperor Justinian took a major part in this process of growing congruence through the revision of the *Theodosian Code* and subsequent legal rulings, *Novellae*, which introduced many Christian elements and turned the full force of imperial legislation against deviants of all kinds, particularly religious. This effectively established the word of God on the same level as Roman law, combining an exclusive monotheism with a persecuting authority. Thereafter, conformity with Christian Scripture became the yardstick for more than religious affiliation, for it also measured loyalty to the empire.

The supremacy of Christian belief involved considerable destruction. Decades after the decree of AD 528 that barred pagans from state office, Justinian ordered a persecution of surviving Hellenes, accompanied by the burning of pagan books, pictures, and statues.[37] This bonfire took place in the *Kynêgion*, an area associated with ancient beliefs and practices, and that later became a dumping ground for the bodies of convicts condemned to death.[38] All the bad elements of the old world were here connected and they symbolically identified what was no longer acceptable. As so much pagan literature was recorded on papyrus and perished before it could be recopied onto more durable parchment, it is hard to assess the degree of Christian responsibility for losses of ancient documents. But in the mid-sixth century, active persecution in Constantinople probably destroyed many ancient texts. For the authorities, the bonfires of metal statues had the added bonus of providing additional supplies for the mint.

Similar methods were used to secure the utter obliteration of Arian theology after the conversion of the Gothic tribes to the Catholic faith. In AD 589, the Council of Toledo returned the Visigothic church of Spain to orthodoxy, and the subsequent destruction of Arian Bibles was so efficient that none survives.[39] Only a couple of deluxe manuscripts made in sixth-century Italy for Arian Ostrogoths preserve the beauty of Gothic Bibles (for example, the purple-dyed parchment written in silver ink now in Uppsala). In this passion to obliterate the vestiges of wrong religious beliefs, whether heretical or pagan, the Christians could find no better method than the old imperial system of destruction formerly employed against themselves. Yet here they faced a major contradiction. Like the ancients who claimed that their poetry was immortal, believers held that correct Christian texts would survive even the flames, like the three young men in the fiery furnace, a popular theme in Byzantium. In this metaphor for the eternal power of revealed truth, they knew that their efforts to destroy the views of their opponents would fail.

If their own holy books could be reconstructed or replaced by other copies, so could other writings. Since they could not contemplate the irrevocable destruction of their own holy texts, why did they not understand that burning would not remove unorthodox books? The answer may lie in the radical change experienced by Christian leaders, once their belief had become the dominant ideology and they had recourse to the means available to the highest secular authority. Christianity was gradually absorbed by the older imperial system and abandoned its self-conscious identity as a minority faith. This integration endowed the Roman Empire with a Christian ideology that endured to the fall of the capital to the Ottoman Turks in AD 1453. It also ensured the high status of the book in Byzantium.

But even without the aid of strong secular power, book burning also became an established practice in the medieval West. The Council of Chalon-sur-Sâone held in AD 815 "denounced the *libelli* called Penitentials, of which the errors are certain, the authors uncertain." And fourteen years later in Paris, bishops were ordered to seek out these "booklets written against canonical authority and give them to the flames, that through them unskilled priests may no longer deceive men."[40] In all parts of Christendom, the authorities tried to make sure that only the approved texts circulated. Their restriction of writings not authorized or considered inappropriate can therefore be seen as a form of censorship. But they lived in a world of infinite variety, where uniformity was unachievable. Regional traditions, limited access to libraries, and local cults guaranteed a wide range of Christian texts. The canon of the Christian Bible took many centuries to become established, and communities continued to use their own versions and to read unauthorized additions. Even in the ninth century, the wording of the Gospels was not completely fixed, so it was extremely difficult to ensure correct readings.

Yet from an early period, church leaders had stipulated that the passions of the Early Christian heroes who had died for their faith were to be read on the anniversaries of their deaths as an inspiration to later generations (for example, canon 46 of the Council of Carthage held in AD 419).[41] These positive directions rapidly gave rise to an opposing tendency to prohibit the reading of unauthorized texts, such as the false martyrology of Longinus.[42] Equally, an ancient tradition, attributed to Pope Clement, banned the public reading of "false writings of unholy books" and ordered that anyone found reading these *pseudepigrapha* in church should be deposed. This ruling may in fact be apocryphal; it is found in the 60th of the Apostolic Canons, and was never accepted in the West.[43] Although it does not order the destruction of false writings, it reflects a concern over reading impious books in church.

❧

In the late seventh century, the Byzantine Emperor Justinian II summoned an ecumenical council to meet in Constantinople. It is variously identified as the *Quini-Sext* (because it sought to complete the work of the Fifth and Sixth Councils) or the Council in Trullo (because it met in a hall under the dome [*troullos*] of the Palace).[44] No disciplinary canons had been issued for the entire church since the Fourth Council, held at Chalcedon in AD 451. After 240 years, conditions had changed dramatically, notably with the collapse of Roman imperial authority in the West and the advance of the Arabs, who had occupied the three great Eastern patriarchates of Jerusalem, Alexandria, and Antioch. Although the acts of the council are lost, the preliminary address to the emperor signed by all present, and the text of 102 canons are preserved. It is clear from their content that many bishops journeyed to the capital city with pressing local problems to which they wanted a decisive and authoritative solution. Since all of them, apart from the papal legates, came from the East and some from regions recently conquered by the Muslims, these concerns were often quite specific.

The Trullan Council makes one reference to book burning, in canon 63. This extends book burning to any writing that might lead the simpleminded (*haplousteroi*) to lose their faith (*apistia*):

> We ordain that stories of the martyrs, which have been falsely concocted by the enemies of the truth so as to dishonour the martyrs of Christ and to cause those listeners to lose faith, should not be read publicly in churches but are to be given over to the flames [*puri paradidôsthai*]. As for those who receive them or accept them as true, we anathematize them.[45]

The question of how to distinguish true from false martyrologies is not addressed, merely the fate of those judged to be false. Nor are books actually mentioned, though the public reading, *demosieuesthai*, implies reading from a text, as does the order to destroy them by burning.

Part of the reason for this anxiety lay in the nature of early Christian martyrologies. Since the passions of the saints and martyrs often included "real life" stories, they were immensely popular, even or perhaps especially those with the most gruesome accounts of torture and death at wild-beast shows. Details of the dismemberment of Blandina or Febronia make grisly reading today but may have entranced earlier audiences. In the seventh century, for the first time, anxieties about invented stories, forgeries, and misleading writings led to an important change: an order to burn those pseudo-martyrologies.

Even as late as the twelfth century, the reading of certain books in church was prescribed. In about AD 1105, Patriarch Sergios responded to a question raised by a group of Athonite monks, decreeing that "the

Apostolic Books of Clement and the *Life* of St. Niphon are not to be read, because they are corrupted." The *Apostolic Constitutions* could be read in private but not out aloud in public; and the *Life* was prohibited because "it has not come down to us in the traditional form."[46] Patriarchs of this date were still condemning the books of heretics to be burned, and in AD 1063, efforts to bring the inhabitants of Melitene back into the Orthodox faith were accompanied by the burning of their books. Michael the Syrian comments that Patriarch Constantine Leichoudes's death shortly after this decree proved that it did not carry divine approval.[47]

The Council in Trullo issued one additional canon that relates to book destruction. Canon 68 states:

> Absolutely no one is to be allowed to destroy any volume of the Old or New Testament, or of our holy and approved preachers and teachers, nor to cut it up, nor to give it to the book sellers [*bibliokapelois*] nor to the so-called perfumers [*myrepsois*] or to anyone else who will destroy it, unless it has been completely ruined by worms or dampness or by some other manner.[48]

There is no mention of destruction by burning, which seems to have been reserved for heretical books. But both the person found handing over or selling Christian writings for destruction and the recipient are to be anathematized for one year. Similarly, anyone who buys a copy of such writings must prove that he intends to keep them for his own edification, or to give them to another as a benefaction and for safekeeping. If he plans to destroy them, he will be excommunicated.

Judging from the commentaries on this canon made by twelfth-century legal experts, the so-called perfumers and booksellers would probably have scraped down the old parchments in order to create new writing material (palimpsests).[49] The key phrase is *heteron en tois apaleipheisi metagraphein*, that is, writing another text over Holy Scripture.[50] The church does not permit any reuse of Scripture until the manuscript is totally destroyed. Presumably the so-called perfumers had a line in cleaning parchment for reuse (perhaps with chemical materials resembling perfumes), while booksellers knew all about the resale value of parchment.

This rule makes it clear that no biblical text can ever be reused until it has been completely worn away, or destroyed by water or some other way such as by fire, or eaten by worms. The existence of many palimpsests confirms the expense of preparing parchment and reflects its continuous reuse. Among the most interesting recently discovered texts are classical ones like Archimedes' "The Theory of Floating Bodies," "The

Method of Mechanical Theorems," and "The Stomachion" found underneath a thirteenth-century collection of Orthodox prayers copied by the monk Johannes Myronas in Jerusalem. The original had been written on goatskin parchment by an anonymous Byzantine monk in the tenth century. It is interesting to note that this is one of a great many copies of ancient Greek scientific works made during the Macedonian Renaissance, when even clerical scribes realized the importance of preserving pre-Christian texts (for instance, the *Greek Anthology*, complete with the most erotic epigrams, or the *Geography* of Strabo). Three centuries later, there was less concern, and so the texts of Archimedes were scraped off and the skin reused.

Taken in the context of such persistent concern about the circulation of unauthorized writings, these two canons of AD 692 provoke a few observations about book burning, purification, and the status of written texts in early Byzantium. First, in the late seventh century, holy writings, copies of the Bible and the works of Church Fathers, saints, holy people, teachers, and preachers, were highly revered in Byzantium.[51] Any intentional damage to such books, of whatever kind, was condemned, and the care of copies that had been accidentally damaged was recommended. When ecclesiastical texts became too worn to be used, they were to be copied. Sometimes even secular texts were rebound to prevent further deterioration; the oldest known copy of Strabo's *Geography*, preserved in a minuscule hand from ca. AD 950–1000, was rebound with an uncial commentary on the Old Testament, a judicial text and fragments of the historian Dio Cassius.[52]

Conversely, apocryphal or false stories about the martyrs, which might mislead people, now could and should be burned. Their existence suggests fabrication of texts to prove miracles, or to adduce sanctity in individuals who were not acknowledged as saints. Forgery and alteration to established texts were well-known practices in Byzantium, as in the medieval West.

Second, while some people kept even damaged copies of the Bible for their own use, implying private study, personal reading, or merely the desire to possess Holy Scripture (whether for pride, social concern, or superstition), others might be misled simply by hearing false martyr stories read in church (suggesting that they did not read for themselves and relied on public performance). Traditions of literacy coexisted with oral culture, which is not at all surprising, though it is not usually emphasized.[53] Overall, the written word had immense power and was treated with great respect. The two Trullan canons draw attention to the importance attached to written records while demonstrating the dangers of other types of documents—unreliable, inaccurate, or heretical books that had to be destroyed. This is the *verso* of the *recto* that represents the book's significance. Drastic action was necessary to curb the spread of any writing that might mislead.

Further implications about the status of readers and nonreaders in Byzantium emerge: those who are dependent on literate, educated people to read to them are identified as the more simple-minded (*haplousteroi*), those of lesser capacity, childlike people who are easily misled. The assembled bishops probably meant "women and children." Yet many activities performed "through ignorance" by both clerics and lay people are also condemned, suggesting that it is not only females who fall into the category of "simple-minded." In canon 79, for example, clerical and lay people seem to take part in an inappropriate celebration of the Nativity.[54] Similarly, canon 96 points out that *asteriktoi psychai*, "unstable souls," are all too easily seduced by fancy plaited hair styles, and forbids them. Apparently men are considered most responsible, but the masculine participle *tous* can also cover women.[55]

Third, the destruction of images that might corrupt or encourage licentious feelings is authorized in canon 100.[56] This censorship of pictures is novel and requires explanation. I think it may be related to statues, frescoes, and images of pagan gods, goddesses, and local women, which must have decorated most Late Antique cities.[57] Many licentious paintings decorated private spaces, such as the brothels of Pompeii, and individuals also advertised their services in public in images that could well be described as liable to engender inappropriate feelings. An encaustic portrait described by Agathias may serve as an example: "I was a harlot in Byzantine Rome, granting my venal favors to all, I am Callirhoe the versatile, whom Thomas, goaded by love, set in this picture, showing what great desire he has in his soul, for even as his wax melts so melts his heart."[58] While the portraits may have been removed, the statues still remained a feature of seventh-century cities.

The council's effort to control art reappears in the well-known canon 82 about depicting Christ in his human form.[59] Instead of painting the symbolic image of the Lamb of God, painters are to show the Savior in his earthly incarnation. This regulation is often quoted out of context, with no reference to the other canons designed to direct Christian faith in appropriate directions. It must also be related to the heightened awareness of "barbarian incursions," which at this date is surely connected with the Arab conquests of formerly Byzantine lands. These concerns are made clear by canons 18, 30, 37, 39, and possibly 12, addressed to priests and bishops forced to leave their sees, or to adopt improper behavior in their new circumstances.[60]

One final aspect of the conciliar decrees concerns forms of penance that are to be made appropriate to the status of the sinner (canon 102).[61] This suggests an awareness that sins committed by people who know no better are in a different category from sins committed by those who are well aware of the rules. It is tempting to link this to the preceding canon (101), which stipulates that no lay person is to receive the eucharist in a golden or silver vessel.[62] Everyone should hold their hands in the form of a cross and thus receive the immaculate body. A similar anxiety is expressed about wealthy people who wish to have their children baptized in their private chapels (canon 59); baptisms are to be performed in the local parish church.[63]

༄

The status of the Trullan canons as binding on the entire *Oikoumenê* has long been questioned by some Western theologians, who claim that the basic purpose of the council was anti-Roman and that it was never accepted in the West. They draw attention to three canons in particular, by which the council sought to distance itself from practices reported as common in the church of Rome (and by extension in the West). These relate to the position of the bishop of Rome as the heir of St. Peter and the equivalent status of the bishop of Constantinople, the marriage of lesser clergy, and local practices of fasting and genuflecting.[64] There is no mention of the more serious theological problem: the *filioque* clause added to the creed. Thanks to the conference held on the 1,400th anniversary of the Council in Trullo, published one year later in 1995, it is now possible to take a more balanced view.[65] The rulings that relate to Roman traditions can be seen as the only way the eastern Christians could insist that their own customs were correct. The bishops gathered in Constantinople in AD 692 recognized that certain things were done differently in Rome, and set up their own ways of organizing the calendar of fasting, methods of expressing contrition, clerical celibacy and marriage. They reiterated the decree of Chalcedon that promoted Constantinople to an equal status with Rome and granted precedence of honor to the see of St. Peter. It is important to emphasize that in AD 692 the papal legates accepted the canons, although Pope Sergius did not. After considerable debate, Pope Constantine I journeyed to the East to sign them in AD 711, so they became binding throughout Christendom. Even so, they were never widely diffused in the West.

The council's concern about the influence of books and pictures was clearly serious, even though the example of Islamic nonfigural art was not yet known in Byzantium. Subsequently, under the impact of early eighth-century Muslim advances, which were accompanied by the destruction of Christian art in some areas conquered by the Arabs, this anxiety helped to fuel the most serious episode of destruction of both books and pictures in Byzantium. The period of iconoclasm provoked destruction on both sides, by iconoclasts and iconophiles; it set a clear precedent for later generations and reformers even of the fifteenth century, and was justified by the highest ecclesiastical sanction. If certain writings and images encouraged wrong belief or unsuitable behavior, the church had already issued unequivocal instructions to burn books and destroy art.

Since iconoclast activity under Leo III and Constantine V is the most celebrated example of the destruction of images and texts in Byzantium, I shall draw attention to only one recorded instance of book burning attributed to Michael Lachanodrakon, *stratêgos* of the Thrakesian *thema*. After his infamous persecution of monks and nuns who were paraded in the polo playing field at Ephesos, Lachanodrakon forced them to choose between marriage or blinding and exile to Cyprus. The following year, Theophanes records that he sent one of the former monks to gather up all the things of value in the deserted monasteries and sell them. Any books found "containing stories of monks and fathers of the desert" were burned, together with phylacteries containing the relics of saints.[66] Patriarch Nikephoros confirms that Constantine V had ordered these actions and imposed them on monks rounded up in the capital, but does not mention bonfires of books.[67] While the survival of manuscripts with illustrations cut out demonstrates the iconoclasm exercised by officials to conform to imperial orders, there is no way of evaluating the scale of the destruction.

This style of official suppression of deviant theology was to have a long life in European culture. It gave rise to the first serious efforts to censor writings by drawing up a list of unacceptable books, which were put on the Index of Prohibited Books by the Inquisition. Book burning was instituted as the best method of destroying books of magic and necromancy, which were condemned to the flames together with their owners.[68] This in turn formed the precedent for later censors, who ordered the burning of effigies of wicked individuals, for instance, Sigismondo Malatesta (1417–68), charged with parricide, sacrilege, treason, and heresy by Pope Pius II, Aeneas Sylvius Piccolimini, who had him burnt in effigy twice at Rimini.[69] From the successful destruction of texts and images considered dangerous, the Inquisition established a model followed by all modern dictatorial regimes in their attempts to outlaw freedom of thought by banning books. Yet the Index of Prohibited Books established to control the reading of believers could not prevent the illegal circulation of texts it considered corrupting, and book burning as a method of prevention is quite outdated.

Finally, spontaneous acts of destruction that do not represent official book burning are also found in ancient times. During the Muslim conquest of Syria, Jacob, bishop of Edessa, a famous scholar and translator from Greek into Syriac, quarreled with Patriarch Julian over lapses in clerical discipline, which may have been a consequence of the Arab occupation. Julian favored a more lenient attitude to improper Christian behavior, and Jacob decided to make a symbolic protest. After accusing his superior of "trampling the canons under foot so that they were superfluous and useless," Jacob is reported to have burned a collection of the same canons in a public spectacle, designed to demonstrate the patriarch's disrespect and to restore Christian adherence to church law.[70] His sensational bonfire drew attention to the inherent value and status of the book, especially the written record of ecclesiastical rulings already agreed verbally. It was organized without ecclesiastical support as a personal demonstration of disapproval.

This is not the same as the Bradford burning of *The Satanic Verses*, but it represents a similar style of destruction to make a point rather than to destroy utterly all copies of a reprehensible text. It is a private form of destruction designed to display a personal condemnation rather than an institutional one. In the case of Jacob of Edessa, he chose to burn those very canons that had been overturned by his patriarch, as a symbolic gesture. He wanted the church to abide by its own rulings rather than compromise with the occupying Muslim authorities. So his book burning was not an instance of suppression but of purification: he intended to show how the canons had been neglected.

In the era of handwritten books, civilian and ecclesiastical authorities might attempt to suppress books with improper content. In some cases they seem to have been successful and many texts no longer survive. But once printing extended the availability of books to much wider audiences, such effective removal became almost impossible. Individual acts of destruction serve as a reminder that book burning as purification and ineffective efforts at censorship have been intimately linked for centuries. And in the present conditions of heightened anxiety about the views of others that seems to dominate our world, I fear that they may remain associated for some time to come.[71]

NOTES

1. J. L. Flood, "Varieties of Vandalism," *Common Knowledge* 82 (2002), 366–86; J. Raven, ed., *Lost Libraries: The Destruction of Great Book Collections since Antiquity* (Basingstoke, 2004).

2. J. Goudsblom, *Fire and Civilization* (London, 1992), esp. 100–102, on the possible change to cremation during pandemics, when burial becomes impossible and wild animals may start to scavenge on human flesh.

3. Eusebios, *Praeparatio Evangelium*, 14.3.7, 14.19.10; Edouard des Places, ed., *La Préparation évangélique, XIV–XV*, Sources Chrétiennes, 338 (Paris, 1987), 48–50, 168–70; A. Adler, ed., *Suidae Lexicon*, 5 vols. (Leipzig, 1928–38), s.v. Protagoras, vol. 4, 246–47. Greek text and trans. available at *Suda On Line: Byzantine Lexicography*, ed. D. Whitehead, www.stoa.org/sol/. K. Dover, "The Freedom of the Intellectual in Greek Society," *Talanta* 8 (1976), 24–54, raised doubts about the reliability of the charges against Protagoras and other intellectuals, and also pointed to the impossibility of destroying an author's works by burning. Nonetheless, it was later believed that such bonfires had occurred.

4. A. Hirst and M. Silk, eds., *Alexandria, Real and Imagined* (Aldershot, UK, 2004), esp. the chapters by H. Maehler, "Alexandria, the Mouseion, and cultural identity," 1–14, and M. El-Abbadi, "The Alexandrian Library in history," 167–83; J. Raven, "The Resonances of Loss," in Raven, ed., *Lost Libraries*, 12–21.

5. A. S. Pease, "Notes on Book Burning," in *Munera studiosa: Festschrift W.H.P. Hatch*, ed. M. H. Shepherd and S. E. Johnson (Cambridge, MA, 1946), 158–59. **Update** Daniel Hadas has reminded me of the Old Testament example of the prophet Jeremiah, whose words, dictated to Baruch, were burned by Jehoiakim, king of Judah, and immediately reconstructed, Jeremiah 36. He also directed me to Bede's description of books, which were known to exist but do not survive, because they had been consumed by fire, *Quaestiones in Libros Regum*, PL, 91, 720.

6. W. Speyer, *Büchervernichtung und Zensur des Geistes bei Heiden, Juden und Christen* (Stuttgart, 1981), 5, 31–33, 49.

7. F. H. Cramer, "Book Burning and Censorship in Ancient Rome," *Journal of the History of Ideas* 6 (1945), 157–96.

8. Cramer, "Book Burning," 172–77.

9. Speyer, *Büchervernichtung*. **Update** This fact may slightly reduce the force of the dictum, "Better to burn Torah than to allow a woman to handle it," quoted by Peter Brown, *The Body and Society. Men, Women, and Sexual Renunciation in Early Christianity* (New York, 1988), 145.

10. Acts of the Apostles 19.19.

11. J. F. Matthews, *Laying Down the Law: A Study of the Theodosian Code* (London/New Haven, 2000), 194, citing *Cod. Theod.* 9.34.3, 4, 7, 9, 10.

12. Matthews, *Laying Down the Law*, 195, n. 97. This method of spreading rumors and making accusations implies "a high level of public and even literary appreciation of what was said in them [the *famosi*]," and burning was clearly a well-established method of removing writings from circulation and attempting to curb the circulation of unproven charges.

13. Speyer, *Büchervernichtung*, 33, 164–65.

14. Ammianus Marcellinus, 29.1 and 2; in particular 29.1.38–39 (Simonides), 41 (books), and 42 (Maximos). Ammianus claims that the writings destroyed were of a literary and legal character, not the alleged books of magic practices.

15. Zacharias Scholastikos, *Vita Severi*, Syriac text with French trans. by M.-A. Kugener, *PO*, ii, fasc. 1, no. 6 (Paris, 1903), 63, 65.

16. Speyer, *Büchervernichtung*, 76.

17. Eusebios, *Historia ecclesiastica*, 8.2; Lactantius, *De mortibus persecutorum*, ed. J. L. Creed (Oxford, 1984), 12.2. **Update** My thanks to Daniel Hadas, who points out how this persecuting feature can be aligned with the wicked acts of Antichrist as recorded in Lactantius's *Divine Institutes*: 7.17.8: "idem iustos homines obvolvet libris prophetarum atque ita cremabit."

18. H. A. Drake, "Lambs into Lions: Explaining Early Christian Intolerance," *Past and Present* 153 (1996), 3–36.

19. Socrates, *Historia ecclesisastica*, 1.9, esp. the letter of Constantine to the bishops.

20. J. Hastings, *Encyclopedia of Religion and Ethics*, vol. 12 (Edinburgh, 1921), s.v. "Tolerance," 360–65.

21. P. Zagorin, *How the Idea of Religious Toleration Came to the West* (Princeton, 2003); W. Speyer, "Toleranz und Intoleranz in den alten Kirche," in *Christentum und Toleranz*, ed. I. Broer and R. Schluüter (Darmstadt, 1996), 83–106.

22. A. Cameron and J. Herrin, eds., *Constantinople in the Early Eighth Century: The Parastaseis Syntomoi Chronikai* (Leiden, 1984), 10, which also accuses the Arians of burning an icon of the Mother of God with the Christ child (68).

23. *Cod. Theod.* 16.5.34.

24. *Cod. Just.* 1.1.3; Speyer, *Büchervernichtung*, 34, 152–53. **Update** Paul Magdalino, *L'Orthodoxie des astrologues* (Paris, 2006), 28, n. 57, notes that certain mathematicians were also obliged to burn their books in front of the local bishop; see *Cod. Just.* 1.4.10.

25. *Cod. Just.* 1.5.6.12; C. A. Forbes, "Books for the Burning," *Proceedings of the American Philological Association* 67 (1936), 114–25.

26. Socrates, *Historia ecclesistica*, 7.15.

27. B. Caseau, "*Polemein Lithois*: la désacralisation des espaces et des objets religieux païens durant l'antiquité tardive," in *Le Sacré et son inscription dans l'espace à Byzance et en Occident: études comparées*, ed. M. Kaplan (Paris, 2001), 61–123; B. Caseau, "The Fate of Rural Temples in Late Antiquity," in *Recent Research on the Late Antique Countryside*, ed. W. Bowden, L. Lavan, and C. Marchiado (Leiden, 2004), 105–44.

28. Speyer, *Büchervernichtung*, 106–7.

29. C. Roberts, *Buried Books in Antiquity: "Habent sua fata libelli,"* Arundell Esdaile Memorial Lecture, 62 (London, 1963), 5–6; E. Pagels, *Beyond Belief: The Secret Gospel of Thomas* (New York, 2005), 32–39, 96–99, 177–78.

30. Roberts, *Buried Books*, 6–11, on the role of Neleus's successors in burying the papyri to save them from officials trying to build up the Attalids' library at Pergamon, which they intended to rival Alexandria.

31. *The Guardian*, 23 August 2006.

32. *LP*, 51.

33. Ibid., 53.

34. Ibid., 54.

35. *Mansi*, 11, cols. 573, 581.

36. *Theophanes*, AM 6016 (I, 170).

37. Malalas, *Chronographia*, ed. L. Dindorf (Bonn, 1831), 491.

38. Cameron and Herrin, eds., *Constantinople in the Early Eighth Century*, 28 (88–90).

39. *The Fourth Book of the Chronicle of Fredegar with its Continuations*, ed. J. M. Wallace-Hadrill (London, 1960), 8; J. Herrin, *The Formation of Christendom* (Princeton, 1987), 228–31.

40. J. T. McNeil and H. M. Gamer, *Medieval Handbooks of Penance* (repr. New York, 1990), 27.

41. P. P. Joannou, *Discipline générale antique (IIe– IXe s.)*, i, 2: *Les Canons des Synodes Particuliers* (Rome, 1962), 263. (Hereafter Joannou, *Discipline générale*; further references will be to this volume, unless otherwise indicated.)

42. J. K. Elliott, *The Apocryphal New Testament* (Oxford, 1993); Joannou, *Discipline générale*. Canon 24 of Carthage listed the biblical books that were authorized, and forbade the reading of any other books in church (239–40).

43. Joannou, *Discipline générale*, 39. In AD 692, the Council in Trullo addressed this problem in canon 2, pointing out that "certain spurious passages, foreign to true piety have been inserted to the detriment of the church by heretics." Ibid., 120–25, esp. 121.

44. The canons are published by G. A. Ralles and M. Potles, *Syntagma tôn theiôn kai hiereôn kanonôn tôn te hagiôn kai paneuphemôn apostolôn kai tôn hiereôn oikoumenikôn kai topikôn synodôn*, 6 vols. (Athens, 1852–59); by Joannou, *Discipline générale*, i, 1: *Les Canons des conciles oecuméniques* (Rome, 1962), with French trans.; and by G. Nedungatt and M. Featherstone, eds., *The Council in Trullo Revisited*, Kanonika 6 (Rome, 1995), with Eng. trans. **Update** New edition with German trans. H. Ohme, *Concilium Quinisextum* (Turnhout, 2006).

45. Joannou, *Discipline générale*, 200; Nedungatt and Featherstone, *Council in Trullo Revisited*, 144.

46. V. Grumel, ed., *Les Regestes des actes du Patriarchat de Constantinople* (Paris, 1932–79), fasc. 3, no. 982 (63–69).

47. Grumel, *Regestes*, 3, nos. 890–91; *Chronique de Michel le Syrien*, 16.11, ed. with Fr. trans. by J. Chabot (Paris, 1889), 3, 166. In the mid-twelfth century, Patriarch Nikolaos Mouzalon condemned a poorly written version of the *Life* of St. Paraskeve to be burned; Ralles and Potles, *Syntagma*, 2 (Athens, 1852), 453.

48. Joannou, *Discipline générale*, 206–7; Nedungatt and Featherstone, *Council in Trullo Revisited*, 150–51 (although the key word *bibliokapelois* is omitted from the translation).

49. Ralles and Potles, *Syntagma*, 2, 464 (commentaries by Zonaras), 464–65 (Balsamon), and 465 (Aristenos).

50. Ralles and Potles, *Syntagma*, in the commentary of Balsamon, 2, 465.

51. See most recently the splendid survey by G. Cavallo, "Libri in scena," *Proceedings of the 21st International Congress of Byzantine Studies*, ed. E. Jeffreys (Aldershot, UK, 2006), I, Plenary Papers, 345–64.

52. A. Diller, *The Textual Tradition of Strabo's Geography* (Amsterdam, 1975).

53. C. Holmes and J. Waring, eds., *Literacy, Education and Manuscript Transmission in Byzantium and Beyond* (Leiden, 2002).

54. Joannou, *Discipline générale*, 215–16; Nedungatt and Featherstone, *Council in Trullo Revisited*, 159–60.

55. Joannou, *Discipline générale*, 233–34; Nedungatt and Featherstone, *Council in Trullo Revisited*, 177–78.

56. Joannou, *Discipline générale*, 236–37; Nedungatt and Featherstone, *Council in Trullo Revisited*, 190–91. Update Leslie Brubaker and John Haldon, *Byzantium in the Iconoclast Era ca. 680–ca. 850: A History* (Cambridge, UK, 2011), 779–80, 784.

57. For images of local gods, see T. F. Mathews, *Byzantium: From Antiquity to the Renaissance* (New York, 1998), 46–47. I am grateful to Dr. Joe Munitiz for reminding me that these icons would have offended Christians.

58. W. R. Paton, ed., *The Greek Anthology*, 5 (Cambridge, MA, repr. 1979), 16.80. Similar, if not quite so explicit, epigrams dedicated to statues of the goddess Aphrodite, and to pictures of dancing girls, female singers, and lyrists, indicate the range of possibly corrupting paintings, XVI, 159–82, 277–90.

59. Joannou, *Discipline générale*, 218–20; Nedungatt and Featherstone, *Council in Trullo Revisited*, 162–64. Update There is a vast literature on this famous canon, most recently summarized in Brubaker and Haldon, as earlier, 61–62, 91. See also D. Freedberg, *The Power of Images* (Chicago/London, 1989), 206–7, 211–12.

60. Joannou, *Discipline générale*, 149–50, 160–61, 171–72, 173–74, 138–39; Nedungatt and Featherstone, *Council in Trullo Revisited*, 93–94, 104–5, 115–16, 117–18, 82–83.

61. Joannou, *Discipline générale*, 239–41; Nedungatt and Featherstone, *Council in Trullo Revisited*, 183–85.

62. Joannou, *Discipline générale*, 237–39; Nedungatt and Featherstone, *Council in Trullo Revisited*, 181–83; B. Caseau, "L'Abandon de la communion dans la main (IVe–XIIe siècles)," in *Mélanges Gilbert Dagron—Travaux et Mémoires* 14 (Paris, 2002), 79–94.

63. Joannou, *Discipline générale*, 195; Nedungatt and Featherstone, *Council in Trullo Revisited*, 139.

64. Canons 3, 13, 36: Joannou, *Discipline générale*, 125–30, 140–43, 170; Nedungatt and Featherstone, *Council in Trullo Revisited*, 69–74, 84–87, 114.

65. Nedungatt and Featherstone, *Council in Trullo Revisited*; see in particular the contributions of N. Dură, "The Ecumenicity of the Council in Trullo: Witnesses of the Canonical Tradition in the East and in the West," 229–62, and H. Ohme, "Die sogennanten 'anti-römischen' Kanones des Concilium Quinisextum," 307–21. Update H. Ohme, *Concilium Quinisextum* (as earlier).

66. *Theophanes*, AM 6262–63 (ed. de Boor, I, 445–46).

67. Nikephoros, Patriarch of Constantinople, *Short History*, 80; text, trans., and comm. by C. Mango (Washington, DC, 1990), 152–54.

68. R. Kieckhefer, *Magic in the Middle Ages* (Cambridge, UK, 1989), cites two instances of the Dominican Nicholas Eymericus (1320–99) using this style of destruction, 157, 191. Update Of course, it also continued to be the most common

way of trying to remove dangerous books from circulation in Byzantium; see Magdalino, *L'Orthodoxie des astrologues*, 149. From a later period, Louis XV ordered the public hangman to burn copies of books published without royal permission, but when Charles Théveneau de Morande threatened a new book of revelations about Madame du Barry he was able to blackmail the court for a large sum and a substantial annuity. In return he hired a kiln especially for the purpose of burning all 6,000 copies in April 1774. David Coward, "Reasons to Write," *Times Literary Supplement*, 9 July 2010.

69. C. M. Woodhouse, *Gemistos Plethon, the Last of the Hellenes* (Oxford, 1986), 160.

70. K.-E. Rignell, *A Letter from Jacob of Edessa to John the Stylite of Litarab Concerning Ecclesiastical Canons* (Malmö, 1979).

71. Two useful papers came to my attention after completing this chapter, both by D. Sarefield: "Bookburning in the Christian Roman Empire: Transforming a Pagan Rite of Purification," in H. A. Drake, ed., *Violence in Late Antiquity: Perceptions and Practices* (Aldershot, UK, 2006), 287–96; and "The Symbolics of Book Burning: The Establishment of a Christian Ritual of Persecution," in W. E. Klingshirn and L. Safran, eds., *The Early Christian Book* (Washington, DC, 2007), 159–73.

INDEX

❧

Aachen, 225, 233–34
Achaia, 9, 132, 138
Adrianople, 10, 128n32
Aelius Aristides, 28
Agathon, deacon, 183, 185, 194–96, 201
Aigina, 18–19, 39, 47
Aistulf, king of the Lombards, 224
Albania, 11
Alexander of Macedon, xxiii, 48
Alexander of Abonouteichos, 337
Alexandria, xxii, 42, 125n9, 239–41, 243,
    244, 247, 252, 254, 256, 267, 275, 285,
    287, 302, 312, 313, 315–15, 320, 325,
    337, 341, 345
Alexios I Komnenos, emperor, 27, 61, 77,
    83, 86, 87–88, 114–15, 117, 118, 123,
    206
Alexios II Komnenos, emperor, 75, 113,
    119
Alexios III Angelos, emperor, 8, 76, 108,
    118, 123–24
Alexios IV, emperor, 123
Alexiou, Meg, 312
Allard, André, 316
Anatolia, xxii, 7, 10, 12, 23, 212
Anastasios I, emperor, 278, 339
Anastasios II, emperor, 173, 182, 185, 187,
    195, 200, 207, 208, 210, 211, 228. See
    also Artemios
Anatolikon thema, 193, 208, 209, 211,
    212
Anatolios of Alexandria, 315
Andrew of Patras, Saint, 16, 139
Andronikos I, emperor, 75–76, 113, 118,
    122
Andros, 25–26, 43, 318
Anglo-Saxons, 206, 224, 227, 257
Ankara, 10
Anna Komnene, 27

Antioch, 194, 239–40, 241, 243, 244, 247,
    252, 257, 269, 280, 281, 282, 284, 285,
    301, 306, 339, 345
Antonios, patriarch of Constantinople, 246
Antony, Saint, 201, 275
Apollonios of Perga, 320, 325
Apollonios of Tyana, 337
Apsimar, 181, 182, 199, 209. See also
    Tiberios II, emperor
Aquinas, Thomas, Saint, See Thomas
    Aquinas, Saint
Arabs, xx–xxi, xxii, 5, 12, 13, 18, 38–39,
    40, 41, 43, 44, 46, 47–48, 114, 116,
    138–39, 167, 173, 196–98, 206,
    208–210, 211, 212, 222, 225, 227, 233,
    234, 239, 241, 242, 243, 244, 245, 247,
    257–59, 269, 285, 313, 317, 318, 345,
    348, 350–51
Arcadius, emperor, 133, 341
Archimedes, 319–20, 346, 347
Arethas, bishop of Caesarea, 5, 27, 28,
    34–35, 37, 39, 47–48
Argos, 9, 46, 144
Aristotle, 28, 42, 324, 342
Arius, 340
Armenians, 43, 48, 184, 193, 196, 197–98,
    201, 202–3, 208, 317
Artemios, 173, 179, 185–86, 187. See also
    Anastasios II, emperor
Artemios, Saint, 284
Asia Minor, xvii, 10, 23, 38, 47, 68, 74,
    111, 113, 184, 196, 206, 211, 279, 281,
    303
Aston, Margaret, xiv
Athanasios, Saint (bishop of Methone), 15,
    41, 44, 46
Athens, xvii–xviii, 4, 9, 13, 15, 17, 19, 20,
    21, 33, 37, 42, 47, 59, 60, 67, 68–74,
    75–75, 78, 80, 81–82, 84, 86, 87, 89,

Athens (*continued*)
103–108, 119, 121, 122, 141, 146, 160, 162, 279, 336. *See also* Greece
—churches: of the Virgin Theotokos (Parthenon), 19, 47, 69, 70, 71, 73, 77, 119; of St. George (Theseion), 70; of St. John the Baptist, 47
Augustine, Saint, 30, 307
Augustus, 338
Auzépy, Marie-France, 245
Avars, 36, 161, 285
Avlemon, 133, 146

Babylonia, 314
Baghdad, 160, 217n16, 312, 318
Baldwin of Flanders, 8
Barbarossa, Hayreddin, 130, 132, 146, 151
Bardanes, 181–82, 193. *See also* Philippikos, emperor
Bardas, 318, 320
Basil I, emperor, 6–7, 41, 46, 161, 164, 167, 168, 206, 254, 255, 256, 258
Basil II, emperor, 19, 70, 113
Basil of Caesarea, Saint, 279–80, 304
Basileios of Gortyna, 242, 260n5
Bayezid I, Ottoman sultan, 10
Beck, Hans-Georg, 179
Bede, 54n53, 227, 352n5
Behrens, Betty, xiv
Benedict II, pope, 226
Benedict III, pope, 248
Benevento, 230, 231
Benjamin of Tudela, 24, 108
Berroia, 15, 17, 19
Bessarion, xxii, 324–35, 327
Bitha, Ioanna, 131
Black Sea, 9, 19, 116, 181, 193, 197
Blastares, Matthew, 31
Boccaccio, 336
Bombelli, Raphael, 325, 326
Boniface of Montferrat, 8, 9
Book of Ceremonies, 165, 170, 174, 186
Boris/Boris-Michael of Bulgaria, 249, 252, 255–56
Bosphorus, 6, 163, 171 172, 223
Boukellarion, *thema,* 212
Bouraphos, Count of Opsikion, 172, 184, 186–87
Boustronios, George, 30
Bradbury, Ray, 337
Brown, Peter, 268, 274, 335, 337, 340
Browning, Robert, 3, 58

Brubaker, Leslie, xxi
Bryer, Anthony, xviii, xix, 58, 111, 206
Bulgaria, 10, 12, 19, 31, 240, 249, 252–53, 255–56
Bulgars, 9, 16, 18, 19, 34, 36–37, 46, 47, 48, 80, 112, 184, 185, 195, 196, 206, 212, 214, 240, 249, 256
Bursa, 10

Caesarea, 5, 27, 34, 279, 280, 285, 303
Calabria, 5, 35, 39, 41, 45, 123
Cameron, Alan, xix, 159, 179–80, 192
Cameron, Averil, xix, 159, 192
Cappadocia, 5, 28, 48
Carr, E. H., xiii–xiv
Carthage, 180, 209, 275
Carthage, Council of, 344
Catania, 41
Cefalù, 20
Chalcedon, Fourth Ecumenical Council of, 195, 239, 240, 241–42, 245, 250, 251, 253, 345, 349
Chamaretos, Leon, 77, 82, 90, 140
Charles/Charlemagne, xvii, xx, 220–21, 228, 230–32, 233, 244
Chatzedakes, Manolis, 131
Cherson, 181–82, 193, 199
China, xvii, 233, 327
Chios, 19, 24, 115, 120
Choniates, Michael, Archbishop of Athens, xvii–xviii, 24, 58–59, 60, 67, 69–73, 75–76, 78–81, 82, 85, 87, 89–90, 103–4, 108, 111, 113, 119–20, 122–24
Chortasmenus, John, 322, 324
circus factions, 180. *See also* Constantinople: circus factions
Clement of Alexandria, Saint, 275
Clermont, 9
Codex Atheniensis, 103–8, 144
Coldstream, J. Nicholas, 130
Constans II, emperor, 13, 40, 47, 193, 208, 225, 232
Constantine I, emperor, 159–60, 163, 166, 182, 183, 221, 229, 239, 240, 268, 274, 277, 278, 280, 324, 240
Constantine I, pope, 162, 196, 224, 225, 349
Constantine IV, emperor, 13, 194, 226, 242
Constantine V, emperor, 6, 14, 15, 18, 161, 163, 167, 171, 206, 210, 211–12, 214–15, 220–21, 222, 227, 228, 229, 233, 234, 350

Constantine VI, emperor, 15, 18, 230, 231, 232, 245
Constantine VII Porphyrogennitos, 28, 34, 35, 36, 168–69, 173, 229
Constantine IX Monomachos, 19, 23
Constantine XI, 11
Constantine Palaiologos, 9
Constantinople: Baths of Zeuxippos, 172, 183, 185, 187, 199–200, 232; circus factions, 160, 165–70, 172, 173, 174, 179, 180, 183–88, 192–93, 232; Forum of Constantine, 162, 170, 173, 277, 342; Hippodrome, 160, 161–62, 163, 165, 166, 170, 171, 172, 173, 174, 183, 184, 186–87, 188, 193, 232, 270, 277–78, 280, 287, 323; Milion, 185, 194, 199, 200
—Councils: Eighth Ecumenical Council, 241, 254, 256; Sixth Ecumenical Council, 182, 185, 192, 194–95, 200, 202, 242, 342; in Trullo, 197, 335, 345, 346, 349
—churches: Blachernai, 170; Church of St. Irene (Peace), 163; church of the Forty Martyrs, 318; Holy Apostles, 170; New Church, 164; St. Christopher, 170; St. Euphemia, 170; St. Kallinikos, 170; St. Mokios, 170; St. Polyeuktos, 170, 172; St. Sergios, 170; St. Sophia/Hagia Sophia/Holy Wisdom/Great Church, 10, 28, 159, 161, 163, 170, 173, 185, 194, 195, 198, 226, 277, 278, 285–86, 317; Virgin Diaconissa, 170
—monasteries: Chora, 195, 323; Dalmatou, 184; Kallistratos, 182, 196, 200, 202; Metanoia, 283; Stoudios, 26, 28, 179, 245
—palaces: Boukoleon, 164; Great Palace, 35, 159–60, 161–73, 180, 184, 186, 187–88, 194, 196, 198, 200, 207, 213, 232, 233, 285, 289, 345; palace of Placidia, 162, 223, 225; palace of St. Mamas, 162, 171; palace of Hiereia, 162; Eleutherios, 162
—orphanages: of St Paul, 284; orphanage/leprosarium of St Zotikos, 277, 286
Constantius II, emperor, 133, 277
Corfu, 9–10, 18, 24, 43, 69, 72, 84, 145
Corinth, 4, 7, 8, 10–11, 15, 17, 19, 24, 30, 33, 37, 68, 73, 75, 84, 87, 104, 121–22, 140, 144

Cornelius, bishop of Rome, 300
Coron, 121. See also Korone
Cos/Kos, 138, 259n5
Cosmas/Kosmas, 40, 43, 316
Crete, 4, 14, 18–19, 47–48, 79, 83, 86, 114, 130, 131, 132, 138–40, 145–46, 151, 180, 212, 242, 338
Crimea, xxii, 130, 193, 199, 226
Crusades: First, 7; Third, 97n74; Fourth, xvii, 8–10, 22, 24, 58, 77, 112, 123, 132, 144
Cyprian of Carthage, Saint, 275, 276
Cyprus, xvii, xix, 6, 9, 28, 30, 82, 83, 87, 114, 132, 138–39, 145, 151, 212, 246, 304, 308, 350
Cyril, Saint, 27, 37, 48, 249

Damala, 144
Damascus, 40, 209, 308, 316, 322
Dandolo, Andrea, 8
Danube, 4, 6, 16, 36
Daphne/i, 18, 28, 30, 68
Dardanelles, 10, 210
Darrouzès, Père, 103
Davis, Ralph, 58
David of Thessalonike, Saint, 44
Demetrias, 19, 45, 47
Demetrios Chomatenos, 29, 59
Demetrios of Thessalonike, Saint, 24
Dierkens, Alain, 159
Digenes Akritas, 12, 29
Diocletian, emperor, 340
Diophantos/us, xxii, 312–17, 319–28
Dioskorides, 169, 324
Dyrrachion/um, 7, 13, 18, 63, 83, 133

East Illyricum, 14, 132, 224, 227, 248–49, 255
Edict of Milan, 277
Egypt, xxi, 4–5, 13, 38, 44, 81, 116, 269, 282, 285, 287, 314, 327, 341
Eirene. See Irene, empress
Eisenstadt, Shmuel, xiv
Elias, Norbert, 33
Elias, patriarch of Jerusalem, 255
Elias of Sicily, Saint, 43, 45
Elizabeth of Herakleia, Saint, 303
England, 206, 227, 257
Ephesos/us, 160, 162, 278, 305, 338, 339, 350
Epicurus, 337–38
Epiphanios, bishop of Salamis, 303

Epiros, 8, 9, 18, 22, 43, 72, 80, 114

Euboia, 47, 60, 68, 71, 106, 120

Euclid, 27, 35, 315, 316, 318, 319, 322, 323, 325

Eudaimonoioannis family, 131, 141, 145, 146

Eudokia, empress (wife of Theodosius II), 281

Eudoxia, empress, 304

Eugenius IV, pope, 10

Euphrosyne, empress, xxi

Eusebius of Caesarea, 201

Eustathios, Archbishop of Thessalonike, xviii, 29, 67, 70

Euthymios Malakès, Archbishop of Neopatras, 70, 73, 85

Farmers' Law, 20–21, 213

Febronia, Saint, 284, 345

Fermat, Pierre de, xxii, 312–14, 326–27

Filioque, 244–45

France, xxii, 325, 327

Francia, 206, 221, 224–25, 229, 244, 254

Franks, xvii, xxi, 27, 29, 58, 70, 72, 73, 118–19, 128, 131, 141, 144–45, 146, 220–22, 224–25, 227–34, 243–44, 249, 251, 253–54

Galerius, emperor, 340

Gallipoli, 10

Gaul, 36, 284

Genoa, 115, 122, 146

George Bardanès, 71–73

Giovanni of Otranto, 325, 326, 327

Gisela (daughter of Pippin III), 229

Gortyna, 180, 188n4, 242

Goudsblom, Johan, 336

Great Church. *See* Constantinople: churches

Great Palace. *See* Constantinople: palaces

Greece, xvii, 3–4, 181, 273, 289, 336; Byzantine society in, 20–32; the Fourth Crusade and, 8–10; and hellenization of the Slavs, 34–48; Ottoman Turks and, 10–11; reintegration to Byzantine Empire, 6–8, 12–20; transition from ancient world, 4–6
   —Hellas and Peloponnesos: civilian administration of, 74–82; economic organization of, 112–13, 119–23; metropolitan administration of, 32, 68–74, 103–108; military

administration of, 82–88; *thema* of, 58, 60–67, 89–91. *See also* Athens

Greek Anthology, 320, 321, 323, 327, 347

Greenwood, Tim, 202–3

Gregory I, pope, 36, 223, 225, 226, 230

Gregory II, pope, 224

Gregory III, pope, 224, 227

Gregory Asbestas, archbishop of Syracuse, 248, 253

Gregory of Nazianzos, Saint, 47, 201, 279–80, 308

Gregory of Nyssa, Saint, 279, 316

Gregory of Tours, 36

Gregory the Dekapolite, Saint, 26, 44, 242

Gregory the Theologian, Saint. *See* Gregory of Nazianzos, Saint

Grierson, Philip, xiv

Hadas, Daniel, 335

Hadrian I, pope, 230–31, 243

Hadrian II, pope, 254, 256

Hagia Sophia (Constantinople). *See* Constantinople: churches

Hagios Georgios, monastery in Kythera, 133, 146

Haldon, John, xxi, 58

Halmyros, 7, 121

Harmenopoulos, Constantine, 31

Harun al Rashid, caliph, 171, 244, 245

Hiereia, 171; Council of, 227, 243

Helena, 280, 324

Helias, *spatharios*, 181–82

Herakleia, 242, 303

Heraclius, 4, 133, 207, 226. *See also* Herakleios

Herakleios, 180, 193, 194, 274, 285–86, 287, 288. *See also* Heraclius

Hill, Christopher, xiii

Hilton, Rodney, xiv

Hincmar of Rheims, 250–51, 256, 258

Hobsbawm, Eric, xiv

Holy Luke, 17, 19, 28

Holy Sepulchre, church in Jerusalem, 244, 280, 281

Holy Wisdom, church of. *See* Constantinople: churches

Homer, 29, 42, 320

Honorius, pope, 194, 200

Hosios Loukas, monastery of, 68. *See also* Holy Luke

Hosios Theodoros, 131, 139, 140. *See also* Theodore of Kythera, St.

Hosios Meletios, monastery of, 78
Hughes, Kathleen, xiv
Huxley, George W., 33, 130
Hypatia, 315, 316, 322, 324, 341

iconoclasm, xix, xx, xxi, 26, 39, 40, 44,
    45, 132, 167–68, 193, 200, 206–7, 210,
    212–13, 214–15, 220–21, 224, 227,
    230, 241, 243, 246–48, 255, 299, 318,
    350
Ignatios, patriarch of Constantinople, 45,
    248, 253, 254, 256, 258
Innocent III, pope, 8, 68, 106, 107
Imbros, 6, 139
Ioannes Apokaukos, 59, 73
Irene, empress, 15, 21, 26, 163, 171, 213,
    230–31, 232, 243
Isaac II Angelos, emperor, 8, 76, 104, 106,
    112, 118
Isauria, 44, 132

Jacoby, David, 58
Jerusalem, 5, 7, 10, 20, 40, 43, 239–41,
    243, 244, 245, 255, 257, 273, 280–81,
    282, 302, 303, 304, 322, 345, 347; St.
    Sabas, monastery near Jerusalem, 40,
    244, 245, 281, 304
John, patriarch of Alexandria, 287
John, patriarch of Jerusalem, 322
John I Tzimiskes, emperor, 31, 106, 144,
    167
John II Komnenos, emperor, 85, 86, 87,
    115
John V, pope, 13
John V Palaiologos, emperor, 10, 25
John V, patriarch of Constantinople, 286
John VI Kantakouzenos, emperor, 25
John VIII, pope, 256
John Chrysostom/os, Saint, 269, 280, 284,
    301, 303
John Kameniates, 16–17
John Kontzomytes, 22
John of Damascus, Saint, 40, 43, 308, 316,
    322
John the Grammarian, patriarch of Con-
    stantinople, 318
Jovian, emperor, 339
Julian, emperor, 201, 268
Justin I, emperor, 207
Justin II, emperor, 133, 183, 199, 232, 274,
    285
Justin Martyr, 300

Justinian I, emperor, 4, 7, 11, 42, 44, 133,
    159, 161, 164, 213, 222, 250, 274,
    278–79, 281, 284, 304, 342–43
Justinian II, emperor, 13, 164, 180, 181–82,
    184, 193, 194, 196–97, 199–200, 201,
    207, 209, 213, 225, 226, 229, 242, 344

Kaegi, Walter, 185
Kaisareiane, monastery, 68
Karystos, 68, 71, 73
Kastoria, 18, 19, 28, 72
Kastri/o, 130, 132, 133, 141, 145, 146. See
    also Kythera
Kazhdan, Alexander, 268
Kea, xvii, 68, 71, 105
Kephalonia, xxii, 14, 18, 144, 181, 193, 199
Kibyrreot, thema, 139, 211–2
Kiev, 20, 23
Knossos, 130
Kolovou, Photeine, 59
Korone, 7, 15, 41, 140, 144, 145, 151. See
    also Coron
Kydones, Demetrios, 30, 323
Kyros, patriarch of Constantinople, 195,
    196
Kythera, xxiv, 9, 130–32; churches in,
    130–55; in the late Roman period,
    132–139; in the middle Byzantine
    period, 139–144; the Venetian domina-
    tion of, 144–51

Laiou, Angeliki, 111
Lachanodrakon, Michael, 350
Laconia, 131, 139, 140–41
Lakedaimonia, 15, 17, 22, 39, 41, 43, 77,
    121, 122, 132, 140–41
Larissa, 14, 19, 22, 47, 73, 104, 118
Laskaris, Constantine, 316
Lazaros, Saint, 305
Lemerle, Paul, 319
Leo I, pope, 242, 243–46
Leo III, emperor, xxi, 13, 14, 26, 132, 166,
    167, 171, 206–7, 208, 209–15, 224, 227,
    248, 255, 350
Leo III, pope, 230, 232, 244
Leo IV, emperor, 15, 162, 229, 230
Leo IV, pope, 248, 252
Leo V, emperor, 164, 167, 246
Leo VI, emperor, 12, 16, 34–35, 43, 45,
    168, 171, 172, 321
Leo the Mathematician, 25–26, 27, 43,
    318–22, 323, 327

Leontios, emperor, 182, 184, 193, 207–8, 209
Leontios Makhairas, 30
Leontios of Neapolis, 302
Lesbos, 132
Libanius, 280
Licinius, emperor, 340
Liutprand, 172
Lombards, 4, 8, 220, 222, 224, 226–28, 229, 243
Longobardia, 41, 116, 122, 123
Louis the Pious, 233, 234
Lounghis, Telemachos, xv
Lucian, 28
Luke of Steiris, Saint. See Holy Luke
Lyons, 160; Council of, 30

Macedonia, 13, 15, 20, 24, 25, 28, 120, 273, 347
Macrina, Saint, 279
Madrid, 316, 317, 320, 322, 325
Maier, Franz-Georg, xix
Maina, 18, 144
Makarios, patriarch of Antioch, 194
Malalas, John, 183
Maltezou, Chrysa, 131
Mango, Cyril, 316
Mantzikert, 23, 113; Council of, 197
Manuel I Komnenos, emperor, 86, 87, 104, 113, 115, 118, 287
Manuel II, emperor, 30
Marcian, emperor, 279, 341
Maria, empress (wife of Leo III), 171–72
Maria of Amnia, empress, 231
Mark, Saint, 244
Marmara, sea of, 163, 164
Martin I, pope, 223, 226, 283
Marxism, xiii–xvi, 3
Maurice, emperor, 133, 179, 193
Maxentius, emperor, 201
Maximos Margounios, bishop of Kythera, 151
Maximos/us Confessor, 195, 225, 226, 242, 288, 305, 307
Maximus Planudes, 30, 316, 322–24, 325, 327
Megara, 6, 68
Melitene, 196, 197, 198, 346
Messenia, 18
Meteora, 20, 25
Methodios I, patriarch of Constantinople, 40

Methodios of Thessalonike, Saint, 27, 37, 48, 249
Methone, 7, 15, 41, 45, 46, 140, 144, 145, 151. See also Modon
Michael, patriarch of Alexandria, 254, 256
Michael I, emperor, 231, 233, 245
Michael II, emperor, 47, 167
Michael III, emperor, 16, 171, 253–54
Michael VI, emperor, 162
Michael VIII Palaiologos, emperor, 9, 30, 118, 131
Michael Komnenos Doukas, 8, 82
Milan, 206, 277, 316, 323, 340
Mistra, 9, 11, 20, 25, 30, 31, 131
Mitylene, 105
Modon, 121. See also Methone
Monemvasia, 7, 8, 9, 20, 33, 39, 84, 86, 122, 131–32, 139, 140–41, 144, 145, 146, 151
Mongols, 10, 233
Monophysitism, 39, 194, 197–98, 241, 307, 339
Monotheletism, 179, 182, 192–93, 194–96, 197, 198, 200, 201–3, 226, 242, 246, 342
Moore, Barrington, xiv
Moravia, 27, 249
Morea, 9, 11, 25, 29, 30, 131, 144
Morris, Rosemary, 299
Moscow, 164
Mount Sinai, monastery of St. Catherine, 242, 303
Muhammad, xx, 4, 335
Murad I, Ottoman sultan, 10
Murad II, Ottoman sultan, 10

Naples, 225
Naupaktos, 45, 68, 73, 289
Nauplion, 7, 8, 9, 123
Naxos, 132
Neilos Doxapatris, 104–5, 106
Neopatras, 68, 70, 73, 85, 104–6
Nicaea, 8, 30, 70, 72, 80, 302
Councils: First Ecumenical, 239, 240, 252, 340; Seventh Ecumenical, 15, 52n31, 164, 226, 243, 253
Nicholas I, pope, 14, 241, 248–54, 256, 257–58, 259
Nicholas V, pope, 325
Nicopolis, 18, 22
Nika riot, 160, 183, 200
Nikephoros (father of Bardanes), 181, 193

Nikephoros, patriarch of Constantinople, 183, 184, 185, 195, 196, 201, 245, 246, 306, 350

Nikephoros I, emperor, 12, 15–16, 18, 37, 41, 167, 231

Nikephoros II Phokas, emperor, 139, 167, 168, 172

Niketas, patriarch of Constantinople, 48

Nikolaos Mystikos, patriarch of Constantinople, 12, 34–35, 45, 123

Nikon of Lakedaimonia, Saint, 17, 140, 141

Normans, 7, 41, 84, 114, 118, 122, 123, 141

North Africa, xxi, 5, 38, 43, 114, 209, 269, 341

Ohrid, 29, 69

Opsikion, *thema,* 172, 179, 182, 184–85, 187, 208, 212

Orchomenos, 46

Organ, 166, 180, 183, 211, 229, 232–34

Orosios, 169

Orove, 33, 39

Ostrogorsky, George, xiv

Ostrogoths, 343

Otto II, 31

Otto III, 31

Ovid, 336

Oxyrhynchos, 304

Pachymeres, George, 30, 322

Palaiochora, Kythera, 130, 132, 146

Palermo, 6, 20, 43

Palestine, 4–5, 38, 44, 116, 195, 245, 247, 316

Parastaseis Syntomoi Chronikai, xix, 159, 192, 198, 199–202

Paris, 160

Parthenon. *See* Athens: church of the Virgin Theotokos

Pascal, Roy, xiv

Paschal I, pope, 246

Patras, 5, 7, 11, 13, 15–16, 17, 18, 27, 38, 33, 35, 39, 41, 44–45, 104, 106, 139, 144

Paul, Saint, 71, 271, 273, 284, 301, 306, 307, 338

Paul I, pope, 40

Paul of Gortyna, 14

Pausanias, 28, 323

Pepin. *See* Pippin III

Persians, 4, 5, 38, 222, 269, 285, 302, 339

Peter, patriarch of Constantinople, 286

Peter, Saint, 36, 240, 244, 248, 251, 257, 258, 349

Peter of Argos, Saint, 46

Philippikos, emperor, 172–73, 179, 180–88, 192–203, 207, 208, 232. *See also* Bardanes

Phokas, emperor, 179, 221

Photios, patriarch of Constantinople, 27, 35, 45, 47, 241, 248–59

Pippin III, Frankish king, 220–22, 227–28, 229, 230, 232, 234, 243

Pirenne, Henri, xx

Pisa, 115, 116, 121, 122, 123

Plethon, Gemistos, 31

Pliny, 338

Plutarch, 30, 323, 326

Porphyrios, bishop of Gaza, 270, 301, 304

Porphyry, 320, 341

Proclus, 341

Procopius, 283, 284

Protagoras, 336

Psellus, Michael, 317, 322

Ptolemy, 132, 315–16, 319, 322, 323, 325

Pulcheria, empress, 279, 284, 304

Pythagoras, 316

Ravenna, 39, 40, 132, 193, 196, 221, 222, 224, 226, 227, 242, 243

Ravennika, 9

Rendakis, 7

Rhodes, 24, 115, 120, 132, 139

Roger II, king of Sicily, 104

Roilos, Panagiotis, 312

Romanos I Lekapenos, emperor, 16, 48, 167, 169

Romanos II, emperor, 139

Rome, xxi, 11, 29, 36, 39, 40, 43, 159–61, 162, 182, 193, 194, 196, 206, 243, 269, 273, 275, 276, 277, 282, 288, 300, 336, 342, 349; ecclesiastical authority and, 14, 31, 35, 40, 132, 182, 196–97, 220–34; the Franks and, 220–34; iconoclasm and, 26, 39, 44, 220; Lateran palace in, 277; Lateran Synod at, 243, 342; the pentarchy and, xix, 239–59
—churches: Church of San Clemente, 27; monastery of St. Sabas, 245; Santa Maria Maggiore, 342; St. Peter's, 225, 232, 244

Rothad, bishop of Soissons, 250, 251

Rotrud (daughter of Charlemagne), 230, 231

Rouphos, 184, 187
Rushdie, Salman, xxii, 335, 336
Russia, xxiii, 20, 23, 25, 27, 31, 106, 169, 288

Samos, 18
Samothrace, 6, 139
Sansterre, Jean–Marie, 159
Sanudo, Marco, 9
Sardica, Council of, 246, 248, 250, 253
Sardinia, 242
Sarris, Peter, xv
Seljuk Turks, 7, 23, 111, 112, 113
Septimius Severus, emperor, 163
Serbia, 10, 19, 20, 25, 31, 288
Sergios, patriarch of Constantinople, 194, 200, 285, 286, 287, 345
Sergius III, pope, 35
Severus, patriarch of Antioch, 339
Sgouros, Leo/n, 8, 24, 73, 74, 77, 79, 81, 82, 90, 119, 123
Shepard, Jonathan, 220
Sicily, 4–5, 13, 14, 15, 33, 37–43, 107, 114, 122, 138, 210, 211, 222, 225, 227, 231, 312, 319, 321
Silks, 6, 112, 139, 168, 232, 244; the Gunther silk, 19
Singh, Simon, 326
Skripou, 17–18, 46–47
Skyros, 47
Slavs, 4–5, 6, 13, 15–16, 17, 18, 27, 33–48, 138–39, 249
Sophia, empress (daughter–in–law of Romanos I), 48
Sophia, empress (wife of Justin II), 199, 232
Soteriou, Georgios, 133
Southern, R. W., xiv
Sozomen, 201
Spain, 4, 169, 206, 209, 312, 317, 336, 343
Sparta, 75, 77, 90, 131, 132, 139, 140, 141
Speck, Paul, 179, 183
Spiridon of Corfu, Saint, 24
St. Sophia, church of. See Constantinople: churches
Stagoi, 18, 24
Stavrakios, 15, 139
Stephen II, pope, 220, 221, 225, 227, 228, 232, 243
Stephen III, pope, 230
Stephen V, pope, 43
Stephanos Asmiktos, 180

Stone, Lawrence, 267
Strabo, 323, 326, 347
Strymon, 18
Symeon, tsar of the Bulgars, 19, 47
Synesius of Cyrene, 316
Syracuse, 13, 14, 40, 225, 248, 253
Syria, 4–5, 21, 38, 44, 116, 195, 197, 206, 209, 210, 212, 346, 351

Taurus Mountains, xxii, 5
Taygetos Mountains, 12, 138
Tarasios, patriarch of Constantinople, 243, 288, 289, 302
Tenedos, 6, 139
Tertullian, 300
Tervel, 181
Thebes, 7, 9, 17, 20, 21, 47, 60, 68–69, 70, 73, 75, 78, 79, 82, 84, 104, 105, 106, 107, 108, 119, 121, 122; Church of St. Gregory the Theologian, 47; Jewish community at, 60, 108; silk production in, 7, 24, 28, 60, 108, 122, 128n31
Theodora, empress (daughter of Constantine VIII), 162
Theodora, empress (wife of Justinian I), 283
Theodora, empress (wife of Justinian II), 193
Theodora, empress (wife of Theophilos), 172
Theodore Laskaris, emperor, 8
Theodore of Kythera, Saint, 130, 138
Theodore of Tarsus, Archbishop of Canterbury, 42
Theodore of the Stoudios, Saint, 26, 179
Theodore Prodromos, 30
Theodosios I, emperor, 133, 201, 239
Theodosios II, emperor, 281, 341
Theodosios III, emperor, 207, 208, 209
Theon, 316, 320, 325
Theophanes the Confessor, 183, 184, 185, 195, 196, 197, 201
Theophano, empress (wife of Otto II), 31
Theophilos, emperor, 17, 166, 171, 172, 232, 233, 247, 318, 320
Theophylact, archbishop of Ohrid, 29, 71, 302
Thermopylai, 37, 72, 106
Thessalonike, xv, xviii, 4, 7, 9, 13, 14, 16–17, 18–19, 24, 25, 26–27, 28, 29, 30, 31, 37, 38, 43, 44, 47, 70, 77, 78, 87, 121, 187, 211, 242, 318

—churches: Church of St. Demetrios, 24; Hagia Sophia, 15, 27

Thessaly, 13, 16, 18, 22, 24, 25, 37, 45, 60, 77, 90, 120

Thomas, bishop of Kea, 105

Thomas, patriarch of Jerusalem, 244, 245

Thomas II, patriarch of Constantinople, 286

Thomas Aquinas, Saint, 30

Thomas the Slav, 12

Thomson, George, xiv

Thrace, 6, 10, 13, 14, 15, 24, 25, 120, 171, 172, 179, 184, 185, 195, 196, 209, 210, 232

Tiberios/us (son of Justinian II), 182, 193, 213, 225

Tiberios II, emperor, 181, 182, 193, 199, 207, 208, 209

Toledo, Council of, 343

Torcello, 20

Trajan, emperor, 338

Trebizond, xvii, 8, 10, 25, 82, 144, 324

True Cross, 28, 169

Truffaut, François, 337

Trullo, Council in. See Constantinople: Councils

Valens, emperor, 339

Valla, Giorgio, 319

Venice, 8–9, 10, 20, 42, 86, 114, 116, 117, 122, 123, 145, 146, 151, 162, 186, 249, 324, 325, 327

Veniero family, 145–46

Vigilius, pope, 222

Visigoths, 4, 16, 343

Vitalian, pope, 14, 225, 232

Waterhouse, Ellis, 111

Wickham, Chris, xxi

Wiles, Andrew, 312, 313, 326

William of Moerbeke, 30, 320

Wilson, Nigel, 322

Zacharias, pope, 54n53, 224, 230, 234

Zakynthos, 18, 144

Zealots of Thessalonike, xv, 25

Zemaina, 18, 144

Zoe, empress (fourth wife of Leo VI), 34–35, 45

Zoe, empress (daughter of Constantine VIII), 162

Zuckerman, Constantin, 103